THE
unofficial GUIDE®
TO Washington, D.C.

11TH EDITION

THE
unofficial GUIDE®
TO Washington, D.C.

11TH EDITION

EVE ZIBART

Please note that prices fluctuate in the course of time and that travel information changes under the impact of many factors that influence the travel industry. We therefore suggest that you write or call ahead for confirmation when making your travel plans. Every effort has been made to ensure the accuracy of information throughout this book, and the contents of this publication are believed to be correct at the time of printing. Nevertheless, the publishers cannot accept responsibility for errors or omissions, for changes in details given in this guide, or for the consequences of any reliance on the information provided by the same. Assessments of attractions and so forth are based upon the authors' own experiences; therefore, descriptions given in this guide necessarily contain an element of subjective opinion, which may not reflect the publisher's opinion or dictate a reader's own experience on another occasion. Readers are invited to write the publisher with ideas, comments, and suggestions for future editions.

Published by:
John Wiley & Sons, Inc.
111 River Street
Hoboken, NJ 07030-5774

Produced by Menasha Ridge Press

Cover design by Paul Dinovo

Interior design by Vertigo Design

For information on our other products and services or to obtain technical support, please contact our Customer Care Department within the United States at 800-762-2974, outside the United States at 317-572-3993, or by fax at 317-572-4002.

John Wiley & Sons, Inc., also publishes its books in a variety of electronic formats. Some content that appears in print may not be available in electronic formats.

ISBN 978-0-470-88607-6

Manufactured in the United States of America

5 4 3 2 1

CONTENTS

LIST *of* MAPS

ABOUT *the* AUTHOR

Eve Zibart, author of several books, including *The Unofficial Guide to New Orleans, The Unofficial Guide to New York, The Unofficial Guide to Walt Disney World for Grown-ups,* and *The Ethnic Food Lover's Companion,* spent many (many!) years as a feature writer, nightlife columnist, and restaurant critic for the *Washington Post* and now contributes to *Washingtonian* and other magazines. As a frequently chastised aging athlete, she also keeps track of the fun trails, team stats, and hot workout trends—even when she's on the DL, which is more often these days. Her other passions are her black cat (she's a Halloween baby) and her vintage sports car (also black). And when it comes to shopping, she moves as fast as possible—usually in the opposite direction.

ACKNOWLEDGMENTS

EVE WOULD LIKE TO THANK the always patient and encouraging Holly "The Queen" Cross; fact-checkers Andy Sloan and Carla Stec for playing solid follow-up; Joe Surkiewicz, who contributed much to the original version of this book; and Rich Scherr, who personally inspected more than 140 hotels and inns for our accommodations chapter.

THIS BOOK IS FOR DODGER, who has to live with me while I'm working.

PREFACE

GEORGE WASHINGTON MAY HAVE BEEN, FAMOUSLY, "first in the hearts of his countrymen," but no such claim could have been made for the city that bore his name. In fact, strange as it may sound, Washington, D.C. has spent most of its history suffering from a serious inferiority complex.

It has never been given much respect, or at least not until fairly recently. Charles Dickens called it "the City of Magnificent Intentions," filled with "spacious avenues that begin in nothing and lead nowhere." Pierre L'Enfant, who planned the city, died penniless and brokenhearted; his vision was considered too grandiose and was repeatedly amended. In 1809, the British minister Francis Jackson called it "scantily and rudely cultivated." Washington Irving called it a "forlorn . . . desert town." Even John F. Kennedy famously described it as a "city of Northern charm and Southern efficiency," although the massive beautification programs launched by Lady Bird Johnson in the mid-1960s and committed to the National Park Service have done much to change that.

It wasn't the first or second or even fifth city to serve as the capital. Philadelphia was first and foremost: The Continental Congress briefly adjourned to Baltimore when the British threatened, but quickly returned, only to retreat again to York, Pennsylvania, with an overnight session in Lancaster. The representatives returned to Philadelphia in 1778, but an uprising five years later not by British but their own troops (who were still awaiting their promised pay) sent them first to Princeton, New Jersey; then to Annapolis; then to Trenton, New Jersey; then to New York; and—inevitably—back to Philadelphia. (There's a good reason that the city's main boulevard is named Pennsylvania Avenue.)

When Washington was finally established as the nation's capital in 1790, its site was highly problematic—a "foggy bottom," still the nickname given to the Department of State. It had to borrow land from Maryland and Virginia, only to have the latter state renege and request its acreage back. While New York grandly swept to Gilded Age grandeur and Chicago awarded itself the title of "Second City," the seat of the national government couldn't even settle on a name. Designer L'Enfant called it the Capital City; Jefferson referred to it as Federal Town. It was officially dubbed Washington City in 1791, but modest George never used that name himself, continuing to refer to it as the Federal City. (He did, however, allow the city to use his coat of arms as a basis for its flag and to place him on its seal.) Even Annapolis outshone Washington as a social center in its early days, as did Alexandria and Georgetown.

Worse, as Washingtonians frequently point out, it is still more like a colony of the United States, because residents have no voting Representative in Congress (only a nonvoting seat) and no Senator at all—which is why you will see license plates bearing the ironic slogan "Taxation without Representation." (The District's motto, *Justitia omnibus,* or "Justice for all," might also be considered somewhat ironic.) Residents of the District couldn't even vote for President until 1961. Washington was briefly under the administration of a territorial governor after the Civil War, but the office was abolished soon thereafter, and the city remained under the direct rule of Congress until 1975, when the city was allowed to elect a mayor and city council. And although the House of Representatives passed a measure in 1992 approving statehood for "New Columbia," the Senate has consistently refused to consider it.

Perhaps it's appropriate, then, that Washington is a more international city than an American one, housing as it does the scores of embassies and consulates, the headquarters of the World Bank and International Monetary Fund, the Organization of American States, and so on. And of course, repeated waves of immigration have made it if not the melting pot of America, a sizeable and simmering one.

In another way, however, Washington is among the oldest areas to have been developed. The first Europeans to explore the Washington region were Spanish; Admiral Pedro Menendez, who also founded St. Augustine, may have sailed up the Potomac River (which he dubbed the Espiritu Santo) as far as Occoquan, Virginia. Captain John Smith of Pocahontas fame came even farther, to what is now Great Falls, Virginia, in 1608, though it is not clear whether he actually landed. Foragers from the Jamestown colony raided an Indian village in Anacostia in 1622; a few years later, George Calvert, Lord Baltimore, was granted the tract of Virginia north and east of the river—henceforth to be known as Maryland—as a refuge for British Catholics. By the middle of the 17th century, the entire area had been staked out as great tracts and manor seats.

The question of whether the nation's capital should be built in the North or the South was a subject of much debate, and in fact, while the Congress was in Trenton, some members made an attempt to lay out a site on the Delaware River. Vice President John Adams, voting as president of the Senate, favored Germantown, Pennsylvania. A compromise was finally struck, so the legend goes, at a private dinner Thomas Jefferson hosted for Alexander Hamilton and "Light Horse" Harry Lee, former governor of Virginia and father of Robert E. Lee.

The specific site was selected by Washington himself, probably because the former surveyor believed the Potomac River would become a major waterway. The initial design was a diamond shape, 10 miles by 10 miles, or 100 square miles; many of the mile markers around the perimeter, which were laid by Andrew Ellicott and Benjamin Banneker—a farmer, mathematician, astronomer, inventor, and probably the most famous black man in Colonial America—still stand, though badly deteriorated.

Within that 10-mile square lay a confederation of smaller towns: Washington City, which ended at Rock Creek Park on the west and Florida Avenue and Benning Road on the north; Georgetown, or the Port of Georgetown; Alexandria County, which included parts of Alexandria (the city) as well as present-day Arlington County; and the unincorporated County of Washington. (Florida Avenue was then called Boundary Street, which explains why the streetcar exhibit in the American History Museum shows cars with that destination.)

But in 1846 the residents of Alexandria, who feared that the capital would outlaw slavery and thus strangle the slave trade in that busy port, voted to ask Congress to return the portion of the District across the river to the state of Virginia. In July the request was granted. It was just short of a third of the 100 square miles; you can clearly see on a map how the original diamond is cut off at the southwestern corner by the Potomac. (It's even more obvious on the graphically pared-down Metro subway maps.) Eventually the city charters for Washington and Georgetown were revoked and their duties given over to the District of Columbia—in fact, the sector outside Washington City, termed the County of Washington, remains in historical, if not practical, limbo.

The cornerstone of the White House was laid on October 13, 1792, the day after the 300th anniversary of Columbus's arrival in the New World, but Washington never resided there; in fact, the building was still under construction in 1800 when President John Adams moved in. Congress finally convened later that year, too, in the one wing of the Capitol that had been finished. And Washington was officially declared the nation's capital on December 1, 1800.

Even so, the Capitol and White House had barely been completed in 1814 when British troops set both on fire, along with nearly every other public building. A temporary Capitol, at which James Monroe took his oath of office, was built where the Supreme Court Building is now. The President's House, as it was then known, was restored in 1817, and the Capitol reopened at the end of 1819.

(Incidentally, although the map directions of the District—Northwest, Northeast, Southwest, and Southeast—are taken from the Capitol building, the geographical center of the city is nearer the White House—a bit north of the Washington Monument, near 17th Street NW. And the official heart of the District of Columbia, and hence the point from which all those "miles to Washington" are measured, can be found on the Ellipse.)

The city would be invaded once more, in 1864, by Confederate troops under the command of General Jubal A. Early; that raid, which culminated in the battle at Fort Stevens in Northwest Washington, marks the only time in American history that a President of the United States was present at a battle. Abraham Lincoln was reportedly so fascinated that he kept standing up to watch, oblivious to the bullets flying around him. (The young captain who finally yelled, "Get down, you damned fool!" to the civilian he did not recognize has been identified by some historians as future Supreme Court Justice Oliver Wendell Holmes Jr.)

At the beginning of the Civil War, Washington held only about 75,000 residents; the war and the subsequent expansion of federal agencies boosted that number to nearly 132,000. The last part of the 19th century also saw the beginning of what would be a series of ethnic and cultural influxes. In 1900 only 7% of the residents had come from other countries; a century later a fifth were foreign-born, and by 2020 it's estimated that half of Washington's population will be immigrant. Before 1960 most of the incoming were European; since then they have been primarily Hispanic and Asian.

The population peaked at more than 800,000 in 1950, making the city the ninth largest in the country; it's now about 583,000 (the entire metropolitan area comprises over 5,358,000). Now the mix is about 54% Caucasian, 26% African-American, 10% Hispanic, 8% Asian and the rest a variety of minorities, Ethiopian and Eritrean among them.

Today, early in its third century, Washington is again at a cultural and architectural crossroads, considering its massive new Mall development plan, expanding public transportation, embracing of the suburbs, and balancing national dignity with "security" barriers. The astounding revitalization of the Pennsylvania Avenue neighborhood and reuse of historical buildings is a belated testament to the vision of L'Enfant (who was finally reinterred in Arlington National Cemetery). Washington has clearly taken its place among the world's great cities as the center of international policy. Soon, perhaps, Washingtonians will feel lucky to live here.

Meanwhile—it's a great place to visit!

—*Eve Zibart*

INTRODUCTION

WELCOME *to* WASHINGTON

I LIVE IN WASHINGTON NOW, but I came first as a tourist—and later as a sort of Tennessean in exile.

I must have been about six the first time I laid eyes on the Washington Monument. My parents and older brother were equally delighted—we are a sentimental clan—but they were rather more sensible: I begged to be allowed to walk up all those 897 steps; my mother quite intelligently brokered a deal whereby we took the elevator up and walked down. Still, I can recall quite clearly that seemingly endless, mesmerizing downward-spiraling trek; the vision a few hours later of that floodlit spire—it was reflected in the river—from a restaurant along the Southwest Waterfront; the towering gravity of Lincoln's great visage; and the gleaming width of the Mall itself.

When later I moved here to work, I made myself into a sort of professional tourist: I took two months off between jobs to learn my way around, to find my place in the neighborhood (Capitol Hill was my immediate first love), and to luxuriate in the myriad riches of the Smithsonian museums. I was also determined to discover the secrets to negotiating traffic—a process that is much easier now thanks to the increased reach of the Metrorail subway but which at the time forced me to become an intimate of the city's unique and sometimes mysterious layout.

I never really expected to become a Washingtonian, but I eventually succumbed to the strange, almost hybrid spell: a city with Southern charm and manners but New Yorkian attractions, and a life rhythm somewhere in between. I was stubborn, though: It was at least five years before I realized I had shifted allegiance. I was flying in down the Potomac River and past the Mall when I suddenly became aware that I was feeling the "coming home" sensation, not the "back to work" one. I began to feel proud, almost possessive of

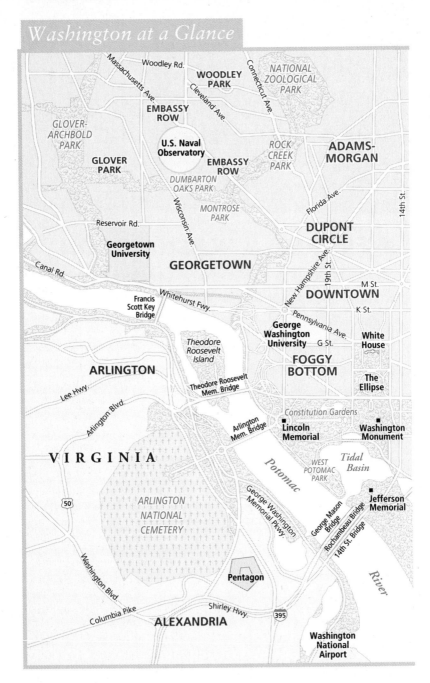

Washington at a Glance

Woodley Rd.

Massachusetts Ave.

WOODLEY PARK

Cleveland Ave.

Connecticut Ave.

NATIONAL ZOOLOGICAL PARK

EMBASSY ROW

GLOVER-ARCHBOLD PARK

U.S. Naval Observatory

ROCK CREEK PARK

ADAMS-MORGAN

GLOVER PARK

EMBASSY ROW

DUMBARTON OAKS PARK

Wisconsin Ave.

MONTROSE PARK

Florida Ave.

14th St.

Reservoir Rd.

DUPONT CIRCLE

Georgetown University

GEORGETOWN

New Hampshire Ave.

19th St.

M St.

Canal Rd.

Whitehurst Fwy.

Francis Scott Key Bridge

DOWNTOWN

K St.

Pennsylvania Ave.

George Washington University

G St.

White House

Theodore Roosevelt Island

FOGGY BOTTOM

ARLINGTON

Lee Hwy.

Theodore Roosevelt Mem. Bridge

The Ellipse

Arlington Blvd.

Arlington Mem. Bridge

Constitution Gardens

■ **Lincoln Memorial**

■ **Washington Monument**

V I R G I N I A

Potomac

WEST POTOMAC PARK

Tidal Basin

50

■ **Jefferson Memorial**

ARLINGTON NATIONAL CEMETERY

George Washington Memorial Pkwy.

George Mason Bridge

Rochambeau Bridge

14th St. Bridge

Washington Blvd.

Pentagon

River

Columbia Pike

Shirley Hwy.

395

ALEXANDRIA

Washington National Airport

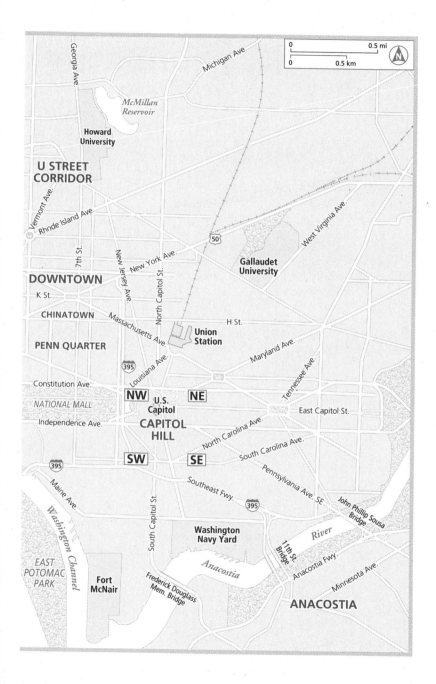

the city's beauty, of the friezes and the statuary and the gardens (and the flower plantings in every leftover bit of ground, a permanent tribute to the graciousness of Lady Bird Johnson), of the cemeteries and cathedrals and historic homes. I walked, and continue to walk, its broad avenues and winding paths; I sit at sidewalk cafés and watch the passersby just as if I were in Paris—and frankly, the celebrity spotting's better here.

Sure, Washington can be hot, but isn't that the point of most of the beach vacations people take? It can be cold, too, which might be more of a surprise: the first week I lived here, it was too cold to recaulk the replacement windows for two that had been taken out. (I spent most of the time with my feet in the fireplace.) The traffic's extraordinary, but so is the scenery. Washington is a living multicultural festival, with infinite chances to make new friends and experience new customs.

Even more astoundingly, Washington has blossomed in the 21st century, the 9/11 chill more than offset by the boom in first-rate restaurants, theater and performing arts, and museum exhibits. And unlike the ones in New York, nearly all the museums here are free!

Sure, Washingtonians make jokes about the tourists, but rarely are they serious. In fact, most Washingtonians came from somewhere else, just as I did, and chose to stay. We're actually pretty friendly: you'll find us smiling at the people on the sidewalk, turning the confused around toward the White House, explaining the intricacies of the Metro farecard machines, and recommending favorite watering holes.

So welcome to Washington. Whether you think of it as the nation's capital, Hollywood on the Potomac, Power Central, the center of the free world, or just a beautiful city, it's well worth the time. This time, and the next.

ABOUT *this* GUIDE

WHY "UNOFFICIAL"?

MOST "OFFICIAL" GUIDES TO WASHINGTON, D.C., tout the well-known sights, promote local restaurants and accommodations indiscriminately, and leave out a lot of good stuff. This one is different.

Instead of pandering to the tourist industry, we'll tell you if the food is bad at a well-known restaurant, we'll complain loudly about D.C.'s notorious high prices, and we'll guide you away from the crowds and lines for a break now and then.

Visiting Washington requires wily strategies not unlike those used in the sacking of Troy. We sent in a team of evaluators who toured each site, ate in the city's best restaurants, performed critical evaluations of its hotels, and visited Washington's wide variety of nightclubs. If a museum is boring, or standing in line for two hours to view a famous attraction is a waste of time, we say so—and, in the process, hopefully make your visit more fun, efficient, and economical.

CREATING A GUIDEBOOK

WE GOT INTO THE GUIDEBOOK BUSINESS because we were unhappy with the way travel guides force the reader to work to get any usable information. Wouldn't it be nice, we thought, if we were to make guides that are easy to use?

Most guidebooks are compilations of lists. This is true regardless of whether the information is presented in list form or artfully distributed through pages of prose. There is insufficient detail in a list, and prose can present tedious helpings of nonessential or marginally useful information. Not enough wheat, so to speak, for nourishment in one instance, and too much chaff in the other. Either way, these types of guides provide little more than departure points from which readers initiate their own quests.

Many guides are readable and well researched, but they tend to be difficult to use. To select a hotel, for example, a reader must study several pages of descriptions with only the boldface hotel names breaking up large blocks of text. Because each description essentially deals with the same variables, it is difficult to recall what was said concerning a particular hotel. Readers generally must work through all the write-ups before beginning to narrow their choices. The presentation of restaurants, nightclubs, and attractions is similar except that even more reading is usually required. To use such a guide is to undertake an exhaustive research process that requires examining nearly as many options and possibilities as starting from scratch. Recommendations, if any, lack depth and conviction. These guides compound rather than solve problems by failing to narrow travelers' choices down to a thoughtfully considered, well-distilled, and manageable few.

HOW *UNOFFICIAL GUIDES* ARE DIFFERENT

READERS CARE ABOUT THE AUTHORS' OPINIONS. The authors, after all, are supposed to know what they are talking about. This, coupled with the fact that the traveler wants quick answers (as opposed to endless alternatives), dictates that authors should be explicit, prescriptive, and above all, direct. The authors of the *Unofficial Guide* try to be just that. They spell out alternatives and recommend specific courses of action. They simplify complicated destinations and attractions and allow the traveler to feel in control in the most unfamiliar environments. The objective of the *Unofficial Guide* authors is not to give the most information or all of the information, but to offer the most accessible, useful information.

An *Unofficial Guide* is a critical reference work; it focuses on a travel destination that appears to be especially complex. Our experienced authors and research team are completely independent from the attractions, restaurants, and hotels we describe. *The Unofficial Guide to Washington, D.C.* is designed for individuals and families traveling for the fun of it, as well as for business travelers and conventioneers, especially those visiting D.C. for the first time. The guide is directed at value-conscious, consumer-oriented travelers who seek a cost-effective, though not spartan, travel style.

SPECIAL FEATURES

THE *Unofficial Guide* OFFERS THE FOLLOWING special features:

- Friendly introductions to Washington's most fascinating neighborhoods.
- "Best of" listings, giving our well-qualified opinions on things ranging from bagels to baguettes, 4-star hotels to 12-story views.
- Listings that are keyed to your interests, so you can pick and choose.
- Advice to sightseers on how to avoid the worst of the crowds; advice to business travelers on how to avoid traffic and excessive costs.
- Recommendations for lesser-known sights that are away from the huge monuments of the Mall but are no less spectacular.
- A neighborhood system and maps to make it easy to find places you want to go to and avoid places you don't.
- Expert advice on avoiding street crime.
- A Hotel Information Chart that helps you narrow down your choices fast, according to your needs.
- Shorter listings that include only those restaurants, clubs, and hotels we think are worth considering.
- A detailed index to help you find things fast.
- Insider advice on crowds, lines, best times of day (or night) to go places, and our secret weapon, Washington's stellar subway system.

What you *won't* get:

- Long, useless lists where everything looks the same.
- Information that gets you somewhere you want to go at the worst possible time.
- Information without advice on how to use it.

HOW THIS GUIDE WAS RESEARCHED AND WRITTEN

WHILE A LOT OF GUIDEBOOKS HAVE BEEN WRITTEN about Washington, D.C., very few have been evaluative. Some guides come close to regurgitating the hotels' and tourist offices' own promotional material. In preparing this work, nothing was taken for granted. Each museum, monument, federal building, hotel, restaurant, shop, and attraction was visited by trained observers who conducted detailed evaluations and rated each according to formal criteria.

While our observers may have some particular expertise, they are independent and impartial. Like you, they visited Washington as tourists or business travelers, noting their satisfaction or dissatisfaction.

The primary difference between the average tourist and the trained evaluator is the evaluator's skills in organization, preparation, and observation. The trained evaluator is responsible for much more than simply observing and cataloging. While the average tourist is gazing in awe at stacks of $20 bills at the Bureau of Engraving and Printing, for instance, the professional is rating the tour in terms of the information provided, how quickly the line moves, the location of restrooms, and how well children can see the exhibits. He or she also checks out things like other attractions close by, alternate places to go if the line at a main attraction is too long, and the best local lunch options. Observer teams use detailed checklists to analyze hotel rooms, restaurants, nightclubs, and attractions. Finally, evaluator ratings and observations are integrated with tourist reactions and the opinions of patrons for a comprehensive quality profile of each feature and service.

In compiling this guide, we recognize that a tourist's age, background, and interests will strongly influence his or her taste in Washington's wide array of attractions and will account for a preference for one sight or museum over another. Our sole objective is to provide the reader with sufficient description, critical evaluation, and pertinent data to make knowledgeable decisions according to individual tastes.

LETTERS, COMMENTS, AND QUESTIONS FROM READERS

WE EXPECT TO LEARN FROM OUR MISTAKES, as well as from the input of our readers, and to improve with each new book and edition. Many of those who use the *Unofficial Guides* write to us asking questions, making comments, or sharing their own discoveries and lessons learned in Washington. We appreciate all such input, both positive and critical, and encourage our readers to continue writing. Readers' comments and observations will frequently be incorporated into revised editions of the *Unofficial Guide* and will contribute immeasurably to its improvement.

How to Write the Author:

Eve Zibart
The Unofficial Guide to Washington, D.C.
P.O. Box 43673
Birmingham, AL 35243
UnofficialGuides@menasharidge.com

If you write by mail, be sure to put your return address on your letter as well as on the envelope—sometimes envelopes and letters get separated. And remember, our work takes us out of the office for long periods of time, so forgive us if our response is delayed.

Reader Survey

At the back of the guide you will find a short questionnaire that you can use to express opinions about your Washington visit. Clip out the questionnaire along the dotted line and mail it to the address on page 7.

The *Unofficial Guide* Website

The website of the *Unofficial Guide* Travel and Lifestyle Series, providing in-depth information on all *Unofficial Guides* in print, is at **www.theunofficialguides.com.**

HOW INFORMATION IS ORGANIZED: BY SUBJECT AND BY LOCATION

TO GIVE YOU FAST ACCESS TO INFORMATION about the *best* of Washington, we've organized material in several formats:

ACCOMMODATIONS Since most people visiting Washington stay in one hotel for the duration of their trip, we have summarized our coverage of hotels in charts, maps, ratings, and rankings that allow you to quickly focus your decision-making process. We do not go on, page after page, describing lobbies and rooms which, in the final analysis, sound much the same. Instead, we concentrate on the specific variables that differentiate one hotel from another: location, size, room quality, services, amenities, and cost. The accommodations are compared by rankings in a concise table (pages 56–61), and the vital information for all accommodations is provided in an extensive chart (pages 67–82).

ATTRACTIONS Attractions—historic buildings, museums, art galleries—draw visitors to Washington, but it's practically impossible to see them all in a single trip. We list them by type (see pages 160–163) as well as map their locations and then evaluate each one, including its appeal to various age groups. These descriptions are the heart of this guidebook and help you determine what to see, and when.

RESTAURANTS We provide a lot of detail when it comes to restaurants. Since you will probably eat a dozen or more restaurant meals during your stay, and since not even you can predict what you might be in the mood for on Saturday night, we provide detailed profiles of the best restaurants in and around Washington. They are also listed by cuisine (see pages 282–285) and their locations mapped.

ENTERTAINMENT AND NIGHTLIFE Visitors frequently try several different clubs or nightspots during their stay. Since clubs and nightspots, like restaurants, are usually selected spontaneously after arrival in Washington, we believe detailed descriptions are warranted. The best nightspots and lounges in Washington are profiled as well (see profiles starting on page 389).

NEIGHBORHOODS Once you've decided where you're going, getting there becomes the issue. To help you do that, we have divided the city into neighborhoods. Generally, we refer to:

- The National Mall and Arlington Memorials
- Capitol Hill
- Downtown
- Foggy Bottom
- Georgetown
- Dupont Circle/Adams Morgan
- Upper Northwest
- Northeast
- Southeast
- Maryland Suburbs
- Virginia Suburbs

However, in specific chapters (nightlife, dining, shopping), we have also referred to some smaller, trendier sections, including U Street, the Atlas District, and Logan Circle. All hotel charts, as well as profiles of restaurants and nightspots, include the neighborhood. If you are staying at the Carlyle Suites, for example, and are interested in Japanese restaurants within walking distance, scanning the restaurant profiles for restaurants in Dupont Circle/Adams Morgan will provide you with the best choices.

PART ONE

PLANNING YOUR VISIT *to* WASHINGTON

▌ WHEN *to* GO

GAUGING THE WEATHER

IF YOU'RE JUST GOING BY THE WEATHER, the best times to visit Washington are in the spring and fall, when the weather is most pleasant and nature puts on a show. The city's fabled cherry blossoms bloom in late March or early April—not necessarily coinciding with the Cherry Blossom Festival fortnight but nevertheless enticing hordes of pedestrian and vehicular traffic—while fall brings crisp, cool weather and, by mid-October, a spectacular display of gold, orange, and red leaves.

The summers—mid-June through September—can be brutally hot and humid. (Remember the summer of 2010? Washingtonians do.) Visitors in July and August not only must contend with the heat as they trudge from building to building but also must then adjust to the city's heavy reliance on X-treme air-conditioning. (Unfortunately, the Metro subway system has a tendency to have trouble with its AC in the summer and its heat in winter.) August, with its predictably oppressive heat, is the month when as many Washingtonians who can follow the lead of those sometime residents, the members of Congress and foreign governments, and flee the city.

However, if you don't mind the humidity, or like an early-and-late schedule with a break in the afternoon, August has its good side: far less traffic and shorter queues, easy restaurant reservations, extended museum hours, and—precisely because Congress is in recess and many federal employees are on vacation—less tedious security. Washington is so much less crowded, in fact, that August is when many of the area's most prominent chefs participate in the summer Restaurant Week, offering bargain-priced three-course lunch and dinner menus at about $20 and $35, respectively.

Though Washington's weather is erratic in winter, it's one of the best times to avoid crowds. On weekdays especially, the Mall is nearly

WASHINGTON'S AVERAGE MONTHLY TEMPERATURES

	HIGH	LOW		HIGH	LOW
January	42° F	27° F	July	87° F	68° F
February	44° F	28° F	August	84° F	66° F
March	53° F	35° F	September	78° F	60° F
April	64° F	44° F	October	67° F	48° F
May	75° F	54° F	November	55° F	38° F
June	83° F	64° F	December	45° F	30° F

deserted, and museums, monuments, and normally crowd-intensive hot spots like the Capitol are almost congenial. There are holiday concerts, lights, and displays galore, which make this season prime for a festive family vacation. And especially if you are staying in or close to the District, you can use the underground subway to crisscross the city without exposing yourself to the weather. (Curiously, despite the obvious advantages of the subway system, Washingtonians tend to climb back into their cars at the first hint of bad weather, driving inexpertly enough that it almost guarantees fender-benders and more back-ups—just one of many reasons not to drive around the city.)

And you may get lucky: Balmy, mid-60s days are possible through December. While it often gets into the teens in January and February—witness the chilly temperatures that attended President Obama's inauguration and forced the wholesale cancellation of President Reagan's—midday temperatures can climb into the 40s and 50s. (Though to be fair, we should also remind you of the blizzard of December 2009 and the back-to-back blizzards of February 2010. Still, according to the law of averages, winter should be a good bet for several years to come—unless you're a global-warming phobe.) And as an added enticement, the other Restaurant Week is in January.

March is tricky. While warm daytime temperatures are frequent, occasionally a large, moist air mass moving north from the Gulf of Mexico will collide with a blast of frigid air from Canada. The result is a big, wet snowfall that paralyzes the city for days. (It should be further noted that the mere prediction of snow, or omission thereof, can wreak surprising havoc on the entire area.)

Still, the best information we can give you is what the meteorologists and statisticians give us. The table above lists the city's average monthly temperatures, in degrees Fahrenheit.

GAUGING THE CROWDS

HERE'S THE SECOND CONSIDERATION: other visitors. A pleasant Washington experience is as much about the "who," or at least the "how many," as the "when." In general, popular tourist sites are busier on weekends than weekdays, Saturdays are busier than Sundays, and summer is busier than winter. The slowest days, generally speaking, are Monday through Wednesday. During the height of the spring and summer tourist seasons, the major attractions are reliably crowded from 9:30 a.m. to 3 p.m. For people in town on business, this tourist influx means heavier traffic, congested airports, a packed Metro, and a tough time finding a convenient hotel room.

And honestly, no additional tourist traffic is required for Washington to be gridlocked. Each day, primarily during rush hours, a quarter-million cars, vans, and buses are struggling to get onto, around, and eventually off of the Capital Beltway, a fate that out-of-town drivers should avoid at all costs. (Driving for those unfamiliar with any part of the Washington area should be avoided anyway, as highway signage is so bad that even locals frequently take wrong turns.) The same prime-time warning applies to riding the Metro, which is not only more crowded but more expensive during peak periods, which now include "peak of the peak" surcharges. (See Part Four: Getting In and Getting Around Washington for a complete explanation of Metro service and fares.)

If you insist on driving to Washington, try to time your arrival on a weekend or during a rather narrow window that opens around 10:30 a.m. and starts to close quickly around 2 p.m. Afternoon traffic doesn't begin to clear up until 7:30 p.m. (and frequently later). Friday afternoon rush hours are the worst—don't even think of driving near D.C. until well after 8 p.m.

As we suggested above, winter can be a great time to avoid crowds. The tourist traffic begins picking up in late March and peaks in early April, when the Japanese cherry trees along the Tidal Basin bloom and Washington is flooded with visitors, cars, buses, and tour vans. Mammoth throngs pack the Mall, and it's elbow-to-elbow in the National Air and Space and American History museums. Despite the undeniable splendor of the cherry trees, it's not the optimum time to tour Washington unless you are uncommonly cheerful and patient (or don't have much choice).

Otherwise, if at all possible, delay your visit until late May or early June. Crowds are more manageable for a few weeks, and the weather is usually delightful. The tourist pace begins picking up again in mid-June as schools let out, and the throngs don't begin to thin out until the last two weeks of August, when kids start returning to school. Between Memorial Day and Labor Day, Washingtonians are regular weekend beach and mountain commuters, which makes the Friday "getaway" traffic (and Sunday evenings) a serious pain in the car seat. After Labor Day, the volume of weekday visitors drops off significantly, but weekends remain busy through October. Washington's elaborate cultural season kicks into full swing mid-September (the second weekend in September is one of the best times for music lovers to visit; see the Calendar of Special Events at the end of this chapter).

Beginning in November, tourist activity slows down dramatically. Though Thanksgiving Day brings hordes of family groups to popular sights on the Mall, car traffic is light. Getting around town from November through March is markedly easier, and it's a very comfortable time to be on the Metro. And the list of music festivals and light shows around the holidays increases every year. If you have no restrictions on your travel time, we suggest you skim the calendar of annual events and see which might lure you.

GATHERING INFORMATION

BEFORE YOU COME

THERE ARE PLENTY OF DEPENDABLE and frequently updated websites that you might want to browse while planning your visit. The official tourism site is **Washington.org,** which lists many family-friendly and free seasonal options, events, some package deals you might compare, and so on. It also offers an official visitor's guide, updated twice a year, with maps and local hotel options that you can download. D.C. also has a visitor's site, **www.thedistrict.com,** which includes hotel and travel information. You might also want to look into **www .vrc.dc.gov/vrc, www.culturaltourismdc.org, www.visitalexandriava .com,** which includes many historical attractions, and **www.visitmaryland .org/capital,** which describes the area closest to the District. We also list some specific sites and downloadable tours in Part Five: Sightseeing Tips, Tours, and Attractions.

Of course, Washington is one of the political hot spots not only of the United States but of the world, and most Washingtonians are news junkies of the first order. (Not surprisingly, the "News Junkie" T-shirt is a popular souvenir at the Newseum's gift shop.)

Washington is not only the home of one of the most famous newspapers in journalism history, *The Washington Post,* it's also the home of CNN and C-Span as well as news bureaus of all the broadcast networks (your hotel will have a menu informing you of which cable channel these are on, depending on the carrier).

Several of the major publications in the area have online editions that you can surf in advance of your visit, including the *Post* (**www .washingtonpost.com**); Washington's free weekly "alternative" newspaper, *City Paper* (**www.washingtoncitypaper.com**); and the area's major monthly magazine, *Washingtonian* (**www.washingtonian.com**).

Incidentally, if you're planning to visit any of the Smithsonian museums—and it's hard to imagine how you wouldn't—their new site, **www.gosmithsonian.com,** will give you a quick first look at the exhibits and floor plans.

APPLY FOR CONGRESSIONAL PAYBACK

A POLITE LETTER TO ONE OF YOUR REPRESENTATIVES or senators well in advance of your trip—and if you expect to arrive in peak season, six months out is not too early—can turn a run-of-the-mill visit into something of a VIP experience: admittance to limited White House tours, reservations to VIP tours of the Library of Congress, the Treasury Department, the Bureau of Engraving and Printing, the Kennedy Center, and even Mount Vernon that can save you hours of time waiting in line, as well as getting you on longer, more informative tours. In addition, the congressperson's constituent services staffers may be able to add some recommendations for restaurants, shopping, and special events.

These "services" are free, but Congress members are only given so many passes for these VIP tours. And, as all members are allocated the same number of passes, this is one time when having to travel a longer way can be an advantage: Maryland legislators, some of whose constituents can literally jump on the Metro to reach D.C., are often booked five and six months in advance for the White House VIP tours. But a family from South Dakota should have a much better chance that their representative will be able to get reservations during their visit. So send off your letter as soon as you know the exact dates of your visit, and the attractions you'd like to see. (Just don't get a Very Inflated Personality: VIP tours still require waiting in line.)

For senators, the Washington address is U.S. Senate, Washington, D.C. 20510, or visit **www.senate.gov** to find your specific senator. For House members, address your letter to the U.S. House of Representatives, Washington, D.C. 20515, or visit **www.house.gov.**

GETTING DOWN TO DETAILS

ONCE YOU ARRIVE, YOU'LL REALIZE that there are dozens of concerts, art shows, and special events going on all the time around Washington—in Part Eight: Entertainment and Nightlife, we point out the many free summer concerts by the armed forces bands and local musicians—so you should be sure to check the local press while you're in town. Those aforementioned news junkies will want to grab the *Washington Post* anyway, but there are lists of events in the Style section, the Thursday Local Living sections (which concentrate on specific areas), and the Friday Weekend section. The *Post* also owns a free quick-read newspaper, called *Express,* handed out at Metro stations and many street corners; its Thursday edition has many listings as well.

The *Washington Times* offers a more conservative slant on national and world events than the *Post* but also has some event listings and reviews, primarily on Thursday. Like *Express,* the *Washington Examiner,* a free tabloid belonging to the media company that owns the conservative *Weekly Standard* magazine, is handed out at most Metro stations.

Serious political junkies should look for the printed newspaper edition of the influential political journal *Politico,* published exclusively in Washington and offered for free in area newsboxes. They should also go online to the widely admired and, though generally liberal, wittily contentious Slate (**www.slate.com**), founded by longtime *New Republic* editor Michael Kinsley and now owned, though not operated, so to speak, by the *Washington Post* Company.

The weekly *Washington City Paper* is another good, and free, source of information on arts, theater, clubs, popular music, and movie reviews. It's available from street-corner vending machines and stores all over town.

The *Washingtonian,* the area's preeminent magazine, is strong on lists (top 10 restaurants, hot shopping boutiques, etc.) and provides a monthly calendar of events, dining information, and feature articles. *Where/Washington* is one of several glossy monthly publications that list popular things to do around town; however, this one is free and generally more egalitarian, and it's usually available in your hotel or at airport racks. Or you can go online to **www.wheretraveler.com** and pick the D.C. link. The *Washington Blade,* the LGBT community's weekly, is available in many restaurants and nightspots, especially around Dupont Circle and Capitol Hill; it also has an extensive website (**www.washingtonblade.com**).

If you don't have time or the inclination for much advance work, there's a sort of one-stop shop for brochures, maps, discount coupons, hotel/restaurant reservation kiosks, and so on: the Visitor Information Center in the Ronald Reagan Building and International Trade Center at 1300 Pennsylvania Avenue NW near the Mall. It's at street level, just inside the Wilson Plaza entrance across the street from the Federal Triangle Metro station. Even handier, the building houses an extensive food court, public phones, and restrooms, and in summer hosts a lot of free concerts as well. From mid-March to Labor Day it's open weekdays 8:30 a.m. to 5:30 p.m. and Saturdays 9 a.m. to 4 p.m.; fall and winter weekdays only, 9 a.m. to 4:30 p.m. For more information call ☎ 202-289-8317 or 866-DC-IS-FUN (324-7386) or go to **www.dcchamber.org.**

unofficial **TIP**
The District of Columbia, Fairfax County, Virginia, and Montgomery County, Maryland, have instituted the 311 information line; within those jurisdictions, call 311 for any non-emergency public information you need.

Information On Air

Of course, print and online are not the only sources of news and entertainment. If you prefer to wake up to the radio, or prefer to pack a potentially disposable radio instead of a more expensive personal media player for exercise, here are some of the major options:

FORMAT	FREQUENCY	STATION
All news	103.5-FM, 103.9-FM, 107.7-FM	WTOP
Black community news/talk	1450-AM	WOL
C-Span	90.1-FM	WCSP
Conservative talk	1260-AM	WWRC
Conservative talk/news	570-AM	WTNT
Federal news	1500-AM	WFED
NPR	90.9-FM	WETA
Sports talk	980-AM	WTEM

WHERE *to* STAY

THE NEIGHBORHOODS

YOU SHOULD ALSO SPEND A LITTLE TIME thinking about what area of Washington you want to stay in so that you can pick the right accommodations for your budget and preferences for the attractions that most interest you. (See Part Two: Accommodations for in-depth advice.) The presence of a Metro stop in many of the areas described below is a real bonus.

When most people think of Washington (and most of them think specifically of the District of Columbia), they conjure up an image of the Mall anchored by the U.S. Capitol at the east end and the Lincoln Memorial on the other. On its east end alone, the Mall features at least 11 major museums and attractions. In the center is the Washington Monument, with the White House just to the north.

While there's much to see and do on the Mall, visitors who don't get beyond the two-mile strip of green are missing a lot of what this vibrant, international city has to offer: brick sidewalks in front of charming colonial-era row houses in Georgetown, the bohemian cafés of Adams Morgan, the stately town houses and mansions near Dupont Circle, the glitter and overflowing street life in the "new downtown" of Penn Quarter, or the "New U," U Street NW around 14th Street. At the very least, a foray off the Mall can elevate your trip beyond the level of an educational grade-school field trip and give you a taste of the lively city itself. Starting from near the Mall, some of the more intriguing areas include:

The Southwest Waterfront

A surprising array of private yachts and houseboats is on view in Washington's waterfront area, a stretch along Maine Avenue that features marinas, seafood restaurants, and the Wharf Seafood Market, where visitors can sample fresh fish and Chesapeake Bay delicacies such as oysters on the half shell. The gorgeous, technically sleek brand-new home of the award-winning Arena Stage is here, and it's also where you can take a scenic river cruise to Mount Vernon. It's easy to get to the waterfront: take the subway to the Waterfront Metro station (Green Line). And the next stop on the Green Line, Navy Yard, is the gateway to the new Nationals Park.

Anacostia

Two decades past, when Washington was slammed as the "Murder Capital of the U.S.," those statistics referred primarily to the swath of Northeast and Southeast Washington across the Anacostia River from downtown. Now, however, there are ambitious plans underway for the Anacostia riverfront, including upgrading the public park facilities and building a new professional soccer arena that will face the new Nationals baseball stadium on the opposite shore, with a pedestrian bridge between. While Anacostia is still off the beaten tourist path—there is a Metro station, but it's not convenient to tourists—there are two attractions visitors should take the time to explore, especially those interested in their ethnic heritage: Cedar Hill, the home of 19th-century abolitionist Frederick Douglass (just emerging from a lengthy restoration), and the Smithsonian's Anacostia Museum. And if you have time, add Kenilworth Park and Aquatic Gardens to your list. These are accessible by public transportation (see details in Part Five, Sightseeing Tips, Tours, and Attractions), but unless you are staying with friends who drive, cabbing or hiring a tour guide might be best.

Capitol Hill

The neighborhood surrounding the Capitol is a mix of residential and commercial, with plenty of restored town houses and trendy bars. Called "The Hill" by locals, it houses a blend of congressional staffers, urban homesteaders, and a mix of middle-class and lower-middle-class families. Among its more famous attractions, in addition to the Capitol itself, are the Supreme Court, the Library of Congress, the old RFK Stadium (no longer used for football or baseball, but still the home of Washington's Major League Soccer team, D.C. United), and Union Station, among others. And of course it abuts the Mall. The area above Union Station along H Street NE, which is becoming known as the Atlas District, is the hottest new hip neighborhood for restaurants and performing arts (see Part Eight: Entertainment and Nightlife). Some residential blocks are still on the edgy side, but if you don't wander far from these major areas you'll have no worries.

Penn Quarter/Downtown

Directly north of the Mall toward K Street NW and roughly between the Capitol and the White House is the "old downtown," an area which in recent years has undergone an almost unimaginable renaissance, fueled by the construction of the Verizon Center, the major sports and events arena; hip and sometimes splendid condo renovations; and the opening of a number of new museums. In fact, this area almost rivals the Mall in that way, with eight museums—although four of them, the Newseum, the International Spy Museum, the Museum of Crime and Punishment (co-owned by "America's Most Wanted" star John Walsh), and Madame Tussauds, require paid admission. (See Part Five for details.) The other four are the Smithsonian's American Art Museum and National Portrait Gallery; the National Building Museum; and Ford's Theater and the Peterson House. The area between Sixth and 10th streets in particular is referred to as Penn Quarter (as in Pennsylvania Avenue, its southern border), which is full of department stores, shops, street vendors, and boutique hotels; the sparkling new Harmon Center for the Arts, home to the acclaimed Shakespeare Theatre Company, and its sibling Lansburgh Theater around the corner; the tiny remnant of the old Chinatown; and the Washington Convention Center. It's also far and away the trendiest restaurant scene in the region; while its western edge, the longtime lobbyist-and-lawyer district, around K and 14th Streets NW, is becoming a high-profile and high-tab nightclub strip.

Foggy Bottom

Located west of the White House, Foggy Bottom got its name from the swampy land on which it was built. And no, it's not true that foreign dignitaries received hazardous duty pay for working here. Today, the neighborhood is home to George Washington University, the U.S. Department of State ("Foggy Bottom" is journalese for "State"), the Daughters of the American Revolution and Decatur House museums, the Kennedy Center for the Performing Arts, the International Monetary Fund (which makes this the center of almost routine street protests), and, for political junkies, the Watergate Hotel. Closer to the Mall, massive government office complexes house the Department of the Interior and the Federal Reserve.

Georgetown

A river port long before Washington was built, famous in the '60s and '70s as home to the political establishment/journalism elite (thanks to the charisma of local residents JFK and Jackie), and in the '80s and '90s as a nightlife center, Georgetown is now less cutting-edge boutique than college-fashion supermall. From a distance, Georgetown is immediately identifiable by its skyline of spires. The neighborhood of restored town houses is filled with crowded bars and (increasingly) familiar name brand shops—though its ornate shopping mall is under-occupied—and the streets pulse with crowds late into the night. An overflow of suburban teens on weekends makes for traffic congestion that's intense, even by Washington standards; but it also makes for good people-watching, especially for the under-30 set, and late-night shopping. It's also a good place for antique and trendy furniture shopping (see the "Great Neighborhoods for Shopping" section in Part Seven). Georgetown University marks the neighborhood's western edge. The Chesapeake & Ohio Canal and its famous towpath begin in Georgetown (at the east end, behind the Four Seasons Hotel) and follow the Potomac River upstream for 184 miles to Cumberland, Maryland, with many options for recreation (see Part Nine: Exercise and Recreation for suggestions).

Dupont Circle/Logan Circle/U Street

Dupont Circle is the center of one of the city's most fashionable residential neighborhoods, where you'll find elegantly restored town houses, boutiques, restaurants, cafés, bookstores, and art galleries. (It's also where the inhabitants of MTV's *Real World* took up temporary residence, if that matters to you.) A stroll down Embassy Row (along Massachusetts Avenue) leads past sumptuous embassies and chancelleries, as well as some of Washington's best visitor attractions: Anderson House, the Phillips Collection, and the Woodrow Wilson House. You can recognize an embassy by the national coat-of-arms or flag; a pack of reporters and TV cameras may indicate that international unrest has erupted somewhere in the world.

Although not as well known outside Washington, there are two very hip up-and-coming neighborhoods east of Dupont Circle. Logan Circle/Shaw, a reviving Victorian-era town house region centered around 14th and P streets NW, is home to a number of restaurants, bars, galleries, small theatrical troupes, and the Studio Theatre. It's also where the former home (now museum) of National Council of Negro Women founder, educator, and FDR confidant Mary McLeod Bethune is located, and the neighborhood where Duke Ellington spent the first 25 years of his life.

The "new-U" Street Corridor a little above and centered around 14th and U Streets NW (accessible from the U Street/African-American Civil War Memorial/Cardozo Metro) is partially a revival of what was known in the early 20th century as the Black Broadway, a moniker bestowed by Pearl Bailey. After decades of decline, it's once again a major music district, home to the restored Lincoln Theater and Howard Theater, the Black Cat and the 9:30 Club, Bohemian Caverns and the BYOB HR-57 jazz clubs. Among the more popular restaurants in the area are Busboys and Poets, Marvin (named for soul singer Marvin Gaye), Café Saint-Ex, Etete Ethiopian restaurant, and Ben's Chili Bowl, once famous as Bill Cosby's favorite D.C. eatery and now more famous as the place President Obama hoisted a chili dog and fries. The new-U also houses a number of smart boutiques (see Part Seven: Shopping in Washington for more information).

Incidentally, though the name is rarely used anymore, the area between 16th and 19th Streets NW and Florida Avenue and Swann Street is the Strivers' Section Historic District, which, like Harlem's Strivers' Row, was the home to many influential black businessmen and professionals, including abolitionist Frederick Douglass and poet

Langston Hughes, in whose honor the local-fave restaurant Busboys and Poets is named.

Adams Morgan

One of Washington's oldest ethnic-chic neighborhoods, with a heavy emphasis on Hispanic and African cultures, Adams Morgan is where young and cool bohemians migrated after the price of real estate zoomed around Dupont Circle in the 1970s and 1980s (though it's now in the shadow of newer, more edgy areas to the south and east). While it doesn't offer much in the way of museums or monuments, the neighborhood is full of ethnic restaurants, eclectic shops, and nightclubs. Parking, alas, is a severe problem. (See a guy standing in a vacant slot? Wave a couple of bucks at him and he'll let you in, and believe us, it's worth that tiny shakedown.) The nearest subway stop is Woodley Park–National Zoo–Adams Morgan, an eight- to ten-minute walk over the Rock Creek Park bridge; depending on the hour or how long you've been walking, you might want to take a cab.

If you hear the term "Columbia Heights," it refers to a rapidly gentrifying neighborhood a little to the northeast of Adams Morgan, following Columbia Road toward Howard University. It's quickly redeveloping around the Columbia Heights Metro station, a Target and Best Buy, and other large retailers and restaurants; its cultural landmarks include the Tivoli Theatre, a former movie palace now home to GALA Hispanic Theatre; the Dance Institute of Washington, just across the street from the Tivoli; and several foreign embassies.

Upper Northwest

Though it sounds a somewhat loose designation, covering everything between Georgetown and Dupont Circle and Friendship Heights, it's immediately recognizable to locals as referring in general to the most affluent quadrant of the city, home to members of Congress, foreign representatives, lobbyists, old-line Washingtonians, and attorneys. This is also where you'll find the Washington National Cathedral, the National Zoo, the Hillwood Museum, the city's best private schools, and so on. Some of the city's most beautiful Victorian homes are in Cleveland Park and Woodley Park (both of which have their own Metro-centered restaurant rows). Other neighborhood names you'll hear from this area are Glover Park, just north of Georgetown; Tenleytown and American University Park above that; and Van Ness, where the University of the District of Columbia is headquartered.

Rock Creek Park

Though it's not a neighborhood per se, the great swath of Rock Creek Park—more than twice as large as New York's Central Park—is one of the great recreational assets of the area. Within its borders are the Carter Barron Amphitheatre, site of many summer concerts; the Fitzgerald Tennis Center, where the top pro–level Legg-Mason tennis tournament is held (and home to 25 clay and hard-surface public courts); a planetarium, equestrian center, golf course, numerous playgrounds, picnic areas, hiking trails, and so on. For more information see Part Nine or go to **www.nps.gov/rocr/**.

Friendship Heights/Chevy Chase

At the five-way intersection of Wisconsin Avenue, Military Road, and Western Avenue, which marks the division between the District of Columbia and the state of Maryland, is the newly revitalized—gilded might a better term—neighborhood centered on the Friendship Heights Metro. This is now a major shopping area, housing not only several malls but also the luxurious Collection at Chevy Chase (the mini-Fifth Avenue of Washington, a must for jewelry addicts in particular). It's also sprouting restaurants, partly to keep up with the sleek new condominium developments; and, should you need to know, home to many medical offices and senior residences as well. See Part Seven: Shopping in Washington for more on this area. (Chevy Chase is actually the neighborhood on the Maryland side of the divide, and a very desirable address.)

Bethesda

You could call Wisconsin Avenue, which becomes Rockville Pike/Route 355 (and eventually Frederick Pike), the Rodeo Drive of Washington—and there have been times when sections of it brought in more retail sales per square foot than that more famous Los Angeles address. (And considering Chevy Chase, it may be true again; see Part Seven: Shopping.) From Georgetown, it runs northwest through Friendship Heights and into Bethesda, long a fairly quiet bedroom community but now a booming young-condo and restaurant site. It's not yet a major draw for out-of-towners, and has little in the way of cultural attractions (mostly sports bars and nightclubs with occasional music), but it does have several large hotels.

Rockville

Continuing up either Route 355 or the Red Line Metro into Maryland, you come to an ambitious new-town/condo development in Rockville that has a lot of mixed-use development buildings and restaurants near the county office buildings, though not so many hotels. Still, it's a busy area for meetings and corporations, and business lunches and cocktails in the neighborhood are quite popular. (Rockville is actually a broad description, including Twinbrook, which has its own Metro, several hotels, and another restaurant and shopping strip; and the reviving White Flint area.)

Clarendon and Ballston

Although not as near to D.C. as Rosslyn, these Northern Virginia suburbs have been redeveloped around Metro stops as trendy and relatively upscale neighborhoods, with lots of condo and apartment developments catering to younger residents, large areas of shopping, and nightclubs.

WHAT *to* **PACK**

WASHINGTON MAY BE A TOURIST TOWN, but it's also an old Southern city, and a cosmopolitan center to boot. Which means that while you'll be tolerated in shorts during the day—and Lord knows you'll be one of many thousands—you might feel a social as well as climatic chill if you wear that Hawaiian shirt to a moderately upscale restaurant for dinner. (Everyone will be too polite to actually comment unless you're a celebrity, in which case you'll be assumed to be making a fashion statement.) After all, most people will still be in office duds—at least long pants, if not suits.

This doesn't mean you have to pack a tuxedo, unless you actually have a formal engagement, but it never hurts to dress up rather than down. A nice sports jacket or even a sweater, for either sex, is not only a way of looking nice but of usefully offsetting either air-conditioning or off-season chill. (Plus, sweaters pack thinner than sweatshirts.)

In general, shorts and polo shirts are fine for day close to half the year (spring and fall are temperate times); a sundress or reasonably neat pair of khakis will make you look downright respectable. A rainproof top of some sort, a lightweight jacket and/or sweater may be all you'll need in the summer.

(It's unhappily true that several of the restaurants that for many years clung to a respectable dress code are retreating. The Prime Rib no longer requires a tie, for example, and several upscale spots now list jackets for gentleman as "requested" rather than "required." But as yet, women in anything nicer than a pub will be hard-pressed to feel comfortable in shorts in the evening, unless they're rhinestone-studded; Corduroy, a popular restaurant across from the Washington Convention Center, stocks wraparound skirts as well as extra sports jackets. In this as in most things, it's better and easier to be safe than to be sorry.)

In winter, you can probably get by with something along the lines of a trench coat with a zip-in lining or a wool walking coat with a sweater. Though they're not much of a protest target these days, fur coats are only likely to be necessary in January or February; and with the hassle of dealing with them on limited-carry-on planes these days (not to mention the choice of checking them at every stop or hauling them around), it's really not worth the effort unless you're staying for some time. Gloves and hats are important, of course, but when choosing headgear make sure to bring something that won't streak colors down your neck or blow off. (You think that doesn't happen? Trust us; it's no Chicago, but the city has some wind tunnels.) And no matter how accustomed you are to wearing that damn ball cap, take it off indoors. *Please.* It's rude in a restaurant, and even a small brim can block someone else's view in a gallery.

Women will find a heavy scarf or shawl a good interim layer in fall, and it will stand in as a sweater (or throw, or seat cushion) in emergencies. Men and women both should take not just polite little pocket squares but decent-sized handkerchiefs or bandanas: they make good seat covers and sun protectors as well as forehead moppers. And both might also seriously consider elastic waistbands, although they don't have to be obvious ones. Even tourists who don't eat a lot may be unhappily surprised by the bloating effects of travel, heat, coffee treats, extra cocktails, etc.

If possible, we recommend you pack any prescription medicines either in their labeled bottles or, if they're too large, in smaller containers but with photocopies of the prescriptions, in your carry-on luggage. If you can't fit, make sure to pack at least as much as you will need for 36 hours in case your packed bag gets lost. The other reason to carry photocopies of the prescriptions is that if the medicine is truly lost or damaged, you can get a pharmacist to confer with your doctor back home and replace or refill it.

unofficial **TIP**
A penlight and magnifying reading glasses may come in handy for perusing small or dimly lit art or museum captions. And if you're staying in a medium-level or basic bargain hotel, a small sewing kit and mini-multi-tool gadget might be really helpful. Just don't try to carry it on board an airplane.

Similarly, if you wear spectacles or contact lenses, pack an extra pair. Sunglasses you can buy on the street.

As for the larger bag, you should definitely pack travel-sized over-the-counter headache and stomach-upset medications. If you're allergic to beestings, don't forget the antihistamines. Though there are no-smoking laws for interiors, there are still plenty of sidewalk smokers, so if you react to that, carry asthma or allergy meds as well. (Washington is famous for people who say, "I never had allergies until I moved here," so be warned—especially in the spring, D.C. is as much pollen central as politico center.)

If you plan to walk a lot, especially in hot weather, you should pack double sets of thin socks rather than wear too-thick ones; also, carry some precut moleskin bandages—they offer the best possible protection, stick great, and won't sweat off.

Zippered plastic bags are one of the great inventions of humanity: they keep dry clothes dry and wet clothes separated, keep your underwear together so the luggage inspector doesn't have to sort through them, prevent jewelry from tarnishing, and prevent shampoos and lotions from leaking. Those stain-removing pens or packets can be very helpful, too.

Frankly, the most important thing to consider when packing is comfortable shoes, and more than one pair of them. This is a culture of concrete and marble, and even if you are using one of the trolleys or shuttles, you're likely to be standing about at monuments and in museums quite a bit. Wearing walking or running shoes during the day is fine—although if you haven't noticed, super-thick high-tops are hotter than Hades—but don't think you're necessarily going to want to pull on those high heels or shiny lace-ups at the end of a long day of sightseeing. Pick your evening shoes (or boots) with reasonable comfort in mind.

Finally, as longtime travelers, we can assure you that the most common mistake tourists make is packing too much—expecting to wear a different outfit every day (and evening). As obvious as those efficient-packing tips in magazines may be—pick a basic color and a few accessories or ties, pack non-wrinkling fabrics, etc.—an astounding number of travelers still can't seem to be convinced not to pack an entire outfit for every meal. Seriously, do you change clothes three times a day? In any case, you're a visitor here—nobody is going to know if you wear the same shirt twice, or the same jeans or khakis. (In fact, the waste-not mini-wardrobe is quite trendy these days.) Little black dress? Maybe, but also think little black skirt—something thin that folds flat. If you do overpack, you're just going to have to lug a heavier suitcase around. Why do you think they call it luggage? And besides, you're probably going to buy a souvenir T-shirt anyway.

TRAVELING *with* CHILDREN
(and Perhaps Grandparents)

MOST VISITORS TO WASHINGTON, whether citizens of the United States or elsewhere, can't help but be impressed and moved when they see such international icons as the U.S. Capitol, the Washington Monument, and the White House. (It's how Americans feel seeing the Eiffel Tower or Westminster Abbey.) And it's a city with almost more all-ages attractions than can be experienced in a school year, much less a spring break. From the President's House to President Kennedy's eternal flame, from the Wright Brothers' biplane to moon rocks, from giant pandas to mounted police, Washington is as much playground as political sanctum.

But there are a few extra factors to consider if you are planning a family vacation, especially with small children (or in some cases, seniors). In particular, you should realize that while there are specific sights that delight toddlers and preschoolers, Washington's attractions are generally oriented to older kids and adults. We believe that children should be a fairly mature 8 years old to get the most out of popular attractions such as the National Museum of Natural History and the Air and Space Museum, and a year or two older to get much out of the art galleries, monuments, and other federal buildings around town. Parents may well be inured to breakdowns and tantrums, but not everyone is. (And as someone whose legs bear the scars of numerous strollers being wielded as weapons by families in must-see exhibitions, Eve begs that you take this seriously.)

In the in-depth profiles of Washington's major attractions in Part Five, we include—right up top—the age groups we think will find each site interesting, and to what degree.

We already pointed out that it's more pleasant if you can avoid the hottest, most crowded months, but it's even more of a consideration if you are traveling with small, easily tired and fractious children. Try to go in late September through November, or mid-April through mid-June. If you have children of varying ages and your school-age kids are good students, consider taking the older ones out of school so you can visit during the cooler, less-congested off-season. Ask their teachers if you can arrange special study assignments so that the visit to Washington isn't just "time off." If your children can't afford to miss school or their various teams and extra-curricular activities, take your vacation as soon as the school year ends in late May or early June. Of course, if your kids are in high school, they may be spending spring break with their classmates and a few thousand other class tours anyway.

Again, especially if your children are younger, you should consider seeing some attractions first thing in the morning and returning to your hotel midday for a swim—if your hotel has a pool, that is—and/or a nap. (A lot of visitors to D.C. assume that, considering the climate, Washington hotels automatically come with a pool, but unhappily, too many do not. Be sure to ask before making hotel reservations or check our hotel information chart and the list of public pools in Part Nine: Exercise and Recreation.) Even during the fall and winter, when the crowds are smaller and the temperature more pleasant, the sheer size of D.C. will exhaust many children, and adults, by lunchtime. Go back and visit more attractions in the late afternoon and early evening.

If you are traveling with children, you won't be able to afford as much time (meaning, energy) commuting to and from downtown as you will traveling with other adults. (And again, it will be harder to get back to your hotel midday or at an unexpected breakdown time.) So you may want to stay inside the District and near a Metro station. The two major areas for sightseeing, especially with kids, are the Mall and the nearby Penn Quarter, so look for accommodations in or near those areas. The older the children, the farther out from downtown you can safely stay.

The best way to avoid arguments and disappointments is to develop a game plan before you go. Establish some general guidelines for the day and get everybody committed in advance. Be sure to include:

1. Wake-up time and breakfast plans.
2. What time you need to depart for the part of Washington you plan to explore.
3. What you need to take with you.

4. A policy for splitting the group up or for staying together.
5. A plan for what to do if the group gets separated or someone is lost. (This is obviously easier in the cell phone age, but only if everyone is carrying one—and if nobody is in a no-phone or no-signal zone.) For instance, tell small children to look for uniformed guards or information desks, the Lost and Found, etc.
6. How long you intend to be out and what you want to see, including fallback plans in the event an attraction is too crowded.
7. A policy on what you can afford for snacks, lunch, and refreshments.
8. A target time for returning to your hotel to rest, change clothes, etc.
9. What time you want to go back out and how late you will stay.
10. Plans for dinner.
11. A policy for shopping and buying souvenirs, including who pays.

Despite these precautions, families become separated, especially in crowded spaces. Consider dressing young children in a distinctive color T-shirt and sewing a label into each child's shirt that states his or her name, your name, and the name of your hotel. (The same thing can be accomplished less elegantly by writing the information on a strip of masking tape: hotel security professionals suggest that the information be printed in small letters and that the tape be affixed to the outside of the child's shirt five inches or so below the armpit.)

Children are more susceptible than adults to overheating, sunburn, and dehydration. A small bottle of sunscreen will help you take precautions against overexposure to the sun. Be sure to put some on children in strollers, even if the stroller has a canopy. Some of the worst cases of sunburn we have seen were on the exposed foreheads and feet of toddlers and infants in strollers. (That, and the back of the neck of their fathers.) To avoid overheating, rest at regular intervals in the shade or in an air-conditioned museum, hotel lobby, or federal building. Also, since small children don't always tell their parents about a developing blister until it's too late, consider using some of those breaks to check their feet.

Similarly, excited children may not inform you or even realize that they're thirsty or overheated. Carry plastic water bottles (there are plenty of vendors, but you should hold off on spending the extra money for when you can't find a fountain), keep the kids drinking, and always follow the Chicago rule: drink early and often. You, too.

TIPS *for* INTERNATIONAL TRAVELERS

VISITORS FROM WESTERN EUROPE, the United Kingdom, Japan, or New Zealand who stay in the United States fewer than 90 days need only a valid, machine-readable passport, not a visa; and a round-trip or return ticket. Canadian citizens need a passport if arriving by air, but most do not need a visa to enter the United States (though if you have any doubts, you can certainly apply for one). Canadian visitors' passports do not have to be machine-readable. If arriving by land or sea, Canadian citizens can get by with an Enhanced Driver's License, Enhanced ID, or Trusted Traveler Program or Registered Traveler card. Citizens of other countries must have a passport good for at least six months beyond the projected end of the visit, and a tourist visa as well, available from any U.S. consulate. Contact consular officials for application forms; some airlines and travel agents may also have forms available.

If you are taking prescription drugs that contain narcotics or require injection by syringe, be sure to get a doctor's signed prescription and instructions (good advice for all travelers). Restrictions on HIV-positive visitors have been lifted, but again, make sure all syringes are sterile and intact. Pacemakers, metal implants, and surgical pins may set off security machines, so a letter from your doctor describing your condition is a wise precaution (again, this applies to domestic travelers as well). Also check with the local consulate to see whether travelers from your country are currently required to have any inoculations; there are no set requirements to enter the United States, but if there has been any sort of epidemic in your homeland, there may be temporary restrictions.

International visitors should also remember that the United States does not have a national medical program and that if medical treatment is required it will have to be paid for; you may wish to investigate medical and/or travel insurance. However, throughout the United States, if you have a medical, police, or fire emergency, dial ☎ 911, free even on a pay telephone, and an ambulance or police cruiser will be dispatched to help you. (For non-emergency police aid, dial ☎ 311.) You can also contact the Traveler's Aid Society International at ☎ 202-546-1127 (**www.travelersaid.org**).

If you arrive by air, be prepared to spend as much as two hours entering the country and getting through U.S. Customs. Canadians and Mexicans crossing the borders either by car or by train will find a much quicker and easier system. Every adult traveler may bring in, duty-free, up to 1 liter of wine or hard liquor; 200 cigarettes, 100 non-Cuban cigars, or 3 pounds of loose tobacco; and $100 worth of gifts, as well as up to $10,000 in U.S. currency or its equivalent in foreign currency. No food or plants may be brought in, and the contents of personal laptops and other electronic devices may be examined. For information on sales tax refunds, see Part Seven: Shopping in Washington.

Credit cards are by far the most common form of payment in Washington, especially American Express, VISA (also known as Barclaycard in Britain), and MasterCard (Access in Britain, Eurocard in Western Europe, and Chargex in Canada). Other popular cards include Diners Club and Discover. Traveler's checks will be accepted at most hotels and restaurants if they are in American dollars; other currencies should be taken to a bank or foreign exchange and turned into dollars.

The dollar is the basic unit of monetary exchange, and the entire system is decimal. The smaller sums are represented by coins. One hundred cents (or pennies, as the 1-cent coin is known) equal one dollar; 5 cents is a nickel (20 nickels to a dollar); 10 cents is called a dime (10 dimes to a dollar); and the 25-cent coin is called a quarter (4 quarters to a dollar). There are two types of dollar coins—Sacagawea and presidential. Both are nearly the same size as the quarter but are gold in color, not silver, so they are easily distinguished. Beginning with one dollar, money is in currency bills (there are both one-dollar coins and bills). Bills come in $1, $2 (uncommon), $5, $10, $20, $50, $100, $500, and so on, although you are unlikely to want to carry $1,000 or more. Stick to $20s for taxicabs and such; drivers rarely can make change for anything larger.

One last reminder: Although there have been attempts to lower the legal drinking age in the United States to 18, at press time it remains at 21, something many European travelers forget. And again, we remind you that most of Washington's restaurants and all of its cultural facilities are nonsmoking venues.

TRAVELERS *with* SPECIAL NEEDS

WASHINGTON IS ONE OF THE MOST ACCESSIBLE CITIES in the world for those with disabilities. With the equal-opportunity federal government as the major employer in the area, Washington provides a good job market for disabled people. As a result, the service sector—bus drivers, waiters, ticket sellers, retail clerks, cab drivers, tour guides, and so on—are somewhat more attuned to the needs of people with disabilities than are service-sector employees in other cities. It doesn't hurt that a number of organizations that lobby for physically challenged people are headquartered in Washington.

The White House, for instance, has a special entrance on Pennsylvania Avenue for tourists using wheelchairs (you can also borrow one there), and White House guides frequently allow visually impaired visitors to touch some of the items described during the tour. Go to the website at **www.nps.gov/whho/planyourvisit/accessibility.htm** for more information. The U.S. Capitol offers a variety of special services, including wheelchair loans, interpreters for the hearing impaired, Braille and large-type brochures and sensory aides; go to **www.visitthecapitol.gov** and select "Visitors with Disabilities" for information.

The Metro was designed to meet federal standards for accessibility from the beginning. As a result, the stations and trains provide optimal services to a wide array of people with special requirements. Elevators provide access to the mezzanine, or ticketing areas platform, and street level; call the Metro's 24-hour elevator hotline at ☎ 202-962-1825 to check if the elevators at the stations you plan to use are operating. When elevators are out of service (and Metro is constantly struggling with mechanical timeouts and repairs), shuttle buses are provided between the stations that bookend the outage; but depending on your stamina or comfort, you may not wish to go that route.

The edge of the train platform is built with a 14-inch smooth, light-gray granite strip that's different in texture from the rest of the station's flooring so that visually impaired passengers can detect the platform edge with a foot or cane. Flashing lights embedded in the granite strip alert hearing-impaired passengers that a train is entering the station. Handicapped-only parking spaces are placed close to station entrances. While purchasing a farecard is a strictly visual process (unless the station is equipped with the talking vending machines), visually impaired passengers can go to the nearby kiosk for assistance. Priority seating for senior citizens and passengers with disabilities is located next to doors in all cars.

unofficial **TIP**
Be aware that in many parts of Washington, particularly Capitol Hill, Dupont Circle, Georgetown, Adams Morgan, and Old Town Alexandria, restaurants, historic house museums, etc. are in older buildings that may not be wheelchair accessible. On the other hand, some that at press time were not accessible may have been renovated by the time you visit. Be sure to check in advance.

Visitors with disabilities who possess a transit ID from their home city can pick up a courtesy Metro ID or half-fare SmarTrip card that provides substantial fare discounts; the ID is good for a month. Schedule an appointment (mandatory) and go to Metro Headquarters, 600 Fifth Street NW, from 8 a.m. to 4 p.m. weekdays (until 2:30 p.m. Tuesdays) to pick one up; call ☎ 202-962-1245 or visit **www .wmata.com/accessibility** for more information. If you want to ride the Metro to get there, the nearest station is Judiciary Square (F Street exit), a half block away. For a free guide with information on Metro's rail and bus system for the elderly and physically disabled, call ☎ 202-637-1328. To request forms for fare discounts, contact the Office of ADA Programs at ☎ 202-962-1100. They also offer system orientations for individuals or groups on using the rail and bus system.

The Smithsonian and the National Park Service, agencies that run the lion's share of popular sights in Washington, offer top-notch services to people with disabilities. Museums are equipped with entrance ramps, barrier-free exhibits, elevator service to all floors, and accessible restrooms and water fountains. (There are some designated handicapped parking spaces located along Jefferson Drive on the Mall, though they fill up quickly.) Visually impaired visitors can pick up large-print brochures, audio tours, and raised-line drawings of museum artifacts at many Smithsonian museums. For special tours or information about accessibility for visitors with disabilities, contact the individual museum or the Smithsonian Accessibility Office at ☎ 888-783-0001 or 202-633-2921; more information is available also at **www.si.edu.** For a copy of the National Zoo's guide for disabled visitors call ☎ 202-633-4480.

Public telephones at the National Air and Space Museum are equipped with amplification, and the briefing room is equipped with audio loop.

Tourmobile offers a special van equipped with a wheelchair and scooter lift for disabled visitors. The van visits all the regular sites on the tour; in fact, visitors can usually specify what sites they want to see in any order during regular tour hours, and the van will wait until they are finished touring. The service is the same price as the standard Tourmobile rate ($27 for adults and $13 for children). Call ☎ 703-979-0690 at least a day in advance to reserve a van. Information is available at **www.tourmobile.com.**

In spite of all the services available to disabled visitors, it's still a good idea to call ahead to any facility you plan to visit and confirm that services are in place and that the particular exhibit or gallery you wish to see is still available.

International visitors to Washington who would like a tour conducted in their native language can contact the Guide Service of Washington (see "Get Up Close and Personal" on page 150).

PICKING *a* FLIGHT PLAN
(or Not)

PEOPLE PLANNING A TRIP TO OUR NATION'S CAPITAL have several options when it comes to getting there: by car, train, bus, or plane. We explore these in detail in Part Four: Getting In and Getting Around, but here are some quick points:

- A lot of people who live within a 12-hour drive of Washington assume that the car is the easiest mode of transportation, which seems to make sense, as a number of state and interstate highways converge on or near there. However, there are two major road-blocks: the notorious Capital Beltway, which surrounds the city in the Maryland and Virginia suburbs and is only slightly less congested than New York and Los Angeles; and the road map inside the Beltway, a seemingly logical grid overturned with diagonals, traffic circles, one-way streets, massive construction, and reversible lanes.

Street parking near popular tourist sites is severely limited, and garage parking is expensive and often inconvenient. Our recommendation: If at all possible, leave the car at home. Washington's air-and-rail connections are excellent, and its Metro subway system is one of the best in the world. And where the Metro won't take you—Georgetown, Mount Vernon, and the Washington National Cathedral—plentiful cabs, shuttle buses, and commercial touring outfits will. If you do drive, park it and forget it until you leave.

- Washington's gleaming Union Station, the city's most visited tourist attraction (the National Air and Space Museum is number two), is the second-best reason to take the train; the best is convenience. East Coast cities from Boston to Miami are served daily by Amtrak, and lots of people living east of the Mississippi are close to direct rail service into the nation's capital. In some cases you can board the train in the evening and arrive in Washington in the morning. From Union Station you're only minutes from a downtown hotel by subway—the Union Station Metro is right alongside the tracks and covered from the weather—or, if your hotel isn't near a Metro stop, you can easily hail a cab.

- If you're looking for a bargain, let someone else do the driving. There are a number of well-equipped, inexpensive, and easily booked bus lines these days, and they are *not* your grandfather's Greyhound.

- Washington is understandably well served by the airline industry. (Would you want to annoy either the Congress members who hold the purse strings or the federal regulators?) Ronald Reagan Washington National Airport is the closest, and has a dedicated Metro station, but its very proximity to the city means that it has limited hours of operation and the size of air vehicles allowed to use it are also limited. Dulles International Airport is about 45–60 minutes outside town, and although a Metro link is under construction, for the time being you'll have to take a cab or shuttle bus. Baltimore/Washington International Thurgood Marshall Airport, universally known as BWI, is a little closer to Baltimore than to D.C., but it is accessible by commuter trains and Amtrak as well as cabs. In many cases, using the train to BWI rather than one of the closer-in airports will save you money; see Part Four for full details.

A **CALENDAR** *of* FESTIVALS *and* EVENTS

January

WASHINGTON RESTAURANT WEEK EARLY TO MID-JANUARY. More than 150 restaurants offer fixed-price lunch ($20) and dinner ($35) menus; **www.washington.org/restaurantwk.**

February

CHINESE NEW YEAR PARADE EARLY FEBRUARY TO EARLY MARCH. Marching bands, lion and dragon dancers, and other performers celebrate through Chinatown and around Verizon Center; ☎ 202-393-7838.

WASHINGTON, D.C. INTERNATIONAL WINE AND FOOD FESTIVAL MID-FEBRUARY. Sample wines from around the world and watch demonstrations by celebrity chefs at the Ronald Reagan Building and International Trade Center; tickets required; ☎ 888-665-6069; **www.wineandfooddc.com.**

ABRAHAM LINCOLN'S BIRTHDAY FEBRUARY 12. A wreath-laying ceremony, music, and a dramatic reading of the Gettysburg Address at the Lincoln Memorial; ☎ 202-619-7222; **www.nps.gov/linc.**

FREDERICK DOUGLASS'S BIRTHDAY FEBRUARY 14. A wreath-laying ceremony, musical tributes, and other activities honor the birthday anniversary of the abolitionist leader at Cedar Hill, the Frederick Douglass National Historic Site; ☎ 202-426-5961; **www.nps.gov/frdo.**

GEORGE WASHINGTON'S BIRTHDAY MID-FEBRUARY. Mount Vernon celebrates the first president's birthday anniversary with parades and a sample of Washington's favorite breakfast, "hoecakes swimming in butter and honey"; music; and a wreath-laying ceremony; ☎ 703-780-2000; **www.mountvernon.org.**

WASHINGTON'S BIRTHDAY PARADE MID-FEBRUARY. The nation's largest, with marching bands, floats, military reenactors, and other units on the streets of Old Town Alexandria; ☎ 703-991-4474; **www.washingtonbirthday.net.**

March

WASHINGTON ANTIQUARIAN BOOK FAIR FIRST WEEKEND. About 75 exhibitors from across the United States offer rare books, manuscripts, documents, maps, and other memorabilia in this annual benefit for Concord Hill School at the Holiday Inn Rosslyn, 1900 North Fort Myer Drive, Arlington; ☎ 301-654-2626; **www.wabf.com.**

ALEXANDRIA ST. PATRICK'S DAY PARADE FIRST SATURDAY. The annual parade of floats, bands, Irish dancers, and other units through the streets of Old Town Alexandria; ☎ 703-237-2199 or 703-838-5005; **www.ballyshaners.org.**

WASHINGTON, D.C. ST. PATRICK'S DAY PARADE SUNDAY BEFORE MARCH 17. Dancers, bagpipers, and marching bands salute Ireland and all things Irish along Constitution Avenue NW from Seventh to 17th streets; ☎ 202-619-7222; **www.dcstpatsparade.com.**

SMITHSONIAN KITE FESTIVAL LATE MARCH. The Smithsonian Associates and NASM host a free annual festival on the Mall with competitions in design, performance, and other categories; ☎ 202-633-3030 or 202-619-7222; **www.kitefestival.org.**

NATIONAL CHERRY BLOSSOM FESTIVAL LATE MARCH TO EARLY APRIL. The blooming cherry trees surrounding the Tidal Basin are the centerpiece of this annual two-week festival of concerts, cooking and dance demonstrations, art, children's activities, and restaurant specials. Also featured are the Parade of the annual National Cherry Blossom Festival along Constitution Avenue NW and the Sakura Matsuri Street Festival on Pennsylvania Avenue; ☎ 877-442-5666 or 202-619-7222; **www.nationalcherryblossomfestival.org.**

WHITE HOUSE EASTER EGG ROLL LATE MARCH TO MID-APRIL, ALWAYS THE MONDAY AFTER EASTER. Colored-egg collecting and entertainment held Easter Monday, rain or shine. Open to children age 12 and younger and their families; children must be accompanied by adults. Free tickets are distributed through an online lottery system; ☎ 202-456-2200; **www.whitehouse.gov/easterEggRoll.**

AFRICAN AMERICAN FAMILY CELEBRATION LATE MARCH TO MID-APRIL. The free annual Easter Monday jubilee offers an Easter egg hunt, gospel music, storytellers, and food vendors at the National Zoo; ☎ 202-633-4800; **nationalzoo.si.edu.**

April

THOMAS JEFFERSON'S BIRTHDAY APRIL 13. Speakers, a military honor guard, and a wreath-laying ceremony mark the birthday anniversary of the third president, noon at the Jefferson Memorial; ☎ 202-426-6841; **www.nps.gov/thje.**

WHITE HOUSE SPRING GARDEN TOURS MID-APRIL (weather permitting). Free, timed tickets distributed each day on first-come basis at Ellipse Visitor Pavilion, 15th and E streets NW, at 7:30 a.m.; ☎ 202-456-2200 or 202-208-1631; **www.whitehouse.gov.**

WASHINGTON INTERNATIONAL FILM FESTIVAL MID- TO LATE APRIL. Scores of new American and foreign films are screened in theaters across town during the annual Filmfest D.C.; ☎ 202-234-FILM (3456); **www.filmfestdc.org.**

SMITHSONIAN CRAFT SHOW MID- TO LATE APRIL. About 120 artists and artisans display their museum-quality creations in 12 juried media categories at the National Building Museum; ☎ 888-832-9554 or 202-633-5006; **www.smithsoniancraftshow.com.**

EARTH DAY LATE APRIL. Earth Day is actually April 22, but the celebration on the Mall, one of the nation's largest, is generally the weekend closest to that date. Music, demonstrations of green technology, celebrity speakers, and vendors; ☎ 202-518-0044; **www.earthday.net.**

SHAKESPEARE'S BIRTHDAY THE CLOSEST SUNDAY TO APRIL 23. Annual open house with free cake, children's activities, theater tours, dramatic readings, medieval crafts, and entertainment at the Folger Shakespeare Library; ☎ 202-544-4600; **www.folger.edu.**

MARYLAND DAY LAST SATURDAY. The University of Maryland holds a free open house with exhibits, lectures, demonstrations, tours, and performances throughout the campus in College Park; ☎ 877-868-3777 or 301-405-1000; **www.marylandday.umd.edu.**

GEORGETOWN HOUSE TOUR LAST SATURDAY. Tour private homes in Washington's Georgetown district; ☎ 202-338-1796; **www.george townhousetour.com.**

May

VIRGINIA GOLD CUP FIRST SATURDAY. Annual running of this popular, classic steeplechase race at Great Meadow near The Plains, Virginia; ☎ 540-347-1215; **www.vagoldcup.com.**

CHESAPEAKE BAY BRIDGE WALK FIRST SUNDAY (weather permitting). 4.3-mile Chesapeake Bay Bridge is closed to vehicles for pedestrian crossing. *Note:* the event was cancelled in 2010 due to construction and budgetary reasons; ☎ 410-537-1017; **www.baybridge.com.**

MOUNT VERNON'S SPRING GARDEN PARTY MID-MAY. Celebrate spring at the first president's estate with music, wagon rides, and gardening demonstrations; ☎ 703-780-2000; **www.mountvernon.org.**

MARY LOU WILLIAMS WOMEN IN JAZZ FESTIVAL MID-MAY. Performances at multiple stages at The Kennedy Center; ☎ 202-467-4600 or 800-444-1324; **www.kennedy-center.org/programs/jazz/womeninjazz.**

NATIONAL ZOO ZOOFARI MID-MAY. This annual fund-raising gala features tastings by more than 100 area restaurants, international wines, entertainment, animal demonstrations, and a silent auction at the National Zoo; ☎ 202-633-4800; **nationalzoo.si.edu.**

MOUNT VERNON SPRING WINE FESTIVAL AND SUNSET TOUR MID- TO LATE MAY. Taste wines from Virginia vineyards, learn more about George Washington's winemaking efforts, and enjoy live jazz at the first president's estate. Tickets are required, and advance purchase is recommended; ☎ 202-397-7328 (tickets) or 703-780-2000 (information); **www.mountvernon.org.**

D.C. CHILI COOK OFF MID-MAY. The area's leading chili chefs compete for a place in the International Chili Society's world championships, featuring music and other food and refreshments at the RFK Stadium parking lot; ☎ 202-244-7900; **www.kidneywdc.org.**

PREAKNESS STAKES THIRD SATURDAY. Running of the second jewel in thoroughbred horse racing's Triple Crown at Pimlico Race Course in Baltimore; ☎ 410-542-9400; **www.preakness.com.**

JOINT SERVICE OPEN HOUSE AND AIR SHOW ARMED FORCES WEEK-END, MID- TO LATE MAY. Aerial demonstrations by precision flying teams and other aircraft, a mass paratroop drop, sky diving by the Golden Knights, and ground displays of vintage and modern warplanes are featured at Andrews Air Force Base; ☎ 301-981-4600; **www.jsoh.org.**

ROCKVILLE HOMETOWN HOLIDAYS LAST WEEKEND. Three-day street festival in Rockville includes Memorial Day parade, Rockville restaurant vendors, children's activities, and local and national entertainers; **www.rockvillemd.gov.**

NATIONAL MEMORIAL DAY CONCERT LAST SUNDAY. The National Symphony Orchestra and guest performers from Broadway, pop, R&B, country music, and more in a free concert on the West Lawn of the U.S. Capitol; ☎ 202-619-7222.

MEMORIAL DAY CEREMONIES LAST MONDAY. Commemorative events and wreath layings are scheduled at Arlington National Cemetery, the Vietnam Veterans Memorial, World War II Memorial, National Law Enforcement Officers Memorial, Navy Memorial, Air Force Memorial, and the Women in Military Service for America Memorial; ☎ 202-619-7222.

NATIONAL MEMORIAL DAY PARADE LAST MONDAY. Marching bands and veteran units from all over the country parade down Constitution Avenue; ☎ 703-302-1012.

MEMORIAL DAY NAVY BAND CONCERT LAST MONDAY. The U.S. Navy Band performs a free concert at the U.S. Navy Memorial; ☎ 202-433-2525; **www.navyband.navy.mil.**

June

UPPERVILLE COLT AND HORSE SHOW EARLY JUNE. More than 1,000 horse-and-rider teams compete in the nation's oldest jumpers competition (more than 150 years old) at the show grounds in Upperville, Virginia; ☎ 540-687-5740, or 540-592-3858 during show only; **www .upperville.com.**

D.C. JAZZ FESTIVAL EARLY TO MID-JUNE. More than 100 concerts at nearly 50 venues around town, including the Kennedy Center and the Mall; ☎ 202-232-3611; **www.dcjazzfest.org.**

U.S. OPEN JUNE 13–19. The second of the four major professional golf tournaments will be played at Bethesda's Congressional Country Club in 2011; **www.usopen.com.**

COLUMBIA FESTIVAL OF THE ARTS MID-JUNE. International, national, and regional music, stage, and dance stars perform over two weeks at venues throughout the city of Columbia; ☎ 410-715-3044; **www.columbiafestival.com.**

CAPITAL PRIDE FESTIVAL MID-JUNE. A parade Saturday in the Dupont Circle area and a street festival Sunday along Pennsylvania Avenue with crafts and food vendors winding up a weeklong celebration by the area's gay, lesbian, bisexual, and transgender residents; ☎ 202-797-5304; **www.capitalpride.org.**

ANTIQUE AND CLASSIC BOAT FESTIVAL MID-JUNE. Displays of antique and classic boats, wooden boat building demonstrations, artists and artisans, a crafts fair, music, and food vendors at the Chesapeake Bay Maritime Museum in St. Michaels, Maryland; ☎ 410-745-2916; **www.chesapeakebayacbs.net.**

SAFEWAY'S NATIONAL CAPITAL BARBECUE BATTLE LATE JUNE. Teams from across the country compete to win prizes for best barbecued pork, chicken, and beef. Entertainment on multiple stages, cooking demonstrations by celebrity chefs, children's activities, and food vendors, along Pennsylvania Avenue between Ninth and 14th streets NW; purchase tickets in advance to avoid lines; ☎ 202-828-3099; **www.bbqdc.com.**

D.C. CARIBBEAN CARNIVAL LATE JUNE. Parade along Georgia Avenue NW Corridor on Saturday winds up near Howard University with food, dance, arts and crafts, and entertainment; festival continues Sunday; ☎ 202-726-2204; **www.dccaribbeancarnival.org.**

SMITHSONIAN FOLKLIFE FESTIVAL LATE JUNE TO EARLY JULY. Annual two-week festival celebrates the food, music, arts, and culture of a specific nation, region, state, or theme; on the Mall between Seventh and 14th streets; ☎ 202-633-1000; **www.folklife.si.edu/center/ festival.html.**

July

FOURTH OF JULY CELEBRATION INDEPENDENCE DAY is commemorated with the National Independence Day Parade along Constitution Avenue NW, the "Capitol Fourth" concert by the National Symphony Orchestra, and guest musical celebrities on the West Lawn of the U.S. Capitol, culminating in fireworks over the Washington Monument grounds; ☎ 800-215-6405; **www.july4thparade.com.**

WASHINGTON KASTLES THROUGHOUT JULY. Washington's professional mixed men's and women's World Team Tennis franchise, which has included stars such as Venus and Serena Williams, plays its home matches of the three-week season; ☎ 202-4-TENNIS; **www.washington kastles.com.**

CONTEMPORARY AMERICAN THEATER FESTIVAL SECOND WEEKEND THROUGH THE REST OF THE MONTH. New American plays are performed in rotating repertory at Shepherd University in Shepherdstown, West Virginia; ☎ 304-876-3473; **www.catf.org.**

USA/ALEXANDRIA BIRTHDAY CELEBRATION EARLY TO MID-JULY. The Alexandria Symphony Orchestra celebrates the City of Alexandria's birthday (it's older) and America's birthday with a free concert that includes Tchaikovsky's 1812 Overture with cannon fire followed by fireworks at Oronoco Bay Park on the Potomac; ☎ 703-746-3301; **www.visitalexandriava.com.**

BASTILLE DAY CELEBRATION JULY 14. Live entertainment and a race by tray-bearing waiters and waitresses down Pennsylvania Avenue from 12th Street to the U.S. Capitol and back; ☎ 202-319-1800.

SCREEN ON THE GREEN MID-JULY TO MID-AUGUST. Monday-night outdoor screenings of classic movies on the Mall between Fourth and Seventh streets; ☎ 877-262-5866.

CHINCOTEAGUE PONY SWIM LATE JULY. Wild ponies are rounded up and "herded" across the Assateague Channel for auction in Chincoteague Island, Virginia—the event made famous by "Misty of Chincoteague"; ☎ 757-336-6161; **www.chincoteague.com/pony.**

August

LEGG MASON TENNIS CLASSIC FIRST WEEK. The U.S. Open men's tennis tour (and young women pros) stop at FitzGerald Tennis Center in Rock Creek Park in preparation for New York, complete with top-ranked players; ☎ 202-397-7328 (tickets), ☎ 202-721-9500 (information); **www.leggmasontennisclassic.com.** (*Note:* This and all pre-Open tournaments change dates as Labor Day shifts.)

WASHINGTON RESTAURANT WEEK EARLY TO MID-AUGUST. More than 150 area restaurants offer fixed-price lunch ($20) and dinner ($35) menus; **www.washington.org/restaurantwk.**

COMCAST OUTDOOR FILM FESTIVAL MID-AUGUST. Watch free family feature films on a giant outdoor screen nightly on the lawn of the Universities at Shady Grove in North Bethesda; ☎ 301-816-6958; **www.filmfestnih.org.**

MARYLAND STATE FAIR LATE AUGUST TO LABOR DAY. Huge old-fashioned fair features livestock shows and demonstrations, home and garden exhibits, thoroughbred racing, carnival rides, and entertainment at the Maryland State Fairgrounds in Timonium; ☎ 410-252-0200; **www.marylandstatefair.com.**

MARYLAND RENAISSANCE FESTIVAL LATE AUGUST TO MID-OCTOBER. Entertainment, food, crafts, music, juggling school, and jousting in a re-creation of a 16th-century English village; weekends and Labor Day in Crownsville, just outside Annapolis; ☎ 800-296-7304 or 410-266-7304; **www.rennfest.com.**

September

LABOR DAY CONCERT SUNDAY BEFORE LABOR DAY. National Symphony Orchestra performs a free concert on the West Lawn of the U.S. Capitol; ☎ 202-619-7222.

NAVY BAND CONCERT FIRST MONDAY. The U.S. Navy Band and Sea Chanters commemorate Labor Day with a free concert at the U.S. Navy Memorial; ☎ 202-433-2525; **www.navyband.navy.mil.**

ALEXANDRIA FESTIVAL OF THE ARTS SECOND WEEKEND. An outdoor festival features sculptures, paintings, photography, fused glass, jewelry, and other works by nearly 200 artists and artisans along King Street in Old Town Alexandria; ☎ 703-838-5005 or 703-746-3301; **www.visit alexandriava.com.**

BLACK FAMILY REUNION SECOND WEEKEND. Annual cultural celebration of the African American family, with live entertainment, exhibits, an arts-and-crafts marketplace, and food vendors on the Mall; ☎ 202-737-0120; **www.ncnw.org/events.**

NATIONAL CAPITAL CAT SHOW EARLY SEPTEMBER. More than 500 cats compete in one of the nation's largest feline shows at Dulles Expo Center in Chantilly, Virginia; ☎ 703-378-0910; **www.national capitalcatshow.com.**

SHAKESPEARE THEATRE "FREE FOR ALL" EARLY TO MID-SEPTEMBER. The Shakespeare Theatre Company presents free performances of Shakespeare plays at the troupe's Sidney Harman Hall. Free tickets are distributed day of show; ☎ 202-547-1122 or 202-334-4790; **www.shakespearetheatre.org/about/free.aspx.**

ROSSLYN JAZZ FESTIVAL EARLY TO MID-SEPTEMBER. Daylong free outdoor concerts by local and national jazz stars at Gateway Park (near the Rosslyn Metro station); ☎ 703-276-7759; **www.rosslynva.org.**

KENNEDY CENTER OPEN HOUSE ARTS FESTIVAL MID-SEPTEMBER. Free daylong celebration of music, ballet, theater, storytelling, and other performance arts on multiple stages at The Kennedy Center for the Performing Arts; ☎ 202-467-4600; **www.kennedy-center.org/ openhouse.**

SILVER SPRING JAZZ FESTIVAL MID-SEPTEMBER. Daylong free outdoor concerts by local and national jazz stars at the Silver Spring Civic Building, Veterans Plaza (near Silver Spring Metro station); ☎ 240-777-5300; **www.silverspringdowntown.com.**

ADAMS MORGAN DAY FESTIVAL MID-SEPTEMBER. Daylong celebration of Washington's most famous multicultural neighborhood with entertainment, children's activities, food vendors, and more; ☎ 202-232-1960; **www.adamsmorgandayfestival.com.**

ARTS ON FOOT MID-SEPTEMBER. Free performances, artist demonstrations, cooking demonstrations, hands-on activities, open rehearsals, and theatrical events in Washington's Penn Quarter; ☎ 202-661-7592; **www.artsonfoot.org.**

18TH-CENTURY CRAFT FAIR MID-SEPTEMBER. Crafts displays and demonstrations by artisans in Colonial attire, 18th-century entertainment, food, and children's activities at Mount Vernon; ☎ 703-780-2000; **www.mountvernon.org.**

INTERNATIONAL CHILDREN'S FESTIVAL MID-SEPTEMBER. Children's performers from around the world entertain on multiple stages at Wolf Trap National Park in Vienna, Virginia; ☎ 703-642-0862; **www.internationalchildrensfestival.com.**

KALORAMA HOUSE AND EMBASSY TOUR THIRD SUNDAY. Visit embassies, ambassadors' residences, and other sites; advance purchase only; ☎ 202-387-4062, ext. 18; www.woodrowwilsonhouse.org.

MOUNTAIN HERITAGE ARTS AND CRAFTS FESTIVAL MID- TO LATE SEPTEMBER. Displays by about 200 artists and artisans, music by bluegrass bands, and food vendors; between Charles Town and Harpers Ferry, West Virginia; ☎ 304-725-2055 or 800-624-0577; www.jeffersoncountywv.org/festival.

COLUMBIA CLASSIC GRAND PRIX LATE SEPTEMBER. World-class and Olympic-caliber riders compete in this annual equestrian event at Howard Community College in Columbia; ☎ 410-772-4450; www.howardcc.edu/grandprix.

NATIONAL BOOK FESTIVAL LAST SATURDAY. More than 70 authors of all types gather for readings, signings, and literacy exhibits along the Mall; www.loc.gov/bookfest.

ALEXANDRIA SEAPORT DAY LAST SATURDAY. Boat-building demonstrations, model boat–building workshops, exhibits, and boat rides at Waterfront Park in Old Town Alexandria; ☎ 703-549-7078; www.alexandriaseaport.org.

October

MOUNT VERNON FALL WINE FESTIVAL AND SUNSET TOUR EARLY OCTOBER. Taste wines from Virginia vineyards, learn more about George Washington's winemaking efforts, and enjoy live jazz at the first president's estate. Tickets are required, and advance purchase is recommended; ☎ 202-397-7328 (tickets) or 703-780-2000 (information); www.mountvernon.org.

WATERFORD HOMES TOUR AND CRAFTS EXHIBIT FIRST WEEKEND. The annual festival on the streets of this village, founded in 1733, with music, a crafts fair, crafts demonstrations, and tours of Colonial homes in Waterford, Virginia; ☎ 540-882-3018 or 540-882-3085; www.waterfordva-wca.org/waterford-fair.htm.

TASTE OF BETHESDA FIRST SATURDAY. This street festival features samples from area restaurants, entertainment on multiple stages, and kids' activities in downtown Bethesda; ☎ 301-215-6660; www.bethesda.org/bethesda/taste-bethesda.

ART ON THE AVENUE FIRST SATURDAY. A multicultural arts and music festival, with exhibits by more than 300 artists, entertainment, interactive kids' activities, and food vendors along Mount Vernon Avenue in Alexandria; ☎ 703-683-3100; www.artontheavenue.org.

FESTIVAL OF THE BUILDING ARTS EARLY TO MID-OCTOBER. Hands-on activities for all ages illustrate the skills used in the building arts at the National Building Museum; ☎ 202-272-2448; www.nbm.org.

GRAND MILITIA MUSTER EARLY TO MID-OCTOBER. Competitions and pageantry by St. Maries City Militia and other 17th-century military reenactment units in Historic St. Mary's City, Maryland's first capital; ☎ 800-762-1634 or 240-895-4990; **stmaryscity.org.**

COLUMBUS DAY CEREMONY SECOND MONDAY. A celebration of the explorer's achievements at the Columbus Memorial Statue at Union Station; ☎ 202-619-7222.

WHITE HOUSE FALL GARDEN TOURS MID-OCTOBER (weather permitting). Free, timed tickets distributed each day on first-come basis at the Ellipse Visitor Pavilion, 15th and E streets NW, at 7:30 a.m.; ☎ 202-456-2200 or 202-208-1631; **www.whitehouse.gov.**

INTERNATIONAL GOLD CUP THIRD SATURDAY. Annual running of this fall classic steeplechase race at Great Meadow near The Plains, Virginia; ☎ 540-347-2612; **www.vagoldcup.com.**

BETHESDA ROW ARTS FESTIVAL THIRD WEEKEND. More than 180 artists and artisans display their creations along four blocks in downtown Bethesda; ☎ 301-637-5715; **www.bethesdarowarts.org.**

WASHINGTON INTERNATIONAL HORSE SHOW LATE OCTOBER. Hundreds of horses and riders from around the world compete in hunter and jumper events at the Verizon Center; ☎ 202-397-7328 (tickets); ☎ 202-628-3200 or 202-525-3679 (information); **www.wihs.org.**

"BOO AT THE ZOO" LAST WEEKEND. Halloween trick-or-treating, animal demonstrations, and zookeeper talks at the National Zoo; ☎ 202-633-4800; **www.nationalzoo.si.edu.**

MARINE CORPS MARATHON LAST SUNDAY. Tens of thousands of runners start at the Iwo Jima Memorial in Arlington and follow a course into Washington, along the Mall, and back to the Memorial; ☎ 800-786-8762; **www.marinemarathon.com.**

November

VETERANS DAY CEREMONIES NOVEMBER 11. Commemorations and wreath-laying ceremonies at Arlington National Cemetery, the Navy Memorial, the Air Force Memorial, National Marine Corps Museum, the World War II Memorial, the Vietnam Veterans Memorial, the Vietnam Women's Memorial, and the Women in Military Service for America Memorial; ☎ 202-619-7222.

D.C. METROPOLITAN COOKING & ENTERTAINING SHOW SECOND WEEKEND. Celebrity chef (Bobby Flay, Paula Deen, Giada DeLaurentis, Guy Fiere, the Neelys, etc.) demonstrations and book signings; gadget and specialty food vendors; plus seminars on food and wine (or beer) pairings, festive occasions, an over-21 spirits pavilion, tastings, kids' cooking classes, and more. At the Washington Convention Center; ☎ 703-321-4890; **www.metrocooking.com.**

WASHINGTON CRAFT SHOW EARLY TO MID-NOVEMBER. Nearly 200 artists from across the country display their glasswork, furniture, textiles, and other creations at the Washington Convention Center; ☎ 202-249-3000 or 203-254-0486; **www.craftsamericashows.com.**

WATERFOWL FESTIVAL MID-NOVEMBER. The annual festival celebrates ducks, geese, and other wildlife in photographs, paintings, carvings, sculpture, and other media, with music, duck-calling contests, children's activities, and food vendors in Easton, Maryland; ☎ 410-822-4567; **www.waterfowlfestival.org.**

MOUNT VERNON BY CANDLELIGHT THANKSGIVING WEEKEND THOUGH EARLY DECEMBER. Tour the first president's estate by candlelight, along with music and fireside caroling; ☎ 703-780-2000; **www.mountvernon.org.**

December

KENNEDY CENTER HOLIDAY FESTIVAL ALL MONTH. The Kennedy Center celebrates the holidays with free performances and ticketed concerts; ☎ 202-467-4600; **www.kennedy-center.org.**

SCOTTISH CHRISTMAS WALK FIRST SATURDAY. More than 100 Scottish clan units parade through Old Town Alexandria; ☎ 703-549-0111; **www.scottishchristmaswalk.com.**

HOLIDAY SING-A-LONG FIRST SUNDAY. Free family carol-singing at the Filene Center at Wolf Trap Park in Vienna; ☎ 877-965-3872 or 703-255-1900; **www.wolftrap.org.**

PAGEANT OF PEACE EARLY DECEMBER. The lighting of the National Christmas Tree on the Ellipse, usually by the President and First Lady, kicks off a month of free holiday activities, including nightly choral performances and a display of lighted trees representing the states and territories; free passes issued in early November; ☎ 202-208-1631 or 202-619-7222; **www.thenationaltree.org.**

PEARL HARBOR DAY DECEMBER 7. A ceremony commemorates the 1941 attack on Pearl Harbor at the Navy Memorial; ☎ 202-737-2300; **www.navymemorial.org.**

HISTORIC ALEXANDRIA CANDLELIGHT TOURS MID-DECEMBER. Sites include the Lee-Fendall House, Gadsby's Tavern Museum, and the Carlyle House in Old Town Alexandria, with music, colonial dancing, seasonal decorations, and light refreshment; ☎ 703-838-4242; **oha.alexandriava.gov.**

NEW YEAR'S EVE Family-oriented, alcohol-free "First Night" festivals with concerts, children's entertainers, and other activities are in Alexandria (☎ 703-746-3299), Fredericksburg (☎ 540-372-1086, press 2), Leesburg (☎ 703-777-6306), and Warrenton (☎ 703-777-6306).

PART TWO

ACCOMMODATIONS

DECIDING WHERE *to* STAY

ON WEEKDAYS, DRIVING AND PARKING IN DOWNTOWN Washington can be nightmarish. On weekends there is less traffic congestion, but parking is extremely difficult, particularly in the area of the Mall. Because the best way to get around Washington is on the Metro, we recommend a hotel within walking distance of a Metro station. With two rather prominent exceptions, all of Washington's best areas, as well as most of the Virginia and Maryland suburbs, are safely and conveniently accessible via this clean, modern subway system. In fact, **Penn Quarter,** which lies between the U.S. Capitol and the White House and is Washington's most rapidly revitalizing neighborhood, is served by a handful of stations, with several more (if you don't want to bother to transfer) only a few more blocks away. If you are subway-savvy, look into the name-chain hotels in Crystal City, which has its own Metro station in between Washington National Airport and D.C. itself—cutting commute time in both directions—an impressive restaurant neighborhood, and better nightly rates. Only historic **Georgetown** and the colorful, ethnically diverse **Adams Morgan** neighborhood are off-line (and even they are only a few blocks' walk from a stop or connector bus; see Part Four: Getting In and Getting Around).

Most of Georgetown's hotels are on the pricey side. Adams Morgan, a great neighborhood for dining and shopping, does not offer much in the way of lodging, though there are increasing numbers of B&B options in Logan Circle and Dupont Circle. If you go to Adams Morgan, especially at night, take a cab.

SOME CONSIDERATIONS

1. When choosing your Washington lodging, make sure your hotel is situated in a location convenient to your recreation or business needs, and that it is in a safe and comfortable area. Please note that while it can

be a substantial walk to the Washington Convention Center (the major convention venue) from many of the downtown hotels, larger conventions and trade shows provide shuttle service.

2. Find out how old the hotel is and when the guestrooms were last renovated. Check out guestroom photos on the hotel's website. Ask if photos on the website are accurate and current.

3. If you plan to take a car, inquire about the parking situation. Some hotels offer no parking at all, some charge dearly for parking, and a few offer free parking.

4. If you are not a city dweller, or if you are a light sleeper, try to book a hotel on a more quiet side street. Ask for a room off the street and high up.

5. Much of Washington is quite beautiful, as is the Potomac River. If you are on a romantic holiday, ask for a room on a higher floor with a good view.

6. When you plan your budget, remember that there is a 14.5% hotel tax (including sales tax) in the District of Columbia.

7. Washington is one of the busiest convention cities in the United States. If your visit to Washington coincides with one or more major conventions or trade shows, hotel rooms will be both scarce and expensive. If, on the other hand, you are able to schedule your visit to avoid big meetings, you will have a good selection of hotels at reasonably competitive prices. If you happen to be attending one of the big conventions, book early and use some of the tips listed on the following pages to get a discounted room rate. To assist in timing your visit, check the convention and trade-show calendar at **www.dcconvention.com.**

GETTING *a* GOOD DEAL *on a* ROOM

THOUGH WASHINGTON, D.C., IS A MAJOR TOURIST DESTINATION, the economics of hotel room pricing is driven by business, government, and convention trade. This translates to high "rack rates" (a hotel's published room rate) and very few bargains. The most modest Econo Lodge or Days Inn in Washington charges from $75 to $149 a night, and midrange chains, such as Holiday Inn and Radisson, ask from $129 to $419.

The good news is that Washington, D.C., and its Virginia and Maryland suburbs offer a staggering number of unusually fine hotels, including a high percentage of suite properties. The bad news, of course, is that you can expect to pay dearly to stay in them.

In most cities, the better and more expensive hotels are located close to the city center, with less expensive hotels situated farther out. There is normally a trade-off between location and price: if you are willing to stay out off the interstate and commute into downtown, you can expect to pay less for your suburban room than you would for a downtown room. In Washington, D.C., unfortunately, it very rarely works this way.

In the greater Washington area, every hotel is seemingly close to something. No matter how far you are from the Capitol, the Mall, and downtown, you can bank on your hotel being within spitting distance of some bureau, agency, airport, or industrial complex that funnels platoons of business travelers into guestrooms in a constant flow. Because almost every accommodation has its own captive market, the usual proximity/price trade-off doesn't apply. The Marriott at the Beltway and Wisconsin Avenue, for example, is 30 to 40 minutes away by car from the Mall but stays full with visitors to the nearby National Institutes of Health.

SPECIAL WEEKEND RATES

ALTHOUGH WELL-LOCATED WASHINGTON HOTELS are tough for the budget-conscious, it's not impossible to get a good deal, at least relatively speaking. For starters, some hotels that cater to business, government, and convention travelers offer special weekend discount rates that range from 15 to 40% below normal weekday rates. You can find out about weekend specials by calling individual hotels or by consulting your travel agent.

GETTING CORPORATE RATES

MANY HOTELS OFFER DISCOUNTED CORPORATE RATES (5 to 20% off rack). Usually you do not need to work for a large company or have a special relationship with the hotel to obtain these rates. Simply call the hotel of your choice and ask for their corporate rates. Many hotels will guarantee you the discounted rate on the phone when you make your reservation. Others may make the rate conditional on your providing some sort of bona fides, for instance a fax on your company's letterhead requesting the rate, or a company credit card or business card on check-in. Generally, the screening is not rigorous.

THE INTERNET REVOLUTION

PURCHASING TRAVEL ON THE INTERNET has revolutionized the way both consumers and hotels do business. For you, it makes shopping for a hotel and finding good deals much easier. For the hotel, it makes possible a system of room inventory management often referred to as "nudging." Here's how it works. Many months in advance, hotels establish rates for each day of the coming year. In developing their rate calendar, they take into consideration all of the variables that affect occupancy in their hotel as well as in Washington, D.C., in general. They consider weekend versus weekday demand; additional demand stimulated by holidays, major conventions, trade shows, and sporting events; and the effect of the four seasons of the year on occupancy.

After rates for each date are determined, the rates are entered into the hotel's reservation system. Then hotel management sits back to see what happens. If the bookings for a particular date are in accord with management's expectations, no rate change is necessary. If demand is greater than management's forecast for a given date, they might raise the rate to take advantage of higher than expected bookings. If demand eases off, the hotel can revert back to the original rate.

If demand is less than expected, the hotel will begin nudging, that is, incrementally decreasing the rate for the day or days in question until booking volume increases to the desired level. Though this sort of rate manipulation has been an integral part of room inventory management for decades, the Internet has made it possible to rethink and alter room rates almost at will. A hotel can theoretically adjust rates hourly on its own website. Major Internet travel sellers such as Travelocity, Hotels.com, and Expedia, among others, are fast and agile and quite capable of getting a special deal (that is, a lower rate) in front of travel purchasers almost instantaneously. For the hotel, this means they can manage their inventory on almost a weekly or daily basis, nudging toward full occupancy by adjusting their rates according to demand.

Of course, hotels don't depend entirely on the Internet. Lower rates and various special deals are also communicated by e-mail to preferred travel agents, and sometimes directly to consumers via e-mail, print advertisements, or direct-mail promotions.

Finding Deals on the Internet

By far the easiest way to scout room deals is on the Internet search engine **www.kayak.com.** Kayak is a straightforward, easy-to-navigate site that scans not only Internet sellers but also national hotel-chain websites and sometimes individual hotel websites. You can organize your search by price, location, star rating, brand, and amenities. Detailed descriptions of each property along with photos, customer reviews, and a map are also available. Kayak provides a direct link to the lowest-price sellers.

Also, for Internet shopping, consider **www.priceline.com.** There you can tender a bid for a room. You can't bid on a specific hotel, but you can specify location and the quality rating expressed in stars. If your bid is accepted, you will be assigned to a hotel consistent with your location and quality requirements, and your credit card will be charged in a nonrefundable transaction for your entire stay. Notification of acceptance usually takes less than an hour. We recommend bidding $45 to $60 per night for a three-star hotel and $65 to $90 per night for a four-star. To gauge your chances of success, check to see if any major conventions or trade shows are scheduled during your preferred dates. Reduce your bid for off-season periods.

RESERVATION SERVICES

Capitol Reservations   ☎ 800-847-4832; www.hotelsDC.com

Hotel Discounts   ☎ 800-715-7666; www.hoteldiscounts.com

Hotels.com   ☎ 800-964-6835; www.hotels.com

Quikbook   ☎ 800-789-9887; www.quikbook.com

Washington, D.C., Accommodations   ☎ 800-503-3330; www.wdcahotels.com

RESERVATION SERVICES

WHEN WHOLESALERS AND CONSOLIDATORS DEAL DIRECTLY with the public, they frequently represent themselves as "reservation services." When you call, you can ask for a rate quote for a particular hotel, or, alternatively, ask for their best available deal in the area where you prefer to stay. If there is a maximum amount you are willing to pay, say so. Chances are, the service will find something that will work for you, even if they have to shave a dollar or two off their own profit. Sometimes you will have to pay for your room in advance, with a credit card, when you make your reservation. Other times you will pay at the usual time, when you check out.

BED-AND-BREAKFASTS (B&BS)

B&Bs offer a lodging alternative based on personal service and hospitality that transcend the sterile, predictable product of chain hotels; however, they can be quirky. Most, but not all, B&Bs are open year-round. Some accept only cash or personal checks, while others take all major credit cards. Not all rooms come with private baths. Some rooms with private baths may have a tub but not a shower, or vice versa. Some allow children but not pets, others pets but not children. Many B&Bs provide only the most basic breakfast, while some provide a sumptuous morning feast. Still others offer three meals a day. Most B&Bs are not wheelchair accessible, but it never hurts to ask.

unofficial **TIP**
Because staying at a B&B is like visiting someone's home, reservations are recommended, though B&Bs with more than ten rooms usually welcome walk-ins.

To help you sort out your B&B options, we recommend the following guides. Updated regularly, these books describe B&Bs in more detail than is possible in the *Unofficial Guide*.

Inspected, Rated, and Approved: Bed and Breakfasts and Country Inns, by Beth Burgreen Stuhlman, published by the American Bed & Breakfast Association. Covers the entire United States. Visit **www.abba.com.**

Bed & Breakfasts and Country Inns by Deborah Sakach, published by American Historic Inns, Inc. Covers the entire United States. To order, call ☎ 800-397-4667 or 949-499-8070 or visit **www.iloveinns.com.**

Recommended Country Inns, Mid-Atlantic and Chesapeake Region, by Suzi Forbes Chase, published by The Globe Pequot Press. Covers Virginia, Delaware, Maryland, Pennsylvania, New Jersey, New York, and West Virginia. To order, phone ☎ 800-243-0495.

For Washington-area B&B reservations, check out **www.bedand breakfastdc.com** or call **Bed and Breakfast Accommodations, Ltd.** at ☎ 202-328-3510.

HELPING YOUR TRAVEL AGENT HELP YOU

WHEN YOU CALL YOUR TRAVEL AGENT, ask if he or she has been to Washington. If the answer is no, be prepared to give your travel agent some direction. Do not accept any recommendations at face value. Check out the location and rates of any suggested hotel and make certain that the hotel is suited to your itinerary.

Because some travel agents are unfamiliar with Washington, your agent may try to plug you into a tour operator's or wholesaler's preset package. This essentially allows the travel agent to set up your whole trip with a single phone call and still collect an 8 to 10% commission. The problem with this scenario is that most agents will place 90% of their Washington business with only one or two wholesalers or tour operators. In other words, it's the line of least resistance for them, and not much choice for you.

Travel agents will often use wholesalers who run packages in conjunction with airlines, like Delta's Dream Vacations or American's Fly-Away Vacations. Because of the wholesaler's exclusive relationship with the carrier, these trips are very easy for travel agents to book. However, they will probably be more expensive than a package offered by a high-volume wholesaler who works with a number of airlines in a primarily Washington market.

To help your travel agent get you the best possible deal, do the following:

1. Determine where you want to stay in Washington and, if possible, choose a specific hotel. This can be accomplished by reviewing the hotel information provided in this guide and by writing or calling hotels.
2. Check out the hotel deals and package vacations advertised in the Sunday travel section of the *Washington Post*. Often you will be able to find deals that beat the socks off anything offered in your local paper. See if you can find specials that fit your plans and include a hotel you like.
3. Call the hotels, wholesalers, or tour operators whose ads you have collected. Ask any questions you have concerning their packages, but do not book your trip with them directly.
4. Tell your travel agent about the deals you find and ask if she can get you something better. The deals in the paper will serve as a benchmark against which to compare alternatives proposed by your travel agent.
5. Choose from among the options that you and your travel agent

uncover. No matter which option you elect, have the agent book it. Even if you go with one of the packages in the newspaper, it will probably be commissionable (at no additional cost to you) and will provide the agent some return on the time invested on your behalf. Also, as a travel professional, your agent should be able to verify the quality and integrity of the deal.

IF YOU MAKE YOUR OWN RESERVATION

AS YOU POKE AROUND TRYING TO FIND A GOOD DEAL, there are several things you should know. First, always call the specific hotel as opposed to the hotel chain's national toll-free number. Quite often, the reservationists at the national toll-free number are unaware of local specials. Always ask about specials before you inquire about corporate rates. Do not be reluctant to bargain. If you are buying a hotel's weekend package, for example, and want to extend your stay into the following week, you can often obtain at least the corporate rate for the extra days. Do your bargaining, however, before you check in, preferably when you make your reservations.

HOW TO EVALUATE A TRAVEL PACKAGE

HUNDREDS OF WASHINGTON PACKAGE VACATIONS are offered to the public each year. Packages should be a win-win proposition for both the buyer and the seller. The buyer has to make only one phone call and deal with just one salesperson to set up the whole vacation: transportation, rental car, lodging, meals, tours, attraction admissions, and even golf and tennis. The seller, likewise, has to deal with the buyer only once, eliminating the need for separate sales, confirmations, and billing. In addition to streamlining sales, processing, and administration, some packagers also buy airfares in bulk on contract like a broker playing the commodities market. Buying a large number of airfares in advance allows the packager to buy them at a significant savings from posted fares. The same practice is also applied to hotel rooms. Because selling vacation packages is an efficient way of doing business, and because the packager can often buy individual package components (airfare, lodging, etc.) in bulk at a discount, savings in operating expenses realized by the seller are sometimes passed on to the buyer. In addition to being convenient, such packages can be exceptional values. In any event, that is the way it is supposed to work.

All too often, in practice, the seller cashes in on discounts and passes none on to the buyer. In some instances, packages are loaded up with extras that cost the packager next to nothing but inflate the retail price sky-high. As you may expect, the savings to be passed along to customers evaporate.

When considering a package, choose one that includes features you are sure to use. Whether you use all the features or not, you will certainly pay for them. Second, if cost is of greater concern than convenience, make a few phone calls and see what the package would cost if you booked its individual components (airfare, rental car, lodging, etc.) on your own. If the package price is less than the à la carte cost, the package is a good deal. If the costs are about the same, the package is probably worth buying just for the convenience.

If your package includes a choice of rental car or "airport transfers" (transportation to and from the airport), take the transfers unless you are visiting Washington for the weekend and don't plan to visit the Mall. During the weekend, it is relatively easy to get around by car as long as you don't visit the dreaded "Monument Alley." During the week, forget it—a car is definitely *not* the way to go. If you do take a car, be sure to ask if the package includes free parking at your hotel.

TIPS *for* BUSINESS TRAVELERS

THE PRIMARY CONSIDERATIONS FOR BUSINESS TRAVELERS are affordability and proximity to the site or area where you will transact your business. Identify the areas where your business will take you on the maps on pages 64–66, and then use the Hotel Information Chart on pages 67–82 to cross-reference the hotels located in that area. Once you have developed a short list of possible hotels that are conveniently located, fit your budget, and offer the standard of accommodations you require, you (or your travel agent) can make use of the cost-saving suggestions discussed earlier to obtain the lowest rate.

LODGING CONVENIENT TO WASHINGTON CONVENTION CENTER

IF YOU ARE ATTENDING A MEETING or trade show at **Washington Convention Center,** look for convenient lodging in downtown Washington, where at least a half dozen hotels are within walking distance. From most downtown hotels, Washington Convention Center is at most a five- to eight-minute cab or shuttle ride away. Parking is available at the convention center, but it is expensive and not terribly convenient. We recommend that you leave your car at home and use shuttles and cabs.

The Washington Convention Center is served directly by the Mount Vernon Square/Seventh Street–Convention Center Metro Station and is only about five blocks from Metro Center. The walk passes through a section of town that is safe during daylight hours.

Commuting to Washington Convention Center from the suburbs or the airports during rush hour is something to be avoided if possible. If you want a room downtown, book early—very early. If you screw up and need a room at the last minute, try a wholesaler, reservation service, or one of the strategies that follow.

CONVENTION RATES:
HOW THEY WORK AND HOW TO DO BETTER

IF YOU ARE ATTENDING A MAJOR CONVENTION or trade show, it is probable that the meeting's sponsoring organization has negotiated "convention rates" with a number of hotels. Under this arrangement, hotels agree to "block" a certain number of rooms at an agreed-upon price for convention-goers. Sometimes, as in the case of a small meeting, only one hotel is involved. In the event of a large citywide convention at Washington Convention Center, however, almost all downtown and airport hotels will participate in the room block.

Because the convention sponsor brings a lot of business to the city and reserves a large number of rooms, it usually can negotiate a volume discount on the room rates, a rate that should be substantially below rack rate. However, some conventions and trade shows have more clout and negotiating skill than others. Hence, your convention sponsor may or may not be able to obtain the lowest possible rate.

Once a convention or trade show sponsor has completed negotiations with participating hotels, it will send its attendees a housing list with all the hotels serving the convention and the special convention rate for each. When you receive the list, compare the convention rates with the rates obtainable using the strategies covered in the previous section. If the negotiated convention rate doesn't sound like a good deal, try to reserve a room using a reservation service or a tour operator. Remember, however, that many of the deep discounts are available only when the hotel expects to be at less than 80% occupancy, a condition that rarely prevails when a big convention is in town.

Here are some tips for beating convention rates:

1. Reserve early. Most big conventions and trade shows announce meeting sites one to three years in advance. Get your reservation booked as far in advance as possible using a half-price club. If you book well before the convention sponsor sends out its hotel list, chances are much better that the hotel will have space available.

2. If you've already got your convention's housing list, compare it with the list of hotels presented in this guide. You might be able to find a hotel not on the convention list that better suits your needs.

3. Use a local reservation agency. This strategy is useful even if you need to make reservations at the last minute. Local reservation agencies almost always control some rooms, even during a huge convention or trade show. (See our section on reservation services on page 47.)

4. Book a hotel somewhat distant from the convention center but situated close to the Metro. You may save money on your room rate, and your commuting time underground to the convention center will often be shorter than if you take a cab or drive from a downtown hotel.

5. Stay in a bed and breakfast, either downtown or near a Metro line. Bed and Breakfast Accommodations, Ltd. (at ☎ 202-328-3510; **www.bedandbreakfastdc.com**) can help you locate one.

ACCOMMODATIONS:
Rated and Ranked

WHAT'S IN A ROOM?

EXCEPT FOR CLEANLINESS, STATE OF REPAIR, AND DECOR, most travelers do not pay much attention to hotel rooms. There is, of course, a discernible standard of quality and luxury that differentiates Motel 6 from Holiday Inn, Holiday Inn from Marriott, and so on. In general, however, hotel guests fail to appreciate that some rooms are better engineered than others. Making the room usable to its occupants is an art, a planning discipline that combines both form and function.

Decor and taste are important, certainly. No one wants to spend time in a room where the decor is dated, garish, or even ugly. But beyond the decor, certain variables determine how livable a hotel room is. The next time you stay in a hotel, pay attention to the details and design elements of your room. Even more than decor, these are the things that will make you feel comfortable and at home.

When the *Unofficial Guide* researchers inspect a hotel room, here are a few of the things we check that you may want to start paying attention to:

ROOM SIZE While some smaller rooms are cozy and well designed, a large and uncluttered room is generally preferable, especially for a stay of more than three days.

TEMPERATURE CONTROL, VENTILATION, AND ODOR The guest should be able to control the temperature of the room. The best system, because it's so quiet, is central heating and air-conditioning controlled by the room's own thermostat. The next best system is a room module heater and air-conditioner, preferably controlled by an automatic thermostat, but usually by manually operated button controls. The worst system is central heat and air without any sort of room thermostat or guest control.

Most hotel rooms have windows or balcony doors that have been permanently secured shut. Though there are some legitimate safety and liability issues involved, we prefer windows and balcony doors that can be opened to admit fresh air. Hotel rooms should be odor-free and smoke-free and should not feel stuffy or damp.

ROOM SECURITY Most rooms these days have locks that require a plastic card instead of the traditional lock and key. Card-and-slot systems allow the hotel to change the combination or entry code of the lock with each new guest who uses the room. A burglar who has somehow acquired a room key to a conventional lock can afford to wait until the situation is right before using the key to gain access. Not so with a card-and-slot system.

In addition to an entry-lock system, the door should have a dead-bolt and preferably a chain that can be locked from the inside. A chain by itself is not sufficient. Doors should also have a peephole. Windows and balcony doors should have secure locks.

SAFETY Every room should have a fire or smoke alarm, clear fire instructions, and preferably a sprinkler system. Bathtubs should have a nonskid surface, and shower stalls should have doors that either open outward or slide side-to-side. Bathroom electrical outlets should be positioned high on the wall and not too close to the sink. Balconies should have sturdy, high rails.

NOISE Better hotels are designed with noise control in mind. Wall and ceiling construction are substantial, effectively screening out routine noise. Carpets and drapes, in addition to being decorative, also absorb and muffle sounds. Mattresses mounted on stable platforms or sturdy bed frames do not squeak. Televisions with volume governors rarely disturb guests in adjacent rooms. The air-conditioning and heating system is well maintained and operates without noise or vibration. Likewise, plumbing is quiet and positioned away from the sleeping area. Doors to the hall, and to adjoining rooms, are thick and well fitted to better keep out noise.

DARKNESS CONTROL Ever been in a hotel room where the curtains would not quite come together in the middle? In cities where many visitors stay up way into the wee hours, it's important to have a dark, quiet room where you can sleep late without the morning sun blasting you out of bed. Thick, lined curtains that close completely in the center and extend beyond the dimensions of the window or door frame are required.

LIGHTING Poor lighting is an extremely common problem in American hotel rooms. The lighting is usually adequate for dressing, relaxing, or watching television, but not for reading or working. Lighting needs to be bright over tables and desks and alongside couches or easy chairs. Since many people read in bed, there should be a separate light for each person. A room with two queen beds should have an individual light for four people. Better bedside reading lights illuminate a small area, so if you want to sleep and someone else prefers to stay up and read, you will not be bothered by the light. The worst situation by far is a single lamp on a table between the beds. This deficiency is often compounded by lightbulbs of insufficient wattage.

In addition, closet areas should be well lit, and there should be a switch near the door that turns on lights in the room when you enter. A seldom seen but desirable feature is a bedside console that allows a guest to control all or most lights in the room from the bed.

FURNISHINGS At bare minimum, the bed(s) must be firm. Pillows should be made with nonallergenic fillers and, in addition to the sheets and spread, a blanket should be provided. Bedclothes should be changed daily. Better hotels usually provide extra blankets and pillows in the room or on request and sometimes use a second top sheet between the blanket and the spread.

There should be a dresser large enough to hold clothes for two people during a five-day stay. A small table with two chairs, or a desk with a chair, should be provided. The room should be equipped with a luggage rack and a three-quarter- to full-length mirror.

The television should be cable-connected and have a remote control. The telephone should be touch-tone, conveniently situated for bedside use, and should have, on or near it, easily understood dialing instructions and a rate card. Local white and yellow pages should be provided. Better hotels have phones in the bath, equip room phones with long cords, and have Internet connections or wireless access in every room.

Well-designed hotel rooms usually have a plush armchair or a sleeper sofa for lounging and reading. Better headboards are padded for comfortable reading in bed, and there should be a nightstand or table on each side of the bed(s). Nice extras in any hotel room include a small refrigerator, a digital alarm clock, and a coffeemaker.

BATHROOM Two sinks are better than one, and you cannot have too much counter space. A sink outside the bath is a great convenience when one person dresses as another bathes. Better bathrooms have both a tub and a shower with a nonslip bottom. Tub and shower controls should be easy to operate. Adjustable shower heads are preferred. The bath needs to be well lit and should have an exhaust fan and a guest-controlled bathroom heater. Towels should be large, soft, and fluffy and provided in generous quantities, as should hand towels and washcloths. There should be an electrical outlet for each sink, conveniently and safely placed. Complimentary shampoo, conditioner, and lotion are a plus, as are robes and bathmats. Luxurious baths feature a phone, a hair dryer, and sometimes a small television or a jacuzzi.

VENDING There should be complimentary ice and a drink machine on each floor. Welcome additions include a snack machine and a sundries (combs, toothpaste) machine. The latter are seldom found in large hotels that have 24-hour restaurants and shops.

ROOM RATINGS

TO SEPARATE PROPERTIES ACCORDING TO the relative quality, tastefulness, state of repair, cleanliness, and size of their standard rooms, we have grouped the hotels and motels into classifications denoted by stars (see table on the next page).

Star ratings in this guide do not necessarily correspond to ratings awarded by Mobil, AAA, or other travel critics. Because stars have little relevance when awarded in the absence of commonly recognized standards of comparison, we have tied our rating to expected levels of quality established by specific American hotel corporations.

Star ratings apply to *room quality only* and describe the property's

★★★★★	Superior Rooms *Tasteful and luxurious by any standard*
★★★★	Extremely Nice Rooms *What you would expect at a Hyatt Regency or Marriott*
★★★	Nice Rooms *Holiday Inn or comparable quality*
★★	Adequate Rooms *Clean, comfortable, and functional without frills (like a Motel 6)*
★	Super-Budget

standard accommodations. For most hotels and motels a "standard accommodation" is a hotel room with either one king bed or two queen beds. In an all-suite property, the standard accommodation is a one- or two-room suite. In addition to standard accommodations, many hotels offer luxury rooms and special suites that are not rated in this guide. Star ratings for rooms are assigned without regard to whether a property has restaurant(s), recreational facilities, entertainment, or other extras.

In addition to stars (which delineate broad categories), we also employ a numerical rating system. Our rating scale is 0 to 100, with 100 the best possible rating and 0 the worst. Numerical ratings are presented to show the difference we perceive between one property and another that may be in the same star category. Rooms at the Hotel Topaz, the Hotel Monaco, and the Melrose Hotel, for instance, are all rated as ★★★★ (four stars). In the supplemental numerical ratings, the Hotel Topaz and the Hotel Monaco are rated 87 and 86, respectively, while the Melrose Hotel is rated 84. This means that within the four-star category, the Hotel Topaz and the Hotel Monaco are comparable, and that both have somewhat nicer rooms than the Melrose Hotel.

The location column identifies the greater Washington area (by neighborhood) where you will find a particular property.

HOW THE ACCOMMODATIONS COMPARE

COST ESTIMATES ARE BASED ON THE HOTEL'S published rack rates for standard rooms. Each "$" represents $50. Thus, a cost symbol of "$$$" means a room (or suite) at that hotel will cost about $150 a night.

Below is a hit parade of the nicest rooms in town. We've focused strictly on room quality and excluded any consideration of location, services, recreation, or amenities. In some instances, a one- or two-room suite is the same price or less than a regular hotel room.

If you used previous editions of this guide, you may notice that many of the ratings and rankings have changed. These changes reflect

continued on page 60

How the Hotels Compare in Washington, D.C.

HOTEL	STAR RATING	QUALITY RATING	COST ($=$50)	ZONE NAME
Elden Luxury Suites	★★★★½	93	$$$$$$+	Downtown
Jefferson Hotel	★★★★½	92	$$$$$$$+	Downtown
Mandarin Oriental	★★★★½	92	$$$$$$$$+	National Mall
Ritz-Carlton Georgetown	★★★★½	92	$$$$$$$$	Georgetown
Ritz-Carlton Washington, D.C.	★★★★½	92	$$$$$$$$$+	Dupont Circle/ Adams Morgan
St. Regis	★★★★½	92	$$$$$$$$–	Downtown
Gaylord National	★★★★½	91	$$$$$$$–	Maryland Suburbs
Hay-Adams Hotel	★★★★½	91	$$$$$$$–	Downtown
Park Hyatt	★★★★½	91	$$$$$$$$–	Georgetown
Hotel Monaco Alexandria	★★★★½	90	$$$$$$$–	Virginia Suburbs
Hotel Palomar Arlington	★★★★½	90	$$$–	Virginia Suburbs
Four Seasons Hotel	★★★★	89	$$$$$$$$$$+	Georgetown
Morrison House	★★★★	89	$$$$–	Virginia Suburbs
Doubletree Washington, D.C.	★★★★	88	$$$+	Upper Northwest
Embassy Suites Chevy Chase	★★★★	88	$$$$	Upper Northwest
Georgetown Suites Hotel	★★★★	88	$$$$	Georgetown
Hotel Helix	★★★★	88	$$$+	Upper Northwest
Hotel Madera	★★★★	88	$$$$–	Dupont Circle/ Adams Morgan
Ritz-Carlton Pentagon City	★★★★	88	$$$$+	Virginia Suburbs
Ritz-Carlton Tysons Corner	★★★★	88	$$$$–	Virginia Suburbs
River Inn	★★★★	88	$$$$$–	Foggy Bottom
Sofitel Lafayette	★★★★	88	$$$$$$–	Downtown
St. Gregory Lauxury Hotel & Suites	★★★★	88	$$$$$$	Dupont Circle/ Adams Morgan
Westin Grand	★★★★	88	$$$$$–	Georgetown
Westin Washington, D.C. City Center	★★★★	88	$$$$–	Downtown
Willard Inter-Continental	★★★★	88	$$$$$$$–	Downtown
Aloft Washington National Harbor	★★★★	87	$$$$	Maryland Suburbs
Grand Hyatt Washington	★★★★	87	$$$$–	Downtown
Hotel Topaz	★★★★	87	$$$$–	Dupont Circle/ Adams Morgan

HOTEL	STAR RATING	QUALITY RATING	COST ($=$50)	ZONE NAME
Residence Inn Dupont Circle	★★★★	87	$$$$$–	Dupont Circle/ Adams Morgan
Washington Suites Alexandria	★★★★	87	$$$	Virginia Suburbs
Carlyle Suites Hotel	★★★★	86	$$$$$+	Dupont Circle/ Adams Morgan
Hotel Monaco	★★★★	86	$$$$$	Downtown
One Washington Circle Hotel	★★★★	86	$$$$–	Foggy Bottom
Residence Inn Bethesda	★★★★	86	$$$–	Maryland Suburbs
Courtyard Chevy Chase	★★★★	85	$$+	Maryland Suburbs
Embassy Suites Conv. Center	★★★★	85	$$$$+	Downtown
Embassy Suites Crystal City	★★★★	85	$$$+	Virginia Suburbs
Embassy Suites Tysons Corner	★★★★	85	$$+	Virginia Suburbs
Fairmont Washington, D.C.	★★★★	85	$$$$+	Georgetown
Hotel George	★★★★	85	$$$$$+	Downtown
Hotel Palomar Washington	★★★★	85	$$$$$$+	Dupont Circle/ Adams Morgan
Hyatt Arlington	★★★★	85	$$+	Virginia Suburbs
Renaissance M Stree Hotel	★★★★	85	$$$$$	Dupont Circle/ Adams Morgan
Sheraton Suites Alexandria	★★★★	85	$$$$	Virginia Suburbs
Churchill Hotel	★★★★	84	$$$$$$–	Dupont Circle/ Adams Morgan
Crowne Plaza Silver Spring	★★★★	84	$$+	Maryland Suburbs
Doubletree Bethesda	★★★★	84	$$$+	Maryland Suburbs
Embassy Suites Alexandria	★★★★	84	$$$+	Virginia Suburbs
Embassy Suites Downtown	★★★★	84	$$$$$$	Dupont Circle/ Adams Morgan
Fairfax Embassy Row	★★★★	84	$$$$$$$$+	Dupont Circle/ Adams Morgan
Georgetown Inn	★★★★	84	$$$$+	Georgetown
Hawthorn Suites	★★★★	84	$$$+	Virginia Suburbs
Hotel Monticello	★★★★	84	$$$$$–	Georgetown
Hotel Rouge	★★★★	84	$$$+	Dupont Circle/ Adams Morgan
Hyatt Regency Crystal City	★★★★	84	$$$$	Virginia Suburbs
L'Enfant Plaza Hotel	★★★★	84	$$$$$–	National Mall

How the Hotels Compare (continued)

HOTEL	STAR RATING	QUALITY RATING	COST ($=$50)	ZONE NAME
Madison Hotel	★★★★	84	$$$$+	Downtown
Marriott Hotel Bethesda	★★★★	84	$$+	Maryland Suburbs
Marriott Wardman Park Hotel	★★★★	84	$$$$$+	Upper Northwest
Melrose Hotel	★★★★	84	$$$$$$$+	Georgetown
Morrison-Clark Inn	★★★★	84	$$$–	Upper Northwest
Omni Shoreham Hotel	★★★★	84	$$$$$$	Upper Northwest
Radisson Hotel Reagan National	★★★★	84	$$+	Virginia Suburbs
Renaissance Mayflower Hotel	★★★★	84	$$$$+	Downtown
Residence Inn Pentagon City	★★★★	84	$$$–	Virginia Suburbs
The Quincy	★★★★	84	$$$	Downtown
Washington Court Hotel	★★★★	84	$$$$+	Downtown
Washington Suites Georgetown	★★★★	84	$$$+	Georgetown
Westin Tysons Corner	★★★★	84	$$$$$–	Virginia Suburbs
Beacon Hotel	★★★★	83	$$$$$+	Dupont Circle/ Adams Morgan
Bethesda Court Hotel	★★★★	83	$$$$+	Maryland Suburbs
Capitol Hilton	★★★★	83	$$$$$–	Downtown
Courtyard Silver Spring Downtown	★★★★	83	$$+	Maryland Suburbs
Crowne Plaza Hotel Old Town	★★★★	83	$$$$+	Virginia Suburbs
Donovan House	★★★★	83	$$$$	Downtown
Doubletree Hotel Crystal City	★★★★	83	$$$+	Virginia Suburbs
Embassy Row Hilton	★★★★	83	$$$$+	Dupont Circle/ Adams Morgan
Hilton Arlington and Towers	★★★★	83	$$$$$+	Virginia Suburbs
Sheraton Premiere Tysons Corner	★★★★	83	$$$–	Virginia Suburbs
W Washington D.C.	★★★★	83	$$$$$$$–	Downtown
Washington Marriott Hotel	★★★★	83	$$$$$+	Dupont Circle/ Adams Morgan
Courtyard Embassy Row	★★★½	82	$$$$–	Dupont Circle/ Adams Morgan
Hampton Inn & Suites Reagan National Airport	★★★½	82	$$+	Virginia Suburbs

HOTEL	STAR RATING	QUALITY RATING	COST ($=$50)	ZONE NAME
Hampton Inn Alexandria	★★★½	82	$$+	Virginia Suburbs
Hilton Alexandria at Mark Center	★★★½	82	$$$+	Virginia Suburbs
Hilton Washington	★★★½	82	$$$$$$$−	Dupont Circle/ Adams Morgan
Holiday Inn Arlington	★★★½	82	$$$−	Virginia Suburbs
Hotel Lombardy	★★★½	82	$$$+	Foggy Bottom
Hyatt Regency Capitol Hill	★★★½	82	$$$$$$+	Downtown
J.W. Marriott Pennsylvania Avenue	★★★½	82	$$$$$$−	Downtown
Liaison Capitol Hill	★★★½	82	$$$$$	Downtown
Residence Inn Washington, D.C.	3½	82	$$$$−	Downtown
The Normandy Hotel	★★★½	82	$$$$−	Dupont Circle/ Adams Morgan
Tysons Corner Marriott	★★★½	82	$$−	Virginia Suburbs
American Inn of Bethesda	★★★½	81	$$$$−	Maryland Suburbs
Courtyard Washington Convention Center	★★★½	81	$$$$−	Downtown
Dupont Hotel	★★★½	81	$$$$$$$+	Dupont Circle/ Adams Morgan
Henley Park Hotel	★★★½	81	$$$	Downtown
Hyatt Regency Bethesda	★★★½	81	$$$−	Maryland Suburbs
Courtyard Crystal City	★★★½	80	$$$+	Virginia Suburbs
Courtyard New Carrollton	★★★½	80	$$+	Maryland Suburbs
Courtyard Rosslyn	★★★½	80	$$$−	Virginia Suburbs
Hilton of Silver Spring	★★★½	80	$$+	Maryland Suburbs
Marriott Crystal Gateway	★★★½	80	$$$	Virginia Suburbs
Marriott Hotel Key Bridge	★★★½	80	$$$$	Virginia Suburbs
Savoy Suites Hotel	★★★½	80	$$$+	Upper Northwest
Sheraton National Hotel	★★★½	80	$$$$−	Virginia Suburbs
Washington Plaza Hotel	★★★½	80	$$$$+	Downtown
Marriott Crystal City	★★★½	79	$$$+	Virginia Suburbs
Washington National Airport Hilton	★★★½	79	$$	Virginia Suburbs

How the Hotels Compare (continued)

HOTEL	STAR RATING	QUALITY RATING	COST ($=$50)	ZONE NAME
Best Western Georgetown Hotel & Suites	★★★½	78	$$$$–	Dupont Circle/ Adams Morgan
Comfort Inn Pentagon	★★★½	78	$$$–	Virginia Suburbs
Courtyard Alexandria	★★★½	78	$$$–	Virginia Suburbs
Courtyard Alexandria Pentagon South	★★★½	78	$$+	Virginia Suburbs
Courtyard Washington Northwest	★★★½	78	$$$$$$–	Dupont Circle/ Adams Morgan
Hamilton Crowne Plaza	★★★½	78	$$$$$–	Downtown
Hilton Garden Inn Washington Downtown	★★★½	78	$$$$+	Downtown
Holiday Inn Georgetown	★★★½	78	$$$+	Upper Northwest
Sheraton Crystal City	★★★½	78	$$$$–	Virginia Suburbs
State Plaza Hotel	★★★½	77	$$$+	Foggy Bottom
Washington Renaissance Hotel	★★★½	77	$$$$$$$$+	Downtown
Crowne Plaza National Airport	★★★½	76	$$$–	Virginia Suburbs
Holiday Inn Capitol	★★★½	76	$$$$+	Capitol Hill
Holiday Inn Rosslyn at Key Bridge	★★★½	76	$$$–	Virginia Suburbs
Marriott Metro Center	★★★½	76	$$$$$–	Downtown

continued from page 55

the inclusion of new properties, as well as guest-room renovations or improved maintenance and housekeeping in previously listed properties. A failure to properly maintain guestrooms or a lapse in house-keeping standards can negatively affect the ratings.

Finally, before you begin to shop for a hotel, take a hard look at this letter we received from a couple in Hot Springs, Arkansas:

> *We canceled our room reservations to follow the advice in your book [and reserved a hotel room highly ranked by the* Unofficial Guide]. *We wanted inexpensive, but clean and cheerful. We got inexpensive, but [also] dirty, grim, and depressing. I really felt disappointed in your advice and the room. It was the pits. That was the one real piece of information I needed from your book! The room spoiled the holiday for me aside from our touring.*

HOTEL	STAR RATING	QUALITY RATING	COST ($=$50)	ZONE NAME
Four Points Sheraton Downtown	★★★½	75	$$$$$–	Downtown
Phoenix Park Hotel	★★★½	75	$$$$$$$–	Capitol Hill
Holiday Inn National Airport	★★★	74	$$$	Virginia Suburbs
Latham Hotel	★★★	74	$$$$+	Georgetown
Best Western Pentagon Hotel	★★★	73	$$$–	Virginia Suburbs
Holiday Inn Hotel and Suites	★★★	72	$$$–	Virginia Suburbs
Best Western Rosslyn Iwo Jima	★★★	71	$$$+	Virginia Suburbs
Days Inn Connecticut Ave	★★★	70	$$$+	Upper Northwest
Holiday Inn Alexandria	★★★	70	$$$–	Virginia Suburbs
Holiday Inn Central	★★★	70	$$$+	Upper Northwest
Comfort Inn Arlington Blvd/Falls Church	★★★	68	$$$+	Virginia Suburbs
Comfort Inn Landmark	★★★	68	$$$–	Virginia Suburbs
Best Western Tysons Westpark	★★½	62	$$$$+	Virginia Suburbs
Channel Inn Hotel	★★½	62	$$$	National Mall
Comfort Inn Downtown DC/Convention	★★½	62	$$$	Downtown
Embassy Inn	★★½	60	$$$$–	Dupont Circle/ Adams Morgan
Windsor Park Hotel	★★½	56	$$$$–	Dupont Circle/ Adams Morgan

Needless to say, this letter was as unsettling to us as the bad room was to our reader. Our integrity as travel journalists, after all, is based on the quality of the information we provide our readers. Even with the best of intentions and the most conscientious research, however, we cannot inspect every room in every hotel. What we do, in statistical terms, is take a sample: We check out several rooms selected at random in each hotel and base our ratings and rankings on those rooms. The inspections are conducted anonymously and without the knowledge of the management. Although it is unusual, it is certainly possible that the rooms we randomly inspect are not representative of the majority of rooms at a particular hotel. Another possibility is that the rooms we inspect in a given hotel are representative but that by bad luck a reader is assigned a room that is inferior. When we rechecked the hotel our reader disliked, we discovered that our rating was correctly representative but that he and his wife had unfortunately been assigned to one of a small number of threadbare rooms scheduled for renovation.

The key to avoiding disappointment is to snoop around in advance. We recommend that you check out the hotels guestrooms on their website before you book, or at least get a copy of the hotel's promotional brochure. Be forewarned, however, that some hotel chains use the same guestroom photo in their promotional literature for all hotels in the chain; a specific guestroom may not resemble the brochure photo. When you or your travel agent call, ask how old the property is and when your guestroom was last renovated. If you arrive and are assigned a room that does not live up to the brochure's promises, demand to be moved to another room.

GOOD DEALS AND BAD DEALS

HAVING LISTED THE NICEST ROOMS IN TOWN, let's reorder the list to rank the best combinations of quality and price in a room—in other words, its value. Using a mathematical formula that factors in a hotel's quality and star ratings as well as the rack rate, we derive a list of hotels ranked by value. As before, the rankings are made without consideration of location or the availability of restaurants, recreational facilities, entertainment, or amenities. We list only the top 30 hotel values because, as consumers, value-conscious readers are simply concerned with finding the best deals.

We use the hotels' rack rates as a level playing field, so to speak, when calculating value. However, most hotels offer special rates and incentives; they also increase rates to capitalize on periods of peak demand. If you're looking for a room on short notice most times of the year, then the value chart on page 63 should serve you well. If, however, you're planning a value-conscious vacation well in advance, use the chart as a guide but by no means as a substitute for the advice listed under "Getting a Good Deal on a Room," on pages 44–50.

A reader recently complained to us that he had booked one of our top-ranked rooms in terms of value and had been very disappointed in the room. We noticed that the room the reader occupied had a quality rating of ★★½. We remind you that the value ratings are intended to give you some sense of value received for dollars spent. A ★★½ room at $90 may have the same value rating as a ★★★★ room at $200, but that does not mean the rooms will be of comparable quality. Regardless of whether it's a good deal or not, a ★★½ room is still a ★★½ room.

Listed on the next page are the best room buys for the money, ordered without regard to quality or star ratings. Note that sometimes a suite can cost less than a hotel room.

The Top 30 Best Deals in Washington, D.C.

HOTEL	STAR RATING	QUALITY RATING	COST ($=$50)	ZONE NAME
1. Tysons Corner Marriott	★★★½	82	$$–	Virginia Suburbs
2. Hyatt Arlington	★★★★	85	$$+	Virginia Suburbs
3. Radisson Hotel Reagan National	★★★★	84	$$+	Virginia Suburbs
4. Embassy Suites Tysons Corner	★★★★	85	$$+	Virginia Suburbs
5. Hotel Palomar Arlington	★★★★½	90	$$$–	Virginia Suburbs
6. Courtyard Chevy Chase	★★★★	85	$$+	Maryland Suburbs
7. Crowne Plaza Silver Spring	★★★★	84	$$+	Maryland Suburbs
8. Marriott Hotel Bethesda	★★★★	84	$$+	Maryland Suburbs
9. Courtyard Silver Spring Downtown	★★★★	83	$$+	Maryland Suburbs
10. Washington National Airport Hilton	★★★½	79	$$	Virginia Suburbs
11. Hampton Inn & Suites Reagan National Airport	★★★½	82	$$+	Virginia Suburbs
12. Hampton Inn Alexandria	★★★½	82	$$+	Virginia Suburbs
13. Morrison-Clark Inn	★★★★	84	$$$–	Upper Northwest
14. Courtyard New Carrollton	★★★½	80	$$+	Maryland Suburbs
15. Residence Inn Bethesda	★★★★	86	$$$–	Maryland Suburbs
16. Residence Inn Pentagon City	★★★★	84	$$$–	Virginia Suburbs
17. Sheraton Premiere Tysons Corner	★★★★	83	$$$–	Virginia Suburbs
18. Hilton of Silver Spring	★★★½	80	$$+	Maryland Suburbs
19. Washington Suites Alexandria	★★★★	87	$$$	Virginia Suburbs
20. Courtyard Alexandria Pentagon South	★★★½	78	$$+	Virginia Suburbs
21. Hotel Helix	★★★★	88	$$$+	Upper Northwest
22. Hyatt Regency Bethesda	★★★½	81	$$$–	Maryland Suburbs
23. Doubletree Washington, D.C.	★★★★	88	$$$+	Upper Northwest
24. The Quincy	★★★★	84	$$$	Downtown
25. Courtyard Rosslyn	★★★½	80	$$$–	Virginia Suburbs
26. Embassy Suites Crystal City	★★★★	85	$$$+	Virginia Suburbs
27. Hawthorn Suites	★★★★	84	$$$+	Virginia Suburbs
28. Holiday Inn Arlington	★★★½	82	$$$–	Virginia Suburbs
29. Holiday Inn Rosslyn at Key Bridge	★★★½	76	$$$–	Virginia Suburbs
30. Doubletree Bethesda	★★★★	84	$$$+	Maryland Suburbs

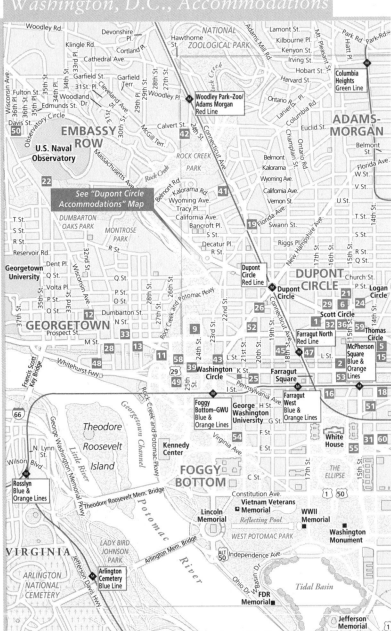

Washington, D.C., Accommodations

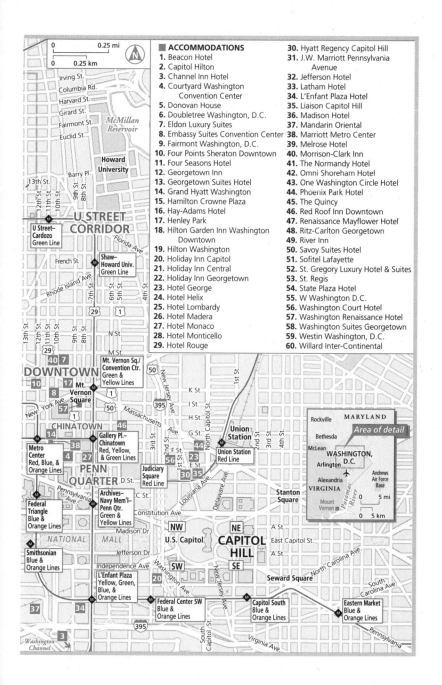

■ **ACCOMMODATIONS**
1. Beacon Hotel
2. Capitol Hilton
3. Channel Inn Hotel
4. Courtyard Washington Convention Center
5. Donovan House
6. Doubletree Washington, D.C.
7. Eldon Luxury Suites
8. Embassy Suites Convention Center
9. Fairmont Washington, D.C.
10. Four Points Sheraton Downtown
11. Four Seasons Hotel
12. Georgetown Inn
13. Georgetown Suites Hotel
14. Grand Hyatt Washington
15. Hamilton Crowne Plaza
16. Hay-Adams Hotel
17. Henley Park
18. Hilton Garden Inn Washington Downtown
19. Hilton Washington
20. Holiday Inn Capitol
21. Holiday Inn Central
22. Holiday Inn Georgetown
23. Hotel George
24. Hotel Helix
25. Hotel Lombardy
26. Hotel Madera
27. Hotel Monaco
28. Hotel Monticello
29. Hotel Rouge
30. Hyatt Regency Capitol Hill
31. J.W. Marriott Pennsylvania Avenue
32. Jefferson Hotel
33. Latham Hotel
34. L'Enfant Plaza Hotel
35. Liaison Capitol Hill
36. Madison Hotel
37. Mandarin Oriental
38. Marriott Metro Center
39. Melrose Hotel
40. Morrison-Clark Inn
41. The Normandy Hotel
42. Omni Shoreham Hotel
43. One Washington Circle Hotel
44. Phoenix Park Hotel
45. The Quincy
46. Red Roof Inn Downtown
47. Renaissance Mayflower Hotel
48. Ritz-Carlton Georgetown
49. River Inn
50. Savoy Suites Hotel
51. Sofitel Lafayette
52. St. Gregory Luxury Hotel & Suites
53. St. Regis
54. State Plaza Hotel
55. W Washington D.C.
56. Washington Court Hotel
57. Washington Renaissance Hotel
58. Washington Suites Georgetown
59. Westin Washington, D.C.
60. Willard Inter-Continental

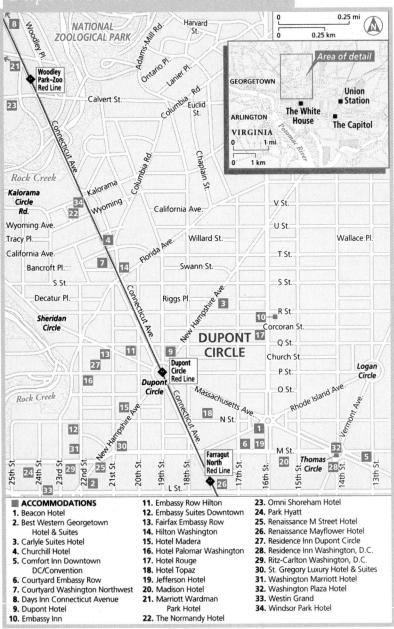

Dupont Circle Accommodations

■ ACCOMMODATIONS

1. Beacon Hotel
2. Best Western Georgetown Hotel & Suites
3. Carlyle Suites Hotel
4. Churchill Hotel
5. Comfort Inn Downtown DC/Convention
6. Courtyard Embassy Row
7. Courtyard Washington Northwest
8. Days Inn Connecticut Avenue
9. Dupont Hotel
10. Embassy Inn
11. Embassy Row Hilton
12. Embassy Suites Downtown
13. Fairfax Embassy Row
14. Hilton Washington
15. Hotel Madera
16. Hotel Palomar Washington
17. Hotel Rouge
18. Hotel Topaz
19. Jefferson Hotel
20. Madison Hotel
21. Marriott Wardman Park Hotel
22. The Normandy Hotel
23. Omni Shoreham Hotel
24. Park Hyatt
25. Renaissance M Street Hotel
26. Renaissance Mayflower Hotel
27. Residence Inn Dupont Circle
28. Residence Inn Washington, D.C.
29. Ritz-Carlton Washington, D.C.
30. St. Gregory Luxury Hotel & Suites
31. Washington Marriott Hotel
32. Washington Plaza Hotel
33. Westin Grand
34. Windsor Park Hotel

Hotel Information Charts

Aloft Washington National Harbor ★★★★
156 Waterfront Street
National Harbor, MD 20745
☎ 301-749-9000
TOLL-FREE ☎ 877-GO-ALOFT
www.aloftnationalharbor.com

ROOM QUALITY	87
COST ($=$50)	$$$$
LOCATION	Maryland Suburbs
NO. OF ROOMS	190
PARKING	Self $11
ROOM SERVICE	—
BREAKFAST	—
ON-SITE DINING	•
POOL	•
SAUNA	—
EXERCISE FACILITIES	•

American Inn of Bethesda ★★★½
8130 Wisconsin Avenue
Bethesda, MD 20814
☎ 301-656-9300
FAX 301-656-2907
TOLL-FREE ☎ 800-323-7081
www.american-inn.com

ROOM QUALITY	81
COST ($=$50)	$$$$–
LOCATION	Maryland Suburbs
NO. OF ROOMS	76
PARKING	Free lot
ROOM SERVICE	—
BREAKFAST	Continental
ON-SITE DINING	•
POOL	•
SAUNA	—
EXERCISE FACILITIES	—

Beacon Hotel ★★★★
1615 Rhode Island Avenue, NW
Washington, DC 20036
☎ 202-296-2100
FAX 202-331-0227
TOLL-FREE ☎ 800-821-4367
www.capitalhotelswdc.com/
BeaconHotelWDC_com

ROOM QUALITY	83
COST ($=$50)	$$$$$+
LOCATION	Dupont Circle/ Adams Morgan
NO. OF ROOMS	199
PARKING	Valet $32
ROOM SERVICE	•
BREAKFAST	•
ON-SITE DINING	•
POOL	Access
SAUNA	—
EXERCISE FACILITIES	•

Best Western Georgetown Hotel & Suites ★★★½
1121 New Hampshire Ave., NW
Washington, DC 20037
☎ 202-457-0565
FAX 202-331-9421
TOLL-FREE ☎ 800-762-3777
www.bestwesternwashingtondc.com

ROOM QUALITY	78
COST ($=$50)	$$$$–
LOCATION	Dupont Circle/ Adams Morgan
NO. OF ROOMS	76
PARKING	Self $20 (off site)
ROOM SERVICE	—
BREAKFAST	Continental
ON-SITE DINING	—
POOL	—
SAUNA	—
EXERCISE FACILITIES	—

Best Western Pentagon Hotel ★★★
2480 S. Glebe Road
Arlington, VA 22206
☎ 703-979-4400
FAX 703-979-0189
TOLL-FREE ☎ 800-426-6886
www.bestwestern.com

ROOM QUALITY	73
COST ($=$50)	$$$–
LOCATION	Virginia Suburbs
NO. OF ROOMS	205
PARKING	Free lot
ROOM SERVICE	—
BREAKFAST	Continental
ON-SITE DINING	•
POOL	•
SAUNA	—
EXERCISE FACILITIES	•

Best Western Rosslyn Iwo Jima ★★★
1501 Arlington Boulevard
Arlington, VA 22209
☎ 703-524-5000
FAX 703-522-5484
TOLL-FREE ☎ 877-424-6423
www.bestwestern.com

ROOM QUALITY	71
COST ($=$50)	$$$+
LOCATION	Virginia Suburbs
NO. OF ROOMS	141
PARKING	Free lot
ROOM SERVICE	•
BREAKFAST	•
ON-SITE DINING	•
POOL	•
SAUNA	—
EXERCISE FACILITIES	•

Best Western Tysons Westpark ★★½
8401 Westpark Drive
McLean, VA 22102
☎ 703-734-2800
FAX 703-734-0521
TOLL-FREE ☎ 800-336-3777
www.comfortinntysons.com

ROOM QUALITY	62
COST ($=$50)	$$$$+
LOCATION	Virginia Suburbs
NO. OF ROOMS	301
PARKING	Free lot
ROOM SERVICE	•
BREAKFAST	—
ON-SITE DINING	•
POOL	•
SAUNA	•
EXERCISE FACILITIES	•

Bethesda Court Hotel ★★★★
7740 Wisconsin Avenue
Bethesda, MD 20814
☎ 301-656-2100
FAX 301-986-0375
TOLL-FREE ☎ 800-874-0050
www.bethesdacourtwashdc.com

ROOM QUALITY	83
COST ($=$50)	$$$$+
LOCATION	Maryland Suburbs
NO. OF ROOMS	74
PARKING	Self $14
ROOM SERVICE	—
BREAKFAST	Continental
ON-SITE DINING	—
POOL	—
SAUNA	•
EXERCISE FACILITIES	•

Capitol Hilton ★★★★
1001 16th Street, NW
Washington, DC 20036
☎ 202-393-1000
FAX 202-639-5784
TOLL-FREE ☎ 800-HILTONS
www.hilton.com

ROOM QUALITY	83
COST ($=$50)	$$$$$–
LOCATION	Downtown
NO. OF ROOMS	544
PARKING	Self and valet $42
ROOM SERVICE	•
BREAKFAST	•
ON-SITE DINING	•
POOL	—
SAUNA	—
EXERCISE FACILITIES	•

Hotel Information Charts (continued)

Carlyle Suites Hotel ★★★★
1731 New Hampshire Avenue, NW
Washington, DC 20009
☎ 202-234-3200
FAX 202-387-0085
TOLL-FREE ☎ 866-468-3532
www.carlylesuites.com

ROOM QUALITY	86
COST ($=$50)	$$$$$+
LOCATION	Dupont Circle/ Adams Morgan
NO. OF ROOMS	170
PARKING	Free lot
ROOM SERVICE	—
BREAKFAST	—
ON-SITE DINING	•
POOL	—
SAUNA	—
EXERCISE FACILITIES	Free access

Channel Inn Hotel ★★½
650 Water Street, SW
Washington, DC 20024
☎ 202-554-2400
FAX 202-863-1164
TOLL-FREE ☎ 800-368-5668
www.channelinn.com

ROOM QUALITY	62
COST ($=$50)	$$$
LOCATION	National Mall
NO. OF ROOMS	100
PARKING	Self, free
ROOM SERVICE	•
BREAKFAST	—
ON-SITE DINING	•
POOL	•
SAUNA	—
EXERCISE FACILITIES	Access

Churchill Hotel ★★★★
1914 Connecticut Avenue, NW
Washington, DC 20009
☎ 202-797-2000
FAX 202-462-0944
TOLL-FREE ☎ 800-424-2464
www.thechurchillhotel.com

ROOM QUALITY	84
COST ($=$50)	$$$$$–
LOCATION	Dupont Circle/ Adams Morgan
NO. OF ROOMS	144
PARKING	Valet $32
ROOM SERVICE	•
BREAKFAST	—
ON-SITE DINING	•
POOL	—
SAUNA	—
EXERCISE FACILITIES	•

Comfort Inn Pentagon ★★★½
2480 S. Glebe Road
Arlington, VA 22206
☎ 703-682-5500
FAX 703-682-5505
TOLL-FREE ☎ 800-325-3535
www.comfortinn.com

ROOM QUALITY	78
COST ($=$50)	$$$–
LOCATION	Virginia Suburbs
NO. OF ROOMS	120
PARKING	Free lot
ROOM SERVICE	•
BREAKFAST	Continental
ON-SITE DINING	•
POOL	•
SAUNA	—
EXERCISE FACILITIES	•

Courtyard Alexandria ★★★½
2700 Eisenhower Avenue
Alexandria, VA 22314
☎ 703-329-2323
FAX 703-329-6853
TOLL-FREE ☎ 800-321-2211
www.marriott.com

ROOM QUALITY	78
COST ($=$50)	$$$–
LOCATION	Virginia Suburbs
NO. OF ROOMS	176
PARKING	Free lot
ROOM SERVICE	—
BREAKFAST	—
ON-SITE DINING	•
POOL	•
SAUNA	—
EXERCISE FACILITIES	•

Courtyard Alexandria Pentagon South ★★★½
4641 Kenmore Avenue
Alexandria, VA 22304
☎ 703-751-4510
FAX 703-751-9170
TOLL-FREE ☎ 888-298-2054
www.marriott.com

ROOM QUALITY	78
COST ($=$50)	$$+
LOCATION	Virginia Suburbs
NO. OF ROOMS	203
PARKING	Self $10
ROOM SERVICE	—
BREAKFAST	—
ON-SITE DINING	•
POOL	•
SAUNA	—
EXERCISE FACILITIES	•

Courtyard New Carrollton ★★★½
8330 Corporate Drive
Landover, MD 20785
☎ 301-577-3373
FAX 301-577-1780
TOLL-FREE ☎ 800-321-2211
www.marriott.com

ROOM QUALITY	80
COST ($=$50)	$$+
LOCATION	Maryland Suburbs
NO. OF ROOMS	150
PARKING	Free lot
ROOM SERVICE	•
BREAKFAST	—
ON-SITE DINING	•
POOL	•
SAUNA	—
EXERCISE FACILITIES	•

Courtyard Rosslyn ★★★½
1533 Clarendon Boulevard
Rosslyn, VA 22209
☎ 703-528-2222
FAX 703-528-1027
TOLL-FREE ☎ 800-321-2211
www.marriott.com

ROOM QUALITY	80
COST ($=$50)	$$$–
LOCATION	Virginia Suburbs
NO. OF ROOMS	162
PARKING	Self $10
ROOM SERVICE	•
BREAKFAST	—
ON-SITE DINING	•
POOL	•
SAUNA	—
EXERCISE FACILITIES	•

Courtyard Silver Spring Downtown ★★★★
8506 Fenton Street
Silver Spring, MD 20910
☎ 301-589-4899
FAX 301-589-4898
TOLL-FREE ☎ 800-321-2211
www.marriott.com

ROOM QUALITY	83
COST ($=$50)	$$+
LOCATION	Maryland Suburbs
NO. OF ROOMS	184
PARKING	Self $8.25
ROOM SERVICE	•
BREAKFAST	—
ON-SITE DINING	•
POOL	Access
SAUNA	—
EXERCISE FACILITIES	Access

Comfort Inn Arlington Blvd/Falls Church ★★★

6111 Arlington Boulevard
Falls Church , VA 22044
☎ 703-534-9100
FAX 703-534-5589
TOLL-FREE ☎ 800-228-5150
www.ichotelsgroup.com

ROOM QUALITY	68
COST ($=$50)	$$$+
LOCATION	Virginia Suburbs
NO. OF ROOMS	111
PARKING	Free lot
ROOM SERVICE	–
BREAKFAST	Continental
ON-SITE DINING	–
POOL	•
SAUNA	–
EXERCISE FACILITIES	•

Comfort Inn Downtown DC/Convention ★★½

1201 13th Street, NW
Washington, DC 20005
☎ 202-682-5300
FAX 202-408-0830
TOLL-FREE ☎ 800-787-6589
www.comfortinn.com

ROOM QUALITY	62
COST ($=$50)	$$$
LOCATION	Downtown
NO. OF ROOMS	100
PARKING	Self $27
ROOM SERVICE	–
BREAKFAST	Continental
ON-SITE DINING	–
POOL	–
SAUNA	–
EXERCISE FACILITIES	•

Comfort Inn Landmark ★★★

6254 Duke Street
Alexandria, VA 22312
☎ 703-642-3422
FAX 703-642-1354
TOLL-FREE ☎ 877-424-6423
www.comfortinn.com

ROOM QUALITY	68
COST ($=$50)	$$$–
LOCATION	Virginia Suburbs
NO. OF ROOMS	150
PARKING	Free lot
ROOM SERVICE	–
BREAKFAST	Continental
ON-SITE DINING	•
POOL	•
SAUNA	–
EXERCISE FACILITIES	–

Courtyard Chevy Chase ★★★★

5520 Wisconsin Avenue
Chevy Chase, MD 20815
☎ 301-656-1500
FAX 301-656-5766
TOLL-FREE ☎ 800-321-2211
www.marriott.com

ROOM QUALITY	85
COST ($=$50)	$$+
LOCATION	Maryland Suburbs
NO. OF ROOMS	226
PARKING	Free lot
ROOM SERVICE	•
BREAKFAST	–
ON-SITE DINING	•
POOL	•
SAUNA	–
EXERCISE FACILITIES	•

Courtyard Crystal City ★★★½

2899 Jefferson Davis Highway
Arlington, VA 22202
☎ 703-549-3434
FAX 703-549-7440
TOLL-FREE ☎ 800-847-4775
www.marriott.com

ROOM QUALITY	80
COST ($=$50)	$$$+
LOCATION	Virginia Suburbs
NO. OF ROOMS	272
PARKING	Self $16
ROOM SERVICE	•
BREAKFAST	–
ON-SITE DINING	•
POOL	•
SAUNA	–
EXERCISE FACILITIES	•

Courtyard Embassy Row ★★★½

1600 Rhode Island Avenue, NW
Washington, DC 20036
☎ 202-293-8000
FAX 202-293-0085
TOLL-FREE ☎ 800-321-2211
www.courtyardembassyrow.com

ROOM QUALITY	82
COST ($=$50)	$$$$–
LOCATION	Dupont Circle/ Adams Morgan
NO. OF ROOMS	156
PARKING	Valet $28
ROOM SERVICE	•
BREAKFAST	–
ON-SITE DINING	•
POOL	•
SAUNA	–
EXERCISE FACILITIES	•

Courtyard Washington Convention Center ★★★½

900 F Street
Washington, DC 20004
☎ 202-638-4600
FAX 202-638-4601
TOLL-FREE ☎ 800-393-3063
www.marriott.com

ROOM QUALITY	81
COST ($=$50)	$$$$–
LOCATION	Downtown
NO. OF ROOMS	188
PARKING	Self and valet $32
ROOM SERVICE	•
BREAKFAST	–
ON-SITE DINING	•
POOL	•
SAUNA	–
EXERCISE FACILITIES	•

Courtyard Washington Northwest ★★★½

1900 Connecticut Avenue, NW
Washington, DC 20009
☎ 202-332-9300
FAX 202-328-7039
TOLL-FREE ☎ 800-321-2211
www.marriott.com

ROOM QUALITY	78
COST ($=$50)	$$$$$–
LOCATION	Dupont Circle/ Adams Morgan
NO. OF ROOMS	147
PARKING	Valet $25
ROOM SERVICE	•
BREAKFAST	–
ON-SITE DINING	•
POOL	•
SAUNA	–
EXERCISE FACILITIES	•

Crowne Plaza Hotel Old Town ★★★★

901 N. FairFAX Street
Alexandria, VA 22314
☎ 703-683-6000
FAX 703-683-7597
TOLL-FREE ☎ 800-333-3333
www.ichotelsgroup.com

ROOM QUALITY	83
COST ($=$50)	$$$$+
LOCATION	Virginia Suburbs
NO. OF ROOMS	253
PARKING	Self $20
ROOM SERVICE	•
BREAKFAST	–
ON-SITE DINING	•
POOL	•
SAUNA	–
EXERCISE FACILITIES	•

Hotel Information Charts (continued)

Crowne Plaza National Airport ★★★½
1480 Crystal Drive
Arlington, VA 22202
☎ 703-416-1600
FAX 703-416-1651
TOLL-FREE ☎ 800-2-CROWNE
www.cpnationalairport.com

ROOM QUALITY	76
COST ($=$50)	$$$–
LOCATION	Virginia Suburbs
NO. OF ROOMS	308
PARKING	Self $19
ROOM SERVICE	•
BREAKFAST	—
ON-SITE DINING	•
POOL	•
SAUNA	—
EXERCISE FACILITIES	•

Crowne Plaza Silver Spring ★★★★
8777 Georgia Avenue
Silver Spring, MD 20910
☎ 301-589-0800
FAX 301-587-4791
TOLL-FREE ☎ 800-972-3159
www.ichotelsgroup.com

ROOM QUALITY	84
COST ($=$50)	$$+
LOCATION	Maryland Suburbs
NO. OF ROOMS	242
PARKING	Self $12, valet $15
ROOM SERVICE	•
BREAKFAST	—
ON-SITE DINING	•
POOL	•
SAUNA	—
EXERCISE FACILITIES	•

Days Inn Connecticut Ave ★★★
4400 Connecticut Avenue, NW
Washington, DC 20008
☎ 202-244-5600
FAX 202-244-6794
TOLL-FREE ☎ 800-952-3060
www.daysinn.com

ROOM QUALITY	70
COST ($=$50)	$$$+
LOCATION	Upper Northwest
NO. OF ROOMS	155
PARKING	Self $22.50
ROOM SERVICE	•
BREAKFAST	—
ON-SITE DINING	•
POOL	—
SAUNA	—
EXERCISE FACILITIES	—

Doubletree Washington, D.C. ★★★★
1515 Rhode Island Avenue, NW
Washington, DC 20036
☎ 202-232-7000
FAX 202-521-7103
TOLL-FREE ☎ 800-222-TREE
www.doubletree.com

ROOM QUALITY	88
COST ($=$50)	$$$+
LOCATION	Upper Northwest
NO. OF ROOMS	219
PARKING	Valet $33
ROOM SERVICE	•
BREAKFAST	—
ON-SITE DINING	•
POOL	—
SAUNA	—
EXERCISE FACILITIES	•

Dupont Hotel ★★★½
1500 New Hampshire Avenue, NW
Washington, DC 20036
☎ 202-483-6000
TOLL-FREE ☎ 866-534-6835
www.doylecollection.com

ROOM QUALITY	81
COST ($=$50)	$$$$$$$+
LOCATION	Dupont Circle/ Adams Morgan
NO. OF ROOMS	327
PARKING	Valet $33
ROOM SERVICE	•
BREAKFAST	—
ON-SITE DINING	•
POOL	—
SAUNA	—
EXERCISE FACILITIES	•

Eldon Luxury Suites ★★★★½
933 L Street, NW
Washington, DC 20001
☎ 202-540-5000
FAX 202-290-1460
TOLL-FREE ☎ 877-463-5336
www.eldonsuites.com

ROOM QUALITY	93
COST ($=$50)	$$$$$$+
LOCATION	Downtown
NO. OF ROOMS	50
PARKING	Valet $25
ROOM SERVICE	•
BREAKFAST	Continental
ON-SITE DINING	—
POOL	—
SAUNA	—
EXERCISE FACILITIES	•

Embassy Suites Chevy Chase ★★★★
4300 Military Road, NW
Washington, DC 20015
☎ 202-362-9300
FAX 202-686-3405
TOLL-FREE ☎ 800-EMBASSY
www.embassysuites.hilton.com

ROOM QUALITY	88
COST ($=$50)	$$$$
LOCATION	Upper Northwest
NO. OF ROOMS	198
PARKING	Self $24
ROOM SERVICE	—
BREAKFAST	Cooked to order
ON-SITE DINING	•
POOL	•
SAUNA	—
EXERCISE FACILITIES	•

Embassy Suites Conv. Center ★★★★
900 10th Street, NW
Washington, DC 20001
☎ 202-739-2001
FAX 202-739-2099
TOLL-FREE ☎ 800-EMBASSY
www.embassysuites.hilton.com

ROOM QUALITY	85
COST ($=$50)	$$$$+
LOCATION	Downtown
NO. OF ROOMS	384
PARKING	Valet $35
ROOM SERVICE	•
BREAKFAST	Cooked to order
ON-SITE DINING	•
POOL	•
SAUNA	—
EXERCISE FACILITIES	•

Embassy Suites Crystal City ★★★★
1300 Jefferson Davis Highway
Arlington, VA 22202
☎ 703-979-9799
FAX 703-920-5947
TOLL-FREE ☎ 800-EMBASSY
www.embassysuites.hilton.com

ROOM QUALITY	85
COST ($=$50)	$$$+
LOCATION	Virginia Suburbs
NO. OF ROOMS	267
PARKING	Self $22
ROOM SERVICE	•
BREAKFAST	Cooked to order
ON-SITE DINING	•
POOL	•
SAUNA	—
EXERCISE FACILITIES	•

Donovan House ★★★★
1155 14th Street, NW
Washington, DC 20005
☎ 202-737-1200
TOLL-FREE ☎ 800-383-6900
www.thompsonhotels.com

ROOM QUALITY	83
COST ($=$50)	$$$$
LOCATION	Downtown
NO. OF ROOMS	193
PARKING	Valet $38
ROOM SERVICE	•
BREAKFAST	—
ON-SITE DINING	•
POOL	•
SAUNA	—
EXERCISE FACILITIES	•

Doubletree Bethesda ★★★★
8120 Wisconsin Avenue
Bethesda, MD 20814
☎ 301-652-2000
FAX 301-664-7317
TOLL-FREE ☎ 800-222-8733
www.doubletreebethesda.com

ROOM QUALITY	84
COST ($=$50)	$$$+
LOCATION	Maryland Suburbs
NO. OF ROOMS	269
PARKING	Valet $20
ROOM SERVICE	•
BREAKFAST	—
ON-SITE DINING	•
POOL	•
SAUNA	—
EXERCISE FACILITIES	•

Doubletree Hotel Crystal City ★★★★
300 Army Navy Drive
Arlington, VA 22202
☎ 703-416-4100
FAX 703-416-4126
TOLL-FREE ☎ 800-222-TREE
www.doubletree.com

ROOM QUALITY	83
COST ($=$50)	$$$+
LOCATION	Virginia Suburbs
NO. OF ROOMS	631
PARKING	Self $22, valet $27
ROOM SERVICE	•
BREAKFAST	—
ON-SITE DINING	•
POOL	•
SAUNA	—
EXERCISE FACILITIES	•

Embassy Inn ★★½
1627 16th Street, NW
Washington, DC 20009
☎ 202-234-7800
FAX 202-234-3309
TOLL-FREE ☎ 877-968-9111
www.embassy-inn.com

ROOM QUALITY	60
COST ($=$50)	$$$$–
LOCATION	Dupont Circle/ Adams Morgan
NO. OF ROOMS	38
PARKING	Self $16
ROOM SERVICE	—
BREAKFAST	Continental
ON-SITE DINING	—
POOL	—
SAUNA	—
EXERCISE FACILITIES	—

Embassy Row Hilton ★★★★
2015 Massachusetts Avenue, NW
Washington, DC 20036
☎ 202-265-1600
FAX 202-328-7526
TOLL-FREE ☎ 800-HILTONS
www.hilton.com

ROOM QUALITY	83
COST ($=$50)	$$$$+
LOCATION	Dupont Circle/ Adams Morgan
NO. OF ROOMS	196
PARKING	Valet $35
ROOM SERVICE	•
BREAKFAST	—
ON-SITE DINING	•
POOL	•
SAUNA	—
EXERCISE FACILITIES	•

Embassy Suites Alexandria ★★★★
1900 Diagonal Road
Alexandria, VA 22314
☎ 703-684-5900
FAX 703-684-1403
TOLL-FREE ☎ 800-EMBASSY
www.embassysuites.hilton.com

ROOM QUALITY	84
COST ($=$50)	$$$+
LOCATION	Virginia Suburbs
NO. OF ROOMS	268
PARKING	Self $24
ROOM SERVICE	—
BREAKFAST	Cooked to order
ON-SITE DINING	•
POOL	•
SAUNA	—
EXERCISE FACILITIES	•

Embassy Suites Downtown ★★★★
1250 22nd Street, NW
Washington, DC 20037
☎ 202-857-3388
FAX 202-293-3173
TOLL-FREE ☎ 800-EMBASSY
www.embassysuites.hilton.com

ROOM QUALITY	84
COST ($=$50)	$$$$$$
LOCATION	Dupont Circle/ Adams Morgan
NO. OF ROOMS	318
PARKING	Self $32
ROOM SERVICE	•
BREAKFAST	Cooked to order
ON-SITE DINING	•
POOL	•
SAUNA	—
EXERCISE FACILITIES	•

Embassy Suites Tysons Corner ★★★★
8517 Leesburg Pike
Vienna, VA 22182
☎ 703-883-0707
FAX 703-760-9842
TOLL-FREE ☎ 800-EMBASSY
www.embassysuites.hilton.com

ROOM QUALITY	85
COST ($=$50)	$$+
LOCATION	Virginia Suburbs
NO. OF ROOMS	232
PARKING	Free lot
ROOM SERVICE	•
BREAKFAST	Cooked to order
ON-SITE DINING	•
POOL	•
SAUNA	—
EXERCISE FACILITIES	•

Fairfax Embassy Row ★★★★
2100 Massachusetts Avenue, NW
Washington, DC 20008
☎ 202-293-2100
FAX 202-293-0641
TOLL-FREE ☎ 888-625-5143
www.starwoodhotels.com

ROOM QUALITY	84
COST ($=$50)	$$$$$$$$+
LOCATION	Dupont Circle/ Adams Morgan
NO. OF ROOMS	259
PARKING	Valet $28
ROOM SERVICE	•
BREAKFAST	—
ON-SITE DINING	•
POOL	•
SAUNA	—
EXERCISE FACILITIES	•

Hotel Information Charts (continued)

Fairmont Washington, D.C. ★★★★
2401 M Street, NW
Washington, DC 20037
☎ 202-429-2400
FAX 202-457-5010
TOLL-FREE ☎ 800-257-7544
www.fairmont.com/washington

ROOM QUALITY	85
COST ($=$50)	$$$$+
LOCATION	Georgetown
NO. OF ROOMS	415
PARKING	Valet $35
ROOM SERVICE	•
BREAKFAST	—
ON-SITE DINING	•
POOL	•
SAUNA	•
EXERCISE FACILITIES	Fee $15

Four Points Sheraton Downtown ★★★½
1201 K Street, NW
Washington, DC 20005
☎ 202-289-7600
FAX 202-349-2215
TOLL-FREE ☎ 888-625-5144
www.fourpointswashingtondc.com

ROOM QUALITY	75
COST ($=$50)	$$$$$–
LOCATION	Downtown
NO. OF ROOMS	265
PARKING	Valet $35
ROOM SERVICE	•
BREAKFAST	—
ON-SITE DINING	•
POOL	•
SAUNA	—
EXERCISE FACILITIES	•

Four Seasons Hotel ★★★★
2800 Pennsylvania Avenue, NW
Washington, DC 20007
☎ 202-342-0444
FAX 202-944-2076
TOLL-FREE ☎ 800-819-5053
www.fourseasons.com

ROOM QUALITY	89
COST ($=$50)	$$$$$$$$$+
LOCATION	Georgetown
NO. OF ROOMS	211
PARKING	Valet $32
ROOM SERVICE	•
BREAKFAST	—
ON-SITE DINING	•
POOL	•
SAUNA	•
EXERCISE FACILITIES	•

Grand Hyatt Washington ★★★★
1000 H Street, NW
Washington, DC 20001
☎ 202-582-1234
FAX 202-637-4781
TOLL-FREE ☎ 800-233-1234
www.grandwashingtonhyatt.com

ROOM QUALITY	87
COST ($=$50)	$$$$–
LOCATION	Downtown
NO. OF ROOMS	888
PARKING	Self $25, valet $35
ROOM SERVICE	•
BREAKFAST	—
ON-SITE DINING	•
POOL	•
SAUNA	•
EXERCISE FACILITIES	•

Hamilton Crowne Plaza ★★★½
1001 14th Street NW
Washington, DC 20005
☎ 202-682-0111
FAX 202-682-9525
TOLL-FREE ☎ 800-980-6429
www.hamiltonhoteldc.com

ROOM QUALITY	78
COST ($=$50)	$$$$$–
LOCATION	Downtown
NO. OF ROOMS	318
PARKING	Valet $35
ROOM SERVICE	•
BREAKFAST	—
ON-SITE DINING	•
POOL	—
SAUNA	—
EXERCISE FACILITIES	•

Hampton Inn Alexandria ★★★½
4800 Leesburg Pike
Alexandria, VA 22302
☎ 703-671-4800
FAX 703-671-2442
TOLL-FREE ☎ 800-HAMPTON
www.hamptoninn.com

ROOM QUALITY	82
COST ($=$50)	$$+
LOCATION	Virginia Suburbs
NO. OF ROOMS	130
PARKING	Free lot
ROOM SERVICE	•
BREAKFAST	Full
ON-SITE DINING	—
POOL	•
SAUNA	—
EXERCISE FACILITIES	•

Henley Park Hotel ★★★½
926 Massachusetts Avenue, NW
Washington, DC 20001
☎ 202-638-5200
TOLL-FREE ☎ 800-222-8474
www.henleypark.com

ROOM QUALITY	81
COST ($=$50)	$$$
LOCATION	Downtown
NO. OF ROOMS	96
PARKING	Valet $35
ROOM SERVICE	•
BREAKFAST	—
ON-SITE DINING	•
POOL	Off-site privileges
SAUNA	—
EXERCISE FACILITIES	Off-site privileges

Hilton Alexandria at Mark Center ★★★½
5000 Seminary Road
Alexandria, VA 22311
☎ 703-845-1010
FAX 703-845-7662
TOLL-FREE ☎ 800-HILTONS
www.hilton.com

ROOM QUALITY	82
COST ($=$50)	$$$+
LOCATION	Virginia Suburbs
NO. OF ROOMS	496
PARKING	Self $15, valet $20
ROOM SERVICE	•
BREAKFAST	—
ON-SITE DINING	•
POOL	•
SAUNA	—
EXERCISE FACILITIES	•

Hilton Arlington and Towers ★★★★
950 N. Stafford Street
Arlington, VA 22203
☎ 703-528-6000
FAX 703-528-4386
TOLL-FREE ☎ 800-HILTONS
www.hilton.com

ROOM QUALITY	83
COST ($=$50)	$$$$$+
LOCATION	Virginia Suburbs
NO. OF ROOMS	208
PARKING	Self $17
ROOM SERVICE	•
BREAKFAST	—
ON-SITE DINING	•
POOL	—
SAUNA	—
EXERCISE FACILITIES	—

Gaylord National
★★★★½
201 Waterfront Street
National Harbor, MD 20745
☎ 301-965-4000
www.gaylordhotels.com

ROOM QUALITY	91
COST ($=$50)	$$$$$$–
LOCATION	Maryland Suburbs
NO. OF ROOMS	2,000
PARKING	Self $19, valet $28
ROOM SERVICE	•
BREAKFAST	–
ON-SITE DINING	•
POOL	•
SAUNA	•
EXERCISE FACILITIES	•

Georgetown Inn ★★★★
1310 Wisconsin Avenue, NW
Washington, DC 20007
☎ 202-333-8900
FAX 202-625-1744
TOLL-FREE ☎ 888-587-2388
www.georgetowncollection.com

ROOM QUALITY	84
COST ($=$50)	$$$$+
LOCATION	Georgetown
NO. OF ROOMS	96
PARKING	Valet $32
ROOM SERVICE	•
BREAKFAST	–
ON-SITE DINING	•
POOL	–
SAUNA	–
EXERCISE FACILITIES	•

Georgetown Suites Hotel ★★★★
1111 30th Street, NW
Washington, DC
☎ 202-298-7800
FAX 202-333-5792
TOLL-FREE ☎ 800-348-7203
www.georgetownsuites.com

ROOM QUALITY	88
COST ($=$50)	$$$$
LOCATION	Georgetown
NO. OF ROOMS	220
PARKING	Self $20
ROOM SERVICE	–
BREAKFAST	Continental
ON-SITE DINING	–
POOL	–
SAUNA	–
EXERCISE FACILITIES	•

Hampton Inn Reagan National Airport ★★★½
2000 Jefferson Davis Highway
Arlington, VA 22202
☎ 703-418-8181
FAX 703-418-4666
TOLL-FREE ☎ 800-HAMPTON
www.hamptoninn.com

ROOM QUALITY	82
COST ($=$50)	$$+
LOCATION	Virginia Suburbs
NO. OF ROOMS	161
PARKING	Self $12
ROOM SERVICE	•
BREAKFAST	Full
ON-SITE DINING	–
POOL	•
SAUNA	–
EXERCISE FACILITIES	•

Hawthorn Suites ★★★★
420 North Van Dorn Street
Alexandria, VA 22304
☎ 703-370-1000
FAX 703-751-1467
TOLL-FREE ☎ 800-368-3339
www.hawthorn.com

ROOM QUALITY	84
COST ($=$50)	$$$+
LOCATION	Virginia Suburbs
NO. OF ROOMS	185
PARKING	Free lot
ROOM SERVICE	–
BREAKFAST	Buffet
ON-SITE DINING	–
POOL	•
SAUNA	–
EXERCISE FACILITIES	•

Hay-Adams Hotel ★★★★½
800 16th St. NW
Washington, DC 20006
☎ 202-638-6600
FAX 202-638-2716
TOLL-FREE ☎ 800-853-6807
www.hayadams.com

ROOM QUALITY	91
COST ($=$50)	$$$$$$$–
LOCATION	Downtown
NO. OF ROOMS	145
PARKING	Valet $35
ROOM SERVICE	•
BREAKFAST	–
ON-SITE DINING	•
POOL	–
SAUNA	–
EXERCISE FACILITIES	–

Hilton Garden Inn Washington Downtown ★★★½
815 14th Street, NW
Washington, DC 20005
☎ 202-783-7800
FAX 202-783-7801
TOLL-FREE ☎ 800-HILTONS
www.hiltongardeninn.com

ROOM QUALITY	78
COST ($=$50)	$$$$+
LOCATION	Downtown
NO. OF ROOMS	300
PARKING	Valet $35
ROOM SERVICE	•
BREAKFAST	–
ON-SITE DINING	•
POOL	•
SAUNA	–
EXERCISE FACILITIES	•

Hilton of Silver Spring ★★★½
8727 Colesville Road
Silver Spring, MD 20910
☎ 301-589-5200
FAX 301-588-1841
TOLL-FREE ☎ 800-445-8667
www.hilton.com

ROOM QUALITY	80
COST ($=$50)	$$+
LOCATION	Maryland Suburbs
NO. OF ROOMS	263
PARKING	Valet $15
ROOM SERVICE	•
BREAKFAST	–
ON-SITE DINING	•
POOL	•
SAUNA	–
EXERCISE FACILITIES	•

Hilton Washington ★★★½
1919 Connecticut Avenue, NW
Washington, DC 20009
☎ 202-483-3000
FAX 202-232-0438
TOLL-FREE ☎ 800-HILTONS
www.hilton.com

ROOM QUALITY	82
COST ($=$50)	$$$$$$$–
LOCATION	Dupont Circle/ Adams Morgan
NO. OF ROOMS	1,119
PARKING	Self $32, valet $37
ROOM SERVICE	•
BREAKFAST	–
ON-SITE DINING	•
POOL	•
SAUNA	–
EXERCISE FACILITIES	•

Hotel Information Charts (continued)

Holiday Inn Alexandria ★★★
2460 Eisenhower Avenue
Alexandria, VA 22314
☎ 703-960-3400
FAX 703-329-0953
TOLL-FREE ☎ 800-315-2621
www.holidayinn.com

ROOM QUALITY	70
COST ($=$50)	$$$–
LOCATION	Virginia Suburbs
NO. OF ROOMS	196
PARKING	Free lot
ROOM SERVICE	•
BREAKFAST	—
ON-SITE DINING	•
POOL	•
SAUNA	—
EXERCISE FACILITIES	•

Holiday Inn Arlington ★★★½
4610 N. FairFAX Drive
Arlington, VA 22203
☎ 703-243-9800
FAX 703-527-2677
TOLL-FREE ☎ 800-315-2621
www.hiarlington.com

ROOM QUALITY	82
COST ($=$50)	$$$–
LOCATION	Virginia Suburbs
NO. OF ROOMS	221
PARKING	Self $10, free Fri. and Sat.
ROOM SERVICE	•
BREAKFAST	—
ON-SITE DINING	•
POOL	•
SAUNA	—
EXERCISE FACILITIES	•

Holiday Inn Capitol ★★★½
550 C Street, SW
Washington, DC 20024
☎ 202-479-4000
FAX 202-479-4353
TOLL-FREE ☎ 800-972-3159
www.ichotelsgroup.com

ROOM QUALITY	76
COST ($=$50)	$$$$+
LOCATION	Capitol Hill
NO. OF ROOMS	532
PARKING	Self $30
ROOM SERVICE	•
BREAKFAST	—
ON-SITE DINING	—
POOL	•
SAUNA	—
EXERCISE FACILITIES	•

Holiday Inn National Airport ★★★
2650 Jefferson Davis Highway
Arlington, VA 22202
☎ 703-684-7200
FAX 703-684-3217
TOLL-FREE ☎ 800-972-3159
www.hinationalairport.com

ROOM QUALITY	74
COST ($=$50)	$$$
LOCATION	Virginia Suburbs
NO. OF ROOMS	280
PARKING	Self $16
ROOM SERVICE	•
BREAKFAST	—
ON-SITE DINING	•
POOL	•
SAUNA	—
EXERCISE FACILITIES	•

Holiday Inn Rosslyn at Key Bridge ★★★½
1900 N. Fort Myer Drive
Arlington, VA 22209
☎ 703-807-2000
FAX 703-522-8864
TOLL-FREE ☎ 888-465-4329
www.ichotelsgroup.com

ROOM QUALITY	76
COST ($=$50)	$$$–
LOCATION	Virginia Suburbs
NO. OF ROOMS	307
PARKING	Free lot
ROOM SERVICE	•
BREAKFAST	—
ON-SITE DINING	•
POOL	•
SAUNA	—
EXERCISE FACILITIES	•

Hotel George ★★★★
15 E Street, NW
Washington, DC 20001
☎ 202-347-4200
FAX 202-346-4213
TOLL-FREE ☎ 800-576-8331
www.hotelgeorge.com

ROOM QUALITY	85
COST ($=$50)	$$$$$+
LOCATION	Downtown
NO. OF ROOMS	139
PARKING	Valet $40
ROOM SERVICE	•
BREAKFAST	—
ON-SITE DINING	•
POOL	—
SAUNA	•
EXERCISE FACILITIES	•

Hotel Monaco ★★★★
700 F Street, NW
Washington, DC 20004
☎ 202-628-7177
FAX 202-628-7277
TOLL-FREE ☎ 800-649-1202
www.monaco-dc.com

ROOM QUALITY	86
COST ($=$50)	$$$$$
LOCATION	Downtown
NO. OF ROOMS	184
PARKING	Valet $38
ROOM SERVICE	•
BREAKFAST	—
ON-SITE DINING	•
POOL	—
SAUNA	—
EXERCISE FACILITIES	•

Hotel Monaco Alexandria ★★★★½
480 King Street
Alexandria, VA 22314
☎ 703-549-6080
FAX 703-684-6508
TOLL-FREE ☎ 800-368-5047
www.monaco-alexandria.com

ROOM QUALITY	90
COST ($=$50)	$$$$$$–
LOCATION	Virginia Suburbs
NO. OF ROOMS	241
PARKING	Valet $24
ROOM SERVICE	•
BREAKFAST	Continental
ON-SITE DINING	•
POOL	•
SAUNA	•
EXERCISE FACILITIES	•

Hotel Monticello ★★★★
1075 Thomas Jefferson Street, NW
Washington, DC 20007
☎ 202-337-0900
FAX 202-333-6526
TOLL-FREE ☎ 800-388-2410
www.monticellohotel.com

ROOM QUALITY	84
COST ($=$50)	$$$$$–
LOCATION	Georgetown
NO. OF ROOMS	47
PARKING	Valet $30
ROOM SERVICE	—
BREAKFAST	Continental
ON-SITE DINING	—
POOL	—
SAUNA	—
EXERCISE FACILITIES	—

Holiday Inn Central ★★★
1501 Rhode Island Avenue, NW
Washington, DC 20005
☎ 202-483-2000
FAX 202-797-1078
TOLL-FREE ☎ 800-972-3159
www.choicehotels.com

ROOM QUALITY	70
COST ($=$50)	$$$+
LOCATION	Upper Northwest
NO. OF ROOMS	212
PARKING	Self $30
ROOM SERVICE	•
BREAKFAST	—
ON-SITE DINING	•
POOL	•
SAUNA	—
EXERCISE FACILITIES	•

Holiday Inn Georgetown ★★★½
2101 Wisconsin Avenue, NW
Washington, DC 20007
☎ 202-338-4600
FAX 202-338-4458
TOLL-FREE ☎ 800-HOLIDAY
www.higeorgetown.com

ROOM QUALITY	78
COST ($=$50)	$$$+
LOCATION	Upper Northwest
NO. OF ROOMS	285
PARKING	Self $20
ROOM SERVICE	•
BREAKFAST	—
ON-SITE DINING	•
POOL	•
SAUNA	—
EXERCISE FACILITIES	•

Holiday Inn Hotel and Suites ★★★
625 First Street
Alexandria, VA 22314
☎ 703-548-6300
FAX 703-548-8032
TOLL-FREE ☎ 800-972-3159
ichotelsgroup.com

ROOM QUALITY	72
COST ($=$50)	$$$–
LOCATION	Virginia Suburbs
NO. OF ROOMS	178
PARKING	Self $20
ROOM SERVICE	•
BREAKFAST	—
ON-SITE DINING	•
POOL	•
SAUNA	•
EXERCISE FACILITIES	•

Hotel Helix ★★★★
1430 Rhode Island Avenue, NW
Washington, DC 20005
☎ 202-462-9001
FAX 202-332-3519
TOLL-FREE ☎ 800-706-1202
www.hotelhelix.com

ROOM QUALITY	88
COST ($=$50)	$$$+
LOCATION	Upper Northwest
NO. OF ROOMS	178
PARKING	Valet $33
ROOM SERVICE	•
BREAKFAST	Continental
ON-SITE DINING	•
POOL	—
SAUNA	—
EXERCISE FACILITIES	•

Hotel Lombardy ★★★½
2019 Pennsylvania Avenue N.W.
Washington, DC 20006
☎ 202-828-2600
FAX 202-872-0503
TOLL-FREE ☎ 800-424-5486
www.hotellombardy.com

ROOM QUALITY	82
COST ($=$50)	$$$+
LOCATION	Foggy Bottom
NO. OF ROOMS	140
PARKING	Valet $30
ROOM SERVICE	•
BREAKFAST	—
ON-SITE DINING	•
POOL	•
SAUNA	—
EXERCISE FACILITIES	•

Hotel Madera ★★★★
1310 New Hampshire Avenue, NW
Washington, DC 20036
☎ 202-296-7600
FAX 202-293-2476
TOLL-FREE ☎ 800-368-5691
www.hotelmadera.com

ROOM QUALITY	88
COST ($=$50)	$$$$–
LOCATION	Dupont Circle/ Adams Morgan
NO. OF ROOMS	82
PARKING	Valet $38
ROOM SERVICE	•
BREAKFAST	—
ON-SITE DINING	•
POOL	—
SAUNA	—
EXERCISE FACILITIES	—

Hotel Palomar Arlington ★★★★½
1121 N. 19th Street
Arlington, VA 22209
☎ 703-351-9170
FAX 703-894-5079
TOLL-FREE ☎ 866-505-1001
www.hotelpalomar-arlington.com

ROOM QUALITY	90
COST ($=$50)	$$$–
LOCATION	Virginia Suburbs
NO. OF ROOMS	154
PARKING	Valet $18
ROOM SERVICE	•
BREAKFAST	—
ON-SITE DINING	•
POOL	—
SAUNA	—
EXERCISE FACILITIES	•

Hotel Palomar Washington ★★★★
2121 P Street, NW
Washington, DC 20037
☎ 202-293-3100
FAX 202-857-0134
TOLL-FREE ☎ 800-333-3333
www.hotelpalomar-dc.com

ROOM QUALITY	85
COST ($=$50)	$$$$$+
LOCATION	Dupont Circle/ Adams Morgan
NO. OF ROOMS	325
PARKING	Valet $40
ROOM SERVICE	•
BREAKFAST	—
ON-SITE DINING	•
POOL	•
SAUNA	—
EXERCISE FACILITIES	•

Hotel Rouge ★★★★
1315 16th Street, NW
Washington, DC 20036
☎ 202-232-8000
FAX 202-667-9827
TOLL-FREE ☎ 800-738-1022
www.rougehotel.com

ROOM QUALITY	84
COST ($=$50)	$$$+
LOCATION	Dupont Circle/ Adams Morgan
NO. OF ROOMS	137
PARKING	Valet $33
ROOM SERVICE	•
BREAKFAST	—
ON-SITE DINING	•
POOL	—
SAUNA	—
EXERCISE FACILITIES	•

Hotel Information Charts (continued)

Hotel Topaz ★★★★
1733 N Street, NW
Washington, DC 20036
☎ 202-393-3000
FAX 202-785-9581
TOLL-FREE ☎ 800-775-1202
www.topazhotel.com

ROOM QUALITY	87
COST ($=$50)	$$$$−
LOCATION	Dupont Circle/ Adams Morgan
NO. OF ROOMS	99
PARKING	Valet $35
ROOM SERVICE	•
BREAKFAST	Buffet
ON-SITE DINING	•
POOL	−
SAUNA	−
EXERCISE FACILITIES	•

Hyatt Arlington ★★★★
1325 Wilson Boulevard
Arlington, VA 22209
☎ 703-525-1234
FAX 703-908-4790
TOLL-FREE ☎ 800-233-1234
www.hyatt.com

ROOM QUALITY	85
COST ($=$50)	$$+
LOCATION	Virginia Suburbs
NO. OF ROOMS	317
PARKING	Self $17, valet $21
ROOM SERVICE	•
BREAKFAST	−
ON-SITE DINING	•
POOL	•
SAUNA	•
EXERCISE FACILITIES	•

Hyatt Regency Bethesda ★★★½
One Bethesda Metro Center
Bethesda, MD 20814
☎ 301-657-1234
FAX 301-657-6453
TOLL-FREE ☎ 800-233-1234
bethesda.hyatt.com

ROOM QUALITY	81
COST ($=$50)	$$$−
LOCATION	Maryland Suburbs
NO. OF ROOMS	390
PARKING	Self $12–$15, valet $17–$20
ROOM SERVICE	•
BREAKFAST	−
ON-SITE DINING	•
POOL	•
SAUNA	•
EXERCISE FACILITIES	•

Jefferson Hotel ★★★★½
1200 16th Street, NW
Washington, DC 20036
☎ 202-347-2200
FAX 202-331-7982
TOLL-FREE ☎ 866-270-8102
www.thejeffersonwashingtondc.com

ROOM QUALITY	92
COST ($=$50)	$$$$$$$+
LOCATION	Downtown
NO. OF ROOMS	100
PARKING	Valet $30
ROOM SERVICE	•
BREAKFAST	•
ON-SITE DINING	•
POOL	−
SAUNA	−
EXERCISE FACILITIES	•

Latham Hotel ★★★
3000 M Street, NW
Washington, DC 20007
☎ 202-726-5000
FAX 202-448-1800
TOLL-FREE ☎ 800-LATHAM-1
www.thelatham.com

ROOM QUALITY	74
COST ($=$50)	$$$$+
LOCATION	Georgetown
NO. OF ROOMS	142
PARKING	Valet $36
ROOM SERVICE	•
BREAKFAST	•
ON-SITE DINING	•
POOL	•
SAUNA	−
EXERCISE FACILITIES	•

L'Enfant Plaza Hotel ★★★★
480 L'Enfant Plaza, SW
Washington, DC 20024
☎ 202-484-1000
FAX 202-646-4456
TOLL-FREE ☎ 800-635-5065
www.lenfantplazahotel.com

ROOM QUALITY	84
COST ($=$50)	$$$$$−
LOCATION	National Mall
NO. OF ROOMS	370
PARKING	Valet $35
ROOM SERVICE	•
BREAKFAST	•
ON-SITE DINING	•
POOL	•
SAUNA	−
EXERCISE FACILITIES	•

Marriott Crystal City ★★★½
1999 Jefferson Davis Highway
Arlington, VA 22202
☎ 703-413-5500
FAX 703-413-0192
TOLL-FREE ☎ 800-228-9290
www.marriott.com

ROOM QUALITY	79
COST ($=$50)	$$$+
LOCATION	Virginia Suburbs
NO. OF ROOMS	343
PARKING	Self $22, valet $27
ROOM SERVICE	−
BREAKFAST	−
ON-SITE DINING	•
POOL	•
SAUNA	•
EXERCISE FACILITIES	•

Marriott Crystal Gateway ★★★½
1700 Jefferson Davis Highway
Arlington, VA 22202
☎ 703-920-3230
FAX 703-271-5212
TOLL-FREE ☎ 800-228-9290
www.crystalgatewaymarriott.com

ROOM QUALITY	80
COST ($=$50)	$$$
LOCATION	Virginia Suburbs
NO. OF ROOMS	697
PARKING	Self $19, valet $25
ROOM SERVICE	•
BREAKFAST	Continental
ON-SITE DINING	•
POOL	•
SAUNA	−
EXERCISE FACILITIES	•

Marriott Hotel Bethesda ★★★★
5151 Pooks Hill Road
Bethesda, MD 20814
☎ 301-897-9400
FAX 301-897-0192
TOLL-FREE ☎ 800-228-9290
www.marriott.com

ROOM QUALITY	84
COST ($=$50)	$$+
LOCATION	Maryland Suburbs
NO. OF ROOMS	407
PARKING	Self $12
ROOM SERVICE	•
BREAKFAST	−
ON-SITE DINING	•
POOL	•
SAUNA	•
EXERCISE FACILITIES	•

Hyatt Regency Capitol Hill ★★★½
400 New Jersey Avenue, NW
Washington, DC 20001
☎ 202-737-1234
FAX 202-737-5773
TOLL-FREE ☎ 800-233-1234
www.washingtonregency.hyatt.com

ROOM QUALITY	82
COST ($=$50)	$$$$$+
LOCATION	Downtown
NO. OF ROOMS	834
PARKING	Valet $42
ROOM SERVICE	•
BREAKFAST	–
ON-SITE DINING	•
POOL	•
SAUNA	–
EXERCISE FACILITIES	•

Hyatt Regency Crystal City ★★★★
2799 Jefferson Davis Highway
Arlington, VA 22202
☎ 703-418-1234
FAX 703-418-1289
TOLL-FREE ☎ 800-233-1234
crystalcity.hyatt.com

ROOM QUALITY	84
COST ($=$50)	$$$$
LOCATION	Virginia Suburbs
NO. OF ROOMS	686
PARKING	Valet $25
ROOM SERVICE	•
BREAKFAST	–
ON-SITE DINING	•
POOL	•
SAUNA	•
EXERCISE FACILITIES	•

J.W. Marriott Pennsylvania Avenue ★★★½
1331 Pennsylvania Avenue, NW
Washington, DC 20004
☎ 202-393-2000
FAX 202-626-6991
TOLL-FREE ☎ 800-228-9290
www.jwmarriottdc.com

ROOM QUALITY	82
COST ($=$50)	$$$$$–
LOCATION	Downtown
NO. OF ROOMS	772
PARKING	Valet $44
ROOM SERVICE	–
BREAKFAST	–
ON-SITE DINING	•
POOL	•
SAUNA	•
EXERCISE FACILITIES	•

Liaison Capitol Hill ★★★½
415 New Jersey Avenue, NW
Washington, DC 20001
☎ 202-638-1616
FAX 202-347-1813
TOLL-FREE ☎ 800-638-1116
www.affinia.com

ROOM QUALITY	82
COST ($=$50)	$$$$$
LOCATION	Downtown
NO. OF ROOMS	343
PARKING	Self $35
ROOM SERVICE	•
BREAKFAST	–
ON-SITE DINING	•
POOL	•
SAUNA	–
EXERCISE FACILITIES	•

Madison Hotel ★★★★
1177 15th Street, NW
Washington, DC 20005
☎ 202-862-1600
FAX 202-785-1255
TOLL-FREE ☎ 800-424-8578
www.loewshotels.com

ROOM QUALITY	84
COST ($=$50)	$$$$+
LOCATION	Downtown
NO. OF ROOMS	353
PARKING	Valet $32
ROOM SERVICE	•
BREAKFAST	–
ON-SITE DINING	•
POOL	–
SAUNA	–
EXERCISE FACILITIES	•

Mandarin Oriental ★★★★½
1330 Maryland Avenue, SW
Washington, DC 20024
☎ 202-554-8588
FAX 202-787-6161
TOLL-FREE ☎ 888-888 1778
www.mandarinoriental.com

ROOM QUALITY	92
COST ($=$50)	$$$$$$$$+
LOCATION	National Mall
NO. OF ROOMS	400
PARKING	Valet $45
ROOM SERVICE	•
BREAKFAST	–
ON-SITE DINING	•
POOL	•
SAUNA	•
EXERCISE FACILITIES	•

Marriott Hotel Key Bridge ★★★½
1401 Lee Highway
Arlington, VA 22209
☎ 703-524-6400
FAX 703-524-8964
TOLL-FREE ☎ 800-228-9290
www.marriott.com

ROOM QUALITY	80
COST ($=$50)	$$$$
LOCATION	Virginia Suburbs
NO. OF ROOMS	582
PARKING	Self $17
ROOM SERVICE	•
BREAKFAST	–
ON-SITE DINING	•
POOL	•
SAUNA	•
EXERCISE FACILITIES	•

Marriott Metro Center ★★★½
775 12th Street, NW
Washington, DC 20005
☎ 202-737-2200
FAX 202-347-5886
TOLL-FREE ☎ 800-228-9290
www.metrocentermarriott.com

ROOM QUALITY	76
COST ($=$50)	$$$$$–
LOCATION	Downtown
NO. OF ROOMS	456
PARKING	Valet $35
ROOM SERVICE	•
BREAKFAST	–
ON-SITE DINING	•
POOL	•
SAUNA	–
EXERCISE FACILITIES	•

Marriott Wardman Park Hotel ★★★★
2660 Woodley Road, NW
Washington, DC 20008
☎ 202-328-2000
FAX 202-234-0015
TOLL-FREE ☎ 800-228-9290
www.marriott.com

ROOM QUALITY	84
COST ($=$50)	$$$$$+
LOCATION	Upper Northwest
NO. OF ROOMS	1,316
PARKING	Self $32, valet $37
ROOM SERVICE	•
BREAKFAST	–
ON-SITE DINING	•
POOL	•
SAUNA	–
EXERCISE FACILITIES	•

Hotel Information Charts (continued)

Melrose Hotel ★★★★
2430 Pennsylvania Avenue, NW
Washington, DC 20037
☎ 202-955-6400
FAX 202-955-5765
TOLL-FREE ☎ 800-635-7673
www.melrosehotelwashingtondc.com

ROOM QUALITY	84
COST ($=$50)	$$$$$$+
LOCATION	Georgetown
NO. OF ROOMS	240
PARKING	Valet $38
ROOM SERVICE	•
BREAKFAST	–
ON-SITE DINING	•
POOL	–
SAUNA	–
EXERCISE FACILITIES	•

Morrison House ★★★★
116 S. Alfred Road
Alexandria, VA 22314
☎ 703-838-8000
FAX 703-684-6283
TOLL-FREE ☎ 866-834-6628
www.morrisonhouse.com

ROOM QUALITY	89
COST ($=$50)	$$$$–
LOCATION	Virginia Suburbs
NO. OF ROOMS	45
PARKING	Valet $24
ROOM SERVICE	•
BREAKFAST	–
ON-SITE DINING	•
POOL	–
SAUNA	–
EXERCISE FACILITIES	–

Morrison-Clark Inn ★★★★
1015 L Street, NW
Washington, DC 20001
☎ 202-898-1200
FAX 202-289-8576
TOLL-FREE ☎ 800-332-7898
www.morrisonclark.com

ROOM QUALITY	84
COST ($=$50)	$$$–
LOCATION	Upper Northwest
NO. OF ROOMS	54
PARKING	Valet $32
ROOM SERVICE	•
BREAKFAST	–
ON-SITE DINING	•
POOL	–
SAUNA	–
EXERCISE FACILITIES	•

Park Hyatt ★★★★½
24th Street at M Street, NW
Washington, DC 20037
☎ 202-789-1234
FAX 202-419-6795
TOLL-FREE ☎ 800-233-1234
www.parkwashington.hyatt.com

ROOM QUALITY	91
COST ($=$50)	$$$$$$$–
LOCATION	Georgetown
NO. OF ROOMS	223
PARKING	Valet $45
ROOM SERVICE	•
BREAKFAST	–
ON-SITE DINING	•
POOL	•
SAUNA	•
EXERCISE FACILITIES	•

Phoenix Park Hotel ★★★½
520 N. Capitol Street, NW
Washington, DC 20001
☎ 202-638-6900
FAX 202-393-3236
TOLL-FREE ☎ 800-824-5419
www.phoenixparkhotel.com

ROOM QUALITY	75
COST ($=$50)	$$$$$$–
LOCATION	Capitol Hill
NO. OF ROOMS	149
PARKING	Valet $40
ROOM SERVICE	•
BREAKFAST	–
ON-SITE DINING	•
POOL	–
SAUNA	–
EXERCISE FACILITIES	•

The Quincy ★★★★
1823 L Street, NW
Washington, DC 20036
☎ 202-223-4320
FAX 202-223-4320
TOLL-FREE ☎ 800-424-2970
www.thequincy.com

ROOM QUALITY	84
COST ($=$50)	$$$
LOCATION	Downtown
NO. OF ROOMS	99
PARKING	Self $30
ROOM SERVICE	•
BREAKFAST	–
ON-SITE DINING	–
POOL	–
SAUNA	–
EXERCISE FACILITIES	Off-site privileges

Residence Inn Bethesda ★★★★
7335 Wisconsin Avenue
Bethesda, MD 20814
☎ 301-718-0200
FAX 301-718-0679
TOLL-FREE ☎ 800-331-3131
www.residenceinnbethesdahotel.com

ROOM QUALITY	86
COST ($=$50)	$$$–
LOCATION	Maryland Suburbs
NO. OF ROOMS	187
PARKING	Self and valet $20
ROOM SERVICE	–
BREAKFAST	Buffet
ON-SITE DINING	–
POOL	•
SAUNA	•
EXERCISE FACILITIES	•

Residence Inn Dupont Circle ★★★★
2120 P Street, NW
Washington, DC 20037
☎ 202-466-6800
FAX 202-466-9630
TOLL-FREE ☎ 800-331-3131
www.marriott.com

ROOM QUALITY	87
COST ($=$50)	$$$$$–
LOCATION	Dupont Circle/ Adams Morgan
NO. OF ROOMS	107
PARKING	Self $28
ROOM SERVICE	•
BREAKFAST	Buffet
ON-SITE DINING	•
POOL	–
SAUNA	–
EXERCISE FACILITIES	•

Residence Inn Pentagon City ★★★★
550 Army Navy Drive
Arlington, VA 22202
☎ 703-413-6630
FAX 703-418-1751
TOLL-FREE ☎ 800-331-3131
www.marriott.com

ROOM QUALITY	84
COST ($=$50)	$$$–
LOCATION	Virginia Suburbs
NO. OF ROOMS	299
PARKING	Self $21
ROOM SERVICE	•
BREAKFAST	Cooked to order
ON-SITE DINING	•
POOL	•
SAUNA	–
EXERCISE FACILITIES	–

The Normandy Hotel ★★★½
2118 Wyoming Avenue, NW
Washington, DC 20008
☎ 202-483-1350
FAX 202-387-8241
TOLL-FREE ☎ 866-534-6835
www.doylecollection.com

ROOM QUALITY	82
COST ($=$50)	$$$$–
LOCATION	Dupont Circle/Adams Morgan
NO. OF ROOMS	75
PARKING	Self $30
ROOM SERVICE	–
BREAKFAST	–
ON-SITE DINING	–
POOL	–
SAUNA	–
EXERCISE FACILITIES	–

Omni Shoreham Hotel ★★★★
2500 Calvert Street, NW
Washington, DC 20008
☎ 202-234-0700
FAX 202-265-7972
TOLL-FREE ☎ 888-444-6664
www.omnihotels.com

ROOM QUALITY	84
COST ($=$50)	$$$$$$
LOCATION	Upper Northwest
NO. OF ROOMS	834
PARKING	Valet $28
ROOM SERVICE	•
BREAKFAST	–
ON-SITE DINING	•
POOL	•
SAUNA	•
EXERCISE FACILITIES	Fee $10 per day, $18 stay

One Washington Circle Hotel ★★★★
One Washington Circle, NW
Washington, DC 20037
☎ 202-872-1680
FAX 202-887-4989
TOLL-FREE ☎ 800-424-9671
www.onewashcirclehotel.com

ROOM QUALITY	86
COST ($=$50)	$$$$–
LOCATION	Foggy Bottom
NO. OF ROOMS	151
PARKING	Valet $30
ROOM SERVICE	•
BREAKFAST	–
ON-SITE DINING	•
POOL	•
SAUNA	–
EXERCISE FACILITIES	–

Radisson Hotel Reagan National ★★★★
2020 Jefferson Davis Highway
Arlington, VA 22202
☎ 703-920-8600
FAX 703-920-2840
TOLL-FREE ☎ 800-395-7046
www.radisson.com/arlingtonva

ROOM QUALITY	84
COST ($=$50)	$$+
LOCATION	Virginia Suburbs
NO. OF ROOMS	251
PARKING	Self $20
ROOM SERVICE	•
BREAKFAST	–
ON-SITE DINING	•
POOL	•
SAUNA	–
EXERCISE FACILITIES	•

Renaissance M Street Hotel ★★★★
1143 New Hampshire Avenue, NW
Washington, DC 20037
☎ 202-775-0800
FAX 202-331-9491
TOLL-FREE ☎ 888-803-1298
www.marriott.com

ROOM QUALITY	85
COST ($=$50)	$$$$$
LOCATION	Dupont Circle/Adams Morgan
NO. OF ROOMS	355
PARKING	Valet $35
ROOM SERVICE	•
BREAKFAST	–
ON-SITE DINING	•
POOL	–
SAUNA	–
EXERCISE FACILITIES	•

Renaissance Mayflower Hotel ★★★★
1127 Connecticut Avenue, NW
Washington, DC 20036
☎ 202-347-3000
FAX 202-776-9182
TOLL-FREE ☎ 800-228-7697
www.marriott.com

ROOM QUALITY	84
COST ($=$50)	$$$$+
LOCATION	Downtown
NO. OF ROOMS	657
PARKING	Valet $42
ROOM SERVICE	•
BREAKFAST	–
ON-SITE DINING	•
POOL	–
SAUNA	–
EXERCISE FACILITIES	•

Residence Inn Washington, D.C. ★★★½
1199 Vermont Avenue, NW
Washington, DC 20005
☎ 202-898-1100
FAX 202-898-1110
TOLL-FREE ☎ 800-331-3131
www.marriott.com

ROOM QUALITY	82
COST ($=$50)	$$$$–
LOCATION	Downtown
NO. OF ROOMS	202
PARKING	Valet $25
ROOM SERVICE	–
BREAKFAST	Buffet
ON-SITE DINING	–
POOL	–
SAUNA	–
EXERCISE FACILITIES	•

Ritz-Carlton Georgetown ★★★★½
3100 South Street, NW
Washington, DC 20007
☎ 202-912-4100
FAX 202-912-4199
TOLL-FREE ☎ 800-241-3333
www.ritzcarlton.com

ROOM QUALITY	92
COST ($=$50)	$$$$$$$$
LOCATION	Georgetown
NO. OF ROOMS	86
PARKING	Valet $39
ROOM SERVICE	•
BREAKFAST	–
ON-SITE DINING	•
POOL	–
SAUNA	•
EXERCISE FACILITIES	•

Ritz-Carlton Pentagon City ★★★★
1250 S. Hayes Street
Arlington, VA 22202
☎ 703-415-5000
FAX 703-415-5061
TOLL-FREE ☎ 800-241-3333
www.ritzcarlton.com

ROOM QUALITY	88
COST ($=$50)	$$$$+
LOCATION	Virginia Suburbs
NO. OF ROOMS	366
PARKING	Valet $29
ROOM SERVICE	•
BREAKFAST	–
ON-SITE DINING	•
POOL	•
SAUNA	•
EXERCISE FACILITIES	•

Hotel Information Charts (continued)

Ritz-Carlton Tysons Corner ★★★★
1700 Tysons Boulevard
McLean, VA 22102
☎ 703-506-4300
FAX 703-506-2694
TOLL-FREE ☎ 800-241-3333
www.ritzcarlton.com

ROOM QUALITY	88
COST ($=$50)	$$$$–
LOCATION	Virginia Suburbs
NO. OF ROOMS	398
PARKING	Valet $30
ROOM SERVICE	•
BREAKFAST	—
ON-SITE DINING	•
POOL	•
SAUNA	•
EXERCISE FACILITIES	•

Ritz-Carlton Washington, D.C. ★★★★½
1150 22nd Street, NW
Washington, DC 20037
☎ 202-835-0500
FAX 202-835-1588
TOLL-FREE ☎ 800-241-3333
www.ritzcarlton.com

ROOM QUALITY	92
COST ($=$50)	$$$$$$$$$+
LOCATION	Dupont Circle/ Adams Morgan
NO. OF ROOMS	300
PARKING	Valet $45
ROOM SERVICE	•
BREAKFAST	—
ON-SITE DINING	•
POOL	•
SAUNA	•
EXERCISE FACILITIES	Access $15

River Inn ★★★★
924 25th Street, NW
Washington, DC 20037
☎ 202-337-7600
FAX 202-337-6520
TOLL-FREE ☎ 888-874-0100
www.theriverinn.com

ROOM QUALITY	88
COST ($=$50)	$$$$$–
LOCATION	Foggy Bottom
NO. OF ROOMS	125
PARKING	Valet $30
ROOM SERVICE	•
BREAKFAST	—
ON-SITE DINING	•
POOL	—
SAUNA	—
EXERCISE FACILITIES	•

Sheraton Premiere Tysons Corner ★★★★
8661 Leesburg Pike
Vienna, VA 22182
☎ 703-448-1234
FAX 703-610-8293
TOLL-FREE ☎ 888-625-5144
www.starwoodhotels.com

ROOM QUALITY	83
COST ($=$50)	$$$–
LOCATION	Virginia Suburbs
NO. OF ROOMS	443
PARKING	Free lot
ROOM SERVICE	•
BREAKFAST	—
ON-SITE DINING	•
POOL	•
SAUNA	•
EXERCISE FACILITIES	•

Sheraton Suites Alexandria ★★★★
801 N. St. Asaph Street
Alexandria, VA 22314
☎ 703-836-4700
FAX 703-548-4518
TOLL-FREE ☎ 888-625-5144
www.starwoodhotels.com

ROOM QUALITY	85
COST ($=$50)	$$$$
LOCATION	Virginia Suburbs
NO. OF ROOMS	247
PARKING	Free lot
ROOM SERVICE	•
BREAKFAST	•
ON-SITE DINING	•
POOL	•
SAUNA	•
EXERCISE FACILITIES	•

Sofitel Lafayette ★★★★
806 15th Street, NW
Washington, DC 20005
☎ 202-730-8800
FAX 202-730-8500
TOLL-FREE ☎ 800-763-4835
www.sofitel.com

ROOM QUALITY	88
COST ($=$50)	$$$$$–
LOCATION	Downtown
NO. OF ROOMS	237
PARKING	Valet $42
ROOM SERVICE	•
BREAKFAST	—
ON-SITE DINING	•
POOL	—
SAUNA	—
EXERCISE FACILITIES	•

Tysons Corner Marriott ★★★½
8028 Leesburg Pike
Vienna, VA 22182
☎ 703-734-3200
FAX 703-734-5763
TOLL-FREE ☎ 800-228-9290
www.marriott.com

ROOM QUALITY	82
COST ($=$50)	$$–
LOCATION	Virginia Suburbs
NO. OF ROOMS	396
PARKING	Free lot
ROOM SERVICE	—
BREAKFAST	—
ON-SITE DINING	•
POOL	•
SAUNA	•
EXERCISE FACILITIES	•

W Washington D.C. ★★★★
515 15th Street, NW
Washington, DC 20004
☎ 202-661-2400
TOLL-FREE ☎ 800-424-9540
www.whotels.com

ROOM QUALITY	83
COST ($=$50)	$$$$$$$–
LOCATION	Downtown
NO. OF ROOMS	317
PARKING	Valet $50
ROOM SERVICE	•
BREAKFAST	—
ON-SITE DINING	•
POOL	•
SAUNA	—
EXERCISE FACILITIES	•

Washington Court Hotel ★★★★
525 New Jersey Avenue, NW
Washington, DC 20001
☎ 202-628-2100
FAX 202-879-7918
TOLL-FREE ☎ 800-321-3010
www.washingtoncourthotel.com

ROOM QUALITY	84
COST ($=$50)	$$$$+
LOCATION	Downtown
NO. OF ROOMS	267
PARKING	Valet $35
ROOM SERVICE	•
BREAKFAST	—
ON-SITE DINING	•
POOL	•
SAUNA	—
EXERCISE FACILITIES	•

Savoy Suites Hotel ★★★½
2505 Wisconsin Avenue, NW
Washington, DC 20007
☎ 202-337-9700
FAX 202-337-3644
TOLL-FREE ☎ 800-944-5377
www.savoysuites.com

ROOM QUALITY	80
COST ($=$50)	$$$+
LOCATION	Upper Northwest
NO. OF ROOMS	150
PARKING	Free garage
ROOM SERVICE	•
BREAKFAST	—
ON-SITE DINING	•
POOL	—
SAUNA	•
EXERCISE FACILITIES	Access

Sheraton Crystal City ★★★½
1800 Jefferson Davis Highway
Arlington, VA 22202
☎ 703-486-1111
FAX 703-769-3970
TOLL-FREE ☎ 888-625-5144
www.sheraton.com/crystalcity

ROOM QUALITY	78
COST ($=$50)	$$$$–
LOCATION	Virginia Suburbs
NO. OF ROOMS	217
PARKING	Self $20
ROOM SERVICE	•
BREAKFAST	—
ON-SITE DINING	•
POOL	•
SAUNA	•
EXERCISE FACILITIES	•

Sheraton National Hotel ★★★½
900 South Orme Street
Arlington, VA 22204
☎ 703-521-1900
FAX 703-271-6626
TOLL-FREE ☎ 800-325-3535
www.sheratonnational.com

ROOM QUALITY	80
COST ($=$50)	$$$$–
LOCATION	Virginia Suburbs
NO. OF ROOMS	408
PARKING	Self $20, valet $29
ROOM SERVICE	•
BREAKFAST	—
ON-SITE DINING	•
POOL	•
SAUNA	—
EXERCISE FACILITIES	•

St. Gregory Luxury Hotel & Suites ★★★★
2033 M Street NW
Washington, DC 20036
☎ 202-530-3600
FAX 202-466-6770
TOLL-FREE ☎ 800-829-5034
www.capitalhotelswdc.com

ROOM QUALITY	88
COST ($=$50)	$$$$$
LOCATION	Dupont Circle/ Adams Morgan
NO. OF ROOMS	154
PARKING	Valet $20, weekend $32
ROOM SERVICE	•
BREAKFAST	—
ON-SITE DINING	•
POOL	—
SAUNA	—
EXERCISE FACILITIES	•

St. Regis ★★★★½
923 16th Street & K Street, NW
Washington, DC 20006
☎ 202-638-2626
FAX 202-683-4231
TOLL-FREE ☎ 800-562-5661
www.starwoodhotels.com

ROOM QUALITY	92
COST ($=$50)	$$$$$$$$–
LOCATION	Downtown
NO. OF ROOMS	175
PARKING	Valet $45
ROOM SERVICE	•
BREAKFAST	—
ON-SITE DINING	•
POOL	—
SAUNA	•
EXERCISE FACILITIES	•

State Plaza Hotel ★★★½
2117 E Street, NW
Washington, DC 20037
☎ 202-861-8200
FAX 202-659-8601
TOLL-FREE ☎ 800-424-2859
stateplaza.com

ROOM QUALITY	77
COST ($=$50)	$$$+
LOCATION	Foggy Bottom
NO. OF ROOMS	230
PARKING	Valet $32
ROOM SERVICE	•
BREAKFAST	—
ON-SITE DINING	•
POOL	—
SAUNA	—
EXERCISE FACILITIES	•

Washington Marriott Hotel ★★★★
1221 22nd St. and M Street, NW
Washington, DC 20037
☎ 202-872-1500
FAX 202-872-1424
TOLL-FREE ☎ 800-393-3053
www.marriottwashington.com

ROOM QUALITY	83
COST ($=$50)	$$$$$+
LOCATION	Dupont Circle/ Adams Morgan
NO. OF ROOMS	470
PARKING	Self $32, valet $36
ROOM SERVICE	•
BREAKFAST	—
ON-SITE DINING	•
POOL	•
SAUNA	•
EXERCISE FACILITIES	•

Washington National Airport Hilton ★★★½
2399 Jefferson Davis Highway
Arlington, VA 22202
☎ 703-418-6800
FAX 703-418-3763
TOLL-FREE ☎ 800-HILTONS
www.hilton.com

ROOM QUALITY	79
COST ($=$50)	$$
LOCATION	Virginia Suburbs
NO. OF ROOMS	386
PARKING	Self $24
ROOM SERVICE	•
BREAKFAST	—
ON-SITE DINING	•
POOL	•
SAUNA	—
EXERCISE FACILITIES	•

Washington Plaza Hotel ★★★½
10 Thomas Circle, NW
Washington, DC 20005
☎ 202-842-1300
FAX 202-371-9602
TOLL-FREE ☎ 800-424-1140
www.washingtonplazahotel.com

ROOM QUALITY	80
COST ($=$50)	$$$$+
LOCATION	Downtown
NO. OF ROOMS	340
PARKING	Self $32
ROOM SERVICE	•
BREAKFAST	—
ON-SITE DINING	•
POOL	—
SAUNA	—
EXERCISE FACILITIES	•

Hotel Information Charts (continued)

Washington Renaissance Hotel ★★★½
999 Ninth Street, NW
Washington, DC 20001
☎ 202-898-9000
FAX 202-289-0947
TOLL-FREE ☎ 888-236-2427
www.marriott.com

ROOM QUALITY	77
COST ($=$50)	$$$$$$$$+
LOCATION	Downtown
NO. OF ROOMS	807
PARKING	Self $28, valet $40
ROOM SERVICE	•
BREAKFAST	–
ON-SITE DINING	•
POOL	•
SAUNA	•
EXERCISE FACILITIES	•

Washington Suites Alexandria ★★★★
100 S. Reynolds Street
Alexandria, VA 22304
☎ 703-370-9600
FAX 703-370-0467
TOLL-FREE ☎ 877-736-2500
www.washingtonsuitesalexandria.com

ROOM QUALITY	87
COST ($=$50)	$$$
LOCATION	Virginia Suburbs
NO. OF ROOMS	222
PARKING	Free lot
ROOM SERVICE	•
BREAKFAST	Continental
ON-SITE DINING	–
POOL	•
SAUNA	–
EXERCISE FACILITIES	•

Washington Suites Georgetown ★★★★
2500 Pennsylvania Avenue
Washington, DC 20037
☎ 202-333-8060
FAX 202-955-5765
TOLL-FREE ☎ 877-736-2500
www.washingtonsuitesgeorgetown.com

ROOM QUALITY	84
COST ($=$50)	$$$+
LOCATION	Georgetown
NO. OF ROOMS	124
PARKING	Valet $33
ROOM SERVICE	–
BREAKFAST	Continental
ON-SITE DINING	–
POOL	–
SAUNA	–
EXERCISE FACILITIES	•

Westin Grand ★★★★
2350 M Street, NW
Washington, DC 20037
☎ 202-429-0100
FAX 202-429-9759
TOLL-FREE ☎ 888-937-8461
www.westin.com

ROOM QUALITY	88
COST ($=$50)	$$$$$–
LOCATION	Georgetown
NO. OF ROOMS	263
PARKING	Self $28, valet $40
ROOM SERVICE	•
BREAKFAST	–
ON-SITE DINING	•
POOL	•
SAUNA	•
EXERCISE FACILITIES	•

Westin Tysons Corner ★★★★
7801 Leesburg Pike
Falls Church, VA 22043
☎ 703-893-1340
FAX 703-847-9520
TOLL-FREE ☎ 888-625-5144
www.starwoodhotels.com

ROOM QUALITY	84
COST ($=$50)	$$$$–
LOCATION	Virginia Suburbs
NO. OF ROOMS	405
PARKING	Free lot
ROOM SERVICE	•
BREAKFAST	–
ON-SITE DINING	•
POOL	•
SAUNA	•
EXERCISE FACILITIES	•

Westin Washington, D.C. City Center ★★★★
1400 M Street, NW
Washington, DC 20005
☎ 202-429-1700
FAX 202-785-0786
TOLL-FREE ☎ 800-WYNDHAM
www.starwoodhotels.com

ROOM QUALITY	88
COST ($=$50)	$$$$–
LOCATION	Downtown
NO. OF ROOMS	406
PARKING	Valet $30
ROOM SERVICE	•
BREAKFAST	•
ON-SITE DINING	•
POOL	–
SAUNA	–
EXERCISE FACILITIES	•

Willard Inter-Continental ★★★★
1401 Pennsylvania Avenue, NW
Washington, DC 20004
☎ 202-628-9100
FAX 202-637-7326
TOLL-FREE ☎ 800-980-6429
www.intercontinental.com

ROOM QUALITY	88
COST ($=$50)	$$$$$$$–
LOCATION	Downtown
NO. OF ROOMS	332
PARKING	Valet $40
ROOM SERVICE	•
BREAKFAST	–
ON-SITE DINING	•
POOL	–
SAUNA	•
EXERCISE FACILITIES	•

Windsor Park Hotel ★★½
2116 Kalorama Road, NW
Washington, DC 20008
☎ 202-483-7700
FAX 202-332-4547
TOLL-FREE ☎ 800-247-3064
www.windsorparkhotel.com

ROOM QUALITY	56
COST ($=$50)	$$$$–
LOCATION	Dupont Circle/ Adams Morgan
NO. OF ROOMS	43
PARKING	Street, free
ROOM SERVICE	–
BREAKFAST	Continental
ON-SITE DINING	–
POOL	–
SAUNA	–
EXERCISE FACILITIES	–

PART THREE

VISITING WASHINGTON *on* BUSINESS

NOT ALL VISITORS ARE HEADED *for the* MALL

WHILE MOST OF THE 16-MILLION-PLUS PEOPLE who come to Washington each year are tourists—it's the favorite metropolitan destination for visitors from other parts of the United States—not everyone visiting the city has an itinerary centered around the National Mall.

About 40% of those 16.2 million are business travelers, at least 1½ million of whom are headed to the **Washington Convention Center,** located in downtown Washington. However, it has a burgeoning rival. In 2008, the 41-acre **Gaylord National Hotel & Convention Center** opened in the National Harbor development in Prince George's County, adding another 470,000 feet of convention space, including more than 100,000 square feet of ballroom space, 180,000 square feet of exhibit space, 18 executive meeting rooms, and 17 dedicated loading docks. As Gaylord puts it, the largest exhibit hall is the size of three football fields and could house 400 tractor-trailer trucks.) (We'll treat these two in more detail below.)

The **Ronald Reagan Building and International Trade Center** near Federal Triangle, where the main downtown visitor center is, and where the Woodrow Wilson Plaza hosts outdoor concerts and festivals, also has conference and meeting facilities, although somewhat smaller—15 meeting rooms that can be configured into five suites that accommodate up to 1,000 people each. However, because of the federal and international agencies housed here, tightened post-9/11 security has limited public access somewhat; many of the functions held there are smaller social events. There are several smaller convention hotels and expo centers in the region as well, but most of those are either in suburban complexes or day centers with shuttle service provided by the companies involved.

In addition to the convention traffic, Washington, as the seat of the United States government, hosts approximately 1½ million visitors from around the world who fly in to conduct business with both federal agencies and the wide array of private organizations headquartered here. (As mentioned before, the meetings of global organizations such as the International Monetary Fund become semi-regular endurance tests for local office workers.)

The city is also a center of higher education. The District is home to **George Washington University, Georgetown University, American University, Howard University, Gallaudet University** (the world's only university with an entire curriculum for the deaf and hard-of-hearing), the **University of the District of Columbia**, and the **Catholic University of America,** among others. And, although they are perhaps less visible to tourists, it is also home to a large number of specialized institutions, ranging from arts, museum, and conservation schools to social and political think tanks, financial and diplomatic policy institutes, medical schools, design and innovation companies, security and military concerns, and theological faculties, just to name a few. As a result, Washington attracts a lot of visiting academics, college administrators, scholars, government advisors, theoreticians, and advocates, as well as "ordinary" students and their families.

In most ways, the problems facing business and policy visitors on their first trip to Washington don't differ much from the problems of folks in town intent on hitting the major tourist attractions. People visiting on business need to locate a hotel that's convenient, want to avoid the worst of the city's traffic, face the same problems getting around an unfamiliar city, must figure out how to buy a Metro ticket, and want to know the locations of the best restaurants and whatever sightseeing they can squeeze in. (And of course, many business travelers have family members with them who aren't working during the day.)

The main difference is probably that business travelers are less likely to have much say in the timing of their visit. Still, a lot of the advice and information in the *Unofficial Guide* can make the trip smoother and more enjoyable—and perhaps make squeezing in those extra few recreational hours easier.

The WASHINGTON CONVENTION CENTER

IN THE FALL OF 1998, WHEN IT BECAME CLEAR that the existing convention center had been eclipsed by at least 30 larger spaces around the country, ground was broken for the $800-million Washington Convention Center near Mount Vernon Square, located two blocks from the previous center. The existing building, which opened in 2003, has more than 2 million square feet of space, including 725,000 square feet of exhibit space, 500,000 square feet of contiguous space, and 150,000 square feet of meeting space—plus a 120-piece permanent art collection, complete wheelchair access, and 65 loading docks. It's the largest building in D.C. (Although many locals don't realize it, either, the complex is named not for the city but for the District's first elected major, Walter E. Washington.)

The Washington Convention Center is a four-level structure located on a 17-acre site bounded by Mount Vernon Place, Ninth, N, and Seventh streets NW. The center contains 66 meeting rooms (some divisible); a 52,000-square-foot ballroom that can be divided into three smaller spaces; and five exhibit halls (with 151,000 square feet, 194,000 square feet, 128,000 square feet, 111,000 square feet, and 119,000 square feet of space). The center provides all food and beverage services on the premises, including catered meals by an in-house catering service partner and brand-name partners such as Wolfgang Puck and Starbucks. In 2009, the center won a Guinness World Record for hosting the largest sit-down dinner—serving 16,206 members of Alpha Kappa Alpha sorority.

For both exhibitors and attendees, the Washington Convention Center is an excellent site for a meeting or trade show and attracted nearly 1 million visitors in its first year. Large and small exhibitors alike can set up their exhibits with minimal effort. Sixty-five loading docks and huge bay doors make unloading and loading quick and simple for large displays arriving by truck. Smaller displays transported in vans and cars are unloaded in the same area, entering from N Street. Equipment can be carried or wheeled directly to the exhibit area. The exhibit areas and meeting rooms are well marked and easy to find. For more information, call ☎ 202-249-3000 or 800-368-9000, or visit **www.dcconvention.com.**

LODGING WITHIN WALKING DISTANCE OF THE CONVENTION CENTER

WHILE PARTICIPANTS IN CITYWIDE CONVENTIONS lodge all over town, a number of hotels are within four or five easy-walking blocks of the convention center, including the Renaissance Washington at Ninth and K streets NW, on the south side of Mt. Vernon Square (☎ 202-898-9000); the Henley Park Hotel, at 926 Massachusetts Avenue NW (☎ 202-582-1234); the Grand Hyatt at 10th and H Streets NW (☎ 202-582-1234); and the Embassy Suites Convention Center (☎ 202-739-2001) at 10th and K Streets NW. And there are many more only a few minutes farther away; see Part Two: Accommodations for more information.

PARKING AROUND AND WHEELCHAIR ACCESS TO THE CONVENTION CENTER

WHILE THERE'S NO PARKING IN THE CONVENTION CENTER itself, the surrounding area offers eight parking lots and garages within a three-block walk. There are a dozen public parking spaces reserved for vehicles with wheelchair permits or license tags in the area. There are ramps for wheelchairs from surrounding sidewalks and several drop-off ramps; go to **www.dcconvention.com/Visitors/ Accessibility.aspx** for details.

METRO SERVICE, CABS AND SHUTTLES TO THE CONVENTION CENTER

THE MOUNT VERNON SQUARE/SEVENTH STREET–CONVENTION CENTER Metro stop is on the Yellow and Green Line. The Yellow Line connects directly with Ronald Reagan Washington National Airport. The Gallery Place–Chinatown station is one stop away, which connects to the Red Line two stops from Union Station and with destinations to several of the major Maryland suburbs; the Metro Center stop, one stop farther west than Gallery Place on the Red Line, connects to the Blue and Orange Lines toward the Virginia suburbs and also connects to Reagan National (via the Blue Line). For more information on the subway system see Part Four: Getting In and Getting Around Washington.

Large convention planners often arrange for complimentary bus or shuttle service from major hotels to the convention center. If you are staying at a smaller hotel and wish to use the shuttle bus, get a copy of the pick-up map and walk to the nearest large hotel on the shuttle route.

Metrobus route 79 stops at the corners of Seventh and Ninth Streets NW, running north past Logan Circle to Silver Spring, and south through Penn Quarter toward the Mall and Constitution Avenue, with many other connections available; go to **www.wmata .com/bus** for details. The DC Circulator bus service, which is only $1 per ride (and can be free if you're transferring from Metro), runs daily from 7 a.m. to 9 p.m.; it has a circuit that passes around the convention center and goes south through Penn Quarter and across the Mall to the Southwest waterfront area. It also connects to other Circulator routes toward Georgetown, around the Mall, Capitol Hill, Dupont Circle and Adams Morgan; for more information see Part Four or go to **www.dccirculator.com.**

The main taxi stand is on Mount Vernon Place, though cabs are relatively cheap and easy to flag down, especially around downtown. (If you have traveled to Washington before, you may wish to know that taxi fares have changed from a zone system to a metered system; see Part Four.)

DINING ALTERNATIVES FOR CONVENTION CENTER ATTENDEES

PRICES OF FOOD FROM THE CONVENTION CENTER'S food service are on the high side, but convention attendees needn't feel trapped: plenty of good eating establishments are within a few blocks. Among those near and nice enough to entertain a prospective client are: **Bobby Van's Grill** (1201 New York Avenue NW; ☎ 202-589-1504), the New Orleans–style **Acadiana** (901 New York Avenue NW; ☎ 202-408-8848), the Belgian beer-and-mussels favorite **Brasserie Beck** (1101 K Street NW; ☎ 202-408-1717), the new American **Corduroy** (1122 Ninth Street NW; ☎ 202-589-0699), and the surf-and-turf **Finn & Porter** (900 Tenth Street NW; ☎ 202-719-1600). The convention center neighborhood is also home to two of the most popular, though least formal, hotspots in D.C.: **Matchbox** (713 H Street NW; ☎ 202-289-4441), originally famous as one of downtown's most popular wood-fired pizza joints but also offering unusual upscale bistro-pub fare (scallops with fried green tomatoes, seared salmon with cheddar grits, short ribs, and a sort of super-Cuban sandwich with roast turkey, serrano ham, and manchego cheese), and **Againn** (1099 New York Avenue NW; ☎ 202-639-9830), which takes an irreverent attitude toward Scots-Irish pub fare (pork belly, frog legs, fish and chips, oysters, salmon, black pudding) and pulls it off. However, if you have a little more time to walk (or jump the subway), the convention center is only five or six blocks from the many choices of Penn Quarter; see "Hot Restaurant Districts" in Part Six: Dining and Restaurants (pages 266–267) for more suggestions.

GAYLORD NATIONAL HOTEL & CONVENTION CENTER

THE MASSIVE GAYLORD HOTEL is only the fourth resort property from the Opryland-centric company and the keystone of the ambitious 300-acre National Harbor development (the 20,000-square-foot spa and fitness center, complete with 24-meter lap pool, tells you it's serious about claiming a slice of the tourism pie). Being a Gaylord property, it not surprisingly has plenty of entertainment options, including an increasingly popular display of Christmas trees, a dancing water-lights show, a family arcade, etc. The conservatory-like glass-sided atrium, a labyrinth of water features, bridges, shops, and more, is large enough to house the Space Shuttle. The Gaylord offers bus shuttle service to Reagan National Airport and water taxi service to Mount Vernon, Old Town Alexandria, and Georgetown (via Old Town). The National Harbor complex authority, which operates a second marina nearby for non-Gaylord visitors, has similar service.

National Harbor, which is across the Potomac River in Maryland and about eight miles south of the White House, was at one point considered an "outsider" venue, and unlikely to attract tourists. However, because of the increasing number of restaurants and shopping opportunities at National Harbor, and particularly because of its special events calendar—it hosts a large food and wine festival, an Oktoberfest, a sunset concerts series, and is now the Washington home for the traveling Cirque du Soleil shows—it is acquiring a reputation as a destination in itself.

In addition to the hotels already on site, the Walt Disney Company is building a freestanding resort hotel here, which may be part of the Disney Vacation Club properties, and which will likely include some amusement facilities, though not a park per se. Even without a Disney park, National Harbor boasts an outdoor-adventure complex with a pirate ship rope climb, climbing wall, a giant swing, and a 400-foot-long zip line course (open Friday–Sunday, May through November). The long-closed National Children's Museum, formerly on Capitol Hill, is relocating to a Cesar Pelli–designed 150,000-square-foot facility at National Harbor near the Disney parcel, scheduled to open in 2013. The five-piece aluminum sculpture of a giant writhing out of the sand called "The Awakening," which was formerly across from the Jefferson Memorial Tidal Pool, is now installed on the National Harbor waterfront, along with the 85-foot "Beckoning," fountains, restored indigenous habitats, and so on. If you fly into Reagan National Airport from the south, you'll have a fairly impressive view of the hotel's 18-story atrium's glass-wall view—not only of the Potomac River and Old Town Alexandria but of, say, Fourth of July fireworks.

LODGING AT NATIONAL HARBOR

THE NATIONAL HARBOR COMPLEX SO FAR (i.e., in advance of the Disney development) includes six hotels: the Gaylord, the Westin National Harbor, a Hampton Inn and Suites, a Marriott Residence Inn, a Wyndham vacation resort, and a W Hotels boutique property called Aloft, plus a number of condo buildings. The Gaylord Hotel alone has 2,000 rooms (which includes 300 VIP Tower spots). There will eventually be a total of a million square feet of dining, retail, and entertainment space, as well as office buildings and commercial marinas. Already several riverboat and cruise companies use the marinas here for water taxis and tourist cruises; see Part Four: Getting In and Getting Around for more details.

TRANSPORTATION TO AND FROM NATIONAL HARBOR

NATIONAL HARBOR HAS A DEDICATED EXIT from Interstate 95/495 (the Beltway), Exit 2A; it also has an exit (1A) from I-295, Route 210, and Oxon Hill Road. (Long-running reconstruction of the Woodrow Wilson Bridge, which made access from I-95 difficult, has been completed.) Taxi fare from Reagan National is approximately $30, from Dulles International $75, and from BWI $85.

Dedicated Gaylord SuperShuttle service runs about every 20 minutes between the hotel and Reagan National Airport (near the baggage claim area) between 6 a.m. and 8 p.m.; tickets are $18 one way and $32 round-trip. (Exclusive van service, booked in advance, is $78, but might be worth it for some convention groups.) Shuttle service from Washington Dulles or BWI airports to Gaylord is $43 ($125 exclusive); call 800-660-8000 and press 2 for reservations.

There is fairly continuous shuttle service from the Gaylord Resort to Union Station and the Old Post Office Pavilion, leaving every half-hour from 8 a.m. to 9 p.m.; one-way tickets are $13, round-trip tickets $20, and unlimited-use three-day passes are $49. Shuttles to the Old Town Alexandria waterfront and to the King Street Metro station run every 45 minutes on a constant loop from 6:30 a.m. to 9 p.m. (later departure Friday and Saturday nights). Tickets are $7, $14 round-trip.

Gaylord also has a contract with ExecuCar for private car, SUV, and/ or limo services. At press time, service from Reagan to Gaylord is $59; the return trip is $35. Service from Dulles or BWI is $125, return $95.

For water taxi service to Old Town and Mount Vernon, see Part Four: Getting In and Getting Around.

PARKING AT NATIONAL HARBOR

COUNTING TEMPORARY SHIFTING SPACES, there are about 9,500 public parking spaces at National Harbor, mostly indoor (with car washes available) but some outdoor meters. Parking starts at $3 per hour and $11 for 24 hours or after 6 p.m. Cash and credit cards are accepted, but there are no attendants in the three main garages.

At the Gaylord hotel, for instance, daily rates are $5 for the first hour, $12 for the first three hours, and $19 overnight; valet parking is $28 overnight. However, some hotels and restaurants have validation stamps that lessen the cost.

DINING AT NATIONAL HARBOR

INSIDE THE GAYLORD RESORT are two high-end restaurants—the **Old Hickory Steakhouse** and **Moon Bay Coastal Cuisine,** plus an Italian restaurant, a coffee bar/sandwich pub, a huge sports bar and grill complex with a 30-foot-wide HD video wall, a martini-champagne-cocktail lounge, and a VIP-style nightspot and lounge that boasts 18-foot glass walls, fiber-optic color effects, a second-floor VIP level, dancers in glass "pods," and a small-bites menu.

Among the other notable restaurants in the National Harbor complex are a branch of New York's **Bond 45** Italian steak-and-seafood house, **Elevation Burger** (a regional chain emphasizing organic beef and bison), a branch of Warren Brown's **CakeLove,** a couple of Maryland-style crab-and-lobster grills as well as **McCormick and Schmick, Rosa Mexicano** (another New York import), a Los Angeles catchall called **Ketchup, Ben & Jerry's,** and restaurants specializing in Thai, Chinese, American grill, *hefty* American grill (i.e., the **Cadillac Ranch,** complete with '80s-style mechanical bull), a dueling-pianos bar (**Bobby McKey's**), and various pubs and lounges.

PART FOUR

GETTING *In*
and
GETTING *Around*

COMING *into the* CITY

WE'VE ALREADY TRIED TO PERSUADE YOU NOT TO DRIVE to Washington, or at least to come only as close as you have to; but we realize that there are many factors (cost, number of people traveling together, distance, time, etc.) involved in choosing a mode of transportation, and if you must, you must. But there are several options, and we'll try to lay out the pros and cons of all of them—even driving—as clearly as possible.

ARRIVING BY CAR

IF YOU DRIVE, YOU WILL MOST LIKELY ARRIVE on one of four major highways: Interstate 95 (I-95) from the north or the south; I-66 from the west (likely off I-81 between New York and Pennsylvania or Virginia and Tennessee); or I-70/270 from the northwest. Other routes that converge in Washington are US 50 (which hooks up with Annapolis, Maryland, US 301, and Maryland's Eastern Shore) and US 1 and the Baltimore-Washington Parkway, which parallel I-95 between the two cities' beltways (and in some places actually coincide).

All of these routes have one common link: they connect with Washington's Capital Beltway (I-495), a ribbon of concrete encircling the city.

Remember how we warned you about the traps poor signage can lay for unsuspecting motorists? Exhibit A: Part of the Beltway is numbered both I-95 and I-495. Why? Since the main interstate artery, I-95, doesn't cut (yet) directly through Washington as it does in Richmond to the south and Baltimore to the north, it's rerouted along the southern half of the Beltway, i.e., 495. One section that does continue into the city, past and occasionally underneath the Mall, is marked I-395; though it ends only halfway through the District, converging with New York Avenue NE, someday it *may* become the "real" I-95. Another section that slices off part of the

Washington, D.C., and Vicinity

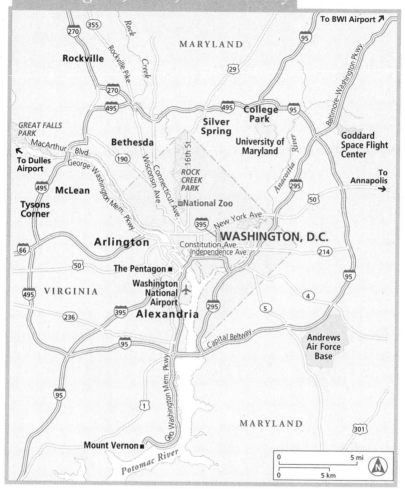

Beltway on the eastern side of the Anacostia River and hooks back up to the Baltimore-Washington Parkway is labeled I-295. Then there are signs that say take this ramp onto 495 toward Virginia and that one onto 495 toward Maryland, which seem helpful—except that, depending on exactly where you're going, they may lure you into taking the much longer way around. Another famous den of driving iniquity—call it Exhibit B—is the George Washington

continued on page 95

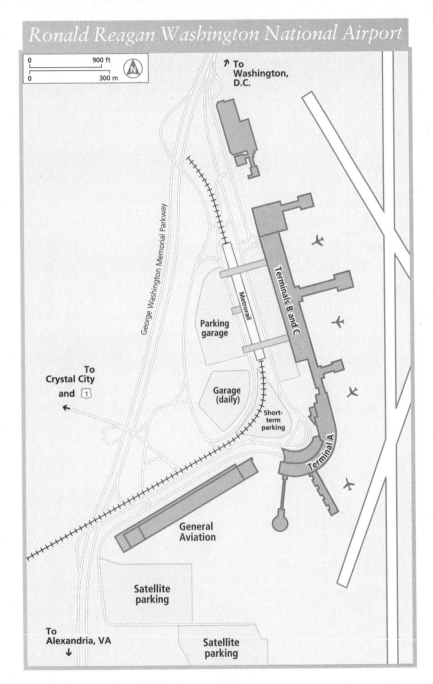

Ronald Reagan Washington National Airport

0 900 ft
0 300 m
N

↑ To
Washington,
D.C.

George Washington Memorial Parkway

Metrorail

Parking
garage

Garage
(daily)

Short-
term
parking

To
Crystal City
and ①
←

Terminals B and C

Terminal A

General
Aviation

Satellite
parking

To
Alexandria, VA
↓

Satellite
parking

Washington-Dulles International Airport

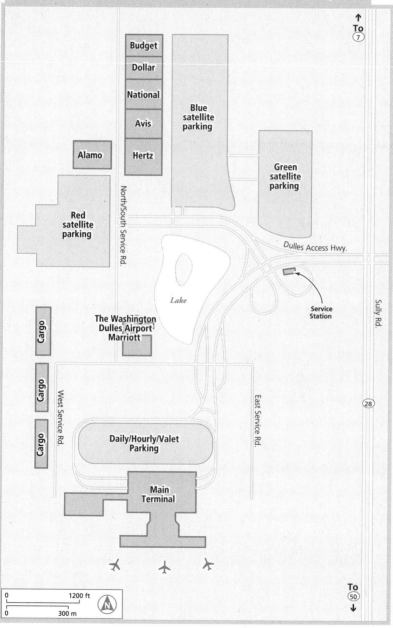

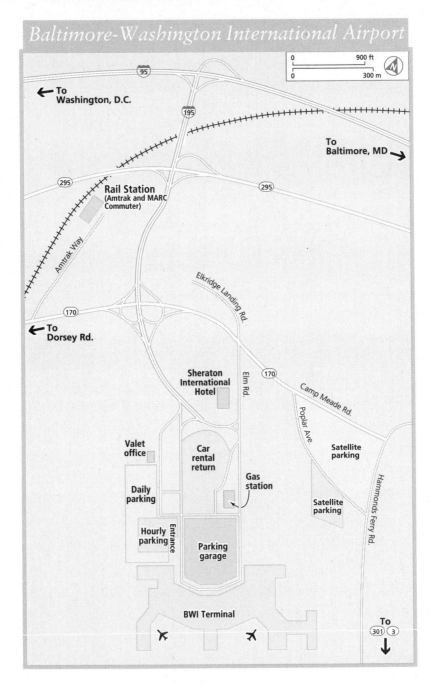

continued from page 91

Memorial Parkway, where those attempting to visit GW himself at Mount Vernon might well find themselves headed either to see Lincoln and Jefferson instead or south into unknown Virginia. However, as we said, if you must drive, you must.

Drivers coming from I-70/270 headed downtown should take the Beltway east to the Baltimore-Washington Parkway and exit south. Bear right onto New York Avenue where the Parkway splits; it goes straight to downtown, near Union Station. If you're going to the Maryland suburbs of Bethesda or Silver Spring, stay on I-270 to I-495 West. If you're going to Northern Virginia or the more westerly neighborhoods such as Reston or Potomac, take I-495 south toward Virginia and use the rather prettier George Washington Memorial Parkway. Just pay close attention to those signs.

From the south and west, motorists can take either I-66 (into the Beltway at about 9 o'clock) or I-95/395 (that section of the "straight" I-95 at about 7 o'clock) into Washington. Both cross the Potomac into the center of the tourist hubbub. But look at the map; the "clock" is not exact. If, from I-66, you are going toward Maryland, you will head north on I-495. That seems fairly obvious; however, if you are going to Tysons Corner, a huge "edge city," you will also go north on I-495, albeit briefly.

Our advice to drivers unfamiliar with Washington: Sit down with a map before you leave home and carefully trace out the route to your destination. If you need to make a phone call or two for directions, do it then. And we say again: avoid rush-hour traffic (5:30 to 10 a.m. and about 2:30 to 8 p.m.).

unofficial **TIP**
You'll hear constant references to the "Inner Loop" and "Outer Loop," especially in regard to traffic jams. These refer to the twin circles of the Beltway. Since Americans drive on the right, the Inner Loop runs clockwise and the Outer Loop counterclockwise. (Those of you from the UK, grit your teeth.)

ARRIVING BY PLANE

Ronald Reagan Washington National Airport Of the area's three airports, this—variously shorthanded as Reagan or National—is by far the most convenient, located a few miles south of D.C. on the Virginia side of the Potomac River. This means that some of the flight patterns offer a breathtaking up-close-and-personal view of the Mall monuments, and others a similarly breathtaking view, though not for the same reasons, of the river as the plane lands on its banks.

Yet its close proximity to the city has resulted in some restrictions. No aircraft are allowed to fly over the White House or other sensitive areas, which makes for a few roundabout approaches and takeoffs (which won't really affect you); nor are any aircraft allowed to take off or land late at night—which might affect you if, like Eve, you are seriously delayed by bad weather, in which case you may find yourself being delivered not to National but to BWI or Dulles.

In addition, only about three dozen larger jets are allowed to land or take off in an hour; and a "perimeter rule" restricts nonstop flights to and from National to a distance of 1,250 miles or less, so it serves no international airlines (except for Air Canada, which is almost domestic, and an occasional business charter to Mexico or the Bahamas, etc.). So National is more of an East Coast short-hop airport, a U.S. Airways hub (broadly contracted out to smaller "express" jet lines). Of course, if you can't get a direct flight into National, you can search out a connection that will get you into National. It will probably be faster—and almost certainly more convenient—than flying into either of the other two airports.

Expanded and lavishly refurbished (for about $1 billion) in the late 1990s, National is very user-friendly. There are three levels, so that pickup and drop-off traffic coexist calmly. There are dozens of shops and vendors for those who find themselves without a clean shirt, silver drop earring, hostess gift, or working cell phone; and you'll find more than 40 restaurants, bars, and snack bars, including Gordon Biersch, Samuel Adams, Sam & Harry's steakhouse, Matsutake Steak and Sushi, TGI Friday's, and Cibo wine bar. The entire airport has wireless Internet service. There are Traveler's Aid booths, ATMs, and currency exchanges. The USO lounge here is in the main lobby of Terminal A and is open 6 a.m.–10 p.m.; follow the signs to gates 10–45 and the lounge is on the left across from the Lost and Found.

unofficial **TIP**
All three Washington regional airports now have designated animal relief areas for those traveling with four-legged companions. All three also have USO lounges for members of the armed services and their families (and service animals if needed).

Reagan National offers several options for getting into the city or suburbs. The airport's own Metro station is the most obvious (both the Blue and Yellow lines stop here, offering connections to other lines at Rosslyn, Gallery Place–Chinatown, L'Enfant Plaza, and MetroCenter). Two mezzanines connect the Metro to the main terminal via pedestrian bridges, although if you're going to the farther end, have extra baggage, are transferring terminals, etc., there is free shuttle service. On weekend mornings Metrobus numbers 13F and 13G shuttle between downtown, circling around Federal Triangle, Penn Quarter, the Smithsonian, and the airport (for details call ☎ 202-637-7000 or go to **www.wmata.com**). Two ground-transportation centers located on the baggage claim level provide information on Metro, taxi service, SuperShuttle vans, and rental cars.

(For some travelers, it might be worth noting that Union Station is also on the Metro, although on the Red Line, which means you'd have to transfer at Gallery Place or MetroCenter; but if Washington is only one stop on your vacation, or a hop-off point, the subway-train connection might be useful.)

Cab fares are reasonable (about $12 to Georgetown, downtown or Capitol Hill, for example). You could certainly rent a car here, but—here we go again—you'll have to negotiate some of the busiest sections of highway just to get out of the immediate airport area.

SuperShuttle shared-service vans leave every 15 (or fewer) minutes to any destination in the D.C. area. Fares start at $14 (additional members of the party are $10 each) for travel into the District of Columbia. Three SuperShuttle ticket counters are located at National; look for the "Washington Flyer/SuperShuttle" signs posted through-out the airport. For more information, exact fares, and reservations, call ☎ 800-BLUE VAN (258-3826) or go to **www.supershuttle.com.**

Although it may only apply when you are returning home, Reagan National Airport participates in the Registered Traveler Program.

For detailed information about Reagan National Airport, call ☎ 703-417-8000 or go to **www.metwashairports.com/reagan.**

WASHINGTON DULLES INTERNATIONAL AIRPORT Located 26 miles west of downtown in the sprawling Virginia suburbs, in a soaring landmark building designed by Eero Saarinen (which was copied by the Taiwan airport authorities), Dulles International is 45 minutes to an hour from the city by car. There is no direct public transportation downtown (although a light-rail connection to the Vienna Metro is finally under construction). Dulles is primarily known as an international hub—more than 20 international companies fly here—but a dozen domestic airlines do so as well. United Airlines, which has a major hub at Dulles, handles nearly two-thirds of the airport traffic; discount carriers such as AirTran (formerly ValuJet) and JetBlue have increased the airport's domestic traffic volume considerably in the last few years.

The building covers more than a million square feet, with four terminals, two of which have been renovated and the other two of which are scheduled to be replaced entirely by a more ergonomic building. Dulles has recently inaugurated smoother underground passenger traffic between terminals, though there are still some elevated van-like "people movers" in use, which will gradually be retired. It has separate levels of traffic for drop-off and pick-up, which is where ground transportation is located.

With all its space, Dulles offers nearly four dozen dining options, including Vino Volo Wine Room, Harry's Tap Room, Old Dominion Brewing Co., Gordon Biersch, and a tequila bar. There are 40 retail shops, nine currency exchange booths, plenty of ATMs, and even a bank branch. It also has wireless

unofficial **TIP**
The Smithsonian National Air and Space Museum's Steven F. Udvar-Hazy annex just outside Dulles houses a Concorde, the space shuttle Enterprise, and the Enola Gay, among other aviation and aerospace legends. Unfortunately, you'll probably have to take a cab from the airport.

Internet throughout, along with some public computer terminals, and Travelers Aid bureaus.

The Dulles USO Lounge for military and their families is located on the Arrivals level opposite baggage claim carousel 12 and is open daily 6 a.m.–10 p.m. Like Reagan National Airport, Dulles participates in the Registered Traveler program. For complete information on the airport and services, call ☎ 703-572-2700 or go to **www.met washairports.com/dulles.**

Until direct light-rail service from D.C. is complete (the so-called Silver Line), Dulles remains the least convenient of the three airports serving Washington, about a 45-minute drive from downtown—longer during rush hour, despite the existence of the airport-only Dulles Access Road, which connects with the Capital Beltway and I-66. Cab fare is about $55–$65 to downtown Washington.

Washington Flyer coach service to the West Falls Church Metro station leaves about every 30 minutes, seven days a week ($10 one-way, $18 round-trip); it's a 25-minute bus trip to the subway station. (As a comparison, a cab ride between Dulles and the West Falls Church station costs about $40, so the better bargain might depend on the number of people in the party.) For more information, call ☎ 888-927-4359 or visit **www.washfly.com.** SuperShuttle shared-ride vans will take you anywhere in the D.C. metropolitan area; there's usually about a 30-minute wait and fares start at about $29 to the downtown area (additional members of the party are $10 each). For more information, exact fares, and reservations for pickup for your return trip to Dulles, call SuperShuttle at ☎ 800-BLUE VAN (258-3826) or go to **www.supershuttle.com.**

Metrobus has service from the L'Enfant Plaza Metro Station with stops at the Rosslyn Metro and the Tysons-Westpark Transit Station, which might be handy for those staying in the Virginia suburbs. The 5A bus leaves L'Enfant Plaza every 25–45 minutes weekdays and on the hour between 6:30 a.m. and 11:40 p.m. on weekends; the trip takes about 50 minutes and costs $3.20 each way ($3.10 with a SmarTrip card; see explanation on page 117). For information call ☎ 202-637-7000 or go to **www.wmata.com.**

If you happen to be staying or working near Dulles Town Center, there is also bus service from there to the airport, with five stops in between. The Dulles 2 Dulles Connector leaves from the town center every 45-60 minutes between 7:30 a.m. and 6 p.m. The trip takes about 30 minutes and costs only 50 cents. For more information call ☎ 877-777-2706 or go to **www.vatransit.org.**

BALTIMORE/WASHINGTON INTERNATIONAL THURGOOD MARSHALL AIRPORT In a series of remarkably prescient marketing moves, Baltimore's old Friendship Airport was renamed, first Baltimore/Washington International Airport (BWI), and then Baltimore/Washington International Thurgood Marshall Airport—and is (for obvious reasons) universally referred to as BWI.

There's a reason "Baltimore" comes first in the name; it's located only 10 miles south of Baltimore's Inner Harbor but about 35 miles—a 50-minute drive in the best of traffic conditions—from downtown D.C. On the other hand, Thurgood Marshall himself is not forgotten; there's an exhibit tracing the life of the great civil rights advocate and Supreme Court Justice.

The USO lounge here is in the lower level of the terminal between Concourses D and E.

Although it is a true international port (British Airways flies into BWI as well as into Dulles), BWI handles primarily domestic air traffic. A Southwest Airlines hub, which accounts for more than half the traffic, BWI is also a secondary hub for AirTran. Its popularity as a lower-cost, high-efficiency airport has kept business booming; nearly 21 million passengers came through BWI in 2009, making it the 24th busiest airport in North America. It has also won awards from Aviation.com as one of the Top 10 easiest airports to get to, and from the Airports Council International as the top airport for service quality in its size group. It's also been something of a test lab for TSA check lines, and as a result the queues usually proceed quite smoothly.

The easy-to-get-to nod comes in great part because despite its out-of-the-way location, it has public transportation links both south and north, on Amtrak to Washington and light rail to Baltimore.

If you decide to use four-wheel transportation, go to the lower level, where you will find the SuperShuttle van service, taxicabs, and Metrobuses. Vans run from BWI to the Washington Convention Center daily on the hour from 6 a.m. to 7 p.m. ($37 each way, $12 for additional passengers, children up to 2 years old free). No reservation is required; for information call ☎ 800-BLUE VAN (258-3826) or go to **www.supershuttle.com**). Metrobus B30 offers express service to the Greenbelt Metro station, which may be the ideal transfer point for you. (If you are going all the way into the city, Greenbelt is also a stop for the MARC Camden line, below, which terminates at Union Station.) The bus leaves every 40 minutes from about 6 a.m. to 10 p.m. weekdays and 9 a.m.–10 p.m. weekends; the fare is $6 ($3 for seniors and disabled passengers), and the transfer onto the subway system is free. For more information call ☎ 202-637-7000 or go to **www.wmata.com.**

unofficial **TIP**
Although at press time BWI did not participate in the Registered Traveler program, the airport authority has expressed interest in being approved for RT queues.

Cab fare from BWI to downtown starts at about $70 without tip, but if you have several people in your party and/or a lot of luggage, it might be a better bargain than the van. (And of course there are those car rental desks, but do we have to go through that again?)

Amtrak has a designated station at BWI, and the free shuttle ride from the airport over to the station takes only a few minutes.

Depending on the time of day, day of week, and the particular train (unreserved, Acela, etc.), one-way tickets to Union Station range from $13 to $39, but there is also an Amtrak stop at New Carrollton, which is a subway stop and might be closer to some Maryland destinations such as College Park, home of the University of Maryland. Travel time from BWI to Union Station is about 30 minutes, and 15 minutes to New Carrollton; for information call ☎ 800-USA-RAIL (872-7245) or go to **www.amtrak.com.** MARC trains, which use the same stations as Amtrak, are inexpensive ($4 from Greenbelt to Union Station), but it's primarily a commuter service that is only available on weekdays and infrequently at that; for schedule information call ☎ 866-743-3682 or go to **mta.maryland.gov/services/marc.** Also see the next section for more information.

Among the dining choices at BWI are a number of regional names, such as California Tortilla (yup, from Maryland), the Greene Turtle, DuClaw Brewing Company, Varsity Grill, Obrychi's, Ram's Head Tavern, plus the usual franchise names. It also has ATMs and a bank, wireless Internet, and UPS and FedEx drop-off points as well as postal boxes. For more information on Baltimore/Washington International Airport, go to **www.bwiairport.com.**

ARRIVING BY TRAIN

UNION STATION, LOCATED NEAR CAPITOL HILL, is the central Amtrak connecting point in Washington. From here, trains go out all over the country. For most routes you can choose either Acela Express, Metroliner, or a regular train. Once inside the newly restored train station (which also houses restaurants, a multiplex, a food court, and plenty of shopping, in case you missed a meal or your best suit), you can jump on the Metro, located on the lower level. To reach cabs, limousines, buses, and open-air tour trolleys, walk through Union Station's magnificent Main Hall to the main entrance.

For information and schedules for Amtrak, the national passenger train service, call ☎ 800-872-7245 (TTY 800-523-6590) or visit **www.amtrak.com.**

In addition to Amtrak, Washington's Union Station is served by the Maryland commuter system (MARC) and Virginia Railway Express (VRE), which might be useful for those staying with family or friends farther out or who wish to make a day trip to some of the regional attractions.

MARC train service operates three lines: the Penn Line, connecting Washington with Baltimore's Pennsylvania Station (the Amtrak terminal) with stops at the New Carrollton Amtrak/Metro stations, Laurel Racetrack, and BWI airport; the Camden Line, which ends in downtown Baltimore near the Inner Harbor and the Baltimore Orioles' and Ravens' stadiums; and the Brunswick Line, going northwest through the Montgomery County suburbs along the Potomac River into western Maryland with a stop at Harper's Ferry and

Amtrak Passenger-train Service to Washington

REGION/CITY	DISTANCE	TRAVEL TIME	FREQUENCY
NORTHEAST			
Philadelphia	115 miles	1½–2 hours	more than 1 per hour
New York City	225 miles	3–4½ hours	more than 1 per hour
Boston	400 miles	8–9¾ hours	11 per day
SOUTH			
Richmond	110 miles	2 hours	8 per day
Newport News	187 miles	4 hours	2 per day
Raleigh-Durham	305 miles	6 hours	2 per day
Charlotte	376 miles	8½–10 hours	2 per day
Charleston, S.C.	503 miles	9–9½ hours	2 per day
Atlanta	633 miles	13½ hours	1 per day
Birmingham	799 miles	18 hours	1 per day
New Orleans	1,155 miles	25–36 hours	1 per day
Jacksonville	753 miles	13½–15 hours	3 per day
Tampa	996 miles	18 hours	1 per day
Orlando	1,129 miles	16½–18½ hours	2 per day
Miami	1,166 miles	22½–24 hours	3 per day
WEST			
Pittsburgh	300 miles	7½ hours	1 per day
Cleveland	440 miles	11 hours	1 per day
Toledo	550 miles	13 hours	1 per day
Cincinnati	602 miles	14 hours	3 per week
Chicago	780 miles	18 hours	10 per week

an extension to Frederick, Maryland. Note, however, that MARC operates Monday through Friday only. For schedules and more information, go to **www.mtamaryland.com/services/marc** or call ☎ 800-325-RAIL (TTY 410-539-3497).

VRE operates two commuter lines, one from Fredericksburg (to the south) and the other from Manassas (to the west). Most service is inbound in the mornings and outbound in the afternoons, but some trains serve day trippers as well. VRE also operates only Monday through Friday. For more information call ☎ 703-684-1001 (TTY 703-684-0551) or 800-RIDE VRE (743-3873) or visit **www.vre.org.**

ARRIVING BY BUS

Greyhound MAY BE THE VETERAN on the block and have the most memorable slogan, but it's not up (yet) to the standards of some of the hipper modern bus lines, the routes aren't always direct, and it's not even always a bargain. Instead, if you happen to be traveling from New York, Philadelphia, or along the Northeast Corridor, you might also check into some of the new "luxury" bus lines, several of which offer free wireless access, bottled water, and/or video screens. Tickets start as low as $1, and though that's obviously a very limited promotional rate, most tickets range from $20 to $50; departure and arrival points vary.

As noted in Part 1: Planning Your Visit, the Greyhound bus terminal is near Union Station, which gives you easy access to the subway or taxis, but if you have much more than a carry-on, it's something of a schlep. Those new coach lines along the corridor mentioned above have various arrival points, all of them at or very near major Metro subway stops. The **DC2NY** (☎ 202-332-2691 or **www.dc2ny.com**) stops at Dupont Circle; **Washington Deluxe Bus** (☎ 866-287-6932 or **www .washny.com**), which makes a 20-minute pit stop and runs family-friendly movies, will drop you off near the Farragut North, Dupont Circle, or Union Station Metro stops (the route depends on the time you leave New York); **Vamoose Bus** (☎ 877-393-2828 or **www.vamoose bus.com**) stops in Bethesda and Arlington. The gimmick at **BoltBus** (**www.boltbus.com**), which arrives at the Metro Center subway station, is that the earlier you make reservations, the cheaper the seats—starting at $1—and if you buy four trips, the fifth is free. **Megabus** also terminates at Metro Center, and fares can also dip to the bargain bin if you book several weeks ahead (☎ 877-462-6342 or **www.megabus.com**). The new **MVP** bus runs between New York, Baltimore, and D.C., with fares starting at $20 (**www.mvpbus.com**)

The easiest way to compare these is to go to Bus Junction (**www .busjunction.com**), which monitors a dozen bus lines, including the old grey dog.

All these bus companies hook up with the Metro, which is crucial to getting around town. With few exceptions (most obviously Georgetown and Adams Morgan), the subway delivers visitors within a comfortable walking distance of everywhere they might want to go inside the city and into the suburbs. And even those two neighborhoods aren't a particularly long walk from one stop or another. The trains are generally clean, quiet, carpeted, virtually crime free (except for those kids who can't resist noshing on board), and (in theory, at least) air-conditioned. They run so often that carrying a schedule isn't really necessary; just remember that trains run more frequently at rush hours (5 to 10 a.m. and 2:30 to 7 p.m.) than at other times—as much as ten minutes more frequently. For complete information on taking Metro and other mass transportation, see pages 108–124.

GETTING *Around* WASHINGTON

THE LAY OF THE LAND

IN WASHINGTON, GEOGRAPHY ISN'T SO MUCH DESTINY as destination. Washington itself is a city of nearly 600,000 people, located near the southern end of the East Coast megalopolis stretching from Boston to Richmond. However, what is generally considered the Washington metropolitan area (or the National Capital Region) includes Arlington County, the town of Alexandria, Prince William, Fairfax, and Loudoun counties in Virginia, and the Maryland counties of Montgomery, Prince George's, and parts of Howard and Frederick, totaling nearly 5.4 million residents. All the suburbs surrounding D.C. are experiencing exponential growth. Rockville, for example, a few miles north of the D.C. line, has become Maryland's second-largest city, after Baltimore. Loudoun County, west of Fairfax County, is the fastest-growing and, according to some surveys, wealthiest county in the nation.

Washington's most important geographical features, the Potomac River and, to a slightly lesser degree, the Anacostia River, are natural impediments to both tourists and suburban commuters. The few bridges that cross the river are rush-hour bottlenecks, and the high concentration of government and tourist sites near the river make getting into the city a challenge. Much of the rest of the downtown area is office-heavy, and there are a number of particular driving challenges—alternating one-way streets, streets that are two-way most of the time but one-way at certain hours, and of course the two blocks of Pennsylvania Avenue immediately in front of the White House, tourist central, that are closed to vehicles—that just add to the confusion. Not to mention constant construction obstructions and detours, accidents, official motorcades. . . .

unofficial **TIP**
Although it isn't technically accurate, residents generally use "Washington" to refer to the entire metropolitan region, and "D.C." or "the District" to indicate the central city.

On the other hand, while it's routinely exhausting to drive around Washington, the street layout—i.e., what tourists need to know on the ground—is more logical than it might seem. (Poor Pierre L'Enfant, he was just ahead of his time.)

Many of Washington's streets, especially downtown, are arranged in a grid, with numbered streets running north–south and lettered streets going east–west. The Capitol is the grid's center (although if you look at the map, you'll see that the White House is much closer to the geographical heart), with North Capitol, South Capitol, and East Capitol streets spoking out in those directions. What would be West Capitol Street, in effect, is the green swath of the Mall.

What takes getting used to are the avenues—Wisconsin, Massachusetts, New York, New Hampshire, etc.—which are named after states and which cut across the grid diagonally; they tend to lead into traffic circles or park squares that, though picturesque on a map, are the nemesis of many drivers. To make it worse, those diagonal state place names will disappear for the space of the square: Vermont Avenue temporarily vanishes at either end of McPherson Square, Connecticut Avenue runs toward, and away from, Farragut Square, and so on.

Our advice is to look at the map long enough to understand that underlying pattern—and to mutter the alphabet to yourself once in a while. If you are trying to find an address on a lettered street, such as the National Building Museum, at 401 F Street NW, it's on F Street between Fourth and Fifth streets NW; the International Spy Museum at 800 F Street NW is quite simply at the corner of Eighth and F streets in the NW quadrant. (Those NWs are important, because there can be multiple examples of the same address; there is, for instance, an Eighth and F streets SE, a similarly named intersection in NE, and despite the Southwest Freeway and a few office buildings, you could find yourself wandering very near the old Eighth and F streets SW as well.)

unofficial **TIP**
Although longstanding legend has it that it was because Pierre L'Enfant so disliked U.S. Supreme Court Chief Justice John Jay that he refused to acknowledge even the homonym, it was actually because in those days the letters "I" and "J" looked so much alike that it would have caused confusion.

If you are looking for an address on a numbered street, such as 1150 15th Street NW, the address of *The Washington Post*, you can pretty much count on your fingers to get the right cross street. A 300 address, for example, is between C and D streets. However, there is no J Street, so the *Post* building, which according to the address should be between K and L Streets NW, is actually between L and M streets NW.

Even if your destination is, in fact, on a street named after a state, the underlying grid of number- and letter-named streets will get you there and can even help you locate your block. An example: A popular destination for both tourists and power seekers is 1600 Pennsylvania Avenue NW. Because this well-known street snakes a course from the poor neighborhoods of Southeast Washington through downtown and into Georgetown, pinpointing an exact address can be tough. The clue, however, is in the street address: the White House is near the intersection of Pennsylvania Avenue and 16th Street. (And that's relatively easy; Eve spent a whole week learning to drive Massachusetts Avenue all the way across town without getting off on the wrong spoke of a traffic circle.)

Here are some of the major avenues that visitors will likely encounter in the city (or at least in directions):

- **Connecticut Avenue** runs from the northwest corner of Lafayette Square, in front of the White House, through Dupont Circle, past the National Zoo, and into Chevy Chase, Maryland.

- **Constitution** and **Independence** avenues run east–west as the northern and southern boundaries of the Mall.
- **Florida Avenue** starts in the busiest area of Northeast Washington and goes northwest past Gallaudet and Howard universities before making a peculiar hook down toward Dupont Circle.
- **Massachusetts Avenue** runs from near the Anacostia River on Capitol Hill through Dupont Circle, up Embassy Row, and past Washington National Cathedral and American University on its way to its terminus in Glen Echo, Maryland.
- **New York Avenue** is a major artery that runs from the White House to Northeast Washington and turns into US 50 and the Baltimore–Washington Parkway.
- **Pennsylvania Avenue** runs from Southeast and Capitol Hill through downtown and into Georgetown. The two blocks of Pennsylvania Avenue immediately in front of the White House are closed to vehicles.
- **Wisconsin Avenue** starts in Georgetown, about four blocks west of where Pennsylvania Avenue terminates, and leads north to the Maryland suburbs of Bethesda, Rockville (where it's called Rockville Pike and Route 35S), and Gaithersburg (Frederick Road), eventually going all the way through Frederick, Maryland.

Among those aforementioned circles and squares are some that are major landmarks or reference points, and often lend their name to the entire neighborhood. Among the most important are:

- **Dupont Circle** (at the convergence of Connecticut, Massachusetts, and New Hampshire avenues NW, 19th and P streets NW)
- **The Ellipse** (bounded by 15th and 17th streets NW, and Constitution Avenue and State Place NW)
- **Farragut Square** (bounded by 17th and 18th streets NW, and I and K streets NW)
- **Lafayette Square** (bounded by Jackson and Madison places NW, and H Street NW and Pennsylvania Avenue NW)
- **Logan Circle** (at the convergence of Rhode Island and Vermont avenues NW, and 13th and P streets NW)
- **Mount Vernon Square** (bounded by Massachusetts and New York avenues NW, and K Street and Mount Vernon Place NW)
- **Scott Circle** (at the convergence of Massachusetts and Rhode Island avenues, and 16th and M streets NW)
- **Washington Circle** (at the convergence of New Hampshire and Pennsylvania avenues NW, and 23rd and K streets NW)

These are some of the more famous streets worth being familiar with:

- **14th Street** is a major point of access to and egress from the Virginia suburbs, but it's also a major theatrical, restaurant, and shopping area linking Logan Circle, the new-U district, and Columbia Heights.
- **16th Street NW** heads due north from the White House through

Adams Morgan, edges Rock Creek Park, and merges with Georgia Avenue in Silver Spring, Maryland.

- **K Street NW** is a major east–west downtown business artery running from Florida Avenue NW past the Convention Center area to the Georgetown waterfront.
- **P Street** is an east–west street linking trendy Logan Circle, Dupont Circle, and Georgetown.

You'll also hear the names of several scenic parkways that do double duty as major thoroughfares:

- **Canal Road/Cabin John/Clara Barton Parkway** Connecting with M Street NW just west of the Key Bridge in Georgetown and edging the C&O Canal toward the Potomac River, Canal Road becomes the Clara Barton Parkway in Glen Echo, Maryland; shortly beyond that, where the Clara Barton Parkway merges with the Capital Beltway northbound toward Maryland, the Cabin John Parkway forks off and turns toward the southbound Beltway into Virginia.
- **The George Washington Memorial Parkway,** known as the "GW Parkway," runs from Mount Vernon through Old Town Alexandria (Washington Street), past National Airport, the 14th Street, Arlington Memorial, and Theodore Roosevelt bridges, McLean, Virginia, the CIA headquarters in Langley, Virginia, and out to the Capital Beltway/I-495.
- **Rock Creek Parkway,** formally designated (but almost never referred to as) the Rock Creek and Potomac Parkway, runs generally north–south from the Lincoln Memorial Bridge (connecting to Ohio Drive around the Tidal Basin and Jefferson and Lincoln Memorials) past the Kennedy Center, between Dupont Circle and Georgetown, and through Rock Creek Park to Beach Drive near the National Zoo.
- **Whitehurst Freeway** is fairly short but centrally located; it's an elevated highway that diverges from K Street NW to run over K Street in Georgetown to Canal Road and the Key Bridge into Rosslyn.

Incidentally, if you do find yourself driving these parkways, *watch your watch!* Sections of Rock Creek Parkway and Canal Road are one-way at rush hour (following the commuter traffic). Some of the busier in-town roads have one-way periods as well, including 15th Street NW (as Eve discovered her first week in Washington) and 17th Street NW, or have lanes that change direction.

Here's another thing to remember; the entire region is rife with red-light cameras, so speeding isn't the only thing to avoid.

IT'S NOT JUST THE DRIVING, IT'S THE PARKING

IF WE HAVEN'T ALREADY MADE IT CLEAR why you don't want to be driving around Washington, especially anywhere near a tourist attraction, we'll drop the other shoe: You have to park somewhere, and that's even harder, *and* more complicated, than it used to be.

Many neighborhoods have shifted to a park-by-space system, where you have to check the number of your space, either on the street or in a garage, and plug that number into a machine to pay. Street meters likely only provide two hours' parking anyway. But not only does street parking space continue to shrink, many street meters and lots now require you to pay via credit card or have a cell phone–debit charge account; and more confusingly, within the metropolitan area, various neighborhoods use different companies for that. And police are quick to issue tickets for expired meters. Also, a lot of legal spaces turn illegal during rush hour. The lingering hope is to find a space after 5:30 p.m., when many become free—although increasingly, meters in high-demand areas run until 7 p.m. or, as in Bethesda, until 10 p.m. Be sure to check the times on parking signs; they may not be right alongside the money box. And if your car is in a traffic lane at rush hour, no matter how much you put in that box, you're outta there, so don't even think about it. In 2009, D.C. towed nearly 20,000 cars for rush-hour violations alone.

The old-fashioned (so to speak) parking garages charge $12–15 a day or $7 an hour, and many of those are moving toward automated payment as well. Valet parking for dinner at a hot spot can easily cost you $10.

In popular residential neighborhoods such as Georgetown and Adams Morgan, parking gets even worse at night. Unless you've got a residential parking permit on your windshield—not likely if you're from out of town—street parking is limited to two or three hours, depending on the neighborhood.

(Incredibly, there's free parking along the Mall beginning at 10 a.m. weekdays; the limit is three hours. Needless to say, competition for the spaces is fierce, and the possible repercussions are, too.)

Here are some of the parking options in play in the Washington area. Around Dupont Circle, Union Station, and the K Street business corridor, as well as in Bethesda, you can pay by cell phone, but only if you have signed up with **www.parkmobile.com** or in Montgomery County, Maryland, **www.goparknow.com,** and set up an account using a credit card before-

unofficial **TIP**
All the area jurisdictions take parking violations very seriously; a $40 ticket for an elapsed meter is about the lowest fine you'll see, and that's if you haven't been towed. Towing fees can add over $100.

hand. Most places you find the space number you're in by reading the street square, then go to a central unit, pay, and get a receipt. (A few blocks have live attendants, but they're rare.) Some places you enter your license plate number and pay the meter with that ID, which the police can check. Along U Street NW in the Atlas District, you can pay by any of the three. But there are an increasing number of garages where you need either large numbers of coins or a prepaid system; and there are no longer humans to explain it to you, so you may drive in and find yourself stuck. We say again: just don't do it.

If you do make the ultimate mistake (or go running to get more quarters to feed the meter) and your vehicle is towed—or if you're not sure if it was towed or you're just lost—you can call the D.C. Dispatch Center at ☎ 202-576-6071 and find out where it is. Just remember, where you pay isn't the same place as where the car is likely to be— and all these divisions keep day hours. Note that in D.C. ticket fees double after 30 days, and after 60 days you'll be booted, which is *really* expensive. (Parking fines double in Montgomery County after only 15 days.)

ALTERNATIVE WHEELS

THERE IS ONE POSSIBLE EXCEPTION to our don't-drive rule, and that is if you (intelligently) get into Washington by some other means but really want to take a day trip or go outside the tourmobile/mass transit circuit. If you are already an urbanite who happens to be a member of the Zipcar auto-sharing nation, there are dozens of pickup locations; go to **www.zipcar.com** for details.

There is also a bike-share network, which will become increasingly useful as Washington tests bicycle-only lanes along tourist-friendly routes such as Pennsylvania Avenue between the White House and the Capitol. For bike sharing, you'll have to pay a membership fee, etc., but if that's how you get around back home, or if you want to build a little exercise into your touring, you might want to check into it. It's possible to sign up for a 30-day or annual membership ($25 and $75, respectively), which require advance registration and a credit card, or you can also get a 24-hour membership for only $5 at one of the kiosks; go to **www.capitalbikeshare.com** for detailed info on usage fees. For information on suggested commuter routes, maps, and expanded bike lanes go to **www.waba.org** or **www.bikewashington.org.**

In fact, Metro is rather bike-friendly. There are free bicycle racks at most Metro parking lots (available on a first-come basis); but you can actually take your bike on the subway at non-rush hours during the week and all day on weekends and *most* holidays. (Those super-sized crowd days such as the Fourth of July are a no-go.) Use the first and last cars only. This only applies to the classic two-wheeler, however: no trikes, tandems, recliners, etc. You can also rack your bike on the front of many Metrobuses. For more information go to **www.wmata .com/getting_around/bike_ride/.**

TAKING *the* METRO:
Just Do It

LEAVE THE DRIVING TO METRO

IT SHOULD BE CLEAR BY NOW THAT VISITORS who would prefer to spend their time doing something more pleasant and productive than sitting in traffic jams shouldn't drive in or around Washington. Thanks to the underground Metrorail system—nearly always called the Metro, though theoretically that could refer to the Metrobus system as well—visitors can park their cars and forget them. Just remember you need a SmarTrip card to exit most parking lots (see Parking at the Metro, page 112); cash or paper tickets are not accepted for this purpose. You can purchase a Metro pass in advance if you go to **www.wmata.com/fares/purchase/store;** they are available in denominations of $10 and $20. You can also buy a one-day pass for $9 online; see "Figuring the Cost," page 113.

There are farecard vending machines at all Metro stations that have daily parking (which eliminates most downtown locations); you can also purchase regular SmarTrip cards, though not the seniors' version, at Washington-area CVS pharmacies and many Safeway and Giant grocery stores. (For more on the SmarTrip system, see page 117.)

For trivia freaks, Washington's Metrorail system might be a tourist attraction in its own right, because the Wheaton station boasts the Western Hemisphere's longest escalator: a 508-foot-long behemoth that takes 2¾ minutes to ride. (The Forest Glen station, which is nearly 200 feet underground, doesn't even have escalators, only elevators.)

What might be even more useful for a first-time visitor would be the official Metro Visitors Kit, which includes a pocket guide complete with Metrorail system map, sites of interest near Metrorail stations, and hours and fare information. You can download the kit, along with Metrobus routes for the District, Virginia, and Maryland, at **www.wmata.com/getting_around/visitor_info/visitorkit.cfm**. If you prefer to have it mailed, call ☎ 888-METROINFO (638-7646) or 202-962-2773, but you need to allow about three weeks for delivery.

Five color-coded subway lines connect downtown Washington to the outer reaches of the city and beyond to the Maryland and Virginia suburbs. It's a clean, safe, and generally efficient system that saves visitors time, money, and energy; most will find it the ideal mode of transportation.

The trains are well maintained and quiet, with carpeting, cushioned seats, and air-conditioning. (Successive generations of new cars have been shuffled into the system, and more than 400 additional cars were ordered in May 2010.) The stations are clean, if somewhat stark; constructed with high, arching ceilings paneled with sound-absorbing, lozenge-shaped concrete panels.

unofficial **TIP**
The Metro Pocket Guide and map is available for downloading in English and 10 additional languages.

The wide-open look of the stations has been criticized as sterile and monotonous, but the design may explain why the Metro has managed to limit the sort of pickpocketing and petty crime often associated with subways: there's no place for thieves to hide. Cars and stations are nearly graffiti free, again thanks to the design, because the walls are rarely within reach over the electrified tracks.

In addition, the entire system is monitored by closed-circuit TV cameras, and each car is equipped with passenger-to-operator intercoms, as are rail platforms and elevators.

Metrorail is the second-busiest rapid transit system in the country, after New York City, transporting nearly 800,000 passengers every weekday along 106 miles of track and through 86 stations (more extensions and a Silver Line are under construction).

Trains operate so frequently that carrying a schedule is unnecessary. During peak-fare hours (weekdays 5 a.m. to 9:30 a.m. and 3 p.m. to 7 p.m.), trains enter the stations every three to six minutes. During off-peak hours, the interval increases to an average of 12 minutes; it can go to 20 minutes on weekends. To maintain the intervals

BRONZE PYLONS identify Metro stations; colored stripes at top show the line or lines served by that station.

throughout the year, the Metro adds and deletes trains to compensate for holidays and peak tourist season. Hours of operation are 5 a.m. to midnight Monday through Thursday, 5 a.m. to 3 a.m. on Friday, 7 a.m. to 3 a.m. on Saturday, and 7 a.m. to midnight on Sunday. (Holiday schedules vary; check the schedule at **www.wmata.com.**)

In 2010, Metro instituted "peak of the peak" fares that apply 7:30–9 a.m. and 4:30–6 p.m.; this only amounts to 20 cents more, so it's more of an annoyance for commuters for whom that means an extra $1 every week; but for tourists it's just a tenth of a cup of coffee.

Similarly, use of cash on buses and for transfers is sometimes a dime or so more expensive than use of a SmarTrip card, but since a card costs $5 before you can even put money on the account—i.e., a $30 card gets your $25 to use for riding or parking—you have to decide how much you'll use it.

Metro Do's and Don'ts

Right off the bat, you can make yourself obvious as an outsider. We don't mean perusing a system map, and in fact most locals will be courteous enough to help you find your way; many will actually volunteer if you look confused. We mean littering the system. Most international

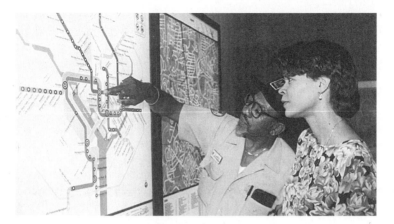

METRO SYSTEM AND NEIGHBORHOOD MAPS are located in the mezzanine of each station, as are automated Farecard vending machines (*below*).

visitors (and New Yorkers) are used to being able to eat and drink on their subway systems, but consumption is illegal in the Metro. In fact, you can be arrested for indulging on board (and don't think all those teenagers get away with it, either). You can carry water or coffee or a burger in a bag, but keep it closed. Smoking is also illegal, which might surprise some international visitors; and although some people cheat and light up as they're running up the escalator, technically that's off-limits, too, and you may get some feedback about it. Also: You must use earphones for music and/or video devices and observe the signs for seating reserved for seniors and disabled riders.

Most importantly, don't shove your arm in between doors as they are closing. These do not respond like elevator doors, and *will not reopen* because of the obstruction. Make sure you don't let a purse strap or briefcase get caught, either, because you're likely to see it dragged away.

And here is something that not only marks you as a tourist but makes you the target of hundreds of disgruntled fellow travelers: standing on the left side of the escalators. Washingtonians (among others) are divided into those who stand on the escalators—to the right—and those who walk up on the left. If you block the left half of the moving stairs, you are seriously asking for trouble.

Although Metro in general is a very safe vehicle, it does serve as a major people-mover, and that sometimes means teenagers and others prone to extravagant gestures. Usually, it means a group of students, who—like most kids—seem required to talk at the top of their lungs. Occasionally, however, it means rival teams and even, though rarely, gangs. There have been isolated incidents of violence at downtown stations, including a seemingly spontaneous but rather large fistfight at Gallery Place–Chinatown, and one at Union Station that apparently concerned a fight over an iPod. As we said, these are isolated incidents, but you should never be taken unaware.

PARKING AT THE METRO

THERE ARE A FEW THINGS TO KNOW before you drive to the Metro station. First, there are only a few stations—Franconia-Springfield, Huntington, Largo Town Center, Anacostia, New Carrollton, Shady Grove, Vienna-Fairfax-GMU—where you can simply swipe a credit card to exit the parking lot. Everywhere else, you must have a SmarTrip card to get your car out of the lot on weekdays after 10:30 a.m. (Parking fees are supposed to apply until the system closes, but in fact they vary somewhat; still, it's best to assume you're going to pay.) Lot parking ranges from $3.25 to $7 (depending on the station) except on Saturdays, Sundays, and federal holidays, when you can get out of jail (so to speak) for free.

unofficial **TIP**
There are a dozen or so spots at the Greenbelt, Huntington, and Franconia-Springfield lots that allow you to park for up to 10 days, and at a single-day rate, if you exit with a SmarTrip card. This might work well for some lucky family groups; for specific directions go to **www .wmata.com/rail/parking.**

There are a limited number of metered spaces that you may be able to grab, and that allow you to pay in coin, but these are short-term spots (follow the "Short-Term Parking" signs), usually limited to two hours and costing $1 per hour. In a few cases, such as Rockville, there are meters on the streets and in lots just outside the main parking lot as well; though these have longer allowable hours, they are still $1 for 60 minutes. Even trickier, these meters accept only quarters and $1 coins.

Incidentally, if you pull into a Metro parking lot or garage, you may see areas of parking spaces marked "Reserved." These require a monthly permit, but are only reserved for permit holders until 10 a.m., after which you may grab an empty space. (Don't try to get in too early; Metro police keep an eye out for that—and you'll likely have competition from savvy locals.)

MASTERING THE METRO

IT'S REALLY BETTER TO START OUT with a system map (again, check out **www.wmata.com**) or directions from a friend, but if you have a fairly good idea where you're going, you can probably find a station. (Or ask someone for help; we don't bite.) Many, though unfortunately not all, street signs in Washington indicate the direction and number of blocks to the nearest Metro station. Station entrances are identified by brown columns or pylons with an "M" on all four sides and the newer ones are marked with a combination of colored stripes in red, yellow, orange, green, or blue that indicate the line or lines serving that station. (To find the elevator, look for the wheelchair symbol near the station entrance; it won't be on all the pylons, only the "correct" one.)

Since most stations are underground, users usually descend on escalators to the mezzanine or ticketing part of the station. At above-ground and elevated stations outside of downtown Washington, you most often walk into the ticketing area at ground level or go down a short set of stairs or escalator to the main floor.

Figuring the Cost

The Metro system uses a fare system based on distance, unlike New York, for example, where all trips cost the same regardless of how many stops you pass. If you expect to make only one or two subway trips during your visit, look at the chart at each station (attached to the attendant kiosk) that tells you the cost of a trip between your starting place and destination. (It also tells you the difference between peak and off-peak fares.) These fares are also listed at the bottom of the color-coded system in the station, along with the estimated time of travel.

One-way fare is a minimum of $1.95 and a maximum of $5 at rush hour, and a minimum of $1.60—the least amount you can purchase a paper farecard for—and a maximum of $2.75 at non-rush hour. Check with the station agent about your return trip if you aren't sure. (A reminder: Peak fares are in effect from 5 a.m. to 9:30 a.m. and from 3 p.m. to 7 p.m. weekdays and from midnight to closing on weekends; peak of the peak fares, which add another $.20, are from 7:30 to 9 a.m. and 4:30 to 6 p.m. weekdays.)

Some lines have shorter routes within them at rush hour, so that the busiest stations get more service. If you are staying in Bethesda, for example, you can take a Red Line train marked either Grosvenor-Strathmore or Shady Grove, because both are beyond Bethesda. If you're going to Rockville, however, you'd have to disembark at

STEP 1: (*left*) To purchase a farecard, insert bills and/or coins.

STEP 2 (*right*): Use toggle switches to add or decrease the farecard's value. Plug in enough cash to buy at least a round-trip ticket (or more, if desired).

STEP 3 (*left*): Press the "Push for Farecard" button; the farecard appears at the "Used Farecard Trade-in" slot.

Grosvenor-Strathmore and wait for a Shady Grove–bound train—not unpleasant in nice weather but chilly in the snow! (Or, cleverly, get off at Medical Center and await the next train under cover.) Also, some stations are served by more than one line—both the Blue and Yellow lines will bring you from National Airport into town; and the Orange and Blue lines and Yellow and Green lines run together for several stops. Check the map or ask the agent.

Here's another useful trick: Even though the Red and Green/Yellow lines don't correspond, they do intersect, twice: at Gallery Place–Chinatown and at Fort Totten. If you hear of a service disruption on the Red Line— say, at Union Station—and you're in Silver Spring headed for a meeting in Dupont Circle, you could use the other line to bypass the problem altogether. Similarly, if you're on Capitol Hill taking the Blue Line to the Pentagon and there's a problem, you could swap to the Yellow Line at L'Enfant Plaza. Spend a little time studying the options.

If you have time to purchase a pass in advance, you might benefit by choosing a one-day pass for $9, which is good any weekday

unofficial **TIP**
You can use the routes with shorter internal routes to your advantage. For instance, if you get on a train at Rockville that is full, get off at Grosvenor-Strathmore and wait for a train that originates there; you'll have plenty of seats to choose from.

after 9:30 a.m. or all day weekends and holidays; an unlimited weekly pass for $47; or a "short-ride" weekly pass for in-town travel for $32.35 (though there may be an additional charge for the longest trips in the system). Seniors and passengers with disabilities are eligible for discounted fares; for information, go to **www.wmata.com/fares.**

Farecard Vending Machines

Though the machines can seem rather imposing in their long square-shouldered ranks, buying a pass from the farecard vending machines in Metro stations is fairly obvious: You stick in cash or a credit card, and out comes either a SmarTrip card or a paper ticket with a magnetic stripe that you will use to get in and out of the subway.

Notice that we said in *and* out. If you are used to a subway system that has a one-price-fare for all trips, you may be in the habit of stashing the ticket in your pocket or even disposing of it once you're on board; but here you must hold onto it, whether you are using a paper farecard or a SmarTrip pass; otherwise, like poor Charlie in that Kingston Trio song, you may ride forever 'neath the streets and never return. (Not really, of course, but it will be a pain.)

To buy a farecard from the vending machine, you start alongside the large orange circle marked, not surprisingly, "1." Next to that are buttons that point to ligthed choices on a screen (pretty much like an ATM); you decide if you want a SmarTrip card or a paper farecard. Info circle number 2 leads you through the payment process (cash, coin, credit card) and if you're using cash, allows you to adjust the actual value—if you put in three $1 bills but only need $2.60, for example. (Most of the paper farecard-only machines now have charts across the top that tell you how much a particular trip will be at rush hour and/or off-peak; if you don't see it, there is a large one on the front of the attendant's kiosk.) However, try not to stick in a $5 bill if you only want a $1.60 farecard; the machines only dispense coins, no bills, so you'll have a pocketful of change to lose. (The maximum change dispensed is $4.95, so definitely don't put in a $20 bill for a low fare, or you'll have a high-balance card whether you wanted it or not.)

When you're finished, your pass will emerge, and any change will drop down into the bin near the bottom.

RUSH HOUR AND NON-RUSH HOUR FARES are listed alphabetically at each station's kiosk.

AUTOMATED FAREGATES, which control access in and out of spacious Metro stations, are located near the kiosk. The woman pictured here is exiting the station.

Like all machines that accept paper money, these occasionally turn snarky, spitting back bills they don't like, so use new, stiffer greenbacks whenever you can or try smoothing wrinkled bills before inserting them. Inserting coins is nearly foolproof, though not terribly practical if you're riding the Metro a lot.

You can save yourself both time and aggravation by inserting or charging $10 or $20 at a time, which means you're buying a ticket good for several trips at least. (You can put as much as $45 on a single farecard at a time and $300 on a SmarTrip card.) The computerized turnstiles print the remaining value on the farecard after each use, which lets you know when it's time to buy a new one.

SmarTrip Cards

For the past several years, Washington-area transit authorities have been working toward a unified system for paying fares, like the one in New York. **SmarTrip,** as the pass is called, is already a mainstay of the subway system; can be used to exit any Metro-station parking lot; can be used on any Metro bus and nearly every regional bus and shuttle system (including, most importantly for tourists, the DC Circulator, described below). The downside is that it costs $5 in the beginning, but it can be reused indefinitely, which could be a great convenience to business travelers who return frequently or those who have family members in the Washington area. Plus, SmarTrip riders get a discount of 25 cents per trip. If you expect to be in town a lot—say, working on a major project or bid—it's worth knowing that you can store as much as $300 on your SmarTrip card at a time. If you register the card when you buy it—and if you buy it online or by mail, it is automatically registered—you can replace a lost card for $5, and all the money that was still on it will be restored. You can also register your card by going to **www.smartrip.com.**

You can buy the passes online or in Metro stations at the same machines that sell paper tickets, and if you expect to do extensive travel by public transportation, they are both sturdier and faster than paper passes. Instead of inserting them and waiting for them to reemerge, you simply press the face of the SmarTrip card to the large round plate so marked, and it calculates the fare electronically. All Metrobuses are equipped with SmarTrip readers that work the same way—

*un*official **TIP**
SmarTrip cards for those with disabilities cost $5 as well, but automatically deduct only the half-price fare when passed by the reader. For information on eligibility, go to www .wmata.com/accessibility.

touch and go—except that you only touch it once and the fare is automatically counted. If you have used the card at a Metrorail station or other Metrobus within the past two hours, the SmarTrip box automatically registers your fare as a transfer, and the second trip is free. And if you use the SmarTrip card on another related shuttle, you'll get a discount over the cash price.

For more information about SmarTrip, visit **www.wmata.com/fares/smartrip.**

Entering the Station

Now that you have your farecard or SmarTrip in hand, you can pass the gate into the Metro station proper. If you have a paper farecard, hold it in your right hand (sorry, but the machines are right-handed) with the brown magnetic stripe facing up and on the right. Walk up to one of the waist-high faregates with the green light and white arrow (not one that reads "Do Not Enter" and has a red light—they are for passengers exiting the station) and insert your card into the slot. It will be sucked in, the gate will open, and as you walk through, the card will pop back up for you to retrieve.

The SmarTrip card is not inserted into the machine but pressed onto a magnetic reader on the side of the gate (clearly marked). When you exit, press the card against the identical reader on the other side; when the gate opens, the machine will read out your remaining balance.

WHEN ENTERING OR EXITING, INSERT THE FARECARD (*face up with the magnetic strip on the right*) into the slot on the front of the faregate.

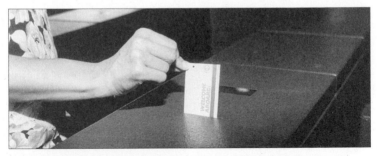

THE FARECARD REAPPEARS AT THE TOP OF THE FAREGATE; remove it and the faregate opens. On faregates for disabled people, the farecard reappears at the front of the gate.

NOTE: Remember to hang on to the farecard—you need it to exit the system.

Negotiating the Platform

Once you're inside the gate, look to the right and left; there will be escalators with arrows and the name of the end station indicating which platform your train will be on. Most stations have a single, middle platform, though some have dual platforms framing the tracks. You can confirm that you're on the correct side of the platform by reading the list of stations printed on the pylons located there. The route and the appropriate stations are marked with the route color; if there are two routes that use that station but diverge farther on, make sure the station you want to get off at is marked with the correct color, or both.

Above the platform are electronic signs on either track side that tell you how long the wait will be for the next several trains—the estimations are pretty accurate—and how far each particular train is going (Grosvenor vs. Shady Grove, Glenmont vs. Silver Spring, etc.) "Approaching" means the train has left the previous station and is within about a minute of arriving; "arriving" means just that. The signs also say how many cars are in each train, four being the shortest and eight the longest, which gives you an idea of how many seats there will be but also how far out toward the edges of the platform you can stand and still be near the doors when they open. Trains go in one direction only (like cars, on the right side forward), so you can tell which way your train is coming.

*un*official **TIP**
The anomalies are the Wheaton and Forest Glen stations, which are so far underground that they have individual tunnels for the north- and southbound trains; so you have less chance of getting on the wrong train.

If you are in a station with multiple levels, and you almost certainly will be at some point, the arrow signs directing you around can be a little confusing. The main thing to sort out is that if an arrow is pointing straight ahead but down, it may mean either descend (the obvious answer) or continue straight ahead if you are in a flat area; an arrow with the point up means actually ascend the stairs or escalator. Sideways or angled, you can probably guess.

Boarding and Exiting the Train

As a train approaches a station, lights embedded in the floor along the granite edge of the platform begin flashing. As the train comes out of the tunnel, look for a sign over the front windshield that states the train's line (Blue, Red, Green, Orange, or Yellow) and usually destination. The terminus, but not the color, is also shown on the side of the train. Double-check to make sure the approaching train is the one you want.

Then approach the doors, but stand a little off to the side to let departing passengers exit the train. Then move smartly; the train stops for only a few seconds before the chimes and warning voice indicate that the doors are about to close. Remember, if you're trying

WHEN THE VALUE OF A FARE-CARD DROPS BELOW $1, trade it in for a new one at a fare-card machine.

EMERGENCY INTERCOMS are located on all station platforms.

to squeeze into a train and hear the chimes, back off; if the doors close on you, you will seriously feel it. Just wait for the next train. In fact, because of the usual subway lemming syndrome—everybody trying to get on as fast as possible—there is often a much less crowded train only a couple of minutes behind.

Inside, take a seat (if possible) or grab a hanging strap; you may be able to study the system map located near the doors. The trains all have real operators who announce the next station over a PA system and give information for transferring to other lines, but you can't always hear them over the din and the static. The newer cars have electronic signs at the front and rear that list the next station. Also, those large station signs on the walls over the tracks are visible through the car windows, so if you check the map and see which stop is just before the one where you want to get off, you'll have a couple of minutes to gather your belongings (or kids).

Directions are given as if you are facing forward, even though some seats face the side or the back. So if the conductor says, "Doors opening on the right," he or she means the right if you are facing forward. However, if you are getting off at one of the stations that has a central platform, you will have to exit on the left; at a few stations, especially the ones at the ends of routes, trains may alternate sides. Try to hear what the conductor is saying, or just watch the crowd shifting to one side or the other.

When you get off the train, in most stations, you will have a choice of turning left or right to an escalator, and the signs are not always terribly instructive. At the Smithsonian station, for example, the choices are "The Mall" (which is almost certainly the one you want) and "Independence Avenue," which means you tunnel beneath the street and come up over on the side with federal buildings. That's not too hard to figure out. At Dupont Circle, on the other hand, one says "Q Street"—which brings you out north of the circle—and the other says "Dupont Circle," which lets you up south of it. The problem is, you might have much rather been above the traffic. So if you aren't sure of the exit in advance, it might be a good idea to ask the kiosk attendant at the first station so you don't have to go through the turnstile before discovering you're taking the long way around. But worse comes to worst, you'll still only be a few blocks away.

Changing from One Line to Another

Sooner or later you will probably need to transfer from one Metro line to another. Metro Center is the intended giant of the transfer stations, where the Red, Orange, and Blue lines converge in downtown Washington; but as the system has grown, several other stations have gained muscle. Other transfer stations tourists are likely to hit are Gallery Place–Chinatown (Red, Yellow, and Green); L'Enfant Plaza (Yellow, Blue, Orange, Green); Rosslyn (Orange and Blue); and Pentagon (Yellow and Blue).

You don't need your farecard or SmarTrip to transfer. Simply get off the first train, take the escalator to the correct platform, and board the other train. Try to listen to the PA system as your train enters the station: the driver recites where different lines are located in the approaching station (for example, "Transfer to the Red Line on the lower level"). If you can't hear the driver's instructions, look for the color-coded pylons with arrows that point toward the platforms, and look for the one with your destination listed on it.

The Gallery Place–Chinatown station and Metro Center are especially complicated. Frequently, you're routed down and up escalators to reach your platform. Remember that what looks like a straight-ahead arrow means go forward, but an up-arrow at an angle means look for an escalator.

Exiting the Station

Once you've taken the escalator or stairs up to the gates, you'll have to present your farecard or SmarTrip card again to pay the correct fare. If you used a paper farecard, you'll repeat the process—with the card in right hand, magnetic stripe up and on the right, insert it in the slot in the gate. If you have a SmarTip card, press it against the round reader on the side. (In either case, remember to check that the light is green on your side, not red, or you won't be able to pass through the gate regardless.) If your farecard still has money left on it, it will pop up as the gate opens and the sign will flash "Take Farecard." If you bought exact fare, you won't get your card back, but the gate will open and a little sign will flash "Exact Fare." You will just walk through and out.

However, if your farecard doesn't have enough value to cover your trip, the gate won't open and the card will pop back out (or, with a SmarTrip card, the light will flash a warning that you have insufficient funds). In that case, look around and find an Exitfare machine, which looks pretty much like a farecard vending machine, somewhere just behind you. Insert the paper farecard or press the SmarTrip to the reader light and the digital readout will tell you how much more money you need to exit the station. If you are short 40 cents, that's exactly how much you can add, and no more. If you stick a $5 bill into the Exitfare machine, you'll get $4.60 in change back. If you have a SmarTrip card, you'll be able to add on as much as you like; but if you have a farecard, and have to add on, the machine will swallow the card and let you go, but without the card, just as an exact fare card would. But note: Exitfare machines only accept cash. To add value with a credit card, you'll have to go back to the main farecard machines.

Also remember: A paper farecard will not get your car out of the parking lot. You must have a SmarTrip card except in those few stations mentioned above.

Discounts and Special Deals

Up to two children aged 4 or younger can ride free when accompanied by a paying passenger. Senior citizens and those with disabilities are eligible for reduced fares. Seniors should call ☎ 202-637-7000 or go to **www.wmata.com/fares/reduced.cfm** for more information. People with disabilities should call ☎ 202-962-1245 or 202-962-1558, or go to the same website.

Boarding the Wrong Train

Unless you're concerned about being a few minutes late for a job interview or tough restaurant reservation, boarding a train going in the wrong direction is not cause for panic. Simply get off at the next station, and if the platform is located between the tracks, cross to the other side of the platform to wait for the next train running in the opposite direction. If both tracks run down the center of the station, take the escalator or stairs (up at Dupont Circle, down at Metro Center, etc., but it will be fairly obvious) and cross the tracks to the other side, where you can catch the next train going the other way.

If you realize you've boarded the wrong color train (the Yellow Line to Pentagon City instead of the Blue Line to Arlington Cemetery) before the terminus, you may be able to get off at the next station, stay on the same platform, and take the next Blue Line train. If you're already beyond the split, you'll have to backtrack, but so long as you don't actually exit the station, it won't cost you extra.

What to Do with Low-Balance Farecards

After a few days in Washington, you may start accumulating farecards that don't have enough value for even a $1.95 one-way trip; but don't throw them away. Just remember that you can insert the used farecard into one of the machines at a Metro station and add enough money for more trips; you'll get a new card with the added value.

Those Red-Green Genes ...

Like approximately 8% of men, and a very few women, *Unofficial Guide* buddy Joe Surkiewicz is afflicted with red-green color blindness. On a map, he sees the Metro's Red and Green Lines as nearly identical, and the Orange Line looks a lot redder than it ought to. The only lines on the system map he can distinguish by color are the Blue and Yellow ones.

Don't let this worry you. For visitors suffering from color-blindness, the simple solution is to ignore the pretty graphics and stick to the facts—that is, find the station you want to travel to and then be sure of the names of the stations at the ends of the lines. For instance, the Red Line is the "Glenmont–Shady Grove" line, while the Green Line is the "Greenbelt–Branch Avenue" line. That way, when you see the station name on the front of the train, you'll know immediately that it's your train—depending on which way you're going at the time, of course. You'll need to know the other one for your return trip. And in fact, even this is just a precaution: The train cars have signs reading "red" or "green" (in the usual yellowish electronic lights). Just don't forget that the Red Line also has some trains that run only between Grosvenor-Strathmore and Silver Spring. Double-check by reading those pylons.

Oh, and don't be embarrassed if you are red-green colorblind: Scientists now theorize that you are actually better at seeing through certain types of camouflage, so it might have been an evolutionary benefit. And you can quote us on that.

METROBUS AND OTHER BUS SYSTEMS

WASHINGTON'S EXTENSIVE BUS SYSTEM, known as Metrobus, serves Georgetown, downtown, and the suburbs. Racks recently installed on metro buses as part of the new Bike-on-Bus program further increase commuter flexibility. There is no additional charge for passengers with bicycles. However, with 400 routes and more than 1,500 buses, Metrobus is an extremely complicated system to figure out how to use. As a result, we feel that visitors to Washington should leave Metrobus to the commuters and stick to the Metro except when the route is fairly simple—the 30s from downtown to Georgetown, for instance—or your concierge has written it down for you.

If you plan to transfer from the Metro to a Metrobus in D.C. or Virginia, get a SmarTrip card; it will contribute a small discount. (A single trip is $1.50 with a SmarTrip but $1.70 in cash, and $.75 for seniors and riders with disabilities; express routes are $3.65 using SmarTrip but $3.85 in cash, and $1.90 (cash) or $1.80 (SmarTrip) for seniors and people with disabilities). Most of Washington's suburbs have good subsidiary bus or shuttle systems that connect to the subway and thence into the District of Columbia, and if you are staying with friends, they'll probably show you the nearest stop; otherwise, these systems are probably too complicated for most tourists.

However, there is a system of limited shuttle routes called **DC Circulator** that may be useful to tourists, especially those staying downtown or doing sustained sightseeing. (Some newer Metro maps show these shuttle routes as well, which is extremely helpful.)

The Circulator buses follow six routes that can be very convenient. One connects Union Station to Georgetown by way of the Washington Convention Center and K Street NW; the section from downtown (17th and K streets NW) and Georgetown runs until midnight weekdays and 2 a.m. Fridays and Saturdays. A second route runs north and south from around the Convention Center to the Southwest Waterfront and back along Seventh and Ninth Street NW, putting it through the heart of the Penn Quarter–Chinatown neighborhood and also crossing the Mall. These two lines intersect at Mount Vernon Square. A third line shuttles between Dupont Circle and Rosslyn through Georgetown, primarily along M Street NW; a fourth connects McPherson Square with Woodley Park and Adams Morgan via the trendy 14th Street area and has late-night service (until 3:30 a.m. Fridays and Saturdays and midnight the rest of the week).

There are also two more limited routes. One connects Union Station to the Navy Yard by way of Capitol Hill; this runs weekends only from 6 a.m. to 7 p.m. unless there is a Nationals ball game, when there is later service. The fifth route runs east and west around the National Mall between Fourth and 17th streets NW, but this one operates only on summer weekends.

unofficial **TIP**
Circulator stop signs are also marked with a fish-shaped red-and-gold logo, while Metrobus stop markers are red, white, and blue. They are often, but not always, at the same intersections.

The bright-red Circulator buses, with a distinctive fish-shaped gold route map on the side, run from 7 a.m. to 9 p.m. daily (except where noted) every ten minutes. A single trip is $1. Seniors and riders with disabilities pay $0.50, or ride free if transferring; children 4 and under ride free. You can pay cash (exact change) or touch the SmarTrip reader at the front driver's door. Just as on Metrobus, a SmarTrip passage on the Metrorail within three hours will be registered as a transfer and cost $0.50.

You can purchase single-day, three-day, weekly, or monthly passes in advance at **www.commuterdirect.com** or at some CVS pharmacies. You can also get an all-day pass for $3 from one of the machines along the routes, which take change or credit cards but no paper bills. There are ticket machines all along the way (and also at the Gallery Place, Waterfront, and Mount Vernon Square–Convention Center Metro stations). For route maps and more information go to **www.dccirculator.com.**

▌ TAXIS

WASHINGTON TAXIS ARE PLENTIFUL—there are 150 companies licensed in the District alone—and relatively cheap. Many companies also have wheelchair-accessible vans, but it's a good idea to reserve those a day in advance (and get a confirmation number).

Although repeat visitors may remember an archaic fare system based on zones, in 2009 D.C. cabs shifted to the meter system used almost everywhere else, including the Maryland and Virginia suburbs. Rates start at $3 for the first sixth of a mile range and increase $.25 for every succeeding sixth-mile; there's also a 25-cent add-on per minute if you're just sitting in traffic. Within the District of Columbia, the maximum fare is $19 absent emergency add-ons (25% in snow emergencies) or the $1.50 extra-passenger fee.

The suburban taxi companies have their own rates; if you expect to use them, it is probably a good idea to call or go online to see what they are.

In Washington, cab drivers can pick up other fares as long as the original passenger isn't taken more than five blocks out of the way of the original destination. That's good news if you're the second or third rider and it's raining; it's not so hot if you're the original passenger and are trying to catch a train.

*un*official **TIP**
Unlike many other major metropolitan cities, Washington has not yet required all taxicabs to install charge-card machines, perhaps because D.C. is still new to the meter system, so if you don't have cash, ask the driver before you get in.

MAJOR WASHINGTON TAXI COMPANIES	
Action Taxi	☎ 301-840-1000
Barwood (Montgomery County)	☎ 301-984-1900
Red Top (Arlington and Alexandria)	☎ 703-522-3333
Silver Cab (Prince George's County)	☎ 301-277-6000
Yellow Cab (general)	☎ 202-544-1212

▌ THINGS *the* NATIVES *Already* KNOW

WHERE THERE'S SMOKE, THERE'S FINES

IF YOU HAVEN'T ALREADY REALIZED IT, Washington—the District of Columbia in particular—is predominantly public territory. And since the federal government, and the surrounding jurisdictions (even tobacco-proud

*un*official **TIP**
In contrast to New York's subway system, food and drink are prohibited on the Metro.

Virginia), have finally conceded that indoor tobacco smoke is as hard on art, archival materials, and even infrastructure and support services as it is on the human body, smoking is prohibited in all public facilities, including, but not limited to: federal buildings, including all the Smithsonian museums (and all other museums as well), memorials, and federal offices; Metrorail and Metrobus, as well as most smaller transit services, including tour buses and trolleys; performing arts venues and educational facilities, cinemas, the Verizon Center, and other indoor arenas; airports and train terminals; stores and shopping malls; restaurants; and hotel lobbies (and most hotel restrooms). Most open-air facilities—football and baseball stadiums, for instance—have restricted, designated smoking areas.

Consequently, if you are a habitual smoker, you'll need to factor that in to your itineraries, or at least calculate where and when you can take a butt break. And that's not a bathroom joke.

CUSTOMS AND PROTOCOL

DINING OUT We've already discussed the general dress taboos in town (which is to say, there aren't too many), and will speak more specifically about particular restaurants in Part Six. However, in terms of restaurant manners, respect is still the rule (regardless of the less-cultured people around you). Washington, as an international city, is full of ethnic restaurants at all price points and clientele. Many are casual, though quite a number are at least business class; and while you needn't feel intimidated about unfamiliar menus or customs, it never hurts to move cautiously when it comes to waving about knives or (much worse) drumming on the table with chopsticks. Yes, this means you as well as your kid. If the cuisine is new to you, feel free to ask your server for a recommendation. Or just watch what's going on around you; dining out is nearly a professional activity for a lot of Washingtonians.

TIPPING Is the tip you normally leave at home appropriate in Washington? Probably, but bear in mind that while a tip is a reward for good service, Washington waiters in particular tend to be a bit

Porters, redcaps, and bellmen	At least $1–$2 per bag and $5 for a lot of baggage
Cab drivers	15%–20% of the fare; add an extra dollar if the cabbie does a lot of luggage handling
Valet parking	$1–$2
Waiters	15–20% of the pretax bill
Bartenders	10–15% of the pretax bill
Chambermaids	$1–$2 per day
Checkroom attendants in restaurants or theaters	$1 per garment
Shoeshine guys	$2 for shoes, $3–$4 for boots

spoiled, so be sure you're making a point if you tip lightly. Also, consider your hotel's schedule: if your room is serviced twice a day, it would be nice to leave a tip for both the day and night staff—one of Eve's golden rules—and it might earn you extra attention. It's been known to happen. Above are some general guidelines, but in truth, we recommend the high end.

TELEPHONES

THE WASHINGTON AREA IS SERVED BY SEVERAL AREA CODES: ☎ 202 inside the District; ☎ 301 and ☎ 240 for the Maryland suburbs; ☎ 703 and ☎ 571 for the closer Northern Virginia suburbs across the Potomac River; ☎ 540 for the outer Virginia suburbs; and ☎ 410 and ☎443 for Baltimore, Annapolis, and the ocean resorts. (The Delaware ocean resorts use the ☎ 302 area code.) To dial out of D.C. to suburbs beyond the city's limits, it's necessary to dial the right area code. While calls to Arlington, Alexandria, and most of Fairfax County in Virginia and to Montgomery and Prince George counties in Maryland are dialed as if they're long distance, they are charged as local calls (50¢ from most pay phones—if you can still find one).

RESTROOMS

THE *UNOFFICIAL GUIDE* FAMILY IS LEGENDARILY on guard for travelers with small bladders, a legacy from UG patriarch Bob Sehlinger. (And someday we'll stop kidding him about it.) When we enter a marble edifice, you can be sure we're not just scrutinizing the layout, the flow of the crowd, and the aesthetics: we're also eyeing the real estate for the nearest public facility where we can unload that second cup of coffee.

So how does Washington rate in the restroom department? Actually, pretty well. That's because of the huge number of museums, monuments, federal office buildings, restaurants, bars, department stores, and hotels that cover the city, nearly all of which have clean and conveniently located restrooms.

Leading any list of great restroom locations should be the National Air and Space Museum on the Mall. For women who claim there's no justice in the world when it comes to toilet parity, consider this: there are three times as many women's restrooms as there are men's restrooms. "And the men don't seem to notice," says a female Smithsonian employee who works at the information desk.

Other facilities of note on the Mall include those at the National Gallery of Art, the Arthur M. Sackler Gallery, the Hirshhorn Museum and Sculpture Garden, and the National Museum of African Art. At the Arts and Industries Building, facilities are located far away from the front entrance (which means they aren't as frequently, um, frequented). The restrooms in The Castle, the Smithsonian's visitor center, are easier to find and also usually not very crowded—perhaps because tourists tend to go there earlier in the day.

Nearly all the monuments have restrooms equipped for wheelchair users, including the Lincoln and Jefferson memorials (which are downstairs by the museum stores and something of a secret) and the Washington Monument (in the ticket lodge). The new restrooms at the National World War II Memorial on the Mall and the FDR Memorial are very nice. The new U.S. Capitol Visitor Center has more than two dozen restrooms, and there are more at both the Ellipse Visitor Pavilion and the White House Visitor Center. Downtown hotels, restaurants, department stores, coffee shops, and bars are good bets. You won't find restrooms in Metro stations, although a few stations are located in complexes that do provide restrooms, including Union Station, Metro Center, Farragut North, Friendship Heights, and L'Enfant Plaza; ask the attendant which exit to take.

THE HOMELESS

IF YOU'RE NOT FROM A BIG CITY or haven't visited one in a while, you may be shocked by the number of homeless in Washington. Many street corners and even medians are filled with people—women and men, many claiming to be veterans (and who's to disagree?)—asking for money. All along the Mall, near the national monuments, on downtown sidewalks, and in parks and gardens, you will see people sleeping in blankets and sleeping bags, their possessions piled up next to them. On crowded Georgetown streets lined with restaurants and shops, homeless women with small children beg for money. Drivers are approached at stoplights by people carrying cardboard signs reading "Homeless—Will Work for Food." Many Metro exits are populated by people begging for money.

Most are lifelong D.C. residents who are poor, according to home- less advocacy groups. A disproportionate number are minorities and people with disabilities, mental or physical. And despite any stereo- types, studies show that the homeless have lower conviction rates for violent crimes than the population at large.

Giving the homeless money is a choice, but civility should not be. Whatever you decide, you should be polite; even if the answer is no, look the person in the eye and say calmly that you can't help right now. We believe that most of these people are what they claim to be: home- less. (If you watch closely, you'll see that begging is a very embarrassing and difficult thing to do.) We tend to carry a few dollar bills in outside pockets so that it's not necessary to open a purse or wallet to donate.

Be honest: The cost of giving those homeless who approach you a dollar really does not add up to all that much in the great scheme of things—how much was that double latte you had at Starbucks?—and it is much better for the psyche to respond to their plight than to deny or ignore their presence. A little kindness regarding the homeless goes a long way in both directions. We are not suggesting a lengthy conver- sation or prolonged involvement, just something simple like, "Sure, I can help a little bit. Take care."

And a smile is always well spent. From Eve's point of view, the "God bless you" of a person in such dire straits is worth a thousand times more than some clichéd "have a good one"—whatever one that is.

There is a notion, perhaps valid in some instances, that money given to a homeless person generally goes toward the purchase of alcohol or drugs. If this bothers you excessively, carry granola bars for distribution or buy some inexpensive gift coupons that can be redeemed at a McDonald's or other fast-food restaurant for coffee or a sandwich. Frankly, we think whatever gets you through the night. . . .

Just don't play psychologist. All the people you encounter on the street are strangers. They may be harmless, which is highly likely, or they might possibly be dangerous. Just be aware.

HOW *to* AVOID CRIME *and* KEEP SAFE *in* PUBLIC PLACES

CRIME IN WASHINGTON

TWENTY YEARS AGO, THE COMBINATION of a widespread crack epidemic and the availability of high-powered weaponry put Washington on the map for a dubious distinction: "Murder Capital of the United States"—a phrase a lot of people seem to think is Washington's official slogan. Since then, however, many of the neighborhoods that were associated with the worst of the violence have been re-developed and gentrified; and networks of surveillance cameras have been mounted in high-crime areas. Strict gun-control laws helped curtail violent crime, although recent court rulings have eased handgun regulations while maintaining the assault weapons ban. (This is locally a hot-button issue: the National Rifle Association and its primarily Republican beneficiaries in Congress have seen fit to threaten to overturn even that restriction should District residents have the gall to continue to insist they vote for themselves.)

Between 1995 and 2008, violent crime and property crime rates in D.C. each dropped nearly by half, although tourists should remember that trendier nightlife neighborhoods tend, by definition, to be a little edgy. In fact, Washington now ranks 16th among major U.S. cities, behind such other tourist magnets as St. Louis, New Orleans, Cleveland, Baltimore, and Memphis, and only one step above Orlando. Close to 17 million visitors come to the nation's capital each year, making it one of the most visited destinations in the United States, and very few have a problem during their visit.

In fact, local law enforcement officials call Washington very safe for tourists. Washington's various police departments take the patrolling of the main visitors attractions extremely seriously, not only because of the city's high public profile (and all that implies) but frankly because of the importance of tourism to the area economy. And there are so many of these law enforcement layers, public and private, that the District might well be the most closely patrolled 68 square miles in the United States.

In addition to the Metropolitan Police Department, there are the U.S. Park Police, which patrols all the monuments and parks, including the Mall; the U.S. Capitol Police, which has jurisdiction over not only the Capitol itself but the 20-square-block area around it; the Secret Service, which patrols the area around the White House, including the Treasury Building, as well as the Vice-President's residence and foreign embassies and diplomats; the Marshals Service, which ensures the safe conduct of the federal judiciary, jurors, and any judicial proceedings; and the D.C. Protective Services, which guards all city buildings and agencies. The Metro transit system has its own police force, patrolling public transportation. Many federal agencies—the FBI, the ICE, the TSA, and the now-famous NCIS, among others—have their own armed officers. On top of that, many museums hire their own police and security guards—the Smithsonian has its own federally trained police force patrolling inside the buildings and around the grounds—as do most embassies, corporations, and international associations. (Which is why you should get in the habit of traveling security gate–friendly.)

Aside from all the officers on the ground (and horseback, bicycles, motorcycles, Segways, etc.), a network of security cameras has been added around the Mall by the Park Police, and the Metropolitan Police has installed a similar network in high-traffic areas such as Georgetown, Union Station, and around the White House. And none of that even takes into account the ever-upgraded high-tech security measures that have become standard since 9/11.

However, there are still sections of Washington, mostly low-income residential areas removed from the city center and business/tourist districts, that outsiders should avoid. These include sections of Northeast and Southeast Washington, the outer sections of Anacostia, and some areas of Prince George's County. (This is, as is all crime advice, general.) But since most tourists tend to spend their time downtown and around the Mall, Georgetown, upper Northwest, Dupont Circle, Adams Morgan, and the more affluent Maryland and Virginia suburbs, these concerns shouldn't come into play.

Not that any area is entirely safe under every circumstance. Both Georgeown and Capitol Hill have had brushes with violence. But as one former Metropolitan police officer (now a private security consultant) put it, "Too many powerful congressmen live in Capitol Hill for it not to be well patrolled." And too many wealthy people in Georgetown.

Over the last decade a new force of uniformed city employees, armed only with clipboards, walkie talkies, and perhaps litter sticks, has been making Washington both safer and cleaner: downtown SAM (Safety and Maintenance) Teams, easily recognized by their bright red attire. By cleaning streets and sidewalks, removing graffiti, and assisting visitors, SAM Teams are creating a safer environment downtown. Visitors are encouraged to stop a SAM Team member and ask for directions, get a restaurant recommendation, or obtain directions to a landmark.

BEING PREPARED

AS WE SAID, REGARDLESS OF THE NUMBER OF SECURITY OFFICERS, random violence and street crime are facts of life in any large city— or subway system. You just need to be reasonably cautious and consider preventive measures that will keep you out of harm's way, as well as an escape plan just in case. Don't make yourself attractive as a target—or, put another way, make potential assailants see you as a bad risk. Good general strategies include:

- Don't play solitaire. You're always less appealing as a target if you're with other people. Don't let shyness deter you: If you're in an area you don't know well, and feel at all unsure, ask a nearby couple if you can walk with them. If you explain that you're a stranger, it's unlikely that they'll turn you down.

  If you must be out alone, act alert, be alert, and always have at least one of your arms and hands free. Thieves gravitate toward preoccupied people—those plodding along, staring at the sidewalk, with both arms encumbered by briefcases or packages. Visible jewelry (on either men or women) attracts the wrong kind of attention, as do expensive cameras slung on straps. Men, keep your billfolds in your front trouser or coat pocket, from which it's harder for someone else to extract. Women, keep your purses tucked securely under your arm; if you're wearing a coat, put it on over your shoulder bag strap. Both men and women can assemble a fake wallet, with about $20 in cash and some expired credit cards—actually, the fake ones you get in the mail that read "your name here" are really good for this—while keeping the real money hidden in a pocket or money belt. But many thieves are getting wise to that particular maneuver; if you are confronted, it's best not to argue.

- Know where you're going in advance, and if you get lost, be careful about whom you ask for directions. This isn't much of a problem during the day, when almost everyone you see is either a local or another tourist, who may have a map; but after dinner, and especially after showtime, it's important. When in doubt, ask a shopkeeper, theater manager, bartender—what *aren't* bartenders good for?—Metro station attendant, or one of those various patrol officers.

- Don't count your money in public, and carry as little cash as possible, leaving the bulk of it in your hotel safe, etc. If you need to use an ATM, either choose one that is inside a bank lobby or station a friend or family member behind you to make sure nobody reads your PIN. And stay away from any ATM that looks temporary (at a festival) or exposed or in any way odd; sophisticated scammers have figured out how to put false fronts and magnetic strip readers on less closely guarded machines.

- Guard your personal information. If you are an international visitor and need to use your passport for identification or cash-exchange purposes, you should make a photocopy and keep the original in the hotel safe or at least your room safe. If you bring your laptop or notebook computer—and this is equally applicable to smart phones or the like— be absolutely sure you don't have any bank account or charge-card password information on it. And as an extra precaution, double-check that you haven't checked "remember me" after entering your computer user name and password, either.

  If you are making any transaction requiring you to tell the last four numbers of your Social Security number, try to dial it in rather than speak it out loud. And please don't spend a lot of time Twittering or posting Facebook entries about your vacation or where you are at a particular time; not only are you advertising that you are not at home (or in your hotel room), you are likely providing a criminal information that might allow him to pretend he knows you, and gain more information.

- Don't let yourself be surprised, or you cede the advantage. Police will tell you that a felon has the least amount of control over his intended victim during the few moments of his initial approach. A good strategy, therefore, is to short-circuit the crime scenario as quickly as possible. If a felon starts by demanding your money, either take out your billfold (preferably the fake one) or a $20 dollar bill and hurl it in one direction while you run shouting for help in the opposite direction. The odds are greatly in your favor that the felon will prefer to collect your money rather than pursue you. If you hand over your purse or wallet and just stand there, the felon will likely ask for your watch and jewelry next. If you're a woman, the longer you hang around, the greater your vulnerability to personal injury or rape.

- Stay put. Under no circumstance should you allow yourself to be taken to another location—a "secondary crime scene" in police jargon—without a battle. This move, police warn, provides the felon more privacy and consequently more control. A felon can rob you on the street very quickly and efficiently. If he tries to remove you to another location, whether by car or on foot, it is a certain indication that he has more in mind than robbery. Even if the felon has a gun or knife, your chances are infinitely better running away. If the felon grabs your purse, let him have it. If he grabs your coat, come out of the coat. Hanging onto your money or coat is not worth getting mugged, raped, or murdered. However, in a worst-case scenario, you may have to submit in hopes of finding a way of escaping en route; keep your cool as much as possible.

  The corollary to this is, never believe anything a felon tells you, especially, "I won't hurt you if you come with me." No matter how logical or benign he sounds, assume the worst. Always, always break off contact as quickly as possible and run.

- Cocoon. Public transportation usually means you have company. When riding a bus, always take a seat as close to the driver as you can. Likewise, on the subway, sit near the driver's compartment, which on the Washington Metro is up front. Drivers have phones and can summon help in the event of trouble.

  Similarly, a cab driver is good company—if *his* company is. Meaning, make sure it is a licensed taxi. While there aren't as many gypsy or illicit taxi drivers as there are in New York, and it's fairly easy to hail a cab on the street in Washington any time of day, late at night it's best to hail one along the busier commercial routes or approaching the doorman of a hotel with a dollar or so and asking him to summon one for you. Otherwise, call a reliable cab company and stay inside while they dispatch a cab to your door. When your cab arrives, check the driver's certificate, which must, by law, be posted on the dashboard. Address the cabbie by his last name (Mr. Jones or whatever) or mention the number of his cab. This alerts the driver to the fact that you are going to remember him and/or his cab. Not only will this contribute to your safety, it will also keep your cabbie from trying to run up the fare. Absolutely never skip the official taxi queue, or accept an offer for a cab or limo made by a stranger in the terminal or baggage claim. At best, you will be significantly overcharged for the ride. At worst (though it's unlikely), you may be abducted.

- Image is not everything. *Play it safe.* Never assume or pretend you know everything about your surroundings. You can be the victim of a crime, and it can happen to you anywhere. Women leaving a restaurant or club alone should never be reluctant to ask to be escorted to their car, and men, particularly gay men, shouldn't either; the new bump in D.C. personal crime recently has been hate crime. Never let pride or indignation imperil your survival. It makes no difference whether you are approached by an aggressive drunk, a mentally ill street person, or an actual felon, the rule is the same: Break off contact as quickly as possible. Who cares whether the drunk insulted you if everyone ends up back at the hotel safe and sound? If you or one of your party winds up injured, it's too late to decide that the drunk's filthy remark wasn't really all that important.

  The other thing to remember is that this is not a level playing field, from either side. Druggies, some street people, the mentally unbalanced, and even some "simple" drunks can go off in a way you never have bargained for. And from their point of view, you may seem unduly affluent, cheery, indulgent, etc., fueling their resentment. (Another good reason not to wear your best jewelry.)

- Arm yourself—and we don't mean with a gun. Regardless of shifting laws, concealed weapons are still illegal in D.C., though legal in Virginia and Maryland, and most police officers say you're more likely to have your gun turned on you than be able to defend yourself successfully.

  The best self-defense device for the average person, aside from some basic physical training and mental clarity, is Mace spray, which is legal in most states, nonlethal, and easy to use. (However, it must be registered with the D.C. Police Department.) When you shop for Mace, look for two things: it should be able to fire about eight feet, and it should have a protector cap so it won't go off by mistake in your purse or pocket. Carefully read the directions that come with your device, paying particular attention to how it should be carried and stored, and how long the active ingredients will remain potent. Wearing a rubber glove, test-fire your Mace, making sure that you fire downwind.

When you are out about town, make sure your Mace is someplace easily accessible, say, attached to your keychain. (A loud whistle or alarm is another good keychain "charm.") And don't drop it deep into a purse or briefcase; hook it to a strap or make sure you have it in hand before you go out.

- Although carjacking episodes are now rare, they do occur—yet another reason not to drive in the city. Be aware of those around you, leave enough space between the car in front of you and yours in case you need make a U-turn, and stash your purse of briefcase under your knees or in the trunk, not on the seat beside you.

- Scam I am. Every tourist city has its particular scams, and Washington is no exception. One involves charging for a map or brochure about the Smithsonian, an especially popular dodge around the top of the Smithsonian Metro. Don't fall for it; the brochures are free in Smithsonian museums. And then there are always those asking for money for train fare or the like: Use your common sense. If they look like they need money, make your own choice. Otherwise, point them toward the information desk or a police officer and move on.

- Always have an exit strategy. Be aware of all the public and federal facilities around you. If, despite your precautions, you are attacked, head for any federal office building for help. The entrances are all patrolled by armed guards who can offer assistance—and even though many (such as embassy guards) are forbidden to leave their posts in case the "emergency" is a ruse, their presence is enough to ward off the perpetrator.

PART FIVE

SIGHTSEEING TIPS, TOURS, *and* ATTRACTIONS

SO MUCH *to* SEE, SO LITTLE TIME

WE'VE ALREADY DISCUSSED THE "WHEN" and the "how" of visiting Washington, and the "how much" insofar as it affects your travel and lodging arrangements. But there is another big "how much" you ought to consider, and that's the staggering number of "whats" you have to choose from—preferably in advance, but at least on the trip and at the very latest as you're unpacking and settling in.

Regardless of how it looks on screen, Washington is a big, sprawling metropolis with attractions in all directions. The long promenade of the National Mall between the Capitol and the Lincoln Memorial alone is two miles long, with a baker's dozen museums and nearly as many monuments and statues. And as even the briefest skimming of a list of attractions will show you, that's just the bare beginning. If you don't have some idea of which and how many attractions you want to visit–*and* how much time and energy it will require—you can find your trip going sour in a hurry.

Even if you have a whole a week to spend (and only about a third of visitors do), you will still have to calculate how many sights you can visit, and how best to arrange your itinerary. If your visit is shorter, say only two or three days, which is the average stay, it makes even more sense to outline your visit as soon as possible, as you won't have as much time to relax once you arrive. (We know that you know this in theory, but like over-packing, putting off the detail work is a universal tendency.)

Let's face it: Most visitors to Washington, especially first- and even second-timers, have a pretty good idea of the places they want to visit. You might call them the Three Must-seers: the Mall, the monuments, and Mount Vernon. Sounds fun—but it's a much more strenuous itinerary than it sounds. And that's not even counting the fourth M: the many, many museums *not* on the Mall, such as the Newseum, the International Spy Museum, the private collections, and the historic homes, which are increasing in popularity. (Or the fifth: the military parades and concerts. . . .)

So the first thing to do is decide whether you want to go general or specific—that is, see the famous sights or the ones of personal interest. The second choice is whether you want to take a guided tour or a self-directed one. But you don't have to give up your first choice for your second choice.

For example: If you want to take a fairly broad tour, or just get the lay of the land, you can easily sign up for a go-round that will give you a glimpse of the most famous sights—but you can do that in almost any sort of vehicle you like. In fact, even Paul Revere would have a hard time signaling for a Washington monuments tour these days, whether by land or by sea (at least by the Potomac River). You can tour by day or by night, get around via bike or Segway, hop on and off a trolley, hire a horse-drawn carriage, or hoof it yourself. You can even travel on your stomach, as military historians would say, via an eating tour. (There was a time when you could sightsee by air, too, but most of official Washington is under restricted airspace these days.)

Or you could choose something more specialized that emphasizes American history, ethnic roots, architecture, etc. Then you need to decide whether you need just a fairly routine tour guide or someone with particular expertise; or whether you're happier doing it yourself. (And DIY tours these days, what with the abundance of information online and even downloadable, are easier than ever.) In fact, many of the city's most interesting places are not tall, pale, and handsome, although the Washington Monument might not like to hear that.

If you are interested in a specific area (or era), you might want to arrange a day trip outside the city. You might even have a quirkier itinerary in mind: to visit the scenes of famous movies or television series (and corny though it may be, that nighttime view of the Lincoln Memorial that brought tears to Jimmy Stewart's eyes in *Mr. Smith Goes to Washington* more than 60 years ago is still pretty affecting), track notorious political scandals, retrace the "clues" in Dan Brown's Masonic-mythical *Lost Symbol,* or notch a few more minor-league baseball stadiums off your to-see list. You might be a military-history buff, a budding inventor, an ambitious gardener, or a Food Network groupie chasing the latest hot chefs.

So we seriously recommend that you try to reach some decisions about what your preferences are—and make some realistic choices about time and stamina—before you leave for Washington. Are you curious about how the government makes (or takes) your tax money? Are you looking to celebrate your ethnic roots in America? Are you a military buff? Does technology fascinate you? Do you love exploring art museums? Gardens? Historical houses? Washington offers places to explore for people with all these interests; we have assembled some categorical recommendations for special-interest tours below.

The other advantage of thinking outside the tour bus is that you are less likely to encounter repeated crowds of tourists visiting the same famous places as you are at the same time (and hearing the same canned info). As we pointed out in Part One, unless you have taken the time to write your congressperson to get access to a VIP tour, you'll be standing under the Capitol dome listening to the same routine as a hundred or so of your fellow citizens—whereas, if you head for one of the smaller, less frequented spots, you are likely to hear a much more detailed presentation, *and* find yourself touring with people who share your interests. You might be able to swap information on other places worth seeing; you might even make friends. And after all, making new friends is one of the most enjoyable fringe benefits of traveling.

Also, by following your own interests instead of just the "must-sees," you can make some intriguing discoveries as you visit Washington:

- A collection of miniature Revolutionary soldiers fighting a mock battle (Anderson House);
- A four-sided colonial-era mousetrap that guillotines rodents (Daughters of the American Revolution building);
- A tropical rain forest–type garden located just off the Mall (Organization of American States building);
- Fabergé eggs encrusted with diamonds (Hillwood Museum and Gardens)
- The tomb of the only president, Woodrow Wilson, actually buried in the District (Washington National Cathedral);
- A garden filled with flowers mentioned in the plays of William Shakespeare (the Folger Shakespeare Library);
- A 350-year-old miniature white pine tree (National Arboretum);
- Dorothy's ruby slippers from *The Wizard of Oz* (National Museum of American History)
- Abraham Lincoln's top hat with a bullet hole through it (President Lincoln's Cottage)
- A pub that shows how typical colonial-era Americans lived (Gadsby's Tavern).

As you travel around Washington, you'll discover sights like these and many others that most visitors miss. To help you on your way, we've selected major categories and listed the best destinations for visitors to explore. As you read the list, keep in mind that many attractions overlap. For example, the National Air and Space Museum might appeal to technology and military buffs as well as stargazers, while the Woodrow Wilson House is of interest to history fans, lovers of the decorative arts, and folks curious about how the high and mighty conducted their day-to-day lives in the 1920s.

Most of the attractions mentioned here are profiled in detail later in this chapter, particularly the ones most visitors have on the must-see list and that are more easily accessible (see also the list of sights grouped specifically by Metro station.) But we have also listed some museums and collections that you will likely only get to if you have special interests or are making a return visit. We just thought you might want to have an idea of the variety of options.

NOT SO FAST . . .

JUST BECAUSE SOMETHING IS FREE doesn't mean it's easy. In the post-9/11 era, there are a lot of places we, the people are not welcome to walk in, at least not without a reservation. Tickets to the White House tours, as we mentioned in Part One, must be obtained through a member of Congress, at least 30 days in advance. However, you should really try six months in advance, as the tours are limited. And they're first-come, first-served, *and* are offered only until lunchtime Tuesday through Saturday, so you have to be organized. You can, however, tour the White House Visitor Center at 15th and E Streets NW without a reservation, and it's open daily from 7:30 a.m. to 4 p.m. except Thanksgiving, Christmas, and New Year's Day.

You also have to have Congressional support to take the tour of the Treasury Building—which is not the same as the Bureau of Engraving—but it's definitely worth it: see the description in "The Best Inside Tours in Town."

Unless you're a member of the military, you will also need a reservation to tour the Pentagon, with at least two weeks' advance notice, and again, your member of Congress can be helpful; but you can make your own arrangements online at **pentagon.afis.osd.mil/tour**. Be sure to fill out all security information.

The U.S. Capitol is a little easier to tour; again, advance passes are available through your Congressperson, or you can book them at **www.visitthecapitol .gov;** but a few same-day passes are issued at the tour kiosks at the east and west fronts of the Capitol and at the information desk on the lower level of the visitor centers.

The J. Edgar Hoover FBI building remains closed to tours, however, and there's no indication of any relaxing of the guard.

*un*official **TIP**
It's important to check the websites of the major government sites before you arrive, as the list of forbidden items grows all the time; you can't take cameras, water bottles, a backpack, or even a comb into the White House or Capitol, so travel light.

OPERATING HOURS

BY AND LARGE, WASHINGTON'S MAJOR attractions keep liberal operating hours, making it easy for visitors to plan their itineraries without worrying about odd opening and closing times. Most Smithsonian museums—those on the Mall—are open every day except Christmas, and most hold the hours of 10 a.m. to 5:30 p.m. (During the summer, hours at certain museums may be extended into the evening if operating budgets allow.) There are, however, a few exceptions. One pair of Smithsonian museums, the National Portrait Gallery and the American Art Museum, which are a sort of Siamese twin museum in the Penn Quarter, are open 11:30 a.m.–7 p.m. every day except Christmas. The National Zoo is open until 6 p.m. from April to October (it closes at 4:30 p.m. the rest of the year). The National Archives, which is not part of the Smithsonian, despite its proximity, is open until 7 p.m. on Sundays mid-March to Labor Day (it closes at 5:30 p.m. the rest of the year); and the National Gallery of Art, also not part of the Smithsonian, is open until 6 p.m. on Sundays.

Here's another thing to consider: While the exhibits close at the Smithsonian's Natural History and Air and Space museum (both locations) at 5:30 p.m., these three have IMAX theaters with later screenings; check those schedules so you don't waste daylight hours on what you can see later. The Air and Space museum on the Mall also has a planetarium with extended hours.

The private museums, such as the Corcoran Gallery of Art and the Phillips Collection, are generally open 10 a.m.–5 p.m. plus one late night a week, but are more likely to be closed Sundays and Mondays. What might be called the for-profit museums, such as the International Spy Museum, are likely to stay open a little later. We have listed the hours of the attractions profiled in this chapter as they were known at press time, but it's always best to call or check the website for details.

Of all the major tourist attractions, the Bureau of Engraving and Printing keeps the most European hours: It allows visitors to view its money-printing operation Monday through Friday from 9 to 10:45 a.m., from 12:30 to 2 p.m., and again from 2 to 3:45 p.m. and 5 to 7 p.m. in the summer (a free time-ticket system is in effect in the spring and summer but you have to get in line early). And while the most lavishly decorated of the three Library of Congress buildings, the Jefferson, closes at 4:30 p.m., the Madison building stays open until 9:30 p.m. weekdays, and the Adams is open that late Monday, Wednesday, and Thursday. All LOC buildings are closed on Sunday.

Most monuments, on the other hand, are open 24 hours a day. We strongly recommend you visit the Lincoln and Jefferson memorials after dark. Lit up by floodlights, the marble edifices appear to float in the darkness, and the Reflecting Pool and Tidal Basin dramatically reflect the light. It's much more impressive than by day—and a lot less crowded, and Park Rangers are on duty as late as midnight to answer questions. (The Korean War Veterans Memorial, which is near the Lincoln memorial, was partly designed to be seen at night.) However, this isn't as much of an insider's secret as it used to be; as you will see below, many of the organized tour companies, of all types of vehicles, offer sunset or even moonlight tours.

Of course, while the outdoor sites are visible all the time, many indoor attractions are closed on federal holidays: New Year's Day,

Martin Luther King Jr. Day (the third Monday in January), Presidents' Day, Memorial Day, Independence Day, Labor Day (the first Monday in September), Columbus Day (the second Monday in October), Veterans Day, Thanksgiving, and Christmas Day, when virtually everything except outdoor monuments and Mount Vernon is closed. Again, check the profiles or websites.

If you do want to get an early start, we have a few specific tricks.

GOING WITH, OR RATHER AGAINST, THE FLOW

AS WE MENTIONED IN PART ONE, the ebb and flow of crowds follows *something* of a pattern throughout the day and the week (and the season) at major tourist attractions. Some of this is anecdotal, and certainly not ironclad; but by being aware of the general tendencies, you can sometimes avoid the worst of the crowds.

Mornings start slow, and the quietest time to visit most museums and sights is when they open. As lunchtime approaches, the number of people visiting a popular attraction begins to pick up, peaking around 3 p.m. Then the crowds begin to thin, and after 4 p.m. things start to get quiet again. So the best times to visit a wildly popular place like the National Air and Space Museum is just after it opens and/or (if you missed the IMAX, for example, or had an afternoon jet arrival) just before it closes.

Conversely, midday, when there are hordes of visitors at the Museum of Natural History, you can find a cool retreat at the Sackler Gallery and the National Museum of African Art, which are connected underground. Or, depending on the demographics of your group, you could circumvent the conventional wisdom—have an early breakfast, hit two museums, then break for lunch and a nap—by sticking it out a little longer, having a later lunch, and getting back into the swing as the family groups are winding down.

Among days of the week, Monday, Tuesday, and Wednesday see the lowest number of visitors. If you plan to visit the Washington Monument, the Bureau of Engraving and Printing, the National Air and Space Museum, the National Museum of American History, or the National Museum of Natural History, try to do so early in the week. Attempt to structure your week so that Thursday, Friday, and the weekend are spent visiting sights that are away from the Mall.

unofficial **TIP**
Although nearly every major attraction in Washington closes for the major holidays, there's one important exception: Mount Vernon, which is open every day of the year.

Also, since it's no longer much of a secret that some of the popular "commercial" attractions, such as the International Spy Museum and the Museum of Crime and Punishment, are open later than the Mall museums, more and more families plan to end their afternoons there; you might do better to go at lunchtime. Even better, consider buying your tickets in advance online; in many cases, prepaid tickets will save you a few dollars, and you can guarantee your admission time as well.

The one pay-per-view museum, so to speak, that lets you view it more than once is the Newseum, which offers two days' admission in one; so another strategy might be to visit in the afternoon and then at closing (5 p.m.) head to the Spy or Crime and Punishment museums, which are just a few blocks away. That way, you don't feel rushed, because if you don't get to see it all, you can go back the next day.

EARLY BIRD SPECIALS

AGAIN, WE RECOMMEND GETTING A HOTEL ROOM close to a Metro station, especially in spring and summer. If you're driving, get there early—and we mean really early, because most lots fill up by 7 a.m.—and head to your first destination. If you're going to the Mall, there's a coffee kiosk in the Castle that opens at 8:30 a.m. You can easily be at door of any of the mall museums before 10 a.m. (Take your coffee to the Hirshhorn Sculpture Garden; it opens at 7:30.)

The café at the Holocaust Museum at the other end of the Mall also opens at 8:30, so if you're going to the big monuments, the nearby Bureau of Engraving and Printing, or planning to get in line for tickets to the Washington Monument, you might want to start there. If you're really an early bird, remember all those outdoor monuments at the west end of the Mall and get a real head start on the day.

If you're doing the Penn Quarter museums, you'll have plenty of breakfast carryouts and coffee shops to choose from; but if you're with a group and want to get into the mood, the Spy City Café at the International Spy Museum opens at 8 a.m. during the week and 9 a.m. Saturdays and Sundays.

If you're planning to duck the usual noontime crush, you can certainly make reservations at a downtown restaurant (if you're starting at one of the Penn Quarter attractions, it wouldn't be a bad idea); but many of the museums have attractive dining options; see "The Best Museum Restaurants" in Part Six: Dining and Restaurants. Indeed, while it isn't a museum eatery in the usual sense, the Source at the Newseum is one of Washington's highest rated restaurants, period.

HAPPY HOURS
(The Sightseeing Kind)

WE POINTED OUT THAT SOME OF THE MUSEUMS have extended hours or theaters. The Museum of Natural History stays open until 7:30 p.m. in summer. There are also a couple with outdoor gardens and/or ice rinks (depending on the season) whose cafés also stay open.

The National Gallery of Art's sculpture garden stays open late from about Memorial Day through Labor Day and hosts jazz on Fridays from 5 to 8:30 p.m.; during the coldest months, when it becomes a rink, it's open even later (**www.nga.gov**). In both cases, the Pavilion Café stays open late as well.

The tower at the Old Post Office Pavilion, which offers as fine a view as the Washington Monument, is open until 8 p.m. weekdays during the summer, and the food court will still be cooking when you come down.

The Bureau of Engraving and Printing is open until 7 p.m. from May through August, but you'll have to have the timed tickets, released at 8 a.m.; its visitor center is open until 7:30 p.m. in summer.

Also, there is plenty of free entertainment around town: see Part Eight: Entertainment and Nightlife for more information.

SIGN UP *for a* GROUP TOUR *or* FLY SOLO?

FIRST-TIME VISITORS TO WASHINGTON CAN'T HELP BUT NOTICE the regular procession of open-air, multicar tour buses—"motorized trolleys" is probably a more accurate term—that prowl the streets along the Mall, the major monuments, Arlington Cemetery, downtown, Georgetown, and Upper Northwest Washington. These regularly scheduled shuttle buses drop off and pick up paying customers along a route that includes the town's most popular attractions. Between stops, passengers listen to a tour guide point out the city's monuments, museums, and famous buildings.

We recommend the big charter companies mostly for those who like to get the big picture layout in their heads first and then focus in on the specifics; for those with children; for visitors with a somewhat short time frame; and for those who have mobility or breathing problems such as allergies or asthma. (Remember to check with your hotel staff or the Weather Channel about air quality; Washington is prone to pollution and irritant buildup, especially in the summer, and health officials will issue alerts on those days.)

Chartered tours are also handy if you don't like to read and ride at the same time, since the conductor or driver passes along the primary facts about each building or memorial and tosses in a few jokes and perhaps some intriguing trivia. Not as much as your friendly neighborhood *Unofficial Guide,* of course, but some. On the other hand, some narrations are just recordings, so you may have to scribble down any questions you have for future research.

If you're already pretty familiar with the major monuments, you should look into the special-interest tours, whether guided or do-it-yourself. We have listed a good sampling of the variety available in both camps in "Far(ther) From the Madding Crowd," page 147. If you'd like a customized tour, there are specialists aplenty. If you're the self-directed type, several good online resources, including those mentioned in Part One, can help you customize your own route. What's more, many of the national monuments have park rangers on site who know everything—and who talk for free. Government buildings, religious sites, and historic houses are likely to offer docent-led tours and/or detailed recorded versions.

Certain types of tours are more common at particular seasons: ghost tours around Halloween, candlelight tours from Thanksgiving to New Year's, garden tours in early summer, and the like; check newspapers or local websites. And, obviously, some types of tours—kayaks, Segways, open-air vessels—are likely to be warmer-weather options. Reserve well ahead if you plan to try one of those.

And finally, although some are probably on your to-do list, we have selected some of our favorite attraction tours in the area, and we'll explain why. Just in case you're waffling on one. . . .

TAKING *an* ORIENTATION TOUR

LET'S FACE IT: TOURS ARE BIG BUSINESS THESE DAYS. In fact they're one of the industries in Washington that seem to flourish even in tough times. And with increasing competition come not only the professionals but also the PR experts hoping to lure you on board with hooks, shticks, novelties, etc. The only tour we haven't seen advertised yet is an all-musical one—that, and maybe a mime version. (Hmmm; a pantomime recreation of some of Washington's most famous scandals . . . you read it here first.) From our point of view, a tour that includes a stop at a bagel shop on Capitol Hill isn't quite the same as a deli tour of the Lower East Side in New York. Having said that, there is no completely wrong way to see Washington, except the ways you don't enjoy.

What follows is not a compendium, it's just a broad sampling; so if you pass a van with a logo painted on the side and you're inspired to jump in, just make sure there's some form of license attached, either to the person or the vehicle.

GET ON THE BUS, GUS

IF YOU CHOOSE ONE OF THE BIG DRIVE-AROUND TOURS, you can either stick to the bus for the whole circuit or hop on and off at more than a dozen hot spots. These on–off tours circulate every 20 to 30 minutes, so you can pretty much set your own rhythm. On the other hand, even tour operators suggest not trying to see more than a half-dozen sites in a day, so you might want to make a list of the ones you really care about. Also note that although most of the bus drivers

Washington Old Town Trolley

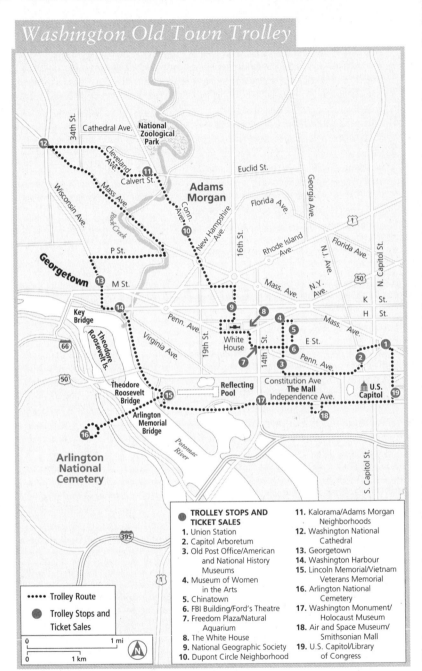

TROLLEY STOPS AND TICKET SALES

1. Union Station
2. Capitol Arboretum
3. Old Post Office/American and National History Museums
4. Museum of Women in the Arts
5. Chinatown
6. FBI Building/Ford's Theatre
7. Freedom Plaza/Natural Aquarium
8. The White House
9. National Geographic Society
10. Dupont Circle Neighborhood
11. Kalorama/Adams Morgan Neighborhoods
12. Washington National Cathedral
13. Georgetown
14. Washington Harbour
15. Lincoln Memorial/Vietnam Veterans Memorial
16. Arlington National Cemetery
17. Washington Monument/Holocaust Museum
18. Air and Space Museum/Smithsonian Mall
19. U.S. Capitol/Library of Congress

•••• Trolley Route

● Trolley Stops and Ticket Sales

0 _____ 1 mi
0 _____ 1 km

have credit card machines on board so you can start at the nearest point, you might want to have cash just in case of snafus. (Also ask whether your AAA or AARP card is good for a discount; it often is.)

Tourmobile has the franchise for operating on National Park Service territory and shuttles open-air buses around the Mall from Capitol Hill past the Tidal Basin and to Arlington National Cemetery. You can get on at any red-white-and-blue route marker along the way between 9:30 a.m. and 4:30 p.m. ($27 adults, $13 ages 3–11; ☎ 202-554-5100; **www.tourmobile.com**). Tourmobile also has a twilight circuit that leaves Union Station at 6:30 p.m. and some seasonal tours. (For specifics on the Arlington Cemetery route alone, see the profile of the cemetery on page 170.)

The **Old Town Trolley** routes include a couple of stops—Washington National Cathedral and Georgetown—that, unlike most of the other points are not near a Metro stop ($35 adults, $18 ages 4–12; 9 a.m.–5:30 p.m.; ☎ 202-832-9800; **www.oldtowntrolleytours .com**) Old Town Trolley also offers a 2 1/2-hour "Monuments by Moonlight" version that leaves Union Station at 7:30 p.m. (6:30 p.m. in fall and winter) and includes a few ghostly anecdotes. Tickets for Old Town Trolley tours are also available at many hotels. (There is a 10% discount for online purchases.)

Martz Gray Line offers some of the longest, farthest ranging tours, such as the eight-hour version that takes in Mount Vernon, Old Town Alexandria, Arlington Cemetery, and the Iwo Jima memorial; eight hours sounds like a lot, but the off-the-bus portions—the changing of the guard at Arlington Cemetery, the farm at Mount Vernon, and so on—will keep even restive kids busy (prices vary according to tour; ☎ 202-289-1995; **www.graylinedc.com**).

All About Town has bus tours that range from half- and whole-day ($36) itineraries to two-day treks ($102) that cover just about all the major sites and offers pickup from many downtown hotels; it also offers after-dark monument tours (☎ 301-856-5556; **www.allabouttown.net**).

The **Circulator** bus is not a tour shuttle per se, and you won't hear any stories, but the tour routes will carry you to more than a dozen attractions along the Mall as well as to Penn Quarter (Verizon Center, National Portrait Gallery–Smithsonian American Art Museum [route suspended until April 2011], International Spy Museum), the Convention Center, and the Waterfront, so it may serve you just as well. Fares are 50¢ to $1, and you can get off and back on within three hours at no charge if you pay with a SmarTrip card (or, get a day pass for $3). See more information on the Circulator in Part Four: Getting In and Getting Around Washington.

GET YOUR FEET WET

WATER TOURS GO IN BASICALLY TWO DIRECTIONS: up and down the Potomac with pretty but passing views of the Capitol, the Washington Monument, the Kennedy Center, Georgetown, the Southwest

Waterfront, and Old Town Alexandria. The newest is actually a water taxi between Old Town Alexandria and the new National Harbor complex in Prince George's County; even if you aren't staying at one of the hotels there, the $8 adult/$5 child (one way), 20-minute ride might be fun—the views back toward Washington are impressive— and plans are underway to add a terminal from National Airport. Water taxis run between Georgetown and the Gaylord Resort or indirect service with Old Town Alexandria in between. They also run to Mount Vernon as well. For information call ☎ 703-684-0580 or visit **www.potomacriverboatco.com.**

That same **Potomac Riverboat Company** has a varied and intriguing fleet, including a couple of double-deckers, an authentic split sternwheeler, and a 1906 skipjack that takes 90-minute cruises from National Harbor. PRC also offers a "Washington by Water" cruise from Old Town or Georgetown up to the Capitol and back down toward Alexandria (round-trip $26 adults, $14 ages 2–11); and for those who can't leave the pooch at home, there are weekly canine cruises in warm weather.

From April through October, **Capitol River Cruises** leave on the hour from Washington Harbour for a 45-minute narrated cruise past the Kennedy Center, the Capitol building, the LBJ and Maritime memorials, the Custis-Lee Mansion, and other points of interest ($14 adults, $7 ages 3–12; ☎ 800 405-5511; **www.capitolrivercruises.com**). **National River Tour Co.** (☎ 202-369-7077) runs a quick, pleasant 45-minute pontoon tour from Washington Harbour to the Pentagon every hour from 11:45 a.m. to 6:45 p.m. seven days a week, April through October; tours may run later on weekends. Tours carry a maximum of 42 passengers and include live narration ($12 adults, $6 11 and under).

If you can stand the "wise quacks," or if your party includes kids, take the **DC Ducks** tour aboard renovated WWII amphibious vehicles ($35 adults, $33 ages 4–12; ☎ 800-213-2474 or 202-832-9800; **www .dcducks.com**). Ducks leave Union Station every hour between 10 a.m. and 4 p.m., roll through the Mall, then plop into the Potomac River near Georgetown and cruise down to Gravely Point, under the National Airport flight path. These are 90-minute, seasonal tours, running only from mid-March to the end of October, and only if the weather permits. You can buy advance tickets online at **www.trustedtours.com**.

If you love the water, try the **American Spirit** schooner tour. This two-and-a-half-hour cruise aboard a 65-footer goes along the Anacostia and Potomac rivers and past Fort McNair and Bolling Air Force Base, the Alexandria waterfront, and so on. Tours leave at 5:30 p.m. from the SW Waterfront at the Gangplank Marina every other Friday night from the end of April through mid-September. Reservations are required ($50; ☎ 202-547-1250; **www.nmhf.org**).

They're a little more limited in focus and season (late March until the end of October), but the **National Park Service**'s hour-long barge trips, drawn 19th-century–style by mules through the locks of the C&O Canal at Georgetown and Great Falls, Virginia, are wonderful family excursions. Park Service rangers in costume explain the workings of the lock system and the history of the canal. In Georgetown, board at the landing across from the Foundry Mall at 1057 Thomas Jefferson Street NW ($5 ages 4 and up; ☎ 202-653-5190). For information about the Great Falls stop, call ☎ 301-767-3714. Visit **www.nps.gov/choh** for more information. These trips are particularly fun on summer weekends when there are sometimes free canal-side concerts.

Personally, we think drinking-dining cruises aren't the way to go, only because the sights tend to be mere window dressing (you're glassed in most of the time). But if you're touring for more than one day or you've been to Washington before, you might like them. **Odyssey** offers brunch, lunch, and dinner cruises from two to three hours long, departing from the Gangplank Marina at Sixth and Water streets SW or from National Harbor ($44–$104 adults; tickets for children ages 3–11 are half price; ☎ 866-306-2469; **www.odyssey cruises.com**). **Dandy Restaurant Cruises** berths two ships at Old Town Alexandria that cruise for brunch, lunch, or dinner and dancing (Sunday brunch $55, lunch $45–$50, dinner $66 and up, not counting drinks; ☎ 703-683-6076; **www.dandydinnerboat.com**). And **Spirit Cruises,** which also docks at Pier 4 in Southwest, offers a Saturday brunch with gospel music (from $50 adults, $23 ages 3–12; **www.spirit cruises.com/Washington-DC/home**).

FAR(THER) FROM THE MADDING CROWD

YOU CAN STILL GET A PRETTY BROAD OVERVIEW of the Washington landscape without hearing the same old story about why there's a line around the bottom section of the Washington Monument and so on. There are plenty of special-interest bus and van tours that have a fringe benefit or funnier style.

On Board DC Tours (formerly known as DC Party Shuttle Tours) has a hop-on–hop-off system with a difference: the tour guide hops off with you and continues the narration until you all hop back on. And it's unusually extensive, stopping at a dozen points and passing two dozen more. If you have the time—it's a six-hour, $80 circuit ($50 ages 3–11) with a lunch stop at the Pentagon City Mall food court—this tour will get you far better situated than the others. It also offers a three-hour "nightlights" tour starting at 7:30 p.m. for $50 adults/$40 children (**www.washingtondcpartyshuttle.com**).

Scandal Tours takes a slightly different tack. It covers much of the same geography—the Tidal Basin (remember Fanne Foxe and Wilbur Mills?), the White House (specifically, the Lincoln Bedroom, favorite haunt of Friends of Bill and of Abraham Lincoln's ghost), the U.S. Capitol (John and Rita Jenrette's not-so-private trysting spot)—but with "celebrity" guides (members of the political comedy troupe

Gross National Product). Tours by advance reservation (☎ 202-783-7212; **www.gnpcomedy.com**).

On Location Tours runs a two-and-a-half-hour tour of more than 30 locales used in *The Exorcist, The West Wing, X-Files, Forrest Gump, Wedding Crashers,* and other productions. Local actors are scheduled to do the narration (although Linda Blair's head-turning part hasn't been cast). Tours depart from near Union Station Saturdays at 10 a.m. ($38 adults, $22 children 6–10; ☎ 800-979-3370; **www.screentours.com**).

WHEELING AROUND WASHINGTON

BIKE TOURS HAVE A FEW ADVANTAGES, and getting on and off in a second is just one. And it's certainly closer than a drive-by ("Every seat is a window seat," goes the sales pitch). You get some exercise, you don't have to get your old bike in order (rental and helmets are included), and you can bring the kids—tandem trailers are available—so long as they're old enough to wear helmets and hold their heads up. On the other hand, bike tours are subject to the whims of weather (generally closed January and February in any case) and require advance bookings.

Bike and Roll offers three-hour tours of the monuments by day and night, plus a larger Capitol Hill–Mall tour, and, by prior arrangement, private tours down to Mount Vernon and other locations. Tours depart from 12th Street NW between Pennsylvania and Constitution (the Old Post Office Pavilion) at 10 a.m. and 2:30 p.m., with evening tours at 6:30 p.m. (prices start at $40 adults, $30 for kids ages 12 and under; includes hybrid bike and helmet rental; ☎ 202-842-2453; **www.bikethesites.com**).

Bike and Roll also rents wheelchairs and mobility scooters: wheelchairs, $15 for two hours, $25 for up to four hours, and $35 per day; scooters, $35 for two hours, $50 for up to four hours, and $65 per day.

Segways are great fun, but you do have to learn how to drive one first, so tours begin with training sessions and safety checks. (Segways are not suited to children under age 16 or anyone over 260 pounds.) Tours are also somewhat seasonal, obviously, as the surfaces are weather susceptible.

City Segway Tours leads three-hour tours that leave from the office at 624 9th Street NW at 10 a.m. and 2 p.m. ($70; ☎ 202-626-0017 or 877-734-8687; **www.citysegwaytours.com/washington-dc**). City Segway has also begun to branch out into more specialized tours; the newest recreates the route John Wilkes Booth took in escaping from Ford's Theatre after assassinating President Lincoln ($60).

Segs in the City, which shares a kiosk behind the Old Post Office Pavilion with Bike and Roll, offers two-hour tours at 10 a.m. and 2:30 p.m. as well as some mini-tours and specialty routes, such as a Sunday morning roll from Dupont Circle up to Washington National Cathedral (☎ 800-734-7393; **www.segsinthecity.com/segs_in_dc.htm**). **Capital Segway** runs its own tours that leave from its showroom at

14th and I streets NW at various times Monday through Sunday ($70–$80; ☎ 202-682-1980; **www.capitalsegway.com**). Capital is an authorized Segway dealership, so if you fall in love with your ride and want to buy it, your tour fee will be shifted to the bill.

WHEELS WITH REAL HORSEPOWER

WHILE THEY MAY NOT BE AS FAMOUS or ubiquitous as the carriages of Central Park, horse-drawn buggy tours are available in Washington. Six people is usually the limit, but it would be a prime possibility for romance. **Charley Horse Carriage Company** (☎ 202-488-1155) usually picks up night rides outside the Hyatt Regency Hotel on Capitol Hill starting about 7:30. Walk-up rides vary in price depending on length of ride starting at the half-hour ride for $20 adults, $10 kids under 12 with a minimum of $75; prices go up from there depending upon length of ride and the season (holiday pricing and times are different, and rides booked in advance are more expensive). Christmas rides depart from near the Hyatt, the Capitol, and the White House. Rides near the ice-skating rink at the National Gallery of Art may afford a sighting of Santa. Daytime rides are available as well.

    Carriages of the Capital ($150 per hour and up for a group of six; ☎ 202-841-4135; **www.carriagesofthecapital.com**) generally depart from the Willard Hotel at 6:30 p.m. (other hours by reservation).

HOOFING IT YOURSELF

THERE ARE PLENTY OF REGULARLY SCHEDULED walking tours you can hook up with. **Washington Walks** (☎ 202-484-1565; **www .washingtonwalks.com**), founded by Carolyn Crouch, who moved to Washington and walked it on her own, is an established organization whose most popular subjects include "Memorials by Moonlight"; the "I've Got a Secret" tour (more trivia game than Scandal Tours, it includes a onetime brothel and the severed leg of a Civil War general); various neighborhood tours; and another tour of local sites that appear in movies and television. (If you don't know yet that there is no Georgetown subway station, despite that scene in *No Way Out*, it's time you learned.) Some Washington Walks are seasonal, and a few are for younger audiences; check the website for a full list. You can also book any Washington Walks tour for times and/or days other than the regularly scheduled ones. Most tours are $15 for ages 4 and up.

    If you're on a budget, you can get a free tour—although you should at least be prepared to tip generously—from the guys at **DC by Foot** (☎ 571-431-7543; **www.dcbyfoot.com**). Guides meet you in the heart of the Federal City near the Washington Monument at 15th Street and Constitution Avenue NW at 10 a.m., 2 and 6 p.m. Tuesday–Saturday spring and summer and give you a 90-minute tour with (good) attitude.

    Once you have a feel for the area, you may want to do it alone, taking it one attraction or area at a time. One extensive online resource is **Cultural Tourism DC** (**www.culturaltourismdc.org**), which offers information on local attractions by neighborhood (Barracks Row, U Street, the Southwest Waterfront, and more); by cultural niche (religious sites, museums, and so on); by historical themes such as black history and the Civil War; and by a few specialized interests, including gardens, cemeteries, and historic houses. Some pages include route maps as well as walking itineraries. If you're packing your iPod or smartphone, you can download a tour of the monuments and the Mall from **www.slate.com/id/2132202, www.dctours.us, or www .audiosteps.com** and wander at your own pace.

GET UP CLOSE AND PERSONAL

IF YOU'RE SERIOUS ABOUT A PARTICULAR FIELD of interest or neighborhood, you may want to hire an expert. The most elaborate of customized tours are likely to be expensive, and you should be sure to ask whether transportation or admission fees and/or gratuities are included (plus, most tours last three or four hours). But rates are generally the same for a solo tour or a small group, so if you have a friend who shares your passion, it might help with the bill. Be sure your guide is licensed by the District government—it's the law.

With a personal guide, you can set your own timetable and mode of transportation, so there's more flexibility. The **Guide Service of Washington, Inc.** (☎ 202-628-2842; **www.dctourguides.com**) and the **Guild of Professional Tour Guides of Washington, D.C.** (☎ 202-298-1474; **www.washingtondctourguides.com**) can steer you to former government employees, professors, historians, and even ex-spies who will spill the beans on Washington history and gossip for about $40 an hour.

One of Washington's better-known tour guides, who calls his walks "anecdotal history tours," is History Channel narrator and historian **Anthony Pitch** (☎ 301-294-9514; **www.dcsightseeing.com**). Tour locations and themes include Georgetown, Adams Morgan, the Capitol Hill neighborhood ("Skirting the Capitol" points out some Congressional bloopers), "The Curse of Lafayette Square," Lincoln's assassination, and the burning of the capital during the War of 1812. These more elaborate tours cost about $100 an hour, so they're better for serious troupers.

Mondays at 10 a.m., just show up near the top of the (outside) Union Station Metro escalator to meet former Hill staffer Steve Livengood, whose **Capitol Historical Society Walking Tour** points out the architecture and landscaping as well as political history of the neighborhood ($10, March through November; **www.uschs.org**).

Jeanne Fogle (☎ 703-525-2948; **www.atourdeforce.com**), a writer and adjunct professor of regional history and tour guiding at Northern Virginia Community College, also takes a raconteur's approach to Washington history. Her "Tour de Force" itineraries are all customized, but she prefers to explore the social history and architectural evolution of the neighborhoods.

Carol Bessette (☎ 703-569-1875; **www.spiesofwashingtontour .com**) is a retired Air Force intelligence officer and Vietnam veteran who's a walking, talking, one-woman international spy museum. She leads group walks ($12 per person) and customized private driving tours. Carol also leads walks for tourists with dogs and for families.

Natalie Zanin Historic Strolls (☎ 301-588-9255; **www.historicstrolls .com**) takes a more dramatic approach, using for the most part professional actors who assume historical identities at key spots along the way. A character from *A Christmas Carol* leads the "Charles Dickens in Washington" tour; "Gussie the Government Gal" adjusts to life in World War II D.C.; a hoop-skirted gossip explores the Civil War sites. And one of the most intriguing tours brings out the pickpockets, con men, cardsharks, and ladies of ill repute of 19th-century Washington. All tours ($10 adults) partly benefit nonprofit groups.

Children's Concierge is more of a middleman (or -woman) that helps design itineraries for family groups but would also be a good resource for something like a reunion or multigenerational gathering (☎ 301-309-6601; **www.childrensconcierge.com**).

And finally, there are the most lighthearted of the neighborhood tours: the food walks. **DC Metro Food Tours** offers itineraries in Capitol Hill, the Eastern Market, Little Ethiopia (around H and 14th streets NW), Old Town Alexandria, Dupont Circle, U Street, and Adams Morgan. Each tour includes at least three stops, up to six "courses," and cooking demonstrations ($27 for the Eastern Market tour, but most are $50 and up; **www.dcmetrofoodtours.com**).

The BEST *Inside* TOURS *in* TOWN

IF YOU'RE MORE INCLINED TO ENJOY A FEW PLACES in depth than to try to make the Big Circuit, you can pretty much have your pick. Government agencies may have tighter restrictions in the post-9/11 era, but plenty of museums, historic homes, and religious sites offer guided tours or detailed brochures and recordings that you can use. Or you can just wander about at your leisure.

Here are some of our favorite places, most of which you can walk into on the spur of the moment. For details on hours and access, see the profiles later in this chapter.

The **Thomas Jefferson Building** of the Library of Congress is a stunning example of lavish public construction, with its mythological murals and sculptures, gilded ceilings, stained-glass skylights, mosaics, allegorical friezes, and grand staircases—and that's not even counting the Gutenberg Bible or the great dome of the main reading room made famous by that vertiginous tracking shot in *All the President's Men*. It's not just a library, it's a work of art.

The **Daughters of the American Revolution Museum** is one of Washington's underrated beauties. It has 31 period rooms, and even though you can peek in from the doors, the wealth of decorative pieces, ceramics, paintings, silver, costumes, and oddities is wonderful. It may not sound kid-friendly, but in fact there is a space upstairs where children can play with real 18th- and 19th-century toys and flags,

The **U.S. Department of State's Diplomatic Reception Rooms** are another lesser-known delight, a stunning geode of 18th- and 19th-century decorative arts—worth close to $100 million—hidden inside that boulder of an office building. You have to reserve a spot in advance, but it's worth it. Use common sense: this is the State Department, so don't pack pointed objects; also, no strollers are allowed, but this attraction isn't recommended for kids younger than 12 anyway.

The **Society of the Cincinnati** at Anderson House in Dupont Circle is a turn-of-the-20th-century fantasia of Florentine architecture, built for an American diplomat whose patriotic fervor extended to hiring muralists and decorators to install historic scenes and symbols throughout the house. The upper floors have their original furnishings and tapestries—check out the crystal chandeliers in the two-story ballroom and the Gilbert Stuart painting in the billiards parlor—while the first floor holds displays of Revolutionary War artifacts.

Anderson House cost $750,000 in 1905; the 13 acres of formal gardens alone at Hillwood Museum, the home of cereal heiress, socialite, and collector Marjorie Merriweather Post, probably cost that much. (One of Post's husbands was the equally wealthy E. F. Hutton, and another was ambassador to the Soviet Union, so they came in handy when she began collecting art and confiscated Romanov treasures.) If you love exquisite silver, ornate Imperial china, impressive portraits with crowns, and, oh yes, Fabergé eggs, this is the place. The bedrooms and closets are pretty astounding, too; even the earliest photos of Post's daughter, actress Dina Merrill, look like Hollywood studio stills. Have a glass of wine or tea and play aristocrat. Reservations are not required, but we recommend them during busier seasons.

It's not an easy tour, but the **U.S. Holocaust Memorial Museum** is one of the most powerful experiences in Washington and an astounding example of how visionary architecture can magnify that power. Just don't try to squeeze this one into a multistop itinerary—it will leave you emotionally drained. However, there are shortcuts and softened children's exhibits.

There's a lot more to **Mount Vernon** than two hours' worth, including a view over the Potomac so fine it explains why Washington was so eager to retire. In fact, there's now even more: an impressive orientation and education center has been added to the mansion, stables, greenhouses, working farm, and slave quarters. The lavish new complex offers state-of-the-art interactive displays; films; life-size recreations of Washington at three points in his life; and rooms full of china, jewelry, rare books and private letters, Revolutionary War artifacts, and family effects that were not previously on display, so unless you have to settle for one of those packaged quick-stop tours, we'd say make a day trip of it.

There are docent-led tours of **Washington National Cathedral** throughout the day, and you can certainly wander about on your own (unless some special event or ceremony is in progress, of course). But the most fun tours combine a special cathedral highlights tour with afternoon tea high in the tower, which affords a stunning view. Reservations are required (Tuesdays and Wednesdays at 1:30 p.m., $25; ☎ 202-537-8993 or **www.tea.cathedral.org**). If you're only making a three-day weekend visit, you can hear a free demonstration of the Great Organ Mondays at 12:30 p.m.

The **U.S. Department of Treasury,** alongside the White House, is a fabulous, almost palatial building that has been renovated to its pre–Civil War state—or, in the case of the Andrew Johnson Suite, post–Civil War, as he used it as his temporary offices just after the assassination of President Lincoln—but access is very limited. You'll have to enlist the help of your senator or representative (only legal residents of the United States are eligible) to get a reservation here as well; expect to show photo IDs and so on. The hour-long guided tours are free but offered only on Saturdays at 9, 9:45, 10:30, and 11:15 a.m.—and don't even think about being late. Enter on the south side of the building facing the Washington Monument (15th Street and Hamilton Place NW).

FIRST-TIMERS' TIPS *and* FAQS

EVERYONE'S A NEWBIE ONCE. Just remember that when someone rolls his eyes at your question.

WHERE'S THE SMITHSONIAN? Well, here, there, and beyond. A lot of visitors assume that the renowned museum complex is located in one building somewhere along the Mall. In reality, the Smithsonian (**www .si.edu**) is a complex of 17 museums (with the 18th, the National Museum of African American History and Culture, under construction) plus a world-class zoo, scattered around the city. (In addition, the Institution operates the Cooper-Hewitt National Design Museum and another branch of the National Museum of the American Indian, both located in New York City.) Some folks are also surprised when they learn that the National Gallery of Art and the Holocaust Memorial Museum are *not* part of the Smithsonian complex. Nor are the International Spy Museum, an incredibly successful but commercial venture, or the Newseum. The great thing—well, one of them— about the Smithsonian institutions are that they are all free to the public, although these days, when budgets are tight and so many of the facilities are in need of major renovations, a small donation is very welcome. This is one place where your tax dollars really are working

THE SMITHSONIAN'S FACILITIES

Anacostia
Anacostia Museum and Center for African American History and Culture

The National Mall
Air and Space Museum
American History Museum
Arts and Industries Building
Freer Gallery of Art
Hirshhorn Museum and Sculpture Garden
National Museum of African American History and Culture (under construction)
National Museum of African Art
National Museum of the American Indian

National Museum of Natural History
Sackler Gallery of Art
Smithsonian Institution Building (the Castle)

Capitol Hill
National Postal Museum

Downtown
American Art Museum
National Portrait Gallery
Renwick Gallery

Upper Northwest
National Zoo

Northern Virginia
Air and Space Museum (Steven F. Udvar-Hazy Center)

for you. In fact, most of the museums with government connections are free, as well, as you will see below.

WHAT'S THE BEST PHOTO OP? What's not? With its impressive memorials and federal buildings, Washington is a photographer's mecca. Just stand in front of a monument and snap away. However, we have favorites to recommend, starting with the fifth-floor terrace of the Newseum, with views of the Capitol, many of the museums, Pennsylvania Avenue, and the old Post Office Pavilion. The statue of Albert Einstein outside the National Academies of Science is a popular perch, with a lap large enough for sitting in; FDR, who's portrayed in his wheelchair, has one as well; and on the south side of the Tidal Basin, George Mason is relaxing on a bench and waiting for company. In front of the British Embassy on Massachusetts Avenue NW, a larger-than-life Winston Churchill raises both hands in his famous victory gesture.

One of the most dramatic views of Washington is from the Iwo Jima Memorial in Arlington, Virginia, near the Netherlands Carillon. At dawn, the sun rises almost directly behind the U.S. Capitol. At dusk, the panorama of twinkling lights includes the Jefferson and Lincoln memorials, the Washington Monument, and, more than two miles away, the U.S. Capitol.

Crowds notwithstanding, it's hard to resist the Tidal Basin when the cherry trees are blossoming. (And no, we didn't mention Madame Tussauds; you want your picture taken with a wax Johnny Depp, be our guest. We'll wait for the real thing.)

HOW CAN I TELL IF THE PRESIDENT IS IN TOWN? A flag flies over the White House when the president is in Washington. At night, one of the facades on the White House stays lit for the benefit of trench coat–clad TV news reporters who intone to the camera, "Live, from the White House . . ." To find out what high diplomatic or royal personages are here, check the flags outside Blair House.

HOW CAN I TELL IF CONGRESS IS IN SESSION? Look for a flag flying over the respective chamber of the U.S. Capitol to determine which, if either, house of Congress is in session. From the Mall, the Senate is to the left of the dome; the House of Representatives is to the right. At night, a light burns on top of the Capitol dome if either chamber is in session. (And before you ask: The figure on the top of the dome is the Statue of Freedom, not Pocahontas, as some people think because of the headdress: see the profile on pages 232–233 for details.)

CAN I GET IN TO SEE CONGRESS IN ACTION? Unlike in the movies (or on C-SPAN), most real legislative action takes place in committee meetings. Check the *Washington Post* "A" section for a list of Congressional hearings open to the public, along with their times and locations (always in one of the buildings near the Capitol).

WHAT'S THE BIGGEST MISTAKE I CAN MAKE? Run afoul of security. Walk-through metal detectors staffed by no-nonsense guards are standard equipment in virtually every federal building in Washington, including the U.S. Capitol, the Supreme Court, all Senate and House office buildings, Mall museums, and nearly all other exhibition sites. Treat these the way you would an airport security check (except that you are not apt to have to take your shoes off): Have all your change and keys in one pocket or bag. Avoid metal-buckled belts and elaborate jewelry. Purses, backpacks, and briefcases will likely have to go through X-ray machines, so keep your carry-ons small and open the zippers and clasps. And we say again, read up on restrictions *before* you leave the hotel. Bringing the queue to a halt will make you a target of your fellow tourists' ire; and if you *really* start alarms ringing, you could face some serious trouble.

LET METRO BE YOUR GUIDE

WITH SO MANY TOURIST ATTRACTIONS LOCATED within walking distance of Metro stations, you can actually pretty much lay out your schedule along its lines—an underground hop-on, in a way. Of course, if you don't mind walking a mile or so in between stations, you can save a couple of bucks, but on the other hand, there's that all-day pass. Although this list shows what attractions are closest to a Metro station, some sights could be as far as 20 minutes away by foot. For example, while the Foggy Bottom–GWU Metro is the closest to the Lincoln Memorial, it's still about a three-quarter-mile hike. (On the other hand, many of the museums, especially along the Mall and in Penn Quarter, are accessible from more than one station.) Also note that some of these are smaller, more special-interest attractions. Check our profiles below for details and check the map.

Red Line

BROOKLAND-CUA The National Shrine of the Immaculate Conception, the Franciscan Monastery (10- and 20-minute walks, respectively)

UNION STATION National Postal Museum, Sewall-Belmont House Women's History Museum, the U.S. Supreme Court, the U.S. Capitol, Senate office buildings, Folger Shakespeare Library, Library of Congress

JUDICIARY SQUARE National Building Museum, National Law Enforcement Officers Memorial, the Lillian and Albert Small Jewish Museum

GALLERY PLACE-CHINATOWN National Portrait Gallery and Smithsonian American Art Museum, Chinatown, National Building Museum, Washington Convention Center, Ford's Theatre/Peterson House, International Spy Museum, National Museum of Crime & Punishment, Koshland Science Museum, Madame Tussauds Wax Museum

METRO CENTER Madame Tussauds Wax Museum, National Museum of Women in the Arts, U.S. Department of the Treasury, the Washington Convention Center

FARRAGUT NORTH The *Washington Post* building, National Geographic Society Museum

DUPONT CIRCLE Embassy Row, the Phillips Collection, Anderson House, the Islamic Center, Woodrow Wilson House, the Textile Museum, House of the Temple, Christian Heurich Mansion

WOODLEY PARK-ZOO/ADAMS MORGAN National Zoo, Washington National Cathedral, Adams Morgan (despite the name, the Zoo is about a ten-minute walk; Adams Morgan is about 15 minutes away on foot; and the Cathedral is a half-hour stroll)

CLEVELAND PARK National Zoo (this way you're walking downhill rather than up)

VAN NESS-UDC Intelsat, Hillwood Museum (20-minute walk)

BETHESDA National Museum of Health and Medicine

ROCKVILLE Beall-Dawson House, Stonestreet Museum of 19th-Century Medicine

Blue and Orange Lines

CAPITOL SOUTH Library of Congress, House office buildings, the U.S. Capitol, Folger Shakespeare Library, the U.S. Supreme Court

FEDERAL CENTER SW U.S. Botanic Garden, the National Air and Space Museum, National Museum of the American Indian

L'ENFANT PLAZA The National Air and Space Museum, the Hirshhorn Museum and Sculpture Garden, the Arts and Industries Building (closed for renovation), National Museum of the American Indian

SMITHSONIAN The National Mall, the Freer and Sackler galleries, the National Museum of African Art, the Bureau of Engraving and Printing, the National Museum of Natural History, the National Museum of American History, the Washington Monument, the Smithsonian Castle visitor center, the Tidal Basin, the Jefferson Memorial (15-minute walk), FDR Memorial (15-minute walk), Korean War Veterans' Memorial (20-minute walk), Lincoln Memorial (20-minute walk), Martin Luther King Jr. Memorial (under construction), the U.S. Holocaust Memorial Museum, National World War II Memorial, National Museum of the American Indian

FEDERAL TRIANGLE The Old Post Office Pavilion, the National Aquarium, Pennsylvania Avenue, National Museum of American History, National Museum of Natural History, the White House Visitors Center, Visitor Information Center (in the Reagan Building)

MCPHERSON SQUARE The White House, the *Washington Post* building, Lafayette Park, Kiplinger's Washington Collection

FARRAGUT WEST Decatur House, Renwick Gallery, the Old Executive Office Building, the White House, the Corcoran Gallery of Art, the DAR Museum, the Ellipse, the Octagon Museum (*closed for renovation*)

FOGGY BOTTOM-GWU The Kennedy Center, U.S. Department of State Diplomatic Reception Rooms, Vietnam Veterans Memorial, Korean War Veterans Memorial, National World War II Memorial, the Reflecting Pool, the Lincoln Memorial, the FDR Memorial, Federal Reserve Board, Georgetown (20- to 30-minute walk)

ARLINGTON CEMETERY Arlington National Cemetery, the Lincoln and FDR memorials (across Memorial Bridge)

PENTAGON The Pentagon, DEA Museum

RONALD REAGAN WASHINGTON NATIONAL AIRPORT Ronald Reagan Washington National Airport

KING STREET Old Town Alexandria (15-minute walk), shops and restaurants, the Torpedo Factory (20-minute walk), the Stabler-Leadbetter Apothecary Museum (15-minute walk), Gadsby's Tavern Museum, the George Washington National Masonic Memorial (20-minute walk)

Yellow Line

GEORGIA AVENUE-PETWORTH President Lincoln's Cottage, Rock Creek Cemetery

U STREET-AFRICAN AMERICAN CIVIL WAR MEMORIAL-CARDOZO Lincoln Theater, Bethune Council House, African-American Civil War Monument and Museum

MOUNT VERNON SQUARE/SEVENTH STREET-CONVENTION CENTER City Museum of Washington, Inter-American Development Bank Cultural Center

GALLERY PLACE–CHINATOWN National Portrait Gallery and Smithsonian American Art Museum, Chinatown, National Building Museum, Washington Convention Center, Ford's Theatre, National Museum of Crime & Punishment, Newseum, International Spy Museum, Koshland Science Museum

ARCHIVES–NAVY MEMORIAL–PENN QUARTER The National Archives, Newseum, National Museum of Crime & Punishment, International Spy Museum, the U.S. Navy Memorial, the National Gallery of Art, the National Museum of Natural History

Green Line

COLLEGE PARK College Park Aviation Museum

GEORGIA AVENUE–PETWORTH President Lincoln's Cottage, Rock Creek Cemetery

WATERFRONT-SEU Washington's Potomac River waterfront area (restaurants, marinas, and river cruises), Fort McNair, Arena Stage

NAVY YARD Washington Navy Yard, Nationals Stadium

IT BEARS REPEATING . . .

ALTHOUGH WE'VE SAID IT BEFORE, there's no quicker way to ruin a vacation than to get overtired or injured. So before you head out, even on one of the least strenuous tours, run over the essentials list. We can lead you to water, but—well, you know.

But you have to use common sense even here, because while carrying a water bottle is a really good idea most of the time, you cannot take any food or beverage into the White House or U.S. Capitol, for instance; and there are no lockers for you to stash them.

Bottle or not, drink up. Even the simplest walk is a form of exercise, especially if it's hot and humid. Even if you're good about hydrating at the gym, being in a strange place can make you forget to water on time. And there's always more temptation to drink alcohol on a vacation, which just adds to the problem.

Don't settle for sunscreen in the morning; you'll sweat it off. And wear sunglasses with protective coating, not just cute logos; Washington's marble quotient is high and reflective, and that's not even counting the pools and rivers.

Wear comfortable clothes, ideally layered for in-and-out AC, and flexible enough for mass transit. Wear shoes that fit (and are already broken in), and that have non-slick soles. Avoid socks with fat seams or bulges, but carry a bandage or two just in case of a surprise blister.

Just don't do it—too much of it, anyway. Make a reasonable schedule, but be flexible. Outside of a movie plot and a whole lot of special effects, the Washington Monument isn't going anywhere overnight.

Don't force everyone into the same itinerary. If young kids need a break, maybe their teenaged siblings want to do a little shopping. What did you give them a cell phone for, anyway? And the older folks may opt for a leisurely lunch rather than another gallery. Just make sure you have settled on a place to regroup and that everyone is very clear about where that is.

And finally, look back at Part One to our suggestions about carrying a full-sized handkerchief, penlight, stain and wine treatments, and so on. Trust us, we have experience.

WASHINGTON'S ATTRACTIONS

NOW WE GET TO THE SPECIFICS OF MANY of the city's most popular or most interesting attractions. And that in itself is a problem. Visitors come to Washington from all over the world—and for a lot of different reasons—so it's difficult for a guidebook to decree to such a diverse group where they should spend their time. Is the National Gallery of Art better than the Air and Space Museum? The answer is yes—if your interests and tastes range more toward Van Gogh than von Braun. House of the Temple or Library of Congress? Well, is your favorite author Dan Brown or Thomas Jefferson? We don't know; we can only offer up the best clues we have to your own personal treasure map.

So, we have prepared in-depth profiles to start you off. In each case, we've included an author's rating from one star (skip it unless you're particularly interested) to five stars (not to be missed), a rating based on age group that reflects the sort of exhibits and relative sophistication of the attraction (and to some extent, the wear and tear involved), and a physical description. Not being included doesn't mean a museum or historical sight isn't worth visiting; some have rotating exhibits that can't be rated, for example.

And the ratings aren't entirely comments on the quality of a particular collection. Occasionally, the attraction's relative accessibility—both in terms of public transportation and disabled comfort—has weighed in its rating. In other cases it is a matter of how narrow or general the institution's attraction may be, so read the entire profile if you're undecided. Also note that a few of the attractions require advance reservations. Often we refer to other attractions whose proximity might recommend them to those who have extra time or are repeat visitors (or who have special interests).

But even beyond those, there are hundreds of "attractions" we haven't specifically listed, partly because they are stand-alone memorials (all those statues in traffic circles), parks, cemeteries with fine statuary; or simply buildings or bridges with elaborate facades, friezes, and carvings. And, of course, there are new memorials and museums going up all the time. Washington is a city worth seeing; so don't find yourself walking with your nose glued to a book, even this one. Art is all around.

continued on page 162

Washington Attractions by Type

CEMETERIES

Arlington National Cemetery ★★★★★   NATIONAL MALL largest U.S. military cemetery

CHURCHES/HOUSES OF WORSHIP

Basilica of the National Shrine of the Immaculate Conception ★★½   NORTHEAST
largest Catholic church in U.S.

Franciscan Monastery and Gardens ★★   NORTHEAST   restored church, catacombs, garden

Islamic Center ★★   DUPONT CIRCLE/ADAMS MORGAN   exotic mosque

Washington National Cathedral ★★★★★   UPPER NORTHWEST
6th-largest cathedral in the world

GOVERNMENT BUILDINGS OPEN FOR TOURS

Bureau of Engraving and Printing ★★★   NATIONAL MALL
where U.S. dollars and stamps are printed

National Archives ★★½   NATIONAL MALL   where the nation's walking papers are kept

U.S. Capitol ★★★★★   CAPITOL HILL   where Congress meets

U.S. Department of State Diplomatic Reception Rooms ★★★★★   FOGGY BOTTOM
decorative arts; reservation only

U.S. Department of the Treasury ★★★★   NATIONAL MALL
restored 19th-century landmark

U.S. Supreme Court ★★★★   CAPITOL HILL   nation's highest court

Voice of America ★★   NATIONAL MALL   radio studios

Washington Navy Yard ★★★   SOUTHEAST   3 military museums and U.S. Navy destroyer;
reservations only

HISTORIC BUILDINGS AND HOMES

Decatur House ★★★   NATIONAL MALL   early D.C. residence near the White House

Dumbarton House ★★★   GEORGETOWN   historic mansion

Ford's Theatre/Petersen House ★★★   DOWNTOWN
where Lincoln was assassinated and died

Frederick Douglass National Historic Site ★★★   SOUTHEAST
preserved Victorian mansion

Gunston Hall ★★★   VIRGINIA SUBURBS   George Mason's plantation

Mount Vernon Estate and Gardens ★★★★★   VIRGINIA SUBURBS   George Washington's
river plantation

The Octagon ★★★   NATIONAL MALL   early D.C. home and museum (*closed for renovation*)

Old Town Alexandria ★★★★   VIRGINIA SUBURBS   restored colonial port town

President Lincoln's Cottage ★★★★★   UPPER NORTHWEST   Lincoln's summer home

Society of the Cincinnati Museum at Anderson House ★★★★   DUPONT CIRCLE/
ADAMS MORGAN   lavish mansion and Revolutionary War museum

Tudor Place ★★★ GEORGETOWN mansion built by Martha Washington's granddaughter

Union Station ★★★ CAPITOL HILL beaux arts palace; food court, shopping mall

The White House ★★ NATIONAL MALL the Executive Mansion, reservation only

Woodrow Wilson House ★★★★ DUPONT CIRCLE/ADAMS MORGAN
final home of the 28th president

LIBRARIES

Folger Shakespeare Library ★★★ CAPITOL HILL bard museum and library

Library of Congress ★★★★ CAPITOL HILL world's largest library

MONUMENTS AND MEMORIALS

Franklin Delano Roosevelt Memorial ★★★★ NATIONAL MALL
open-air memorial to FDR

House of the Temple ★★ DUPONT CIRCLE/ADAMS MORGAN Masonic temple modeled
on an ancient wonder

Jefferson Memorial ★★★ NATIONAL MALL classical-style monument on Tidal Basin

Korean War Veterans Memorial ★★★ NATIONAL MALL "walking" platoon memorial

Lincoln Memorial ★★★★ NATIONAL MALL memorial to 16th president on Reflecting Pool

Martin Luther King Jr. National Memorial N/A NATIONAL MALL meditation garden
and walk (under construction)

National World War II Memorial ★★ NATIONAL MALL tribute to "the greatest
generation"

Old Post Office Tower and Pavilion ★★½ NATIONAL MALL
food court with a great view

Pentagon Memorial ★★★★ NATIONAL MALL outdoor memorial to victims
of 9/11 attacks

Vietnam Veterans Memorial ★★★★ NATIONAL MALL U.S. soldier memorial on the Mall

Washington Monument ★★★ NATIONAL MALL 500-foot memorial to first U.S. president

MUSEUMS AND GALLERIES

Anacostia Museum N/A SOUTHEAST African American history and culture

Arthur M. Sackler Gallery ★★★ NATIONAL MALL Asian art

Arts and Industries Building N/A NATIONAL MALL (*closed for renovation*)

Corcoran Gallery of Art ★★★★ NATIONAL MALL modern and classical art and antiques

DAR Museum ★★★★ NATIONAL MALL decorative U.S. arts and antiques

Dumbarton Oaks and Gardens ★★★★ GEORGETOWN mansion/museum and a
beautiful garden

Freer Gallery of Art ★★★★★ NATIONAL MALL Asian and American art

Washington Attractions by Type (cont'd)

MUSEUMS AND GALLERIES (CONTINUED)

Hillwood Estate Museum and Gardens ★★★★★ UPPER NORTHWEST
mansion with fabulous art treasures, reservation only

Hirshhorn Museum and Sculpture Garden ★★★★★ NATIONAL MALL modern art

International Spy Museum ★★½ DOWNTOWN history and gadgetry of espionage

Koshland Science Museum ★★½ DOWNTOWN for budding researchers

Kreeger Museum ★★★ DUPONT CIRCLE/ADAMS MORGAN modern-art museum

Madame Tussauds ★★½ DOWNTOWN wax museum

NASA/Goddard Space Flight Visitors Center ★★★ MARYLAND SUBURBS
space-flight museum

National Air and Space Museum ★★★★★ NATIONAL MALL chronicles manned flight

National Aquarium ★★ NATIONAL MALL fish tanks in a basement

National Building Museum ★★★ DOWNTOWN architectural marvel and exhibits

National Cryptologic Museum ★★ MARYLAND SUBURBS NSA spook museum

National Gallery of Art: East Building ★★★★★ NATIONAL MALL 20th-century art

National Gallery of Art: West Building ★★★★★ NATIONAL MALL
Euro and American classical art

National Geographic Museum ★★★ DOWNTOWN high-tech exhibition for kids

National Museum of African Art ★★★ NATIONAL MALL traditional arts of Africa

National Museum of American History ★★★★★ NATIONAL MALL
American experience

National Museum of the American Indian ★★★ NATIONAL MALL
native art and artifacts

National Museum of Crime & Punishment ★★½ DOWNTOWN collection of weapons
and gangster memorabilia

National Museum of Health and Medicine ★★ UPPER NORTHWEST medical museum

National Museum of Natural History ★★★★★ NATIONAL MALL treasure chest of
natural sciences

continued from page 159

THE NATIONAL MALL AND ARLINGTON MEMORIALS

AS THE EAST HALF OF THE MALL IS TO MUSEUMS, so the west side is to monuments. Many of them are smallish and open-air, some classical, some modern, some abstract.

But there is a quite strong "generation gap" visible among them. While the older memorials tend to be valedictory and emotionally elevating, if solemn—Washington's Egyptian-Masonic monolith,

National Museum of Women in the Arts ★★★★ DOWNTOWN
modern and classical art by women

National Portrait Gallery–Smithsonian American Art Museum ★★★★★
DOWNTOWN 2 important art collections in one beautifully restored building

National Postal Museum ★★★ CAPITOL HILL philately and exhibits

Newseum ★★★★★ DOWNTOWN salute to media

Phillips Collection ★★★★ DUPONT CIRCLE/ADAMS MORGAN
first U.S. modern-art museum

Renwick Gallery ★★★ NATIONAL MALL American crafts and decorative arts

Smithsonian Institution Building (The Castle) ★★★★ NATIONAL MALL
museum information and display

Textile Museum ★★ DUPONT CIRCLE/ADAMS MORGAN textile arts

U.S. Department of the Interior ★½ FOGGY BOTTOM
old-fashioned museum of parks and outdoors

U.S. Holocaust Memorial Museum ★★★★½ NATIONAL MALL
graphic memorial to WWII holocaust

PARKS, GARDENS, AND ZOOS

Dumbarton Oaks and Gardens ★★★★ GEORGETOWN mansion/museum and a
beautiful garden

Kenilworth Aquatic Gardens ★★★ SOUTHEAST national park for water plants

National Wildlife Visitor Center ★★½ MARYLAND SUBURBS museum on 13,000-acre
wildlife refuge

National Zoological Park ★★★★★ UPPER NORTHWEST world-class zoo

U.S. Botanic Garden ★★★ CAPITOL HILL huge greenhouse and living museum on Mall

U.S. National Arboretum ★★★ NORTHEAST 446-acre collection of trees, flowers, herbs

THEATERS/PERFORMANCES

JFK Center for the Performing Arts ★★ FOGGY BOTTOM stunning performing-arts
center on the Potomac

Jefferson's Pantheon, and Lincoln's impressive Parthenon—those erected in the late 20th century are somewhat grimmer and more realistic. The **Korean War Veterans Memorial,** with its platoon of dogged, almost antiheroic grunts, and the two sculptural appendages to the otherwise-stark **Vietnam Veterans Memorial**—one honoring soldiers and the other the female medical and support troops who tended them—provoke an essentially different emotional response from visitors than do the great temples of the Founding Fathers. The still-under-construction Martin Luther King and Eisenhower memorials are large-scale meditation sites. (Even more intriguingly, the similarly shaped Hirshhorn and American Indian museums, one curved, one actually cylindrical, represent almost opposite philosophies, one a neutral, pragmatic background for artistic creation, the other an organic reverence for natural creation.)

In addition to the monuments and memorials profiled later in this chapter are three others you should stop to examine as you stroll from Washington to Lincoln, so to speak.

Notable for its restrained elegance, the **District of Columbia War Memorial** is an open-sided Doric temple with the names of D.C. residents killed in World War I engraved upon its outer walls. Above the circular colonnade is another inscription, subtle but striking in its irony: a reference to "*the* World War"—the one after which Americans believed there would be no other. President Herbert Hoover and General John Pershing both took part in the dedication ceremony in 1931, and the bandleader, John Phillip Sousa, played not only his own "Stars and Stripes Forever" but also "The Star-spangled Banner," which had just been named the U.S. national anthem by an act of Congress. As befits a monument to what in some ways was the last 19th-century war, the memorial is about halfway between the Lincoln and World War II memorials, on the south side of Constitution Gardens facing Independence Avenue.

Almost directly opposite, between 17th and 20th streets just south of Constitution Avenue, is a pretty figure eight–shaped lake, at one side of which is a small island that houses the **56 Signers of the Declaration of Independence Memorial.** The memorial itself is simply designed, with the final phrase of the Declaration, "We pledge to each other our Lives, our Fortunes, and our sacred Honor," engraved in the base and the 56 signatures reproduced in the granite blocks of a semicircle. Something of the signers' varied personalities seems evident in their handwriting—the self-consciously elegant Thomas Jefferson, the expansive John Hancock, the plain John Adams, and the even plainer Samuel Adams. Dedicated to mark the bicentennial in 1976, the island is also a waterfowl refuge. It is so often overlooked by tour companies that you're more likely to see locals than visitors reading or resting beneath one of its weeping willows.

On the southeast edge of the Tidal Basin is the seated figure of the oft-underappreciated Founding Father **George Mason;** he rests, his cane leaning on the bench alongside, near the memorial to Thomas Jefferson, who borrowed so many ideas from Mason but wound up with most of the credit.

And there is more to come: the **Martin Luther King Jr. National Memorial** is being constructed on the northwest shore of the Tidal Basin in a direct line between the Lincoln and Jefferson memorials,

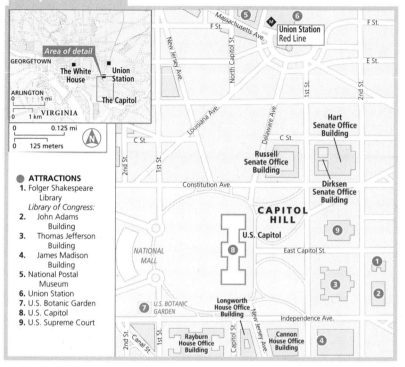

Capitol Hill

Area of detail

GEORGETOWN

The White House — Union Station

ARLINGTON 0 — 1 mi — The Capitol

VIRGINIA 0 — 1 km

0 — 0.125 mi
0 — 125 meters

● **ATTRACTIONS**
1. Folger Shakespeare Library
   Library of Congress:
2. John Adams Building
3. Thomas Jefferson Building
4. James Madison Building
5. National Postal Museum
6. Union Station
7. U.S. Botanic Garden
8. U.S. Capitol
9. U.S. Supreme Court

Union Station Red Line

Hart Senate Office Building

Russell Senate Office Building

Dirksen Senate Office Building

CAPITOL HILL

U.S. Capitol

East Capitol St.

NATIONAL MALL

U.S. BOTANIC GARDEN

Longworth House Office Building

Independence Ave.

Rayburn House Office Building

Cannon House Office Building

emphasizing the long, historic "line of freedom" in America. Much like the FDR Memorial, the King Memorial will combine a meditation walk with statuary and plaques bearing quotations from the civil rights leader.

And back toward the eastern side of the Mall, between Fourth and Sixth streets SE facing the Arts and Industries building across Constitution Avenue, will be the **Dwight D. Eisenhower Memorial,** an open park of oak trees and limestone tablets with quotations from the war leader–turned–President (who, like FDR, did not really want a monument but got one anyway).

Across the Potomac River, partly in the District and partly in Virginia, are several armed-forces and war memorials. Though not within the Mall proper, they are certainly connected to it, and so we have included them here.

At the opposite end of the Memorial Bridge from the Lincoln Memorial, just outside the entrance to Arlington National Cemetery,

continued on page 168

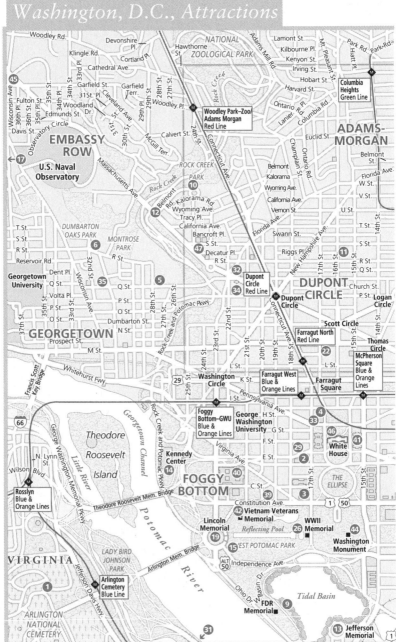

Washington, D.C., Attractions

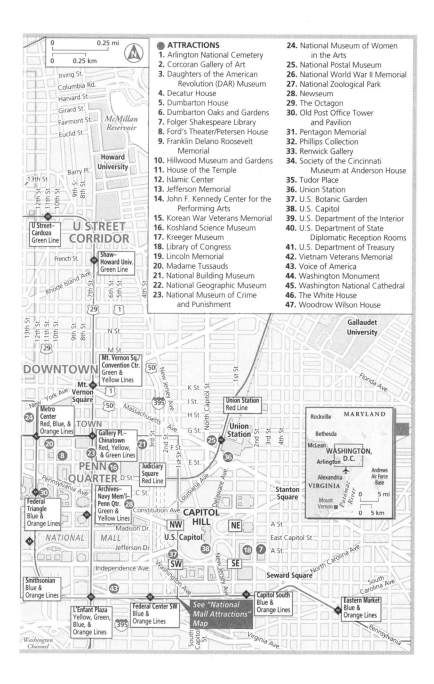

ATTRACTIONS
1. Arlington National Cemetery
2. Corcoran Gallery of Art
3. Daughters of the American Revolution (DAR) Museum
4. Decatur House
5. Dumbarton House
6. Dumbarton Oaks and Gardens
7. Folger Shakespeare Library
8. Ford's Theater/Petersen House
9. Franklin Delano Roosevelt Memorial
10. Hillwood Museum and Gardens
11. House of the Temple
12. Islamic Center
13. Jefferson Memorial
14. John F. Kennedy Center for the Performing Arts
15. Korean War Veterans Memorial
16. Koshland Science Museum
17. Kreeger Museum
18. Library of Congress
19. Lincoln Memorial
20. Madame Tussauds
21. National Building Museum
22. National Geographic Museum
23. National Museum of Crime and Punishment
24. National Museum of Women in the Arts
25. National Postal Museum
26. National World War II Memorial
27. National Zoological Park
28. Newseum
29. The Octagon
30. Old Post Office Tower and Pavilion
31. Pentagon Memorial
32. Phillips Collection
33. Renwick Gallery
34. Society of the Cincinnati Museum at Anderson House
35. Tudor Place
36. Union Station
37. U.S. Botanic Garden
38. U.S. Capitol
39. U.S. Department of the Interior
40. U.S. Department of State Diplomatic Reception Rooms
41. U.S. Department of Treasury
42. Vietnam Veterans Memorial
43. Voice of America
44. Washington Monument
45. Washington National Cathedral
46. The White House
47. Woodrow Wilson House

The National Mall

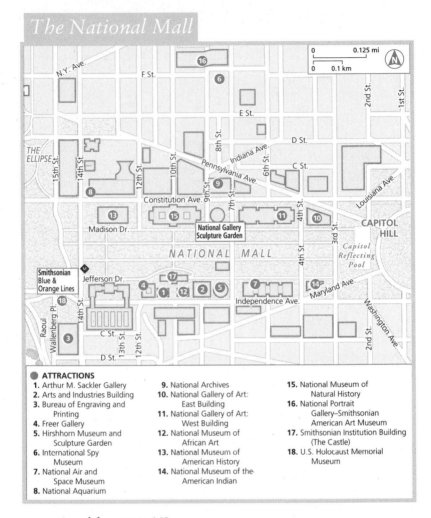

● **ATTRACTIONS**

1. Arthur M. Sackler Gallery
2. Arts and Industries Building
3. Bureau of Engraving and Printing
4. Freer Gallery
5. Hirshhorn Museum and Sculpture Garden
6. International Spy Museum
7. National Air and Space Museum
8. National Aquarium

9. National Archives
10. National Gallery of Art: East Building
11. National Gallery of Art: West Building
12. National Museum of African Art
13. National Museum of American History
14. National Museum of the American Indian

15. National Museum of Natural History
16. National Portrait Gallery–Smithsonian American Art Museum
17. Smithsonian Institution Building (The Castle)
18. U.S. Holocaust Memorial Museum

continued from page 165

is the little island comprising **Lady Bird Johnson Park.** Though not technically a memorial, it is a fittingly green tribute to the First Lady who turned her energies to the beautification of the capital. About a mile south of the Memorial Bridge along the George Washington Parkway is the **Lyndon Baines Johnson Memorial Grove,** which consists of a commemorative monolith and a grove of 500 white pines. (The stream between Lady Bird Johnson Park and the cemetery is **Boundary Channel,** which marks the border between D.C. and Virginia.)

The **Pentagon Memorial** (profiled in detail on pages 224–225), which opened to the public on September 11, 2008, is accessible via the Pentagon Metro; those arriving by car must park in public lots at Pentagon City, about a half-mile away, and walk to the site.

The **U.S. Air Force Memorial,** which opened in October 2006, is a triad of soaring (270-foot-tall) stainless-steel arcs that are illuminated at night and are visible from many of the approaches to Washington. The actual site includes an inscribed glass contemplation wall that represents those who have been killed in action, along with a curving wall that one follows up to the sculpture—at its foot there is a great view of the Washington Monument—and back down. This is also accessible to pedestrians via the Pentagon Metro Station (it's about a half-mile walk); the auto or cab entrance is off Columbia Pike/Route 244.

The **U.S. Marine Corps Memorial,** popularly known as the Iwo Jima Memorial and recently the subject of a major motion picture, *Flags of Our Fathers,* is about a 20-minute walk from the Arlington Cemetery subway stop. The 32-foot-long sculpture, capped by a 60-foot-tall flagpole, was dedicated by President Eisenhower on Veterans Day, November 11, 1954. Alongside the memorial is the **Netherlands Carillon,** a gift from the Dutch people in gratitude for American aid during and after World War II. It plays recorded music—mostly armed-forces themes, marches, "The Star-spangled Banner," and the like—hourly from 10 a.m. to 6 p.m. every day, with some longer concerts in the summer.

ATTRACTION PROFILES

Anacostia Community Museum (*a Smithsonian museum*)

Because the museum features special exhibitions that change throughout the year, it's not really possible to rate this Smithsonian facility's appeal by age group.

Location 1901 Fort Place SE, in Anacostia; No Metro access; ☎ 202-633-4870; anacostia.si.edu

---

Type of attraction Originally a museum focusing on African American history and culture, this now addresses social issues affecting communities of all sorts. **Admission** Free. **Hours** Daily, 10 a.m.–5 p.m.; closed Christmas Day. **When to go** Anytime. But either call first or pick up a brochure at the Castle on the Mall to find out what's on view before making the trip, and it's likely you'll need to arrange for a cab. **How much time to allow** 1 hour.

DESCRIPTION AND COMMENTS Located on the high ground of old Fort Stanton, the Anacostia Museum features changing exhibits on black culture and history and the achievements of African Americans (baseball players, Africans in Mexico), as well as addresses issues of social change. Unfortunately for out-of-town visitors, it's in a location that's difficult to reach.

TOURING TIPS To save yourself the frustration of arriving between major shows, either call the museum first or pick up a flyer at the Castle on the Mall.

OTHER THINGS TO DO NEARBY Frederick Douglass National Historic Site is a short drive, but you should call in advance to make reservations for the house tour.

Arlington National Cemetery ★★★★★

Location **Across the Potomac from Washington via Arlington Memorial Bridge, which crosses the river near the Lincoln Memorial;** Nearest Metro station **Arlington Cemetery; ☎ 703-607-8000; www.arlingtoncemetery.org**

Type of attraction The largest military cemetery in the United States. Admission Free. Hours Daily, April–September, 8 a.m.–7 p.m.; October–March, 8 a.m.–5 p.m. When to go First thing or later afternoon in spring and summer. Special comments No food concessions on site. How much time to allow 2 hours.

DESCRIPTION AND COMMENTS It's not fair to call a visit to Arlington National Cemetery mere sightseeing; as Americans, our lives are too intimately attached to the 200,000 men and women buried here. They include the famous, the obscure, and the unknown: Presidents John F. Kennedy and William Howard Taft, General George C. Marshall and the father and son generals Benjamin O. Davis, war hero Audie Murphy, civil rights martyr Medgar Evers, boxing champ Joe Louis, baseball's popularizer Abner Doubleday, and Supreme Court Justices Thurgood Marshall and Oliver Wendell Holmes are among them. Sights located in the cemetery's 612 rolling acres include the Tomb of the Unknowns (guarded 24 hours a day; witness the changing of the guard on the hour from October to March, and on the half-hour the rest of the year); memorials to the crew of the space shuttle *Challenger;* the Iran Rescue Mission Memorial; and Arlington House, built in 1802. With the ease of touring provided by Tourmobile, Arlington Cemetery should be on every first-time visitor's list of things to see.

TOURING TIPS Private cars are not allowed inside, but there's plenty of parking near the visitor center; still, it's easier to take Metro. Although you can wander around the cemetery on your own, the narrated Tourmobile tour is informative and saves wear and tear on your feet—and at $7.50 for adults, $6.50 for seniors, and $3.75 for children under age 12, it's a good deal. The ticket allows you to get off at all the major sites and reboard at your leisure. The shuttle tours leave the visitor center (where tickets are sold) about every 15 to 20 minutes. If you're touring the entire Mall by Tourmobile, transferring to the cemetery tour is free for that day only. But if you want to tour the cemetery by shuttle bus on a different day, don't pay for another full-circuit ticket. Just subway to the Arlington Cemetery station, walk the short distance to the visitor center and buy the cemetery-only ticket.

OTHER THINGS TO DO NEARBY The 9/11 Pentagon Memorial and the Air Force Memorial are not far, but you'll need to take another subway leg to the Pentagon station. The Iwo Jima Memorial and the Netherlands Carillon are about a 20-minute walk from Arlington House (down Custis Walk and through Weitzel Gate).

Arlington National Cemetery

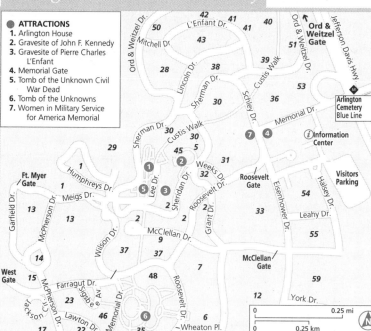

● **ATTRACTIONS**
1. Arlington House
2. Gravesite of John F. Kennedy
3. Gravesite of Pierre Charles L'Enfant
4. Memorial Gate
5. Tomb of the Unknown Civil War Dead
6. Tomb of the Unknowns
7. Women in Military Service for America Memorial

0 ___ 0.25 mi
0 ___ 0.25 km

Arthur M. Sackler Gallery (*a Smithsonian museum*) ★★★

APPEAL BY AGE	PRESCHOOL ★	GRADE SCHOOL ★★	TEENS ★★
YOUNG ADULTS ★★★	OVER 30 ★★★		SENIORS ★★★

Location 1050 Independence Avenue SW, on the Mall near the Castle (the Smithsonian Institution Building); Nearest Metro station Smithsonian; ☎ 202-633-1080 or 202-357-1729 (TDD); www.asia.si.edu

Type of attraction A museum dedicated to Asian art from ancient times to the present. **Admission** Free. **Hours** Daily, 10 a.m.–5:30 p.m.; closed Christmas Day. **When to go** Anytime. **Special comments** Fabulous and exotic art make this a quiet respite when other Mall attractions are jammed with visitors. No food concessions on site. **How much time to allow** 1 hour.

DESCRIPTION AND COMMENTS Descend through a granite-and-glass pavilion to view a collection of Asian (mostly Chinese) treasures, many of them made of gold and encrusted with jewels. The Sackler is full of exotic stuff that will catch the eye of older children, teens, and adults. Barring a strong interest in the Orient, however, first-time visitors on a tight schedule should visit the Sackler another time.

TOURING TIPS Stop at the information desk and ask about the guided tours offered throughout the day. The gift shop is an exotic bazaar featuring

Washington Attractions by Location

THE NATIONAL MALL /MEMORIALS
Arlington National Cemetery
Arthur M. Sackler Gallery
Arts and Industries Building
Bureau of Engraving and Printing
Corcoran Gallery of Art
DAR Museum
Decatur House
Dwight D. Eisenhower Memorial
(under construction)
Franklin Delano Roosevelt Memorial
Freer Gallery of Art
Hirshhorn Museum and Sculpture
Garden
Jefferson Memorial
Korean War Veterans Memorial
Lincoln Memorial
Martin Luther King Jr. National
Memorial (under construction)
National Air and Space Museum
National Aquarium
National Archives
National Gallery of Art: East Building
National Gallery of Art: West Building
National Museum of African Art
National Museum of American History
National Museum of the American
Indian
National Museum of Natural History

National World War II Memorial
The Octagon
Old Post Office Tower and Pavilion
Renwick Gallery
Smithsonian Institution Building
(The Castle)
U.S. Department of Treasury
U.S. Holocaust Memorial Museum
Vietnam Veterans Memorial
Voice of America
Washington Monument
The White House

NORTHEAST
Basilica of the National Shrine of the
Immaculate Conception
Franciscan Monastery and Gardens
U.S. National Arboretum

DUPONT CIRCLE/ADAMS MORGAN
House of the Temple
Islamic Center
Phillips Collection
Society of the Cincinnati Museum at
Anderson House
Textile Museum
Woodrow Wilson House

UPPER NORTHWEST
Hillwood Estate Museum and Gardens

paintings, textiles, ancient games, Zen–rock garden kits, and plenty of other Asian-influenced items. Free walk-in tours are offered daily (except Wednesday) at 11 a.m.

OTHER THINGS TO DO NEARBY The Sackler is connected with its twin, the Museum of African Art, below ground, so that's the logical next stop—especially if it's rainy or blazingly hot outside. Another underground corridor connects the Sackler to the Freer Gallery, making this an Asian art lover's dream.

Arts and Industries Building (*a Smithsonian museum*)
Closed for renovation

National Museum of Health and Medicine
National Zoological Park
President Lincoln's Cottage
Washington National Cathedral

CAPITOL HILL
Folger Shakespeare Library
Library of Congress
National Postal Museum
Union Station
U.S. Botanic Garden
U.S. Capitol
U.S. Supreme Court

FOGGY BOTTOM
JFK Center for the Performing Arts
U.S. Department of the Interior
U.S. Department of State Diplomatic Reception Rooms

GEORGETOWN
Dumbarton House
Dumbarton Oaks and Gardens
Kreeger Museum
Tudor Place

DOWNTOWN
Ford's Theatre/Petersen House
International Spy Museum
Koshland Science Museum

Madame Tussauds
National Building Museum
National Geographic Museum
National Museum of Crime & Punishment
National Museum of Women in the Arts
National Portrait Gallery–Smithsonian American Art Museum
Newseum

SOUTHEAST
Anacostia Museum
Frederick Douglass National Historic Site
Kenilworth Aquatic Gardens
Washington Navy Yard

VIRGINIA SUBURBS
Gunston Hall
Mount Vernon Estate and Gardens
Old Town Alexandria
Pentagon Memorial

MARYLAND SUBURBS
NASA/Goddard Space Flight Visitors Center
National Cryptologic Museum
National Wildlife Visitor Center

Basilica of the National Shrine of the Immaculate Conception   ★★½

APPEAL BY AGE	PRESCHOOL ★	GRADE SCHOOL ★	TEENS ★
YOUNG ADULTS ★		OVER 30 ★	SENIORS ★★

Location **Fourth Street and Michigan Avenue NE, on the campus of the Catholic University of America;** Nearest Metro station **Brookland-CUA;** ☎ **202-526-8300; www.nationalshrine.com**

Type of attraction The largest Catholic church in the U.S. and one of the ten largest religious structures in the world. Admission Free. Hours November 1–March 31, daily 7 a.m.–6 p.m.; until 7 p.m. the rest of the year. Closed

Thanksgiving and Christmas. Guided tours are conducted Monday–Saturday, 9 a.m.,10 a.m., and 2 p.m.; Sunday, 1:30, 2:30, and 3:30 p.m. When to go Anytime. Special comments It's a huge cathedral—lots of marble—and it requires a lot of walking. There is a small cafeteria on the ground level. How much time to allow 1 hour.

DESCRIPTION AND COMMENTS A huge blue-and-gold onion dome lends Byzantine overtones to this massive cathedral, as does the wealth of colorful mosaics and stained glass throughout its interior. But its more formal style is not as generally accessible as the awe-inspiring National Cathedral across town.

TOURING TIPS Skip the guided tour, which stops in every one of the 70 (!) chapels. Instead, grab a map at the information desk on the ground (crypt) level and enter Memorial Hall, which is lined with chapels and houses the great organ. Then go up the stairs (or elevator) to the Upper Church.

OTHER THINGS TO DO NEARBY The Franciscan Monastery is a brisk, 20-minute walk away: continue past the Metro station on Michigan Avenue to Quincy Street, turn right, and walk about four blocks. The Pope John Paul II Cultural Center, an interactive museum open to all faiths, is nearby. Call ☎ 202-635-5400 for hours and directions. A free shuttle service to the center operates from the Brookland-CUA Metro station on weekends.

🏛️ kids Bureau of Engraving and Printing ★★★

APPEAL BY AGE	PRESCHOOL ★★	GRADE SCHOOL ★★★★	TEENS ★★★½
YOUNG ADULTS ★★★	OVER 30 ★★★½		SENIORS ★★★★

Location Raoul Wallenberg Place (formerly 15th Street) and C Street SW (2 blocks south of the Mall); Nearest Metro station **Smithsonian;** ☎ **866-874-2330 or 202-874-2330; www.moneyfactory.gov**

Type of attraction The presses that print U.S. currency and stamps (guided tour). Admission Free. Hours Monday–Friday, 10 a.m.–2 p.m. and (May–August only) 5–7 p.m.; closed on federal holidays, the week between Christmas and New Year's Day, and weekends. The ticket office, located on Raoul Wallenberg Place, opens at 8 a.m. First come, first served and tickets are usually gone by 9 a.m. No tickets are required September–February. A valid ID is required. No book bags, backpacks, or sharp objects are allowed. When to go The earlier, the better. During peak season, try to arrive by 8 a.m. (or earlier) and pick up tickets at the ticket office; they are often gone by 9 a.m. Special comments Small children may have trouble looking over the ledge and down into the press rooms below. Also be aware that when the Department of Homeland Security threat level is elevated to high, all general public tours are canceled. No food concessions on site. How much time to allow About an hour when the ticket system is in effect. In the early fall, when the line snakes out the front door and up 14th Street, figure on at least 2 hours. Count on about 15 minutes for every 100 people in line ahead of you.

DESCRIPTION AND COMMENTS This is a 35- to 45-minute guided tour through the rather cramped glass-lined corridors that go over the government's immense money and stamp printing plant. Visitors look down and gape at the printing presses that crank out the dough and at pallets of greenbacks in various stages of completion. The sign some wag hung on a press, however, says it all: "You have never been so close yet so far away." Kids love this place, so it's a tourist site families should plan on hitting, even if you're only in town for a short period. However, if you do miss out on tickets for the tour, you can still see the exhibits in the visitor center, which stays open late in summer.

TOURING TIPS Arrive early—this is one of D.C.'s most popular attractions. In early spring and summer, get to the ticket booth before 8 a.m. to avoid disappointment. The ticket office distributes about 80 tickets for every tour starting at 15-minute intervals between 9 and 10:45 a.m., and 12:30 and 2 p.m. When all tickets are gone, the ticket office closes. After picking up your tickets, come back for your tour and meet near the ticket office on Raoul Wallenberg Place, where you will be escorted into the building. You have about a 30-minute grace period if you're running late. Check out the bags of shredded money for sale in the visitor center at the end of the tour. For a VIP guided tour, contact your congressperson's office at least two months before your trip. The VIP tours are conducted at 8:15 and 8:45 a.m. and 4 and 4:45 p.m., Monday through Friday.

OTHER THINGS TO DO NEARBY As you exit the building on Raoul Wallenberg Place, the Tidal Basin is a short walk to the left: benches, tables, a lot of greenery, and the calming effect of water make it a great spot to unwind or eat lunch—or rent a paddleboat. And there's a great view of the Jefferson Memorial. Other sights close at hand are the Holocaust Memorial Museum, the Washington Monument, the new National World War II Memorial, and the seven-and-a-half-acre memorial to President Franklin D. Roosevelt. The $52-million series of gardens, sculptures, and granite walls are located between the Lincoln and Jefferson memorials along the Potomac River and the Tidal Basin.

Corcoran Gallery of Art ★★★★

APPEAL BY AGE	PRESCHOOL —	GRADE SCHOOL ★★	TEENS ★★½
YOUNG ADULTS ★★★	OVER 30 ★★★		SENIORS ★★★

Location **17th and E streets NW, a half block west of the White House;** Nearest Metro stations **Farragut West, Farragut North;** ☎ **202-639-1700 or 888-CORCORAN; www.corcoran.org**

Type of attraction A museum that primarily features American art from the colonial period to the present. Admission $10 for adults; $8 for seniors 62 and over, students, and military; free for children under 12. Hours Wednesday, Friday, Saturday, Sunday, 10 a.m.–5 p.m.; Thursday, 10 a.m.–9 p.m.; closed Mondays, Tuesdays, Christmas Day, and New Year's Day. When to go Anytime; Sunday brunch. Special comments Summer Saturdays are free. Free 45-minute tours are offered daily at noon, Thursdays at 7 p.m., and Saturdays and Sundays at 3 p.m. There is a nice café on-site. How much time to allow 2 hours.

DESCRIPTION AND COMMENTS Frank Lloyd Wright called this Beaux Arts museum "the best designed building in Washington." Inside are works by John Singer Sargent, Mary Cassatt, and Winslow Homer, among others. There's also an abundance of cutting-edge contemporary art. It's a big place with a wide range of periods and styles, so you're bound to see something you like.

TOURING TIPS Maybe it's because of the art school next door, but this museum has a distinctly serious atmosphere. (In fact, one reason that a long-planned expansion was abandoned was that many people considered the Frank Gehry–designed addition a bad and even more frivolous match.) For a delightful Sunday museum excursion, take this Smithsonian staffer's suggestion: begin with brunch in the Corcoran's stunning café, which is occasionally accompanied by gospel music from a local choir. Afterward, take a leisurely tour of the art museum and then stroll over to the Renwick Gallery for more first-class art—and, perhaps, some shopping in the Renwick's excellent museum shop. It's a great, laid-back way to spend the day, and you won't be battling the crowds besieging the mega-museums on the Mall. The Corcoran's café hours are Wednesday through Saturday 10 a.m.–3 p.m. and Sunday 10 a.m.–1 p.m. Reservations are suggested; call ☎ 202-639-1786.

OTHER THINGS TO DO NEARBY Duck into the Organization of American States and enter a rain forest: a courtyard filled with palm trees and the sound of falling water awaits you. Walk up the staircase and peek into the opulent Hall of the Americas. Then head to the nearby DAR Museum (see next profile).

Daughters of the American Revolution (DAR) Museum ★ ★ ★ ★

APPEAL BY AGE	PRESCHOOL —		GRADE SCHOOL ★	TEENS ★★★★
YOUNG ADULTS ★★		OVER 30 ★★★★		SENIORS ★★★★★

Location 1776 D Street NW, across from the Ellipse;
Nearest Metro station Farragut West; ☎ 202-628-1776; www.dar.org

Type of attraction The 33 period rooms are a cornucopia of decorative arts and antiques. Admission Free. Hours Monday–Friday, 9:30 a.m.–4 p.m.; Saturday, 9 a.m.–5 p.m.; closed on Sunday, federal government holiday weekends, and the first 2 weeks in July. When to go Anytime. Special comments Expect to do a lot of stair climbing on the tour. You can't enter the rooms, and only two or three visitors at a time can squeeze into doorways to peer inside. A must-see for lovers of antiques and decorative arts. No food concessions on site. How much time to allow 2 hours.

DESCRIPTION AND COMMENTS This Beaux Arts building, completed in 1910, is a knockout. The huge columns that grace the front of the building are solid marble; a special railroad spur was built to transport them to the building site. The DAR Museum, predictably enough, emphasizes the role of women throughout American history and includes fine examples of furniture, ceramics, glass, paintings, silver, costumes, and textiles.

It's a small museum filled with everyday items out of America's past. From the interior of a California adobe parlor of 1850, to a replica of a 1775 bedchamber in Lexington, Massachusetts, to the kitchen of a 19th-century Oklahoma farm family, the period rooms display objects in a context of time and place. Kids will get a kick out of the four-sided mousetrap that guillotines rodents, the foot-controlled toaster, and the sausage stuffer that looks like an early-19th-century version of a NordicTrack machine.

To make the museum more attractive to children accompanying parents, docents drop kids off at the Touch Area on the third floor. While their parents tour nearby period rooms, kids can play with authentic 18th- and 19th-century toys and objects, including miniature Chippendale tables and chairs, real powder horns, butter molds, candle snuffers, and flags. The museum and period rooms are sleepers that a lot of visitors to Washington overlook. But for lovers of antiques and decorative arts, the rooms provide an opportunity to view beautiful objects in authentic period settings.

TOURING TIPS Finding the entrance is a bit tough, although the DAR building itself is easy enough to find. At D and 17th (across from the Ellipse), walk about half a block down D Street; the museum-and-tour entrance is on the side of the building. During the busy spring and summer, the period-room tours can get crowded, especially on Saturday, so try to arrive before noon.

OTHER THINGS TO DO NEARBY If you have time to make a reservation in advance (tours@usa.redcross.org or ☎ 202-303-7066), decorative arts lovers should visit the national headquarters of the American Red Cross, next door on 17th Street. Though you can only visit Wednesdays and Fridays between 10 a.m. and 2 p.m., it's worth it. A grand staircase leads to the second-floor ballroom, which holds three 25-foot Tiffany stained-glass Memorial Windows, reputed to be the largest suite of Tiffany panels still in their original location (except in churches). The three, which represent the organization's three missions—Hope, Charity, and Love—were donated to the Red Cross by Union and Confederate nursing agencies, and their theme is ministry to the sick and wounded. Next door to DAR, the lobby of the Organization of American States building is a bit of a tropical paradise; around back is the Art Museum of the Americas, a small gallery featuring art from Latin America and the Caribbean.

Decatur House ★ ★ ★

APPEAL BY AGE	PRESCHOOL ★	GRADE SCHOOL ★	TEENS ★
YOUNG ADULTS ★★	OVER 30 ★★		SENIORS ★★★

Location **1610 H Street NW, on Lafayette Square;**
Nearest Metro stations **Farragut West, Farragut North;**
☎ **202-842-0920; www.decaturhouse.org**

Type of attraction One of Washington's earliest surviving important residences (guided tour). Admission Free. Hours Monday–Saturday, 10 a.m.–5 p.m.; Sunday, noon–4 p.m.; closed Thanksgiving and Christmas days. When to go

Anytime. **Special comments** An interesting yet narrow slice of early Americana; the tour involves descending a steep, curving staircase. Guided tours Friday and Saturday 10:15 a.m.–4:15 p.m., Sundays 12:15–3:15 p.m. ($5 donation). Cellphone tours available at all times. No food concessions on site. **How much time to allow** 1 hour.

DESCRIPTION AND COMMENTS Stephen Decatur was a naval war hero who defeated the Barbary pirates off the shores of Tripoli (ring a bell?) during the War of 1812. If he hadn't been killed in a duel, some say he might have been president. No doubt he built this house in 1819 with presidential aspirations in mind: it's close to the White House. The first floor is decorated in authentic Federalist style and displays Decatur's furnishings and sword. The formal parlors on the second floor reflect a later Victorian restyling. Famous statesmen who resided in the building include Henry Clay, Martin Van Buren, and Edward Livingston.

TOURING TIPS If you're on a tight schedule, this isn't the place to be blowing your time. But it's an okay rainy-afternoon alternative that gives insight into the early days of Washington.

OTHER THINGS TO DO NEARBY The Renwick Gallery is around the corner on Pennsylvania Avenue; next to it is Blair House, where foreign dignitaries stay. Decatur House faces Lafayette Park, site of frequent political demonstrations, once home to many homeless, and predictably filled with statues. Across the street is the White House.

Dumbarton House ★ ★ ★

APPEAL BY AGE	PRESCHOOL —	GRADE SCHOOL ★	TEENS ★ ★
YOUNG ADULTS ★ ★	OVER 30 ★ ★ ★		SENIORS ★ ★ ★

Location 2715 Q Street NW; No Metro access; ☎ 202-337-2288; www.dumbartonhouse.org

Type of attraction An historic Georgetown mansion that once belonged to one of George Washington's granddaughters (guided tour). **Admission** $5; students with ID free. **Hours** Tours Tuesday–Saturday, 11 a.m., 12 p.m., and 1 p.m. Group tours of 10 or more by reservation only. **Special comments** Wheelchair accessible. No food concessions on site. **How much time to allow** 1 hour.

DESCRIPTION AND COMMENTS This turn-of-the-19th-century Georgetown mansion is not only a particularly fine example of early Federal architecture, it originally had an unimpeded view of the President's House (as the White House was then known) and of its burning by British forces in 1814. It belonged to a high-level Cabinet member, and First Lady Dolley Madison, having rescued Gilbert Stuart's portrait of George Washington and other papers, stopped here to await word from her husband before evacuating across the Potomac to Virginia. Among exhibits are one of only five known copies of the first printing of the 1777 Articles of Confederation, a 100-piece dining set belonging to Martha Washington's granddaughter Eliza, a George III sofa and chairs believed to have come from the Monroe White House, two Charles Willson Peale paintings, and an extraordinary gentleman's washstand with shaving mirror, bowl, bidet, and hidden chamber pot.

TOURING TIPS The house opens 15 minutes before each tour, but there is a smallish formal garden behind and alongside the museum. Strollers are not allowed, and staff recommends kids be at least age 6 for the tour.

OTHER THINGS TO DO NEARBY An even finer mansion with more elaborate gardens and exhibits is Tudor Place, about four blocks away (see profile on page 230). A much simpler historic structure, the 1765 Old Stone House and its garden is at 3051 M Street NW in the heart of Georgetown. Mt. Zion United Methodist Church (1334 29th Street NW; ☎ 202-234-0148) was built in 1816 and served as a stop on the Underground Railroad in the years before and during the Civil War; open 10 a.m.–2 p.m., but you must call ahead for group tour reservations.

Dumbarton Oaks and Gardens ★★★★

APPEAL BY AGE	PRESCHOOL —	GRADE SCHOOL ★	TEENS ★★★
YOUNG ADULTS ★★★★	OVER 30 ★★★★		SENIORS ★★★★

Location 1703 32nd Street NW, between R and S streets, in Georgetown; No Metro access; ☎ 202-339-6400; www.doaks.org

Type of attraction A mansion/museum and a beautiful terraced garden. **Admission** $1 donation suggested for adults for the museum; $8 fee for adults, $5 for seniors and children for the gardens March 15–October; free admission for the rest of the year. **Hours** Museum hours are mid-March through mid-December, Tuesday–Friday, 10 a.m.–4 p.m., Saturday and Sunday, 11 a.m.–3 p.m. The garden is open (weather permitting) November–March 14, Tuesday–Sunday, 2–5 p.m. and until 6 p.m. the rest of the year. Guided tours Tuesdays and Sundays at 11 a.m., noon, and 1 p.m. Both the museum and gardens are closed on federal holidays, Christmas Eve, and Mondays. The gardens area is also closed during inclement weather. **When to go** Anytime. **Special comments** Don't be put off by the hushed surroundings—this is one of the best museums in Washington, intimate and gorgeous. No food concessions on site, and picnics are not allowed. **How much time to allow** 2 hours.

DESCRIPTION AND COMMENTS Most people associate Dumbarton Oaks with the conference held here in 1944 that led to the formation of the United Nations. Today, however, it's a research center for Byzantine and pre-Columbian studies owned by Harvard University. The Byzantine collection is one of the world's finest, featuring bronzes, ivories, and jewelry. The exquisite pre-Columbian art collection is housed in eight interconnected, circular glass pavilions lit by natural light. It's a knockout of a museum. Dumbarton Oaks Gardens is located around the corner on R Street. The terraced ten-acre garden is rated one of the top gardens in the United States. It features an orangery, a rose garden, wisteria-covered arbors and, in the fall, a blazing backdrop of trees turning orange, yellow, and red—not to mention elaborate ironwork, a swimming pool, amphitheater, and tennis court (now a pebble garden). Dumbarton Oaks isn't the kind of museum with much appeal to small children, and some adults may not find much of interest in the collection due to its narrow focus. But combined with the adjacent gardens, it's a worthwhile place to visit when in Georgetown.

TOURING TIPS Because Dumbarton Oaks doesn't open its massive doors until 2 p.m., combine your visit with a morning trip to Georgetown. If it's raining the day you plan to visit, try to rearrange your schedule so you can come on a nice day; the gardens are terrific. Or make reservations to get into Tudor Place, the 1805 home of Martha Washington's granddaughter at 1644 31st Street NW; ☎ 202-965-0400.

OTHER THINGS TO DO NEARBY Oak Hill Cemetery at 30th and R streets boasts a gothic revival chapel designed by James Renwick and fabulous 19th-century funeral sculptures. (Mt. Zion Cemetery and Female Union Band Cemetery at 27th and O streets are parts of a free black internment site going back to 1842.) Also look into Dumbarton House, a showcase of Federal-period architecture, furniture, and decorative arts.

Folger Shakespeare Library ★★★

APPEAL BY AGE	PRESCHOOL ★	GRADE SCHOOL ★	TEENS ★★
YOUNG ADULTS ★★	OVER 30 ★★		SENIORS ★★★

Location 201 East Capitol Street SE; Nearest Metro stations Capitol South, Union Station; ☎ **202-544-4600; www.folger.edu**

Type of attraction A museum and library dedicated to the Bard. **Admission** Free. **Hours** Monday–Saturday, 10 a.m.–5 p.m.; tours at 11 a.m. and 3 p.m. Monday–Friday, and 11 a.m. and 1 p.m. on Saturday; closed on federal holidays. The Reading Room is open Monday–Friday, 8:45 a.m.–4:45 p.m., and Saturday, 9 a.m.–noon and 1–4:30 p.m. Garden is open daily April–October. Garden tours third Saturdays, April–October, 10 a.m. and 11 a.m.; call ☎ 202-675-0395 for group tours. **When to go** Anytime. **Special comments** Parts of the library are available only to accredited scholars. **How much time to allow** 1 hour.

DESCRIPTION AND COMMENTS The Folger Shakespeare Library is the world's largest collection of Shakespeare's printed works, as well as a vast array of other rare Renaissance books and manuscripts—one of its treasures, a copy of the First Folio, published in 1616, is on permanent display at the east end, open to the title page. (The Folger owns 79 copies of the First Folio, about a third of those in existence.) Stroll the Great Hall featuring hand-carved, oak-paneled walls and priceless displays from the museum's collection. You may also visit the three-tiered Elizabethan Theatre, with walls of timber and plaster and carved oak columns, where three productions are mounted each season. The Bard's birthday is celebrated with a popular open house with performances, kids' activities, and stage combat workshops each year on the Saturday closest to April 23.

TOURING TIPS Guided tours of the building, exhibits, and the Elizabethan garden are conducted daily at 11 a.m. Special tours of the garden, featuring herbs and flowers grown in Shakespeare's time, are held every third Saturday from April through October. The Folger still hosts concerts, readings, and some theatrical performances, most recently including some collaborations with the Shakespeare Theatre Company downtown. At the west end of the building, a statue of Puck from *A Midsummer Night's Dream* genially presides over a fountain and pool.

OTHER THINGS TO DO NEARBY The Folger is directly behind the Library of

Congress, which sits in front of the U.S. Capitol. The Supreme Court is less than a block away.

Ford's Theatre/Petersen House ★★★

APPEAL BY AGE	PRESCHOOL ★	GRADE SCHOOL ★★	TEENS ★★
YOUNG ADULTS ★★★		OVER 30 ★★★	SENIORS ★★★

Location 511 Tenth Street NW; Nearest Metro station Metro Center, 11th Street exit; ☎ 202-426-6924; www.fords.org.

Type of attraction The restored theater where Abraham Lincoln was shot, and the house across the street, where he died. **Admission** Free, but tickets required (**www.ticketmaster.com** or ☎ 800-397-SEAT). **Hours** Daily, 9 a.m.–4:30 p.m. (last entrance at 4); Peterson House open 9:30 a.m.–5:30 p.m. (last entrance at 5); both closed Christmas Day. **When to go** Anytime. **Special comments** The theater (but not the museum) is closed to visitors on Thursday and Sunday afternoons, when matinees are in progress. It may also be closed on other afternoons when rehearsals are in progress. No food concession on site. **How much time to allow** 1 hour, plus a 30-minute introduction.

DESCRIPTION AND COMMENTS After a thorough renovation, the newly reopened theater has been focusing on Lincoln's bicentennial with programs, performances, and an expanded collection of Lincolniana. Once a Baptist church, and later an unlucky federal office building (it burned twice), it now boasts new air-conditioning, accessible restrooms, a gift shop, concessions, up-to-date audio and video, and, at long last, elevators. The display includes a replica of the blood-spattered overcoat Lincoln was wearing when he was assassinated on April 4, 1865 (ironically, it was Good Friday), the derringer John Wilkes Booth used to kill him, and other memorabilia. Petersen House across the street, where the dying president was carried, has more exhibits. (Though also undergoing renovation, it was scheduled to reopen in spring of 2011.) The adjoining building is being turned into additional exhibition space.

TOURING TIPS If you're sensitive, keep an eye on Lincoln's black-draped box; many people report seeing his ghost. (Not only his, in fact; in 1893, the interior of the building, which was then being used by the government for storage and office space, collapsed, killing scores of clerks.) An audio tour is available for $5.

OTHER THINGS TO DO NEARBY The International Spy Museum, the National Portrait Gallery, the American Art Museum, and Madame Tussauds are all close.

Franciscan Monastery and Gardens ★★

APPEAL BY AGE	PRESCHOOL —	GRADE SCHOOL ★★★	TEENS ★★
YOUNG ADULTS ★★		OVER 30 ★★	SENIORS ★★

Location 1400 Quincy Street NE; Nearest Metro station Brookland-CUA; ☎ 202-526-6800; www.myfranciscan.org

Type of attraction A working monastery (guided tour). **Admission** Free. **Hours** Grounds open daily, 10 a.m.–5 p.m. Guided tours Monday–Saturday, 10 a.m.,

11 a.m., 1 p.m., 2 p.m., and 3 p.m.; Sunday, 1 p.m., 2 p.m., and 3 p.m. **When to go** Anytime. **Special comments** The tour (also available in Spanish) involves negotiating many narrow, steep stairs and low, dark passageways. A limited number of wheelchairs are available for touring the church and upper grounds. Beautiful architecture, peaceful grounds—and kind of spooky. **How much time to allow** 1 hour.

DESCRIPTION AND COMMENTS Built around 1900 and recently restored, this monastery has everything you'd expect: quiet, contemplative formal gardens; a beautiful church modeled after the Hagia Sophia in Istanbul; and grounds dotted with replicas of shrines and chapels found in the Holy Land. What's really unusual is the sanitized crypt beneath the church, which is more Hollywood than Holy Land. (You almost expect to run into Victor Mature wearing a toga.) It's a replica of the catacombs under Rome and is positively—if inauthentically—ghoulish. As you pass open (but phony) grave sites in the walls, the guide narrates hair-raising stories of Christian martyrs eaten by lions, speared, stoned to death, beheaded, and burned at the stake. Shudder. (Kids love this.)

TOURING TIPS If you're driving, parking is easy. Two parking lots are located across from the monastery on 14th Street. If you're visiting Washington in the spring, the beautiful gardens alone are worth the trip.

OTHER THINGS TO DO NEARBY The lovely Basilica of the National Shrine of the Immaculate Conception is nearby, as is the small Pope John Paul II Cultural Center.

Franklin Delano Roosevelt Memorial ★★★★

| APPEAL BY AGE | PRESCHOOL ★★★ | GRADE SCHOOL ★★★ | TEENS ★★★ |
| YOUNG ADULTS ★★★ | OVER 30 ★★★★ | | SENIORS ★★★★ |

Location **West Potomac Park, between the Tidal Basin and the Potomac River;** Nearest Metro stations **Smithsonian (Independence Avenue exit), a 30-minute walk; also Foggy Bottom–GWU and Arlington Cemetery (across Memorial Bridge in Virginia); ☎ 202-426-6841; www.nps.gov/fdrm**

Type of attraction A 7½-acre, open-air memorial to the 32nd president of the United States. **Admission** Free. **Hours** Staffed daily, 9:30 a.m.–11:30 p.m., except on Christmas Day. **When to go** Anytime, except during inclement weather; the FDR Memorial is not enclosed. It's especially nice in cherry blossom season. **Special comments** Folks old enough to have voted for FDR and disabled people may find it difficult to visit the memorial; nearby parking is scarce and the walk from the nearest Metro station is about a mile. One hundred and sixty unmetered parking spaces are located along Ohio Drive SW eastbound, and three lots with a total of 247 spaces are in East Potomac Park under the 14th Street bridges. Five handicapped spaces and one van space are located at the main entrance to the memorial on West Basin Drive. Except at off-peak times (before noon on weekdays and evenings), competition for the spaces is fierce. Other options for reaching the memorial include cabs and a water taxi from across the Tidal Basin. Washington's newest presidential memorial successfully blends history, texture, drama, nostalgia, landscaping, and flowing water. The result is a dramatic and inspiring memorial to America's best-loved 20th-century leader. **How much time to allow** 30 minutes to 1 hour.

DESCRIPTION AND COMMENTS Unlike the nearby imposing marble edifices to Lincoln and Jefferson, the $52-million FDR Memorial on the Tidal Basin tells a story: four open-air, interconnected "rooms" ("enclaves" or "tableaus" might be better words) represent each of Roosevelt's four terms, his words are carved on granite walls, bronze images depict the alphabet-soup of programs and agencies he created to help millions of Americans devastated by the Depression, and statues depict the average citizens whose lives he touched. One shows a man listening intently to a radio, evoking the days before television—and a time when FDR's strong and vibrant voice gave hope to Americans in his "fireside chats."

Roosevelt himself is represented in the third room in a larger-than-life bronze statue. The president is seated, his body wrapped in a cape, his face lined with weariness as he approaches the final year of his life. His Scottish terrier Fala is at his feet. The fourth room features a statue of Eleanor Roosevelt, widely regarded as America's greatest First Lady for her service as a delegate to the United Nations and as a champion for human rights. This is the only memorial to honor a presidential wife.

Many elements work in harmony to make the memorial a success. Textures of South Dakota granite, brick, rough wood, and falling water combine with ornamental plantings and shade trees to create the ambience of a secluded garden rather than an imposing structure. This is not a "hands-off" memorial: the slightly-larger-than-life figures of FDR and Mrs. Roosevelt, as well as statues of five men in an urban bread line and a rural couple outside a barn door, are placed at ground level. Visitors can easily drape an arm around the first lady, sit in Franklin's lap as he delivers a fireside chat, or join the men in line for a souvenir snapshot. The memorial's many waterfalls (FDR considered himself a Navy man) attract splashers with stepping stones while kids enjoy climbing on giant, toppled granite blocks inscribed with the words "I hate war."

TOURING TIPS While you can enter the memorial from either end, try to start your tour at the official entrance (the one on the Lincoln Memorial side) so you can stroll through the outside rooms in chronological order. Restrooms are located at both entrances. No food concessions on site (except during Cherry Blossom Festival, when there are tents around the other side of the Tidal Basin), but the memorial is a nice spot for a picnic by the water, so bring a lunch.

OTHER THINGS TO DO NEARBY The Lincoln, Korean War, and Jefferson memorials are relatively close; just wear comfortable walking shoes and keep in mind that distances along the Tidal Basin and Mall can be deceiving. The Bureau of Engraving and Printing and the Holocaust Memorial Museum are located on Raoul Wallenberg Place, on the east side of the Tidal Basin just beyond the Jefferson Memorial. During warm weather, paddleboats are available for rent on the east side of the Tidal Basin, and a water taxi service shuttles tourists along the Potomac River from 11 a.m. to 6 p.m. daily.

Frederick Douglass National Historic Site ★★★

APPEAL BY AGE	PRESCHOOL ★	GRADE SCHOOL ★★	TEENS ★★★
YOUNG ADULTS ★★★	OVER 30 ★★★		SENIORS ★★★

Location 1411 W Street SE, in Anacostia; Nearest Metro station Anacostia;
☎ 202-426-5961 or 800-365-2267 for reservations; www.nps.gov/frdo

Type of attraction Cedar Hill, the preserved Victorian home of abolitionist, statesman, and orator Frederick Douglass (guided tour by reservation only). **Admission** $1.50 per person; school groups $5. **Hours** October 16–April 15, daily, 9 a.m.–4:30 p.m.; April 16–October 15, daily, 9 a.m.–5 p.m. Tours are hourly, except noon. Closed Thanksgiving, Christmas, and New Year's days. **When to go** Anytime. While not required, it's a good idea to call and make reservations for the house tour. **Special comments** No food concessions on site. **How much time to allow** 1 hour.

DESCRIPTION AND COMMENTS This lovely Victorian home on a hill overlooking Washington remains much as it was in Douglass's time. The former slave—who, among other achievements, became U.S. ambassador to Haiti—spent the final 18 years of his life in this house. Douglass lived here when he wrote the third volume of his autobiography, *Life and Times of Frederick Douglass.* For people interested in the history of the civil rights movement and genteel life in the late 1800s, Cedar Hill is a find. National Park Service guides provide a detailed commentary on Douglass's life and times. Look for Douglass's barbells on the floor next to his bed.

A late-afternoon visit is almost like stepping back into the 19th century because the house is preserved as it was when Douglass died in 1895. There's no electricity, and the gathering shadows in the house evoke the past. Be sure to see "The Growlery," a small, one-room structure behind the main house that Douglass declared off-limits to the household so he could work alone.

TOURING TIPS From the Anacostia Metro station, take the B2 bus toward Mt. Ranier.

OTHER THINGS TO DO NEARBY The Anacostia Community Museum is a short drive or cab ride away.

Freer Gallery of Art (*a Smithsonian museum*)   ★★★★★

APPEAL BY AGE	PRESCHOOL ★	GRADE SCHOOL ★★	TEENS ★★★
YOUNG ADULTS ★★★	OVER 30 ★★★★		SENIORS ★★★★

Location Jefferson Drive at 12th Street SW, on the Mall; Nearest
Metro station Smithsonian; ☎ 202-633-1000 or 202-357-1729 (TDD);
www.asia.si.edu

Type of attraction A museum featuring Asian and American art. **Admission** Free. **Hours** Daily, 10 a.m.–5:30 p.m.; closed Christmas Day. Free guided tours daily (except Wednesday) at 11 a.m. **When to go** Anytime. **Special comments** Gorgeous art on a human scale in a setting that's not overwhelming. No food concessions on site. **How much time to allow** 1–2 hours.

DESCRIPTION AND COMMENTS Well-proportioned spaces, galleries illuminated by natural light, and quiet serenity are the hallmarks of this landmark on the Mall, with its unusual blend of American paintings (including the world's most important collection of works by James McNeill Whistler) and Asian paintings, sculpture, porcelains, scrolls, and richly embellished household items. Charles Lang Freer, the wealthy 19th-century industrialist who bequeathed this collection to the Smithsonian, saw similarities of color and surface texture in the diverse assemblage. Surrender to the gallery's tranquility and you may too.

TOURING TIPS An underground link to the nearby Arthur M. Sackler Gallery creates a public exhibition space, as well as convenient passage between the two museums. Don't miss the Peacock Room, designed by James McNeill Whistler; a local favorite, it's widely considered to be the most important 19th-century interior in an American museum. Once the dining room of a Liverpool shipping magnate, it was installed in the Freer Gallery after Freer's death. The ornate room was painted by Whistler to house a collection of blue and white Chinese porcelains. Following a restoration that removed decades of dirt and grime, the room has been restored to its original splendor. Free walk-in tours of the Freer are available daily.

OTHER THINGS TO DO NEARBY The Sackler Gallery, the National Museum of African Art, and the Enid A. Haupt Garden are within a few steps of the Freer Gallery. Directly across the Mall are the National Museum of American History and the National Museum of Natural History. Walk up the Mall toward the Capitol to reach the Arts and Industries Building (closed for renovation), the Hirshhorn Museum, and the National Air and Space Museum.

Gunston Hall ★★★

APPEAL BY AGE	PRESCHOOL ★½	GRADE SCHOOL ★★	TEENS ★★
YOUNG ADULTS ★★½	OVER 30 ★★★		SENIORS ★★★

10709 Gunston Road, Mason Neck, VA (just off I-95 and Route 1); No Metro access; ☎ 703-550-9220; www.gunstonhall.org

Type of attraction Historic home of George Mason, 20 minutes south of Washington. **Admission** $9 adults, $5 ages 6–18, and $8 seniors 60+. **Hours** Daily, 9:30 a.m.–5 p.m., except Thanksgiving, Christmas, and New Year's days; 45-minute guided house tours every half hour. Grounds close at 6 p.m. **When to go** During the week if possible. Occasionally the museum also hosts concerts. **Special comments** An underrated destination, the home is of interest to architecture and gardening fans as well as history buffs. No food concessions on site. **How much time to allow** 2 hours.

DESCRIPTION AND COMMENTS Mason is a fascinating character whose role, like those of several other early activists, has only in recent years been fully appreciated. He was highly influential in the years leading up to the American Revolution: he cowrote, with George Washington, the protest instruments later known as the Virginia Association and the Fairfax County Resolutions, and many of the provisions he constructed for the Virginia Declaration of Rights were adopted by Thomas Jefferson for the Declaration of Independence, including these: "that all men are born equally free and independent, and have certain inherent natural Rights . . . among which are the Enjoyment of Life and Liberty, with the Means of acquiring and possessing Property, and pursuing and obtaining Happiness and Safety." After the revolution, however, as a delegate to the Constitutional Convention, Mason came to feel that the Constitution as drafted was deeply flawed. He urged the inclusion of a Bill of Rights, opposed the extension of slave importation, and disagreed on various fine points (such as majority versus two-thirds votes). Ultimately, despite the resulting vilification, he was unable to bring himself to put aside his principles and sign.

The complex includes Mason's house, a first-class example of Georgian Colonial architecture constructed 1755–1760 and replete with elaborate interior carvings; gardens and grounds where archaeological programs are uncovering slave quarters, fences, and other elements; outbuildings such as a kitchen, dairy, laundry, and smokehouse; and a variety of farm animals. (It's the animals, and the occasional chance to "dig in" to the older ruins, that really get kids involved.) The museum shop has a nice collection of handblown glass, hand-turned wooden accessories from the plantation's 200-year-old boxwoods, scented soaps, silver and jewelry, and books.

TOURING TIPS Check the museum's website, which often has discount admission coupons.

OTHER THINGS TO DO NEARBY Mount Vernon is only about 12 miles away, with Woodlawn Plantation and the Pope-Leighey House only a few miles farther, so history buffs could make a day of it.

Hillwood Estate Museum and Gardens ★★★★★

APPEAL BY AGE	PRESCHOOL —	GRADE SCHOOL —	TEENS ★★
YOUNG ADULTS ★★★	OVER 30 ★★★★★		SENIORS ★★★★★

Location 4155 Linnean Avenue NW; Nearest Metro station **Van Ness–UDC (20-minute walk); ☎ 202-686-8500 or 877-HILLWOOD; ☎ 202-686-5807 for reservations; www.hillwoodmuseum.org**

Type of attraction A mansion housing fabulous art treasures and formal gardens on a 25-acre estate. **Admission** $12 for the house tour; $10 seniors 65+, $5 children ages 6–18, and $7 for full-time students; no children under age 6 permitted. **Reservations** required. **Hours** Tuesday–Saturday, 10 a.m.–5 p.m.; open select Sundays 1–5 p.m. Closed Mondays, the month of January, and most federal holidays. **When to go** Spring is the most beautiful season to tour the house and gardens. But these are popular destinations for garden clubs, so you must secure reservations well in advance. Because of Hillwood's wooded location in Rock Creek Park, it's always five degrees cooler here in D.C.'s hot and humid summers. **Special comments** Self-guided audio tours are available. A docent-led tour is offered Tuesday–Saturday at 11:30 a.m. and 1:30 p.m., and some Sundays at 1:30 p.m.; a docent-led garden tour is offered April 8–June 21, Tuesday through Saturday, at 10:30 a.m. and 12:30 p.m.; specify your preference when making reservations. A children's audio tour is also available ($5). Nice café on site. **How much time to allow** 2–3 hours. The guided tour itself is over an hour but doesn't include the formal gardens and auxiliary buildings.

DESCRIPTION AND COMMENTS   She was a girl from Michigan who inherited two things from her father: good taste and General Foods. That, in a nutshell, is the story of Marjorie Merriweather Post, who bought this Rock Creek Park estate in 1955. She remodeled the mansion and filled it with exquisite 18th- and 19th-century French and Russian decorative art. *Fabulous* is the word required to describe the collection of Imperial Russian objects on display. Mrs. Post was married to the U.S. ambassador to Russia in the 1930s—a time when the communists were unloading decadent pre-Revolution art at bargain prices. Mrs. Post bought literally warehouseloads of stuff: jewels, dinner plates commissioned by Catherine the Great, Easter eggs by Carl Fabergé, and chalices and icons. She then had the loot loaded onto her yacht, *Sea Cloud* (then the largest private ship in the world), for shipment home. The very best of the booty is on display here. The tour provides a glimpse into Mrs. Post's lavish lifestyle.

TOURING TIPS   Call at least two months in advance for a spring tour, although you may luck into a cancellation by calling a day or two before your planned visit. Children under age 6 are not admitted on the tour. Plan your visit so that you have enough time to stroll the gardens. The estate also has a café that serves lunch and tea, a gift shop, and a greenhouse you can tour. A "Behind the Scenes" tour is offered Wednesdays at 3 p.m., June through March (except the first Wednesday of the month; $10 per person). Visitors get a glimpse of Hillwood as it was run when Mrs. Post lived here, by touring the fallout shelter, the massage room, the silver-polishing room, and other places not seen on the regular house tour.

OTHER THINGS TO DO NEARBY   Intelsat, near the Van Ness–UDC Metro station, looks like a building out of the late 21st century. That's no surprise, since the firm is an international conglomeration that produces satellites. The lobby features models and prototypes of its products hanging from the ceiling.

Hirshhorn Museum and Sculpture Garden   ★ ★ ★ ★ ★
(*a Smithsonian museum*)

APPEAL BY AGE	PRESCHOOL ★	GRADE SCHOOL ★ ★	TEENS ★ ★ ★
YOUNG ADULTS ★ ★ ★ ★	OVER 30 ★ ★ ★ ★ ★		SENIORS ★ ★ ★ ★ ★

**Location Seventh Street and Independence Avenue SW, on the Mall;
Nearest Metro stations Smithsonian, L'Enfant Plaza; ☎ 202-633-4674;
hirshhorn.si.edu**

Type of attraction A museum of modern art (self-guided tour). **Admission** Free. **Hours** Daily, 10 a.m.–5:30 p.m.; closed Christmas Day. Sculpture Garden open from 7:30 a.m. until dusk daily. **When to go** Anytime. **Special comments** The Hirshhorn is a lot of people's favorite art museum on the Mall; an outrageous collection of 20th-century art—don't miss it. No food concessions on site. **How much time to allow** 2 hours.

DESCRIPTION AND COMMENTS The art found inside is often as bizarre as the circular building that houses it. Works by modern masters such as Auguste Rodin, Winslow Homer, Mary Cassatt, and Henry Moore line the easy-to-walk galleries. The outdoor sculpture garden (set below Mall level) contains works by Rodin, Giacometti, and Alexander Calder, among many others. The sculpture offers a refreshing contrast to the marble palaces that line the Mall. If you visit only one modern-art gallery while in D.C., make it the Hirshhorn.

Students of modern architecture may also be interested to know that an addition has been proposed to Gordon Bunshaft's 1974 blank-disk design—a temporary exhibit space that would sit atop the museum like a blue egg over the courtyard. (Conceptual drawings make it look like a Pop Art pun on the diner special.) A similar, smaller blue egg will bulge out at ground level. If the plan goes forward, they will be temporary installations, scheduled for May and October. Also check the schedule of new films.

TOURING TIPS Group tours are offered between 10:30 a.m. and noon, but you must schedule in advance. Visit their website for scheduling info. From noon to 4 p.m., docents conduct impromptu 30-minute tours; visit the information desk to get started. The museum's outdoor café is open for lunch during the summer only.

OTHER THINGS TO DO NEARBY This is at the heart of the Mall; museums to the left, museums to the right, museums straight ahead. . . .

House of the Temple ★★

APPEAL BY AGE		PRESCHOOL —	GRADE SCHOOL ★	TEENS ★
YOUNG ADULTS ★		OVER 30 ★		SENIORS ★

Location **1733 16th Street NW; Nearest Metro station Dupont Circle;**
☎ **202-232-3579; www.scottishrite.org**

Type of attraction A Masonic temple modeled after one of the Seven Wonders of the World (guided tour). **Admission** Adults $7.33, seniors and students with ID $3.33, under 18 and military with ID free. **Hours** Guided tours Monday–Thursday, 10 a.m.–4 p.m.; abbreviated tours 4–4:30 p.m.; closed New Year's Day, Martin Luther King Day, Thanksgiving Day and the Friday after, Christmas, and Inauguration Day. *Note:* Extensive renovations will close the temple Fridays, Saturdays, and Sundays through 2011. **When to go** Anytime. **Special comments** No food concessions on site. A very few areas are not wheelchair- or stroller-accessible. Some wheelchairs available on site. **How much time to allow** 2 hours.

DESCRIPTION AND COMMENTS Even before Dan (*The Lost Symbol*) Brown came to town, this massive neoclassical edifice—formally known as the Home of the Supreme Council, 33°, Ancient and Accepted Scottish Rite of Freemasonry, Southern Jurisdiction, Washington D.C., U.S.A.—was widely considered a curiosity, in the best sense. It was designed by John Russell Pope, architect of the Jefferson Memorial, in imitation of the tomb of Mausolus at Halicarnassus, from which the very work "mausoleum" is derived, which should tell you something. It won Pope some very prestigious awards. The massive sphinxes that flank the entrance are a hint at the scale; the walls are 8 feet thick; the exterior is surrounded by 33 massive columns that support a magnificent pyramidal roof; and, inside, the Temple Room features a soaring 100-foot ceiling and 1,000-pipe organ. The J. Edgar Hoover Law Enforcement Room is a shrine to the Mason and lifelong FBI chief. This is also home to the largest collection of Scots poet (and Freemason) Robert Burns memorabilia.

TOURING TIPS The tour can be quite detailed, so if you're not seriously interested or are tight on time, you may want to go late in the afternoon for an abbreviated tour.

OTHER THINGS TO DO NEARBY The House of the Temple is just east of Dupont Circle, where you'll find the Phillips Collection. Six blocks west on S Street are the Textile Museum and the Woodrow Wilson House.

kids International Spy Museum ★★½

APPEAL BY AGE	PRESCHOOL ★	GRADE SCHOOL ★★★	TEENS ★★★
YOUNG ADULTS ★★★	OVER 30 ★★★		SENIORS ★★★★

Location 800 F Street NW; Nearest Metro station Gallery Place–Chinatown; ☎ 866-779-6873 or 202-393-7798; www.spymuseum.org

Type of attraction The history and gadgetry of espionage housed in one of Washington's newest museums (self-guided tour). Admission $18 for adults ages 12–64; $17 for seniors 65+, active-duty military, and community and college students; $15 for children ages 5–11. Note: discounted tickets available online. Hours Hours change frequently, so check the website before you go; closed Thanksgiving, Christmas, and New Year's days. When to go After the spook museum opened in the summer of 2002, lines stretched around the block throughout the day, signaling a minimum wait in line of 45 minutes (from the middle of the block on Ninth Street) or longer. Either arrive at least a half hour before 9 a.m. or plan to visit around 5 p.m. weekdays, when there's usually no wait. Special comments Spycraft meets Austin Powers: the museum is slick, manipulative, and dodges some important moral questions (and historical failures) of U.S. intelligence operations. Otherwise, it's fun in a non-challenging way (located in a city full of world-class museums, most of them free). There's a long, steep flight of stairs to descend about halfway through the museum. Café on site. How much time to allow 90 minutes to 2 hours.

DESCRIPTION AND COMMENTS CIA headquarters across the Potomac in Langley isn't offering tours, but this $40-million privately owned museum has made a killing purporting to expose the secret world of intelligence. (Actually, The National Cryptological Museum, profiled on pages 203–204, is free, and "realer.") More than 400 artifacts are on display, dating from Biblical times to the modern age of terror. What you'll see: tools of the trade such as a lipstick pistol developed by the KGB, an Enigma cipher machine used by the Allies to break German secret codes during World War II, an Aston Martin DB 5 sports car decked out like the one used by James Bond in *Goldfinger,* and tributes to celebrity spies such as dancer Josephine Baker (who worked for the French resistance) and late TV chef Julia Child (who worked for the OSS). What you won't see: any mention of spectacular failures of U.S. intelligence, including how the CIA, NSA, DIA, and other alphabet-soup spy agencies missed the fall of the Soviet Union and the Shah of Iran or helped overthrow elected governments around the world. Alas, the museum's us-versus-them mentality spares visitors from the moral ambiguity of intelligence gathering. To get that insight, skip the museum and curl up with a novel by John le Carré (a former spy).

TOURING TIPS This is one of those museums where visitors are herded into an elevator, taken to the second floor, and everyone negotiates their way through narrow corridors—making it difficult to linger or backtrack against the human current. Keep that in mind as you tour.

OTHER THINGS TO DO NEARBY The National Portrait Gallery and the Smithsonian American Art Museum are across the street; the Museum of Crime and Punishment, Madame Tussauds, and Ford's Theatre/Petersen House (where Lincoln was assassinated and died) are nearby.

Islamic Center   ★★

APPEAL BY AGE	PRESCHOOL ★	GRADE SCHOOL ★★	TEENS ★★
YOUNG ADULTS ★★★		OVER 30 ★★	SENIORS ★★

Location **2551 Massachusetts Avenue NW;**
Nearest Metro station **Dupont Circle;** ☎ **202-332-8343**

Type of attraction A mosque (self-guided tour). **Admission** Free. **Hours** Daily, 10 a.m.–5 p.m. **When to go** Anytime. **Special comments** The mosque enforces a strict dress code. Visitors must remove their shoes to go inside, and no shorts or short dresses are allowed. Women must cover their heads and wear long-sleeved clothing. **How much time to allow** 15 minutes.

DESCRIPTION AND COMMENTS A brilliant white building and slender minaret mark this unusual sight on Embassy Row. Visitors must remove their shoes before stepping inside to see the Persian carpets, elegantly embellished columns, decorated arches, tiled walls, and huge bronze chandelier. The small bookstore next to the mosque is filled with Arabic texts and translations of the Koran. Those with a strong interest in the Middle East should call a week in advance for the one-hour guided tour.

TOURING TIPS Make this small, exotic building a part of a walk down Embassy Row.

OTHER THINGS TO DO NEARBY The Textile Museum and the Woodrow Wilson House are nearby; the opulent Anderson House and Phillips Collection are not much farther.

Jefferson Memorial   ★★★

APPEAL BY AGE	PRESCHOOL ★	GRADE SCHOOL ★★	TEENS ★★★
YOUNG ADULTS ★★★		OVER 30 ★★★	SENIORS ★★★

Location **Across the Tidal Basin from the Washington Monument;**
Nearest Metro stations **L'Enfant Plaza, Smithsonian;** ☎ **202-426-6841;**
www.nps.gov/thje

Type of attraction A classical-style monument to the author of the Declaration of Independence and the third U.S. president (self-guided tour). **Admission** Free.

Hours Always open; staffed 9:30 a.m.–11:30 p.m., except on Christmas Day. **When to go** For the best views, go at night or when the cherry trees along the Tidal Basin are in bloom. **Special comments** The view from the steps and across the Tidal Basin is one of the best in Washington. A favorite at night, but not convenient. **How much time to allow** 30 minutes.

DESCRIPTION AND COMMENTS The neoclassical, open-air design of this monument reflects Jefferson's taste in architecture. It's usually less crowded than the monuments on the Mall.

TOURING TIPS Park interpreters staffing the monument frequently give talks and can answer questions about Jefferson and the monument. Visitors can walk to the memorial along the rim of the Tidal Basin from Independence Avenue or along 14th Street SW.

OTHER THINGS TO DO NEARBY The Bureau of Engraving and Printing and the Holocaust Memorial Museum are both on 14th Street. The FDR Memorial is just to the north along the Tidal Basin, and the Hains Point sports complex is to the south.

John F. Kennedy Center for the Performing Arts ★★

APPEAL BY AGE	PRESCHOOL ★	GRADE SCHOOL ★	TEENS ★
YOUNG ADULTS ★★	OVER 30 ★★★		SENIORS ★★★

Location New Hampshire Avenue NW and F Street;
Nearest Metro station Foggy Bottom–GWU; ☎ 202-467-4600 or
800-444-1324 (TTY); www.kennedy-center.org

Type of attraction Both presidential memorial and D.C.'s performing-arts headquarters (guided tour for groups only). **Admission** Free. **Hours** Daily, 10 a.m.– 9 p.m. **When to go** Free tours begin every 15 minutes; Monday–Friday, 10 a.m.– 5 p.m.; Saturday and Sunday, 10 a.m.–1 p.m. There are free concerts every evening at 6 in the Grand Foyer. **Special comments** Sometimes-intriguing art (exhibits change frequently), a huge building, and a great view (without a show ticket). The leisurely tour lasts about 45 minutes but is easy on the feet, as the center is well carpeted. **How much time to allow** 1 hour.

DESCRIPTION AND COMMENTS The white rectilinear Kennedy Center facility boasts four major stages, a film theater, and a sumptuous interior shimmering with crystal, mirrors, and deep-red carpets. The Grand Foyer is longer than two football fields. Nations from around the world contributed art and artifacts on display in halls and foyers, such as African art, Beame porcelain, tapestries, and sculptures. If rehearsals aren't in progress, the tour includes peeks inside the intimate Eisenhower Theater, the Opera House (featuring a spectacular chandelier), and the Concert Hall. Admirers of JFK and culture vultures will love the tour, while kids will probably get bored. But you don't have to take the tour to enjoy the view; take the elevators to the roof terrace; that 360° view, which includes many major monuments and the infamous Watergate Hotel next door, is one of the city's best.

TOURING TIPS Free round-trip shuttle service from the Foggy Bottom Metro station is offered daily from 10 a.m. to midnight every 15 minutes. If you can't book a full show, be sure to drop in on the free performance given every day at 6 p.m. in the Grand Foyer.

OTHER THINGS TO DO NEARBY You can lunch or snack at the KC Café without securing a second mortgage on your house, but the Roof Terrace Restaurant is pricey. (The bar, though small, is lovely in an old-fashioned manner.) A biking and jogging path along the Potomac River is just below the Kennedy Center; follow it upriver to Thompson's Boat Center, which rents canoes and bikes, and through there to Washington Harbour and into Georgetown. But remember that Georgetown lacks a Metro station to get you back to where you started.

Kenilworth Aquatic Gardens ★★★

APPEAL BY AGE	PRESCHOOL ★	GRADE SCHOOL ★★	TEENS ★★
YOUNG ADULTS ★★★	OVER 30 ★★★		SENIORS ★★★

Location 1900 Anacostia Drive NE, across the Anacostia River from the National Arboretum; Nearest Metro station Deanwood; ☎ 202-426-6905; www.nps.gov/kepa

Type of attraction A national park devoted to water plants (self-guided tour). Admission Free. Hours Daily, 7 a.m.–4 p.m.; closed Thanksgiving, Christmas, and New Year's days. When to go June and July to see hardy water plants; July and August to see tropical plants and lotus. On the third Saturday in July a water-lily festival is held. Year-round it's a great place for bird-watching. Special comments The gardens are located in a dangerous neighborhood. Don't take public transportation. How much time to allow 1 hour.

DESCRIPTION AND COMMENTS In addition to pools filled with water lilies, water hyacinth, lotus, and bamboo, the gardens teem with wildlife such as opossum, raccoon, waterfowl, and muskrats. It's an amazing place to visit on a clear summer morning.

TOURING TIPS Come in the morning, before the heat closes up the flowers. Don't take public transportation; the surrounding neighborhood is unsafe. Drive or go by cab.

OTHER THINGS TO DO NEARBY The National Arboretum is only a few minutes away by car.

Korean War Veterans Memorial ★★★

APPEAL BY AGE	PRESCHOOL ★★	GRADE SCHOOL ★★½	TEENS ★★½
YOUNG ADULTS ★★★	OVER 30 ★★★½		SENIORS ★★★★

Location Between the Lincoln Memorial and the Tidal Basin, across the lawn from the Vietnam Veterans Memorial; Nearest Metro stations Smithsonian, Foggy Bottom–GWU; ☎ 202-426-6841; www.nps.gov/kowa

Type of attraction A three-dimensional freeze-frame sculpture of troops crossing a battlefield. Admission Free. Hours Always open; unstaffed, but rangers at the nearby Jefferson and Lincoln memorials are on duty from 9:30 a.m. to 11:30 p.m., except on Christmas Day. When to go Anytime, but it's particularly striking at night. Special comments Perhaps a few too many elements put together, but all are effective. A good companion piece to the Vietnam Veterans Memorial. **How much time to allow** 20–30 minutes.

DESCRIPTION AND COMMENTS The memorial consists of several distinct parts, though it's not particularly large as a whole. The most obvious elements are sculptor Frank Gaylord's 19 larger-than-life steel statues of soldiers. Each is seven feet, three inches tall, with deliberately outsized hands and heads. Represented are 14 Army troops, 3 Marines, 1 Navy recruit, and 1 Air Force serviceman; 12 are white, 3 are black, 2 are Hispanic, 1 is Asian, and 1 is Native American. All are heavily laden with packs and weapons and covered in ponchos; their attire and boots suggest it is winter, an impression that is even stronger at night, when the statues are individually illuminated and seem to move. (Three are a little ways off in the woods, so the sense of the company emerging from cover is very realistic.)

The second major component is a black granite wall. The design complements that of the Vietnam Veterans Memorial, which is almost directly across the Mall (though not visible from this point); instead of names, however, this wall is covered with images: 2,400 of them, created from 15,000 photos. Etched into the wall are guns, rescue helicopters, ambulances, bridges being built, mines being defused, doctors operating. Combined with the reflections of onlookers, the effect is as if you were looking through a window. The wall is made up of 38 panels, symbolizing both the 38th Parallel—the original boundary between North and South Korea—and the 38 months of the war's duration.

The wall alongside the walkway lists the names of the countries that sent troops; a small garden is planted with Rose of Sharon hibiscus, the national flower of South Korea. The memorial was dedicated July 27, 1995, by President Clinton and South Korean President Kim Young Sam.

TOURING TIPS It's interesting to view this memorial and the Vietnam Veterans Memorial one after another; clearly, Maya Lin's striking wall has made a strong impression on other architects and designers, even if some members of the public have been slow to appreciate it.

OTHER THINGS TO DO NEARBY The memorial is in the middle of the west half of the Mall; there's a monument, and a monumental view, on every side.

Koshland Science Museum   ★ ★ ½

| APPEAL BY AGE | PRESCHOOL ★ | GRADE SCHOOL ★ ★ ½ | TEENS ★ ★ ½ |
| YOUNG ADULTS ★ ★ ½ | | OVER 30 ★ ★ ½ | SENIORS ★ ★ |

Location Sixth and E streets NW; Nearest Metro stations Gallery Place–Chinatown, Judiciary Square; ☎ 202-334-1201; www.koshland-science-museum.org

Type of attraction A small museum aimed at teenagers and adults focusing on biologic and environmental scientific research (self-guided tour). **Admission** $5 adults, $3 seniors, active military, and students. **Hours** Daily, 10 a.m.–6 p.m. (last admission 5 p.m.); closed on Tuesday. **When to go** Anytime. **Special comments** Exhibits vary in interest (an exhibit of vintage health posters might have amused kids who didn't even understand them). **How much time to allow** 30 minutes.

DESCRIPTION AND COMMENTS Operated by the National Academy of the Sciences, this museum is slick and high-tech, with many interactive and touchy-feely exhibits. Its focus is environmental and biologic science—it's the perfect place for the budding DNA or global-warming researcher who has exhausted all the (free) science exhibits on the Mall.

TOURING TIPS Make this a fill-in spot before or after lunch downtown, but at least be sure to look up at the building; a huge gyroscope is parked up there.

OTHER THINGS TO DO NEARBY This is the heart of Penn Quarter, so the National Building Museum, the Law Enforcement Memorial, the International Spy Museum, the National Museum of Crime & Punishment, the Newseum, the Portrait Gallery–American Art Museum complex, Madame Tussauds, and Ford's Theatre are all close, and there are dozens of places to eat.

Kreeger Museum ★ ★ ★

| APPEAL BY AGE | PRESCHOOL ½ | GRADE SCHOOL ★ | TEENS ★★ |
| YOUNG ADULTS ★★ | OVER 30 ★★★ | | SENIORS ★★★ |

Location 2401 Foxhall Road NW, Georgetown; No Metro access;
☎ 202-338-3552 or 877-337-3050; www.kreegermuseum.org

Type of attraction Collection of 19th- and 20th-century art in Philip Johnson–designed mansion. Admission $10 adults, $7 students and seniors age 65+. Hours 90-minute guided tours Tuesday–Friday, 10:30 a.m. and 1:30 p.m. for ages 12 and up, by reservation only. Open Saturday, 10 a.m.–4 p.m. with guided tours at 10:30 a.m., noon, and 2 p.m.; no age restrictions and reservations are not required. Closed in August, around December holidays, plus January 20 and July 4. When to go During the week if possible. Occasionally the museum also hosts concerts. Special comments A must-see third stop for modern-art fans (after the Hirshhorn and Phillips Collection) or architecture students. No food concession on site. How much time to allow 2 hours.

DESCRIPTION AND COMMENTS Philanthropist David Lloyd Kreeger and his wife, Carmen, began collecting art in the early 1950s and over the next 15 years acquired works from the 1850s to the 1970s, including Monet, Picasso, Renoir, Cézanne, Chagall, Gauguin, van Gogh, Kandinsky, Miró, Calder, Noguchi, Moore, David Smith, and Gene Davis. In addition to arts fans, anyone interested in modern architecture should be certain to see this museum. The building, which was designed (in 1963, and completed in 1967) to serve as a residence, museum, and recital hall in one, is an architectural book of quotations: though definitively postmodernist, it alludes to Byzantine domes, Egyptian tombs, classical travertine facades, Middle Eastern window screens, and the Roman modular system, with all spaces in some variation of 22 by 22 by 22 feet.

TOURING TIPS The main level of the museum, the sculpture terrace, and the restrooms are wheelchair accessible; you must take a staircase to lower galleries.

Location **First Street SE, on Capitol Hill;** Nearest Metro station **Capitol South;** ☎ 202-707-8000; www.loc.gov

Type of attraction The world's largest library. **Admission** Free. **Hours** Exhibition areas in the Jefferson Building are open Monday–Saturday, 10 a.m.–4:30 p.m. The library is closed Sundays, federal holidays, and Christmas and New Year's days. The Visitors Theater in the Jefferson Building shows a free 12-minute film on the library's mission. Free guided tours are offered Monday–Friday at 10:30 a.m., 11:30 a.m., 1:30 p.m., 2:30 p.m., and 3:30 p.m.; and Saturdays at 10:30 a.m., 11:30 a.m., 1:30 p.m., and 2:30 p.m. Groups (12–60 people) require advance reservations. **When to go** Anytime. **Special comments** A trip to the library might not be on most folks' vacation itineraries, but consider making an exception in this case. Impressive and informative. **How much time to allow** 1 hour for the guided tour and another hour to browse the exhibits.

DESCRIPTION AND COMMENTS Three huge structures make up the Library of Congress: the Jefferson, Madison, and Adams buildings. To understand what goes on here, take one of the guided tours. (To get the most out of the tour, first watch the 12-minute video about the varied workings of the library.) After the tour, which lasts about an hour, you can look at other exhibits in the Jefferson and Madison buildings on your own. Because it's a lecture tour, it may not be suitable for young children or visitors on a tight schedule. But you should at least go in to admire the Jefferson building itself; it's a masterpiece, filled with allegorical murals, statuary, mosaics, memorials, and the incredible domed Reading Room, famous from the opening sequence of *All the President's Men*.

In the spring of 1997 a permanent exhibit called "American Treasures of the Library of Congress" marked the reopening of the Thomas Jefferson Building, under renovation since 1984. The rotating exhibition in the Great Hall features 200 of the library's rarest and most significant items, such as Thomas Jefferson's rough draft of the Declaration of Independence, Abraham Lincoln's first and second drafts of the Gettysburg Address, a Gutenberg Bible, Wilbur Wright's telegram to his father announcing the first heavier-than-air flight, and Bernard Hermann's manuscript score for the film classic *Citizen Kane*.

Library materials available here go way beyond books. For instance, the Library of Congress has an extensive collection of recorded music, broadcast material, and films. While ostensibly these research materials are for "serious" researchers only, almost anyone with a strong interest in, say, the recordings of Jimmy Durante can find valuable information and hear rare recordings. For musical material, go to the Recorded Sound Reference Center, located on the first floor of the Madison Building, where helpful librarians are ready to assist. Another permanent exhibit on copyright, located on the fourth floor of the Madison Building, which is open late (see tip), features the original Barbie and

Ken dolls, Dr. Martin Luther King Jr.'s "I Have a Dream" speech, and the statue of the Maltese Falcon used in the famous film of the same name. More temporary exhibits are located on the sixth floor.

TOURING TIPS Although the Library consists of three buildings, visitors enter at the Jefferson Building on First Street. The tour, with its well-informed guide, is the way to go if you have the time and interest. (These tours are extremely popular, and it's a good idea to arrive early.) Although the most famous exhibits and elaborate design are in the Jefferson building, both the Madison and Adams buildings are open weekdays until 9:30 p.m., so if you have particular exhibits in mind, you can linger. The sixth-floor cafeteria in the Madison Building is popular with congressional staffers, and it's a good deal for visitors, who can grab a cheap bite to eat here from 12:30 p.m. to 3 p.m. while enjoying a million-dollar view.

OTHER THINGS TO DO NEARBY The U.S. Capitol, Supreme Court, and Folger Library are all within a block or two.

Lincoln Memorial ★★★★

APPEAL BY AGE	PRESCHOOL ★★	GRADE SCHOOL ★★★	TEENS ★★★
YOUNG ADULTS ★★★★		OVER 30 ★★★★	SENIORS ★★★★

Location At the west end of the Mall; Nearest Metro stations Smithsonian, Foggy Bottom–GWU; ☎ 202-426-6841; www.nps.gov/lin

Type of attraction A classical-style memorial to the 16th American president (self-guided tour). **Admission** Free. **Hours** Always open; rangers on duty 9:30 a.m.–11:30 p.m., except Christmas Day. **When to go** For the best views, visit in the early morning, at sunset, or at night. **Special comments** At night, facing west across the Potomac River, you can see the eternal flame at John F. Kennedy's grave. Both solemn and scenic. No food concessions on site. **How much time to allow** 30 minutes.

DESCRIPTION AND COMMENTS To see what the Lincoln Memorial looks like from the outside, just pull out a penny. But that doesn't give you any sense of the beautiful murals, which have recently been restored to their original glory (and which have significantly increased the interest value for smaller children). And it's hard to escape the sense of awe this monument inspires. Historic events took place on the steps: Black soprano Marian Anderson sang here in 1939 after being barred from Constitution Hall. Martin Luther King Jr. gave his "I Have a Dream" speech here in 1963. President Obama's Inauguration kicked off here with an all-star concert that drew nearly 400,000. The Lincoln Memorial anchors the Mall and should be on anyone's must-see list.

Those murals, 60 feet wide, 12 feet tall, and 37 feet up over some of Lincoln's most important quotations, are neoclassical allegories, with angels, muses, and goddesses representing Unification (on the north wall) and Emancipation (on the south). The Angel of Truth strikes the shackles from a slave, as Justice and Immortality stand as witnesses.

TOURING TIPS The Legacy of Lincoln museum in the memorial's basement is worth a peek. You'll find exhibits about demonstrations held at the memorial and a video recounting the building's history.

OTHER THINGS TO DO NEARBY The Vietnam Veterans Memorial and the Reflecting Pool are directly across from the Lincoln Memorial. The Korean War Veterans Memorial is between Lincoln and the Tidal Basin, on the way to the FDR Memorial. The Martin Luther King Jr. Memorial, now under development, is on the bank of the Tidal Basin closest to the Lincoln Memorial.

Madame Tussauds ★★½

APPEAL BY AGE	PRESCHOOL ★½	GRADE SCHOOL ★★★	TEENS ★★★
YOUNG ADULTS ★★★		OVER 30 ★★★	SENIORS ★★★

Location **1025 F Street NW; Nearest Metro stations Metro Center, Gallery Place–Chinatown;** ☎ **202-942-7300; www.madametussauds.com**

Type of attraction Classic wax museum with political touches as well as pop heroes. **Admission** $20 ages 13–59, $18 seniors 60+, $15 ages 4–12. **Hours** Opens at 10 a.m. daily; Monday–Wednesday, last tickets sold at 4 p.m.; Thursday–Sunday last tickets sold at 6 p.m.; longer hours possible during peak season (see website). **How much time to allow** 1 hour.

DESCRIPTION AND COMMENTS If you've seen one Madame Tussauds—and with nine locations worldwide, it's getting a lot easier to do—you've pretty much seen them all, so there aren't many surprises here. However, the Washington outpost does have one big advantage over some of the older establishments: lots of room between figures—and not so many historical artifacts—so visitors are not just invited but actively encouraged to take each others' photos with the stars. In some cases there are special setups, such as the empty seat alongside President Lincoln in his box at Ford's Theatre, the "Oval Office desk," the Rat Pack cocktail bar, and an armchair over which Julia Roberts is bending. The hottest ticket recently has been the newly installed Jonas Brothers band, followed closely by an impressively suave Johnny Depp. It's not a large collection, but it apparently is irresistible. There is an intriguing description of how the figures are made, but there is no "chamber of horrors," unless you count the emaciated figure of Madonna.

TOURING TIPS Make sure your cell phone is charged up; even if you didn't bring a camera, you're likely to find someone you'd like to have your picture snapped with.

OTHER THINGS TO DO NEARBY Again, this is the heart of Penn Quarter; the International Spy Museum, National Portrait Gallery–American Art Museum, and National Museum of Crime & Punishment are close.

🏛 Mount Vernon Estate and Gardens ★★★★★

APPEAL BY AGE	PRESCHOOL ★★	GRADE SCHOOL ★★★★	TEENS ★★★
YOUNG ADULTS ★★★★★		OVER 30 ★★★★★	SENIORS ★★★★★

Location **16 miles south of Washington in Mount Vernon, VA; No Metro access;** ☎ **703-780-2000; www.mountvernon.org**

Type of attraction George Washington's 18th-century Virginia plantation on the Potomac River (self-guided tour). **How to get there** To drive from Washington, cross the 14th Street Bridge into Virginia, bear right, and get on the George Washington Memorial Parkway south. Continue past National Airport into Alexandria, where the parkway becomes Washington Street, then the Mount Vernon Memorial Parkway, which ends at the estate. Tourmobile offers 5-hour narrated bus tours to Mount Vernon daily, June 15 through Labor Day. Departure is at noon. Tickets are $32 for adults and $16 for children ages 3–11. The price includes admission to Mount Vernon. Call Tourmobile at ☎ 202-554-5100 for more information. Gray Line offers 6-hour coach trips to Mount Vernon and Old Town Alexandria that depart from Union Station daily at 8:30 a.m. October 23–March 31, and 2 p.m. June 19–October 22. No tours are scheduled on Thanksgiving, Christmas, and New Year's days. Fares are $46.75 for adults and $25.50 for children. For more information, call Gray Line at ☎ 202-289-1995 or visit www.grayline.com. **Admission** Estate and Gardens: $15 adults, $14 seniors 62+, $7 children ages 6–11, free age 5 and under. Gristmill and distillery: adults and seniors, $2 additional to Estate and Gardens tickets or $4 purchased alone; children (6–11), $1.50 additional or $2 purchased alone; free ages 5 and under. **Hours** All areas open daily, including Christmas Day. Estate and Gardens: April–August, 8 a.m.–5 p.m.; November–February, 9 a.m.–4 p.m.; March, September, and October, 9 a.m.–5 p.m. Gristmill: 10 a.m.–5 p.m.; closed November–March. **When to go** Although mornings may be cooler, they're also busier than afternoons; weekdays are less crowded than weekends. Lightest traffic November through March. **Special comments** Mount Vernon is probably the only major D.C. attraction that opens at 8 a.m., making it a prime place to hit early in hot weather—if you have a car to get you there, and can beat the buses. During the holiday season, the decorated mansion's seldom-seen third floor is open to the public. Full-service restaurant (dinner by candlelight) and food concessions. **How much time to allow** 2–5 hours.

DESCRIPTION AND COMMENTS Folks on a quick trip to Washington won't have time to visit Mount Vernon, but everyone else should. The stunning view from the mansion across the Potomac River is pretty much the same as it was in Washington's day. Unlike most historic sites in D.C., Mount Vernon gives visitors a real sense of how 18th-century rural life worked, from the first president's foot-operated fan chair (for keeping flies at bay while he read) to the rustic kitchen and outbuildings. Historic interpreters are stationed throughout the estate and mansion to answer questions and give visitors an overview of the property and Washington's life. However, the major attraction, even for those who have previously visited the site, is the $110-million, state-of-the-art visitor center, with its several real-life models of Washington based on forensic and computer-modeling advances, videos, 23 galleries of artifacts, and interactive exhibits.

Mount Vernon is more than just a big house. Special 30-minute landscape and garden tours leave at 11 a.m., April through October. "Slave Life at Mount Vernon" is a 30-minute walking tour to slave quarters and workplaces that starts at 2 p.m. daily, April through October.

There's no additional charge for these tours. From April through October, a wreath-laying ceremony is held at George and Martha's tomb. The newest tour ($5) is a "National Treasure II" tour, which highlights places used in the filming of the movie.

Mount Vernon has opened several new attractions on the 30-acre plantation to help diffuse huge crowds that throng the mansion, including a four-acre colonial farm site where visitors can view costumed interpreters using 18th-century farm methods and tools, and see hogs, mules, horses, cattle, oxen, and sheep (though this is *not* a petting zoo). Hands-on activities are available March through November, and wagon rides are offered on weekends.

TOURING TIPS Mount Vernon is *very* popular, and tourists pull up by the busload in the spring and summer months—sometimes before the grounds even open. The longest lines are in April and May, thanks partly to school groups. If you want to avoid big crowds, go around 3 p.m., but you have to leave the grounds by 5:30 p.m. When crowds are small in the winter, visitors are frequently given guided tours of the mansion in groups of 20 to 30 people.

Also note that there are a variety of "package" tickets, such as the Presidential package, which includes a brief river cruise, an audio tour, and a 10% discount at the shops ($28 adults, $16 youth, not available on Mondays). However, you should also be aware that there is no direct transportation to the grist mill and distillery, which are three miles away; you must drive or take a Fairfax Connector bus.

OTHER THINGS TO DO NEARBY Visit Woodlawn Plantation, three miles away, which was built by the Custis granddaughter George and Martha raised (see description under "Virginia Suburbs," below). Visit Old Town Alexandria on your way to or from Mount Vernon. To stop at Gadsby's Tavern is appropriate—that's what George Washington used to do.

NASA/Goddard Space Flight Visitor Center ★ ★ ★

APPEAL BY AGE	PRESCHOOL ★	GRADE SCHOOL ★ ★ ★	TEENS ★ ★ ★
YOUNG ADULTS ★ ★ ★		OVER 30 ★ ★ ★	SENIORS ★ ★ ★

Location **8800 Greenbelt Road, Greenbelt, MD; No Metro access;**
☎ **301-286-8981; www.nasa.gov/goddard**

Type of attraction NASA's 1,100-acre campuslike facility in suburban Maryland, including a small museum and other buildings. **Admission** Free. **Hours** July–August: Tuesday–Friday, 10 a.m.–5 p.m., Saturday and Sunday, 12–4 p.m., closed Monday. September–June: Tuesday–Friday, 10 a.m.–3 p.m.; Saturday and Sunday, 12–4 p.m.; closed all federal holidays. **When to go** By reservation. **Special comments** Informative but not convenient for most visitors. Guided tours by reservation only. Foreign nationals must show passport with full name. **How much time to allow** 1 hour.

DESCRIPTION AND COMMENTS The small museum inside the visitor center is loaded with space hardware, including a space capsule kids can play in, space suits, and real satellites; think of it as a mini–National Air and Space Museum. Outside, some real rockets used to put the hardware into outer space are on display. However, new security guidelines make visiting this site, a few miles outside the Beltway, even more difficult, so most folks will get their fill and then some of spacecraft at the museum on the Mall, and even more if they want to travel to its Dulles annex (below).

TOURING TIPS No drop-in visitors are allowed; to schedule a tour for a group call ☎ 301-286-3978. The small gift shop offers interesting NASA-related items such as postcards, 35mm color slides, posters, and publications.

OTHER THINGS TO DO NEARBY Drive through the adjacent Agricultural Research Center, a collection of farms where the U.S. Department of Agriculture studies farm animals and plants. The roads are narrow and quiet—it's a rural oasis in the heart of Maryland's suburban sprawl. The National Wildlife Visitor Center off nearby Powder Mill Road features nature displays and hiking paths.

🏛️ kids National Air and Space Museum
(a Smithsonian museum) ★ ★ ★ ★ ★

APPEAL BY AGE	PRESCHOOL ★★★★	GRADE SCHOOL ★★★★★	TEENS ★★★★★
YOUNG ADULTS ★★★★★		OVER 30 ★★★★★	SENIORS ★★★★

Location On the south side of the Mall near the U.S. Capitol; Nearest Metro stations Smithsonian, L'Enfant Plaza; ☎ 202-357-2700 or 202-633-1000 (TDD); www.nasm.si.edu

Type of attraction A museum that chronicles the history of manned flight. Admission Free; IMAX admission is $9 ages 13–59, $8 for seniors, and $7.50 for children ages 2–12. Hours September–March: daily, 10 a.m.–5:30 p.m.; April–Labor Day: daily, 10 a.m.-7:30 p.m. Depending on the shape of the federal budget, hours may be extended during the summer. When to go First thing or after 4 p.m. Because of metal detectors and baggage checks, waits of up to 20 minutes can occur, especially at opening. Special comments Some special exhibits require passes; check with the information desk in the main lobby. Some rides and simulators require payment. How much time to allow 2 hours minimum—and you still won't see it all. If possible, try to spread your tour of the museum over 2 or more visits.

DESCRIPTION AND COMMENTS This museum is the most visited in the world, drawing about 9 million visitors a year. Entering from the Mall, visitors can touch a moon rock and gaze up at the Wright Brothers' plane and the *Spirit of St. Louis*, which Lindbergh flew across the Atlantic in 1927. Everywhere you look is another full-size wonder. The only drawback to this museum is its size—going to every exhibit becomes numbing after a while. If your length of stay allows it, try to split your time here into at least two visits. But it's a must-see for virtually anyone—not just airplane buffs and space cadets. The newly remodeled ground floor has new flight simulators. Five are tied to exhibits in the museum, giving visitors the chance to fly a World War I plane flown by Eddie Ricken-backer, Amelia Earhart's Lockheed Vega, and more. At the Einstein Planetarium, the starry sky has been replaced by digital projectors, which transport images from space and cast them out onto the 70-foot dome; shows start every half hour. In Space Hall, you can tour Skylab and check out the Apollo-Soyuz spacecraft. You can look through a 16-inch telescope, experience cockpit simulations of takeoff and landing at Reagan National Airport or even of aerial combat. Other icons on display include the Apollo II command module, space suits that flew to the moon, several other space captures, and early, more atmosphere-bound vehicles.

TOURING TIPS Pick up a highlights brochure at the front desk or print it out in advance from the website. If you want tickets for the five-story-high IMAX theater or planetarium, make the box office on the main floor your first stop or buy in advance online at www.si.edu/imax.

Note: If you're seriously intrigued by this museum, and/or crowd-averse, you might consider the museum's other branch, the Steven F. Udvar-Hazy Center outside Dulles International Airport, with more than 80 more aircraft and dozens of space artifacts including the Space Shuttle *Enterprise*, a Lockheed SR-71 Blackbird, and the *Gemini VII* space capsule, as well as flight simulators, an IMAX theater, and an air-traffic observation tower.

OTHER THINGS TO DO NEARBY As an antidote to the crowds here, take a stroll through the U.S. Botanic Garden or the landscaping around the Museum of the American Indian (the café there is much better, incidentally).

kids National Aquarium ★★

| APPEAL BY AGE | PRESCHOOL ★★★★ | GRADE SCHOOL ★★★★ | TEENS ★★★ |
| YOUNG ADULTS ★★ | | OVER 30 ★★ | SENIORS ★★ |

Location **In the basement of the Department of Commerce building on 14th Street NW at Constitution Avenue NW;** Nearest Metro station **Federal Triangle;** ☎ **202-482-2826 (recording); www.nationalaquarium.com**

Type of attraction The oldest aquarium in the United States (self-guided tour). Admission $9 adults, $8 seniors and military, $4 for children ages 3–11. Hours Daily, 9 a.m.–5 p.m. (last admission 4:30); closed Thanksgiving Day and Christmas Day. When to go Anytime. Special comments A cool, dark oasis on a sweltering summer afternoon. A basement full of fish tanks. Commerce department cafeteria is open to the public. How much time to allow 1 hour.

DESCRIPTION AND COMMENTS Essentially a long room lined with big fish tanks in the basement of an office building, this aquarium is not in the same league with other, newer fish-and-dolphin emporiums that are springing up all over (such as the one in Baltimore). But children will love it. Small and lacking crowd-pleasing sea mammals, the aquarium figures as a minor exhibit for filling in the odd hour or to escape a sweltering afternoon. Otherwise, spend your valuable touring time elsewhere.

TOURING TIPS Daily feedings (sharks, piranhas, or alligators) and talks at 2 p.m. Adopt an animal for a year for $100—give a shark for Christmas?

OTHER THINGS TO DO NEARBY The Washington Monument, the National Museum of American History, and the Old Post Office Pavilion are within a few minutes' walk.

National Archives ★★½

| APPEAL BY AGE | PRESCHOOL ★ | GRADE SCHOOL ★★ | TEENS ★★★ |
| YOUNG ADULTS ★★★ | | OVER 30 ★★★ | SENIORS ★★★ |

Location Seventh Street and Constitution Avenue NW, on the Mall; Nearest Metro station Archives; ☎ 202-357-5450; www.archives.gov

Type of attraction The magnificent rotunda where the Big Three of American government—the Declaration of Independence, the U.S. Constitution, and the Bill of Rights—are displayed (self-guided tour). **Reservations** Required 6 weeks in advance for guided tours. **Admission** Free. **Hours** March 15–Labor Day: weekdays, 10 a.m.–7 p.m.; day after Labor Day–March 14: weekdays, 10 a.m.–5:30 p.m.; closed Christmas Day and Thanksgiving. **When to go** Before noon or after 4 p.m. during spring and summer. If you happen to be in Washington on July 4, you can catch costumed patriots reading the Declaration aloud on the steps. **Special comments** Small children may need a lift to see the documents; skip it if the line is long. Café on site. Use the entrance on Constitution Avenue. **How much time to allow** 30 minutes.

DESCRIPTION AND COMMENTS In addition to trying to decipher the faint and flowing script on the sheets of parchment mounted in bronze and glass cases, visitors can stroll through a temporary exhibit of photos and documents covering various aspects of Americana. Most visitors seem as fascinated by the written description of the elaborate security system that lowers the sacred documents into a deep, nuclear-explosion-proof vault each night as they are by seeing the charters themselves—and you can't even see the contraption. The 75-foot-high rotunda is an impressive backdrop for our founding documents, but most people are surprised at how little there is to see inside this huge building. In fact, there *is* a lot more to see—but you've got to call in advance to arrange a tour. If the line to get in is long, skip it and come back later. It's really not worth the wait.

However, if you have been bitten by the genealogical bug, and have the time to devote to it, this is a wonderful place to do research.

TOURING TIPS Some visitors say the documents on display in the exhibition areas outside the rotunda are more interesting—and certainly easier to read—than the better-known parchments under the big dome. For a behind-the-scenes view of the workings of the National Archives, arrange to take a reserved tour. During spring and summer, six weeks' notice is recommended. Or take a chance and show up at the Pennsylvania Avenue entrance (across from Eighth Street NW) at tour time. If there's a cancellation or a no-show, you're in. The reserved tours begin at 9:45 a.m. Monday through Friday and last about an hour. On the reserved tour, visitors take a tour of the building, including the stacks, microfilm viewing rooms, and exhibits and models that show how researchers preserve documents. The tour ends at the Rotunda. Oh, and don't miss the gift shop, where the best-selling item is a photograph of President Nixon and Elvis Presley embracing. It's a scream.

OTHER THINGS TO DO NEARBY The U.S. Navy Memorial and its underground exhibit area are across the street on Pennsylvania Avenue. Mall museums and Penn Quarter attractions are a few minutes walk.

National Building Museum ★★★

APPEAL BY AGE	PRESCHOOL ★★	GRADE SCHOOL ★★★	TEENS ★★★
YOUNG ADULTS ★★★★	OVER 30 ★★★★		SENIORS ★★★★

Location **401 F Street NW;** Nearest Metro station **Judiciary Square;**
☎ **202-272-2448; www.nbm.org**

Type of attraction A museum dedicated to architecture and the construction arts that's an architectural marvel in its own right (self-guided and guided tours). **Admission** Free; suggested donation of $5 for adults. **Hours** Monday–Saturday, 10 a.m.–5 p.m.; Sunday, 11 a.m.–5 p.m.; closed Thanksgiving, Christmas, and New Year's days. **When to go** Anytime. **Special comments** The Great Hall is eye-popping. Tours are given daily at 11:30 a.m., 12:30 p.m., and 1:30 p.m. **How much time to allow** 45 minutes.

DESCRIPTION AND COMMENTS The ideal way to visit this museum would be to walk in blindfolded, then have the blindfold removed. Rather unimposing on the outside, the Pension Building (as this museum is better known to Washingtonians) offers one of the most imposing interiors in Washington, if not the world. The Great Hall measures 316 feet by 116 feet, and at its highest point the roof is 159 feet above the floor. Eight marbleized Corinthian columns adorn the interior. It's a must-see, even if all you do is poke your head inside the door. And the gift shop has some very nice cards, for those tired of the humorous Hallmark kind.

TOURING TIPS The exhibits in the museum are on the thin side: the main attraction is the building itself. But if you're interested in architecture and building construction, check out the permanent and temporary exhibits on the first and second floors. The Courtyard Café is open weekdays, 9 a.m.–4 p.m.; Saturday, 10 a.m.–4 p.m.; and Sunday, 11 a.m.–4 p.m.

OTHER THINGS TO DO NEARBY The three-acre National Law Enforcement Officers Memorial is directly across from the National Building Museum's entrance on F Street. Engraved on blue-gray marble walls are the names of 12,500 law enforcement officers who died in the line of duty throughout U.S. history. Four groups of striking statues, each showing a lion protecting her cubs, adorn the parks.

The Lillian and Albert Small Jewish Museum, which houses the Adas Israel Synagogue on the second floor, will be "in residence" on the museum grounds while its permanent site, at Third and F Streets NW, is being redeveloped.

National Cryptologic Museum ★★

APPEAL BY AGE	PRESCHOOL —	GRADE SCHOOL ★	TEENS ★★
YOUNG ADULTS ★★★	OVER 30 ★★		SENIORS ★★

Location **The National Security Agency, on the grounds of Fort George G. Meade, about 30 minutes north of Washington and east of Laurel, MD (Route 32 and the Baltimore-Washington Parkway); No Metro access;**
☎ **301-688-5849; www.nsa.gov/about/cryptologic_heritage/museum/**

Type of attraction A small museum offering a glimpse into the secret world of spies, national defense, and ciphers (self-guided tour). **Admission** Free.

Hours Weekdays, 9 a.m.–4 p.m.; the first and third Saturdays of each month, 10 a.m.–2 p.m.; closed federal holidays and Sundays. **When to go** Anytime. **Special comments** This tiny museum's greatest appeal may be its very existence: the National Security Agency (NSA) is the nation's largest spy organization—and its most secretive. **How much time to allow** 1 hour.

DESCRIPTION AND COMMENTS Tourists are barred from Central Intelligence Agency headquarters in Langley, across the river from Washington in suburban Virginia. Yet all is not lost for visitors lusting for a peek into the world of cloaks and daggers. The ultra-hush-hush National Security Agency operates this tiny museum dedicated to codes, ciphers, and spies in a former motel overlooking the Baltimore-Washington Parkway.

All the displays are static; they include items such as rare books dating from 1526, Civil War signal flags, KGB spy paraphernalia, and the notorious Enigma, a German cipher machine (it looks like an ancient Underwood on steroids) whose code was "broken" by the Poles and British during World War II. (*Spies*, a film on code breaking during World War II, tells the story continuously on a TV in a small theater in the museum.) There is an extensive library of codebooks and deciphered cables, and some artifacts of the Navajo "code talkers."

Don't miss the "bugged" Great Seal of the U.S. that hung in Spaso House, the U.S. ambassador's residence in Moscow (the microphone-equipped seal was uncovered in 1952). The new high-tech room features spy devices used to guard against computer hackers. The adjoining open-air National Vigilance Park is more like a parking lot for two reconnaissance jets, a Vietnam-era Army RU-8D and a cold war–era Air Force C-130. Outside, you'll also get a glimpse of the huge NSA headquarters complex from Route 32. NSA is called "The Puzzle Palace" for its secretiveness and worldwide electronic eavesdropping capability. The agency's budget, by the way, is a secret.

TOURING TIPS There are vending machines on site, but be sure to carry plenty of change.

OTHER THINGS TO DO NEARBY South on the Baltimore-Washington Parkway are the National Wildlife Visitor Center and the NASA/Goddard Space Flight Center (Powder Mill Road exit).

National Gallery of Art: *East Building*   ★ ★ ★ ★ ★

| APPEAL BY AGE | PRESCHOOL ★ | GRADE SCHOOL ★ ★ | TEENS ★ ★ ★ |
| YOUNG ADULTS ★ ★ ★ ★ ★ | OVER 30 ★ ★ ★ ★ ★ | | SENIORS ★ ★ ★ ★ ★ |

**Location Fourth Street and Constitution Avenue NW, on the Mall;
Nearest Metro stations Archives, Judiciary Square, Smithsonian;
☎ 202-737-4215; www.nga.gov**

Type of attraction A museum housing 20th-century art and special exhibitions (self-guided tour). **Admission** Free. **Hours** Monday–Saturday, 10 a.m.–5 p.m.; Sunday, 11 a.m.–6 p.m.; closed Christmas and New Year's days. **When to go** Anytime. **Special comments** Even the building, usually referred to as the "East Wing" of the National Gallery, is a great work of art. Visitors with disabilities may park in available spaces in front of the building. Introductory tours are offered daily and last about an hour; for times call ☎ 202-737-4215. No luggage, backpacks, book bags, or other personal bags allowed. **How much time to allow** 2 hours.

DESCRIPTION AND COMMENTS Both the interior and exterior of this I. M. Pei–designed building are spectacular, so it's worth a visit even if you hate modern art. Outside, the popular 1978 building consists of unadorned vertical planes. Inside, it's bright, airy, and spacious. Look for art by modern masters such as Picasso, Matisse, Mondrian, Miró, Magritte, Warhol, Lichtenstein, and Rauschenberg. The exhibits change constantly, so there's no telling which of these is on display.

TOURING TIPS Occasionally, temporary exhibits (such as a van Gogh show) are extremely popular and may require a free "time ticket" that admits you on a certain day at a specific hour. You may pick up such tickets in advance; tickets are available as much as a month before a show opens. If you don't have a ticket on the day you visit the East Wing, you're not completely out of luck: a number of tickets are set aside every day for distribution that day only. If you want one, arrive at the ticket counter on the main floor by noon (or 2 p.m. during the week). Then come back later to see the exhibit. When you exit the museum, turn left and check out the high, knife-edge exterior corner wall of the gallery near the Mall—it's almost worn away from people touching their noses to it.

The six-acre National Gallery Sculpture Garden on the Mall side of the West Building holds works from the gallery's permanent collection, as well as temporary exhibits. A variety of shade trees provide welcome relief in the summer, and there's free jazz on Friday evenings; in winter the central pool serves as a public ice-skating rink. The Art Deco subway gate arching over the café is from the Paris Metro.

TOURING TIPS Don't write this off for all young children; some find the huge Calder mobile in the lobby fascinating, there are sometimes Pop Art or "western" exhibits they'll like—and they'll love running around the gleaming pyramid between the museum wings.

OTHER THINGS TO DO NEARBY The West Wing, with its more traditional European art, is connected to the East Building by an underground concourse. The Capitol and the U.S. Botanic Garden are nearby, as well as the National Archives. The Cascade Café/Buffet, a cafeteria along the concourse with a waterfall wall, and the Sculpture Garden's Pavilion Café are good bets.

National Gallery of Art: *West Building* ★★★★★

APPEAL BY AGE	PRESCHOOL ★	GRADE SCHOOL ★★★	TEENS ★★★
YOUNG ADULTS ★★★★	OVER 30 ★★★★★		SENIORS ★★★★★

Location Sixth Street and Constitution Avenue NW, on the Mall; Nearest Metro station Archives; ☎ 202-737-4215; www.nga.gov

Type of attraction Museum featuring European and American art from the 13th through the 19th centuries (self-guided and guided tours). **Admission** Free. **Hours** Monday–Saturday, 10 a.m.–5 p.m.; Sunday, 11 a.m.–6 p.m.; closed Christmas and New Year's days. **When to go** Anytime. **Special comments** Art with a capital "A."

Introductory tours are offered daily and last about an hour. For times call ☎ 202-737-4125. It's usually referred to as the "West Wing" of the National Gallery. **How much time to allow** 2 hours for a light skimming, but you could spend a week.

DESCRIPTION AND COMMENTS This is where you find the heavy hitters: Dutch masters such as Rembrandt and Vermeer, plus Raphael, Monet, and Jacques-Louis David, just to name a few. And it's all housed in an elegant neoclassical building designed by John Russell Pope. It's a world-class art museum; first-time visitors should make at least one stop.

The Micro Gallery, 13 computer stations featuring high-tech computers and 20-inch touch-screen color monitors, provides visitors with images and information on about 1,700 paintings, sculptures, and decorative arts; 650 artists; and more than 530 art-related subjects. Modeled after a similar system at the National Gallery in London, the Micro Gallery lets visitors with little or no computer experience expand their appreciation of the gallery's permanent collection. You can even create a personal tour of the museum and print a map showing the locations of works of art you've selected.

TOURING TIPS Most of the museum's paintings are hung in many small rooms, instead of a few big ones, so don't try to speed through the building or you'll miss most of them. When museum fatigue begins to set in, rest your feet in one of the atriums located between the museum's many galleries. If you plan on dragging kids through this massive place, try bribing them with a later trip to the National Zoo.

Some special exhibits require a free "time ticket" that admits you on a certain day at a specific hour, and a few will cost you. You may pick up such tickets in advance; they are available as much as a month before a show opens. If you don't have a ticket on the day you want to visit the West Wing, you're not completely out of luck: a number of tickets are set aside every day for distribution that day only. If you want one, arrive at the ticket counter on the main floor by noon (or 2 p.m. on a weekday). Then come back later to see the exhibit.

OTHER THINGS TO DO NEARBY Take the connecting corridor (an underground concourse) to the gallery's East Building. The Air and Space Museum is directly across the Mall, while the National Archives are in the other direction, across Constitution Avenue. One of the more attractive museum cafeterias on the Mall is located along the concourse, and the more elegant (and quiet) Garden Court near the museum shop often has special menus to complement exhibits—Provençal fare for the Cézanne show, for instance. The Pavilion Café at the National Gallery's Sculpture Garden (located next door, across from the National Archives) has indoor and outdoor seating.

kids National Geographic Museum ★ ★ ★

APPEAL BY AGE	PRESCHOOL ★ ★ ★	GRADE SCHOOL ★ ★ ★ ★	TEENS ★ ★ ★ ★
YOUNG ADULTS ★ ★ ★		OVER 30 ★ ★	SENIORS ★ ★

Location 17th and M streets NW, 4 blocks north of the White House;

Nearest Metro stations Farragut North, Farragut West; ☎ 202-857-7588; www.nationalgeographic.com/museum

Type of attraction A small, high-tech exhibition that delights children (self-guided tour). **Admission** Free. **Hours** Daily, 9 a.m.–5 p.m.; closed Christmas Day. **When to go** Anytime. **Special comments** Well-done exhibits that aren't overpowering and sometimes engrossing. The downtown exhibit is handy in an area that's spotty on entertaining things for kids. **How much time to allow** 1 hour.

DESCRIPTION AND COMMENTS It's like walking through a couple of National Geographic TV specials. Located on the first floor of the National Geographic Society's headquarters, this small collection of exhibits showcases weather, geography, astronomy, biology, exploration, and space science. Temporary exhibits range from huge scale models of Crusades-era castles under siege, to imaginary monsters and manipulated photographs. The society also hosts concerts, films, and ethnic cultural events.

TOURING TIPS Don't miss the extensive museum shop offering books, ethnic clothes and jewelry, videos, maps, and magazines. The courtyard on M Street, a great spot for a brown-bag lunch, is filled with whimsical animal sculptures. Free films are shown on Tuesdays at noon.

OTHER THINGS TO DO NEARBY The still-imposing Russian embassy is around the corner on 16th Street; you can't go in, but check out the array of antennas on the roof. The Washington Post is on 15th Street NW two blocks away; the House of the Temple (Scottish Rite) is a ten-minute walk up 16th Street. The Cathedral of St. Matthew on N Street has served many politicians.

National Museum of African Art ★★★
(a Smithsonian museum)

APPEAL BY AGE	PRESCHOOL ★	GRADE SCHOOL ★★	TEENS ★★
YOUNG ADULTS ★★★	OVER 30 ★★★		SENIORS ★★★

Location 950 Independence Avenue SW, on the Mall near the Castle (the Smithsonian Institution Building); Nearest Metro station Smithsonian; ☎ 202-633-4600 or 202-357-4814 (TDD); www.nmafa.si.edu

Type of attraction A museum specializing in the traditional arts of Africa (self-guided tour). **Admission** Free. **Hours** Daily, 10 a.m.–5:30 p.m.; closed Christmas Day. **When to go** Anytime. **Special comments** Provides a quiet respite when other Mall attractions are jam-packed; an excellent museum shop. Exquisite sculpture and fascinating household items. No food concessions on site. **How much time to allow** 1 hour.

DESCRIPTION AND COMMENTS This elegant subterranean museum is paired with the Sackler Gallery, a museum of Asian art, and separated by an above-ground garden. Inside is an extensive collection of African art in a wide range of media, including sculpture, masks, household and personal items, and religious objects. The museum also mounts special exhibitions. Intellectually, this museum transports museumgoers far away from the Mall. It's a good destination for older children, teens, and adults looking for some non-European cultural history and art, and it's a great alternative on hot or crowded days in Washington.

TOURING TIPS Ask at the information desk if there are any gallery tours scheduled. If you don't have to take the elevator, don't, or at least walk down; there are artworks all around the staircase. Don't miss the excellent museum shop, where you'll find textiles, jewelry, scarves and sashes, wood carvings, and a wide selection of African music on CD and DVD.

OTHER THINGS TO DO NEARBY This museum is twinned with the Arthur M. Sackler Gallery, and even connects with it below ground—a nice feature on a sweltering Washington afternoon. If the weather's mild, stroll the Enid A. Haupt Garden, which separates the two museums at ground level. Neither museum has a cafeteria; check the options at the National Gallery or Museum of the American Indian.

kids National Museum of American History
(a Smithsonian museum) ★★★★★

APPEAL BY AGE	PRESCHOOL ★★★	GRADE SCHOOL ★★★★	TEENS ★★★★★
YOUNG ADULTS ★★★★★		OVER 30 ★★★★★	SENIORS ★★★★★

Location 14th Street and Constitution Avenue NW, on the Mall;
Nearest Metro stations Smithsonian, Federal Triangle; ☎ 202-633-1000 or 202-357-1563 (TDD); www.americanhistory.si.edu

Type of attraction An extensive collection of artifacts reflecting the American experience—historical, social, and technological (self-guided tour). **Admission** Free. **Hours** Daily, 10 a.m.–5:30 p.m.; extended summer and holiday hours depend on budget constraints; closed Christmas Day. **When to go** To avoid the worst crowds, visit before noon or after 3 p.m. **Special comments** A collection of national treasures; don't miss it. The immensity of this museum almost demands that visitors try to see it in more than one visit. **How much time to allow** At least 2 hours on a first pass; it would take a week to see it all. Café (with ice cream parlor) and food court on site.

DESCRIPTION AND COMMENTS After a two-year renovation, this irresistibly eclectic museum—affectionately nicknamed "the nation's attic," its entire collection tops 3 million items—gives full due to such treasures as the original 30-by-42-foot Star-Spangled Banner (the veteran of an eight-year conservation, it was one of the prime inspirations for the renovation and atrium-opening of the museum, and now has its own gallery on the second floor), the desk on which Thomas Jefferson wrote the Declaration of Independence, centuries of military uniforms, steam locomotives, printing presses, a Model T Ford, children's toys from past decades, a pendulum three stories high that shows how the earth rotates, a collection of ball gowns worn by First Ladies, letters by Washington, a group of roots community exhibits, a house in which five families lived over a period of two centuries, a pair of Dorothy's ruby slippers (spoiler alert: there were three altogether), and Archie Bunker's chair. A new five-story-high atrium floods the museum with light, and thanks to the glass staircase you can see all the way through the museum from Constitution Avenue to the Mall. If you can't find something of interest here, you may need mouth-to-mouth resuscitation. For a lot of people, this ranks as their favorite Mall museum. No wonder—it offers viewers a dizzying array of history, nostalgia, technology, and culture. And kids love it. It's a must-see for virtually all visitors.

At most museums, you look at *stuff*, but a lot of the collection at American History is arranged so that viewers can learn about *people* in the context of their times. To see what we mean—and to help you organize yourself in this bewilderingly large museum—make it a point to see these exhibits: the First Ladies' Inaugural Gown Exhibition; uniforms and arms from the American wars; and a collection of television objects and ephemera that includes Fonzie's jacket, one of Mr. Rogers' sweaters, Jim Henson's original Oscar the Grouch and Kermit the Frog, and the (real) kitchen, pots, pans, and all, from Julia Child's Cambridge, Massachusetts, home, where she began her TV career. No doubt the knife that gave her that infamous on-camera cut is there, too.

The Hall of Musical Instruments houses a Stradivarius quartet—ornamented instruments, that is. There's a science lab on the first floor with experiments every half hour, a statue of George Washington as a Roman general, and a single Dumbo flying car. The spectacular doll house on the third floor, donated in 1951, had already had 50 years of care and furnishing. The array of fully rigged model ships on the first floor is a child-pleaser too. And, of course, there are simulator rides, on the lower level ($7).

TOURING TIPS Check at the information desk for a schedule of tours (usually at 10 a.m. and 1 p.m. daily), demonstrations, concerts, lectures, films, and other activities put on by the museum staff. Some final hints: A lot of people touring the museum on their own overlook the Hall of Transportation in the museum's east wing, which features an excellent collection of cars, trains, trolleys, and motorcycles that will fascinate all ages.

OTHER THINGS TO DO NEARBY If you've exhausted the Mall, try the National Aquarium across Constitution Avenue.

National Museum of the American Indian
(*a Smithsonian museum*) ★★★

APPEAL BY AGE	PRESCHOOL ★	GRADE SCHOOL ★★	TEENS ★★
YOUNG ADULTS ★★★	OVER 30 ★★★		SENIORS ★★★

Location Fourth Street and Independence Avenue SW (on the Mall between the Air and Space Museum and the U.S. Botanic Gardens); Nearest Metro stations Federal Center, L'Enfant Plaza; ☎ 202-633-1000 or 202-357-1729 (TDD); www.americanindian.si.edu

Type of attraction One of the largest and most diverse collections of Indian art and artifacts in the world. **Admission** Free. **Hours** Daily, 10 a.m.–5:30 p.m.; closed Christmas Day. Free highlights tours Monday–Friday at 1:30 and 3 p.m., Saturdays and Sundays 11 a.m., 1:30 p.m., and 3 p.m. **When to go** Avoid lunch hour. **Special comments** Fabulous setting and expensive shop. Popular cafeteria on site. **How much time to allow** 1–1½ hours.

DESCRIPTION AND COMMENTS Opened in 2004, this is the Smithsonian's newest museum on the Mall, at least until the Museum of African-American History opens. It cost $219 million, features four levels and 250,000 square feet of exhibition space, and is a good example of 21st-century museum design, in that it refers outside to what it holds inside. Architecturally, it honors traditional methods of worship and natural conservation as well as showcases arts and traditional crafts. Here the term "American Indian" means much more than those of the United States; it also includes indigenous tribes from Canada, Alaska, Mexico, and Central and South America (though less heavily). The exhibits are relatively small, but the shop is one of the most alluring—silver and turquoise, wood carvings, feather masks, fine pottery and glass, and ivory and stone carvings—and the café is a popular draw. The museum sits on a 4.25-acre site with natural rock formations and native plants set in a forest, wetlands, meadowlands, and croplands.

TOURING TIPS The museum's Mitsitam Café, an undulating and quite upscale cafeteria featuring regional dishes from salmon and tacos to venison and bison, is one of the best around the Mall, so at prime lunchtime it's filled with federal workers as well as tourists. Eat early or later—it's open 10 a.m. to 5 p.m. daily.

OTHER THINGS TO DO NEARBY The Air and Space Museum is next door; the Botanic Garden beyond that.

National Museum of Crime & Punishment   ★ ★ ½

APPEAL BY AGE	PRESCHOOL ★½	GRADE SCHOOL ★★½	TEENS ★★½
YOUNG ADULTS ★★★		OVER 30 ★★★	SENIORS ★★½

Location 575 Seventh Street NW; **Nearest Metro stations** Gallery Place–Chinatown, Archives–Navy Memorial–Penn Quarter; ☎ 202-393-1099; www.crimemuseum.org

Type of attraction Half-exhibits, half-games collection of real and replica weapons, gangster memorabilia, and with a live studio view of *America's Most Wanted*. **Admission** $18 adults; $15 military and law enforcement officers, seniors, and ages 5–11; children 4 and under free. *Note:* discounted tickets available online. **Hours** Vary; check the website listed above for hours on the date of your visit. **Special comments** There are plenty of interactive games, so adjust the time required if you or your companions insist on playing them all. No food concessions on site. **How much time to allow** 1½ hours.

DESCRIPTION AND COMMENTS The style of this theatrical and sometimes garish attraction was clearly inspired by the nearby International Spy Museum, and likely if you enjoy one, you'll enjoy the other. You can put your head into a pillory and have your photo taken, video-drive a cop car in pursuit of a perp, attempt to hack a computer system, and so on. *Chamber of Horrors* fans can peruse the medieval torture items, while *CSI* addicts can try to solve the murder from a crime scene. If you're here for education, however, pay close attention to the exhibits; some are authentic and some are simply Hollywood hoopla, such as the touring car from the movie *Bonnie and Clyde*, not the gangsters themselves.

TOURING TIPS The gift shop is only marginal; the one at the Spy Museum around the corner is better.

OTHER THINGS TO DO NEARBY In addition to the International Spy Museum, you're within sight of the Navy Memorial, the National Portrait Gallery/American Art Museum, and so on.

National Museum of Health and Medicine ★★

APPEAL BY AGE	PRESCHOOL —	GRADE SCHOOL ★★	TEENS ★★★
YOUNG ADULTS ★★★		OVER 30 ★★★	SENIORS ★★★

Location On the grounds of Walter Reed Army Medical Center, located between 16th Street and Georgia Avenue NW, near Takoma Park, MD; **Nearest Metro station** Takoma (15-minute walk); ☎ 202-782-2200; nmhm.washingtondc.museum

Type of attraction A medical museum (self-guided tour). **Admission** Free. **Hours** Daily, 10 a.m.–5:30 p.m.; closed Christmas Day. Docent-led tours are offered on the second and fourth Saturdays of the month at 1 p.m. **When to go** Anytime. **Special comments** Some excellent exhibits, but a bit unsettling. Though not as gruesome as it used to be, it's still not a place for the squeamish, and it's hard to get to. Some teenagers will love it, however. **How much time to allow** 1 hour.

DESCRIPTION AND COMMENTS Excellent exhibits on the human body make this museum a worthwhile destination. Although there are still plenty of bottled human organs, skeletons, and graphic illustrations of the effects of disfiguring diseases, the emphasis has shifted from the bizarre to education. Exhibits on medicine in the Civil War and an extensive microscope collection (including huge electron microscopes) will probably have more appeal to physicians, scientists, and other health professionals (unless you're addicted to forensic-thriller TV or slasher films).

TOURING TIPS The museum is in the south end of Building 54 (behind the large hospital building). There's a small parking lot next to the museum.

OTHER THINGS TO DO NEARBY No recommendation due to lackluster location.

kids National Museum of Natural History (*a Smithsonian museum*) ★★★★★

APPEAL BY AGE	PRESCHOOL ★★★★	GRADE SCHOOL ★★★★★	TEENS ★★★★★
YOUNG ADULTS ★★★★★		OVER 30 ★★★★★	SENIORS ★★★★★

Location On the Mall at Tenth Street NW and Constitution Avenue; **Nearest Metro stations** Smithsonian, Archives, Federal Triangle; ☎ 202-633-1000 or 202-357-1729 (TDD); www.mnh.si.edu

Type of attraction America's treasure chest of the natural sciences and human culture (self-guided tour). **Admission** Free; IMAX admission is $8.50 ages 13–59, $7 for seniors and children ages 2–12; butterfly pavilion $6 adults, $5.50 ages 60 and up, $5 ages 2–12. **Hours** Daily, 10 a.m.–5:30 p.m.; open until 7:30 p.m.

during the summer months; closed Christmas Day. **When to go** Before noon and after 4 p.m. Free highlight tours Tuesday–Friday (except federal holidays) at 10:30 a.m. and 1:30 p.m. (except July and August). Ocean Hall tours Saturdays and Sundays at 11 a.m. and 2 p.m. **Special comments** Dinosaurs, dioramas, and diamonds make this museum a classic—that, and an IMAX theater. Cafeteria on site. **How much time to allow** 2 hours is enough time to see the really cool stuff (not including the IMAX), but you could easily spend an entire day here.

DESCRIPTION AND COMMENTS Distinguished by its golden dome and the towering bull elephant in the rotunda, the Museum of Natural History is a Washington landmark. It's also old-fashioned, with long halls filled with dioramas, display cases, and hanging specimens that reflect the Victorian obsession with collecting things. This museum, along with Air and Space across the Mall, is immensely popular with families, and for a good reason—folks of all ages and tastes will find fascinating things to see here.

The Janet Annenberg Hooker Hall of Geology, Gems, and Minerals—home, most famously, to the supposedly cursed 45.52-carat Hope Diamond—but also to a blue diamond that may have inspired *Titanic*'s fictional "Heart of the Ocean" gem—features meteorites, emeralds, a 23,000-carat topaz, crystals, a walk-through mine, a re-creation of a cave, and a plate tectonics gallery showing how the earth's surface shifts, plus the now-requisite interactive computers, animated graphics, film and video presentations, and hands-on exhibits.

A new mammal hall premiered in 2003, with state-of-the-art dioramas; an even more impressive renovation, the 23,000-square-foot Ocean Hall, opened in the fall of 2008, combining oceanographic, sea life, and weather exhibits. Its unofficial mascot is the 45-foot replica of a North Atlantic right whale hanging overhead, a scale model of a real whale named Phoenix whom scientists have been tracking since her birth in 1987. (Right underneath her in a metal case is a 24-foot female giant squid, a real one; the male is nearby, and not so large.) The 1,500-gallon aquarium holds a living coral reef. Then there's the great white shark, extinct, and a good thing too; the jaw alone, seen here, is six feet across. In the modernized Discovery Room, kids ages 4 years and up can touch nearly everything. Hours: Tuesday–Thursday, noon–2:30 p.m.; Friday, 10:30 a.m.–2:30 p.m.; weekends, 10:30 a.m.–3:30 p.m.

In addition to the big guys, animal and mineral, check out the little ones in the Insect Zoo, which features a wide array of (live) bugs. Don't overlook the very real spoils of Troy, 5,000-year-old finds from the real city's ruins. Special exhibits are located on the ground level (Constitution Avenue entrance).

TOURING TIPS Save time by buying IMAX tickets in advance at **www.si.edu/ imax** or calling ☎ 202-633-4629. On Tuesdays the live butterfly pavilion is free, but timed tickets are required; ☎ 877-932-4629 or 202-633-4629 up to two weeks in advance. If you have kids, make the popular Discovery Room your first stop; if it's busy, pick up free timed tickets, tour the rest of the museum, and return at the time stamped on your ticket.

OTHER THINGS TO DO NEARBY The National Museum of American History is next door; the Old Post Office Pavilion is about a block away on 12th Street NW. In good weather, there is free music on the Woodrow Wilson Plaza at 13th and Pennsylvania Avenue NW.

National Museum of Women in the Arts ★★★★

APPEAL BY AGE	PRESCHOOL ★	GRADE SCHOOL ★★	TEENS ★★★
YOUNG ADULTS ★★★	OVER 30 ★★★★		SENIORS ★★★★

Location 1250 New York Avenue NW; Nearest Metro station Metro Center; ☎ 202-783-5000 or 800-222-7270; www.nmwa.org

Type of attraction The world's single most important collection of art by women (self-guided tour). Admission $10 adults, $8 seniors 65+ and students, free for ages 18 and under. Hours Monday–Saturday, 10 a.m.–5 p.m.; Sunday, noon–5 p.m.; closed Thanksgiving, Christmas, and New Year's days. When to go Anytime. Special comments Both the building and the art are superb, and under-attended. Café on site. How much time to allow 1–2 hours.

DESCRIPTION AND COMMENTS This groundbreaking gendercentric museum has a permanent collection of paintings and sculpture that includes art by Georgia O'Keeffe, Frida Kahlo, and Helen Frankenthaler, as well as art by women from the 16th century to the present. From the outside, it looks like any other office building along crowded New York Avenue. But inside the former Masonic Grand Lodge are striking architectural features such as a crystal chandelier, a main hall and mezzanine, and the Grand Staircase. The second-floor balcony hosts temporary exhibits; the third floor is where you'll find the permanent collection. The annex showcases sculpture and contemporary works by lesser-known women artists. While this beautiful museum a little off the beaten path deserves to be seen by more people, first-time visitors can wait and enjoy it on a later trip.

TOURING TIPS Take the elevator to the fourth (top) floor and work your way down. Admission is free the first Sunday of each month.

OTHER THINGS TO DO NEARBY A block away is the old Greyhound Bus Station, now a fully restored Art Deco masterpiece with a brewpub inside. The City Museum of Washington is a couple of blocks away on New York Avenue at Mount Vernon Square.

National Portrait Gallery–Smithsonian American Art Museum ★★★★★

APPEAL BY AGE	PRESCHOOL ★	GRADE SCHOOL ★★	TEENS ★★½
YOUNG ADULTS ★★★½	OVER 30 ★★★★		SENIORS ★★★★

Location Eighth and F streets NW; Nearest Metro stations Gallery Place–Chinatown, Archives–Navy Memorial–Penn Quarter; ☎ 202-633-8300; americanart.si.edu/reynolds_center/

Type of attraction Two major American art collections joined in one beautifully restored building. Admission Free. Hours Daily, 11:30 a.m.–7 p.m.; closed Christmas Day. When to go Anytime. Special comments The museums are housed in a beautiful historic space. A great collection, both modern and traditional. Free MP3 and cellphone tours available. Café in the courtyard. **How much time to allow** 2 hours.

DESCRIPTION AND COMMENTS After a six-year, $283-million renovation, these twin institutions—now collectively known as the Donald W. Reynolds Center for American Art and Portraiture, in honor of the philanthropist whose donations made the renovation possible (and who also paid for most of the new Mount Vernon museum and visitor center)—are housed in one of Washington's great buildings: the 1836 Patent Office, which in Pierre L'Enfant's plan for the city marks the central point between the White House and Capitol building. The original architect, Robert Mills, had studied with Jefferson, designed the Washington Monument, and took much of his inspiration from the Parthenon. The third floor Great Room in the National Portrait Gallery was believed to be the largest room in the country when it was built.

After decades of ill-advised additions, including false ceilings, walls and window barriers, linoleum, fluorescent lights, and the like, the structure has been elegantly returned to its airy self, with vaulted ceilings, dozens of skylights, a huge central courtyard covered by a glass ceiling and with a water walk running through it, and cantilevered double staircases.

In its time, the building has housed the Declaration of Independence, Ben Franklin's printing press, Matthew Perry's Japanese mementos, and various inventions of the times (such as false teeth and sewing machines), along with several presidential inaugural balls—not to mention serving as a Union Army hospital, where volunteer nurse Walt Whitman tended the wounded and dying and wrote letters for them and poems about them. It was very nearly demolished in 1953 until preservationists prevailed, and is now one of the city's most popular local museums. Both museums are first-class and house a combination of permanent and shifting exhibitions (the Steven Spielberg and George Lucas collections of Norman Rockwell originals, portraits of Elvis, etc.). Among must-sees are the Gilbert Stuart portrait of Washington in the Presidents gallery (Portrait Gallery), the model of the Statue of Liberty, a casting of the famous Clover Adams memorial, and the stunning "The Throne of the Third Heaven of the Nations' Millennium General Assembly," a huge folk-art piece made of found materials, scavenged furniture, and chewing gum wrappers by illiterate handyman James Hampton; it was discovered in his room after his death (SAAM).

TOURING TIPS The museum complex is so centrally located, and so near a subway stop, that it's a good refuge on a rainy or very hot day; also, since it's open later than most museums, it can become your afternoon destination. Limited but nice, the fourth floor Luce Center has been hosting "Take Five" evenings—live jazz and five new acquisitions—on second Thursdays. There is sometimes entertainment in the courtyard as well.

OTHER THINGS TO DO NEARBY The International Spy Museum is directly across the street, as is the Monaco Hotel, which was built in 1839 to house the city's first general post office. Covering an entire city block and copied from a Roman palazzo, complete with marble columns and facia, the hotel has been beautifully restored. Its restaurant, Poste Moderne (profiled in Part Six: Dining and Restaurants), has a nice open-air bar and lounge that make for a restful break.

kids National Postal Museum ★★★ (a Smithsonian museum)

APPEAL BY AGE	PRESCHOOL ★★	GRADE SCHOOL ★★★	TEENS ★★
YOUNG ADULTS ★★	OVER 30 ★★★		SENIORS ★★★

Location Washington City Post Office building, 2 Massachusetts Avenue NE, next to Union Station; Nearest Metro station Union Station; ☎ 202-633-5555 or 202-633-9849 (tdd); www.postalmuseum.si.edu

Type of attraction Displays from the largest philatelic collection in the world and exhibits about the social, historical, and technological impact of the U.S. postal system, and a few of the planes that set it up (self-guided tour). **Admission** Free. **Hours** Daily, 10 a.m.–5:30 p.m.; closed Christmas Day. Occasional hour-long tours; ask at the information desk. **When to go** Anytime. **Special comments** Nifty. And the building that houses the museum is stunning. No food concession on site. **How much time to allow** 1–2 hours.

DESCRIPTION AND COMMENTS It's more interesting than it sounds, even if you're not one of America's 20 million stamp collectors. Kids will love the real airplanes hanging from the ceiling in the atrium (going back to the 1911 biplane), plus hands-on fun like the chance to sort mail on a train and track a letter from Kansas to Nairobi. One exhibit tells the story of Owney, the stray dog who became the mascot of the Railway Mail Service and rode thousands of miles around the country. Exhibits are arranged so that children and adults are entertained while they're in relative proximity to each other. Themes focus on the history of mail service, how the mail is moved, the social importance of letters, and the beauty and lore of stamps. Serious collectors can call in advance for appointments to see any stamp in the museum's world-class collection or to use the extensive library.

TOURING TIPS Due to its small size (at least when compared to museums on the Mall), it's easy to whiz through it in a half hour or so. And because it's right across the street from Union Station, many folks will find it convenient to drop in while waiting for a train. Ask at the information desk about docent-led "drop-in" tours. *Note:* There's no food concession within the museum itself, but there is a restaurant in the same building.

OTHER THINGS TO DO NEARBY Union Station is next door; the U.S. Capitol is two blocks away.

kids National Wildlife Visitor Center ★★½

APPEAL BY AGE	PRESCHOOL ★★★★	GRADE SCHOOL ★★★★	TEENS ★★★
YOUNG ADULTS ★★★	OVER 30 ★★★		SENIORS ★★★

Location Off Powder Mill Road, 2 miles east of the Baltimore-Washington Parkway, south of Laurel, MD; No Metro access; ☎ 301-497-5760; patuxent.fws.gov/vcdefault.html

Type of attraction A museum featuring wildlife research exhibits located in a 13,000-acre national wildlife refuge about 30 minutes north of Washington. **Admission** Free. **Hours** Daily, March–November, 10 a.m.–5:30 p.m.; closed Christmas Day. **When to go** Anytime. Weekends are busier than weekdays. **Special comments** No food concession on site. Static exhibits and stuffed animals, but a tranquil setting in the heart of the hectic Washington-Baltimore corridor. **How much time to allow** 1–2 hours.

DESCRIPTION AND COMMENTS This large, airy museum operated by the U.S. Department of the Interior is filled with attractive exhibits—dioramas, mostly—focusing on a wide range of wildlife and environmental topics. While the static displays won't accelerate the pulse rates of adults weary from traipsing through Smithsonian edifices on the Mall, children are fascinated by this place. Large dioramas on pollution, overpopulation, forest and ocean degradation, wildlife habitats, wolves, whooping cranes, and other endangered species demonstrate the value of wildlife research.

TOURING TIPS A "viewing pod" equipped with spotting scopes and binoculars lets youngsters (and adults) observe wildlife through a picture window overlooking acres of pond and natural wildlife habitat. If it's a nice day, enjoy the sights and sounds of real wildlife by taking a stroll on paved trails through woods and around ponds populated by geese, ducks, and other animals that find refuge on the refuge. Thirty-minute narrated tram rides with a wildlife interpreter are offered on weekends in the spring and fall and daily from the end of June through August ($3 for adults, $2 for seniors, and $1 for children). On weekends documentary wildlife films are shown in the center's movie theater.

Folks looking for additional outdoor enjoyment and the opportunity to see more wildlife can drive a few miles north to the North Tract of the Patuxent Research Refuge; take the Baltimore-Washington Parkway north two exits to Route 198 east, drive one mile, and turn right onto Bald Eagle Drive to the Visitor Contact Station. The 8,100-acre tract features forest, wetlands, a wildlife viewing area (with an observation tower), and eight miles of paved roads for car touring and bicycling. There are another ten miles of graded gravel roads for hiking, mountain biking, and horseback riding. For more information call ☎ 301-776-3090.

OTHER THINGS TO DO NEARBY The National Cryptologic Museum is located next to the huge National Security Agency complex near the intersection of Baltimore-Washington Parkway and Route 32; drive north on the parkway a few miles and follow the signs. For a large selection of fast-food options, take the parkway north a few miles to Route 197.

National World War II Memorial ★★

APPEAL BY AGE	PRESCHOOL ★	GRADE SCHOOL ★★	TEENS ★★
YOUNG ADULTS ★★★	OVER 30 ★★★	SENIORS ★★★★★	

Location At 17th Street NW and the Mall, between the Washington

Monument and the Lincoln Memorial; Nearest Metro station **Smithsonian; www.wwiimemorial.com and www.nps.gov/nwwm**

Type of attraction A memorial on the National Mall to the 16 million Americans who served in uniform during World War II. **Admission** Free. **Hours** Park rangers on site each day except Christmas Day. The monument may be closed during July 4th celebrations. **When to go** Anytime (except during inclement weather). **Special comments** A limited number of handicapped parking spaces are available. Impressive, but a little stodgy, not in the same ballpark as the FDR Memorial. **How much time to allow** 30 minutes to an hour.

DESCRIPTION AND COMMENTS The "greatest generation" gets its due in this new memorial, dedicated in May 2004, for its contributions in winning the most devastating war in human history (which killed 50 million people). Two 43-foot arches, a 17-foot pillar for each state and territory, and 4,000 gold stars honor the more than 400,000 soldiers who died in the conflict. The assemblies of white granite surround a large pool, fountains, and a piazza located in a spectacular setting. However moving to some, the overall effect is oddly stilted, even militaristic (and not in an appropriate way).

TOURING TIPS In the summer, go in the morning or evening to avoid the worst heat of the day. Clean, modern, and air-conditioned restrooms—a scarce commodity on the Mall—are located behind the visitor center (on the Pacific pavilion side of the memorial).

OTHER THINGS TO DO NEARBY You're in the heart of tourist Washington. The Lincoln Memorial, the Washington Monument, and the Vietnam Veterans Memorial are nearby, as are the Martin Luther King Jr. Memorial (under construction) and the Korean War Veterans Memorial. The Smithsonian museum complex is on the other side of the Washington Monument. The Bureau of Engraving and Printing and the National Holocaust Memorial are on 15th Street, south of the Washington Monument. The FDR Memorial is on the Tidal Basin, across Independence Avenue (to the south).

kids National Zoological Park ★★★★★
(part of the Smithsonian Institution)

APPEAL BY AGE	PRESCHOOL ★★★★★	GRADE SCHOOL ★★★★★	TEENS ★★★★
YOUNG ADULTS ★★★★	OVER 30 ★★★★		SENIORS ★★★★

Location 3001 Connecticut Avenue NW; Nearest Metro stations **Woodley Park–Zoo/Adams Morgan, Cleveland Park;** ☎ **202-673-4800 (24-hour recording) or 202-673-7800 (TDD); nationalzoo.si.edu**

Type of attraction The Smithsonian's world-class zoo. **Admission** Free. **Hours** April–October: grounds are open 6 a.m.–8 p.m. and buildings are open 10 a.m.–6 p.m.; October–March: Grounds open 6 a.m.–6 p.m. and buildings are open 10 a.m.–4:30 p.m. The Pollinarium and the invertebrate exhibits are closed Tuesdays. The park is closed Christmas Day only. **When to go** Anytime. In the summer, avoid going during Washington's sweltering afternoons. In the spring, avoid visiting between 10 a.m. and 2 p.m. weekdays, when many school buses full of children arrive. **Special comments** Many sections of the paths winding through the Zoo's 163 acres are steep. A first-rate operation in a beautiful setting. **How much time to allow** 2 hours just to see the most popular attractions; a whole day to see it all. Better yet, see the Zoo over several visits.

DESCRIPTION AND COMMENTS The National Zoo emphasizes natural environment, with many animals roaming large enclosures instead of pacing in cages. And it's all found in a lush woodland setting in a section of Rock Creek Park. Two main paths link the many buildings and exhibits: Olmstead Walk, which passes all the animal houses, and the steeper Valley Trail, which includes all the aquatic exhibits. They add up to about two miles of trail. The Zoo's nonlinear layout and lack of sight lines make a map invaluable; pick one up at the Education Building near the entrance for a buck. The most popular exhibits include the elephants (a $60-million expansion of the Asian elephant house, including more elaborate and authentic terrain, should be complete by 2011); the great apes; the white tiger; the cheetahs; and the giant pandas, Tian Tian and Mei Xiang (their famously photogenic cub, Tai Shan, had to be returned to China) in their new 12,000-square-foot habitat, complete with Chinese-style "mist" and rocky landscapes. The panda habitat is part of the Asia Trail, also stocked up with sloth bears, giant Japanese salamanders, otters, and the endangered clouded leopards.

For diversity and a good chance of seeing some animal activity, check out the Small Mammal House, the invertebrate exhibit (kids can look through microscopes), and the huge outside bird cages (the condors look the size of Volkswagens).

Don't miss three permanent exhibits: Pollinarium, Think Tank, and the Amazonia Science Gallery. Pollinarium, a lush garden housed in a 1,250-square-foot greenhouse, features hundreds of zebra long-wing butterflies that flutter around as visitors get a firsthand look at animal pollinators, plants, and the process of pollination. A glass-enclosed beehive gives an up-close glimpse of the activities of thousands of honeybees.

Think Tank, a 15,000-square-foot exhibit that opened in late 1995, attempts to answer the question, "Can animals think?" Scientists conduct demonstrations on language, tool use, and social organization. Displays, artifacts, graphics, and videos cover topics such as problem-solving ability, brain size, and language. Four animal species are featured in the exhibit: orangutans, Sulawesi macaque monkeys, hermit crabs, and leaf-cutter ants.

Amazonia is a 15,000-square-foot rain forest habitat; a biodiversity demonstration lab is equipped with a working electron microscope and with displays of living beetles, frog eggs, tadpoles, and boas. (What kid could resist?) The two-meter-diameter "Geosphere" globe uses projectors, satellite imagery, and computer data to show seasonal changes, weather and land cultivation patterns, population distribution, and other factors that affect life on earth.

TOURING TIPS Plan to visit either early or late in the day. Animals are more active, temperatures are cooler, and crowds are thinner. During busy periods, some exhibits are subject to "controlled access" to prevent crowding; in other words, you may have to wait in line. If it is rainy, most of the indoor exhibits can be found along Olmstead Walk. Feedings and demonstrations occur throughout the day at the cheetah, elephant, seal, and sea lion exhibits; check at the Education Building for times. Despite the fact that one Metro station is called Woodley Park/National Zoo, you should actually take the Cleveland Park Metro *to* the Zoo and then head downhill to the Woodley Park station when you're through.

Newseum ★★★★★

APPEAL BY AGE	PRESCHOOL ★½	GRADE SCHOOL ★★★	TEENS ★★★½
YOUNG ADULTS ★★★★		OVER 30 ★★★★	SENIORS ★★★★

Location 555 Pennsylvania Avenue NW; Nearest Metro stations Archives– Navy Memorial–Penn Quarter, Gallery Place–Chinatown; ☎ 888-6397386; www.newseum.org

Type of attraction Wide-ranging salute both to the power of the media (traditional and high-tech) and to the importance of journalism itself. **Admission** $20 adults, $13 ages 7–18, and $18 ages 65+; children 6 and under free. **Hours** Daily, 9 a.m.–5 p.m.; closed Thanksgiving Day, Christmas Day, and New Year's Day. **How much time to allow** 2–3 hours.

DESCRIPTION AND COMMENTS The mission of this museum is literally right up front: the words of the First Amendment are chiseled into the façade of the striking glass and steel six-story museum, and there are 80 front pages culled from 600 newspapers worldwide on display every day. Among the major attractions are the studio from which Christiane Amanpour hosts *This Week with . . .* (and no, that view isn't fake—it's just one of the museum's several extraordinary views of the Mall and government buildings), a 4-D film about the history of investigative reporting, a huge display of front pages from noteworthy events (the hanging of Jesse James, the bombing of Pearl Harbor, the sinking of the *Titanic*, Nixon's resignation, the 1890 "J'Acusee!" page, etc.), Pulitzer Prize–winning photographs, and special exhibits on loan from the FBI collection, the first being on "G-Men and Journalists." There are also more sobering displays, including a wall of honor listing journalists killed in the course of reporting (and some of the blood-stained reminders), a section of the Berlin Wall, and a piece of the transmission tower from the World Trade Center. A 100-foot crawl wall keeps you up to date with breaking news. Younger visitors will be thrilled by the interactive games (adults can play the ethics quiz as well), and the blue-wall video technology that allows them to play reporter (for an additional charge).

TOURING TIPS There is a food court, but the Newseum is also home to one of Washington's celebrity restaurants, Wolfgang Puck's Source. Do bring a camera; although you can't take pictures of the exhibits, you should send home photos from the outdoor walkways of yourself with the Capitol in the background.

OTHER THINGS TO DO NEARBY   Again, this is the heart of Penn Quarter; the International Spy Museum, National Portrait Gallery–American Art Museum, and National Museum of Crime & Punishment are the closest.

The Octagon   ★ ★ ★ *(closed for renovation)*

APPEAL BY AGE	PRESCHOOL ★	GRADE SCHOOL ★★	TEENS ★★
YOUNG ADULTS ★★★		OVER 30 ★★★	SENIORS ★★★

Location 1799 New York Avenue NW; Nearest Metro station Farragut West; ☎ 202-638-3221; www.archfoundation.org/octagon

Type of attraction One of the first great homes built in Washington; a museum showcasing American architecture and historic preservation (guided tour). **Admission** $5 adults, $3 students and seniors. **Hours** Tuesday–Sunday, 10 a.m.– 4 p.m.; closed Mondays, Thanksgiving, Christmas, and New Year's days. **When to go** Anytime. **Special comments** This museum belongs to the American Architectural Foundation, and only prearranged group tours are available. **How much time to allow** 1 hour.

DESCRIPTION AND COMMENTS   This elegant building is where President James Madison and First Lady Dolley Madison took up temporary residence after the British burned the White House during the War of 1812. Built in 1801 (when Washington was mostly swamp), this early Federalist building is undergoing a $5-million, six-year renovation; it's owned by the American Architectural Foundation. Period rooms on the first floor offer visitors a glimpse of how the upper crust lived in the early days of Washington; the coal stoves in the entrance hall are original. The former bedrooms upstairs are now galleries displaying temporary exhibits on architecture and design.

TOURING TIPS   Interpreters give half-hour tours of the building that provide additional glimpses into the past—and tell fascinating anecdotes about the building and the city's early days. For example, President Madison signed the Treaty of Ghent, which ended the war that had driven him from the White House, in the upstairs parlor. Later the building served as a girls' school and was subdivided into ten apartments before it was acquired by the American Architectural Foundation in 1899.

OTHER THINGS TO DO NEARBY   The Corcoran Gallery of Art is a block away. The Renwick Gallery and the White House are also nearby.

 **kids   Old Post Office Tower and Pavilion**   ★ ★ ½

APPEAL BY AGE	PRESCHOOL ★★★	GRADE SCHOOL ★★★★	TEENS ★★★★
YOUNG ADULTS ★★★		OVER 30 ★★★	SENIORS ★★★

Location 12th Street and Pennsylvania Avenue NW; Nearest Metro station Federal Triangle; ☎ 202-289-4224 or 202-606-8691 for the tower; www.oldpostofficedc.com or www.nps.gov/opot

Type of attraction A multiethnic food court in a spectacular architectural setting; home of the second-best view in Washington; trendy shops (guided tour of the tower). **Admission** Free. **Hours** *General:* Labor Day–March 27: Monday–Saturday, 10 a.m.–7 p.m.; Sunday, noon–6 p.m. March 28–Labor Day: Monday–Saturday, 10 a.m.–8 p.m.; Sunday, noon–7 p.m. *Tower:* Labor Day–Memorial Day: Monday–Saturday, 9 a.m.–5 p.m.; Sunday, 10 a.m.–6 p.m. Memorial Day–Labor Day: Monday–Saturday, 9 a.m.–8 p.m.; Sunday, 10 a.m.–6 p.m. **When to go** Anytime to take the glass elevator up the clock tower; beat the worst of the crowds in the food court after 1 p.m. **Special comments** This is the place to come when they run out of time tickets at the Washington Monument. The food court is a favorite stop for tour buses, making it difficult at times to find a table. Frequent live entertainment at lunchtime. *Note:* the federal government is considering redeveloping the building, so check the website before visiting. **How much time to allow** 1 hour for the clock tower.

DESCRIPTION AND COMMENTS This fine old building, a Pennsylvania Avenue landmark, was slated for demolition, but preservationist groups intervened to save it. Today, the 315-foot clock tower offers a spectacular view of Washington, while the multiethnic food court occupies a stunning glass-roofed architectural space ten stories high. It offers a complete tourist experience for people of all ages: a view to kill for (through large plate glass windows, not tiny windows like at the Washington Monument), great food, and a shopping mall. And with its proximity to the Mall and White House, the Pavilion is a convenient place to visit for a quick lunch or snack.

TOURING TIPS It's elbow-to-elbow in the small elevator to the observation deck. Beware of clumps of screaming teenagers in the food court—it's a popular destination for school groups. To reach the glass-enclosed elevators to the observation deck, go to the patio area in the food court. The National Park Service rangers on duty in the tower are a great source of advice about D.C. touring. Ask one to show you the lay of the land from the observation deck. Or, if you want to get out and about, check the kiosks for bike and Segway rental.

OTHER THINGS TO DO NEARBY It's a short walk to the National Aquarium or the Mall.

Old Town Alexandria ★★★★

APPEAL BY AGE	PRESCHOOL ★★	GRADE SCHOOL ★★★	TEENS ★★★
YOUNG ADULTS ★★★★★	OVER 30 ★★★★★		SENIORS ★★★★★

Location In suburban Virginia, 8 miles south of Washington; Nearest Metro station King Street; for more information on Old Town, call the Alexandria Convention and Visitors Association at ☎ 800-388-9119 or 703-838-4200; www.visitalexandriava.com

Type of attraction A restored colonial port town on the Potomac River, featuring 18th-century buildings on cobblestone streets, trendy shops, bars and restaurants, parks, and a huge art center (guided and self-guided tours). **Admission** Some historic sites charge about $5 for adults. Admission to the Torpedo Factory Art Center, the Lyceum, and the George Washington Masonic National Memorial is free. A "key to the city" that offers half-price admission to

9 local attractions, plus discounts to restaurants and shops, is available at Ramsay House, the main visitor center on King Street. **Hours** Historic houses, shops, and the Torpedo Factory Art Center open by 10 a.m. and remain open through the afternoon. Note that many of these attractions may be closed on Mondays. **When to go** Anytime. **Special comments** Though this isn't an attraction in the usual sense, it makes for a fun neighborhood stroll, and free trolley service makes it easy. Also see the Calendar of Special Events in Part One. **How much time to allow** At least half a day. If it's the second half, stay for dinner; Old Town Alexandria has a great selection of restaurants.

DESCRIPTION AND COMMENTS   Alexandria claims both George Washington and Robert E. Lee as native sons, so history buffs have a lot to see. Topping the list are several period revival houses that rival those in Georgetown, another old port up the river. Start with the 1753 Georgian Paladian mansion **Carlyle House,** a living history museum at 121 North Fairfax Street (☎ 703-549-2997; **www.carlylehouse.org**) where Washington not only slept, he was a frequent dinner guest and relation by marriage. Several times a year, reenactors participate in events based on details from Washington's diaries, among other sources. Washington celebrated his birthday at **Gadsby's Tavern Museum** (134 North Royal Street; ☎ 703-838-4242), where you can dine in colonial splendor; and he attended services at **Christ Church** (118 North Washington Street; ☎ 703-544-5883). The **Lee-Fendall House** (614 Oronoco Street; ☎ 703-548-1789), built by a cousin of Revolutionary General Henry "Light Horse Harry" Lee in 1785, remained in Lee family hands until 1902; it has been restored to period glory. The newly restored four-story **Stabler-Leadbetter Apothecary Museum** (105–107 South Fairfax Street; ☎ 703-836-3713), where receipts show Martha Washington and James Monroe both purchased items, is also the site where in 1859 Lt. J. E. B. Stuart, then at the U.S. Army, handed Col. Robert E. Lee—then also an officer in the national force—his orders to quell John Brown's insurrection at Harper's Ferry. (Googlers, save your fingers: "Light Horse" was Robert E. Lee's father.)

This hip, revitalized city on the Potomac is crammed with restaurants (including the five-star Restaurant Eve) and shops (art, jewelry, children's books, antiques, Persian carpets). And, unlike those in Georgetown, the eating and drinking establishments in Old Town aren't overrun by sub-urban teenagers on weekends. There are frequently special or seasonal tours available; go to **www.visitalexandriava.com** for information.

As you exit the King Street Metro station, either board the free Old Town Trolley, which circulates between the station and the waterfront, or walk along King Street for a pleasant 25-minute stroll toward the river. The closest visitor center is at the **Lyceum** (201 South Washington Street; ☎ 703-838-4994), where two exhibition galleries and a museum of the area's history are featured; from King Street, turn right onto Washington Street and walk a block. There's a small museum featuring prints, documents, photographs, silver, furniture, and Civil War memorabilia. Farther down King on the left is **Ramsay House** (221 King Street; ☎ 703-746-3301), built in 1724 and now Alexandria's official visitor center, open

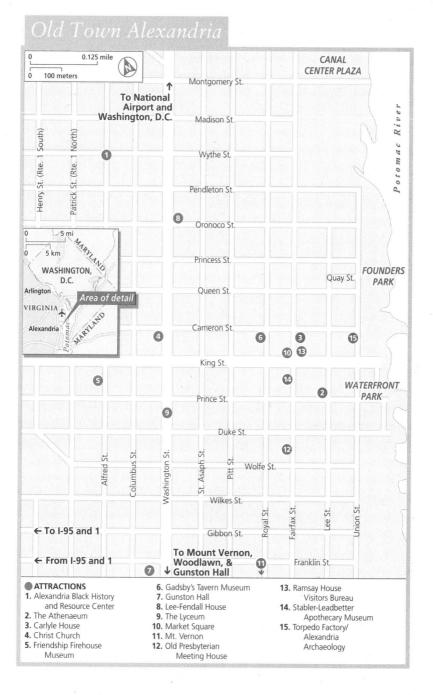

Old Town Alexandria

To National Airport and Washington, D.C.

← To I-95 and 1

← From I-95 and 1

To Mount Vernon, Woodlawn, & Gunston Hall

CANAL CENTER PLAZA

FOUNDERS PARK

WATERFRONT PARK

Potomac River

Montgomery St.

Madison St.

Wythe St.

Pendleton St.

Oronoco St.

Princess St.

Queen St.

Quay St.

Cameron St.

King St.

Prince St.

Duke St.

Wolfe St.

Wilkes St.

Gibbon St.

Franklin St.

Henry St. (Rte. 1 South)

Patrick St. (Rte. 1 North)

Alfred St.

Columbus St.

Washington St.

St. Asaph St.

Pitt St.

Royal St.

Fairfax St.

Lee St.

Union St.

0   0.125 mile
0   100 meters

WASHINGTON, D.C.

Arlington

VIRGINIA

Alexandria

MARYLAND

Area of detail

0   5 mi
0   5 km

● **ATTRACTIONS**

1. Alexandria Black History and Resource Center
2. The Athenaeum
3. Carlyle House
4. Christ Church
5. Friendship Firehouse Museum

6. Gadsby's Tavern Museum
7. Gunston Hall
8. Lee-Fendall House
9. The Lyceum
10. Market Square
11. Mt. Vernon
12. Old Presbyterian Meeting House

13. Ramsay House Visitors Bureau
14. Stabler-Leadbetter Apothecary Museum
15. Torpedo Factory/ Alexandria Archaeology

daily from 10 a.m. to 8 p.m. April through December; 10 a.m.–5 p.m. January through March, except Thanksgiving, Christmas, and New Year's days. Ramsay House is the best starting point for a walking tour of Old Town Alexandria, where you can pick up brochures, walking tours, and tickets to museums. The **Torpedo Factory Art Center** at the foot of King Street features more than 150 painters, printmakers, sculptors, and other artists and craftspeople. Visitors can watch artists at work in their studios housed in the former munitions factory.

TOURING TIPS If you drive to Alexandria, park your car in a two-hour metered space, feed it a nickel or a dime, and go to a visitor center to pick up a pass that lets you park free for 24 hours in any two-hour metered zone inside Alexandria city limits (renewable once); you'll need your vehicle's license plate number. But parking is scarce and the King Street Metro is conveniently located.

OTHER THINGS TO DO NEARBY About a mile west of the center of Alexandria at 101 Callahan Street is the ziggurat-like **George Washington National Masonic Memorial** (☎ 703-683-2007; **www.gwmemorial.org**). A free tour features a view from the 333-foot tower, Washington memorabilia, a 370-year-old Persian rug valued at $1 million, and extensive information about masonry. *Note:* There's a $5 fee for those ages 13 and up to tour the tower exhibits and observation deck. Tours are given Monday through Saturday on the half hour in the mornings and on the hour in the afternoons; the memorial is open October through March, Monday through Saturday, 10 a.m. to 4 p.m. and Sunday 12–4 p.m., and May through September, Monday through Saturday, 9 a.m. to 4 p.m. and Sunday 10 a.m.–4 p.m. Mount Vernon, George Washington's plantation on the Potomac, is eight miles downriver.

Pentagon Memorial ★★★★

APPEAL BY AGE	PRESCHOOL ★	GRADE SCHOOL ★★½	TEENS ★★★
YOUNG ADULTS ★★★★		OVER 30 ★★★★	SENIORS ★★★★

Location Near the south parking area of the Pentagon in Arlington, VA; Nearest Metro station Pentagon

Type of attraction Outdoor memorial to victims of the 9/11 attacks. **Admission** Free. **Hours** Daily 24 hours. **Special comments** Obviously an emotionally loaded site that may have even deeper meaning for anyone who lost family or friends, but its symbolism is quiet enough that young children should not be disturbed. Paved walkways ensure its accessibility. There are no metal detectors or security checkpoints to pass. **How much time to allow** 1 hour.

DESCRIPTION AND COMMENTS This intentionally low-key memorial is designed to encourage visitors to meditate on the enormity of the attacks and of the human toll. As you approach from the plaza, you step across the Zero Line, inscribed "September 11, 2001 9:37 a.m."; the border was cut from the original limestone walls and still shows scorch marks from the fire that followed the impact. There are 184 benches, one for each of those killed when Flight 777, traveling at a speed of 550 mph, struck the building. Under each bench, which resembles a jet wing, is a small pool; during the day they reflect sunlight and at night are lit from beneath the water. Each bench has been oriented so that if you read the name and you're looking at the sky, he or she was actually on the airplane; if the viewpoint is the Pentagon, the victim was in the building. (There is a slab with all the names and years of birth, which is also a locator for benches.) There is a point-of-impact marker, and an "age wall" rises along an arc and reflects the ages of the victims, ranging from 3-year-old Dana Falkenberg, who was in a day care center, to 71-year-old John D. Yamnicky.

TOURING TIPS You are not allowed to take photographs of the Pentagon building itself, or to enter the building without clearance.

OTHER THINGS TO DO NEARBY The Air Force Memorial is a fairly easy walk from here. Pentagon City, just across Army-Navy Drive, is a mall filled with shops and eateries; it also has its own Metro station.

Phillips Collection ★ ★ ★ ★

APPEAL BY AGE	PRESCHOOL —	GRADE SCHOOL ★	TEENS ★★
YOUNG ADULTS ★★★★	OVER 30 ★★★★		SENIORS ★★★★

Location 1600 21st Street NW; Nearest Metro station **Dupont Circle;**
☎ **202-387-2151; www.phillipscollection.org**

Type of attraction The first museum dedicated to modern art in the United States. Admission Weekends: All visitors pay varying special-exhibition fee or $12 ($10 students) if no special exhibition. Admission to the permanent collection is by donation Tuesday–Friday. (Since a fire in 2010, which damaged some of the mansion infrastructure, additional donations are requested.) Hours Tuesday–Saturday, 10 a.m.–5 p.m.; Sunday, 11 a.m.–6 p.m. (5 p.m. June–September). Open Thursday until 8:30 p.m. Closed Mondays, New Year's Day, Fourth of July, plus Thanksgiving and Christmas days. When to go Anytime; Saturdays at 2 p.m. for free guided tours. Special comments With lots of carpeting and places to sit, the Phillips Collection is a very comfortable museum to tour. The café is open Tuesday–Saturday 10 a.m.–4 p.m. and Sunday 11 a.m.–4 p.m. One of the best art museums in Washington. How much time to allow 2 hours.

DESCRIPTION AND COMMENTS Founded by Duncan Phillips, grandson of the founder of the Jones and Laughlin Steel Company, the Phillips Collection is partially set in the family's former mansion (which helps explain its intimate and comfortable feeling) and partly in an airy, well-lit addition. The collection is too large for everything to be on display at once, so the art is constantly rotated, although what is probably its most famous painting, Renoir's "Luncheon of the Boating Party," is a staple. Expect to see works by Monet, Picasso, Miró, Renoir, and Van Gogh, among other modern masters. The large and ornate Music Room is as spectacular as the art hanging on its walls. Over the past several years, the Phillips has expanded twice into adjoining town houses to allow for larger visiting exhibits, and the café is expanding as well. If you've seen the Hirshhorn and the National Gallery of Art's East Wing, this should be on your agenda. It's a classy museum on a human scale.

TOURING TIPS Take advantage of the Saturday tours; the well-informed guides do a good job of giving a context for the paintings and sculptures, the building, and its founder's taste in modern art. In good weather, the café has outdoor seating.

OTHER THINGS TO DO NEARBY Cross Massachusetts Avenue and see another eye-popping mansion, the Anderson House (open Tuesday through Saturday from 1 to 4 p.m.). The Woodrow Wilson House is ten minutes away.

President Lincoln's Cottage ★★★★★

APPEAL BY AGE	PRESCHOOL ★	GRADE SCHOOL ★★★	TEENS ★★★
YOUNG ADULTS ★★★★	OVER 30 ★★★★★		SENIORS ★★★★★

Location **Rock Creek Church Road and Upshur Street NW; No Metro access; ☎ 202-829-0436; www.lincolncottage.org**

Type of attraction Summer home and effectual second White House for President Lincoln and his family (guided tour). Admission $12 adults, $5 ages 6–12. Hours November–March: Monday–Saturday, guided tours, 10 a.m.–3 p.m. (on the hour); visitor center, 9:30 a.m.–4:30 p.m. Sunday, guided tours, noon–3 p.m. (on the hour); visitor center, 11:30 a.m.–4:30 p.m. Open 1 hour later April–October. Special comments Food concession on site. How much time to allow 2 hours.

DESCRIPTION AND COMMENTS This Gothic Revival home—called a cottage and fairly simple, but with 34 rooms—served five chief executives as a summer retreat (including James Buchanan, Rutherford B. Hayes, and Chester A. Arthur), but the length of time Lincoln spent there (from June to November each year from 1862 to 1864) and the fact that several crucial historical events happened here, including the drafting of the Emancipation Proclamation, have indelibly linked it to the Civil War leader. The campus was the original Retired Soldiers' Home, so the mural in the visitor center across the driveway shows both the President and his son Tad engaging the veterans. The visitor center also has an orientation video and a four-room exhibition center with interactive maps and anecdotes (the President once barely escaped assassination riding from the White House to the cottage, and a bullet hole in his stovepipe hat attests to it) and signed copies of the Emancipation Proclamation and the 13th Amendment outlawing slavery. In the cottage itself, guides provide part of the narration and dramatic readings and theatrical lighting provide the rest. (An elevator has been added to make most of the cottage accessible.)

TOURING TIPS Of the several Lincoln-centric sites (Ford's Theatre, the Lincoln Memorial, Museum of American History), this might be the last on the list, but only because of its limited accessibility. Serious Abe fans should weigh taking a cab.

OTHER THINGS TO DO NEARBY Just north of the main gate is Rock Creek Cemetery, where many cabinet members, congressmen, Supreme Court justices, and presidential relations (Henry Adams, Alice Roosevelt Longworth, etc.) are buried; but its most famous monument is the statue and grove dedicated to John Quincy Adams' wife Clover, with the hooded figure by Saint-Gauden often called "Grief" and setting by famed architect Stanford White. St. Paul's Church in the cemetery, built in 1712, is the only surviving colonial church in Washington, its 18-inch brick walls and stained-glass windows have survived many trials.

Renwick Gallery (*a Smithsonian museum*) ★★★

APPEAL BY AGE	PRESCHOOL ★	GRADE SCHOOL ★★	TEENS ★★
YOUNG ADULTS ★★	OVER 30 ★★★		SENIORS ★★★

Location **17th Street and Pennsylvania Avenue NW (diagonally across from the White House);** Nearest Metro station **Farragut West;** ☎ **292-633-1000 or 202-633-2850** (TTY); **www.americanart.si.edu/renwick**

Type of attraction A museum dedicated to American crafts and decorative arts (self-guided tour). Admission Free. Hours Daily, 10 a.m.–5:30 p.m.; closed Christmas Day. When to go Anytime. Special comments From Mid-June to mid-September, free tours Friday at noon and Saturdays and Sundays at 1 p.m.; the rest of the year, free tours weekdays at noon and weekends at 1 p.m. An elegant setting, yet a bit dull. How much time to allow 1 hour.

DESCRIPTION AND COMMENTS This branch of the American Art Museum features a wide array of mixed-media sculptures, tapestries, and constructions by major contemporary artists, which makes for an especially attractive museum shop. It's named for the building's architect, James Renwick, who also designed the Smithsonian's whimsical Arts and Industries Building (and St. Patrick's Cathedral in New York City). Both the art and the Second Empire architecture of the mansion make this Smithsonian museum worth a stop when you're near the White House. Works on display are constructed in glass, ceramics, wood, fiber, and metal. However, it might be a second-trip listing except for those with special interest.

TOURING TIPS Glide up the Grand Staircase to enter the elegant Grand Salon, now an art gallery featuring floor-to-ceiling oil paintings, velvet curtains, and traditional furniture. On the same floor is the elegant Octagon Room, which faces the street and is used as exhibition space. The first floor hosts temporary exhibits. A family scavenger-hunt map is available at the information desk.

OTHER THINGS TO DO NEARBY Next door is Blair House, where visiting foreign dignitaries stay; you can't get in, but look for Secret Service agents and diplomatic limos. A plaque on the wrought-iron gates honors a guard who saved President Truman from a would-be assassin.

Smithsonian Institution Building ★★★★ *aka* the Castle

APPEAL BY AGE	PRESCHOOL —	GRADE SCHOOL ★★	TEENS ★★
YOUNG ADULTS ★★★	OVER 30 ★★★★	SENIORS	★★★★

Location **1000 Jefferson Drive SW, on the Mall;** Nearest Metro station **Smithsonian;** ☎ **202-633-1000 or 202-357-1729** (TDD); **www.si.edu**

Type of attraction Information desks and displays, and a continuously running movie that introduces visitors to the vast number of Smithsonian museums. **Admission** Free. **Hours** Daily, 8:30 a.m.–5:30 p.m.; closed Christmas Day. **When to go** Anytime. **Special comments** A must for first-time Mall visitors. Food concession on site. **How much time to allow** 30 minutes.

DESCRIPTION AND COMMENTS This redbrick building—you can't miss it—contains no exhibits. Known as "the Castle" for obvious architectural reasons, it is the original Smithsonian museum, and was designed by James Renwick, who also designed St. Patrick's Cathedral in New York (and the nearby Renwick Gallery). It now serves as an information center that will help you save time and trouble and reduce the frustration of visiting the Smithsonian's large and perplexing museum complex. Step into one of the two theaters to see the ten-minute film featuring Ben Stiller (he of *Night at the Museum: Battle of the Smithsonian*) that highlights some of the riches each museum has to offer. Then you can talk to someone at the information desk for specific directions and advice (including multilingual assistance). Among the many interactive exhibits is a map that lights up the location of each of the museums on the Mall, as well as other popular D.C. sights, when you press the corresponding button.

Society of the Cincinnati Museum at Anderson House ★★★★

APPEAL BY AGE	PRESCHOOL ★	GRADE SCHOOL ★★	TEENS ★★
YOUNG ADULTS ★★	OVER 30 ★★★★		SENIORS ★★★★

Location 2118 Massachusetts Avenue NW; Nearest Metro station Dupont Circle; ☎ 202-785-2040; www.societyofthecincinnati.org

Type of attraction A combination mansion and Revolutionary War museum. **Admission** Free. **Hours** Tuesday–Saturday, 1–4 p.m.; closed New Year's Day, Thanksgiving, and Christmas. **When to go** Anytime. **Special comments** Robber-baron decadence. Children will love the Revolutionary War figurines fighting battles; older folks will marvel at the opulence. Guided tours at 1:15 p.m., 2:15 p.m., and 3:15 p.m. **How much time to allow** 1 hour.

DESCRIPTION AND COMMENTS This mansion along Embassy Row is a real sleeper that few visitors ever see. Built in 1906 by Larz Anderson, a diplomat, it's a reflection of fabulous turn-of-the-century taste and wealth. The two-story ballroom is a stunner: tapestries line the crystal chandeliered dining room, and paintings by Gilbert Stuart and John Trumbull hang in the billiard room. Anderson was a member of the Society of the Cincinnati, co-founded by George Washington and whose members are descendants of French and American officers who served in the Revolutionary Army. After his death, his widow donated the mansion to the society. Today the building serves the society as both headquarters and museum. Even first-time visitors to D.C. should make the effort to see this spectacular mansion, which is located a block or so from Dupont Circle.

The first floor contains displays of Revolutionary War artifacts. On the second floor, the mansion remains as it was originally furnished, with 18th-century paintings, 17th-century tapestries from Brussels, and huge chandeliers. (See the section above on "Best Inside Tours" for more on the exhibits.)

TOURING TIPS This is the heart of what was once called "Millionaire's Row," now called Embassy Row; the Indonesian Embassy at 2020 Massachusetts Avenue belonged to Evalyn Walsh McLean, last private owner of the Hope Diamond. Take the 15-minute tour; it's like Hillwood in Dupont Circle.

OTHER THINGS TO DO NEARBY Within walking distance are the Phillips Collection, the Christian Heurich Mansion, the Textile Museum, and the Woodrow Wilson House.

Textile Museum ★★

APPEAL BY AGE		PRESCHOOL —		GRADE SCHOOL ★		TEENS ★★
YOUNG ADULTS ★★★			OVER 30 ★★★			SENIORS ★★★

Location **2320 S Street NW;** Nearest Metro station **Dupont Circle;**
☎ **202-667-0441; www.textilemuseum.org**

Type of attraction A museum dedicated to textile arts (self-guided tour). Admission Free; $5 donation suggested. Hours Monday–Saturday, 10 a.m.–5 p.m.; Sunday, 1–5 p.m.; closed federal holidays and December 24. When to go Anytime. Special comments Interesting, but small and esoteric, the museum is wheelchair accessible but not barrier-free. Call ahead if you have special needs. Introductory tours are offered weekends at 1:30 p.m., September through May. How much time to allow 1 hour.

DESCRIPTION AND COMMENTS Cloth, a mass-produced commodity in the West, no longer enjoys much prestige as an art form. But it's a different story in the rest of the world. The museum's collection ranges from countries as diverse as India, Indonesia, and China to Mexico, Guatemala, and Peru. Intricate designs and rich colors grace more than 14,000 textiles and 1,400 carpets dating from ancient times to the present day. Because the items can't be exposed to light for long periods of time, the exhibits are constantly rotated. This museum is much more interesting than it sounds—the rich colors derived from natural dye processes and elaborate details in the fabrics are subtly beautiful. Definitely for distinct tastes, but not to be missed if it appeals to you.

TOURING TIPS In the new second-floor Textile Learning Center, visitors can touch, feel, and examine textiles close up. It's an opportunity to get a better grip on how and why textiles are cultural carriers that reveal a lot about how people live. Don't miss the pleasant garden behind the museum. The gift shop is chock-full of books and items related to textiles and rugs.

OTHER THINGS TO DO NEARBY The Woodrow Wilson House is next door. The Islamic Center is around the corner on Massachusetts Avenue. In the other direction, S Street crosses Connecticut Avenue, where you can shop and dine to your heart's content.

Tudor Place ★★★

APPEAL BY AGE	PRESCHOOL ★½	GRADE SCHOOL ★★	TEENS ★★½
YOUNG ADULTS ★★★	OVER 30 ★★★		SENIORS ★★★½

Location 1644 31st Street NW; No Metro access; ☎ 202-965-0400; www.tudorplace.org

Type of attraction Beautifully maintained early-19th-century mansion built by Martha Washington's granddaughter and containing the greatest concentration of Washingtonia outside Mount Vernon. **Admission** $8 adults, $5 seniors 62+ and military, $3 students ages 7–18 (with ID), $2 children ages 6–12, children under 6 free. **Hours** Open for guided tours on the hour Tuesday–Saturday from 10 a.m. to 3 p.m.; Sundays on the hour from noon to 3 p.m. **Special comments** There are plenty of things to entrance kids, but strollers must be left outside. Tour is not recommended for children under age 6. **How much time to allow** 1½ hours.

DESCRIPTION AND COMMENTS Martha Custis Peter and her husband Thomas Peter began construction on this stucco-faced neoclassical mansion in 1806 with the $8,000 she inherited from the first president. It was designed by William Thornton, who also designed the U.S. Capitol; and its circular domed portico is unique. Like nearby Dumbarton House, Tudor Place had a clear view of the burning of the town in 1814. Andrew Jackson visited here on the anniversary of the Battle of New Orleans, and Robert E. Lee, whose wife was Martha Custis's niece, often slept here. Among the items of historical interest are an affectionate note from George Washington to Martha that was found in a secret drawer of her desk, a miniature painting of George on ivory, swords, and antique toys. The grounds are lovely. Here's a funny bit of trivia: The Peter children were patriotically named America, Britannia Wellington, George Washington, and Columbia.

TOURING TIPS There is no café, but the gift shop has many nice items. The gardens are open daily from 10 a.m.–4 p.m.; you cannot enter the house except just before each tour to buy your tickets, but you can pick up a free garden tour and walk about.

OTHER THINGS TO DO NEARBY If George's note to Martha has you in a romantic mood, stop by the house where John and Jackie Kennedy lived at 3307 N Street NW and then head over to Martin's Tavern (Wisconsin Avenue at N Street NW) where he proposed to her as they dined in Booth 3.

Union Station ★★★

APPEAL BY AGE	PRESCHOOL ★	GRADE SCHOOL ★★	TEENS ★★★
YOUNG ADULTS ★★★★	OVER 30 ★★★★		SENIORS ★★★★

Location Massachusetts Avenue and North Capitol Street NE; Nearest Metro station Union Station; ☎ 202-289-1908; www.unionstationdc.com

Type of attraction A spectacular interior space housing a transportation hub, upscale shops, a multiplex, and a food court. **Admission** Free. **Hours** Shops open Monday–Saturday, 10 a.m.–9 p.m.; Sunday, noon–6 p.m. **When to go** Anytime.

Special comments A Beaux-Arts palace and a great lunch stop. The food court's fare is on the expensive side, but the vast selection justifies the extra cost; a handy rainy-day destination. **How much time to allow** 1 hour to wander; longer for shopping or eating.

DESCRIPTION AND COMMENTS The Main Hall, with a 90-foot barrel-vaulted ceiling, is breathtaking. Shops run the gamut: chic clothing stores, The Great Train Store, bookstores, Brookstone, the Nature Company—130 stores altogether. In the food court you'll find everything from sushi to ribs, while a nine-screen cinema complex offers solace on a rainy day. There are also seven restaurants for dining or private functions, an international currency exchange, three sightseeing companies, and three rental-car companies on-site. First-time visitors to D.C. shouldn't miss this magnificent structure. With more than 25 million visitors a year, Union Station is the most-visited tourist attraction in Washington (the National Air and Space Museum is surprisingly only number two).

TOURING TIPS Union Station is a great jumping-off point for touring Washington. Capitol Hill is a few blocks away (step out the front and walk toward the big dome), and Tourmobile, Gray Line, and Old Town Trolley tours stop in front. Monday through Friday, Maryland commuter trains (called MARC) regularly shuttle between D.C. and Baltimore, stopping at points between (a round-trip from Baltimore is $14). Virginia Railway Express shuttles commuters and day-trippers from Fredericksburg, Manassas, and points in between to Union Station weekdays. To top it off, there's a Metro station in the basement. It's hard to believe that Washington functioned before Union Station's rebirth (at a cost of more than $100 million) in 1988.

OTHER THINGS TO DO NEARBY The Postal Museum is next door to Union Station; the U.S. Capitol, the Supreme Court, and the Library of Congress are also close.

U.S. Botanic Garden ★★★

APPEAL BY AGE	PRESCHOOL ★	GRADE SCHOOL ★★	TEENS ★★
YOUNG ADULTS ★★★	OVER 30 ★★★		SENIORS ★★★★

Location 100 Maryland Avenue SW (on the Mall near the U.S. Capitol); Nearest Metro station Federal Center SW; ☎ 202-225-8333; www.usbg.gov

Type of attraction A permanent collection of tropical, subtropical, and desert plants housed in a stunning, fully renovated, 38,000-square-foot greenhouse (self-guided tour). **Admission** Free. **Hours** Conservatory and garden: daily, 10 a.m.–5 p.m. **When to go** Anytime. **Special comments** An excellent and comprehensive collection of plant life. Skip it on a sweltering summer afternoon. **How much time to allow** 30 minutes.

DESCRIPTION AND COMMENTS The Conservatory, a building that reflects the grand manner of Victorian architecture (even though it was constructed in the 1930s), houses a living museum on the Mall. The central jungle resembles an abandoned plantation in a tropical rain forest under a dome that rises to 93 feet. Other sections display orchids, ferns, cacti, and other types of plants in naturalistic settings. While people with green thumbs will want to put these gardens on their first-visit itinerary, most folks will just want to know it's nearby for a quiet break from more hectic sights along the Mall. You can sit down here, relax, read a book—or just do nothing in a magnificent setting.

TOURING TIPS Before or after strolling though this giant greenhouse, visit Frederic Bartholdi Park (open from dawn until dusk), located across Independence Avenue from the Conservatory and named for the designer of the Statue of Liberty. The park features displays of bulbs, annuals, and perennials. The focal point is Bartholdi Fountain, originally exhibited at the 1876 Centennial Exhibition in Philadelphia.

OTHER THINGS TO DO NEARBY The National Air and Space Museum and the Hirshhorn Museum and Sculpture Garden are close, as is the U.S. Capitol (although to tour the building requires time tickets handed out early each morning). L'Enfant Plaza, about five blocks away, has a shopping mall loaded with restaurants and fast-food outlets.

U.S. Capitol ★★★★★

| APPEAL BY AGE | PRESCHOOL ★ | GRADE SCHOOL ★★★ | TEENS ★★★ |
| YOUNG ADULTS ★★★★ | OVER 30 ★★★★★ | | SENIORS ★★★★★ |

Location **East end of the Mall;** Nearest Metro stations **Capitol South, Union Station;** ☎ **202-225-6827 for a recording or 202-225-3121 for the Capitol switchboard; www.visitthecapitol.gov**

Type of attraction The building where Congress meets (guided tours only). Admission Free. Hours The building is open Monday–Saturday, 8:45 a.m.–3:30 p.m., and tours are conducted 8:50 a.m.–3:20 p.m.; visitor center open 8:30 a.m.–4:30 p.m.; closed Thanksgiving, Christmas Day, New Year's Day, and Inauguration Day. Free tickets required. A limited number of same-day tickets are available at the kiosks on the East and West Fronts and the visitor center starting at 8:30 a.m.; reserve in advance at www.visitthecapitol.gov. Special comments Prohibited items include knives, pointed objects, pepper spray, duffel bags, backpacks, aerosol cans, bottles, food, and beverages. The newly opened visitor center is underground on the east side. It houses a cafeteria, gift shop, and restrooms, as well as exhibit spaces. Interesting and beautiful. How much time to allow 2 hours.

DESCRIPTION AND COMMENTS The U.S. Capitol manages to be two things at once: an awesome monument to democracy and one of the most important places in the world, as the frequent presence of reporters and film crews outside attests. The rather brief public tour, however, takes visitors through only a small part of the Capitol: the Rotunda and a few other rooms, which may include Statuary Hall, the House or Senate chambers (when they're not in session), and the low-ceilinged crypt. From the soaring Rotunda to the opulent rooms where the House and Senate meet, the Capitol is both physically beautiful and packed with historical significance. For first-time visitors, the tour is both awe-inspiring and relatively quick (after you've picked up tickets). After a longer-than-expected eight-year construction project, the Capitol's underground visitor center, which has a glorious skylight view of the Capitol dome, has also made space for the many statues and artifacts that were in storage; it also has two videos on the history of the building.

As for the statue atop the dome, whose costume is sometimes the source of disagreement: She is Freedom, who holds a sword in her right hand and a laurel wreath of victory in the right. Her shield bears 13 stripes, and the helmet, encircled with stars, is adorned with an eagle's head, feathers, and talons. (It's these decorations that has led to Freedom sometimes being identified as a Native American maiden.) Just under 20 feet tall, she rises 300 feet above the east plaza.

TOURING TIPS If your plans include viewing a session of Congress, don't make the time-consuming mistake thousands of other visitors make: coming to the Capitol without a gallery pass. Go first to the office of your senator or representative to pick one up. (Don't forget to ask for maps and other helpful touring goodies while you're there.) Don't know the name of your representative or of your senators? Then call ☎ 202-224-3121 for help locating an office. The free tour is heavy on the history of the building, but if your group makes it to either the House or Senate chambers, you'll get a good rundown on how Congress operates. (Stick close to the guide if you expect to hear the entire spiel.)

OTHER THINGS TO DO NEARBY Explore the rest of Capitol Hill: The Supreme Court and Library of Congress face the Capitol's east front. On the other side, the east end of the Mall features the U.S. Botanic Garden and the East Wing of the National Gallery of Art. Capitol Hill is famous for its bars and restaurants. To find them, walk toward Constitution Avenue and past the Library of Congress's Madison Building, located between Independence Avenue and C Street NE.

U.S. Department of the Interior ★ ½ *(closed for renovation)*

APPEAL BY AGE	PRESCHOOL ★	GRADE SCHOOL ★★	TEENS ★
YOUNG ADULTS ★		OVER 30 ★	SENIORS ★

Location 1849 C Street NW between 18th and 19th streets;
Nearest Metro station Farragut West; ☎ 202-208-4743; www.doi.gov

Type of attraction A museum located inside a square-mile chunk of government bureaucracy (self-guided tour). Admission Free; adults must show a photo ID to enter. Hours Monday–Friday, 8:30 a.m.–4:30 p.m., and every third Saturday, 1–4 p.m.; otherwise, closed weekends and federal holidays. When to go Anytime. Special comments Boring. Go on a rainy day. How much time to allow 45 minutes.

DESCRIPTION AND COMMENTS This six-wing, seven-story limestone edifice includes 16 acres of floors and two miles of corridors—along with an old-fashioned museum. Dioramas of mines and geothermal power plants, Native American artifacts, and a historical exhibit of the National Park Service crowd the rather dark and quiet exhibition hall.

This is definitely a rainy-day kind of a museum, unless you have a strong interest in national parks.

TOURING TIPS Outdoors people and map lovers shouldn't miss the U.S. Geological Survey map store, located off the lobby on the E Street side of the building. You can also load up on brochures on any (or all) U.S. national parks at the National Park Service office here. The Indian Craft Shop, across from the museum entrance, sells turquoise and silver jewelry, baskets, and other handicrafts made by Native Americans. The basement cafeteria can seat 1,200 people (open weekdays, 7 a.m. to 2:45 p.m.).

OTHER THINGS TO DO NEARBY The DAR Museum and the Corcoran Gallery of Art are around the corner on 17th Street; the Mall is about two blocks south.

U.S. Department of State Diplomatic Reception Rooms ★ ★ ★ ★ ★

APPEAL BY AGE	PRESCHOOL —	GRADE SCHOOL —	TEENS ★★★★
YOUNG ADULTS ★★★★	OVER 30 ★★★★★		SENIORS ★★★★★

Location 2201 C Street NW; Nearest Metro station Foggy Bottom–GWU; ☎ 202-647-3241, 202-736-4474 (TDD); https://receptiontours.state.gov

Type of attraction The rooms where visiting foreign dignitaries are officially entertained (guided tour). Admission Free. Hours Tours are given Monday–Friday at 9:30 a.m., 10:30 a.m., and 2:45 p.m. by reservation only, which should be made 4 weeks in advance. Special comments See what $90 million in decorative arts can buy. Children under age 12 are not permitted on the tour, nor are strollers, briefcases, or backpacks. Reservations are accepted up to 90 days in advance of your visit. A short, optional public affairs tour is offered after the main tour. Although most tourists miss this, you shouldn't. How much time to allow 1 hour.

DESCRIPTION AND COMMENTS While the State Department goes about its important work in a building with architecture best described as "early airport," the interiors on the eighth floor are something else entirely: A fabulous collection of 18th- and early-19th-century fine and decorative arts fills stunning rooms that are used daily to receive visiting heads of state and foreign dignitaries. This is a tour for almost anyone: antique and fine arts lovers, history buffs, and just casual visitors. It's also a sight that the overwhelming majority of D.C. tourists miss. First-time visitors should make the effort to get reservations well in advance of their trip. Then forget about visiting the White House. (See "Best Inside Tours" above for more information.)

TOURING TIPS By guided tour only; reservations are required and should be made at least four weeks in advance of your visit.

OTHER THINGS TO DO NEARBY The Lincoln Memorial and Vietnam Veterans Memorial are a short walk away, down 23rd Street toward the Mall.

U.S. Department of the Treasury ★ ★ ★ ★

APPEAL BY AGE	PRESCHOOL ★½	GRADE SCHOOL ★★½	TEENS ★★★
YOUNG ADULTS ★★★★	OVER 30 ★★★★★		SENIORS ★★★★

Location Alongside the White House at the corner of 15th Street NW

and Pennsylvania Avenue; Nearest Metro stations **Farragut Square, Federal Triangle; www.ustreas.gov**

Type of attraction Restored 19th-century landmark to American dream of capitalism. **Admission** Free, but reservations available only through Congressional offices. **Hours** Tours Saturdays at 9, 9:45, 10:30 and 11:15 a.m. only (except for some holidays). **Special comments** These are very limited tickets, obviously, and latecomers will not be accommodated. Be sure to bring identification. **How much time to allow** 1 hour.

DESCRIPTION AND COMMENTS After an elaborate renovation, this Gilded Age beauty has been carried back to its glory days but given all the modern electrical and insulation services it had long needed. The renovation exposed a three-story cast iron ceiling dome with gilded trim which had been obscured by a bank of elevators. Among the highlights of the tour are the Andrew Johnson Room, which was where Johnson ran the nation for six weeks after Lincoln's assassination to allow Mary Todd Lincoln time to move out (the black hangings are gone but a portrait of the dead president remains); the two-story Cash Room with its three enormous chandeliers and seven types of marble, which was originally a bank—Lincoln was among those who used it—and also served as the reception site for Grant's inaugural; the Salmon P. Chase suite, which has two fabulous allegorical murals of "Treasury" and "Justice"; and diplomatic reception rooms.

TOURING TIPS Get there on time. Seriously.

OTHER THINGS TO DO NEARBY The White House is next door, but you'll have to have tickets for that too. Otherwise, the Renwick Gallery, Decatur House, and the Corcoran Gallery are a short walk away.

U.S. Holocaust Memorial Museum ★★★★½

| APPEAL BY AGE | PRESCHOOL — | GRADE SCHOOL ★★ | TEENS ★★★ |
| YOUNG ADULTS ★★★½ | OVER 30 ★★★★ | SENIORS ★★★★ |

Location 100 Raoul Wallenberg Place SW (formerly 15th Street), near the Mall between the Washington Monument and the Bureau of Engraving and Printing; entrances are on Raoul Wallenberg Place and 14th Street; Nearest Metro station **Smithsonian (Independence Avenue exit);** ☎ **202-488-0400; www.ushmm.org**

Type of attraction A museum and memorial presenting the history of the persecution and murder of 6 million Jews and others by Nazi Germany during World War II. **Admission** Free; timed tickets for permanent exhibit March to September; no tickets required for the special exhibitions. **Hours** Daily, 10 a.m.–5:20 p.m. (until 6:30 p.m. weekdays around April and May); closed Christmas Day and Yom Kippur. **When to go** Anytime. **Special comments** For mature audiences. The Museum Annex on Raoul Wallenberg Place has a small deli/café that offers vegetarian and some prepackaged and certified-kosher fare. **How much time to allow** 2 hours.

DESCRIPTION AND COMMENTS As its designers intended, this $168-million museum is ugly, forbidding, and grim—and it delivers a stern message about the evils of racial persecution. It also packs an emotional punch that may not fit some folks' vacation plans. Technologically and emotionally, it's a stunning experience: audiovisual displays, advanced computer technology, and a model of a Nazi death camp recreate one of the darkest periods in human history. (In fact, this would be a five-star attraction if emotional weight and age issues were put aside.) But that's not all. As part of the museum experience, museumgoers are cast as "victims" of Nazi brutality. Visitors receive an identity card of a real Holocaust victim matched to their sex and age—a demographic double. The building attacks the emotions of visitors in other, more subtle ways. The interior of the museum, while spotless, is relentlessly industrial and forbidding—pipes are exposed and rough surfaces of brick and concrete are cold and unwelcoming. Diagonal walls in the exhibition areas create a disorienting effect. Ghostly shapes pass overhead on glass-bottomed walkways, suggesting Nazi prison guards patrolling a camp. (Actually, they are visitors walking on footbridges linking the permanent exhibit spaces.) Every moment spent inside the museum is orchestrated to impart the horror of Nazi persecution. In fact, the primary, and essential, difference between this museum and the Holocaust Museum in New York is that in Manhattan, the mood is "We will survive." This says, "We will never forget."

According to Holocaust Museum officials, the main (permanent) exhibit is inappropriate for children under age 11—and we agree. In fact, almost everyone can pinpoint the spot where their throat begins to feel tight. However, a special exhibit on the museum's first floor, "Daniel's Story: Remember the Children," is designed for visitors ages 8 and older. It gives a child's perspective on the Holocaust, but without the shocking graphics of the permanent exhibit, and serves as a sort of kid's parking lot while the adults continue.

While many exhibits focus on Jewish life prior to the Holocaust and the political and military events surrounding World War II, the most disturbing displays are graphic depictions of Nazi atrocities. Large TV screens scattered throughout the exhibits present still and motion pictures of Nazi leaders, storm troopers rounding up victims, and life inside Jewish ghettos. Some of the TV screens are located behind concrete barriers to prevent younger (and, inadvertently, shorter) visitors from seeing them. They show executions, medical experiments on Jewish prisoners, and suicide victims. It's very strong, grim stuff, and given the unrelenting horror of its subject matter, the Holocaust Museum is at best sobering and, at worst, depressing. There's no bright gloss to put on a museum chronicling the systematic murder of 6 million people . . . and anyone visiting the Holocaust Museum during a vacation should keep that in mind before placing it on his or her touring agenda, especially if traveling with small children.

TOURING TIPS During the busiest months (generally March through August), the Holocaust Museum employs a time-ticket system to eliminate long lines at its permanent exhibits. While the ticket office opens at 10 a.m., plan on getting in line no later than 9 a.m. to be sure of getting a ticket (which are given out for that day only). If you want to be sure of getting on a morning tour during the busy spring and summer months, get in line by 8:30 a.m. A limited number of advance reservations tickets (with a $1 per pass fee) are available at the website (www.ushmm.org/visit) or by calling ☎ 877-80-USHMM (877-808-7466).

OTHER THINGS TO DO NEARBY The Holocaust Memorial Museum occupies some prime real estate near the Mall, the Bureau of Engraving and Printing, the Washington Monument, the Tidal Basin, the FDR Memorial, and the Jefferson Memorial, so finding things to do before or after a tour of the museum is easy.

U.S. National Arboretum ★★★

APPEAL BY AGE	PRESCHOOL ★	GRADE SCHOOL ★★	TEENS ★★
YOUNG ADULTS ★★	OVER 30 ★★★		SENIORS ★★★

Location **3501 New York Avenue NE (near Bladensburg Road); No Metro access;** ☎ **202-245-2726; www.usna.usda.gov**

Type of attraction A 446-acre collection of trees, flowers, and herbs (self-guided tour). Admission Free. Hours Daily, 8 a.m.–5 p.m. The information center is open weekdays, 8 a.m.–4:30 p.m. (until 5 p.m. in summer); the gift shop is open weekdays, March–mid-December, 10 a.m.–3 p.m. The National Bonsai and Penjing Museum is open daily, 10 a.m.–4 p.m. Closed on federal holidays and Christmas Day. When to go Anytime; for information on what's in bloom, visit the website. Special comments The arboretum is mobbed in the spring; the rest of the year it's usually tranquil. Though interesting and beautiful, it requires a car or cab to visit. Food service is limited to some weekends and holidays; call the day of your visit to check if the food cart is open. How much time to allow 1 hour to half a day.

DESCRIPTION AND COMMENTS With nine miles of roads and more than three miles of walking paths, the U.S. National Arboretum offers visitors an oasis of quiet and beauty for a drive or a stroll. Even people without green thumbs will marvel at the bonsai collection, whose dwarf trees are more like sculptures than plants. One specimen, a Japanese white pine, is 350 years old. In the spring, fields of azaleas are in bloom—although at press time, there was a proposal, and public opposition, to remove the azalea landscape. Flowering dogwood and mountain laurel bloom well into May. The world-class bonsai collection is a treat all year. Late July and August feature blooming aquatic plants. Folks with limited time who aren't gardening enthusiasts, however, shouldn't spend their touring hours on a visit.

TOURING TIPS A tram tour with recorded narration (including space for two wheelchairs) is offered weekends only at 11:30 a.m., 1 p.m., 2 p.m., and 3 p.m., with additional 10:30 a.m. and 4 p.m. tours Mid-April through October; $4 adults, $3 seniors, $2 ages 4–16.

OTHER THINGS TO DO NEARBY The Kenilworth Aquatic Gardens are only a few minutes away by car.

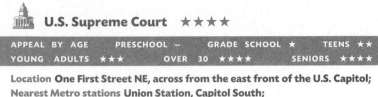

U.S. Supreme Court ★★★★

Location **One First Street NE, across from the east front of the U.S. Capitol;**
Nearest Metro stations **Union Station, Capitol South;**
☎ **202-479-3211; www.supremecourtus.gov**

Type of attraction The nation's highest court. **Admission** Free. **Hours** Monday–Friday, 9 a.m.–4:30 p.m. Free lectures are offered every hour on the half hour between 9:30 a.m. and 3:30 p.m. when the court isn't in session. Closed Saturdays, Sundays, and federal holidays. **When to go** Anytime to tour the building. To see the Court in session, the public may attend oral arguments held Mondays, Tuesdays, and Wednesdays, 10 a.m. to 2 p.m., in 2-week intervals from October through April; check the "A" section of the *Washington Post* for specifics. **Special comments** Seeing an oral argument here is probably your best chance of witnessing one of the 3 branches of the government in operation while in D.C. Extremely interesting and enlightening. Cafeteria on site. **How much time to allow** 1 hour to tour the building; plan on at least 2 hours total to see an oral argument.

DESCRIPTION AND COMMENTS This magnificent faux Greek temple is where the nine-member Supreme Court makes final interpretations of the U.S. Constitution and laws passed by Congress. When the Court's not in session, visitors may enter the stunning courtroom and hear a short lecture on its workings. An excellent 25-minute film explains the workings of the Supreme Court in more detail. A visit to the Supreme Court is a must for anyone interested in how the federal government works, or how the law works in general, though it may not be flashy enough for some.

TOURING TIPS To see an oral argument, plan on arriving no later than 9 a.m. to get in line. Two lines form: a regular line, for those wishing to hear an entire argument (an hour), and a three-minute line, for folks who just want to slip in for a few moments. Bring quarters: you will have to place personal belongings like backpacks and cameras in coin-operated (quarters only) lockers. Security here is no-nonsense: visitors pass through *two* X-ray machines before entering the courtroom, where very serious-looking security people patrol the aisles. Small children are not allowed in the courtroom during oral arguments. The comfortable cafeteria on the ground level of the Supreme Court is one of the better government eateries. It's open for breakfast from 7:30 to 10:30 a.m. and for lunch from 11:30 a.m. to 2 p.m. except at noon and 1 p.m. when only Court employees may enter. There is also a snack bar.

OTHER THINGS TO DO NEARBY The U.S. Capitol, the Library of Congress, the National Postal Museum, and the Folger Shakespeare Library are all nearby.

Vietnam Veterans Memorial ★★★★

APPEAL BY AGE	PRESCHOOL ★	GRADE SCHOOL ★★	TEENS ★★
YOUNG ADULTS ★★★	OVER 30 ★★★★		SENIORS ★★★★

**Location On the west end of the Mall near the Lincoln Memorial;
Nearest Metro station Foggy Bottom–GWU; ☎ 202-426-6841;
www.nps.gov/vive/**

Type of attraction A memorial to U.S. soldiers who died in Vietnam. **Admission**
Free. **Hours** Open 24 hours a day; staff is on site 9 a.m.–11:30 p.m.; closed
Christmas Day. **When to go** Anytime. **Special comments** At night this memorial
is especially moving as people light matches to search for names inscribed on the
wall. Deeply moving. No food concessions on site. **How much time to allow** 30
minutes to 1 hour.

DESCRIPTION AND COMMENTS "The Wall," as it is known, is a black, V-shaped
rift in the earth, nearly 494 feet long and ranging from 8 inches tall at
its outer edges to 10 feet tall at its center. The design competition for
the memorial, which was open to the public, was won by Maya Lin,
then a 21-year-old in her third year at Yale. Both her concept and her
inexperience were the subject of great controversy; to placate those
veterans and their families who thought it too severe and abstract, an
additional sculpture depicting three soldiers was also commissioned.
The Wall was dedicated on Veterans Day, November 13, 1982. Fre-
drick Hart's *Three Servicemen* sculpture, which now dominates the
entrance to the memorial (and, in our opinion, compromises the
concept visually), was dedicated two years later, also on Veterans Day.
Tucked more inconspicuously to one side is a tribute to the women
who served in Vietnam, sculpted by Glenna Goodacre and dedicated
on Veterans Day in 1993.

TOURING TIPS At both ends of the Wall, visitors will find books that list the
inscribed names and panel numbers to help them locate an inscription.

OTHER THINGS TO DO NEARBY The Lincoln Memorial, the Reflecting Pool,
the Korean War Veterans Memorial, and Constitution Gardens are
close. Across from the Mall, the National Academy of Sciences features
science exhibits and a statue of Albert Einstein with a lap that's large
enough to sit in for picture-taking.

Voice of America ★★

APPEAL BY AGE	PRESCHOOL –	GRADE SCHOOL ★	TEENS ★½
YOUNG ADULTS ★★½	OVER 30 ★★★		SENIORS ★★★

**Location Tours meet at the C Street entrance between Third and Fourth
streets SW;** Nearest Metro station **Federal Center SW; ☎ 202-203-4990;
www.voatour.com**

Type of attraction The U.S. Government's overseas radio broadcasting studios
(guided tour). **Admission** Free; reservations are required and no groups larger
than 20 people are allowed. **Hours** The 45-minute tours are Monday–Friday at

noon and 3 p.m., except holidays. **Special comments** A "must" for news junkies; a special kids' tour is available for families and school groups. Fascinating and informative. **How much time to allow** 45 minutes.

DESCRIPTION AND COMMENTS After a short video about the VOA, the knowledgeable tour guide walks you through some of the agency's 34 studios, where you see and hear radio announcers reading newscasts in languages such as Arabic, Estonian, and Urdu. Worldwide, the VOA operates more than 100 shortwave radio transmitters, and all broadcasts originate in this building. You'll also see some murals painted by noted artist Ben Shahn in the 1940s. But mostly this is a tour for people interested in media and world events; or immigrant or foreign visitors intrigued to hear news in the vernacular.

TOURING TIPS You should call to reserve a place on a tour, but individuals and small groups won't have trouble joining a tour by just showing up a few minutes before a scheduled departure.

OTHER THINGS TO DO NEARBY The U.S. Botanic Garden is around the corner on Maryland Avenue SW, and the Mall is two blocks away.

Washington Monument ★★★

| APPEAL BY AGE | PRESCHOOL ★★★ | GRADE SCHOOL ★★★★ | TEENS ★★★★ |
| YOUNG ADULTS ★★★★ | | OVER 30 ★★★★ | SENIORS ★★★★ |

Location **On the Mall between 15th and 17th streets NW;** Nearest Metro station **Smithsonian; ☎ 202-426-6841; www.nps.gov/wamo**

Type of attraction An abstract but iconic monument to the first U.S. president. **Admission** Free, timed tickets required. **Hours** Daily, 9 a.m.–4:45 p.m. (may be open until 10 p.m. Memorial Day–Labor Day). Closed July 4 and Christmas Day. *Note:* The monument and grounds may be closed in thunderstorms and during periods of sustained high winds because of visitor exposure; or during security alerts; use the 15th Street entrance. The ticket kiosk is open 8:30 a.m.–4:30 p.m.; first come, first served. **When to go** At 8 a.m. to pick up a timed ticket. **Special comments** No food, drinks, or large bags are allowed into this monument. Food concession on site. **How much time to allow** Once you make it to the top, 15 minutes.

DESCRIPTION AND COMMENTS For most people, a first-time trip to Washington isn't complete without an ascent of this famous landmark. But even icons have feet of, well, concrete, and to be frank, this one is somewhat overrated. The view is irrefutably grand—at the top you're 500 feet up, and D.C.'s absence of other tall buildings (by law) guarantees a glorious, unobstructed view of Washington—but if it's raining, it's just more gray. And most visitors are surprised by the cramped observation deck and small windows: you almost have to elbow your way over to see anything. The outlook from the Old Post Office Pavilion tower is better, and the one from the balconies at the Newseum nearly as fine.

TOURING TIPS The year-round time-ticket system eliminates the old three-hour waits in line for the elevator trip to the top of the monument; the wait in line is now reduced to about half an hour for most visitors. In general, people take the tickets they get for the soonest time, so early morning tours fill up first. However, if you want to visit at a specific time later in the day, you should still plan to pick up your tickets early, not when you want to go up; except during the slowest of seasons, all tickets are gone by mid- to late morning. The ticket kiosk is on 15th Street on the edge of the monument grounds. Show up 5 minutes before the time printed on your ticket.

OTHER THINGS TO DO NEARBY The Mall museums are on one side, the great Presidential memorials on the other. If you're tired of both, find the nearby Constitution Gardens lake and chill out.

Washington National Cathedral ★ ★ ★ ★ ★

APPEAL BY AGE	PRESCHOOL ★	GRADE SCHOOL ★★	TEENS ★★★★
YOUNG ADULTS ★★★★★	OVER 30 ★★★★★		SENIORS ★★★★★

Location **Massachusetts and Wisconsin avenues NW;**
Nearest Metro station **The Woodley Park–Zoo/Adams Morgan station is about a half-hour walk;** ☎ **202-537-6200 for guided-tour information; www.nationalcathedral.org**

Type of attraction The sixth-largest cathedral in the world. Admission Free; suggested donations are $5. Hours Monday–Friday, 10 a.m.–5:30 p.m., tours 10 a.m.–4 p.m.; Saturday, 10 a.m.–4:30 p.m., tours 10–11:30 a.m. and 12:45–3:30 p.m.; Sunday, 8 a.m.–6:30 p.m., tours 1–4 p.m. Summer hours: open weekdays until 8 p.m. When to go Anytime. Special comments A Gothic masterpiece. Take the optional 30- to 45-minute, docent-led tour. How much time to allow 1 hour.

DESCRIPTION AND COMMENTS If you've been to Europe, you'll experience déjà vu when you visit this massive 102-year-old Gothic cathedral, formally titled the Cathedral Church of Saint Peter and Saint Paul, official seat of the Presiding Bishop of the Episcopal Church in the United States (and of the Bishop of the Episcopal Diocese of Washington). There are 233 stained-glass windows (including the great rose windows in the south transept, displaying scenes from the Book of Revelations, and in the west, showing the Creation), a 53-bell carillon (each bell, including the 12-toner, is carved with a Bible verse), a 10,250-pipe organ, nine chapels (many with fine murals or mosaics), dozens of wrought-iron gates, hundreds of elaborate carvings, and scores of gargoyles—including Darth Vader, devils, golfers, and caricatures of the famous and the humble. There's even a piece of moon rock, brought back by Neil Armstrong and Buzz Aldrin aboard the *Apollo 11*, embedded in a glass bubble of what is called the Space Window. Those familiar with the Al Pacino movie *The Devil's Advocate* will recognize the Frederick Hart carving *Ex Nihilo* in the west façade.

It's a tenth of a mile from the nave to the high altar; the ceiling is 100 feet high, the central tower over 300. Don't miss the Bishop's Garden, designed by Frederick Law Olmstead and modeled on a medieval walled garden, or the Pilgrim Observation Gallery and a view of Washington from the highest vantage point in the city. Small children may not enjoy being dragged around this huge cathedral, but just about anyone else will enjoy its magnificent architecture and stone carvings. Bring binoculars; many are high up, but fascinating—such as the one that shows a young boy with a baseball bat and glove and his sister with a rag doll.

TOURING TIPS Docent-led tours are offered on weekdays. The high tea and highlights tour is fabulous; see details in the "Best Inside Tours," above. You should also try to catch the free organ demonstration Mondays noon to 3 p.m. Carillon recitals are given on Sundays; times vary so call ahead. You can also visit the grave of Woodrow Wilson, the only president buried in Washington. The Cathedral isn't well served by public transportation, but walking there takes you through safe, pleasant neighborhoods that are home to Washington's elite: it's about a half-hour stroll up Cathedral Avenue from the Woodley Park–Zoo/ Adams Morgan Metro.

OTHER THINGS TO DO NEARBY The National Zoo is about a half-hour walk from the National Cathedral, but it's mostly downhill through a pretty residential area.

 **Washington Navy Yard** ★★★

APPEAL BY AGE	PRESCHOOL ★	GRADE SCHOOL ★★★	TEENS ★★★
YOUNG ADULTS ★★		OVER 30 ★★	SENIORS ★★★

Location 9th and M streets SE, on the waterfront; Nearest Metro stations **Navy Yard, Eastern Market; Navy Museum, ☎ 202-433-4882; Navy Art Gallery, 202-433-3815; USS** *Barry,* **202-433-3377; www.history.navy.mil**

Type of attraction Military museum complex and a U.S. Navy destroyer (self-guided tours by reservation only; call ☎ 202-433-6897). **Admission** Free; reservations required for nonmilitary personnel. **Hours** Monday–Friday, 9 a.m.– 5 p.m.; closed weekends and all federal holidays. Navy Art Gallery open until 5 p.m. in the summer and until 4 p.m. in the winter; closed Monday and Tuesday. **When to go** Anytime. But unless you have military ID, advance reservations are required. **Special comments** A nice contrast to the look-but-don't-touch Mall museums. Hands-on fun for kids; informative for adults. No food concession on site. **How much time to allow** 2 hours.

DESCRIPTION AND COMMENTS Exhibits in the Navy Museum include 14-foot-long model ships, undersea vehicles *Alvin* and *Trieste,* working sub periscopes, and, tied up at the dock, a decommissioned destroyer to tour. The Navy Art Gallery is a small museum with paintings of naval actions painted by combat artists. A strong interest in the military is a prerequisite for making the trek to the Washington Navy Yard, and it's not a side trip that many first-time visitors make. But kids will love it. For current exhibition information visit www.history.navy.mil.

TOURING TIPS If you are traveling with kids, make their day and take in a game as well (plenty of concessions there). Or you could pack a swimsuit and head to the aquatic center at Eastern Market.

OTHER THINGS TO DO NEARBY Nationals Park, the Washington Nationals' baseball stadium, is a few blocks away; a new boardwalk area with an ice-skating rink, 60-foot light tower, and pedestrian bridge over the Anacostia is under construction between the Navy Yard and stadium.

 The White House   ★★

APPEAL BY AGE   PRESCHOOL ★★   GRADE SCHOOL ★★★   TEENS ★★★★
YOUNG ADULTS ★★★★   OVER 30 ★★★★   SENIORS ★★★★

Location 1600 Pennsylvania Avenue NW; **Nearest Metro station** Federal Triangle; ☎ 202-456-7041 or 202-456-2121 (TDD); www.whitehouse.gov

Type of attraction The official residence of the president of the United States. **Special comments** Public tours of the White House are available for groups of 10 or more people, but requests must be submitted through one's member of Congress and are accepted up to 6 months in advance. These free, self-guided tours are scheduled Tuesday through Thursday 7:30 a.m.–11 a.m., Friday 7:30 a.m.–12 p.m., and Saturday 7:30 a.m.–1 p.m. (excluding federal holidays), and are scheduled on a first-come, first-served basis approximately one month in advance of the requested date. You should submit your request as soon as possible since there are only a limited number of tours available. *Note:* White House tours may be subject to last-minute cancellation. All visitors should call the 24-hour Visitors Office information line at ☎ 202-456-7041 to determine if any last-minute changes have been made in the tour schedule. No food concessions on site. **How much time to allow** Block out an entire morning, even though there's time to do something else (like eat breakfast) before your scheduled tour.

DESCRIPTION AND COMMENTS Though this is the Executive Mansion, home to the First Family, you have only an infinitesimal chance of seeing any member thereof, unless you luck into a news event or photo op. This 20-minute, hands-off tour passes through the ubiquitous metal detectors and into the East Wing lobby, with a glimpse of the Rose Garden. Then it's up the stairs to the East Room, the Green Room, the Blue Room, the Red Room, and the State Dining Room, and out. It's hard to dispute the emotional pull of the presidential residence or its sumptuous beauty, but if you're on a first-time visit to Washington and on a limited schedule, consider visiting the White House on another trip, preferably in the fall or winter.

The visitor center is large and attractive, featuring lots of carpeting, places to sit, nice restrooms (but no food concessions), static displays on the White House, a gift shop, and a video tour of the mansion.

TOURING TIPS Check the White House website to see if your visit coincides with one of the occasional Garden Tours. Even if you can't visit the Executive Mansion itself, you can go into the visitor center without reservation.

OTHER THINGS TO DO NEARBY Across from the White House on Lafayette Square is St. John's Episcopal Church, known as "The Church of the Presidents," because every president from Madison to Obama has attended services here. Step inside the small church to view its simple design; on most Wednesdays at noon there's an organ recital.

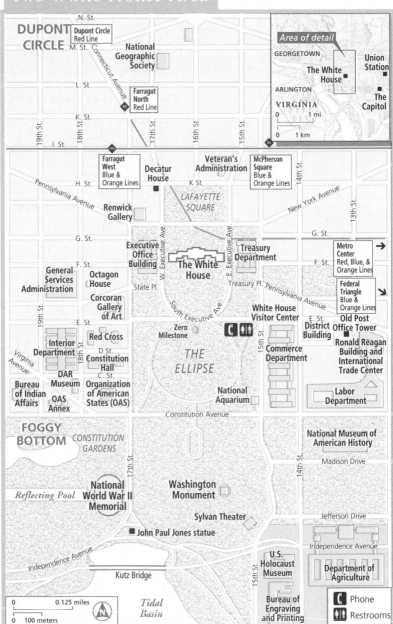

The White House Area

Woodrow Wilson House   ★★★★

| APPEAL BY AGE | PRESCHOOL ★ | GRADE SCHOOL ★★ | TEENS ★★★ |
| YOUNG ADULTS ★★★ | OVER 30 ★★★★ | | SENIORS ★★★★ |

Location **2340 S Street NW; Nearest Metro station Dupont Circle;**
☎ **202-387-4062; www.woodrowwilsonhouse.org**

Type of attraction The final home of the 28th U.S. president (guided tour).
Admission $7.50 adults, $6.50 seniors 62+, $3 students, free ages 6 and under.
Hours Tuesday–Sunday, 10 a.m.–4 p.m.; closed Mondays and national holidays.
When to go To avoid a crowded tour during spring and summer, arrive before
noon. **Special comments** Interesting and informative. Lots of stairs, including a
steep, narrow descent down a back staircase (though there is an elevator). **How
much time to allow** 1–2 hours.

DESCRIPTION AND COMMENTS After Woodrow Wilson left office in 1921, he
became the only former president to retire in Washington, D.C.—and
he did so in this house. The tour starts with a 25-minute video narrated
by Walter Cronkite that puts this underrated president in perspective
and fires you up for the tour. Ninety-six percent of the items in this
handsome Georgian Revival town house are original, so visitors get an
accurate picture of aristocratic life in the 1920s. On the tour you'll see
Wilson's library (his books, however, went to the Library of Congress
after his death), his bedroom (he so admired Lincoln's seven-foot-long
bed that he had one made for himself), his old movie projector, and
beautiful furnishings. Among other curiosities are his medicine chest;
rollout bed, like a cruise ship deck chair; electric "shock box" designed
to treat his paralyzed muscles (he never fully recovered from a serious
stroke); graphoscope (an antique movie projector), kangaroo-fur coat;
six-piece Tiffany desk set; and a mosaic of St. Peter given him by Pope
Benedict XV.

TOURING TIPS The basement kitchen is virtually unchanged from Wilson's
day, with original items such as an ornate wooden icebox and a coal and
gas–fired stove. Peek inside the pantry, still stocked with items from
the 1920s such as Kellogg's Corn Flakes ("wonderfully flavored with
malt, sugar, and salt"). This is another tour that gives visitors the feeling
they've been somewhere special and off the beaten tourist track. Even
the gift shop has unusual items.

OTHER THINGS TO DO NEARBY The Textile Museum is next door. The Phillips
Collection is a short walk.

▌MARYLAND SUBURBS

MARYLAND'S HISTORICAL ATTRACTIONS ARE FAMOUS, and
both Annapolis and Baltimore are easy day trips (below); but it's also
home to some less serious amusements, so to speak. **Six Flags America**
in Bowie (**www.sixflags.com/america**) is the biggest amusement park

nearby, with more than 100 attractions and thrill rides and a water park to boot; and it's accessible by public transportation: Take the Metro to Addison Road and take the C21 bus to the park.

An amusement park of an older, simpler time is **Glen Echo Park** (**www.glenechopark.org**), just inside the Beltway in the Palisades near Cabin John. A long-neglected family favorite, it has been renovated in recent years and now offers children's theater with both live and (quite accomplished) marionette shows; a fine carousel; a small viewing tower; and the Discovery Creek children's recreational area, which has climbing trees, some live animals, nature trails, and more. The Art Deco Spanish Ballroom hosts contra and folk dances on weekends. Glen Echo is also home to several artist studios (photography, glassblowing, pottery) and galleries that may be open, and offers arts and crafts classes. There are sometimes ranger-led park tours. (The **Clara Barton National Historic Site,** the home and original office of the founder of the American Red Cross, is across a parking lot.)

VIRGINIA SUBURBS

NOT SURPRISINGLY, THE NORTHERN VIRGINIA SUBURBS are filled with historical sites, many that would be of special interest to families or veterans. Just off I-395 south on West Braddock Road is **Fort Ward** (☎ 703-838-4848; **www.fortward.org**), a well-preserved Civil War fort and living-history museum with frequent reenactments and exhibits portraying Washington and Alexandria in wartime.

Often overlooked in the Mount Vernon hoopla, in spite of its close connections (and collections, some of which came from Mount Vernon), is **Woodlawn Plantation** (9000 Richmond Highway/Route 1, Alexandria; ☎ 703-780-4000; **www.woodlawn1805.org**). Constructed in 1800–05 for Major Lawrence Lewis (George Washington's nephew and social secretary) and his wife, Nelly Custis Lewis (Martha Washington's granddaughter), the estate is only about three miles from Mount Vernon. The Lewises were married at Mount Vernon on Washington's last birthday, in 1799, and he gave them 2,000 acres from the Mount Vernon estate on which to build a home (and engaged the architect of the U.S. Capitol to design it). The Palladian mansion, with a two-story central block and one-and-a-half-story wings, was sheathed in brick baked by slaves on the plantation grounds. The Lewises and Nelly's brother were Washington's executors, and there is plenty of Washingtonia here, as well as a bedroom that was furnished for a visit from the Marquis de Lafayette in 1824.

A second major attraction at Woodlawn is the **Pope-Leighey House** (☎ 703-780-4000; **www.popeleighey1940.org**), an intact Frank Lloyd Wright Usonian home, built in 1941 and moved from Falls Church to Woodlawn when highway construction threatened its preservation. Tiny but impressive, it is complete with all the furniture Wright designed for it and is constructed entirely of cypress, brick, glass, and concrete. The house is open from March to December.

The **Claude Moore Colonial Farm at Turkey Run** in McLean (6310 Georgetown Pike; ☎ 703-442-7557; **www.1771.org**) is a living-history museum that recreates a low-income tenant family farm just before the Revolutionary War. Staff dressed in period costumes answer questions as they work the land and do the chores, tend the turkeys and hogs, and do the mending. Visitors are encouraged to pitch in and/or to dress the part.

If you head toward the big Leesburg Outlet Malls and the historical town of Leesburg, stop by **Oatlands Historic House and Gardens** (20850 Oatlands Plantation Road, Leesburg; ☎ 703-777-3174 or **www .oatlands.org**), an early-19th-century wheat plantation and stuccoed-brick Greek Revival mansion with an octagonal family room, half-octagonal interior stairs at either end, and a grand portico (the mansion is closed to the public January through March).

The new **National Museum of the Marine Corps,** near the Marine Corps base in Quantico and dedicated in November 2006 by President George W. Bush, has a striking design that echoes the famous Iwo Jima flag-raising memorial, only in abstract, angular steel. The 210-foot "mast" also evokes the image of a sword half-pulled from its sheath, cannons poised for firing, and aircraft takeoffs—all scenarios familiar to members of the nearly 250-year-old corps. Exhibits range from Civil War photos, sniper rifles, and medals of honor to a World War II Curtiss Jenny, a Huey helicopter, a supersonic jet, and Persian Gulf tank. There are several hands-on and immersion opportunities: target ranges and flight simulators, plus a cold-air room that recalls the wintry environment of the Korean War. You can also go through a mini boot camp or be immersed in the sound of troops approaching that Iwo Jima beachhead. The museum also incorporates artifacts from the former Marine Corps Center at the Washington Navy Yard and the Marine Corps Air-Ground Museum at Quantico.

Finally, if you have thrill-seekers in the party, **King's Dominion,** a 400-acre amusement park with 15 roller coasters, several highly rated among adrenaline freaks, is about 75 miles south of Washington on I-95. If the Drop Tower, with its 372-foot, 72-mph fall doesn't shut the kids up, nothing will. Are you there yet?

EXCURSIONS *beyond* *the* BELTWAY

IF YOU'VE GOT THE TIME OR IF YOUR VISIT to Washington is a repeat trip, consider exploring outside the city. With mountains to the west and the Chesapeake Bay to the east, there's plenty to see. Furthermore, a look at something that's not made of marble or granite can be a welcome relief to eyes wearied by the constant onslaught of Washington edifices and office buildings.

In addition to the day or even overnight trip destinations below, wine lovers should note that both Maryland and Virginia have thriving wine industries. To see some of the possible tour routes—and this might be a good time to hire a driver—and tasting room hours go to **www.virginiawine.org** or **www.marylandwine.com.**

Annapolis

Maryland's capital for more than 300 years, Annapolis is more than a quaint little town on the Chesapeake Bay: it's one of the biggest yachting centers in the United States. Often called the sailing capital of the country, it welcomes 10,000 boats a year—and it has also become a major bedroom community or weekend retreat for well-off Washingtonians. Acres and acres of sailboats fill its marinas. A steady parade of sailboats moves past the **City Dock** during the sailing season, April through late fall. (If you want to try it yourself, you can take a harbor cruise aboard the two-masted schooner *Woodwind;* ☎ 410-263-7837 or **www.schoonerwoodwind .com**). You'll see oyster and crab boats that work the bay, in addition to pleasure boats, cruise ships, and old sailing ships. Annapolis has a fine old state office building and is home to the **U.S. Naval Academy** (John Paul Jones is buried in the huge century-old chapel) and the even older fine-arts college of **St. John's,** whose domed 1742 McDowell Hall was admired by Thomas Jefferson. The two schools are old rivals, particularly when it comes to croquet; a high-level match takes place at St. John's every April, the local equivalent of the Harvard-Yale football game.

The historic area of town, from **State Circle** down to the harbor, is a rapidly upscaling area with fine restaurants, fancy shops, bars, and jazz clubs. (If you're Segway-savvy, contact Annapolis Segway Tours at ☎ 410-280-1557 or **www.annapolissegwaytours.com.**) The **Banneker-Douglass Museum** documents the history of African Americans in Maryland. It includes a reproduction of the September 29, 1767 newspaper notice advertising a shipment of slaves including Kunta Kinte. The **Annapolis Maritime Museum** across the harbor bridge in Eastport also operates tours of the Thomas Point Shoal Lighthouse at the mouth of the South River. The town is about a one-hour drive from Washington on US 50; parking can be tough, but most of the time you can park at the Navy–Marine Corps Memorial Stadium and take a free shuttle to City Dock.

Baltimore

Steamed crabs, H. L. Mencken, the Orioles baseball team (or the NFL Ravens), and the National Aquarium are just a few of the reasons Washingtonians trek north one hour on a regular basis to this industrial city on the Chesapeake Bay, affectionately known as Charm City.

Day-trippers can explore **Inner Harbor**, a short walk away from the Orioles Park at Camden Yards, dominated by a bi-level shopping mall that's heavy on restaurants and boutiques, and where you can often sign up for a paddleboat ride on a dragon-shaped boat. The **National Aquarium** across the harbor (you can walk around or take a water taxi) features a tropical rain forest and a sea mammal pavilion—and it's a much larger and finer attraction than the National Aquarium in Washington.

Kids will love the **Maryland Science Center** (with its IMAX theater) and **Port Discovery Children's Museum,** also on the Harbor; the **U.S.S. Constellation,** the last Civil War fighting vessel afloat, the **Top of the World** observation tower, and nearby **Fort McHenry,** where Francis Scott Key wrote the national anthem from a ship anchored offshore. (The Federal Hill neighborhood is another booming residential and restaurant neighborhood.) **Geppi's Entertainment Museum** is a treasure trove of comic books and superhero stuff. On the Aquarium side of the Harbor are the old **Little Italy; Pier Six Pavilion,** site of summer concerts and a restaurant center; and **Power Plant Live!** entertainment complex. Art lovers should stop into the **American Visionary Art Museum** alongside the Science Center, and more serious art lovers should check out the **Walters Art Gallery** in the burgeoning Mount Vernon arts and entertainment neighborhood and the **Baltimore Museum of Art** uptown. One of Eve's personal favorites is **Evergreen Museum,** a treasure trove of decorative arts. Other Baltimore attractions near the Inner Harbor and Orioles Stadium include the **B&O Railroad Museum,** the **Edgar Allan Poe House,** and the **Babe Ruth Birthplace and Museum.**

unofficial **TIP**
If you plan to see several of these attractions, look into purchasing a discounted Harbor Pass in advance (☎ 877-225-8466; www.baltimore.org.)

Middleburg

This most picturesque of horse country towns, about an hour west of town on Route 50, has almost everything going for it: history (George Washington ate here, at what is now the well-known **Red Fox Inn,** as did Jeb Stuart, John Mosby, Elizabeth Taylor, and John and Jackie Kennedy, among other celebs), art galleries and spas, boot and saddle makers, boutiques and antique shops—and fine and casual dining options, most clustered along or around Washington Street in beautiful 18th- and 19th-century buildings. Oh, and celebrity residents. Keep your eyes open. Parking can be a little tough in prime tourist (or hunt) season, but this is a fabulous window-shopping town. The visitor center is on North Madison Street; pick up a walking tour.

Aldie Mill, which is a working 1809 gristmill, is five miles east of Middleburg; several wineries are nearby, including Swedenburg and Crysalis. (This is one of Virginia's busiest wine regions.)

Shenandoah National Park

Although it makes for a long day, a drive to Shenandoah National Park in Virginia is a treat for outdoors lovers, featuring some of the prettiest mountain scenery in the eastern United States. A drive along a portion of the 105-mile-long Skyline Drive takes visitors to a nearly endless series of mountain overlooks where you can get out of the car and walk on well-maintained trails. In early June, the mountain laurel blooms in the higher elevations, and in the fall, it's bumper-to-bumper as hordes of Washingtonians rush to see the magnificent fall foliage. It's about a two-hour drive from Washington, one-way.

Harpers Ferry National Historical Park

This restored 19th-century town at the confluence of the Shenandoah and the Potomac rivers in West Virginia offers visitors history and natural beauty in equal doses—one reason that hikers, bikers, kayakers and tubers pack the parking lots. At the park's visitor center you can see a film about radical abolitionist John Brown's 1859 raid on a U.S. armory here, an event that was a precursor to the Civil War. Then you can tour a renovated blacksmith's shop, ready-made clothing store, and general store. The winding main road climbs past taverns and boutiques to a glorious hilltop view. A short hike to Jefferson Rock is rewarded with a spectacular mountain view of three states (Maryland, Virginia, and West Virginia) and two rivers (the Potomac and the Shenandoah). Thomas Jefferson said the view was "worth a voyage across the Atlantic." Luckily, the trip by car from Washington is only about 90 minutes (don't miss the lovely village of Hillsborough or Breaux Vineyards), and this is one of the destinations accessible by MARC train.

Civil War Battlefields

From the number of battlefield sites there, it would seem that the entire Civil War was fought in nearby Virginia, Maryland, and Pennsylvania—which is not all that far from the truth. Visitors with an interest in history and beautiful countryside can tour a number of Civil War sites within a day's drive of Washington. Several of the larger touring companies such as Gray Line offer bus excursions to some of these sites.

One of the closest Civil War museums is at **Fort Ward,** a 40-acre site just south of King Street and Interstate 395 in Alexandria (4801 West Braddock Street; ☎ 703-838-4848), which is often staffed by volunteer reenactors. **Ball's Bluff** in Leesburg is one of Loudoun County's largest battlefields, with a one-mile walking trail, interpretive signs, and a military cemetery.

Gettysburg, where the Union turned the tide against the South, is about two hours north of D.C. While the overdeveloped town is a testament to tourist schlock gone wild, the National Battlefield Park features a museum, a tower that gives sightseers an aerial view of the battlefield, and many acres of rolling countryside dotted with

monuments, memorials, and stone fences. It's a popular tourist destination and worth the drive. In summer, there are kid's programs that
include learning marching formation and the discomforts of 19th-
century soldiering.

The first battle of the Civil War took place at Bull Run near
Manassas, on the fringe of today's Virginia suburbs. The **Manassas
National Battlefield Park** features a visitor center, a museum, and
miles of trails on the grounds.

The Confederate victory set the stage for the next major battle,
at Antietam, across the Potomac River in Maryland. **Antietam
National Battlefield,** near Sharpsburg, is the site of the bloodiest day
of the Civil War: on September 17, 1862, there were 12,410 Union
and 10,700 Confederate casualties in General Robert E. Lee's failed
attempt to penetrate the North. The battlefield, about a 90-minute
drive from Washington, is 15 miles west of Frederick, Maryland.

A number of later Union campaigns are commemorated at
Fredericksburg and **Spotsylvania National Military Park** in Virginia,
halfway between Washington and Richmond. Included in the park are
the battlefields of Fredericksburg, Chancellorsville, the Wilderness,
and Spotsylvania. The park is about an hour's drive south of D.C.

PART SIX

DINING *and* RESTAURANTS

The WASHINGTON CUISINE SCENE

WELCOME (INDEED) TO THE 21ST CENTURY

IN THE LAST 15 YEARS, AND EVEN MORE RAPIDLY over the past 8 or 10, Washington has evolved from an extremely predictable restaurant town, one in which dining out was more a matter of convenience and expense account than pleasure, to one of the top ten culinary centers in the country—a city where it's really fun to be a restaurant critic.

The sorts of heavy French and Italian (or "Continental") dishes to which a generation of Washingtonians was inured have been replaced by market-fresh, innovative, and nutritionally informed recipes, many of them combining elements of the older classic cuisines (often lumped together as "modern eclectic"), which in turn influenced the development of what is, for lack of a better term, often called modern American.

Ethnic cuisines—Vietnamese, Japanese, Korean, Greek, Indian, Middle Eastern, Chinese (of all regions), Central and South American (of many regions), Thai, and Ethiopian, among others—have progressed from first-generation mom-and-pop immigrant eateries to professional, critically acclaimed restaurants. Among the Washington area's four- and five-star restaurants are kitchens turning out Mediterranean, Pan-Asian, Indian, French, South American, and Belgian cuisine (both haute and homey). Several kitchens are also run by adepts of the difficult, imaginative, technically stunning, and—most important—finely balanced style broadly referred to as molecular gastronomy or deconstruction.

It would be impossible in the space of one chapter, and difficult in a whole book, to describe the variety and quality of Washington dining going into the 20-teens. But even a basic primer—an A-B-C (and more)—should be evidence of its maturation and sophistication. Among the major trends are, for short: **A**ll-in-Ones, **B**istros, **C**elebrity chefs, **D**rink-meisters, **E**thnic (especially upscale), **F**latbreads and pizzas, **G**astropubs and wine bars, and (**H**am)burgers. For a start.

All-in-One Menus

Tasting menus have been a feature of many ambitious Washington chefs for several years, most of whom (Cathal Armstrong at Restaurant Eve; Eric Ziebold at CityZen; Robert Wiedmaier at Brasserie Beck; Frank Ruta at Palena; Robert Weland at Poste Moderne Brasserie; Bernard Chemel at 2941; Vikram Sunderam at Rasika; Yannick Cam at the now-shuttered Le Paradou; Roberto Donna, who has just reopened his seminal Galileo downtown; and Morou Ouattara, whose Farrah Olivia has just emerged as Kora in Crystal City) offered them in addition to more familiar à la carte options. In some cases these were even served in separate rooms from the more relaxed, democratic menus. A few of the better Japanese restaurants offered *omakase* (chef's choice) dinners, but never dispensed with the sushi bar or tempura batter.

But a growing number of restaurants now offer *only* prix-fixe or tasting menus, an almost imperial edict previously limited to the most famous of culinary figures such as Michel Richard at Citronelle, Patrick O'Connell at the Inn at Little Washington, or José Andrés at Minibar.

Johnny Monis of Komi, who has risen to rival these internationally known chefs as a local superstar, offers only one fixed-price meal, a *degustazione* tour de force that allows him to indulge his intensely focused take on Mediterranean classics. Popular chef R. J. Cooper, who tried out a 24-course tasting menu toward the end of his long tenure at Vidalia, was, at press time, preparing to open his own restaurant near Mount Vernon Square, Rogue 24, which will only offer his supersized fixed-price fiesta for $130 (plus $40 for wine pairings). And Nobu Yamazaki, owner-chef of Sushi Taro, has revamped that long-respected but predictable restaurant into a cutting-edge vision of Japanese classics (if that's not a contradiction), with fresh fish flown in daily from Tokyo's Tsukiji market and offering three kaiseki-styled menus. All of these menus start in the three-figure range, not including beverages or tips. . . . It makes one almost nostalgic for Obelisk chef Peter Pastan, who has stuck to his five-course fixed-price menu for more than 20 years, and still holds at $75.

The Bistro Boom

The flip side of this food-centric and rather pricey culinary self-consciousness is what might be called the post–baby-boomer bistro. With the slowing of the stock market and the ripples of economic

continued on page 256

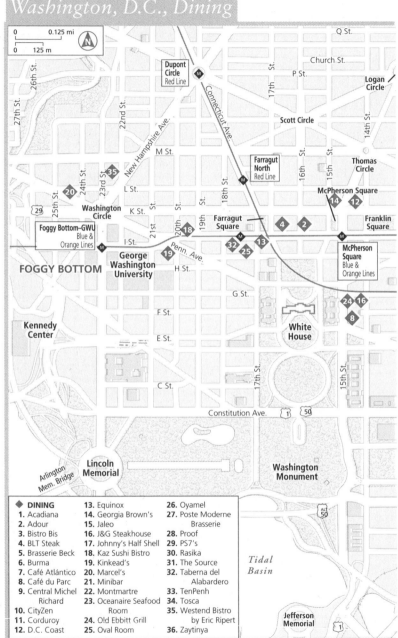

Washington, D.C., Dining

Dupont Circle Dining

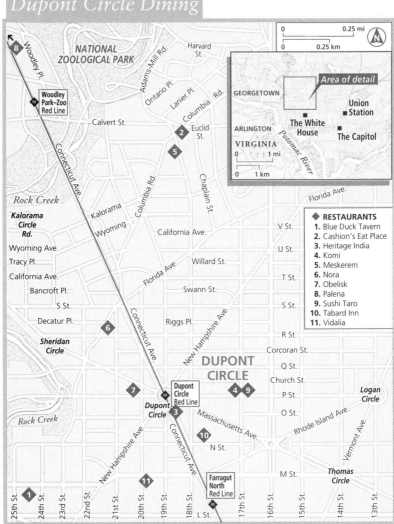

◆ **RESTAURANTS**

1. Blue Duck Tavern
2. Cashion's Eat Place
3. Heritage India
4. Komi
5. Meskerem
6. Nora
7. Obelisk
8. Palena
9. Sushi Taro
10. Tabard Inn
11. Vidalia

continued from page 253

"correction," even Washington's "recession-proof" restaurant industry has taken something of a hit from customer efforts to economize.
Several of the more upscale establishments, caught between the pin-
cers of exorbitant rent and declining expense-account business, have
closed; several have had to take advantage of Chapter 11 or similar

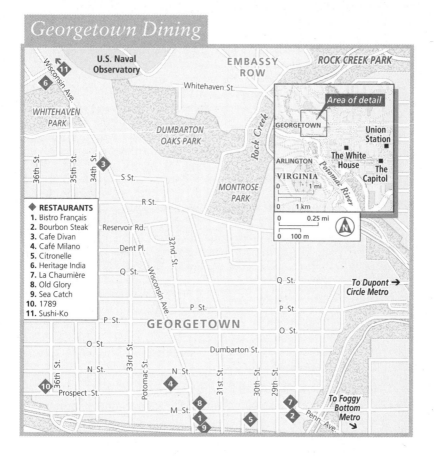

Georgetown Dining

U.S. Naval
Observatory

EMBASSY
ROW

ROCK CREEK PARK

Wisconsin Ave.

Whitehaven St.

WHITEHAVEN
PARK

DUMBARTON
OAKS PARK

Rock Creek

Area of detail

GEORGETOWN

Union
Station

ARLINGTON

The White
House

VIRGINIA

Potomac River

The
Capitol

0   1 mi

0   1 km

36th St.

35th St.

34th St.

S St.

MONTROSE
PARK

0   0.25 mi

R St.

0   100 m

N

◆ RESTAURANTS
1. Bistro Français
2. Bourbon Steak
3. Cafe Divan
4. Café Milano
5. Citronelle
6. Heritage India
7. La Chaumière
8. Old Glory
9. Sea Catch
10. 1789
11. Sushi-Ko

Reservoir Rd.

Dent Pl.

32nd St.

Q St.

Wisconsin Ave.

Q St.

**To Dupont →
Circle Metro**

P St.

P St.

P St.

P St.

GEORGETOWN

O St.

O St.

33rd St.

Dumbarton St.

Potomac St.

N St.

N St.

31st St.

30th St.

29th St.

36th St.

Prospect St.

M St.

**To Foggy
Bottom
Metro**

Penn. Ave.

restructuring. Partly in reaction to the changing financial times, and partly due to a genuine but paradoxical interest in exploring less-ornate food, several influential chefs have opened less formal second or third restaurants: cafés, bistros, brasseries, trattorias, even pizze-rias. (Teatro Goldoni went so far as to fire its highly regarded chef, Fabrizio Aielli, because he and his menu cost too much.)

Michel Richard's **Central Michel Richard** is certainly more straight-forward than the elaborate Citronelle (though admittedly, its prices are still relatively high), and at press time was about to unveil the similar **Michel by Michel Richard** at the Ritz-Carlton Tysons Corner. Robert Wiedmaier of Marcel's opened **Brasserie Beck,** a more relaxed Belgian-beer-and-comfort-food hangout, then **Brabo/Brabo Tasting Room by Robert Wiedmaier** in Old Town Alexandria. Cathal Armstrong of Restaurant Eve opened a Dublin-style fish-and-chipper called **Eamonn's** (728 King St., Old Town Alexandria; ☎ 703-299-8384), restored an American home-style favorite in the **Majestic** (911 King St., Old Town Alexandria; ☎ 703-837-9117), and went on to Irish pub fare at **Virtue Feed & Grain** (named for the warehouse it's in) on South Union Street near the riverfront. They are also sketching out a gourmet-kitchen wine bar, **Society Fair,** nearby. Michelin-star chef Gerard Pangaud shifted his longtime classic-French restaurant into bistro mode before closing it to teach cooking. Yannick Cam, who along with Jean-Louis Palladin brought fine French cooking to Washington 30 years ago—and who has been in and out of ambitious restaurants ever since, most recently Le Paradou downtown—has reappeared at **Bistro Provence** in Bethesda.

And the group behind Laurent Tourondel's BLT Steak near Farragut Square is opening a family-style Italian restaurant, **Casa Nonna,** a few blocks away.

Some chefs have bar or bistro menus that are entirely distinct from their dining room offers. **Restaurant Eve** has a "tasting room," a light-fare bar, and a bistro, all with separate menus; **Palena** has a bar menu distinct from its main list, as do **Kinkead's, The Source, Black's Bar and Kitchen,** and **Marcel's,** among others.

(On top of it all, Armstrong and Ruta are opening markets and developing carryout options—a new type of vertical thinking.)

But equally pleasant, several old-style, smallish bistros—the kind that gave French comfort food such a good name—have opened, including **Bistro Cacao** (320 Massachusetts Ave. NE; ☎ 202-546-4737), **Bistro le Bonne,** and **Eola.**

Celebrity Chefs and Kitchens

The Washington palate has become demanding enough (and, to be frank, the expense accounts have rebounded sufficiently) to inspire, first, a trickle, and more recently a tidal wave of chefs and restaurateurs from other dining capitals—New York, Las Vegas, Chicago, even international centers—to open branches in the nation's capital.

Michel Richard abandoned his L.A. haute-haute Citronelle to make Washington his home base, starting with **Citronelle** and expanding to **Central** and now **Michel.** Charlie Palmer of New York's Aureole fame opened **Charlie Palmer Steak.** Washington gained an offshoot of California's landmark French Laundry, albeit at one degree's remove; its longtime chef de cuisine Eric Ziebold presides over the Mandarin Oriental Hotel's ambitious **CityZen** restaurant. Eric Ripert of the four-star Le Bernardin created **Westend Bistro** in the midtown Ritz-Carlton; Strasbourg's three-Michelin-star chef Antoine Westermann has put his stamp on **Café du Parc** at the Willard Hotel. L.A.'s other pioneer, Wolfgang Puck, designed **The Source** restaurant for the Newseum, and international superstar Alain Ducasse created **Adour** for the St. Regis Hotel downtown (in the space that once housed an offshoot of Lespinasse). Laurent Tourondel added Washington to his **BLT Steak** empire, and former Mexican top chef turned Vegas, Denver, and Dubai chain master Richard Sandoval created a new fusion style, Latino-Asian, for **Zengo** (781 Seventh St. NW; ☎ 202-393-2929) in the Penn Quarter, and persuaded opera superstar Placido Domingo to invest in it.

Two of the biggest names are in the super-, or perhaps supra-, steak houses: Jean-Georges Vongerichten created **J&G Steakhouse** in the W Hotel, which almost immediately staked out a high place in restaurant circles; and L.A. multi-tasker Michael Mina's **Bourbon Steak** is located in the Georgetown Four Seasons Hotel.

unofficial **TIP**
Don't expect to stumble on these super chefs themselves—Michael Mina owns 16 restaurants around the country—so most make only sporadic appearances.

(We should point out that José Andrés, a star of both Spanish and American television and a protégé of El Bulli's Ferran Adria, considered by many to be the world's greatest chef, is also here, at the head of a fistful of restaurants, including the groundbreaking Minibar and Zaytinya. But Washington claims him as an adopted hometown hero, not an import, since he was a celebrity here before he was a TV legend and expanded to highly ranked restaurants in, where else, Las Vegas and Los Angeles. Similarly, although it's a 90-minute drive away, Washingtonians gladly claim pride of place for the five-star **Inn at Little Washington**—little because it's in Washington, Virginia—whose chef, Patrick O'Connell, has for 30 years been admired in print in every culinary journal of note.)

Local favorite Fabio Trabocchi, whose Maestro Restaurant was a destination before he moved to Manhattan to open the critically acclaimed Fiamma (unfortunately just in time for the recession), has returned to Washington to open **Fiola** in the former Bice/Le Paradou space in Penn Quarter.

Susur Lee, whose chic Pan-Asian restaurants range from Toronto to Singapore and New York, has taken over the menu duties at **Zentan** in the Donovan House hotel. Miami-based Guillermo Pernot, a less-famous but insiders' fave ceviche specialist, is heading up the recently opened **Cuba Libre** (801 Ninth St. NW, Ste. A; ☎ 202-408-1600), his fourth along the East Coast, in the Penn Quarter. Danny Meyer (Union Square Cafe, Gramercy Park Tavern, Madison 21) is preparing to open a branch of his hip Manhattan **Shake Shack** in Dupont Circle.

Other New York imports include **Carmine's** family-style Italian "mangiaria" (425 Seventh St. NW; ☎ 202-737-7770) and **Rosa Mexicano,** famous for table-side guacamole and margaritas, in Penn Quarter (575 Seventh St. NW; ☎ 202-783-5522); **Bond 45** (149 Waterfront St.; ☎ 301-839-1445) at National Harbor (and its more casual sibling **Redeye Grill**); **Kellari Taverna** (1700 K St. NW; ☎ 202-535-5274) downtown; and **Hill Country Barbecue** in Penn Quarter. Legendary Manhattan watering house **P. J. Clarke's** (☎ 202-463-6610) is moving to 16th and K streets NW—in the building that formerly housed an outpost of Todd English's Boston Olives. Long-rumored to be scouting Washington locations are Bobby Flay, Nobu Matsuhisa, and Gordon Ramsay.

As part of the burger boom (see below), the New Orleans **Desperados Burger and Bar** (1342 U St.; ☎ 202-299-0443) has expanded to the New-U neighborhood. And among second-line international hot spots moving into Washington are the London-based **Wagamama,** the South African-based **Nando's Peri-Peri** (for locations, see **nandosperiperi.com**), the Hong Kong–based **Ping Pong Dim Sum** (900 Seventh St. NW; ☎ 202-506-3740; with other outposts in Dubai and Brazil, strangely) in Penn Quarter; and the **Buddha-Bar** (455 Massachusetts Ave. NW; ☎ 202-377-5555) of almost everywhere.

There is also a mini-constellation of chefs, famous to TV food network shows, who have taken up Washington residence. *Top Chef* contestant Spike Mendelsohn opened an upscale diner called **Good Stuff Eatery** and a pizza joint called **We, the Pizza** on Capitol Hill. Warren Brown, now a Food Network star, opened his first **CakeLove** bakery (1506 U St. NW; ☎ 202-588-7100) in Washington in 2002 and now has outposts. Sisters Sophie LaMontagne and Katherine Kallinis, whose already successful **Georgetown Cupcake** business went ballistic when they won a Martha Stewart–inspired cupcake contest, have expanded to a bigger location (with longer lines) in Georgetown (3301 M St. NW; ☎ 202-333-8448) and a small, less-famous outpost in Bethesda (4834 Bethesda Ave.; ☎ 301-907-8900). Oprah's former personal chef Art Smith, whose Table 52 restaurant in Chicago was a favorite of the First Family back home, opened the **Art and Soul** restaurant in the Liaison Hotel on Capitol Hill (415 New Jersey Ave. NW; ☎ 202-393-7777). Gray Koonz's protégé Jon Mathieson left New York's Lespinasse to open **Poste Moderne Brasserie** in the Hotel Monaco; after a stint at the fine but financially ill-timed Inox with Jonathan Krinn, the original chef-owner of 2941, both are shopping projects around town.

Other *Top Chef* vets include then-Zaytinya chef Mike Isabella, who is preparing to open the Italian **Graffiato** in the Penn Quarter, and Bryan Voltaggio of **Volt** (228 N Market St.; ☎ 301-696-8658) in Frederick, Maryland (who came in second to his own brother, Michael, of Pasadena, California's Dining Room restaurant).

Even more intriguing is the number of chefs who, like Ziebold and Richard, have been permanently lured away from big-name eateries to positions elsewhere in the nation's capital. Longtime Café Boulud chef Bertrand Chemel is now in charge of **2941** in Falls Church; Jamie Leeds, a veteran of such Manhattan hot spots as Tribeca Grill and Union Square Café, now runs seafood restaurants in Dupont Circle (1624 Q St. NW; ☎ 202-462-4265) and Old Town Alexandria (1026 King St.; ☎ 703-739-4265) called **Hank's Oyster Bar.** In fact, it's rare to read the résumé of the chef at a new opening who can't squeeze Daniel Bouloud, David Bouley, Guy Savoy, Thomas Keller, or Jean-Georges Vongerichten into his CV somewhere. Or a James Beard Award, or a Best New Chef award from a magazine such as

Food & Wine, the latest being Clayton Miller of **Trummer's on Main** in Clifton, Virginia (formerly of Keller's French Laundry), one of the class of 2010.

Drinks, Anyone?

Thanks in large part to noted mix master Todd Thrasher of Restaurant Eve, whose PX "speakeasy" above Eamonn's was the first bar seriously dedicated to the creative cocktail revival, Washington has developed several bars dedicated to the making of original and authentic classic cocktails (as opposed to the sugary shots and chocolate martini generation).

Among the most innovative places to enjoy considered cocktails are **PX** in Old Town Alexandria (728 King St.; ☎ 703-299-8385); **Passenger** near Mount Vernon Square (1021 Seventh St. NW; ☎ 202-393-0220); **Proof** and **PS7's** in the Penn Quarter, both of which are also highly regarded restaurants; **Wisdom** on lower Capitol Hill (1432 Pennsylvania SE; ☎ 202-543-2323); and **Policy** (1904 14th St. NW; ☎ 202-387-7654) and the aptly named **Gibson** in the heart of the U Street neighborhood (14th and U streets NW; ☎ 202-232-2156).

Of course, in the era of *Mad Men*, there are hundreds of fine, more traditional bars, many with history to boot: the **Round Robin** in the Willard InterContinental (1401 Pennsylvania Ave.; ☎ 202-628-9100) lays claim to being the place where the mint julep was formalized; and in the aptly named **Off the Record** lounge (16th and H streets NW; ☎ 202-638-6600) in the basement of the Hay-Adams Hotel, cocktail historian John Boswell holds forth, and/or keeps, a lot of local secrets. Mo Taheri has been tending bar at **701** downtown (701 Pennsylvania Ave. NW; ☎ 202-393-0701) for 20 years; and the legendary Sam Lek has been pouring perfect (giant) martinis, 101 varieties of them, at the **Town & Country Lounge** (1127 Connecticut Ave. NW; ☎ 202-347-3000) in the Mayflower Hotel (currently under renovation). As for those who take their vodka straight, the **Russia House** in Dupont Circle (1800 Connecticut Ave. NW; ☎ 202-234-9433) stocks more than 100 brands (which means you'll see a lot of hockey imports hanging out as well).

Ethnic for Everyone

As we said earlier, Washington has been the beneficiary of a surge in high-quality ethnic restaurants, and for their part, ethnic chefs are finally receiving the critical and public attention they deserve. For many years, "foreign" restaurants were somehow considered separately from "fine dining" establishments, as if only certain kinds of cooking could be considered "cuisine." (The obvious fact that Italian, French, and Chinese styles are all "ethnic" seems to have failed to strike a lot of critics.) As a capital that naturally attracts immigrant professionals, military and diplomatic personnel, students, and refugees, Washington can now boast chefs from around the globe, though not (yet) from every region.

And the greater quantity of choices means better quality as well: each successive ethnic boom, such as the recent one in Thai food, educates diners to the delicacy as well as the potency of that cuisine; then importers ramp up the amount and quality of supplies, and the unauthentic kitchens either upgrade or go out of business.

Not that authenticity in itself is the only criterion; there are some cuisines that may be, by certain standards, better as they are practiced in the United States or Europe because of more dependable storage, electricity, higher-quality meats, and so on. (And where would we be without the Japanese-American hybrid known as California roll?) There are few rigid "purists" among great chefs; influences and creativity are highly prized these days. Many of the chefs mentioned above—Johnny Monis, José Andrés, and Jean-Georges Vongerichten, to name a few—have developed cuisines that are more characteristic than classic, but all are grounded in a real and respectful understanding of a cuisine's basic tenets.

Just as there are elementary school classes in the region where 20 languages may be spoken, there are few neighborhoods where one would have to drive far to find at least a half-dozen ethnic flavors. As just one example, consider Rockville Town Center, a semi-"new town" development near the Rockville metro station: around a fairly small pedestrian square are situated Thai, Indian, Japanese, Lebanese, Vietnamese, Italian, and Peruvian restaurants, as well as a branch of the Gordon Biersch brewpub chain, a hot wings hangout, a burger joint, and a crab cake house (and the public library, where the computers are manned by a melting pot of locals). And within another block are a Hong Kong–style shabu-shabu joint, a Pan-Asian restaurant, pizza, tortillas, Tex-Mex, and a Taiwanese noodle restaurant with a menu more than 200 (big) dishes long. And this is a planned, young-urban town house development.

Here's one other point to consider: there are generally three stages in the evolution of ethnic restaurants in the United States. The first tends to be opened by immigrants who are trying to get along by offering rather Americanized fare—and many of whom are likely never to have cooked for a living before. (What percentage of any population is comprised of trained chefs? You're as likely to have a doctor or engineer cooking for you, and we have.) The second stage tends to the mom-and-pop-style eateries, where the food is more authentic but not particularly fancy. By the third generation, you have chefs who have actually trained in other countries or studied in a kitchen or culinary academy, have access to quality ingredients, and open white-table restaurants. Voila: "ethnic cuisine." Fortunately, an increasing number of Washingtonians can recognize the real thing these days—if only because so many read food blogs or watch food channels.

The ethnic-fare boom is almost certain to continue: national surveys show that younger consumers are developing tastes for a variety of ethnic flavors early in life, and consider them as much a part of the American buffet as the Italian, Mexican, and Chinese fare—generally of middling authenticity—that older diners tend to stick to. And continued immigration naturally means greater cultural diversity, which is why there are increasing numbers of African and Eastern European restaurants in this country.

Flatbreads and Pizzas

We're not going to belabor the point, but the sudden tsunami of pizzerias, many of them "celebrity" connected, is impossible to ignore. Forget the debate about deep-dish versus thin crust; now you have adherents arguing the merits of Neapolitan versus New Haven–style, wood-fired versus coal-fired, classic versus "creative," and on and on.

Among the pizzerias offering the greatest variety (whether to everyone's taste or not) are: **Pizzeria Paradiso** in Dupont Circle, which could be called the patriarch of the Washington gourmet pizza movement, thanks to its being founded by Peter Pastan of Obelisk, its twin in Georgetown, and its semi-sibling **2Amys** in Upper Northwest; the expanding **Matchbox** family of bar-turned-gastropubs in Penn Quarter, Capitol Hill, and Rockville; the New Haven–style **Pete's Apizza** in Columbia Heights and Friendship Heights; **Moroni & Brother's** in Petworth (founded by former Pizzeria Paradiso staffers); **Pizzeria Orso** in Falls Church, sourdough pies from another Pizzeria Paradiso and 2Amy's veteran; **Comet Ping Pong** in Upper Northwest; the coal-fired **Tagolio Pizzeria & Enoteca** in Crystal City; and on Capitol Hill, **We, the Pizza** from *Top Chef* contestant Spike Mendelsohn, and **Seventh Hill Pizza,** thin-crust Neapolitan-inspired pies from the folks who brought you Montmartre. It also shows up on the menus at such bubbling-under spots as **Liberty Tavern** in Clarendon and **Bibiana Osteria and Enoteca** in Penn Quarter.

As for flatbreads, we'll just mention (to give you a sense of their growing popularity) that you should expect them at such disparate spots as the Mediterranean **Zaytinya** and the playful American **PS7's** in Penn Quarter, the Belgian **Brabo Tasting Room** in Old Town Alexandria, and the New England nostalgic **Liberty Tree** (1016 H St. NE; ☎ 202-396-8733) in the Atlas District. Oh, and (obviously) at the Vermont import **American Flatbread** in Arlington and Ashburn, Virginia.

Gastropubs and Wine Bars

One of the most successful and happy trends in recent years has been the gastropubs—beer- and/or bar-centric restaurants that see beyond snack food, frequently with British overtones—and wine bars, where the food is the complement rather than the other way around.

Among them are serious-foodie **Birch & Barley** (with its upstairs twin, ChurchKey, in the New-U neighborhood), which is one of the best beer-list destinations in the city; the simpler Brit-allegiant **CommonWealth** in Columbia Heights and **Againn** in Penn Quarter and Rockville; the

Irish-hearted **Virtue Feed & Grain** in Old Town Alexandria, which boasts cocktail legend Todd Thrasher's "hoptails"; the sustainability- and craft beer–minded **Meridian Pint** in Columbia Heights; and the almost theme-parkish **Biergarten Haus** with oompah music in the Atlas District. Although its menu is limited to the pies from Pizzeria Paradiso upstairs, **Birreria Paradiso** retains a loyal following thanks to its rotating 16 taps and 150 bottled choices; and the beloved grungy **Quarry House Tavern** in Silver Spring, Maryland, though now owned and "fed" by local Southern home-style fave Jackie Greenbaum (Jackie's), stocks 300 beers—and almost as many whiskeys.

Wine bars are increasingly laying out sophisticated, if sometimes short, menus: try **Veritas** in Dupont Circle, which sticks to the char- cuterie and cheese tradition; the real French **Bistro Lepic** in Glover Park (which offers Wi-Fi); **Ripple** in Cleveland Park, with former Maestro saucier Teddy Diggs at the stove and dessert chef and star David Guas consulting (and for Italian lovers in particular, **Dino** down the block); **Evo Bistro** in McLean (1313 Old Chain Bridge Rd.; ☎ 703-288-4422); **Dickson Wine Bar,** one of many kitchens turning out versions of Vietnamese *banh mi* sandwiches (903 U St. NW; ☎ 202-332-1779); the combination wine shop and tapas café **Grand Cru** in Ballston; **Cork** in the New-U; and the wine-first-and-foremost **Grapeseed** in Bethesda and **Proof** in the Penn Quarter, with high-ranking fare that makes *wine bar* an understatement.

(Ham) Burgers and Other Patties

With the trend back to bistro and comfort foods, along with a burgeoning hint of American nostalgia (Philly sandwiches, New England lobster rolls, New Haven pizza, Southern soul food, and the like), more and more chefs are playing culinary games with the most basic of childhood standards, including hot dogs (notably the house-made dogs at **Komi, Palena,** and **PS7's** and tater tots). Oh, and think we're kidding about the lobster rolls? The Brooklyn-based **Red Hook Lobster Pound** vendor cart empire has opened an, um, branch in Washington that trolls Farragut Park; reach them at ☎ 202-341-6263 or on Twitter or Facebook.

The logical end of this trend, perhaps, is the boutique burger joint, and Washington suddenly has several of those as well, notably **Butcher Burgers** in Arlington, also known as Ray's Hell-Burger, where President Barack Obama and Russian President Dmitry Medvedev downed the primo *del primi* patties made from the leftovers of Ray's the Steaks; Spike Mendelsohn's **Good Stuff Eatery** on Capitol Hill, which makes Michelle Obama's favorite turkey burger (domestic détente?); **Hank's Tavern & Eats** in Hyattsville, from local chain-in- the-making "Chef Geoff" Tracy; **Thunder Burger** in Georgetown, which offers bison, venison, Kobe (Wagyu), turkey, tuna, and porto- bello burgers; and **BGR The Burger Joint** in Dupont Circle, Bethesda, Arlington, and Alexandria, which offers a choice of turkey, lamb, lobster (in warm weather), a sort of burger Cubano, and vegetarian in addition to its beef and cheeseburgers. (And a nine-pounder. If you can eat it by yourself, it's free.)

Other kitchens are also turning out multiple-choice patties: turkey, bison, lamb, and, of course, sliders. Tuna tartare sliders. Lamb sliders. How serious is this trend? Rumor has it that Michel Richard himself, whose most famous version of "burgers" involved lobster (still a mainstay of Central), might open a prime-burger joint himself.

Other Trends (in short)

Here's what else is bubbling up on menus all over Washington:

Moules frites, the Belgian-style pot of mussels and fries, used to be rare enough that people regularly drove to Olney, Maryland, to Mannequin Pis. Now they can head to the Palisades, where **Sur La Place** and **Et Voila!** face each other across MacArthur Boulevard; to **Marvin** *and* **Bistro le Bonne** at 14th and U; to Bethesda, where top local chef Robert Wiedmaier, who helped popularize the dish at **Brasserie Beck,** has opened the bluntly named **Mussel Bar** (and also serves them at **Brabo** in Alexandria); **Granville Moore's** in the Atlas District; **Belga Café** on Capitol Hill; and any seafood-centric dining room, of course.

Sustainability is a hot term around Washington these days, along with eco-friendly and farm-to-table. Organic-cooking maven Nora Pouillon of **Nora** may not be able to claim all the credit for the number of menus with additive-free or heart-healthy entries, but as founder of a national organic network, Chefs Collaborative, she has inspired many other chefs to demand the freshest ingredients. Todd Gray of **Equinox** and the itinerant Barton Seaver, both local boys, are among the prime movers in the national sustainable seafood movement. (Although Seaver no longer heads up the kitchen at Hook in Georgetown, he left his sustainable mark on it.) **Restaurant Eve's** Cathal Armstrong was growing his own veggies, curing his own bacon, and scouring local markets almost before the word *locavore* was coined. At **Poste,** chef Rob Weland not only tends his own organic garden (and makes seasonal menus that spotlight it), but he also employs only recycled paper, recycles and filtrates water, and composts the food waste into said garden. Two downtown restaurants, **Founding Farmers** in the IMF Building in Foggy Bottom and **Farmers & Fishers** on the Georgetown waterfront (3000 K St. NW; ☎ 202-298-0003), are tied directly into the North Dakota Farmers Co-op, serving only sustainable, free-range, organic fare. (They are also vegan-friendly.) And, of course, Washington is the home of the Center for Science in the Public Interest, the folks who told you that fettuccine Alfredo was just as bad for you as you always knew it was.

And without getting into detail, you'll also stumble on duck-fat fries, triple-fried fries, and truffle-oil fries; house-made charcuterie (once a rarity but almost a requisite these days); shrimp and grits;

upscale soul food; po'boys; and pho and *banh mi*—in non-Vietnamese places. Think of it as a treasure hunt.

Hot Restaurant Districts

Along with the awakening of the Washington palate has come a rearrangement of the dining map. While Georgetown remains a busy shopping and nightlife area, it is no longer the dominant restaurant strip; and the ethnically mixed Adams Morgan neighborhood, though still intriguing, is gentrifying and "graying" slightly. Upscale redevelopment around various suburban Metro stations—most notably **Crystal City, Ballston,** and **Clarendon** in Virginia, and **Bethesda** and **Rockville** in Maryland—have lured both established and first-time restaurateurs to those mini-cities.

At the same time, restaurant dining has become so diversified that one no longer needs to go to the Little Saigon neighborhood around Clarendon for very good Vietnamese cooking or to Chinatown for dim sum; the "older" Little Ethiopia of Adams Morgan has given way to a second, more lively neighborhood around 14th and U streets. In fact, it's hard to imagine that anyone living in the Washington metropolitan area is more than a mile from five or six different ethnic restaurants. (Much of the best ethnic food is still in the outlying suburbs, especially in still-emerging areas where rents are lower and zoning is less restrictive, but they are also less accessible except by car.)

By far the most energized areas for dining are what is known as **Penn Quarter,** the revitalized downtown arts and entertainment district, and the **U Street to Logan Circle** area north of that. (The Atlas District on H Street NE is more of a draw as a nightlife area—see Part Eight: Nightlife and Entertainment—but it includes plenty of restaurant options as well.)

Penn Quarter, a fairly recent nickname but one that has already been enshrined in a Metro subway station, refers to an area from around the Verizon Center at Seventh Street west to about Tenth Street north of Pennsylvania Avenue; it's gradually spreading into the old law-and-lobby office downtown district just to its west from Pennsylvania Avenue north toward K Street NW. These are at long last becoming residential areas as well, with upscale condos and apartments attracting both younger occupants and empty nesters (as well as corporate types who use Washington as a part-time base), so the longtime curse of downtown—little street traffic after office hours—has largely been exorcised. (Indeed, another new nightclub strip has emerged along K Street itself, formerly a post–rush hour graveyard.)

Among the best restaurants in the downtown dining scene are the Middle Eastern **Zaytinya,** the Mexican *tapatia* **Oyamel,** the traditional *tapatia* **Jaleo,** the Nuevo Latino **Café Atlántico,** and the *laboratorio* of deconstruction **Minibar** (all, astonishingly, under the watchful eye of Catalonian super chef José Andrés); Michel Richard's **Central,** Robert Wiedmaier's **Brasserie Beck,** the Manhattan Greek import **Kellari**

Taverna, the mod-Japanese **Sei, The Source** (the Puck-deluxe diner at the Newseum), **Zola** (600 F St. NW, next to the International Spy Museum; ☎ 202-654-0999), the fine modern-Italian **Tosca** and **Siroc,** the clever modern-American **PS7's** and **701,** French-Indian **Rasika,** the Creole-homesick **Acadiana,** the Low Country–nostalgic **Georgia Brown's, Oceanaire Seafood Room** (the steak house for fish lovers), the modern seafood **D.C. Coast, Poste Moderne Brasserie** in the Hotel Monaco opposite the Verizon Center, **Café du Parc** in the Willard InterContinental, and **Matchbox** for pizza. Most of the above are profiled later in this chapter.

Other flavor options include the Nuevo Latino **Ceiba** (701 14th St. NW; ☎ 202-393-3983) and **Cuba Libre,** sort of retro Havana cafés. Fabio Trabucchi, formerly one of Washington's premier chefs, has returned and plans to reopen in Penn Quarter, as does R. J. Cooper, ex-chef of Vidalia, who hopes to go full out with a 24-course menu.

Not surprisingly, given its long history of lobbying habits, Washington has rediscovered the big steak and big-ticket business meals, and put the two together at the 21st-century version of the saloon, the platinum-card chophouse. These are now so popular, and their formats so similar—prime beef, creamed spinach, Caesar salad, and hefty wine lists—that we have simply listed the biggest cow palaces and their wine menus later in this chapter under "The Best Steak," so that you can browse by location. The big-name **Bourbon Steak, BLT Steak,** and **J&G Steakhouse,** which aren't really chophouses of the same sort, are profiled later.

In the blocks of U Street NW between about 10th and 14th streets, and on the blocks of 14th Street from just above U Street down toward P, you'll find the new-American **Café Saint-Ex,** named for aviator and *The Little Prince* author Antoine de Saint-Exupéry (1847 14th St. NW; ☎ 202-265-7839), and its sibling, the dim but tasty **Bar Pilar,** named for Ernest Hemingway's boat (1833 14th St. NW; ☎ 202-265-1751); the Belgian-inflected pub fare at **Marvin,** named for local-boy soul star Marvin Gaye, who lived in Belgium toward the end of his life; **Busboys and Poets** (for locations, see **busboysandpoets.com**), a combination bookstore, café, bar, and poetry lounge (named for black poet Langston Hughes, who was working as a busboy at the Wardman Park Hotel when he began writing); the New Orleans-flavored **Eatonville** (2121 14th St. NW; ☎ 202-332-9672), named for black novelist Zora Neale Hurston's hometown. More straightforwardly named are **Dickson Wine Bar** and **The Gibson,** the semi-hidden sidecar to Marvin; the **Saloon,** a transplanted Georgetown beer haven (1205 U St. NW; ☎ 202-462-2642); **Locolat,** a first-rate Belgian chocolate and sandwich shop (1781 Florida Ave. NW; ☎ 202-518-2570); and **Cork,** one of the nicest wine bars in town on the basis of its intriguing and wide-ranging menu.

Bistro le Bonne is an old-fashioned bistro in the most comfortable fashion; **Policy** is an aspiring mod-American cocktail bar with eclectic cuisine; **Dukem** (1114–1118 U St. NW; ☎ 202-667-8735), **Little Ethiopia** (1924 Ninth St. NW; ☎ 202-319-1924), and **Etete** are well-regarded Ethiopian restaurants. **DC Noodles** is a laid-back version of an Asian soup kitchen (1410 U St. NW; ☎ 202-232-8424); **Masa 14** (☎ 202-328-1414), on 14th between S and T, is a collaboration between Richard Sandoval of Zengo and Kaz Okochi of Kaz Sushi Bistro.

And, of course, this area is home to the legendary **Ben's Chili Bowl** (1213 U St. NW; ☎ 202-667-0909) and the equally long-lived **Florida Avenue Grill** (1100 Florida Ave. NW; ☎ 202-265-1586), as well as the much younger but soulfully similar **Oohh's and Aahh's** (1005 U St. NW; ☎ 202-667-7142) and **Crème** (1322 U St. NW; ☎ 202-234-1884).

unofficial **TIP**
U Street has replaced the old Chinatown as the place to appease late-night hunger pangs; many of these places are open until the wee hours on weekends—some even during the week.

Just a few blocks south of this cluster, and gradually beginning to merge with it, is Logan Circle, which is actually at 13th and P streets NW but which also serves as the shorthand name for the growing P Street restaurant and 14th Street theater district. Among the top names there are **Estadio,** a Spanish tapas extravaganza from the folks who brought you Proof; the very stylish gastropub **Birch & Barley/ChurchKey** (the one named for the makings, the other for the opener); **Posto,** which offers more than 110 bottles of Italian wine to go with its wood-fired pizza (1515 14th St. NW; ☎ 202-332-8613); and **Logan Tavern,** a very casual but often surprisingly deft neighborhood hangout (1423 P St. NW; ☎ 202-332-3710).

And while both Bethesda and Clarendon have been restaurant centers for years, each has recently received fresh transfusions of high-quality cooking that have further raised the bars. In Bethesda, Robert Wiedmaier has muscled his **Mussel Bar** into the busy Woodmont Avenue dining strip, near **Raku** (7240 Woodmont Ave.; ☎ 301-718-8680) and **Jaleo;** the third branch of the popular local meze family **Cava** is on Bethesda Avenue just around the corner near up-and-comers **Redwood** (7121 Bethesda Ln.; ☎ 301-656-5515) and **Assaggi** and a branch of the TV-centric **Georgetown Cupcake;** and Yannick Cam, who along with Jean-Louis Palladin brought fine French cooking to Washington 30 years ago—and who has been in and out of restaurants ever since—has reappeared in (what else) a bistro setting, **Bistro Provence,** in the "golden triangle" of Bethesda restaurants between Old Georgetown Road and Wisconsin Avenue.

And in Clarendon, where the Metro station always served as an anchor for neighborhood restaurants (and which earned its first critical stripes as the Little Saigon of the area), modern American dining is once again making this a dining destination. In the same block of Wilson Boulevard facing the Clarendon Metro plaza are **Liberty Tavern** and **Eventide,** with Liberty Tavern's new **Lyon Hall** brasserie at the west point of the plaza (3100 N Washington Blvd.; ☎ 703-741-7636).

Tallula is a few blocks east on Wilson, **3 Bar & Grill** is two blocks east on Clarendon, and yet another branch of **Cava** is planned for the neighborhood as well.

Oh, and if you're really just the steak-and-potatoes type? Head to Tysons Corner; it could be a cattle ranch. Just check "The Best Steak" list on page 276.

The Hotel-dining Scene

When it comes to hotel dining rooms, Washington contradicts the conventional wisdom that hotel restaurants are not worth seeking out. As is clear from the preceding list of incoming celebrity chefs, many of Washington's best restaurants are in hotels. This is a mutually beneficial arrangement, allowing the chefs to concentrate on managing a kitchen, not a business, and providing an extra attraction to potential clients. (Although that has a downside: because Washington's hotels count on a great deal of expense-account business, they generally offer menus on the expensive side.) On the other hand, being in a hotel with a house restaurant also means that you're likely to be able to get a really good breakfast.

In addition to the ten or so hotel restaurants profiled later, we recommend those at One Washington Circle (**Circle Bistro;** ☎ 202-293-5390), the secondary restaurant at the Mandarin Oriental (**Sou'Wester** at 1330 Maryland Ave. SW; ☎ 202-787-6140), the Lorian Hotel in Old Town Alexandria (**Brabo/Brabo Tasting Room**), Fairfax at Embassy Row (**Jockey Club** at 2100 Massachusetts Ave. NW; ☎ 202-835-2100), Donovan House (Susur Lee's **Zentan**), and the Marriott Courtyard Embassy Row (**Nage** at 1600 Rhode Island Ave. NW; ☎ 202-448-8005).

Diners' Special Needs

The following profiles attempt to address the special requirements of diners who use wheelchairs or leg braces. Because so many of Washington's restaurants occupy older buildings and row houses, options for wheelchair users are unfortunately more limited than in the newer developments. In most of these cases, wheelchair access is obviously prevented right at the street, but many restaurants offering easy entrance to the dining room keep their restrooms up or down a flight of stairs. In either case, we list them as having "no" disabled access. "Fair" access suggests that there is an initial step or small barrier to cross, or that passage may be a bit tight, but that once inside the establishment, dining is comfortable for the wheelchair user. Here again, hotel dining rooms are good bets—the same wide halls and ramps used for baggage carts and deliveries serve wheelchair users as well. Newer office buildings and mixed shopping and entertainment complexes have ramps and elevators that make them wheelchair accessible; the ones above subway stations even have their own elevators.

Aside from a list of restaurants emphasizing vegetarian and/or vegan dishes, we have not categorized restaurants as offering vegetarian or other restricted diets because almost all Washington restaurants now either offer vegetarian entrées on the menu or will make low-salt or low-fat dishes on request, although some are particularly amenable to doing this, and we have said so. Use common sense: a big-ticket steak house is unlikely to have many nonmeat options (though many have become accustomed to making veggie plates), but because few countries in the world feature as much meat in their cuisine as America, most ethnic cuisines are good bets for vegetarians.

No Smoke Except for the Grill

They said that it couldn't be done—that restaurants couldn't survive no-smoking bans—but after New York City survived, and more pointedly Washington's next-door-neighboring suburbs of Maryland, including restaurant centers Bethesda, Rockville, Wheaton, Silver Spring, and so on, proved "them" wrong, opponents' arguments were largely snuffed out. On New Year's Day 2007, the District of Columbia made good on its resolution to ban smoking in restaurants and nightclubs, and even many bars, though there are a few cigar bars in town (and hookah bars as well). And finally, even Virginia, a huge tobacco state, followed suit.

Also, as mentioned in Part Four: Getting In and Getting Around, the ban also covers the public transportation you may be planning to take to the restaurant. (Be alert: dedicated smokers often snatch out and light cigarettes on the escalators of the Metro, so leave space between you and them.) The ban also covers most restrooms, so you'll likely have to step outdoors for a smoke.

In general, regulations limit smoking to the lounge areas of restaurants or establish separate nonsmoking dining rooms, but if you prefer to avoid any secondhand chemicals (or aromas), it would be a good idea to call ahead.

PLACES TO SEE FACES

WASHINGTON MAY NOT REALLY BE HOLLYWOOD on the Potomac (although so many movie stars come to town to lobby for their pet causes that it's getting very close), but there are celebrity faces aplenty. Consequently, out-of-towners often list "famous people" right after the Air and Space Museum on their required-viewing list. Because being seen is part of the scene—and getting star treatment is one of the perks of being famous—celebrities and politicians tend to be visible in dependable places, particularly at lunch.

For several years now, **Café Milano** in Georgetown has emerged as probably the single most celeb- and socialite-centric restaurant, with politicians, diplomats, royals, actors, and even media types. George Clooney, Bill Clinton, Michael Jordan, and Tom Brokaw have dined here. And owner Franco Nuschese prepared lunch for the

Pope and his cardinals. The decor is based on the best-known roles of frequent drop-in Placido Domingo, director of the Washington National Opera.

Actually, steak houses almost always seem to draw power diners, perhaps because of the titanium-card bills. Both Clintons are regulars at **Charlie Palmer Steak,** which boasts an all-American wine list (and a rooftop view of the Capitol).

unofficial **TIP**
Let's just get this out of the way: Among the places the Obamas have dined are Komi, Equinox, Blue Duck Tavern, Acadiana, Good Stuff, and Sei.

The newest hot spot is **Bourbon Steak,** which has already served Paul McCartney and Brangelina, among others. And the venerable steak-and-lobster **Palm,** with its wall-to-wall caricatures of famous customers and its bullying waiters, is still a popular media and legal-eagle hangout (1225 19th St. NW; ☎ 202-293-9091). The old-clubby **Monocle** on Capitol Hill (107 D St. NE; ☎ 202-546-4488), the unofficial transfer point between the Senate and its office buildings, has long drawn the Republican money men, but more recently it's seen a number of power women happy to break the gender bar, including Secretary of State Hillary Clinton and California Senator Dianne Feinstein. **Johnny's Half Shell** is a favorite of Hill staffers from both sides, as much for the food as for the generous martinis. **Oceanaire Seafood Room** draws plenty of media faces, including former CNN talk-show host Larry King and Fox News Channel's Chris Wallace. **Tosca** has become a sort of unofficial Democratic hangout: regulars include many younger pros from the Kennedy-Shriver-Townsend clan (it was a favorite of the late Senator Edward Kennedy, who preferred to dine in the kitchen), long-time presidential alter ego and sometime cause célèbre Martin Sheen of NBC's *The West Wing*, and power couple NBC reporter Andrea Mitchell and former Federal Reserve Chairman Alan Greenspan.

Perhaps the most unassuming celebrity eatery, however, is near neither the Capitol nor the White House: **Ben's Chili Bowl,** a 50-year survivor of riots and recessions, is still dishing out chili half-smokes (half pork and beef smoked sausage on a bun topped with mustard, onions, and chili) to the likes of Bill Cosby (who reportedly courted wife Camille here), Chris Rock, the Rev. Jesse Jackson, Russell Crowe, and most famously, President Barack Obama.

The RESTAURANTS

RECOMMENDED WASHINGTON RESTAURANTS

THE RESTAURANT PROFILES that follow are not strictly the best restaurants; rather, it's intended to give you a sense of the atmosphere and advantages of a particular establishment as well as its cuisine. None should be taken as gospel, because one drawback of Washington's new appetite for adventure is that restaurants open and close—and promising chefs play musical kitchens—with breathtaking speed. We have for the most part profiled only restaurants that have been in operation for at least a year, or that have chefs with such strong track records that they are of special interest. We have also in most cases given preference to establishments with easy access to the subway or cabs because we realize that the majority of visitors to Washington stay (if not with family or friends) in the major business or tourist areas.

And, blame it on yuppie consciousness, gourmet magazine proliferation, or real curiosity, but the increased interest in the techniques of cooking has also produced a demand for variety, constantly challenging presentations, and guaranteed freshness. Consequently, many of the fancier restaurants change their menus or some portion thereof daily, and many more change seasonally, so the specific dishes recommended at particular places may not be available on a given night. Use these critiques not as menu pages (that's what the Internet is for) but as a guide, an indication of the chef's interests and strengths, rather than a hard-and-fast ordering chart. And truth to tell, the waitstaff often has pretty good advice, if you ask sincerely.

Each profile features an easily scanned heading that allows you, in just a second, to check out the restaurant's name, overall star rating, cuisine, cost, quality rating, and value rating.

OVERALL STAR RATING The star rating is an overall rating that encompasses the entire dining experience, including style, service, and ambience in addition to the taste, presentation, and quality of the food. Five stars is the highest rating possible and connotes the best of everything. Four-star restaurants are exceptional, and three-star restaurants are well above average. Two-star restaurants are good. One star is used to indicate an average restaurant that demonstrates an unusual capability in some area of specialization—for example, an otherwise unmemorable place that has great barbecued chicken.

CUISINE This is actually less straightforward than it sounds. A couple of years ago, for example, "Pan-Asian" restaurants were generally serving what was then generally described as "fusion" food—Asian ingredients with European techniques, or vice versa. Since then, there has been a Pan-Asian explosion in the area, but nearly all specialize in what would be street food back home: noodles, skewers, dumplings, and soups. Modern American sounds pretty broad, and it is—part "new Continental," part "regional," and part "new eclectic." Like art (or pornography), you know it when you see it. Where there are major subdivisions of cuisine, we have tried to put it in the most obvious place; Marcel's is French-Belgian, while its sibling Brasserie Beck is definitely Belgian. And Nuevo Latino is distinctly different from traditional Spanish or South American. Again, though, experimentation and "fusion" is ever more common, so don't hold us, or the chefs, to too strict a style.

COST To the right of the cuisine type in the ratings bar is an expense description that provides a comparative sense of how much a complete meal will cost. A complete meal for our purposes is an appetizer and entrée with side dish; desserts, drinks, and tip are excluded.

Inexpensive	$25 and less per person
Moderate	$26–$40 per person
Expensive	$41–$60 per person
Very expensive	More than $60 per person

QUALITY RATING The food quality is rated on a five-star scale, five being the best rating attainable. The quality rating is based solely on the food served, taking into account taste, freshness of ingredients, preparation, presentation, and creativity. There is no consideration of price. If you want the best food available, and cost is not an issue, look no further than the quality ratings.

VALUE RATING If, on the other hand, you are looking for both quality and value, then you should check the value rating, also expressed in stars. The value ratings are defined as follows:

★★★★★	Exceptional value; a real bargain
★★★★	Good value
★★★	Fair value; you get exactly what you pay for
★★	Somewhat overpriced
★	Significantly overpriced

PAYMENT We've listed the type of payment accepted at each restaurant using the following code: AMEX equals American Express (Optima), CB equals Carte Blanche, D equals Discover, DC equals Diners Club, MC equals MasterCard, JCB equals Japan Credit Bank, T equals Transmedia, and VISA is self-explanatory.

WHO'S INCLUDED Because restaurants are opening and closing all the time in Washington, we have tried to confine our list to establishments with a proven track record over a fairly long period of time. Franchises and national chains are rarely included, although we have included a list of the most dependable locally based chains, especially those that are located in accessible neighborhoods where businesspeople and visitors may find themselves. Also, the list is highly selective. Noninclusion of a particular place does not necessarily indicate that the restaurant is not good, but only that it's relative ranking in its genre may not have been balanced by its accessibility. We've also weighted some choices in favor of a geographic spread. Detailed profiles of individual restaurants follow in alphabetical order at the end of this part.

BUBBLING *Under the* HOT 100

- **Acacia** 4340 Connecticut Ave. NW; ☎ 202-537-1040
- **Assaggi** 4838 Bethesda Ave., Bethesda, MD; ☎ 301-951-1988
- **Bibiana Osteria and Enoteca** 1100 New York Ave. NW; ☎ 202-216-9550
- **BlackSalt** 4883 MacArthur Blvd. NW; ☎ 202-342-9101
- **Brabo by Robert Wiedmaier/Brabo Tasting Room** 1600 King St., Alexandria, VA (in the Lorien Hotel); ☎ 703-894-3440/703-894-5252
- **Cava** 527 Eighth St. SE; ☎ 202-543-9090
  9713 Traville Gateway Dr., Rockville, MD; ☎ 301-309-9090
- **8407** 8407 Ramsey Ave., Silver Spring, MD; ☎ 301-587-8407
- **Eola** 2020 P St. NW; ☎ 202-466-4441
- **Estadio** 1520 14th St. NW; ☎ 202-319-1404
- **Eventide** 3165 Wilson Blvd., Clarendon, VA; ☎ 703-276-3165
- **Galileo III** 600 14th St. NW; ☎ 202-783-0083
- **Kora** 2250-B Crystal Dr., Crystal City, VA; ☎ 571-431-7090
- **Liberty Tavern** 3195 Wilson Blvd., Clarendon, VA; ☎ 703-465-9360
- **PassionFish** 11960 Democracy Dr. (Reston Town Center), Reston, VA; ☎ 703-230-FISH (3474)
- **Present** 6678 Arlington Blvd., Falls Church, VA; ☎ 703-531-1881
- **Ris** 2275 L St. NW; ☎ 202-730-2500
- **Sei** 444 Seventh St. NW; ☎ 202-783-7007
- **Siroc** 915 15th St. NW; ☎ 202-628-2220
- **701** 701 Pennsylvania Ave. NW; ☎ 202-393-0701
- **Tallula** 2761 Washington Blvd., Clarendon, VA; ☎ 703-778-5051
- **3 Bar and Grill** 2950 Clarendon Blvd., Clarendon, VA; ☎ 703-524-4440
- **Vermilion** 1120 King St., Alexandria, VA; ☎ 703-684-9669
- **Willow** 4301 N Fairfax Dr., Ballston, VA; ☎ 703-465-8800
- **Zentan** 1155 14th St. NW (in the Donovan House hotel); ☎ 202-379-4366

The BEST . . .

The Best Gastropubs and Wine Bars

- **Againn** 1099 New York Ave. NW; ☎ 202-639-9830
  12256 Rockville Pike, Rockville, MD; ☎ 301-230-9260
- **Alliance Tavern** 3238 Wisconsin Ave. NW; ☎ 202-362-0362
- **Bier Baron** 1523 22nd St. NW; ☎ 202-293-1885
- **Biergarten Haus** 1355 H St. NE; ☎ 202-388-4053
- **Birreria Paradiso** 3282 M St. NW; ☎ 202-337-1245
- **Birch & Barley/ChurchKey** 1337 14th St. NW; ☎ 202-567-2576
- **Bistro Lepic** 1736 Wisconsin Ave. NW; ☎ 202-333-0111
- **Brasserie Beck** 1101 K St. NW; ☎ 202-408-1717

- **CommonWealth Gastropub** 1400 Irving St. NW; ☎ 202-265-1400

- **Cork** 1720 14th St. NW; ☎ 202-265-CORK (2675)

- **Grand Cru** 4401 Wilson Blvd., Ballston, VA; ☎ 703-243-7900

- **Grapeseed** 4865 Cordell Ave., Bethesda, MD; ☎301-986-9592

- **Meridian Pint** 3400 11th St. NW; ☎ 202-588-1075

- **Proof** 775 G St. NW; ☎ 202-737-7663

- **Quarry House Tavern** 8401 Georgia Ave., Silver Spring, MD;
  ☎ 301-587-8350

- **Ripple** 3417 Connecticut Ave. NW; ☎ 202-244-7995

- **Rock Creek** 1523 22nd St. NW; ☎ 202-293-1885

- **Rustico** 827 Slaters Ln., Alexandria, VA; ☎ 703-224-5051

- **Society Fair** 227 S Washington St., Alexandria, VA; (*no phone yet*)

- **Veritas** 2031 Florida Ave. NW; ☎ 202-265-6270

- **Virtue Feed & Grain** 106 S Union St., Alexandria, VA; (*no phone yet*)

The Best Burgers

- **BGR The Burger Joint** 1514 Connecticut Ave. NW; ☎ 202-299-1071
  106 N Washington St., Old Town Alexandria, VA; ☎ 703-299-9791
  3129 Lee Hwy., Arlington, VA; ☎ 703-812-4705
  4827 Fairmont Ave., Bethesda, MD; ☎ 301-358-6137

- **Good Stuff Eatery** 303 Pennsylvania Ave. SE; ☎ 202-543-8222

- **Hank's Tavern & Eats** 6507 America Blvd., Hyattsville, MD;
  ☎ 301-209-0572

- **Pizzeria Orso** 400 S Maple Ave., Falls Church, VA; ☎ 703-226-3460

- **Ray's Hell-Burger** 1725 Wilson Blvd., Rosslyn, VA; ☎ 703-841-0001

- **Ray's Hell-Burger Too** 1713 N Wilson Blvd., Rosslyn, VA;
  ☎ 703-841-0001

- **Ray's the Classics** 8606 Colesville Rd., Silver Spring, MD;
  ☎ 301-588-7297 (*bar only*)

- **Thunder Burger** 3056 M St. NW; ☎ 202-333-2888

The Best Mussel Bars

- **Belga Café** 514 Eighth St. SE; ☎ 202-544-0100

- **Bistro le Bonne** 1340 U St. NW; ☎ 202-758-3413

- **Brabo by Robert Wiedmaier** 1600 King St., Alexandria, VA;
  ☎ 703-894-3440

- **Brasserie Beck** 1101 K St. NW; ☎ 202-408-1717

- **Et Voila!** 5120 MacArthur Blvd. NW; ☎ 202-237-2300

- **Granville Moore's** 1238 H St. NE; ☎ 202-399-2546

- **Le Mannequin Pis** 18064 Georgia Ave., Olney, MD; ☎ 301-570-4800

- **Marvin** 2007 14th St. NW; ☎ 202-797-7171

- **Mussel Bar** 7262 Woodmont Ave., Bethesda, MD; ☎ 301-215-7817
- **Sur La Place** 5105 MacArthur Blvd. NW; ☎ 202-237-1445

The Best Steak

- **BLT Steak** 1625 I St. NW; ☎ 202-689-8999
- **Bobby Van's** 809 15th St. NW; ☎ 202-589-0060
- **Capital Grille** 601 Pennsylvania Ave. NW; ☎ 202-737-6200
  1861 International Dr., Tysons Corner, VA; ☎ 703-448-3900
- **Caucus Room** 401 Ninth St. NW; ☎ 202-393-1300
- **Charlie Palmer Steak** 101 Constitution Ave. NW; ☎ 202-547-8100
- **Don Shula's** 8028 Leesburg Pike, Tysons Corner, VA; ☎ 703-506-3256
- **Fleming's Steakhouse & Wine Bar** 1960 Chain Bridge Rd.,
  Tysons Corner, VA; ☎ 703-442-8384
- **J. Gilbert's** 6930 Old Dominion Dr., McLean, VA; ☎ 703-893-1034
- **Morton's The Steakhouse** 3251 Prospect St. NW; ☎ 202-342-6258
  8075 Leesburg Pike/Route 7, Tysons Corner, VA; ☎ 703-883-0800
  1050 Connecticut Ave. NW; ☎ 202-955-5997
  1750 Crystal Dr., Crystal City, VA; ☎ 703-418-1444
  11956 Market St. (Reston Town Center), Reston, VA; ☎ 703-796-0128
- **Palm** 1225 19th St. NW; ☎ 202-293-9091
  1750 Tysons Blvd., Tysons Corner, VA; ☎ 703-917-0200
- **Prime Rib** ☎ 2020 K St. NW; ☎ 202-466-8811
- **Ruth's Chris Steakhouse** 1801 Connecticut Ave. NW; ☎ 202-797-0033
  724 Ninth St. NW; ☎ 202-393-4488
  7315 Wisconsin Ave., Bethesda, MD; ☎ 301-652-7877
  2231 Crystal Dr., Arlington, VA; ☎ 703-979-7275
  8571 Leesburg Pike, Tysons Corner; ☎ 703-848-4290
  4100 Monument Corner Dr., Ste. 101, Fairfax, VA; ☎ 703-266-1004
- **Sam & Harry's** 1200 19th St. NW ☎ 202-296-4333
- **Smith & Wollensky** 1112 19th St. NW; ☎ 202-466-1100

The Most Dependable Local Chains

- **Austin Grill** 750 E St. NW; ☎ 202-393-3776
  36-A Maryland Ave. (Rockville Town Center), Rockville, MD;
      ☎ 301-838-4281
  801 King St., Alexandria, VA; ☎ 703-684-8969
  8430-A Old Keene Mill Rd., Springfield, VA; ☎ 703-644-3111
  919 Ellsworth Dr., Silver Spring, MD; ☎ 240-247-8969
- **Chef Geoff's** 13th St. between E and F streets NW; ☎ 202-464-4461
  3201 New Mexico Ave. NW; ☎ 202-237-7800
  4435 Willard Ave., Chevy Chase, MD (**Lia's**); ☎ 240-223-5427
  8045 Leesburg Pike, Vienna, VA; ☎ 571-282-6003

- **Clyde's** 707 Seventh St. NW; ☎ 202-349-3700
    3236 M St. NW; ☎ 202-333-9180
    5441 Wisconsin Ave., Chevy Chase, MD; ☎ 301-951-9600
    1700 N Beauregard St. (Mark Center), Alexandria, VA; ☎ 703-820-8300
    11905 Market St. (Reston Town Center), Reston, VA; ☎ 703-787-6601
    8332 Leesburg Pike, Tysons Corner, VA; ☎ 703-734-1901

- **Jaleo** 480 Seventh St. NW; ☎ 202-628-7949
    7271 Woodmont Ave., Bethesda, MD; ☎ 301-913-0003
    2250-A Crystal Dr., Crystal City, VA; ☎ 703-413-8181

- **Lebanese Taverna** 2641 Connecticut Ave. NW; ☎ 202-265-8681
    1605 Rockville Pike (Congressional Plaza), Rockville, MD; ☎ 301-468-9086
    115-A Gibbs St. (Rockville Town Center), Rockville, MD; ☎ 301-309-8681
    933 Ellsworth Dr., Silver Spring, MD; ☎ 301-588-1192
    4400 Old Dominion Dr., Arlington, VA; ☎ 703-276-8681
    5900 Washington Blvd., Arlington, VA; ☎ 703-241-8681
    1101 S Joyce St., Pentagon City, VA; ☎ 703-415-8681
    1840-G International Dr. (Tysons Galleria), McLean, VA; ☎ 703-847-5244
    7141 Arlington Rd., Bethesda, MD; ☎ 301-951-8681

Best Museum Restaurants

- **National Air and Space Museum Wright Place Food Court** Sixth Street and Independence Ave. NW; ☎ 202-633-1000 (best for kids)
- **National Gallery of Art Sculpture Garden Pavilion Café** Seventh St. and Constitution Ave. NW; ☎ 202-289-3360
- **National Gallery of Art West Building Garden Café** Sixth St. and Constitution Ave. NW; ☎ 202-712-7454
- **National Museum of American History Constitution Café** 14th St. and Constitution Ave. NW; ☎ 202-633-1000
- **National Museum of the American Indian Mitsitam Cafe** Fourth St. and Independence Ave. NW; ☎ 202-633-1000
- **National Museum of Natural History Fossil Cafe** Tenth St. and Constitution Ave. NW; ☎ 202-633-9501 (best for kids)
- **Newseum's The Source** 575 Pennsylvania Ave. NW; ☎ 202-637-6100
- **United States Holocaust Museum Cafe** 100 Raoul Wallenberg Place (15th St. NW); ☎ 202-488-6151 (vegetarian, kosher)

The Best Pizza and Flatbreads

- **American Flatbread** 1025 N Fillmore St., Arlington, VA; ☎ 703-243-9465
    43170 Southern Walks Plaza, Ashburn, VA; ☎ 703-723-7003
- **Comet Ping Pong** 5037 Connecticut Ave. NW; ☎ 202-364-0404
- **Ella's Wood-Fired Pizza** 901 F St. NW; ☎ 202-638-3434
- **Matchbox** 713 H St. NW; ☎ 202-289-4441
    521 Eighth St. SE; ☎ 202-548-0369
- **Moroni & Brother's** 4811 Georgia Ave. NW; ☎ 202-829-2090

- **Pete's Apizza** 1400 Irving St. NW; ☎ 202-332-PETE (7383);
  4940 Wisconsin Ave. NW; ☎ 202-237-PETE (7383)

- **Pizzeria Orso** 400 S Maple Ave., Falls Church, VA; ☎ 703-226-3460

- **Pizzeria Paradiso** 2003 P St. NW; ☎ 202-223-1245
  3282 M St. NW, Georgetown; ☎ 202-337-1245
  124 King St., Old Town Alexandria, VA; ☎ 703-837-1245

- **Seventh Hill Pizza** 327 Seventh St. SE; ☎ 202-544-1911

- **Tagolio Pizzeria & Enoteca** 549 23rd St., Arlington, VA;
  ☎ 703-553-2070

- **2Amys** 3715 Macomb St. and Wisconsin Ave. NW; ☎ 202-885-5700

- **We, the Pizza** 305 Pennsylvania Ave. SE; ☎ 202-544-4008

The Best Raw Bars

- **Black's Bar and Kitchen** 7750 Woodmont Ave., Bethesda, MD;
  ☎ 301-652-5525

- **Kinkead's** 2000 Pennsylvania Ave. NW; ☎ 202-296-7700

- **McCormick & Schmick's**
  11920 Democracy Dr., Reston, VA; ☎ 703-481-6600
  7401 Woodmont Ave., Bethesda, MD; ☎ 301-961-2626
  1652 K St. NW; ☎ 202-861-2233
  8484 Westpark Dr., Tysons Corner, VA; ☎ 703-848-8000
  901 F St. NW; ☎ 202-639-9330
  2010 Crystal Dr., Crystal City, VA; ☎ 703-413-6400

- **Oceanaire Seafood Room** 1201 F St. NW; ☎ 202-347-BASS (2277)

- **Old Ebbitt Grill** 675 15th St. NW; ☎ 202-347-4800

- **Sea Catch** 1054 31st St. NW, Georgetown; ☎ 202-337-8855

The Best Sushi Bars

- **Kaz Sushi Bistro** 1915 I St. NW; ☎ 202-530-5500

- **Kotobuki** 4822 MacArthur Blvd. NW; ☎ 202-281-6679

- **Murasaki** 4620 Wisconsin Ave. NW; ☎ 202-966-0023

- **Kushi Izakaya & Sushi** 465 K St. NW; ☎ 202-682-3123

- **Niwano Hana** 887 Rockville Pike (Wintergreen Plaza), Rockville, MD;
  ☎ 301-294-0553

- **Sei** 444 Seventh St. NW; ☎ 202-783-7007

- **Sushi-Ko** 2309 Wisconsin Ave. NW; ☎ 202-333-4187
  5455 Wisconsin Ave., Chevy Chase, MD; ☎301-961-1644

- **Sushi Taro** 1503 17th St. NW; ☎ 202-462-8999

- **Tako Grill** 7756 Wisconsin Ave., Bethesda, MD; ☎ 301-652-7030

The Best for Vegetarians/Vegans

- **Café Green** 1513 17th St. NW; ☎ 202-234-0505

- **En Asian Bistro and Sushi Bar** 19833 Century Blvd., Germantown, MD; ☎ 301-916-2258

- **Founding Farmers** 1924 Pennsylvania Ave. NW; ☎ 202-822-TRUE (9783)

- **Indique Heights** 2 Wisconsin Circle, Chevy Chase, MD; ☎ 301-656-4822

- **Java Green** 1020 19th St. NW; ☎ 202-775-8899

- **Mark's Kitchen** 7006 Carroll Ave., Takoma Park, MD; ☎ 301-270-1884

- **Rasika** 633 D St. NW; ☎ 202-637-1222

- **Restaurant Eve** 110 S Pitt St., Old Town Alexandria, VA; ☎ 703-706-0450

- **Vegetable Garden** 11618 Rockville Pike, Rockville, MD; ☎ 301-468-9301

The Best Wine Lists Not at a Steak House

- **Blue Duck Tavern** 1201 24th St. NW (Park Hyatt Hotel); ☎ 202-419-6755

- **Central Michel Richard** 1001 Pennsylvania Ave. NW; ☎ 202-626-0015

- **Citronelle** 3000 M St. NW (Latham Hotel); ☎ 202-625-2150

- **Corduroy** 1122 Ninth St. NW; ☎ 202-589-0699

- **Dino** 3435 Connecticut Ave. NW; ☎ 202-686-2966

- **Grapeseed** 4865 Cordell Ave., Bethesda, MD; ☎ 301-986-9592

- **The Inn at Little Washington** Middle and Main streets, Washington, VA; ☎ 540-675-3800

- **Kinkead's** 2000 Pennsylvania Ave. NW; ☎ 202-296-7700

- **L'Auberge Chez François** 332 Springvale Rd., Great Falls, VA; ☎ 703-759-3800

- **Mrs. K's Toll House** 9201 Colesville Rd., Silver Spring, MD; ☎ 301-589-3500

- **Obelisk** 2029 P St. NW; ☎ 202-872-1180

- **Proof** 775 G St. NW; ☎ 202-737-7663

- **Taberna del Alabardero** 1776 I St. NW; ☎ 202-429-2200

The Best Sunday Brunches

- **Black Market Bistro** 4660 Waverly Ave., Garrett Park, MD; ☎ 301-933-3000

- **Blue Duck Tavern** 1201 24th St. NW (Park Hyatt Hotel); ☎ 202-419-6755

- **Bombay Club** 815 Connecticut Ave. NW; ☎ 202-659-3727

- **Café Atlántico** 405 Eighth St. NW; ☎ 202-393-0812

- **The Four Seasons Hotel Seasons Restaurant** 2800 Pennsylvania Ave. NW; ☎ 202-342-0444

- **Georgia Brown's** 950 15th St. NW; ☎ 202-393-4499

- **The Irish Inn at Glen Echo** 6119 Tulane Ave. (MacArthur Boulevard and Clara Barton Parkway), Glen Echo, MD; ☎ 301-229-6600

- **Jaleo** 480 Seventh St. NW; ☎ 202-628-7949
  7271 Woodmont Ave., Bethesda, MD; ☎ 301-913-0003
  2250-A Crystal Dr., Crystal City, VA; ☎ 703-413-8181

- **Kinkead's** 2000 Pennsylvania Ave. NW; ☎ 202-296-7700

- **Mrs. K's Toll House** 9201 Colesville Rd., Silver Spring, MD; ☎ 301-589-3500

- **Old Angler's Inn** 10801 MacArthur Blvd., Potomac, MD; ☎ 301-365-2425

- **Old Ebbitt Grill** 675 15th St. NW; ☎ 202-347-4800

- **Poste Moderne Brasserie** 555 Eighth St. NW (Hotel Monaco); ☎ 202-783-6060

- **Tabard Inn** 1739 N St. NW; ☎ 202-331-8528

RESTAURANT PROFILES

Acadiana ★★★

| SOUTHERN   MODERATE   QUALITY ★★★½   VALUE ★★★ |

901 New York Ave. NW; ☎ 202-408-8848;
acadianarestaurant.com Downtown

Reservations Recommended. **When to go** Anytime; lunch for po'boys, happy hour for bargain cocktails. **Entrée range** $21–$29. **Payment** VISA, MC, AMEX, D, DC. **Service rating** ★★★½. **Friendliness rating** ★★½. **Metro** Foggy Bottom. **Parking** Valet at dinner, lot, street meters. **Bar** Full service. **Wine selection** Very good. **Dress** Business casual, casual. **Disabled access** Good. **Customers** Local foodies, arena- or convention-goers, business entertainers. **Hours** *Brunch:* Sunday, 11 a.m.–2:30 p.m.; *Lunch:* Monday–Friday, 11:30 a.m.–2:30 p.m.; *Dinner:* Monday–Thursday, 5:30–10:30 p.m.; Friday–Saturday, 5:30–11 p.m.; Sunday, 5:30–9:30 p.m.

SETTING AND ATMOSPHERE On the ground floor of this very sleek office building is an elegant surprise—a beautiful, Creole-nostalgic dining room with lush banquettes, chandeliers, and platters bought in New Orleans.

HOUSE SPECIALTIES Updated Louisiana classics such as beer-battered soft shell crab étouffée; New Orleans–style barbecued shrimp spiked with Worcestershire sauce; grillades and grits; and panfried duck with dirty rice, collard greens, and red pepper jelly glaze.

OTHER RECOMMENDATIONS Gumbo; trio of deviled eggs (topped with ham, crab, and such); corn, crab, and turtle soup (or a tasting of all three); fried pork boudin balls; fried green tomatoes; grilled redfish with seafood jambalaya-cum-risotto.

SUMMARY AND COMMENTS The bar is particularly popular for quick dining. In good weather there is seating and sometimes crawfish boils on the patio. Among the treats are the basket of hot biscuits with pepper jelly, good mint juleps, and Sazeracs. The same management team owns several other downtown hot spots, including Havana-inspired Ceiba, upscale seafood restaurant D.C. Coast (see profile, page 300), Asian-fusion TenPenh (see profile, page 340), and the new globally inspired seafood at PassionFish in Reston—though each has its own style. Acadiana offers a three-course $29 pre-theater menu 5:30–6:30 p.m. and half-price wines on Sunday.

Addie's ★★★

MODERN AMERICAN   MODERATE   QUALITY ★★★   VALUE ★★★★

11120 Rockville Pike, Rockville; ☎ 301-881-0081;
addiesrestaurant.com   Maryland suburbs

Reservations Recommended. **When to go** Late lunch, midweek. **Entrée range** $18–$25. **Payment** VISA, MC, AMEX, DC. **Service rating** ★★★½. **Friendliness rating** ★★★. **Metro** Grosvenor-Strathmore. **Parking** Free lot. **Bar** Beer and wine. **Wine selection** Good. **Dress** Casual, informal. **Disabled access** Good. **Customers** Locals, area businesspeople. **Hours** *Lunch:* Monday–Friday, 11:30 a.m.–2:30 p.m.; Saturday, noon–2:30 p.m.; *Dinner:* Monday–Thursday, 5:30–9:30 p.m.; Friday, 5:30–10 p.m.; Saturday 5–10 p.m.; Sunday 5–9 p.m.

SETTING AND ATMOSPHERE   This is a simple suburban house turned into the sort of gathering spot that evokes a favorite family vacation home with rooms painted citrusy Key lime and lemon yellow, doorknobs mounted as coat hooks, and mini-pots of herbs as table decorations. A recently added back porch has eased the seating crunch without the traffic noise of the old front deck. Check out the old-fashioned neon "Let's Eat" sign.

HOUSE SPECIALTIES   Classics with a twist: house-made charcuterie, including a fine rabbit pâté; fried oysters with sweet-and-sour pumpkin sauce; fried green tomatoes stuffed with goat cheese; carpaccio; home-style lasagna; fresh tomato panzanella; sautéed hake with eggplant and artisan bacon; sautéed trout with braised cabbage and baby beets.

OTHER RECOMMENDATIONS   Salads with bright offsetting flavors such as fried artichokes with orange segments and pine nuts; plain grilled seafood; and grilled and roasted vegetables.

ENTERTAINMENT AND AMENITIES   Outdoor seating (some with a close view of Rockville Pike traffic).

SUMMARY AND COMMENTS   Owners Barbara (who's a native) and Jeff Black are simply having fun with food, and it shows: the menu is trendy and smart without being overly showy. Flavorings are distinctive but not overwhelming; salt is carefully considered. Comfort food runs to roast chicken or pork chops. Lunch is much simpler, geared to the working/shopping crowds from White Flint Mall across the street who have a Southern sweet tooth, with such offerings as fried-oyster po'boy, shrimp and grits, Cubano, and prosciutto-wrapped mozzarella

continued on page 284

Restaurants by Cuisine

CUISINE AND NAME	OVERALL RATING	PRICE RATING	QUALITY RATING	VALUE RATING
AMERICAN (SEE ALSO MODERN AMERICAN AND SOUTHERN)				
Ray's the Classics	★★★	Mod	★★★★	★★★
Old Ebbitt Grill	★★	Mod	★★½	★★★
BARBECUE				
Old Glory	★★	Mod	★★½	★★★
BELGIAN				
Brasserie Beck	★★★	Mod	★★★	★★★
BURMESE				
Burma	★★	Inexp	★★½	★★★
ETHIOPIAN				
Etete	★★★	Inexp	★★★	★★★★
Meskerem	★★½	Inexp	★★★	★★★½
FRENCH				
Marcel's	★★★★	Exp	★★★★	★★★
Citronelle	★★★★	V. Exp	★★★★	★★★
Adour	★★★½	V. Exp	★★★★	★★½
Café du Parc	★★★½	Mod/Exp	★★★	★★★★
Bistro Bis	★★★½	Exp	★★★	★★★
Bistro Provence	★★★	Mod/Exp	★★★★	★★★
L'Auberge Chez François	★★★	V. Exp	★★★½	★★★★
Montmartre	★★½	Mod	★★★½	★★★½
La Chaumière	★★½	Mod	★★★	★★★
Bistro Français	★★	Mod	★★½	★★★
INDIAN				
Rasika	★★★★	Mod/Exp	★★★★	★★★
Indique Heights	★★★	Mod	★★★½	★★★
Spice Xing	★★½	Inexp	★★★½	★★★★
Heritage India	★★½	Mod	★★★	★★★
ITALIAN				
Obelisk	★★★½	Exp	★★★★½	★★★★
Tosca	★★★½	Exp	★★★★	★★½
Café Milano	★★½	Exp	★★½	★★

CUISINE AND NAME	OVERALL RATING	PRICE RATING	QUALITY RATING	VALUE RATING
JAPANESE				
Sushi Taro	★★★★	V. Exp	★★★★½	★★★★½
Sushi-Ko	★★★½	Mod	★★★★½	★★★★
Kaz Sushi Bistro	★★★½	Mod	★★★★	★★★
Tako Grill	★★★½	Inexp	★★★½	★★★
Makoto	★★★½	V. Exp	★★★½	★★★
Kushi	★★★	Mod/Exp	★★★½	★★★★
Murasaki	★★½	Mod	★★★	★★★
MEXICAN				
Oyamel	★★½	Mod	★★★½	★★★
MIDDLE EASTERN				
Zaytinya	★★★½	Mod	★★★½	★★★½
MODERN AMERICAN				
The Inn at Little Washington	★★★★★	V. Exp	★★★★★	★★★★★
Minibar	★★★★★	V. Exp	★★★★★	★★★★
Komi	★★★★★	V. Exp	★★★★	★★★
CityZen	★★★★½	V. Exp	★★★★	★★★
J&G Steakhouse	★★★★	V. Exp	★★★★	★★★
Restaurant Eve	★★★★	V. Exp	★★★★	★★★
The Source	★★★★	V. Exp	★★★½	★★½
2941	★★★★	V. Exp	★★★	★★★★
Palena	★★★½	Exp	★★★★½	★★★
Bourbon Steak	★★★½	V. Exp	★★★★	★★★½
Proof	★★★½	Mod/Exp	★★★★	★★★
Blue Duck Tavern	★★★½	Exp	★★★★	★★★
Oval Room	★★★½	V. Exp	★★★★	★★★
1789	★★★½	Exp	★★★★	★★★
Vidalia	★★★½	Mod	★★★½	★★★
Corduroy	★★★½	Exp	★★★	★★★
Central Michel Richard	★★★½	Exp	★★★	★★½
PS7's	★★★	Exp	★★★½	★★★★
Equinox	★★★	Exp	★★★½	★★★
Poste Moderne Brasserie	★★★	Exp	★★★½	★★★

Restaurants by Cuisine (continued)

CUISINE AND NAME	OVERALL RATING	PRICE RATING	QUALITY RATING	VALUE RATING
MODERN AMERICAN (CONTINUED)				
Westend Bistro by Eric Ripert	★★★	V. Exp	★★★½	★★★
Addie's	★★★	Mod	★★★	★★★★
Trummer's on Main	★★★	Exp	★★★	★★★★
Grapeseed	★★★	Exp	★★★	★★★
Persimmon	★★½	Mod	★★★★	★★★
Nora	★★½	Exp	★★★½	★★★
D.C. Coast	★★½	Mod	★★★	★★★
Geranio	★★½	Mod	★★★	★★★
Tabard Inn	★★½	Mod	★★½	★★★
Old Angler's Inn	★★	Exp	★★★	★★½
NUEVO LATINO				
Jaleo	★★★	Mod	★★★	★★★
Café Atlántico	★★½	Mod	★★★★	★★★
PAN-ASIAN				
TenPenh	★★½	Mod	★★½	★★½
SEAFOOD				
Kinkead's	★★★	Exp	★★★	★★½
Black's Bar & Kitchen	★★★	Mod	★★½	★★½
Sea Catch	★★	Mod	★★★	★★½
Oceanaire Seafood Room	★★	Exp	★★★	★★½

continued from page 281

sandwich. The Blacks actually have a sort of family empire now, including Black's Bar and Kitchen (see profile, page 289); BlackSalt, a combination fish market and seafood restaurant; and the eclectic Victorian bistro Black Market.

Adour ★★★½

FRENCH   VERY EXPENSIVE   QUALITY ★★★★   VALUE ★★½

923 16th and K streets NW (in the St. Regis Hotel); ☎ 202-509-8000; adour-washingtondc.com Downtown

Reservations Recommended. **When to go** Lunch (in the bar); anytime. **Entrée range** $26–$48. **Payment** VISA, MC, AMEX, D, DC. **Service rating** ★★★★.

CUISINE AND NAME	OVERALL RATING	PRICE RATING	QUALITY RATING	VALUE RATING
SOUTHERN				
Johnny's Half Shell	★★★½	Inexp	★★★	★★★
Acadiana	★★★	Mod	★★★½	★★★
Cashion's Eat Place	★★★	Exp	★★★	★★★
Georgia Brown's	★★	Mod	★★★	★★
SPANISH				
Taberna del Alabardero	★★★	Exp	★★★	★★★
STEAK				
J&G Steakhouse	★★★★	V. Exp	★★★★	★★★
Bourbon Steak	★★★½	V. Exp	★★★★	★★★½
BLT Steak	★★★	V. Exp	★★★★	★★★
THAI				
Bangkok Garden	★★½	Inexp	★★★	★★★★
TURKISH				
Cafe Divan	★★½	Inexp	★★½	★★★★
VIETNAMESE				
Four Sisters	★★★	Inexp	★★★½	★★★★

Friendliness rating ★★★½. **Metro** Farragut North. **Parking** Street, lot, valet. **Bar** Full service. **Wine selection** Very good. **Disabled access** Good. **Customers** Special occasion celebrants, businesspeople. **Hours** *Breakfast:* Daily, 7–11 a.m.; *Dinner:* Tuesday–Thursday, 5:30–10 p.m.; Friday–Saturday, 5:30–10:30 p.m.; *Lounge menu:* Daily, 11 a.m.–1 a.m.

SETTING AND ATMOSPHERE A mix of old and new—cool white walls and white leather chairs with the hotel's original dark and ornate beams overhead—echoes French star chef Alain Ducasse's style: rigorous technique and classic entrées but with a sense of humor. And don't worry about the room being closed for lunch; you can also get what might be Washington's most amazing bar menus (sweetbreads, lobster medallions, or steak) next door, in the dark, book- and Founding Fathers–lined lounge.

HOUSE SPECIALTIES Salmon and foie gras with fresh ginger; pork belly "BLT" with braised lettuces and tomato confit; a sort of Caprese salad with medallions of lobster between buffalo mozzarella and heirloom tomatoes; halibut with grapes; duck breast with pungent roots, including turnips, radishes, and daikon. Because part of the fun is in the quality of the ingredients and in the mix of textures, this is one of those places to splurge on the tasting menus (four courses for $65, five for $75).

OTHER RECOMMENDATIONS All prime meat, including hanger steak; seared sweetbreads with ricotta gnocchi; seasonal vegetable casseroles.

SUMMARY AND COMMENTS You can get a rib eye here—a superb one, as a $48-per-pound steak should be—but why would you waste your money on something you can grill at home? Go for the dishes you don't have the time or the variety of ingredients to mimic. Incidentally, Adour is famous for Ducasse's macaroons, which come out after the entrées, along with house-made truffles, for free. So don't order dessert unless you're addicted to hazelnut soufflé; go for the cheese plate instead.

Bangkok Garden ★★½

THAI   INEXPENSIVE   QUALITY ★★★   VALUE ★★★★

**4906 St. Elmo Ave., Bethesda; ☎ 301-951-0670;
bkkgarden.com**   Maryland suburbs

Reservations Accepted on weekends. **When to go** Anytime. **Entrée range** $7.50–$20.95. **Payment** VISA, MC, AMEX, D, DC. **Service rating** ★★★½. **Friendliness rating** ★★★★. **Metro** Bethesda. **Parking** Street, free lot after 7 p.m.; valet Thursday–Saturday. **Bar** Full service. **Wine selection** House. **Dress** Casual. **Disabled access** Fair. **Customers** Locals, ethnics. **Hours** Monday–Thursday, 11 a.m.–10:30 p.m.; Friday–Saturday, 11 a.m.–11 p.m.; Sunday, 11:30 a.m.–10 p.m.

SETTING AND ATMOSPHERE Small, cheery, and so crowded with brass and plaster animals—giraffes, elephants, temple Foo dogs, peafowl, and deer—that the enshrined young Buddha resembles a Thai St. Francis of Assisi. Enlarged and framed colorful Thai currency and portraits of the royal family are also prominent.

HOUSE SPECIALTIES A rich, skin-and-fat duck in five-flavor sauce; fat "drunken" noodles with beef; hoy jaw (crispy pork-and-crab appetizer cake); squid with basil and chile (unusual, almost pure squid and scarce vegetable filler); the tangy rather than searing seafood combination.

OTHER RECOMMENDATIONS Soft-shell crabs in one of five sauces, including one very light version with asparagus and oyster sauce; steamed crab dumplings; shrimp in chile oil.

SUMMARY AND COMMENTS Though relatively low profile amid the Thai boom—with Americans, that is; it's very popular within the Thai community—this family-run restaurant rewards regular attendance and obvious interest because some of the best dishes aren't on the English menu, but are available to anyone who knows to ask. A particularly delicious example is the Thai steak tartare, a beef version of a Thai pork classic that is rich with garlic, cilantro, and basil and served with a steaming basket of sticky rice intended to be used as the utensil: take a pinch of rice—about a tablespoon—slightly flatten it, grasp a bite of meat with it, and pop the whole morsel into your mouth. At $8, it's a steal of a meal.

Bistro Bis ★★★½

FRENCH   EXPENSIVE   QUALITY ★★★   VALUE ★★★

15 E St. NW (in the Hotel George); ☎ **202-661-2700; bistrobis.com**
Downtown

Reservations Recommended. **When to go** Late lunch, early or late dinner. **Entrée range** $24.50–$33. **Payment** VISA, MC, AMEX, D, DC. **Service rating** ★★★. **Friendliness rating** ★★★½. **Metro** Union Station. **Parking** Free with validation after 5:30 p.m. at pay lot across the street. **Bar** Full service. **Wine selection** Very good. **Dress** Business, informal. **Disabled access** Good. **Customers** Political/media biz, food trendies. **Hours** *Breakfast:* Daily, 7–10 a.m.; *Brunch:* Saturday–Sunday, 11:30 a.m.–2:30 p.m.; *Lunch:* Monday–Friday, 11:30 a.m.–2:30 p.m.; *Dinner:* Daily, 5:30–10:30 p.m.

SETTING AND ATMOSPHERE   Its name is short for bistro, and like that offhand joke, it's sleek, chic, and a touch oblique, its long space divided into a series of step-down semidetached dining "suites" off a hallway. The dark, old Tiber Creek Pub has been transformed into a very blond-wood and etched-glass complex that somehow makes you feel that your companions may be billing you by the hour: zinc-topped bar, cigar-bar mezzanine with lobbylike chairs, and an almost voyeuristic display of exposed-steel kitchen countertop.

HOUSE SPECIALTIES   Intriguingly idiosyncratic, semiclassical French fare: duck liver "parfait" with fig jam; a sort of deconstructed boeuf bourguignon, with the meat braised in individual portions, and a similar mini-cassoulet of lamb shank with flageolets; halibut with lobster; the more traditional bistroesque steak or mussels with *frites*; and old-fashioned onion soup.

OTHER RECOMMENDATIONS   Roast poultry, in generous portions—a half hen even at lunchtime. (Sallie and Jeff Buben claim to have eaten their way across France one roast chicken at a time.) Game specials are carefully tended, too.

SUMMARY AND COMMENTS   *Bis* can also mean "an encore," but while this may be the second fine production from team Buben of Vidalia (see profile, page 343), it resembles that neo-Southern favorite only in its refusal to see traditional fare as limiting. The quantity of food is not so unusual in this business-expense era, but the delicacy of seasoning and the staff's light hand with rich sauces make it hard to leave much on the plate. The all-French wine list has some fine bargains on it.

Bistro Français ★★

FRENCH   MODERATE   QUALITY ★★½   VALUE ★★★

3128 M St. NW; ☎ **202-338-3830; bistrofrancaisdc.com**   Georgetown

Reservations Recommended. **When to go** Pre- or post-theater. **Entrée range** $19–$32; brunch, $25. **Payment** VISA, MC, AMEX, DC. **Service rating** ★★★. **Friendliness rating** ★★★. **Metro** Foggy Bottom–GWU. **Parking** Street. **Bar** Full service. **Wine selection** House. **Dress** Casual. **Disabled access** Good. **Customers** Locals, ethnics. **Hours** Daily, 11 a.m.–3 a.m.; Friday–Saturday, 11 a.m.–4 a.m.; *Brunch*: Saturday–Sunday, 11 a.m.–4 p.m.

SETTING AND ATMOSPHERE This old reliable hasn't changed much since the word *bistro* was new to Washington—hanging pots, rotisserie spits, frankly well-used flatware, and clanking trays.

HOUSE SPECIALTIES This is the sort of place where as nice as the menu is—especially Dover sole, coq au vin, and its signature spit-roasted chicken—the daily specials are even better: for instance, duck confit, roast game birds, or lamb with artichokes.

OTHER RECOMMENDATIONS The steak 'n' fries here is probably the standard against which all others should be measured. And there are fixed-price lunch, $19.95, and pre-theater fixed dinner menus, $24.95, including wine.

SUMMARY AND COMMENTS For all its many pleasures—its famous late-night service and the especially telling fact that many local chefs eat here after hours—it sometimes seems as if this old favorite gets the Rodney Dangerfield treatment from the fashionable crowds, and is feeling a little bedraggled in response.

Bistro Provence ★★★

FRENCH   MODERATE/EXPENSIVE   QUALITY ★★★★   VALUE ★★★

4933 Fairmont Ave., Bethesda; ☎ 301-656-7373; bistroprovence.org
Maryland suburbs

Reservations Strongly recommended. **When to go** Anytime. **Entrée range** $19.50–$29. **Payment** VISA, MC, AMEX. **Service rating** ★★½. **Friendliness rating** ★★½. **Metro** Bethesda. **Parking** Street, pay lot. **Bar** Full service. **Wine selection** Good. **Disabled access** Good. **Customers** Locals, businesspeople, foodies. **Hours** *Lunch*: Monday–Friday, 11:30 a.m.–2:30 p.m.; Saturday–Sunday, 11 a.m.–3 p.m.; *Dinner*: Monday–Friday, 5:30–10:30 p.m.; Saturday, 5–10:30 p.m.; Sunday, 5–9:30 p.m.

SETTING AND ATMOSPHERE This is easily the most striking restaurant in Bethesda, one that looks as if it were transported whole from some old Manhattan brownstone firehouse, but is in fact a new building. (The penguins carved into the overhead arch commemorate the icehouse that once stood on the site.) The decor is true bistro—chandeliers and honey gold walls—with a stone courtyard in the back. This is not a big space (and it can be loud), so call ahead.

HOUSE SPECIALTIES Roast lobster over tiny lentils; duck confit over sautéed potatoes; a delicate seviche of scallops in grapefruit; saffron risotto with shrimp; veal chop when available.

OTHER RECOMMENDATIONS Foie gras; hanger steak in red wine sauce; grilled shrimp with pear-flavored sauce; walnut-stuffed clams.

SUMMARY AND COMMENTS Yannick Cam's first Washington restaurant, Le Pavillon, was a sensation 30 years ago, and really a revelation of nouvelle cuisine in what was then a pretty heavy Continental cream-sauce town.

He's a perfectionist, and even though he calls this a bistro, the fare is inherently upscale. (He has said he plans to put a more expensive tasting room upstairs.) Cam has since been in and out of a series of Provençal, Brazilian, Catalonian-Spanish, and French–country inn establishments—most recently a five-year run in the super-ritzy Le Paradou—and that's the second big caveat. Cam is notoriously restless (and inconsistent) and might well head off again before he celebrates many anniversaries. Still, there's no denying that when he's good, he's very, very good.

Black's Bar and Kitchen ★★★

SEAFOOD   MODERATE   QUALITY ★★½   VALUE ★★½

7750 Woodmont Ave., Bethesda; ☎ 301-652-5525; blacksbarandkitchen.com   Maryland suburbs

Reservations Recommended. **When to go** Anytime; happy hour. **Entrée range** $13–$32. **Payment** VISA, MC, AMEX, DC. **Service rating** ★★★. **Friendliness rating** ★★★½. **Metro** Bethesda. **Parking** Pay lot, street meters, valet. **Bar** Full service. **Wine selection** Good house list. **Dress** Business casual. **Disabled access** Yes. **Customers** Locals, businesspeople. **Hours** *Brunch:* Sunday, 11 a.m.–2:30 p.m.; *Lunch:* Monday–Friday, 11:30 a.m.–2:30 p.m.; Saturday, noon–3 p.m.; *Dinner:* Monday–Thursday, 5:30–10 p.m.; Friday–Saturday, 5:30–11 p.m.; Sunday, 5:30–9:30 p.m.

SETTING AND ATMOSPHERE   Following an extensive and expensive ($2 million) renovation, this formerly funky fish house is now a stunning, upscale grill with a sleek patio and mini-pond, black glass facade with red logo, burgundy glass dividers in the bar, and a Tuscan-mural dining room with a wine cellar as its centerpiece. The oyster bar and communal table are busy happy hour properties.

HOUSE SPECIALTIES   Grilled whole halibut or roast code; twice-cooked chicken (poached, then deep-fried); Portuguese-style seafood stew; Addie's steamed mussels; wild king salmon tartare or more traditional beef tartare; brandade fritters.

OTHER RECOMMENDATIONS   Soft-shell crabs in season (ask for the market price; it can be a shock); any of a half-dozen wood-grilled options, including rockfish, rib eye, lamb loin, and a double pork chop the size of a small cleaver.

SUMMARY AND COMMENTS   Owner Jeff Black (see profile for Addie's, page 281) has abandoned some culinary fashion frills in favor of a bold, not-quite-retro take on comfort food in share-friendly portions. Who could resist corn cakes with green tomato jam? Light fare (grilled squid, chicken liver mousse, mussels, shrimp roll, and barbecue) is available at the bar all afternoon; oysters and shrimp are among happy hour bargain fare. And that's worth considering, because it often seems as if here—as elsewhere—the appetizers steal more of the kitchen's attention than the entrées. There is also a daily three-course pre-theater menu for $35, available 5:30–6:30 p.m., and half-price wines on Sunday. Black's uses as much local and organic ingredients and renewable energy and recycled products as possible.

BLT Steak   ★★★

STEAK   VERY EXPENSIVE   QUALITY ★★★★   VALUE ★★★

1625 I St. NW; ☎ 202-689-8999; bltsteak.com   Downtown

Reservations Recommended. **When to go** Lunch; anytime. **Entrée range**
$29–$93. **Payment** VISA, MC, AMEX. **Service rating** ★★★. **Friendliness rat-**
ing ★★★½. **Metro** Farragut North. **Parking** Valet (after 5:30 p.m.), pay lots,
street. **Bar** Full service. **Wine selection** Good. **Dress** Business, nice casual.
Disabled access Good. **Customers** Business, power players, media. **Hours** Lunch:
Monday–Friday, 11:30 a.m.–2:30 p.m. Dinner: Monday–Thursday, 5:30–11 p.m.;
Friday–Saturday, 5:30–11:30 p.m.

SETTING AND ATMOSPHERE For a French steak house in an office building,
  it's pretty nice: lots of leather, dim lighting, and the sort of cutesy
  "downscaling"—chicken liver in a Mason jar—that's supposed to keep
  you from choking on a $92 steak.

HOUSE SPECIALTIES The only reason to profile this steak house really is to
  explain its riches (in both senses): a choice of real Japanese Kobe beef,
  priced at $26 an ounce (and generally served in a 5-ounce portion), or
  what's often called Kobe but is really American Wagyu, which will run
  you only about $8 an ounce; an East-West Coast selection of oysters at
  nearly $3 apiece; lobster at $23 a pound.

OTHER RECOMMENDATIONS Braised short ribs, double double-cut racks of
  lamb; hanger steak; ginger-crusted tuna steak; crab cake with Meyer
  lemon sauce.

SUMMARY AND COMMENTS   Actually, there's a second reason to pick this out
  of the steak house crowd: the Gruyère popovers that kick it off and
  that come with the pâté. They're both free, which helps a little with the
  overall bill. It's the ultimate steak house for the cholesterol crowd.

Blue Duck Tavern   ★★★½

MODERN AMERICAN   EXPENSIVE   QUALITY ★★★★   VALUE ★★★

1201 24th St. NW (in the Park Hyatt Hotel); ☎ 202-419-6755;
blueducktavern.com   Downtown

Reservations Recommended. **When to go** Early evening for expert pre-theater
or leisurely dinner, brunch. **Entrée range** $20–$52. **Payment** VISA, MC, AMEX, D,
DC. **Service rating** ★★★½. **Friendliness rating** ★★½. **Metro** Foggy Bottom.
Parking Valet at dinner, lot, street meters. **Bar** Full service. **Wine selection** Very
good. **Dress** Business casual. **Disabled access** Good. **Customers** Local foodies, business entertainers. **Hours** Brunch: Saturday–Sunday, 11 a.m.–2:30 p.m.;
Breakfast: Monday–Friday, 6:30–10:30 a.m.; Lunch: Monday–Friday, 11:30 a.m.–
2:30 p.m.; Dinner: Daily, 5:30–10:30 p.m.

SETTING AND ATMOSPHERE Although it's basically a long, cool, rectangular
  space with glass walls, service bars, and slate walls, the restaurant is
  broken up into several areas (mostly square) but in ways that can be
  confusing at first. The lounge is catty-corner to the kitchen but has half
  the window views (which go around two sides), and in good weather

there is ample seating on the patio, though demand is high. Colors are mostly neutral with "natural" touches of flowers and herbs.

HOUSE SPECIALTIES Roasting or wood grilling occupies a fair amount of the kitchen's attention: roasted salt-crusted veal chop for two, wood-fired chicken or hanger steak, but also scallops (seared or carpaccio), whole fish, and one of the best dishes—roasted rockfish topped with toasted squid with a spicy tomato broth. Look for soft-shell crabs in season, rich short-rib hash or braised short rib, and sweetbreads.

OTHER RECOMMENDATIONS House-smoked mackerel mashed with potatoes into rilletts with wine mustard; roasted bone marrow; and the thick-cut thrice-fried french fries (a dangerous trend; see Brasserie Beck, page 292).

SUMMARY AND COMMENTS It's almost a chicken-and-egg question: did chef Brian McBride design his menu around the giant, 6-by-18-foot, $180,000 custom Moltcni stove, or did the menu demand the stove? Probably both. This is classic American cooking with unabashed pride; the menu, which is divided into categories such as "meat," "grains and potatoes" (which, curiously, includes the baked beans), and "vegetables," also lists the ingredients' "purveyors and artisans." (The stove has a special vat of duck fat for frying those fries—and another fry basket as well.) This also means that everything is à la carte, but many dishes are large enough for sharing. If you are doing several courses, take advantage of the unusually good wines-by-the-glass list. Blue Duck also offers a chef's table, with a maximum of 12 diners, next to the open kitchen.

Bourbon Steak ★ ★ ★ ½

MODERN AMERICAN/STEAK VERY EXPENSIVE QUALITY ★ ★ ★ ★ VALUE ★ ★ ★ ½

2800 Pennsylvania Ave. NW (in the Four Seasons Hotel); ☎ 202-944-2026; bourbonsteakdc.com Georgetown

Reservations Recommended. **When to go** Anytime. **Entrée range** $29–$75. **Payment** VISA, MC, AMEX. **Service rating** ★ ★ ★. **Friendliness rating** ★ ★ ★. **Metro** Foggy Bottom. **Parking** Valet, street. **Bar** Full service. **Wine selection** Good. **Dress** Business casual, designer casual. **Disabled access** Very good. **Customers** Businesspeople, celebrities, celeb-spotters, foodies, other celeb chefs. **Hours** *Lunch:* Monday–Friday, 11:30 a.m.–2:30 p.m.; Saturday, noon–2:30 p.m. *Dinner:* Sunday–Thursday, 6–10 p.m.; Friday–Saturday, 5:30–10:30 p.m.

SETTING AND ATMOSPHERE With its slightly sunken setback, dark and milk chocolate colors, and power-suit diners, this looks like a cross between *Mad Men* and *The Apprentice*. The big room is broken up by overtly intimate booths and windows with canal views. The music is more Coldplay than King Cole, the cocktails are retro-classic (one of the few Corpse Revivers in town), and the liquor list is as long as the wine list.

HOUSE SPECIALTIES Don't miss Mina's signature lobster potpie with brandy and truffles or wild mushrooms (which, being market price, ranges from $85 down to a recession-friendly $65); pan-roasted chicken with country ham and eggs; ahi tuna tartare with ancho chilies and Asian pear; "grass kickin'" chicken liver terrine with pickles. Marrow lovers, here's your spot.

OTHER RECOMMENDATIONS Star chef Michael Mina started in San Francisco, so seafood lovers can safely pile into a shellfish platter of lobster, shrimp, clams, and oysters ($59); smoked trout with creamy cabbage; or vermilion snapper sashimi with Australian finger limes and avocado.

SUMMARY AND COMMENTS Like Charlie Palmer and J&G Steakhouse, two other celeb-chef steak houses in Washington, this is more than just a paean to the bull market, although the Kobe steak, when available, clocks in at about $150. Mina has 18 restaurants in his empire, and the classic dish with a twist, such as the lobster potpie in exquisite pastry, is his shtick. Even the sides are tweaked: pureed (not simply mashed) potatoes with chive pierogies; fried rice with Wagyu beef and Chinese sausage; General Tso's broccoli. His other signature, which he debuted in, where else, Las Vegas, is poaching meat in fat—beef in butter, lamb in olive oil, and pork in bacon fat—and finishing it on the grill. The first dishes to the table are a pair of hefty freebies: a cast-iron skillet of truffle oil–glazed rolls (the second most famous in town, next to CityZen's Parker House roll) and cheddar-dusted duck-fat fries with three house-made condiments (pickle ketchup, for instance).

Brasserie Beck ★ ★ ★

BELGIAN MODERATE QUALITY ★★★ VALUE ★★★

1101 K St. NW; ☎ 202-408-1717; beckdc.com Downtown

Reservations Strongly recommended. **When to go** Late afternoon, late night. **Entrée range** $20–$28. **Payment** VISA, MC, AMEX, D, DC. **Service rating** ★★★½. **Friendliness rating** ★★★½. **Metro** Metro Center or McPherson Square. **Parking** Valet at dinner ($10), street. **Bar** Full service; good beer selection. **Wine selection** Very good. **Dress** Casual. **Disabled access** Good. **Customers** Businesspeople, theatergoers, foodies. **Hours** *Brunch:* Saturday–Sunday, 11:30 a.m.–4 p.m.; *Lunch:* Monday–Friday, 11:30 a.m.–5 p.m.; *Dinner:* Monday–Thursday, 5–11 p.m.; Friday–Saturday, 5–11:30 p.m.; Sunday, 4–8 p.m.

SETTING AND ATMOSPHERE A retro-Belgian bistro that lives up to the name—dining areas are set off by etched glass and high ceilings, and walls are dotted with orange-faced clocks (which echo the copper-bottom pans) timed to Casablanca, Antwerp, and such. Tilted mirrors bring a slightly hectic sense of the sidewalk traffic inside, a glass-walled kitchen is even more hectic, and a long white marble bar bustles at all times. In good weather there's sidewalk seating.

HOUSE SPECIALTIES Reclaiming Belgium's reputation is job one, especially the hearty stuff (paired with suggestions from the lengthy Belgian beer list) that owner Robert Wiedmaier called Flemish redneck: classic waterzooi, roast monkfish with peppers, roasted rabbit, garlicky snails, lamb shanks with white beans, and amazing veal cheek meatballs in pea soup. Charcuterie is job two: lamb sausage with lentils, country pâté, mixed platters, and a liver "parfait" (one layer of duck and one of chicken in Cognac and sea salt) that will change your view of liver forever.

OTHER RECOMMENDATIONS   Classic steak tartare or steak *frites*, mussels (with triple-fried potatoes), chilled seafood platters, classic coq au vin. If goose is on the specials menu, go for it.

SUMMARY AND COMMENTS   This somewhat boisterous but endearing hangout keeps 13 of its 130 or so beers on tap. Beck offers a five-course tasting menu for the table in the kitchen, with a minimum of eight persons. Wiedmaier is also the chef-owner of the highly regarded, more classic Marcel's (see profile, page 316) as well as the Mussel Bar in Bethesda and Brabo in Old Town Alexandria.

Burma ★★

BURMESE   INEXPENSIVE   QUALITY ★★½   VALUE ★★★

740 Sixth St. NW, Ste. 200 (upstairs); ☎ 202-638-1280   Downtown

Reservations Accepted. **When to go** Anytime. **Entrée range** $7–$11. **Payment** VISA, MC, AMEX, D, DC. **Service rating** ★★★½. **Friendliness rating** ★★★. **Metro** Gallery Place–Chinatown. **Parking** Pay lots. **Bar** Beer and wine. **Wine selection** House. **Dress** Casual, informal. **Disabled access** Yes, but call ahead. **Customers** Ethnic South Asians, locals, tourists. **Hours** *Lunch:* Monday–Friday, 11 a.m.– 3 p.m.; *Dinner:* Daily, 6–10 p.m.

SETTING AND ATMOSPHERE   A modest and unobtrusive second-floor warren with only a handful of native art on the walls to advertise its ethnicity.

HOUSE SPECIALTIES   *Kaukswe thoke*, a tangy noodle dish with ground shrimp, cilantro, red pepper, and peanuts; pickled green tea–leaf salad, a slightly sour, spicy slaw with caramelized onions and peanuts dressed in a green tea pesto; squid with ham and scallions; a chile-spiked tofu-and-shrimp stir-fry; and an almost soul-food version of mustard greens with shrimp, pork, or chicken.

OTHER RECOMMENDATIONS   Gold fingers, strips of squashlike calabash in a peppery dipping sauce; chile- and mango-flavored pork; a macrobiotic delight of substantial dried tofu with cruciferous veggies; roast duck (requires 24 hours' notice).

SUMMARY AND COMMENTS   Using familiar ingredients found at any Asian grocery, this Burmese holdout manages to turn out flavors surprisingly distinct from its near relatives: not so "fishy" (no fermented fish sauce or soy) or seafood-conscious as Vietnamese, less purely peppery and more sour-tangy than Thai, and with the concentrated tea and smoke background of classic Chinese and Japanese cuisine. This is not the only Burmese restaurant in town anymore, and perhaps not the best, but it's solid and easily accessible. *Note:* Disabled patrons should call ahead to make sure the elevator is unlocked.

Café Atlántico ★★½

NUEVO LATINO   MODERATE   QUALITY ★★★★   VALUE ★★★

405 Eighth St. NW; ☎ 202-393-0812; cafeatlantico.com   Downtown

Reservations Recommended. **When to go** Anytime. **Entrée range** $22–$29. **Payment** VISA, MC, AMEX, DC. **Service rating** ★★★. **Friendliness rating** ★★★. **Metro** Archives–Navy Memorial–Penn Quarter or Gallery Place–Chinatown.

Parking Street; valet at dinner, $10. **Bar** Full service. **Wine selection** Very good. **Dress** Casual. **Disabled access** Good. **Customers** Locals, businesspeople. **Hours** *Brunch:* Saturday–Sunday, 11:30 a.m.–2:30 p.m.; *Lunch:* Tuesday–Friday, 11:30 a.m.–2:30 p.m.; *Dinner:* Tuesday–Thursday and Sunday, 5–10 p.m.; Friday–Saturday, 5–11 p.m.

SETTING AND ATMOSPHERE A very stylish salon, like the living room of an art collector, with brilliant fabrics, large and vibrant paintings, loftlike balconies and windows, mosaics, and richly oiled wood. The clientele tends to match the decor—very vibrant, very "on," and frequently very loud. This is one of those places that puts the "din" in dinner.

HOUSE SPECIALTIES Foie gras soup with floating corn and chanterelle "island"; squid and scallops with two rices, one seared and one Asian-style with coconut milk; Malbec-braised veal cheeks; conch fritters; duck confit with minced fruit.

OTHER RECOMMENDATIONS The Sunday "Nuevo Latino" dim sum brunch, with 25–30 tapas-sized dishes $2–$8 (deluxe); or pre-theater dinner, $35.

SUMMARY AND COMMENTS Café Atlántico is riding two waves at once: location and cuisine. In the heart of the arts-intelligentsia neighborhood around the Shakespeare Theatre and Lansburg Building, it's also the first major restaurant in this area to specialize in *cocina nueva*, the Latin version of New Continental—lighter fare, more fashionably presented, and, depending on your perspective, less homey and more expensive than the Central and South American originals. Founding chef José Andrés, winner of numerous culinary awards, has designed the menus for Jaleo, Zaytinya, and the new Oyamel as well.

Downstairs from the famed Minibar (profiled on page 318), Café Atlántico is beginning to seem like a tryout for its menu—not that being a guinea pig here is a bad thing. Though Minibar's seating is currently limited to six, meaning that advance reservations are essential, plans are underway to expand it to the entire building and eventually move Café Atlántico somewhere nearby.

Cafe Divan ★★½

TURKISH   INEXPENSIVE   QUALITY ★★½   VALUE ★★★★

1834 Wisconsin Ave. NW; ☎ 202-338-1747; cafedivan.com
Georgetown

Reservations Recommended. **When to go** Thursdays for whole marinated rotisserie lamb. **Entrée range** $5.95–$16.95. **Payment** VISA, MC. **Service rating** ★★★★. **Friendliness rating** ★★★★. **Metro** None nearby. **Parking** Street. **Bar** Full service. **Wine selection** Many Turkish bottlings. **Dress** Business, casual. **Disabled access** Good. **Customers** Locals, homesick Middle Eastern diplomats. **Hours** Monday–Thursday, 11 a.m.–10:30 p.m.; Friday–Saturday, 11 a.m.–11 p.m.; Sunday, 11 a.m.–10 p.m.

SETTING AND ATMOSPHERE A remarkably (and unusually) bright and sunny triangular corner, with windows winging out on both sides, with polished Brazilian cherry flooring, Turkish tile, and pomegranate accents.

HOUSE SPECIALTIES Eggplant-smothered lamb shank; the meze platter of feta, hummus, taramasalata, and stuffed grape leaves. Doner kebab, thin-sliced layers of marinated lamb and veal alternately rolled on a spit and grilled, is a weekend special at most Turkish restaurants, but here it's available at every meal.

OTHER RECOMMENDATIONS *Lahmacun* (Turkish flatbread pizza) topped with chopped lamb and tomatoes or a variety of other toppings; *manti* (the beef-stuffed and yogurt-topped dumplings common to Eastern Asia); a lamb-and-chicken-kebab combo.

SUMMARY AND COMMENTS While not the most accessible in terms of location—the busy stretch of upper Georgetown is rife with restaurants and diners (and residents) struggling for parking—Cafe Divan has made itself a neighborhood favorite by dint of cheery service and Turkish fare far beyond the oily standards.

Café Milano ★★½

ITALIAN   EXPENSIVE   QUALITY ★★½   VALUE ★★

3251 Prospect St. NW; ☎ 202-333-6183; cafemilano.com   Georgetown

Reservations Strongly suggested. **When to go** Late lunch, late dinner. **Entrée range** $14–$43. **Payment** VISA, MC, AMEX. **Service rating** ★★★½. **Friendliness rating** ★★★½. **Metro** None nearby. **Parking** Street, pay lots. **Bar** Full service. **Wine selection** Good. **Dress** Business, hip informal. **Disabled access** Through rear entrance. **Customers** Locals, embassy personnel. **Hours** *Lunch:* Daily, 11:30 a.m.–4 p.m.; *Dinner:* Sunday–Tuesday, 4–11 p.m.; Wednesday–Saturday, 4 p.m.–midnight.

SETTING AND ATMOSPHERE A cross between a haute couturier's salon and a Milan disco, with a subway map painted on the ceiling and a portrait of Placido Domingo as El Cid, too (all of which makes for interesting philosophical speculation on the direction Italian interests have taken since the days of the Sistine Chapel). At Bice, where owner Franco Nuschese was manager, the shadow boxes held wallpaper samples; here they frame the even hip-jokier designer ties—presumably from his closet, as he never seems to be wearing one—and limited-edition scarves. And the pastas are named after designers. There's a terrace for warm-weather dining and a prettier-than-usual long bar.

HOUSE SPECIALTIES Ravioli Cavalli (veal-and-spinach-stuffed ravioli in a butter-sage sauce with shaved porcini mushrooms); zucchini-and-basil-filled half-moon pasta with ricotta cheese; assorted grilled seafood; and for the big boys, steaks and chops with real Italian flavor, no Chicago nakedness. There are even light little pizzas, and lighter courses are available late.

SUMMARY AND COMMENTS Admittedly, this hot hangout is as much about the crowd as the cooking—a few years ago, it was voted Power Spot of the Year by the area restaurant association—but the food has to be at least good enough to bring 'em back. Nuschese is also a partner in two other restaurants: the less-formal pasta-pizzeria Sette Osteria at Connecticut and R streets NW, and the bright and airy Sette Bello, which spotlights wine, antipasti, and crudo (which it calls Italian sushi), near the Clarendon Metro.

Café du Parc ★★★½

FRENCH MOD/EXP QUALITY ★★★ VALUE ★★★★

**1401 Pennsylvania Ave. NW (in the Willard InterContinental Hotel);
☎ 202-942-7000; cafeduparc.com** Downtown

Reservations Suggested. **When to go** Anytime; late afternoon cocktails on the terrace. **Entrée range** $20–$29. **Payment** VISA, MC, AMEX, DC. **Service rating** ★★★. **Friendliness rating** ★★★. **Metro** Federal Triangle. **Parking** Valet, pay lots. **Bar** Full service. **Wine selection** Good. **Dress** Casual, business, nice informal. **Disabled access** Good. **Customers** Locals, area businesspeople. **Hours** *Breakfast:* Monday–Friday, 6:30–10:30 a.m.; Saturday–Sunday, 7–11 a.m.; terrace (weather permitting) 8–10 a.m.; *Lunch:* Monday–Friday, noon–2 p.m.; Saturday–Sunday, noon–2:30 p.m.; *Dinner:* Monday–Friday, 5:30–10 p.m.; Saturday–Sunday, 6–10 p.m.

SETTING AND ATMOSPHERE When weather permits, this is one of the few really pleasant and tasty spots to play at café society, and its light-fare menu 3–5 p.m. is very welcome after a long day on the Mall. Inside there is seating in the bar, which is actually a little nicer than the dining room, which is pretty ordinary.

HOUSE SPECIALTIES Real bistro classics such as steak tartare with a raw quail egg (no one uses mere chicken eggs anymore); a great pot of mussels, even in a mussels town (split it as a first course); and roast chicken. Also roast cod, or rack of lamb with roasted eggplant.

OTHER RECOMMENDATIONS Tomato stuffed with fish tartare with fennel slaw; salmon with smoked salmon butter "crust"; an open-faced burger topped with caramelized sauerkraut and cheese, something like a Reuben burger; veal medallions with ratatouille.

SUMMARY AND COMMENTS Although three-Michelin-star chef Antoine Westermann isn't often on-site (his other restaurants are in Paris and Strasbourg), his classicism is the key to this bistro's consistency. It's delicate and robust at the same time—pâté in flaky pastry and crisp-edged pork belly—and it's one of the few breakfast places worth traveling for, or even making your hotel choice.

Cashion's Eat Place ★★★

NEW SOUTHERN EXPENSIVE QUALITY ★★★ VALUE ★★★

1819 Columbia Rd. NW; ☎ 202-797-1819; cashionseatplace.com
Dupont Circle/Adams Morgan

Reservations Recommended. **When to go** Anytime. **Entrée range** $21–$30. **Payment** VISA, MC, AMEX. **Service rating** ★★★. **Friendliness rating** ★★½. **Metro** Woodley Park–Zoo/Adams Morgan. **Parking** Valet $10. **Bar** Full service. **Wine selection** Good. **Dress** Business, casual. **Disabled access** Not wheelchair accessible. **Customers** Locals, foodies. **Hours** *Brunch:* Sunday, 11:30 a.m.–2:30 p.m.; *Dinner:* Tuesday and Sunday, 5:30–10 p.m.; Wednesday–Saturday, 5:30–11 p.m.

SETTING AND ATMOSPHERE A deliberately low-key, upscale café—jazz and R&B over the sound system and a reclining nude over the bar—in a multiethnic neighborhood that draws its clientele from far and wide (and young and old), even though it's a little pricey for the area (which, admittedly, is rapidly yuppifying). There's sidewalk seating in good weather.

HOUSE SPECIALTIES   Sweetbreads with Catalan spinach; pork souvlaki on grilled flatbread; braised stuffed rabbit leg; duck confit; fried sweetbreads over spinach; duck breast with foie gras; smoked bluefish rilletts.

OTHER RECOMMENDATIONS   Goat cheese ravioli with veal cheeks; roast free-range chicken; almost any pork dish; bison burgers. Late-night fare includes chili dogs and shaved beef sandwiches.

SUMMARY AND COMMENTS   The eponymous chef Ann Cashion, a Mississippi native, made this Southern cuisine-at-the-crossroads establishment a showplace for new Southern fare, and many of her signature flourishes are still on the menu (New Orleans gumbo; duck breast with gooseberries, figs, and foie gras). But longtime kitchen chef and now owner John Manolantos has given the menu a more Mediterranean flavor (witness the souvlaki). He sticks to the mission of using as much regional produce as possible. *Note:* Cashion is now at Johnny's Half Shell, profiled on page 310.

Central Michel Richard   ★ ★ ★ ½

MODERN AMERICAN   EXPENSIVE   QUALITY ★★★   VALUE ★★½

1001 Pennsylvania Ave. NW; ☎ 202-626-0015; www.centralmichelrichard.com Downtown

Reservations Strongly recommended. **When to go** Lunch to save money, late evening for quieter dining. **Entrée range** $18–$31. **Payment** VISA, MC, AMEX, D, DC. **Service rating** ★★★½ **Friendliness rating** ★★½. **Metro** Federal Triangle, Metro Center, or Archives–Navy Memorial–Penn Quarter. **Parking** Valet at dinner, lot, street meters. **Bar** Full service. **Wine selection** Good. **Dress** Business casual, hip. **Disabled access** Good. **Customers** Local foodies, first-date impressors, business entertainers. **Hours** *Lunch:* Monday–Friday, 11:45 a.m.–2:30 p.m.; *Dinner:* Monday–Thursday, 5–10:30 p.m.; Friday–Saturday, 5–11 p.m.; Sunday, 5–9:30 p.m.

SETTING AND ATMOSPHERE   Swedish contemporary meets modern super-bistro: blond woods and wine-colored accents, see-through wine cellars and meat locker, and industrial chic metals. A hugely grinning photo portrait of super chef Michel Richard hangs as paterfamilias on the wall: it's all fun, but it's far from free.

HOUSE SPECIALTIES   Richly indulgent "comfort food" such as 72-hour short ribs that collapse almost before the fork strikes, braised beef cheeks, lamb shanks with polenta and rotisserie chicken, even bangers and mash (charcuterie is a big presence here). Richard's famous lobster burger—really more like a lobster-scallop mousse on brioche—is $29, but the almost-as-good shrimp burger is only $20.

OTHER RECOMMENDATIONS   The often maltreated calf's liver, filet mignon tartare, and mussel chowder.

SUMMARY AND COMMENTS   Richard, whose landmark Citronelle (see next profile) is one of Washington's uber-haute spots, has picked out bits of favorite downscale food from various cuisines (cassoulet, bangers and mash, macaroni and cheese, skate with caper sauce, braised rabbit with spaetzle, fried chicken, scallops a tagliatelle Provençale) and still managed to make them upmarket. Consider the curry-flavored chicken liver mousse bound with bread crumbs that form the fried chicken crust; or the "faux gras" of chicken liver disguised as duck. *Note:* The menu is à la carte.

Citronelle (aka Michel Richard Citronelle)   ★★★★

FRENCH   VERY EXPENSIVE   QUALITY ★★★★   VALUE ★★★

3000 M St. NW (Latham Hotel); ☎ 202-625-2150; citronelledc.com   Georgetown

Reservations Required. **When to go** Before 9 p.m. **Entrée range** Lounge, $8–$70; prix-fixe dinner, $105–$190. **Payment** VISA, MC, AMEX, D, DC, JCB, CB. **Service rating** ★★½. **Friendliness rating** ★★★★. **Metro** Foggy Bottom–GWU. **Parking** Discount at hotel lot. **Bar** Full service. **Wine selection** *Wine Spectator* Award. **Dress** Jackets at dinner. **Disabled access** Excellent. **Customers** Locals, tourists, businesspeople. **Hours** *Dinner:* Tuesday–Thursday, 6–10 p.m.; Friday–Saturday, 6–10:30 p.m.; *Cocktails:* Tuesday–Thursday, 3 p.m.–midnight; Friday–Saturday, 3 p.m.–1 a.m.

SETTING AND ATMOSPHERE Using a series of small level shifts and cutaway ceilings, the designers of this pretty but not showy establishment have made the space seem both intimate and expansive. The upstairs lounge is classic flannel gray and green; the downstairs rooms have a more classic look. Clearly, the star attractions are the exposed kitchen and its six chefs, two prep chefs, and salad chef—and the show does go on, sometimes unreasonably slowly.

HOUSE SPECIALTIES Although listed as French because of chef Michel Richard, this could just as well be called modern American, eclectic, or simply flamboyant, and there's no predicting the menu of the moment. Richard is famous for his food puns, and among his greatest inspirations have been a faux osso buco with veal cheeks and a potato "bone"; rabbit and foie gras–stuffed cannelloni; mushroom "cappuccino"; cuttlefish "fettuccine" with baby beets; "hard-boiled eggs" of mozzarella surrounding yellow-tomato mousse or "scrambled eggs" of diced, saffron-tinted scallops.

OTHER RECOMMENDATIONS Offal is awfully good here; look for sweetbread and foie gras sausage; a very nutrition-of-the-millennium fricassee of sweetbreads, snails, and soybeans; rabbit puzzle dishes mixing loin, limb, and rack of ribs; sautéed foie gras; braised veal in various forms; and game meats.

SUMMARY AND COMMENTS L.A. star chef Michel Richard has become paterfamilias to most of Washington's biggest chefs (no physical insult intended). His menu is inspired by—and in turn inspiring—other creative and engaging chefs, including the other deconstruction humorist, Minibar's José Andrés; and when it's good, it's very, very good. (Most recently he's opened Michel at Ritz-Carlton–Tysons Corner.) Real food-mag addicts should go for the six-course tasting menu—if they can write off the tab. (Check out the bar menu; some of the same dishes can be had for a lot less.)

CityZen ★★★★½

1330 Maryland Ave. NW (in the Mandarin Oriental Hotel);
☎ **202-787-6006; cityzenrestaurant.com**   The National Mall

Reservations Strongly recommended. **When to go** Anytime. **Entrée range** Fixed-price menus: three-course, $80; six-course vegetarian, $95; six-course chef's tasting, $110. **Payment** VISA, MC, AMEX, D, DC. **Service rating** ★★★★. **Friendliness rating** ★★★. **Metro** Smithsonian. **Parking** Valet. **Bar** Full service. **Wine selection** Top flight. **Dress** Business, dressy casual. **Disabled access** Very good. **Customers** Foodies, power brokers, arts benefactors, special-occasion couples, platinum-card business parties. **Hours** Tuesday–Thursday, 6–9:30 p.m.; Friday–Saturday, 5:30–9:30 p.m.; closed Sunday–Monday.

SETTING AND ATMOSPHERE The hotel bows to feng shui principles, so the name—half urban, half Zen—fits well. It's a sleek and showy L-shaped space, with 20-foot-high ceilings; a wall of fire behind the bar; a long, exposed kitchen; and a cool stone- and putty-colored interior with tangerine lanterns and chocolate leather banquettes. On the other hand, there's nothing meditative about the rock-ish soundtrack, or the noise levels.

HOUSE SPECIALTIES The menu changes monthly, but the dash and push-the-envelope style are constants. Sometimes the trick is too cute (a shabu-shabu of foie gras in lukewarm stock) or the service illogically elaborate (the waiter offers a choice of black salt or sea salt while already sprinkling the dish), but when the food is good, it's very, very good. There's a three-course tasting menu, a six-course tasting menu, and a six-course vegetarian menu, but everything comes with extras such as amuse-bouche; the kitchen's signature miniature Parker House rolls, served in a box like fine tea; miniature truffles; and more. (Wagyu beef, also known as American Kobe, is $30 extra.) Look for organ meats such as lamb's brains and liver, grilled or pan-crisped seafood, and game birds such as quail meticulously stuffed with sweetbreads and chard. Most dishes have almost iconoclastic condiments: grain-mustard sabayon, manchego cheese emulsion, celery root–horseradish tapenade, and the like, but always in supporting roles.

OTHER RECOMMENDATIONS Rabbit in any treatment (a recent trio plate combined a tiny rack, a spoonful of diced leg meat, and a slice of loin); rich but concise shoat (also known as piglet) belly; vegetarian choucroute with roasted baby cabbage and "melted" Brussels sprouts; and artisanal cheese.

SUMMARY AND COMMENTS Chef Eric Ziebold is a veteran of Thomas Keller's French Laundry, and it shows. A three-course menu is available in the bar or lounge for $50, although sometimes the staff seems reluctant to admit it. Some hungrier patrons feel the portions are a little small for the price, but the eventual total seems generous. Culinarily speaking, this is one of the city's star attractions. *Note:* Ziebold also oversees the hotel's less formal, Southern-nostalgic but still ambitious restaurant, Sou'Wester, which might be a better fit for some visitor's budgets.

Corduroy ★★★½

MODERN AMERICAN   EXPENSIVE   QUALITY ★★★   VALUE ★★★

1122 Ninth St. NW; ☎ 202-589-0699; corduroydc.com   Downtown

Reservations Recommended. **When to go** Anytime. **Entrée range** $24–$39.
Payment VISA, MC, AMEX. **Service rating** ★★★½. **Friendliness rating** ★★★★.
Metro Mount Vernon Square. **Parking** Street, valet. **Bar** Full service. **Wine selection** Very good. **Dress** Business, Friday casual (jackets requested), shorts prohibited. **Disabled access** Not wheelchair accessible. **Customers** Businesspeople, food-conscious commuters. **Hours** Monday–Saturday, 5:30–10:30 p.m.

SETTING AND ATMOSPHERE This renovated town house has been lightened and brightened with exposed brick and splashy abstract art, blond wood, deep leather chairs, and a small bar upstairs.

HOUSE SPECIALTIES Red snapper bisque; seared scallops over shiitake rice pudding; crispy fluke with warm potato salad; duck leg and egg salad; lobster carpaccio dotted with red roe and chervil; lamb loin with house-made lamb sausage; cinnamon-dusted duck with figs.

OTHER RECOMMENDATIONS Soft-shell crabs; chilled tomato soup with Thai chili and tangy unripe grapes; braised pork belly; veal cheeks osso buco.

SUMMARY AND COMMENTS Chef Tom Power has been through the kitchens of Citronelle (where he learned to value pastry) and the Old Angler's Inn, but seems to have evolved a more subtly elegant manner. He uses local and seasonal ingredients to good effect—thankfully, a growing movement in Washington—and even his more elaborate dishes have a becoming modesty of presentation, so they're easy for all comers to accept; but the little fillips, such as pepper-spiked whipped cream on the chilled pea soup, make even the familiar fresh. Try the $55 three-course tasting menu.

D.C. Coast ★★½

MODERN AMERICAN   MODERATE   QUALITY ★★★   VALUE ★★★

1401 K St. NW; ☎ 202-216-5988; dccoast.com   Downtown

Reservations A virtual necessity. **When to go** Late lunch, dinner. **Entrée range** $22–$29; market price higher. **Payment** VISA, MC, AMEX, D, DC, T. **Service rating** ★★★½. **Friendliness rating** ★★★★. **Metro** McPherson Square. **Parking** Valet after 5 p.m. ($7 minimum), pay lots. **Bar** Full service. **Wine selection** Very good. **Dress** Business, informal. **Disabled access** Good. **Customers** Businesspeople, tourists. **Hours** *Lunch:* Monday–Friday, 11:30 a.m.–2:30 p.m.; *Dinner:* Monday–Thursday, 5:30–10:30 p.m.; Friday–Saturday, 5:30–11 p.m.; Sunday, 5:30–9:30 p.m.

SETTING AND ATMOSPHERE The restaurant's name is a sort of joke on chef Jeff Tunk's previous stints at Washington's "waterfront" River Club, and in New Orleans and San Diego. (His other restaurants run the flavor gamut from Cajun at Acadiana to Pan-Asian at TenPenh to Cuban at Ceiba.) The decor is a low-key pun to match, with a bronze mermaid, a gently rolling ceiling (the curl allows mezzanine diners a view of the bar and kitchen staff), fan-pleated sconces that could have been Neptune's cockle shells, and huge oval mirrors that make the reflected customers seem to swim in and out of your imagination.

HOUSE SPECIALTIES Fresh half-shelled oysters topped with a sorbet of pickled ginger and sake; Chinese-style smoked lobster finished with a soy sauté and Hong Kong–style crispy whole fried fish; caramelized scallops; mushroom-crusted halibut; lobster bisque with lobster-stuffed dumplings; fresh tuna ravioli; chile relleno stuffed with wild mushrooms and goat cheese.

OTHER RECOMMENDATIONS Soft-shell crabs and crab cakes; cornmeal-fried oysters; gratin of artichokes with lump crab; seared foie gras.

SUMMARY AND COMMENTS This smart but not showy restaurant on the 14th Street "fault line" is one of several K Street eateries drawing trend-savvy young types with expense accounts. Even better, it's a light alternative to downtown's preponderance of rich sauces and big-beef chophouses. The wine list is interesting and moderately priced, and the wines by the glass are blessedly unpredictable and refreshing.

Equinox ★★★

MODERN AMERICAN   EXPENSIVE   QUALITY ★★★½   VALUE ★★★

818 Connecticut Ave. NW; ☎ 202-331-8118; equinoxrestaurant.com Downtown

Reservations Required for lunch and dinner. **When to go** Lunch. **Entrée range** $28–$32. **Payment** VISA, MC, AMEX, DC, D. **Service rating** ★★★★. **Friendliness rating** ★★★★. **Metro** Farragut North or McPherson Square. **Parking** Valet, street. **Bar** Full service. **Wine selection** Good. **Dress** Business, casual. **Disabled access** Good. **Customers** Foodies, businesspeople. **Hours** *Lunch:* Monday–Friday, 11:30 a.m.–2 p.m.; *Dinner:* Monday–Thursday, 5:30–10 p.m.; Friday–Saturday, 5:30–10:30 p.m.; Sunday, 5:30–9 p.m.

SETTING AND ATMOSPHERE The best thing about the decor at Equinox is its unobtrusiveness: walls are a pretty mix of cerulean drapes and oversize subway tiles, and gauzy overhead swags lead the eye to the glass-enclosed "patio" and tailored platters. (Actually, it's a good metaphor for chef Todd Gray's polished and reticent technique.) The glass-walled sidewalk area is particularly popular, though better in the evening, after the rush-hour traffic slows.

HOUSE SPECIALTIES Cider-brined rack of Kurobuta pork; potato-crusted scallops or a scallop-oyster mushroom salad; grilled sardines over sweet potato mousse; a chopped salad of figs, house-made pancetta, and quail egg; seared foie gras with duck "crackers"; oyster chowder with parsnips.

OTHER RECOMMENDATIONS Fresh pasta such as lamb sausage-stuffed mezzaluna and hand-rolled farfalle with chanterelles; risotto fritters; and the roasted *branzino* with shellfish.

SUMMARY AND COMMENTS Gray spent many years as the on-site chef at Galileo, and that kitchen's consistently excellent reputation depended heavily on his work (in fact, his leaving in part forced Galileo honcho Roberto Donna to rededicate himself to the art of cooking as well as running a restaurant). But now that he has his own restaurant, he's devoted himself to what he calls mid-Atlantic regional, heavy on fresh seafood. (Gray and wife/partner Ellen are among the leaders of Washington's organic, humane, and sustainable food movement.) And having to close his doors for six months after a kitchen fire gave him time to rethink and refine his style. You'll still see flashes of Italian, of course, but his heart is in the Chesapeake Bay watershed. Gray also enjoys using traditional dishes—polenta, biscuits, grits, and black-eyed peas—in ways guaranteed to earn them new respect. The menu changes frequently, but in general, expect vegetables to be incorporated into the recipes, not relegated to the side; light sauces based on reductions and natural flavors; and a fondness for contrasting sweet and sour, delicate and pungent, or rich and acid within a single dish. Gray is also overseeing development of the tony Salamander Inn and Sheila Johnson resort complex in Middleburg, Virginia.

Etete ★★★

ETHIOPIAN INEXPENSIVE QUALITY ★★★ VALUE ★★★★

1942 Ninth St. NW; ☎ 202-232-7600; eteterestaurant.com
U Street/Logan Circle

Reservations Recommended. **When to go** Early or late; afternoons for the coffee ceremony. **Entrée range** $10–$15. **Payment** VISA, MC, AMEX. **Service rating** ★★★. **Friendliness rating** ★★★★. **Metro** U Street–Cardozo–African American War Memorial. **Parking** Valet, street, pay lots. **Bar** Full service. **Wine selection** House (Ethiopian). **Dress** Casual, informal. **Disabled access** Good. **Customers** Locals, night owls, ethnics, occasional celebrities. **Hours** Daily, 11 a.m.–1 a.m.; bar is open until 2 a.m.

SETTING AND ATMOSPHERE Like a real Ethiopian café, with customers of all ethnicities mixing and laughing. It's especially popular with the pre-nightclub and post-theater crowds. It has become so popular with metrosexual clubgoers that an upstairs dining room has been added.

HOUSE SPECIALTIES Classic dishes such as *doro wat,* the signature dish of spicy stewed chicken legs with hard-boiled eggs; for offal lovers, the *dulet* of lamb tripe and liver; two forms of spicy tartare, *kitfo* (minced with hot peppers and house-made cheese) and *gored gored,* a cubed hotter version; first-rate vegetarian stews of lentils, cabbage and carrots, collard greens, and more.

OTHER RECOMMENDATIONS Marinated short ribs; beef or lentil *sambusas;* lamb chunks in jalapeno-spiked butter; and a sort of beef jerky sauce mixed with shreds of injera (the flatbread that is spoon, napkin, and plate all in one).

SUMMARY AND COMMENTS In one sense, Etete stands in for a neighborhood with several good Ethiopian choices, which also include Dukem and Little Ethiopia. But it has a history here—longtime chef Tiwaltenigus Shenegelegn, known as Etete, or "Mamma," used to cater to the Ethiopian community—and was instrumental in drawing the U Street corridor east (and displacing Adams Morgan as the center of Ethiopian and Eritrean culture). The real Ethiopian roasted coffee is so high-octane that it could fuel a race car.

Four Sisters ★★★

VIETNAMESE   INEXPENSIVE   QUALITY ★★★½   VALUE ★★★★

8190 Strawberry Ln., Ste. 1, Falls Church; ☎ 703-539-8566; four sistersrestaurant.com   Virginia suburbs

Reservations Recommended. **When to go** Late lunch–early dinner, anytime. **Entrée range** $7.95–$29.95. **Payment** VISA, MC, AMEX. **Service rating** ★★★★. **Friendliness rating** ★★★★. **Metro** None nearby. **Parking** Free lot. **Bar** Beer and wine. **Wine selection** House. **Dress** Business casual, casual. **Disabled access** Good. **Customers** Area foodies, ethnic families, locals. **Hours** Daily, 11 a.m.–10 p.m.

SETTING AND ATMOSPHERE The original restaurant put Falls Church's Eden Center on the map, where it was first among its dozens of Vietnamese peers, and it's still among the best in the area. Its new home, a retro–French Colonial mansion with buttery walls, vivid art, and dark rich wood, is just as crowded but says much about the Lai family's understanding of American sensibilities.

HOUSE SPECIALTIES Whole menus of every style—caramelized rice dishes; rice vermicelli; the classic Vietnamese banquet dish, beef seven ways, including sliced rare beef salad, fondue, and steamed meatballs; roast quail with blood oranges; a shredded vegetable salad with shrimp and pork; steamed baby clams with minced pork; elegant shrimp toast; whole steamed black cod, with a layer of fat to keep it moist.

OTHER RECOMMENDATIONS Unusually light spring rolls with herbs for wrapping instead of lettuce; sea bass in black beans; crisp stir-fried asparagus; lightly curried frog's legs in season; grilled beef in grape leaves; caramelized catfish; pork or squid with sour cabbage.

SUMMARY AND COMMENTS For years this was a foodies' insider favorite, the more so because the owners of the five-star Inn at Little Washington used to drive in every Monday, their night off, and have dinner here; but in fact it's just as hospitable to the nonfamous. The Lais have moderated traditional recipes somewhat (though being from Southern Vietnam, they were not heavy on chilies or fish sauce to begin with). But the technique remains impeccable. Despite the name, it's more than just the sisters; it's their two brothers and their parents as well, a mom-and-pop joint to the max (not to mention about a dozen helpers). The menu is almost intimidating, more than 200 entries long and a mix of more and less familiar dishes, but it's hard to go wrong; all the family is more than happy to advise you.

The original sisters were, of course, four; but when the restaurant moved into its new home, the oldest sister, Ly Lai, and her husband, Sly Liao, opened their own place, **Sea Pearl,** next door (8191 Strawberry Ln., Ste. 2; ☎ 703-372-5161). It's sleek and jazzy (literally), so if the lines at Four Sisters seem daunting, step that way.

Georgia Brown's ★★

SOUTHERN   MODERATE   QUALITY ★★★   VALUE ★★

950 15th St. NW; ☎ 202-393-4499; gbrowns.com   Downtown

Reservations Recommended. **When to go** Anytime. **Entrée range** $18–$30. **Payment** VISA, MC, AMEX, DC, D. **Service rating** ★★★½. **Friendliness rating** ★★★½. **Metro** McPherson Square or Farragut North. **Parking** Street; valet (after 6 p.m.), $8. **Bar** Full service. **Wine selection** Very good. **Dress** Business, informal. **Disabled access** Good. **Customers** Businesspeople, locals, tourists. **Hours** *Brunch:* Sunday, 10 a.m.–2:30 p.m.; *Lunch/Dinner:* Monday–Thursday, 11:30 a.m.–10 p.m.; Friday, 11:30 a.m.–11 p.m.; Saturday, noon –11 p.m.; Sunday, 5:30–10 p.m.

SETTING AND ATMOSPHERE An almost too-sophisticated take on Southern garden district graciousness, with vinelike wrought iron overhead, sleek wood curves, and conversation nooks; window tables are prime.

HOUSE SPECIALTIES Real Frogmore stew, with oysters, scallops, clams, shrimp, fish, and potatoes; fried (or grilled) catfish with black-eyed pea succotash; beautiful white shrimp, heads still on, with spicy sausage over grits; kitchen-sink sausage-chicken-shrimp gumbo.

OTHER RECOMMENDATIONS Sugar-and-spice-rubbed pork chop with maple-whipped mashed potatoes and sautéed green beans; grilled lamb chops marinated in garlic oil; Southern fried chicken marinated in buttermilk and served with collard greens and mashed potatoes. Surprisingly, this is a good place to try the veggie plate: red rice, a goat cheese–stuffed fried green tomato, and blue cheese slaw.

ENTERTAINMENT AND AMENITIES Live jazz at Sunday brunch.

SUMMARY AND COMMENTS This is not Low Country cuisine (except perhaps for the high-octane planter's punch); it's hybrid country, with updated versions of dishes you might find in Charleston or Savannah. Presentation is distinctive without being showy, and portions are generous. Homesick Southerners can indulge in the fried chicken livers and the farm biscuit–like scones and still look uptown. The wine list is all-American and fairly priced; barrel-aged bourbons and single-malt scotches are available as well.

Geranio ★★½

MODERN AMERICAN   MODERATE   QUALITY ★★★   VALUE ★★★

722 King St., Old Town Alexandria; ☎ 703-548-0088; geranio.net Virginia suburbs

Reservations Recommended. **When to go** Anytime. **Entrée range** $15–$26. **Payment** VISA, MC, AMEX, DC. **Service rating** ★★★★. **Friendliness rating** ★★★★. **Metro** King Street. **Parking** Street. **Bar** Full service. **Wine selection** Good. **Dress** Business, casual. **Disabled access** Not accessible. **Customers** Locals. **Hours** *Lunch:* Monday–Friday, 11:30 a.m.–2:30 p.m.; *Dinner:* Monday–Saturday, 6–10:30 p.m.; Sunday, 5:30–9:30 p.m.

SETTING AND ATMOSPHERE The exposed brick of this classic Old Town Alexandria town house is softened by richly colored still lifes. Decor also includes the odd hanging implement (a huge old grain scale), majolica-look flooring, and plastered walls painted a soft flaxen that deepens through the evening to a sage green.

HOUSE SPECIALTIES   Giant "free-form" ravioli with lump crab; roast chicken breasts with porcini risotto, favas, and chanterelles; oven-roasted pork loin with creamy polenta, wilted spinach, and crispy onions; osso buco with saffron risotto and broccoli rabe; halibut with globe artichokes and fresh basil; seared rare tuna wrapped in prosciutto.

OTHER RECOMMENDATIONS   Seared scallop with potato pancake; lobster risotto; oven-roasted rib eye with sweet onions, zucchini, and pancetta over a baked potato cake.

SUMMARY AND COMMENTS   As a restaurant town, Old Town is pretty much in the (deserving) grip of Cathal Armstrong, but chef-owner Troy Clayton, who trained with Jean-Louis Palladin, has managed to maintain the neighborhood hospitality of this Old Town beauty without dumbing down the menu. Dishes are complex in pairings but without gratuitous frills; this is a restaurant that remains quiet only by choice. There's a 10% discount on meals ordered before 7 p.m. or after 9:30 p.m.

Grapeseed   ★ ★ ★

MODERN AMERICAN   EXPENSIVE   QUALITY ★ ★ ★   VALUE ★ ★ ★

4865 Cordell Ave., Bethesda; ☎ 301-986-9592;grapeseedbistro.com
Maryland suburbs

Reservations Recommended. **When to go** Early dinner, late on weekends. **Entrée range** $23–$33. **Payment** VISA, MC, AMEX, D, DC. **Service rating** ★ ★ ★ ½. **Friendliness rating** ★ ★ ★. **Metro** Bethesda. **Parking** Pay lots, street meters, valet ($5). **Bar** Full service. **Wine selection** Very good. **Dress** Business, casual chic. **Disabled access** Narrow. **Customers** Food trendies, locals, businesspeople. **Hours** *Lunch:* Tuesday–Friday, 11 a.m.–2 p.m.; *Dinner:* Monday–Thursday, 5–10 p.m.; Friday–Saturday, 5–11 p.m.; closed Sunday.

SETTING AND ATMOSPHERE   This sleek and unfussy space—with its removable front walls onto the sidewalk, sit-to bar, banquettes down the hallway, mini dining rooms, and partially exposed kitchen—makes two points immediately: the wine is up front, and the food goes right behind. Chef-owner Jeff Heineman has designed a modern tapas menu to match his impressive list of wines, about 500 of them, all available by the glass, bottle, or even taste. Both "appetizers" and entrées, which can vary considerably in size and staying power, come listed as accompanying red wine or white, and the pairings are usually quite smart—unless the county's wine imports hit a snag, as they sometimes do. However, the staff is well prepared to make alternate recommendations.

HOUSE SPECIALTIES   Goat cheese–stuffed *piquillo* peppers; crisp tempura shrimp with zucchini blossoms; grilled quail with cheddar corn bread and bourbon barbecue; ethereal smoked trout; grilled monkfish with morels and bacon spoon bread; crisp and delicate cornmeal-fried oysters; a witty and robust pepper-crusted filet mignon with oxtail ragout.

OTHER RECOMMENDATIONS Wild mushroom fricassee; halibut with green tomato marmalade; grilled scallops with eggplant caponata; roast pork with white balsamic vinegar and grapes; seared duck with rosemary and lavender.

SUMMARY AND COMMENTS Allow some time to get the full impact of this menu. The list of dishes is so intriguing that it's difficult not to over-order, which won't at all bother your palate but may surprise you at checkout, especially as the wines can top out at $20 a glass (you can also get a 3-ounce tasting). Nor are the dishes particularly delicate, despite their apparently small size (and Heineman's Southern roots are pretty obvious). Don't mistake this for a wimpy wine bar; this is really hearty stuff.

Heritage India ★ ★ ½

INDIAN   MODERATE   QUALITY ★★★   VALUE ★★★

2400 Wisconsin Ave. NW; ☎ 202-333-3120;
heritageindiausa.com   Georgetown
1337 Connecticut Ave. NW; ☎ 202-333-1414   Dupont Circle

Reservations Recommended. **When to go** Anytime. **Entrée range** $9.95–$24.95.
Payment VISA, MC, AMEX, DC. **Service rating** ★★½. **Friendliness rating** ★★★.
Metro None nearby. **Parking** Street. **Bar** Full Service. **Wine selection** Good. **Dress**
Business, casual. **Disabled access** Good. **Customers** Businesspeople, locals, ethnics.
Hours *Lunch:* Daily, 11:30 a.m.–2:30 p.m.; *Dinner:* Daily, 5:30–10:30 p.m.

SETTING AND ATMOSPHERE Raj traditional, with saffron walls, elaborate wooden screens, romantic sepia-toned photos and Colonial-era lithographs and fabric upholstery.

HOUSE SPECIALTIES Heat freaks look to the lamb vindaloo, a real fire-starter. Moderately spicy choices include fish fillets, any of a half-dozen tandoori dishes, and a tangy but not too spicy dish of sliced grouper in green peppers and tomatoes.

OTHER RECOMMENDATIONS A soothing dish of baby eggplant in sesame sauce; okra and onions in dried mango powder; vegetable fritters..

SUMMARY AND COMMENTS This was one of the first new-age Indian kitchens, so to speak, in the Washington area, ranging into less familiar and more subtle regional fare, and its success has inspired a number of other kitchens to invest in complexity and upscale service. (Though no longer related, Passage to India, once also called Heritage India, retains a very similar menu as well as an even more elegant decor. See also the profile of Spice Xing, page 336.)

Indique Heights ★★★

INDIAN   MODERATE   QUALITY ★★★½   VALUE ★★★

2 Wisconsin Circle, Chevy Chase; ☎ 301-656-4822; indiqueheights.com
Maryland suburbs

Reservations Recommended. **When to go** Anytime. **Entrée range** $8–$22.
Payment VISA, MC, AMEX, D. **Service rating** ★★★½. **Friendliness rating**

★★★★. **Metro** Friendship Heights. **Parking** Street, pay lot. **Bar** Full service. **Wine selection** Good. **Dress** Business casual. **Disabled access** Good. **Customers** Locals, ethnics. **Hours** *Lunch:* Monday–Friday, 11:30 a.m.–2:30 p.m.; Saturday–Sunday, noon–3 p.m.; *Dinner:* Sunday–Thursday, 5:30–10:30 p.m.; Friday–Saturday, 5:30–11 p.m.

SETTING AND ATMOSPHERE A loungy, surprisingly luxe warren of curtain-ringed rooms in an office building, this street snack–smart restaurant is brisk and accommodating. Even dining in the bar is relaxing. Although not exactly enclosed (it's above the Metro escalators), there is a "court-yard" that feels like a second-story mezzanine.

HOUSE SPECIALTIES Anise-flavored crab cakes with coconut flakes; baby egg-plant in a sesame, peanut, and cashew cream; okra with mango powder; shrimp and scallop masala; buttery chicken tikka *makhani;* and a truly "not for the fainthearted!" chicken with toasted tellicherry peppercorns.

OTHER RECOMMENDATIONS As we said, Indique Heights makes street fare a fair: veggie samosas, boneless lamb strips with brown spices, all sorts of fried and stuffed breads and crepes with chutneys, and various regional versions of what might be called Indian trail mix. This is a great place for vegetarians, with a good list of dishes with or without seafood.

SUMMARY AND COMMENTS This upscale and wide-ranging restaurant, with its stunning presentations and carefully attended side dishes, is one of a happily expanding number of serious Indian kitchens in Washington that look beyond the tandoori line. In the heart of the new Friendship Heights–Chevy Chase shopping and condo neighborhood, it's a great place to take a break. It also proves to hotheads that there's plenty of flavor without chili—and vice versa.

Note: Indique Heights is the offshoot of **Indique,** an almost as accom-plished and visually stunning spot above the Cleveland Metro station. The same group also owns the great bargain **Bombay Bistro** in Rockville.

The Inn at Little Washington ★★★★★

MODERN AMERICAN   VERY EXPENSIVE   QUALITY ★★★★★   VALUE ★★★★★

Middle and Main streets, Washington, VA; ☎ 540-675-3800; theinnatlittlewashington.com Virginia suburbs

Reservations Required. **When to go** Anytime. **Entrée range** Prix fixe: $148, Sunday–Thursday; $158, Friday; $178, Saturday. **Payment** VISA, MC, AMEX. **Service rating** ★★★½. **Friendliness rating** ★★★. **Metro** None nearby. **Parking** Free lot. **Bar** Full service. **Wine selection** *Wine Spectator* Award. **Dress** Dressy, informal. **Disabled access** Fair. **Customers** Locals, tourists. **Hours** Monday–Thursday, 6–9 p.m.; Friday–Saturday, seatings at 5:30, 6, 9, and 9:30 p.m.; Sunday, seatings at 4, 4:30, 7, 7:30, 8, and 8:15 p.m.; closed Tuesday except May and October.

SETTING AND ATMOSPHERE An elegantly appointed but unfussy frame build-ing with an enclosed garden (with many romantic seatings on the patio) and rich, hand-painted walls, velvet upholstery, and the clean glint of real crystal and silver in all directions.

HOUSE SPECIALTIES The menu changes continually, but look for dishes such as seafood and wild mushroom risotto; veal or lamb carpaccio; tenderloin of beef that reminds you why that's such a classic entrée; home-smoked trout; sweetbreads with whole baby artichokes; baby lamb morsels with lamb sausage alongside; a duo of hot and cold foie gras; and, more recently, sashimi.

OTHER RECOMMENDATIONS Soft-shell crabs however offered (usually respectfully simple); a signature appetizer of black-eyed peas and Smithfield ham topped with foie gras; that same ham, sliced thin as prosciutto, wrapped around fresh local figs; portobello mushroom pretending to be a filet mignon.

SUMMARY AND COMMENTS A culinary legend—it's been profiled in *The New Yorker* and selected by *Travel + Leisure* as the second-finest hotel in the U.S. and eighth-finest in the world—the Inn at Little Washington is the capital's most popular distant dining destination. Chef Patrick O'Connell is a name to make magic with in gourmet (and gourmand) circles all over the country. O'Connell's strength is a sense of balance: dishes are never overwhelmed or overly fussy; local produce is emphasized (which guarantees freshness); and a lot of fine ingredients are allowed to speak for themselves, which is sadly rare. Everyone remembers his or her first passion here—homemade white-chocolate ice cream with bitter-chocolate sauce or an array of perfect dime-size biscuits with country ham—and for some Washingtonians, driving down to the other Washington becomes an addiction, a compulsion. It's the single biggest reason (besides horses, perhaps) for the boom in yuppie commuting to the hills. Although the dinner is purportedly four courses, here, as at several other top-flight restaurants, there are extras along the way. Incidentally, it was O'Connell who bought up the wine cellar when Le Pavillon (where Yannick Cam used to be chef) went bankrupt, and one can almost not regret it; the wine list is nearly 100 pages long.

Jaleo ★★★

NUEVO LATINO   MODERATE   QUALITY ★★★   VALUE ★★★

480 Seventh St. NW; ☎ 202-628-7949; jaleo.com Downtown
7271 Woodmont Ave., Bethesda; ☎ 301-913-0003 Maryland suburbs
2250-A Crystal Dr., Crystal City; ☎ 703-413-8181 Virginia suburbs

Reservations Lunch, plus 5–6:30 p.m. for pre-theater patrons. **When to go** Early evening. **Entrée range** $6.50–$48. **Payment** VISA, MC, AMEX, D, DC. **Service rating** ★★★. **Friendliness rating** ★★★. **Metro** *Downtown:* Archives–Navy Memorial–Penn Quarter; *Bethesda:* Bethesda; *Crystal City:* Crystal City. **Parking** Street; valet after 5 p.m. except on Sunday, $8. **Bar** Full service. **Wine selection** Good. **Dress** Business, casual. **Disabled access** Good. **Customers** Locals, tourists. **Hours** *Brunch:* Saturday–Sunday, 11:30 a.m.–3 p.m.; *Lunch/Dinner:* Downtown: Sunday–Monday, 11:30 a.m.–10 p.m.; Tuesday–Thursday, 11:30 a.m.–11:30 p.m.; Friday–Saturday, 11:30 a.m.–midnight. Bethesda: Sunday–Thursday, 11:30 a.m.–10 p.m.; Friday–Saturday, 11:30 a.m.–midnight. Crystal City: Tuesday–Thursday,

11:30 a.m.–10 p.m.; Friday–Saturday, 11:30 a.m.–11 p.m.; Sunday, 11:30 a.m.–9 p.m.; closed Monday.

SETTING AND ATMOSPHERE A combination tapas bar and piazza, with bits of wrought iron, a lush suedelike gray decor, and (in the original downtown branch) a partial copy of the John Singer Sargent painting from which it takes its name.

HOUSE SPECIALTIES Paella (in three versions) and tapas—bite-size appetizers (four to a plate) meant to help wash down glasses of sangria and sherry and pass hours of conversation. Among the best regulars: orange peel–marinated mussels; raw tuna with anchovy oil; Cadiz-style marinated fried shark; monkfish with eggplant and black olive oil; grilled quail; spinach with apples, pine nuts, and raisins; salmon with artichokes; eggplant flan with roasted peppers; serrano ham and tomatoes on focaccia; and miniature lamb chops. Daily specials and particularly seasonal rarities, frequently of shrimp or shellfish, are extremely good bets.

OTHER RECOMMENDATIONS Sausage with white beans; grilled portobello mushrooms (getting to be a local staple); lightly fried calamari; paella. There are happy hour specials 4:30–7 p.m. every day but Saturday, and 10 p.m.–midnight at Bethesda only.

SUMMARY AND COMMENTS Jaleo has taken tapas, once just bar food, and built an entire menu around them—there are five times as many tapas as whole entrées. If you're with three or four people, you can just about taste everything in sight. (In fact, the first time, you may want to go extra slow: the plates look so small, and the Palo Cortada goes down so smoothly, that you can overstuff yourself without realizing it.) The bar does a heavy business, too, especially pre- and post-theater.

J&G Steakhouse ★★★★

MODERN AMERICAN/STEAK VERY EXPENSIVE QUALITY ★★★★ VALUE ★★★

515 15th St. NW (in the W Hotel); ☎ 202-661-2440; jgsteakhouse washingtondc.com Downtown

Reservations Strongly recommended. **When to go** Pre-theater. **Entrée range** $17–$54; five-course tasting menu, $68. **Payment** VISA, MC, AMEX, DC. **Service rating** ★★★★. **Friendliness rating** ★★★★. **Metro** McPherson Square or Federal Triangle. **Parking** Valet, pay lots, street. **Bar** Full service. **Wine selection** Very good. **Dress** Business casual, hip informal. **Disabled access** Good. **Customers** Businesspeople, foodies. **Hours** *Breakfast:* Monday–Friday, 7–10:30 a.m.; Saturday–Sunday, 8–11 a.m.; *Lunch:* Daily, 11:45 a.m.–2:30 p.m.; *Dinner:* Sunday–Thursday, 5–10 p.m.; Friday–Saturday, 5–11 p.m.

SETTING AND ATMOSPHERE Manhattan neoclassical decor: white walls and columns, with a vaulted ceiling and chocolate drapes, and easy-back low chairs with tufted banquettes. In fact, there are showier details in the presentation (bone marrow–looking sauce containers) and at the sleek bar, called the Cellar and ringed with wines.

HOUSE SPECIALTIES A lumpy (that's a compliment) crab cake; salmon tartare on a bed of ginger vinaigrette; watermelon as gazpacho or cubed with goat cheese as salad; unusually light fried calamari; hand-ground burgers; seared halibut with scallion-chili sauce; slow-cooked salmon; a side of sautéed *maitake* mushrooms.

OTHER RECOMMENDATIONS Seared scallops with spring peas and bacon; Sichuan peppercorn-crusted tuna; hanger steak and fries. And yes, a token Wagyu steak: a 10-ounce sirloin for $54.

SUMMARY AND COMMENTS The phrase *steak house* is misleading; this is almost the anti–steak house. The menu is almost equally balanced between appetizers, entrées, and "from the grill," and at that there are only a handful of steaks. Which is not surprising: If you think Alain Ducasse's 22-restaurant empire or Michael Mina's 17 are impressive, try 27 (and growing) internationally for Jean-Georges Vongerichten, who may have the widest variety as well (though an Asian fusion tang runs through all). He's infinitely restless in terms of creativity, and although he's rarely in town, he is one of those international chefs who makes sure that he leaves a solid team, including servers, in place. It's the precision of the food here that's impressive. The pre-theater menu, three courses for $35, is available 5–6:30 p.m. There's an unusually good list of wines by the glass.

Johnny's Half Shell ★★★½

SOUTHERN INEXPENSIVE QUALITY ★★★ VALUE ★★★

400 N Capitol St.; ☎ 202-737-0400; johnnyshalfshell.net Capitol Hill

Reservations Accepted. **When to go** Pre- or post-rush. **Entrée range** $18–$30. **Payment** VISA, MC, AMEX. **Service rating** ★★★. **Friendliness rating** ★★★★. **Metro** Union Station. **Parking** Free at night; street, pay lots. **Bar** Full service. **Wine selection** Good. **Dress** Business, casual. **Disabled access** Not accessible. **Customers** Locals, businesspeople. **Hours** *Breakfast:* Monday–Friday, 7–9:30 a.m.; *Lunch:* Monday–Friday, 11:30 a.m.–2:30 p.m.; *Dinner:* Monday–Saturday, 5–10 p.m.

SETTING AND ATMOSPHERE Intentionally low-key, it hearkens back to the New Orleans–style oyster bars and Gulf Coast fish houses: tile floors, waiters in white jackets, a marble-topped pull-up bar, and a raw bar.

HOUSE SPECIALTIES Tequila-cured gravlax; halibut over chanterelles; grilled squid over wilted arugula; fried oyster po'boys (on bread flown in from New Orleans) or charbroiled oysters; soft-shell crabs with corn pudding; fried pork ribs; tuna sliders; spicy lobster.

OTHER RECOMMENDATIONS Barbecued shrimp on cheese grits; a dark and dirty gumbo; sautéed catfish with shrimp and andouille sausage risotto; seafood stew and crab imperial. Breakfast, with grillades and grits, beignets, and eggs Benedict, is fast becoming a Capitol Hill power meal. At the other end of the day, the bar hands out martinis the size of your fist.

ENTERTAINMENT AND AMENITIES Outdoor seating and live jazz Friday and Saturday nights.

SUMMARY AND COMMENTS Executive chef Ann Cashion and co-owner John Fulchino are old friends to Washington foodies (see profile of Cashion's Eat Place, page 296). This newly relocated (and expanded) hangout is a mini-getaway to the sort of old New Orleans bar that is becoming a rarity in the tourist-crazy Big Easy itself: fried oysters, frigid beer, and the sort of couture "comfort food" that Cashion is famous for. There's a $30 pre-theater menu (5–7 p.m.). And now for something completely different: The Half Shell has a first-rate taco annex, **Tacueria Nacional,** with its own breakfast and lunch menu.

Kaz Sushi Bistro ★★★½

JAPANESE MODERATE QUALITY ★★★★ VALUE ★★★

1915 I St. NW; ☎ 202-530-5500; kazsushibistro.com Foggy Bottom

Reservations Recommended. **When to go** Anytime. **Entrée range** $16–$32.
Payment VISA, MC, AMEX, DC. **Service rating** ★★★. **Friendliness rating** ★★★.
Metro Farragut West or Farragut North. **Parking** Pay lots. **Bar** Beer and wine.
Wine selection Fair, several sakes. **Dress** Business, casual. **Disabled access** No.
Customers Food trendies, businesspeople. **Hours** *Lunch:* Monday–Friday, 11:30
a.m.–2 p.m.; *Dinner:* Monday–Saturday, 6–10 p.m.; closed Sunday.

SETTING AND ATMOSPHERE A smart and savvy-funny room, with a mini–fountain wall in front, a smallish sushi bar in the rear, and abstract but oddly *maguro*-ish wallpaper.

HOUSE SPECIALTIES Sake-poached scallops; lobster salad; glazed and grilled baby octopus; spicy broiled green mussels; foie gras infused with plum wine; Japanese-style duck confit in miso; salmon belly with fennel and yogurt sauce; the signature sea trout "napoleon" of chopped fish tossed with peanuts, cilantro, and soy-ginger dressing and layered on crispy wontons. When fugu, the famous blowfish, is in season, Kaz (who is the only one in Washington certified to handle the potentially lethal fish) makes traditional multicourse fugu meals.

OTHER RECOMMENDATIONS Nontraditional sushi such as tuna with foie gras or with Kalamata pesto; lobster with wasabi mayo; asparagus and roasted–red pepper roll; portobello and sun-dried tomato roll.

SUMMARY AND COMMENTS Chef-owner Kaz Okochi earned many of his fans while working at Sushi-Ko, where he originated many of what he calls his original small dishes. He is also fearless about mixing East and West, but not in the usual fusion forms, such as tuna and foie gras. The quality of the more traditional sushi is first-rate, of course. But you can get good sushi in a number of places, as listed in the front of this chapter. So take Kaz's inventions for a spin. Note the number of intriguing vegetarian options as well.

Kinkead's ★★★

SEAFOOD EXPENSIVE QUALITY ★★★ VALUE ★★½

2000 Pennsylvania Ave. NW; ☎ 202-296-7700; kinkead.com
Foggy Bottom

Reservations Recommended (required for the dining room upstairs). **When
to go** Anytime, Sunday brunch. **Entrée range** $17–$32. **Payment** VISA, MC,
AMEX, D, DC. **Service rating** ★★★. **Friendliness rating** ★★★. **Metro** Foggy
Bottom–GWU or Farragut West. **Parking** Validated, pay lots, meters. **Bar** Full

service. **Wine selection** Good. **Dress** Business, informal. **Disabled access** Good. **Customers** Businesspeople, locals. **Hours** *Lunch:* Monday–Friday, 11:30 a.m.– 2:30 p.m.; *Dinner:* Daily, 5:30–10 p.m.

SETTING AND ATMOSPHERE Pleasantly restrained, ranging over two floors and divided into a series of elevated or glass-enclosed areas. The kitchen staff is visible upstairs, as is commonplace these days; it's a little less common to see chef-owner Robert Kinkead on the consumer side of the glass wall, barking at his cooks via headset like a football coach talking to the booth.

HOUSE SPECIALTIES Melting chargrilled squid over polenta with tomato confit (appetizer); roast cod with crab imperial; seared sea scallops with fennel tarte tatin; seared tuna with portobellos and flageolets; lobster specials; roast saddle of rabbit with crispy sweetbreads and fava bean–chanterelle ragout; Brazilian-style pork with black beans; walnut-encrusted snapper.

OTHER RECOMMENDATIONS Ipswich-style fried soft-shell clams; crab and lobster cakes (appetizers); sautéed cod cheeks; Sicilian swordfish with fennel, olives, currants, and arugula.

ENTERTAINMENT AND AMENITIES Live jazz weeknights; nonsmoking raw bar.

SUMMARY AND COMMENTS This is a seafood restaurant for those still a little leery of fish–or rather, fishy flavors. Kinkead's style is simple and straightforward but not shrinking; his sauces are balanced but assured, designed to highlight the food, not the frills. Any available seafood can be ordered broiled or grilled, but simply grilled here is almost an oxymoron. And Kinkead, whose first fame came from his Nantucket restaurant, has installed a little home away from home downstairs by way of a raw bar–plus first-rate chowder, soups, and salads. Kinkead also owns the slightly less formal **Hell Point Seafood** on the Annapolis waterfront, so if you have a day trip in mind, make it part of the itinerary.

Komi ★ ★ ★ ★ ★

MODERN AMERICAN   VERY EXPENSIVE   QUALITY ★ ★ ★ ★   VALUE ★ ★ ★

1509 17th St. NW; ☎ 202-332-9200; komirestaurant.com
Dupont Circle/Adams Morgan

Reservations Required. **When to go** Anytime. **Entrée range** Degustation menu, $135; wine (and beer) pairings, $70 additional. **Payment** VISA, MC, AMEX, D, DC. **Service rating** ★ ★ ★. **Friendliness rating** ★ ★ ★ ★. **Metro** Dupont Circle. **Parking** Street. **Bar** Full service. **Wine selection** Good. **Dress** Business, dressy casual. **Disabled access** No. **Customers** Foodies, after-work business partners. **Hours** Tuesday–Saturday, 5:30 until closing.

SETTING AND ATMOSPHERE With only a dozen tables and buttery walls decorated only with candles, this town house dining room gives *intimate* new meaning.

HOUSE SPECIALTIES There is no longer an à la carte menu, only the 18- to 22-course chef's choice menu, which changes with the market (and which often starts with a huge array of meze). Among recent high points: roast suckling pig; spit-roasted kid; house-made tagliatelle with sea urchin; salmon belly tartare; braised baby octopus; amberjack in a smoked turbot aspic; pork belly souvlaki with pickled cucumber; goat liver ragu.

SUMMARY AND COMMENTS Chef Johnny Monis, a local boy and still in his early 30s, is indisputably one of Washington's best chefs, arguably the most consistently superb, with a cook line that shares his vision (the whole crew looks like a college team). Good things come to those who don't even wait—the moment you're seated, you're likely to get your first little treat (say, roasted dates stuffed with mascarpone and yogurt and dotted with sea salt, now a signature). There is obviously a Greek flavor to the menu—Komi is the name of a small beach town near Monis's Greek grandparents' home—but it's entirely original. However, this is not for the overly prudish; be prepared to eat at least part of your meal by hand—and we don't mean the homemade lollipops that come with the bill.

Kushi ★★★

JAPANESE MOD/EXP QUALITY ★★★½ VALUE ★★★★

465 K St. NW; ☎ 202-682-3123; eatkushi.com   Downtown

Reservations Recommended. **When to go** Anytime; late night. **Entrée range** Sushi/skewers, $12–$37; small plates, $3–$35; seven-course *omakase* menu, $40. **Payment** VISA, MC, AMEX, DC. **Service rating** ★★★½. **Friendliness rating** ★★★★. **Metro** Mount Vernon Square. **Parking** Street, pay lots. **Bar** Full service. **Wine selection** Good. **Dress** Business casual, trendy informal, hip casual. **Disabled access** Good. **Customers** Asian businessmen and hipsters, foodies, locals. **Hours** *Lunch:* Monday–Friday, 11:30 a.m.–2:30 p.m.; Saturday–Sunday, noon–2:30 p.m.; *Dinner:* Sunday–Wednesday, 5:30–11 p.m.; Thursday–Saturday, 5:30 p.m.–2 a.m.

SETTING AND ATMOSPHERE In the emerging NoMa (North of Massachusetts Avenue) neighborhood, this Tokyo-style *izakaya*—the term for small mom-and-pop bars that serve mostly homemade dishes that can be either simple or ornate—is, as the name suggests, two restaurants in one. The *robata* (stone) grill is on one side and the sushi bar on the other side, with a glass-enclosed raw bar in between. It's fairly traditional in decor—hanging *noren* in the doorways, reclaimed-wood tables, paper lanterns, and sake casks—but with a Soho Japanese-club atmosphere, a concrete warehouse with techno-beat backgrounds.

HOUSE SPECIALTIES From the grill, whole *branzino*; quail stuffed with duck sausage; pork belly; crisp duck thighs; foie gras with plum jelly. From the sushi bar, impeccable sea urchin from the shell (no four-day-old gonads here) served in its shell, live scallops, mackerel, and live baby eels.

OTHER RECOMMENDATIONS Check for daily specials: a sort of custard of the day (a take on *chawan mushi*); sake-steamed clams; the fatty tuna belly called *o-toro,* for those who always want the Kobe steak.

SUMMARY AND COMMENTS Kushi is the brainchild of former caterer Darren Lee Norris and his Japanese wife, Ari Kushimoto; and it's a new concept to many (although Bethesda's Tako Grill has had the same dual setup for years). It also serves lunch on the weekends, which is a boon, and late night, which is even better (and more *izakaya* appropriate). Norris has taken a tip from Sushi Taro (profiled on page 337), which upped the seafood-quality steaks by bringing in seafood daily from Tokyo's Tsukiji market. The sushi rice, which in many places is the biggest flaw, is a star here. The fish and shellfish are pristine, and the sake list is a good start. Watch for sports stars here, especially Asian ones.

L'Auberge Chez François ★★★

FRENCH   VERY EXPENSIVE   QUALITY ★★★½   VALUE ★★★★

332 Springvale Rd., Great Falls; ☎ 703-759-3800;
laubergechezfrancois.com   Virginia suburbs

Reservations Required 4 weeks in advance. **When to go** Summer evenings in good weather for the terrace. **Entrée range** $37–$49 (lunch); $59–$75 (dinner). **Payment** VISA, MC, AMEX, D, DC. **Service rating** ★★★★. **Friendliness rating** ★★★★. **Metro** None nearby. **Parking** Free lot. **Bar** Full service. **Wine selection** Very good. **Dress** Dressy, business (jacket required for men at night). **Disabled access** Very good. **Customers** Locals. **Hours** *Lunch:* Tuesday–Saturday, 11:30 a.m.–1:30 p.m.; *Dinner:* Tuesday–Friday, reservations available 5–9 p.m.; Saturday, two seatings at 4:30–6:30 p.m. and 8–9:30 p.m.; Sunday, noon–7:30 p.m.

SETTING AND ATMOSPHERE   This is one of the most beloved and romantic dining sites in the area for more than 50 years, a real country inn with exposed beams, a mix of views of Alsace (home of the late paterfamilias–executive chef Jacques Haeringer), only-a-family-could-love drawings, and a travel-brochure veranda. It's so widely known as an engagement and anniversary mecca that the book *Regrets Only*, Sally Quinn's semi–roman à clef about journalistic and political circles, included a rather improbable but dramatic tryst in the parking lot (in an MG with a stick shift, no less).

HOUSE SPECIALTIES   Classics such as rack of lamb ($50 for one, $98 for two), Chateaubriand for two ($98), and duck foie gras either sautéed with apples or plain; the true choucroute royal garni, with Alsatian sauerkraut, sausages, smoked pork, duck, pheasant, and quail; game in season, such as medallions of venison and roast duck; veal kidneys in a rich, mustardy sauce; sweetbreads with wild mushrooms in puff pastry; roasted boneless duck breast paired with the stuffed leg and fruit-dotted rice; seafood fricassee with shrimp, scallops, lobster, rockfish, and salmon in Riesling.

OTHER RECOMMENDATIONS   Various seafood and game pâtés; red snapper braised in beer; boneless rabbit stuffed with leeks and fennel; soft-shell crabs with extra crabmeat stuffed into the body; big scallops in a bright (but not overwhelming) tomato and bell pepper sauce.

SUMMARY AND COMMENTS   Jacques's son Francois, himself the star of a TV show, has taken over the kitchen, but blood is thicker than broth, and there is no major shake-up in sight. This is a bargain; what look like entrées on the menu are really whole dinners with salads, fancy appetizers, and dessert—not to mention bread and cheese and a bit of sorbet.

Although the two-to-four-weeks' notice rule still applies, competition has increased, along with cancellations: it may be worth it to call in the late afternoon, especially during the week. You can't make reservations for the outdoor terrace, incidentally; just call to make sure it's open (about May–September) and then show up.

La Chaumière ★★½

FRENCH   MODERATE   QUALITY ★★★   VALUE ★★★

2813 M St. NW; ☎ 202-338-1784; lachaumieredc.com   Georgetown

Reservations Recommended. **When to go** Anytime. **Entrée range** $16–$30. **Payment** VISA, MC, AMEX, DC, JCB, CB. **Service rating** ★★★. **Friendliness rating** ★★★. **Metro** Foggy Bottom–GWU. **Parking** Street. **Bar** Full service. **Wine selection** Good. **Dress** Business, informal. **Disabled access** Good. **Customers** Locals, embassy personnel, businesspeople. **Hours** *Lunch:* Monday–Friday, 11:30 a.m.–2:30 p.m.; *Dinner:* Monday–Saturday, 5:30–10:30 p.m.; closed Sunday.

SETTING AND ATMOSPHERE   After 25 years in the often tumultuous Georgetown culinary competition, the cooking in this big-beamed, in-town country inn—with its freestanding fireplace in the center and old iron tools on the wall—has a revived freshness, thanks to the new kitchen broom of chef Patrick Orange.

HOUSE SPECIALTIES   Oysters; seasonal specials of rabbit, choucroute, or venison (as uptown as medallions with chestnut puree or as down-home as potpie); seafood crepes or jumbo shad roe; bouillabaisse; boudin blanc, traditional tripe à la mode in Calvados. Here, as at Bistro Français across the street (see profile, page 287), the daily specials are even more amazing: terrine of duck foie gras or fresh foie gras with cassis; ostrich loin wrapped in bacon; bison osso buco.

OTHER RECOMMENDATIONS   Calf's liver or brains; sweetbreads with turnips and Jerusalem artichokes; medallions of venison; quenelles of pike in lobster sauce; jumbo lump crab cake (lunch).

SUMMARY AND COMMENTS   Part of La Chaumière's charm is its weekly treats: Wednesday it's couscous, and Thursday, cassoulet. Offal can still be hard to find around these parts, but not here.

This is family-style food, and most of its regulars are treated like family. Actually, *regulars* is a key word here; La Chaumière hearkens back to the time when Georgetown was more neighborhood than shopping mall, and a lot of its customers feel as if they graduated into adult dinner-dating here.

Makoto ★★★½

JAPANESE   VERY EXPENSIVE   QUALITY ★★★½   VALUE ★★★

4822 MacArthur Blvd. NW; ☎ 202-298-6866   Upper Northwest

Reservations Recommended. **When to go** Anytime. **Entrée range** Fixed price menu $60. **Payment** VISA, MC, AMEX. **Service rating** 4.5. **Friendliness rating** ★★★. **Metro** None nearby. **Parking** Street. **Bar** Full service. **Wine selection** House. **Dress** Business, casual. **Disabled access** No. **Customers** Ethnic Japanese, locals, businesspeople. **Hours** *Lunch:* Tuesday–Saturday, noon–2 p.m.; *Dinner:* Tuesday–Sunday, 6–10 p.m.

SETTING AND ATMOSPHERE A secret Japanese garden of a spot, hidden behind two wooden doors (with a stone garden between where you exchange your shoes for bedroom slippers) and only two lines of diners long. The kitchen is, in effect, the decor: slightly sunken behind what is now the sushi counter, the chefs busily stir, fry, and slice over the restaurant equivalent of a Pullman stove. There is a small à la carte menu, but it's almost as *omakase* as the rest, with prices that honestly say "from . . ." depending on season and market. Lunch is à la carte.

HOUSE SPECIALTIES A fixed-price *omakase* (chef's choice) dinner based on the market and featuring eight to ten courses of two to six bites each, but generous: sashimi; sushi (perhaps four different pieces, such as a tray of fine miniature desserts); grilled marinated fillet of fish or pork, soft-shell crab; such delicate morsels as *ankimo* (monkfish liver) or rare duck breast with asparagus tips and sesame seeds; salmon with Chinese broccoli; wheat-noodle soup; and sherbet.

OTHER RECOMMENDATIONS Limited à la carte sushi, such as *uni* (sea urchin), *toro*, or fresh sardines; yakitori, skewer-grilled marinated chicken.

SUMMARY AND COMMENTS This is a tiny establishment—perhaps 30 seats, even counting the new sushi bar—which explains how the chefs are able to produce such exquisite and imaginative meals. For the greatest pleasure, order the tasting menu and experience kaiseki cuisine, the formal, Zen-derived technique that salutes both nature and art by using only fresh, seasonal ingredients and a variety of colors, textures, and cooking techniques. (Actually, this is *omakase,* meaning chef's choice, but in the case of Tetsuro Takanashi, the Zen is built in.) Be sure to show your appreciation by admiring each carefully presented dish as it arrives. Note that none of the seats have backs—they're just boxes with removable tops for storing purses, jackets, and cushion lids—and there is no separate nonsmoking area. Cell phones are strictly prohibited, and we mean strictly. Though unrelated, the sushi bar upstairs, **Kotobuki,** is a popular stop.

Marcel's ★ ★ ★ ★

FRENCH-BELGIAN **EXPENSIVE** **QUALITY ★ ★ ★ ★** **VALUE ★ ★ ★**

2401 Pennsylvania Ave. NW; ☎ 202-296-1166; marcelsdc.com
Dupont Circle/Adams Morgan

Reservations Highly recommended. **When to go** Pre-theater. **Entrée range** $26–$39; fixed price, $65–$130; pre-theater three-course, $58. **Payment** VISA, MC, AMEX, DC, D. **Service rating** ★ ★ ★. **Friendliness rating** ★ ★ ★. **Metro** Foggy Bottom–GWU. **Parking** Valet ($8), street meters, lots. **Bar** Full service. **Wine selection** Very good. **Dress** Business, dressy casual. **Disabled access** Very good. **Customers** Businesspeople, foodies. **Hours** Monday–Thursday, 5:30–10 p.m.; Friday–Saturday, 5:30–11 p.m.; Sunday, 5:30–9:30 p.m.

SETTING AND ATMOSPHERE An amber yellow country inn gone upscale, with weathered wood, wrought iron, and stone facades, this is a showplace for classic French fare with a Belgian accent. The long marble bar is a showpiece, and the partially exposed (and elevated) kitchen is not so intrusive as elsewhere.

HOUSE SPECIALTIES The boudin blanc is a signature dish, and a don't-miss. Game dishes in season, such as breast of squab on truffled risotto; pheasant and foie gras in white bean ragout with winter vegetables; or roulade of rabbit stuffed with sausage over caramelized cabbage. Also crispy duck breast with duck confit; pan-fried skate; coriander-seed-crusted salmon; and foie gras–duck liver mousse.

OTHER RECOMMENDATIONS Seared scallops with lardoons of applewood bacon; duck consommé with sweetbreads; and coriander salmon, lobster sauce, and caviar. There are three-, four-, five-, and seven-course menus (plus wine). The brasserie bar menu offers more rustic fare at about $15 a plate.

ENTERTAINMENT AND AMENITIES Outdoor seating; live piano music nightly except Sunday.

SUMMARY AND COMMENTS Chef-owner Robert Wiedmaier gets bigger and more Belgian all the time: confits, root vegetables (including the various endives, of course), artichokes, and flavorful but not heavy sausages. The service is attentive, though at times a trifle educational. Marcel, incidentally, is the owner's older son; the second, Beck, is memorialized at Wiedmaier's Brasserie Beck. As mentioned above, Wiedmaier now has several restaurants, but this is the best.

Meskerem ★ ★ ½

ETHIOPIAN   INEXPENSIVE   QUALITY ★★★   VALUE ★★★½

2434 18th St. NW; ☎ 202-462-4100;
meskeremethiopianrestaurantdc.com   Dupont Circle/Adams Morgan

Reservations Suggested. **When to go** Anytime. **Entrée range** $7–$13. **Payment** VISA, MC, AMEX, DC. **Service rating** ★★★. **Friendliness rating** ★★★★. **Metro** Woodley Park–Zoo/Adams Morgan. **Parking** Street. **Bar** Full service. **Wine selection** Minimal. **Dress** Casual. **Disabled access** Good. **Customers** Locals, tourists. **Hours** Monday–Thursday, 11 a.m.–midnight; Friday–Sunday, 11 a.m.–2 a.m.

SETTING AND ATMOSPHERE Simple but cheerful, with "skylight" rays painted blue and white, musical instruments hung on the walls, and Ethiopian-style seating (for the limber) on leather cushions at balcony basket-weave tables.

HOUSE SPECIALTIES *Kitfo* (tartare with chile sauce, but you can order it lightly cooked or have a similar hot chopped-beef stew called *kay wat*); lamb *tibbs* (breast and leg meat sautéed with onions and green chiles); shrimp watt; beef or lentil and green chile *sambusa* (fried pastries).

OTHER RECOMMENDATIONS Chicken *alicha* for the spice-intimidated; a honey-wine version of *kitfo* called *gored gored*.

SUMMARY AND COMMENTS Washington's many Ethiopian restaurants offer similar menus, in some cases without much distinction between stews, but Meskerem is one of the more dependable, a staple in Adams

Morgan. (It's no longer cutting edge, as Little Ethiopia has moved east to U Street, but it's a safe choice.) If you want a sampler—a tray-sized injera palette—order the *mesob* for $11.95 ($23 for two). *Meskerem*, incidentally, is the first month of the 13-month Ethiopian calendar, the one that corresponds to September, which in Ethiopia is the end of the rainy season and thus is akin to springtime.

Minibar ★ ★ ★ ★ ★

MODERN AMERICAN   VERY EXPENSIVE   QUALITY ★ ★ ★ ★ ★   VALUE ★ ★ ★ ★

405 Eighth St. NW; ☎ 202-393-0812; cafeatlantico.com/minibar
Downtown

Reservations Required. **When to go** Anytime you can get in. **Entrée range** Prix fixe, $150. **Payment** VISA, MC, AMEX, DC. **Service rating** ★ ★ ★ ★ ★. **Friendliness rating** ★ ★ ★ ★. **Metro** Archives–Navy Memorial–Penn Quarter or Gallery Place–Chinatown. **Parking** Street, valet at dinner ($10). **Bar** Full service. **Wine selection** Renowned. **Dress** Business casual, dressy. **Disabled access** Good. **Customers** Local, ethnic. **Hours** Tuesday–Saturday, seatings at 6 and 8:30 p.m. only.

SETTING AND ATMOSPHERE Though as yet it's like the hosts' nook in the kitchen during a party—a tiny six-seat bar inside a three-story town house—turned-restaurant of exposed brick and brilliant wall art (see Café Atlántico, on page 293)—Minibar offers a front-row seat to some of the most imaginative, labor-intensive, ingredient-irreverent, and grin-inducing cuisine in the country. "As yet," because happily for its fans, Minibar is on the verge of expanding its reach—although that very detailed labor makes it a special challenge. If you're new to such creative and frequently comic creations, try to open your mind as much as your mouth.

HOUSE SPECIALTIES The tasting menu may top 30 items, and so is almost impossible to predict, but among the most celebrated and/or recent offerings have been hot-and-cold foie gras soup; cappuccino wrapped in cotton candy; a blown glass–style "lightbulb" of molten sugar; de-and reconstructed guacamole (tomato-cilantro granite wrapped in avocado); prawns in a foamy brioche batter; feta-water linguine; splinter-size fried fish in a London-style cone the size of your little finger; test-tube mojitos; gazpacho poppers; "olives" that are actually like tiny balloons filled with olive essence; and a Caprese salad of cherry tomatoes skewered on a needle of mozzarella cream to be shot into your mouth. While we have categorized the restaurant as modern American, it is really more like haute deconstructed cuisine.

OTHER RECOMMENDATIONS A camera or smartphone; you won't want to forget this, although you will get a copy of the menu.

SUMMARY AND COMMENTS Let us make this clear: Minibar is not for the casual tourist, financially or culinarily. Unless you're a serious foodie, unless you have both respect *and* a broad sense of humor about the art of cooking, and unless you know the phrase *molecular gastronomy* (which makes chef José Andrés wince but is the trendy moniker), the lengths you'll have to go to just to get in may not be worth it. (You must call exactly a month before the evening you hope to get a seat.) Less focused foodies might be just as happy at one of Andrés's other restaurants: Zaytinya, Jaleo, Oyamel, or Café Atlántico.

Andrés, now a star on both American and Spanish public TV, started his cooking career at Ferran Adria's El Bulli, often picked as the world's best restaurant, and he has retained his often frenetic sense of adventure even as the "science" of cooking has ratcheted up to rival the art. And if you're going, let the sommelier do your wine pairings; it may be expensive, but the choices are quite fine (and you'll pay a $25 corkage fee to bring your own, so unless it's a very old Grange, don't bother). Note that Minibar executive chef Ruben Garcia will try to accommodate vegetarian diners (make that clear when you make your reservation), but the kitchen cannot manage vegan versions.

Montmartre ★★½

FRENCH   MODERATE   QUALITY ★★★½   VALUE ★★★½

327 Seventh St. SE; ☎ 202-544-1244; montmartredc.com   Capitol Hill

Reservations Recommended. **When to go** Early or late dinner; brunch. **Entrée range** $17.95–$21.95. **Payment** VISA, MC, AMEX, DC. **Service rating** ★★★★. **Friendliness rating** ★★★★. **Metro** Eastern Market. **Parking** Street. **Bar** Full service. **Wine selection** Short but good. **Dress** Casual, business. **Disabled access** Fair. **Customers** Locals. **Hours** *Brunch:* Saturday–Sunday, 10:30 a.m.–3 p.m.; *Lunch:* Tuesday–Friday, 11:30 a.m.–2:30 p.m.; *Dinner:* Tuesday–Thursday, 5:30–10 p.m.; Friday–Saturday, 5:30–10:30 p.m.; Sunday, 5:30–9 p.m.

SETTING AND ATMOSPHERE This is the sort of place that makes cozy seem like part of the word *café,* a single sunny-sponged room of about 50 seats with a tiny bar at the back, lively views of the sidewalk to the front and the kitchen to the rear, classic French posters, and elbow-to-elbow tables.

HOUSE SPECIALTIES The signature dish here is slow-braised rabbit leg with olives and wide egg noodles in cream sauce, and it's hard to beat. Otherwise, look for hanger steak (*onglet*); a very Parisian salad of frisée with fried gizzards and bacon lardoons; cream of cauliflower soup with mussels; shrimp and lemon risotto; mussels with Ricard; sautéed monkfish over potato cake with anchovy butter.

OTHER RECOMMENDATIONS Daily specials such as venison rib chops with braised endive and a guinea hen confit with Jerusalem artichokes.

SUMMARY AND COMMENTS The owners have spun off a pizza place, **Seventh Hill Pizza,** out of the side door, so to speak.

Murasaki ★★½

JAPANESE   MODERATE   QUALITY ★★★   VALUE ★★★

**4620 Wisconsin Ave. NW; ☎ 202-966-0023; murasakidc.com
Upper Northwest**

Reservations Helpful. **When to go** Anytime. **Entrée range** $11–$20; market price higher. **Payment** VISA, MC, AMEX, D. **Service rating** ★★★★. **Friendliness rating** ★★★★. **Metro** Tenleytown-AU. **Parking** Street. **Bar** Beer and wine.

Wine selection Limited. **Dress** Business, casual. **Disabled access** Good. **Customers** Ethnic Japanese, businesspeople. **Hours** *Lunch:* Monday–Friday, 11:30 a.m.–2:30 p.m.; Saturday, noon–2:30 p.m.; *Dinner:* Monday–Thursday, 5:30–10 p.m.; Friday–Saturday, 5:30–10:30 p.m.; Sunday, 5–9:30 p.m.

SETTING AND ATMOSPHERE *Murasaki* means "purple," but there isn't much of that hue in this elegantly spare room, which tends instead to a clean, partially Deco and only slightly Asian look using wood framing, cream walls, and a pleasant side patio. (Lady Murasaki was also the author of what is sometimes referred to as the first true novel, *The Tale of Genji*). The grill and sushi bars, which run a long L around the rear of the room, are the focal points.

HOUSE SPECIALTIES The real specialties (occult parts of sea creatures, delicate baked dishes, and the like) are not printed on the menu because novice diners too often order dishes they then dislike, so Japanese connoisseurs should consult with the chef about favorite items. On the other hand, even lobster sashimi and lobster miso soup can tickle the trend-addicted. Also look for eggplant *dengaku*, soft-shell crabs tempura, miso-marinated sea bass, white tuna, and *uni* sushi—in fact, any sushi here.

OTHER RECOMMENDATIONS An assortment of seafood tempura that puts all Maine fisherman's platters to shame, and for unregenerate carnivores, pork teriyaki and (seared) beef sushi. For bargain hunters, the bento boxes are first-rate.

SUMMARY AND COMMENTS The chefs here are among the most respected by their peers, and the restaurant's proximity to the Japanese Embassy is probably no accident; large tables of Japanese diners and even wedding parties often crowd the dining room. Should Murasaki be booked, there is a very likeable, though more predictable, Japanese restaurant just down the street called **Yosaku** that should please (4712 Wisconsin Ave. NW; ☎ 202-363-4453).

Nora ★★½

MODERN AMERICAN EXPENSIVE QUALITY ★★★½ VALUE ★★★

2132 Florida Ave. NW; ☎ 202-462-5143; noras.com
Dupont Circle/Adams Morgan

Reservations Recommended. **When to go** Anytime. **Entrée range** $31–$36; tasting menu, $75; vegetarian, $70. **Payment** VISA, MC, AMEX, personal checks. **Service rating** ★★★½. **Friendliness rating** ★★★★. **Metro** Dupont Circle. **Parking** Street, valet. **Bar** Full service. **Wine selection** Good. **Dress** Business, casual. **Disabled access** No. **Customers** Locals. **Hours** Monday–Thursday, 5:30–10 p.m.; Friday–Saturday, 5:30–10:30 p.m.; closed Sunday.

SETTING AND ATMOSPHERE A pretty corner town house with exposed brick walls and a gallery of handicrafts, quilt pieces, and faux-naïf art in the dining rooms; an enclosed greenhouse balcony in the rear is the prettiest area.

HOUSE SPECIALTIES The menu changes frequently, but look for sautéed calf's liver, salmon, and imaginative vegetarian platters.

SUMMARY AND COMMENTS Nora, neighborhood hangout of the Dupont Circle A and B lists, was haute organic before organic was chic: chef-owner Nora Pouillon was a prime mover in the slow-food and renewable-crops forces and founded the Chef's Collaborative, a national organic network. The back of the menu, which changes daily, lists the specific farms where the meat, produce, dairy products, and eggs—naturally low in cholesterol, according to the supplier—are raised. Nora's own all-edible flower and herb garden alongside the restaurant is indicative. The cost of acquiring such specialized ingredients is passed on, but not unreasonably. Nora was also ahead of the crowd by introducing alternative grains and pastas, and it was the first restaurant to make lentils that didn't taste like a Zen penance. Its only drawback is an odd tendency to weightiness—the meals sometimes feel heartier than they taste.

Obelisk ★ ★ ★ ½

ITALIAN   EXPENSIVE   QUALITY ★★★★½   VALUE ★★★★

2029 P St. NW; ☎ 202-872-1180   Dupont Circle/Adams Morgan

Reservations Required. **When to go** Anytime. **Entrée range** Prix fixe (five-course): $70, Sunday–Thursday; $75, Friday–Saturday. **Payment** VISA, MC. **Service rating** ★★★★. **Friendliness rating** ★★★½. **Metro** Dupont Circle. **Parking** Street, valet. **Bar** Full service. **Wine selection** Good. **Dress** Business, informal. **Disabled access** No. **Customers** Locals, businesspeople. **Hours** Tuesday–Saturday, 6–10 p.m.; closed Sunday–Monday.

SETTING AND ATMOSPHERE A cozy room that's elegant and good-humored; the customers, staff, and accoutrements—not only the room's floral centerpiece and silver chest but the astonishingly light breadsticks and bottles of grappa—work intimately elbow to elbow.

HOUSE SPECIALTIES Chef Peter Pastan has figured out the cure for overlong, overrich menus—he offers a fixed-price menu, four to five courses with only three or maybe four choices per course. Among typical antipasti: marinated anchovies and fennel; artichokes with goat cheese; caramel-soft onion and cheese tart; crostini; a thick soup; quail terrine; fresh *burrata* with olive oil and *fleur de sel;* polenta with Gorgonzola; potato or rice balls. The *primi* course is apt to be seafood, pasta (red pepper noodles with crab and pungent chive blossoms; gnocchi with pesto; wheat noodles with rabbit ragout), or soup; the *secondi,* veal (particularly tenderloin prepared with artichokes or chanterelles), fish (pompano with olives; black sea bass with artichokes; grilled shrimp with herb puree), or perhaps game birds or a mixed grill. After that comes a fine bit of cheese, with or without a dessert course following. Whatever the price—it varies with the daily menu—it's a quality bargain in this town.

SUMMARY AND COMMENTS Pastan's hand is so deft that he doesn't need to overdress anything; sauces are more like glazes, and pungent ingredients—olives, pine nuts, garlic, and greens—are perfectly proportioned to their dish. Above all, it shows the value of letting a chef who knows exactly what he likes do as he likes. Pastan, who also owns Pizzeria Paradiso next door and 2Amys, knows the value of a really good bread dough—more than one in fact.

Oceanaire Seafood Room ★★

SEAFOOD EXPENSIVE QUALITY ★★★ VALUE ★★½

1201 F St. NW; ☎ 202-347-BASS (2277); theoceanaire.com Downtown

Reservations Recommended. **When to go** Anytime. **Entrée range** $18.95–$51.95. **Payment** VISA, MC, AMEX, D. **Service rating** ★★★. **Friendliness rating** ★★★. **Metro** Metro Center. **Parking** Valet, pay lots. **Bar** Full service. **Wine selection** Very good. **Dress** Business, dressy casual. **Disabled access** Good. **Customers** Local businesspeople, boutique finance types, lobbyists. **Hours** Monday–Thursday, 11:30 a.m.–10 p.m.; Friday, 11:30 a.m.–11 p.m.; Saturday, 5–11 p.m.; Sunday, 5–9 p.m.

SETTING AND ATMOSPHERE Inspired by the great ocean liners of the 1930s, the room is full of curved surfaces, gleaming cherry- and etched-wood dividers, brass-studded leather booths, and heavy silver. The music is big band, the condiment tray includes oyster crackers, and the raw bar, with its leather-topped stools and great piles of oysters, is a trip in itself. So are the retro cocktails: sidecars, Singapore slings, cosmopolitans, and the like.

HOUSE SPECIALTIES Oysters (up to a dozen varieties a day); even more kinds of fresh fish flown in daily from all directions (Arctic char, Hawaiian spearfish, or North Atlantic cod), all available simply grilled; crab- and shrimp-stuffed gray sole; lobsters by the pound; a huge chilled seafood platter or, for fried seafood fans, the old-fashioned fisherman's platter. If the sushi-grade black grouper is available, head straight for it.

OTHER RECOMMENDATIONS Crab cakes; a "cocktail" of rock lobster–sized shrimp; Ipswich clam or oyster pan roast.

ENTERTAINMENT AND AMENITIES Relish tray of pickled herring, carrot sticks, olives, radishes, giant capers, and such. This even comes with oysters, making a dozen at the bar the steal meal of the new century. In fact, if we were only rating on the oyster bar, Oceanaire would be five stars.

SUMMARY AND COMMENTS This is the seafood chain of the 21st century, the logical outcome (given the ever-increasing size of the portions, steak houses, and expense accounts) of the hefty surf-versus-turf wars. Everything is huge, easily shared, and that goes double for desserts. (The retro look and retro extravagance partly explain some of the retro entrées, such as baked Alaska and oysters Rockefeller.) The asparagus is fat, the frills are a little excessive, and you definitely pay for the quality—even some chophouse veterans might blink at the $32-per-pound tag on the lobsters—and some of the staff can be showily informative, but for a seafood fan, it really is a luxury liner. And for those tired of only a swordfish option at the steak palace, it's funny to see the "not seafood" list hidden at the bottom: one chicken option, a filet mignon, or a cheeseburger.

Old Angler's Inn ★★

10801 MacArthur Blvd., Potomac; ☎ 301-299-9097; oldanglersinn.com
Maryland suburbs

Reservations Required. **When to go** Summer for brunch outside. **Entrée range** $24–$36. **Payment** VISA, MC, AMEX, JCB, CB. **Service rating** ★★★. **Friendliness rating** ★★★. **Metro** None nearby. **Parking** Free lot. **Bar** Full service. **Wine selection** Brief. **Dress** Dressy, business, jacket and tie. **Disabled access** No. **Customers** Locals. **Hours** *Brunch:* Sunday, 11 a.m.–2:30 p.m.; *Lunch:* Tuesday–Saturday, noon–3 p.m.; *Dinner:* Tuesday– Saturday, 6–10 p.m.; Sunday 5–9 p.m.; closed Monday.

SETTING AND ATMOSPHERE A beautiful, old-fashioned inn above the river, with a blazing fireplace in the parlor bar downstairs and a huddle of small dining rooms up a narrow, iron spiral staircase (and bathrooms out of the servants' quarters). The stone terrace and gazebo levels are open in good weather.

HOUSE SPECIALTIES The menu changes seasonally, but in cold weather anticipate game. Also look for squab or duck dishes, caviar (either as an ingredient or in classic service), and fresh fish.

OTHER RECOMMENDATIONS The lounge menu is lighter: salads, burgers, and such. In warm weather a second outdoor bar with live music and light fare (burgers, kebabs, bruschetta) has become popular.

SUMMARY AND COMMENTS This has always been a beautiful site, but its familiar weaknesses—haphazard service and hit-or-miss food—still threaten it occasionally, and the wine list's range doesn't keep up with its prices. The crowd, too, has changed a little: dressing down more, treating it more as a neighborhood restaurant than a special-occasion "inn"—which may be the direction it's headed. Newer versions of the menu are stronger on seafood and less "Continental."

Old Ebbitt Grill   ★★

675 15th St. NW; ☎ 202-347-4800; ebbitt.com   Downtown

Reservations Recommended. **When to go** Sunday brunch, after work for power-tripping. **Entrée range** $9–$24. **Payment** VISA, MC, AMEX, DC, D. **Service rating** ★★★. **Friendliness rating** ★★★. **Metro** Metro Center or McPherson Square. **Parking** Pay lots (validated after 6 p.m. and all day Sunday). **Bar** Full service. **Wine selection** Good; corkage fee, $15 per bottle. **Dress** Business, informal. **Disabled access** Very good (through G Street atrium). **Customers** Businesspeople, feds, locals, tourists. **Hours** *Breakfast:* Monday–Friday, 7:30–11 a.m.; *Brunch:* Saturday–Sunday, 8:30 a.m.–4 p.m.; *Lunch/Dinner:* Monday–Friday, 11 a.m.–midnight; Saturday–Sunday, 4 p.m.–midnight; *Late-night menu:* Daily, midnight–1 a.m.

SETTING AND ATMOSPHERE An updated old-boys' club, but with equal opportunity hospitality: a few horsey accoutrements (bridles, snaffles) in front, lots of greenery and etched-glass dividers in the main room, and a classic oyster bar around back off the atrium.

HOUSE SPECIALTIES Linguine with shrimp, basil, and fresh tomatoes; pork chops with homemade applesauce; black pepper–rubbed leg of lamb with papaya relish; old-fashioned pepper-pot beef; steamed mussels; smoked salmon (a company signature) and smoked bluefish when available. Annually, during the brief halibut season in Alaska, the Old Ebbitt and its Clyde's cousins have a halibut celebration that is a command performance for seafood lovers. For brunch, fat old-style French toast and corned beef hash.

SUMMARY AND COMMENTS This is one restaurant whose whole experience is somehow better than the food might indicate by itself. The Old Ebbitt—actually, the new Old Ebbitt for those who remember the fusty Back Bay–style original around the corner and its stuffed owls and scuffed bar rails—takes its White House neighborhood location seriously, but not too seriously. That is, it gives out pagers to patrons waiting for tables, but the staff democratically seats the ties and T-shirts side by side.

Old Glory ★★

BARBECUE   MODERATE   QUALITY ★★½   VALUE ★★★

3139 M St. NW; ☎ 202-337-3406; oldglorybbq.com Georgetown

Reservations Parties of six or more only, for lunch or weekday dinner. **When to go** Afternoon. **Entrée range** $9.95–$22.95. **Payment** VISA, MC, AMEX, DC, D. **Service rating** ★★½. **Friendliness rating** ★★★. **Metro** Foggy Bottom. **Parking** Pay lots, street. **Bar** Full service. **Wine selection** Minimal. **Dress** Casual, informal. **Disabled access** Good. **Customers** Locals, tourists. **Hours** *Brunch:* Sunday, 11 a.m.–3 p.m.; *Lunch/Dinner:* Monday–Thursday, 11:30 a.m.–2 a.m.; Friday–Saturday, 11:30 a.m.–3 a.m.; Sunday, 11 a.m.–2 a.m.; *Late-night menu:* Daily, 11:30 p.m. until closing.

SETTING AND ATMOSPHERE A chic and cheeky take on roadhouse diner decor with a sort of Six Flags theme: the state colors of Tennessee, Texas, Georgia, Kentucky, Kansas (which used to be Arkansas), and the Carolinas hang overhead, while each table is armed with bottles of six different barbecue sauces—mild, sweet, vinegary, multi-chilies, mustardy, tomatoey—named for the same seven states. A mix of old and new country and honky-tonk music plays on the PA. The bar stocks 80 brands of bourbon.

HOUSE SPECIALTIES Pork ribs or beef spareribs; pulled (shredded rather than chopped) pork shoulder; jerk-rubbed, roasted chicken; slow-smoked leg of lamb; smoked ham; various combinations or sandwich versions thereof. Daily specials often include pit-fired steaks or fresh seafood.

OTHER RECOMMENDATIONS Pit-grilled burgers with cheddar and smoked ham; house-smoked kielbasa; marinated and grilled vegetables; marinated, wood-grilled shrimp; a "smokeshack salad," like a barbecue sampler on greens. The sides include fried okra, collards, mac 'n' cheese, and so on.

ENTERTAINMENT AND AMENITIES The rooftop patio is one of only a few left in Georgetown, and very popular.

SUMMARY AND COMMENTS This trendy finger-lickers' spot is a good stop for families, particularly when it comes to the sort of Southern side dishes that rarely travel well. The biscuits are fine (the corn bread isn't), and the hoppin' John—black-eyed peas and rice—is better than authentic. It's neither mushy nor greasy.

Oval Room ★★★½

MODERN AMERICAN   MOD/EXP   QUALITY ★★★★   VALUE ★★★

800 Connecticut Ave. NW; ☎ 202-463-8700; ovalroom.com   Downtown

Reservations Recommended. **When to go** Anytime; pre-theater for a bargain. **Entrée range** $20–$36; six-course tasting menu, $85, $130 with wines. **Payment** VISA, MC, AMEX, DC. **Service rating** ★★★½. **Friendliness rating** ★★★. **Metro** Farragut North or McPherson Square. **Parking** Valet, pay lots. **Bar** Full service. **Wine selection** Very good. **Dress** Business, business casual, dressy. **Disabled access** Good. **Customers** Politicos, locals, businesspeople. **Hours** *Lunch:* Monday–Friday, 11:30 a.m.–3 p.m.; *Dinner:* Monday–Thursday, 5:30–10 p.m.; Friday–Saturday, 5:30–10:30 p.m.

SETTING AND ATMOSPHERE For many years, this White House–neighborhood restaurant was famous for an upscale Palm-style mural featuring DC power couples of various sorts (Frank Sinatra and Nancy Reagan, then-Senate wife Elizabeth Taylor, Henry Kissinger). It's now cool, sleek, and self-assured, with silvery-green walls and bright abstract paintings—but as it nearly always has been, it's a hangout for executive mansion staffers and watchers.

HOUSE SPECIALTIES Jerk-marinated foie gras with ginger jelly and gingerbread sauce; sweet and sour duck breast with turnips and duck confit "tots"; *kampachi* sashimi cured pastrami-style with tomato jam and spicy mustard; crispy pan-seared rockfish with peekytoe crab chowder and licorice; butter-poached lobster with spiced rum and braised endive or curry rice.

OTHER RECOMMENDATIONS Fat house-made whole wheat pasta with sliced matsutake mushrooms and shaved hazelnuts; and any of the seasonal soups: butternut squash soup with coffee and salted maple, white asparagus soup with Meyer lemon ravioli, or chilled cucumber soup with lime-jalapeno foam.

SUMMARY AND COMMENTS This is one of those places that couldn't have been called new American five years ago, but fusion and deconstruction has lost its food-freak quality and become, if not mainstream, at least not rare. Chef Tony Conte, who spent time with Jean-Georges Vongerichten before returning to DC (where he freshened up 701, which belongs to the same group), tosses in a few foams and culinary quotations: sake *kasu,* which is the leftover, semi-fermented rice dregs of the sake-brewing process, mixed with honey and soy sauce to lacquer duck breast Japanese-style instead of Chinese; foie gras brûlée could be a tip of the toque to Michel Richard's foie gras cappuccino; and the menthol puree with sliced veal loin sounds like a José Andrés experiment. Having the hazelnuts shaved onto the pasta at table-side, while occasionally cute for culinary's sake, can be very good indeed. The $35 pre-theater menu is available 5:30–6:30 p.m.

Oyamel ★★½

MEXICAN   MODERATE   QUALITY ★★★½   VALUE ★★★

401 Seventh St. NW; ☎ 202-628-1005; oyamel.com   Downtown

Reservations Recommended. **When to go** Late lunch, after hours, brunch. **Entrée range** $7.50–$11. **Payment** VISA, MC, AMEX, D, DC. **Service rating** ★★★½. **Friendliness rating** ★★½. **Metro** Foggy Bottom. **Parking** Valet at dinner, lot, street meters. **Bar** Full service. **Wine selection** Good. **Dress** Business Casual. **Disabled access** Good. **Customers** Locals, theatergoers, happy hour office workers. **Hours** *Brunch:* Saturday–Sunday, 11:30 a.m.–3 p.m.; *Lunch/ Dinner:* Sunday–Monday, 11:30 a.m.–10 p.m.; Tuesday–Thursday, 11:30 a.m.– 11:30 p.m.; Friday–Saturday, 11:30 a.m.–midnight.

SETTING AND ATMOSPHERE A sleek modern space in pumpkin and maize colors splashed with cool metal, with wide window views and hordes of butterflies soaring overhead; the smaller dining room is even cheerier, with murals of taco bar menus and platoons of beer bottles.

HOUSE SPECIALTIES Three-bite delights such as seared scallops with pumpkin-seed sauce; airy meatballs in chipotle sauce; braised short ribs with green mole; mussels in tequila; grilled skirt steak with grilled veggie salsa and pickled nopals; grilled half chicken with almond-chocolate-chile mole; huitlacoche tortilla; classic red snapper Veracruzano.

OTHER RECOMMENDATIONS Any of the half dozen seviches, especially the yellowtail kingfish with jalapenos and avocado; fried potatoes with almond-chocolate mole; tacos stuffed with suckling pig confit and pork rinds; chayote salad with crumbled double-cream cheese and peanuts; braised beef tongue and pasilla chilies; shredded duck confit and even Oaxacan-style with grasshoppers and tequila.

SUMMARY AND COMMENTS Don't make the mistake of thinking that this is Tex-Mex—the only similarity might be in the lengthy tequila list. (Just check some of the taco options, above.) This is regional Mexican, both traditional and reconsidered, from *nueva*-tapas king José Andrés. The menu is divided into small plates and large—all bright and bold—and on paper is inexpensive, but in these boisterous communal surroundings, it's almost impossible not to keep adding on those next tastes.

Palena ★★★½

MODERN AMERICAN   EXPENSIVE   QUALITY ★★★★½   VALUE ★★★

3529 Connecticut Ave. NW; ☎ 202-537-9250; palenarestaurant.com
Upper Northwest

Reservations Recommended. **When to go** Anytime; Mondays for homestyle. **Entrée range** $11–$31; three-course prix fixe, $58; four-course, $67; five-course, $76. **Payment** VISA, MC, AMEX, D, DC. **Service rating** ★★★½. **Friendliness rating** ★★★½. **Metro** Cleveland Park. **Parking** Street, pay lot. **Bar** Full service. **Wine selection** Good. **Dress** Business, casual. **Disabled access** Good. **Customers** Local up-and-comers; connected out-of-towners. **Hours** Monday–Saturday, 5:30–10 p.m.

SETTING AND ATMOSPHERE Deceptively low-key from the sidewalk, this is a long, lean, easy, cream-colored space leading back from a chic front lounge past a sort of genteel, faded drawing room to a subtle garden that provides pleasant light over the banquets. This is another dual-menu restaurant: the less formal front room (and in good weather, sidewalk café) is á la carte and lots of fun (try the Asian-spiced roast chicken, house-made hot dog, and the real cheeseburger on house-made brioche, one of the best $10 meals in town); dinner is either three, four, or five fixed-price courses (also available in the café). The newest is a $50-a-head menu for six or more; call 24 hours in advance.

HOUSE SPECIALTIES The menus are seasonal, and also market driven. Examples of the kitchen's work: daring and generally delightful presentations such as lobster and beet salad; guinea hen braised with Pomerol, rutabaga, and foie gras with Brussels sprouts; sea bass braised with Meyer lemon, fennel, and razor clams; rabbit rolled around a quail egg with greens stuffing; fresh sardine en croûte with artichokes, fennel, and olives; sautéed skate, pan-roasted lamb loin, or pig's ears en croquette (which points out the chef's unusually broad repertoire).

OTHER RECOMMENDATIONS Carefully tended duck breast or sometimes sweet-gamy squab; red snapper in a Thai-inflected broth; meaty crab salad; sausage with kabocha-stuffed ravioli topped with almonds and gingerbread crumbs; house-made pasta with duck ragout. All the bread, pasta, and cured meats are prepared in-house. And in this case, the desserts are the equal of the entrées.

SUMMARY AND COMMENTS Chef Frank Ruta ran the White House kitchen through three administrations and spent time at Obelisk and Yannick Cam's Provence—hence the free eclecticism of his combinations. Don't think dining in the café is lowbrow; check out the foie gras-oxtail-celeriac terrine or pappardelle with house-cured duck gizzards and wild mushrooms. (On Mondays, you can mix and match from both menus.)

Persimmon ★★½

MODERN AMERICAN   MODERATE   QUALITY ★★★★   VALUE ★★★

7003 Wisconsin Ave., Bethesda; ☎ 301-654-9860; persimmonrestaurant.com Maryland suburbs

Reservations Recommended. **When to go** Weeknights; brunch. **Entrée range** $25–$32. **Payment** VISA, MC, AMEX, DC, D. **Service rating** ★★½. **Friendliness rating** ★★★½. **Metro** Bethesda. **Parking** Street (metered), pay lots. **Bar** Beer and wine. **Wine selection** Small but good. **Dress** Business, informal. **Disabled access** Good. **Customers** Older suburban couples, young conservative professionals. **Hours** *Lunch:* Monday–Friday, 11:30 a.m.–2 p.m.; *Dinner:* Monday–Saturday, 5–10 p.m.; Sunday, 5–9 p.m.

SETTING AND ATMOSPHERE A real storefront, which has survived various incarnations with its pressed-tin ceiling remarkably intact, now exotically sponged to match its ruby-ripe name and given a "brocade" glitter with clusters of gilt-frame mirrors. The breadbasket comes with homemade pâté.

HOUSE SPECIALTIES Braised short ribs; wasabi-fried oysters; duck confit; crab cakes; pecan-crusted rack of lamb; pan-seared salmon with artichokes and mushrooms.

OTHER RECOMMENDATIONS That retro favorite, roast chicken with mashed potatoes and vegetable ragout; Atlantic bouillabaisse; lobster rolls.

SUMMARY AND COMMENTS This simple but smart eclectic American bistro—actually more mod/Med/fusion—might well fill the Georgetown-chic gap in Bethesda. Chef-owner Damian Salvatore is another Washington chef whose cooking gets more assured and more interesting all the time. And the kitchen (which seems to run more smoothly than in early years) is extremely presentation savvy. Another star seems imminent.

Poste Moderne Brasserie ★★★

MODERN AMERICAN EXPENSIVE QUALITY ★★★½ VALUE ★★★

555 Eighth St. NW (Hotel Monaco); ☎ 202-783-6060
postebrasserie.com Downtown

Reservations Recommended. **When to go** Happy hour; post-show; brunch. **Entrée range** $27–$30. **Payment** VISA, MC, AMEX, D, DC. **Service rating** ★★★½. **Friendliness rating** ★★½. **Metro** Gallery Place–Chinatown or Archives–Navy Memorial–Penn Quarter. **Parking** Valet at dinner, lot, street meters. **Bar** Full service. **Wine selection** Very good. **Dress** Business casual. **Disabled access** Good. **Customers** Local foodies, business entertainers. **Hours** *Brunch:* Saturday–Sunday, 8 a.m.–2 p.m.; *Breakfast:* Monday–Friday, 7–10 a.m.; *Lunch:* Monday–Friday, 11:30 a.m.–2:30 p.m.; *Dinner:* Monday–Thursday 5–10 p.m.; Friday–Saturday, 5–10:30 p.m.; Sunday, 5–9 p.m.

SETTING AND ATMOSPHERE This very modern complex with soaring cast-iron ceilings, pastel walls, and glass dividers stands out against all the renovated 18th-century architecture around it; the glass-enclosed patio bar extends the in-lounge bar with comfy seating (and wireless access) that lures lots of after-work professionals. It's also one of the greenest restaurants in town, using its own leftovers to compost the garden. In summer an outdoor grill provides daily noshing specials and occasionally a pig roast.

HOUSE SPECIALTIES Kobe steak tartare on brioche; red wine–braised rabbit; olive oil–poached halibut; classic pan-roasted chicken with crushed-pea ravioli; wild Alaskan salmon with salmon roe. This may be one of the best bar menus in town, too, complete with foie gras, steak tartare, slider-size croques monsieur and short-rib sandwiches, a smoked duck–sauerkraut Reuben, and great chicken liver pâté.

OTHER RECOMMENDATIONS At brunch the homemade doughnuts and iron-skillet steak and eggs are only surpassed by that smoked duck Reuben (the kitchen makes its own charcuterie).

SUMMARY AND COMMENTS Over the past several years, chef Rob Weyland has consistently raised the standards, emphasizing fresh and local ingredients and putting new twists on comfort foods such as chicken liver bruschetta, roast pork belly, and spit-roasted chicken. He also spotlights the garden with, for example, a tomato tasting menu. Take a break from museum-hopping here; the courtyard and glass-enclosed rear bar are great spots for a cocktail and snack. The bartenders here have the same attitude as Weyland; they like updating classic recipes with house-made ingredients. A pre-theater menu is available 5–6:30 p.m. for $35.

Proof ★★★½

MODERN AMERICAN   MOD/EXP   QUALITY ★★★★   VALUE ★★★

775 G St. NW; ☎ 202-737-7663; proofdc.com   Penn Quarter

Reservations Strongly recommended. **When to go** Lunch; anytime. **Entrée range** $24–$29; four-course tasting menu, $56, $91 with wines. **Payment** VISA, MC, AMEX, DC. **Service rating** ★★★. **Friendliness rating** ★★★. **Metro** Gallery Place–Chinatown. **Parking** Valet, pay lots. **Bar** Extensive. **Wine selection** Very extensive. **Dress** Business, business casual, dressy informal. **Disabled access** Good. **Customers** Locals, businesspeople, hip drinkers. **Hours** *Lunch:* Tuesday–Friday, 11:30 a.m.–2 p.m.; *Dinner:* Monday–Thursday, 5:30–10 p.m.; Friday–Saturday, 5–11 p.m.; Sunday, 5–9:30 p.m.; bar open until midnight Sunday, 1 a.m. Monday–Thursday, 2 a.m. Friday–Saturday.

SETTING AND ATMOSPHERE Despite its proximity to the Verizon Center sports arena, Proof takes its cue more from the arts and hip elements in the neighborhood, showing slides from the National Portrait Gallery as bar background (and using sculptures as bathroom vanities); mixing exposed brick walls with warm wood booths, stainless steel and copper details, and leather chairs; and playing jazz and Motown soundtracks.

HOUSE SPECIALTIES Chilled avocado-cucumber soup with shrimp relish and jalapenos; mushroom tempura; pan-roasted veal sweetbreads with pickled mushrooms, bacon, and poached egg; seared scallops with wild mushroom bread pudding; sherry-glazed sablefish with romesco sauce and chickpeas. The charcuterie list is part house-made (chicken liver terrine with smoked paprika, beef "pho terrine" with star anise), part first-quality imports (prosciutto San Daniele, Serrano ham).

OTHER RECOMMENDATIONS Roasted chicken breast stuffed with goat cheese and wild mushrooms; flatbread with smoked eggplant and chickpeas; spicy lamb meatballs. The cheese selection is as extensive as the charcuterie, and you can taste three for $13 or six for $25.

SUMMARY AND COMMENTS While at first it may seem that Proof has tackled too many trends at once—a bustling bar, a wine list suggested by the walls of bottles, elaborate charcuterie, an exposed glass-enclosed cheese bar, and so on—it manages to keep everything in check, and in balance (except, perhaps, for the elbow-to-elbow bustle and the din). The menu is actually designed to encourage sharing—a little charcuterie, some cheese, some appetizers—so the portions are pretty generous. The tub of Champagnes near the door is one hint to its viniferous tendencies; the vintage wine list, the top of which reaches five figures (though there are plenty of very affordable choices), is another. But the cocktails here are just as extensive, and deservedly popular. You can eat a lot here for a moderate amount, but the plates (and the drinks) can add up. The late night bar fare includes high-class cheesesteaks and subs. A $12 lunch special offers an entrée or sandwich and a glass of wine. The same restaurant group owns the "bubbling under" tapas-style Estadio on Logan Circle.

PS7's ★★★

MODERN AMERICAN　EXPENSIVE　QUALITY ★★★½　VALUE ★★★★

777 I St. NW; ☎ 202-742-8550; ps7restaurant.com　Penn Quarter

Reservations Recommended. **When to go** Late lunch; late night. **Entrée range** $22–$34. **Payment** VISA, MC, AMEX, DC. **Service rating** ★★½. **Friendliness rating** ★★★. **Metro** Gallery Place–Chinatown. **Parking** Pay lots, street. **Bar** Full service. **Wine selection** Good. **Dress** Casual, business, trendy informal. **Disabled access** Good. **Customers** Locals, area businesspeople. **Hours** *Lunch:* Monday–Friday, 11:30 a.m.–2:30 p.m.; Saturday, noon–2:30 p.m.; *Dinner:* Monday–Thursday, 5:30–9:45 p.m.; Friday–Saturday, 5:30–10:45 p.m.; bar with lounge menu open all afternoon.

SETTING AND ATMOSPHERE　Dark and rich in wood tones and deep browns, PS7's is, in those famous words, "like a box of chocolates." For a few years you didn't know exactly what you'd get, but these days you can be pretty sure you'll be happy.

HOUSE SPECIALTIES　Torchon of lobster with truffle gelée; mushroom "carpaccio" with truffle butter and poached quail egg; duck pho with foie gras or short ribs with foie gras baked in pastry; pork shank confit with pistachio-flavored beans; sablefish with miso foam; Arctic char with ginger and baby bok choy; various flatbreads "for the table" (half-price at happy hour).

OTHER RECOMMENDATIONS　A variety of burgers on the lounge menu, including the "buzzed" burger with coffee, porter butter, and wild mushrooms; and the chef's choice with house-cured bacon, fried egg, Gruyère, and marinated tomatoes. Also, house-made Chicago-style hot dogs; a Kobe steak 'n' cheese; tuna (tartare) sliders on Parker House rolls; crisp-fried mac 'n' cheese wrapped in bacon; and mussels and brats.

SUMMARY AND COMMENTS　Chef-owner Peter Smith, a local boy who came up through the ranks of several area restaurants, spent 11 years at Vidalia, which won a James Beard Award during his tenure. After shifting his focus a few times, he has settled into a light and often witty style that makes fun with, not of, regional American classics, and that plays with familiar combinations of flavors in unusual ways. He's also fond of scattering Asian flavorings about. It's not quite deconstructionism; it's closer to reconstructionism. But it's anything but light; check your cholesterol at the door.

Rasika ★★★★

INDIAN　MODERATE/EXPENSIVE　QUALITY ★★★★　VALUE ★★★

633 D St. NW; ☎ 202-637-1222; rasikarestaurant.com　Penn Quarter

Reservations Strongly recommended. **When to go** Anytime. **Entrée range** $10–$30; four-course tasting menu, $58 (vegetarian, $50), wine pairings, $35 additional; six-course tasting menu at chef's table, $75 (vegetarian, $60), wine pairings, $45 additional. **Payment** VISA, MC, AMEX, DC. **Service rating** ★★★½. **Friendliness rating** ★★★★. **Metro** Gallery Place–Chinatown, Archives–Navy Memorial–Penn Quarter, or Judiciary Square. **Parking** Valet, pay lots. **Bar** Full service. **Wine selection** Good. **Dress** Casual, business, informal. **Disabled access** Good. **Customers** Locals, area businesspeople, ethnic professionals. **Hours** *Lunch:* Monday–Friday, 11:30 a.m.–2:30 p.m.; Saturday, noon–2:30 p.m.; *Dinner:* Monday–Thursday, 5:30–10:30 p.m.; Friday, 5:30–10 p.m.; Saturday, 5–11 p.m.; bar open until 11 p.m. Monday–Thursday, midnight Friday–Saturday.

SETTING AND ATMOSPHERE Chef Vikram Sunderam has raised the concept of Indian fare to new heights and has made Rasika one of Washington's very best restaurants. The variety of seating areas—lounge, tables near the exposed kitchen, a communal table, and smaller private areas—and the rich spice colors (cinnabar red, paprika, saffron gold, and twinkling glass) give a nod to this modern Indian's eclectic take on classic ingredients.

HOUSE SPECIALTIES Duck breast with a cashew sauce; tandoori trout with malt vinegar; Bengal fish curry; black cod with fresh dill, honey, and star anise; lobster with cashews and caramelized onions; and chicken tikka masala (described, not entirely incorrectly, as "the national dish of England"). Bet on any seasonal special: curry-pasted skate in banana leaf; ground chestnut and fava bean patties; red chili mahimahi.

OTHER RECOMMENDATIONS Lamb with red chilies or caramelized onions and tomatoes; chicken *makhani* (what is often called butter chicken); tandoori salmon with cinnamon; lamb shank with cardamom and dark rum. Along with the many more familiar breads are versions scented with truffle oil and stuffed with goat cheese.

SUMMARY AND COMMENTS The menu is divided into three major sections: the *tawa* (griddle) dishes; *sigri* (barbecue), more like sautéing or wok-frying; and entrées, which include the curries, tandoori meats, stews, and so on. These go beyond the usual offerings (tandoori-grilled trout, mango shrimp with cashews and coriander, and grilled tuna with mustard and a sort of Indian succotash), so this is the place to try something new. The vegetarian options, which can be ordered in half portions as side dishes, are very good, especially the baby eggplant sauté, the shiitakes with peas and cashews, the okras with dry mango powder, and the cauliflower and green peas with ginger and cumin. Even the chutneys are fresh (in both senses): eggplant ginger, tomato-golden raisin, and the more familiar mango. Three of Rasika's sauces, including the incendiary Goan curry and the rich *makhani* sauce, are bottled for sale. A three-course $30 pre-theater menu is available weekdays 5:30–6:30 p.m. and Saturdays 5–6:30 p.m.

Ray's the Classics   ★★★

AMERICAN STEAK HOUSE   MODERATE   QUALITY ★★★★   VALUE ★★★

8606 Colesville Rd., Silver Spring; ☎ **301-588-7297; raystheclassics.com**
Maryland suburbs

Reservations Strongly recommended. **When to go** Early or late; anytime with a reservation. **Entrée range** $16–$34. **Payment** VISA, MC, AMEX, DC. **Service**

rating ★★★. **Friendliness rating** 4.5. **Metro** Silver Spring. **Parking** Pay lots, street. **Bar** Full service. **Wine selection** Very good. **Dress** Business, casual, informal. **Disabled access** Good. **Customers** Locals, foodies, businesspeople. **Hours** *Dinner:* Sunday–Friday, 5:30–10 p.m.; Saturday, 5–10 p.m.

SETTING AND ATMOSPHERE Oddly anonymous for a local-hero chain, though that's part of the shtick: bistro tables, white linens, red leatherette banquettes, wine crates, and Deco lettering.

HOUSE SPECIALTIES Hand-carved, corn-fed prime Angus and Hereford beef, butchered on-site, including a huge bone-in cowboy rib eye; prime New York strip with black peppercorn crush, brandy mushroom sauce, and blue cheese; Cajun blackened rib eye; signature crab royale; diver scallops wrapped in bacon. The bargains are the old-fashioned cuts, the $20 hanger steak and the $23 *coulotte* (eye of the New York strip) with mushroom ragout. Creamed spinach and mashed potatoes for the tables come free.

OTHER RECOMMENDATIONS Devilishly good eggs (steak tartare served like a deviled egg); smoked salmon with black and red roe; three cheese mac. You can get a Ray's Hell Burger here, but only in the bar (which is first-come, first-seated).

SUMMARY AND COMMENTS This profile is a sort of placeholder for a love-'em-or-hate-'em mini-chain of restaurants owned by local hero Michael Landrum, primarily because this is the only one that takes reservations. Landrum is a veteran of Morton's and Capital Grille, and the original Ray's the Steaks in Arlington was a sort of subversive, take-back-the-steaks movement that kept up the quality but sliced the prices. Ray's Hell Burger and Hell Burger Too in Arlington were launched by a burger that was made from the scraps of the steaks. Landrum has also promised to open Ray's the Game, offering venison, elk, ostrich, wild boar, and duck burgers; and a wine bar called, of course, Ray's the Glass. (Landrum has also landed one of Washington's best sommeliers, Mark Slater, longtime staff member of Citronelle.) The latest offshoot, Ray's the Steaks at East River (across the river in Anacostia), is what can only be called a soul-food kitchen crossed with a steak house. You get the idea: big beef, moderate prices, a lot of attitude. The menu specifies how certain steaks will be served and "requests" that the cowboy steak not be split.

Restaurant Eve ★★★★

MODERN AMERICAN   VERY EXPENSIVE   QUALITY ★★★★   VALUE ★★★

110 S Pitt St., Old Town Alexandria; ☎ 703-706-0450; restauranteve.com   Virginia suburbs

Reservations Strongly recommended. **When to go** Early for quiet, late for energy. **Entrée range** Bistro, $26–$38; Prix fixe: five-course, $110; seven-course, $125; nine-course, $150. **Payment** VISA, MC, AMEX, D, DC. **Service rating** ★★★★. **Friendliness rating** ★★★★. **Metro** King Street. **Parking** Public garage, street. **Bar** Full service and unusually inventive. **Wine selection** Top flight. **Dress** Business, nice casual. **Disabled access** Good. **Customers** Destination-no-issue foodies, Old

Town professionals, cocktail trendies, wine lovers, late-night indulgers. **Hours** *Lunch:* Monday–Friday, 11:30 a.m.–2:30 p.m.; *Dinner:* Monday–Saturday, 5:30–10 p.m. (bistro); 5:30–9:30 p.m. (tasting room); Monday–Thursday, 11:30 a.m.–11:30 p.m.; Friday–Saturday, 11:30 a.m.–12:30 a.m. (lounge).

SETTING AND ATMOSPHERE Simple, elegant, intimate-sized Federal town house with exposed brick, polished wood floors, fruit and veggie paintings for art, and soft background music. There are two menus, or rather three: à la carte or tasting in the form room, à la carte in the bistro.

HOUSE SPECIALTIES From the bistro menu: house-cured gravlax or mixed charcuterie; confit of house-cured pork belly with cranberry beans; pan-roasted sweetbreads with morels and ramps; potato-crusted halibut with fava beans and butter clams; homemade lemon-lobster ravioli and pan-roasted *branzino* with lobster meat; and luxurious bouillabaisse. Among the tasting-room dishes: marinated sardines niçoise; butter-poached lobster; duck foie gras en croûte with figs; sautéed squab with leg confit; Filipino-style slow-roasted Korobuta pork belly; and roasted Oregon wild matsutakes. Among the surprises: morsels of porcini beignet; deviled quail's egg with caviar; chilies in the steak tartare.

SUMMARY AND COMMENTS Chef Cathal Armstrong, one of *Food & Wine* magazine's top chefs of 2006, is Irish by nature, French by nurture—he spent his childhood summers in France—and has cooked Latino fusion, French bistro, modern Southern, and Italian. He also keeps a full-time charcuterie chef on duty. But this ambitious kitchen is all-American, heavy on Virginia produce, artisanal cheeses, organic meats, and sustainable seafood. Eve is actually two (or three) restaurants in one: the formal tasting room, the more casual but still upscale à la carte bistro, plus a very elegant fireside bar and lounge.

The tasting-room menu comprises five, seven, or nine courses: "Creation" (appetizers), "Ocean" (seafood), "Earth and Sky" (meats and poultry), "Age" (cheeses), and "Eden" (desserts). And that doesn't count the couple of preliminary treats. Sommelier and passionately creative bartender Todd Thrasher, who makes his own quinine tonic for gin and tonics, makes the bar a fun scene. In addition, Armstrong and manager-wife Meshelle have opened Eamonn's, a Dublin-style fish-and-chips shop named after their son (Eve is their daughter), at 728 King Street; the knock-and-enter retro "speakeasy" PX—in effect, Thrasher's own exhibition kitchen—above that; Virtue Feed & Grain, an Irish gastropub by the waterfront; and the wine bar/exhibition kitchen called Society Fair.

Sea Catch ★★

SEAFOOD   MODERATE   QUALITY ★★★   VALUE ★★½

1054 31st St. NW; ☎ 202-337-8855; seacatchrestaurant.com
Georgetown

Reservations Recommended. **When to go** Early. **Entrée range** $19–$42, market price higher. **Payment** VISA, MC, AMEX, D, DC. **Service rating** ★★★. **Friendliness rating** ★★½. **Metro** Foggy Bottom. **Parking** Validated for three hours. **Bar** Full service. **Wine selection** Good. **Dress** Casual, business. **Disabled access** Good. **Customers** Locals, businesspeople. **Hours** *Lunch:* Monday–Saturday, 11:30 a.m.–3 p.m.; *Dinner:* Monday–Saturday, 5:30–10 p.m.; closed Sunday.

SETTING AND ATMOSPHERE Sleekly elegant, with a white marble raw bar, polished-wood dining room with fireplace, and, in good weather, a balcony overlooking the Chesapeake & Ohio Canal.

HOUSE SPECIALTIES Jumbo lump crab cakes with vegetable slaw; poached lobster linguine; seared tuna au poivre; seafood gumbo; grilled rainbow trout, flounder, mahimahi, Chilean sea bass, swordfish, and always a whole fish of the day.

OTHER RECOMMENDATIONS A personal "off the menu" favorite is the lobster sashimi, which is only available when the raw bar isn't too busy. Fresh stone crab claws are another seasonal treat.

SUMMARY AND COMMENTS This is an underrated seafood establishment particularly ideal for people who suffer from fear of frying. Those who prefer the straighter stuff may order lobster steamed, grilled, broiled, baked, or poached; a variety of fresh fish (there is no freezer in the kitchen) brushed with oil and grilled; or an updated surf-and-turf of tenderloin and crab-stuffed mushrooms. Ask for guidance with the wine list—it's much more interesting than the usual fish grill's selection. However, for dedicated carnivores, the Thai-marinated roast chicken or the steaks are very dependable. There is also a steamed lobster and shellfish dinner for $42.

1789 ★★★½

| MODERN AMERICAN   EXPENSIVE   QUALITY ★★★★   VALUE ★★★ |

1226 36th St. NW; ☎ 202-965-1789; 1789restaurant.com   Georgetown

Reservations Recommended. **When to go** Anytime. **Entrée range** $10–$35. **Payment** VISA, MC, AMEX, D, DC. **Service rating** ★★★. **Friendliness rating** ★★★. **Metro** None nearby. **Parking** Valet. **Bar** Full service. **Wine selection** Good. **Dress** Jacket required. **Disabled access** Not accessible. **Customers** Locals, businesspeople, tourists. **Hours** Monday–Thursday, 6–10 p.m.; Friday, 6–11 p.m.; Saturday, 5:30–11 p.m.; Sunday, 5:30–10 p.m.

SETTING AND ATMOSPHERE A meticulously maintained Federal town house with blazing fireplaces, gaslight-style sconces, polished silver, and historical poise; a certain formality is implied rather than expressed. Coat and tie are still required, but there are a few extras on hand for the too-casual. The bar is small but very romantic.

HOUSE SPECIALTIES Bay scallops in any form; black cod; veal cheeks with preserved orange; cider-braised pork chop; roast loin of veal with chanterelles; crispy sweetbreads with grilled lobster; bluefin tuna confit with black-eyed peas; scallops with baby beets, blue foot mushrooms, and pistachios.

OTHER RECOMMENDATIONS Rack of lamb with pierogi, fennel, and fontina; torchon of foie gras with peaches, saffron honey, and vanilla salt.

SUMMARY AND COMMENTS This menu, inspired by seasonal availability, showcases regional game and seafood with care and respect. The kitchen aims to recreate and reclaim classic dishes—grilled quail, venison medallions, and rack of lamb—and update them rather than invent novel treatments. In other words, it's more of a culinary tender of the flame than an innovator, which suits its old-money clientele. However, in recent years, the kitchen has moved with increasing confidence into a middle ground, still classic but fresh. Chef Daniel Giusti, who began his career with the Clyde's group, previously worked at Restaurant Guy Savoy in Las Vegas. A $40 pre-theater menu (until 6:45 p.m.) as well as a post-theater version (after 9 p.m. weekdays and after 10 p.m. weekends) is available.

The Source ★★★★

MODERN AMERICAN   VERY EXPENSIVE   QUALITY ★★★½   VALUE ★★½

575 Pennsylvania Ave. NW (in the Newseum); ☎ 202-637-6100; wolfgangpuck.com Downtown

Reservations Recommended. **When to go** Early evening for leisurely dinner, brunch. **Entrée range** $26–$58. **Payment** VISA, MC, AMEX, D, DC. **Service rating** ★★★½. **Friendliness rating** ★★½. **Metro** Archives–Navy Memorial–Penn Quarter. **Parking** Valet at dinner, lot, street meters. **Bar** Full service. **Wine selection** Very good. **Dress** Business casual. **Disabled access** Good. **Customers** Local foodies, business entertainers. **Hours** *Lunch:* Monday–Friday, 11:30 a.m.–2 p.m.; *Dinner:* Monday–Thursday, 5:30–10 p.m.; Friday–Saturday, 5:30–11 p.m.

SETTING AND ATMOSPHERE Very cool and architecturally open, as befits a restaurant tucked into the corner of the glittering Newseum and with showcase views of the Mall; it's also appropriately video-shoot ready. Colors are pale and dividers are unobtrusive, with glass, steel beams, and see-through wine cellars. Even the plates are white, the better to showcase the multicolored, often multilayered dishes. The street-level lounge could be background for a cop show.

HOUSE SPECIALTIES Crispy suckling pig with black plum puree; lacquered duck with tender fat *chow fun* noodles; airy crab-shrimp *shumai*; prawns in a bright citrusy curry; steak au (Sichuan) poivre; meltingly tender Korean-flavored short ribs; really thick double-cut lamb chops with mint-coriander sauce; pan-fried pork-belly dumplings; a layering of roast pork, spinach, and honey-glazed pork belly.

OTHER RECOMMENDATIONS Lobster "spring roll" in daikon radish; surprisingly tangy General Tso's chicken wing; Kobe beef sliders on brioche; or wood-grilled pizzas (in the lounge). The complimentary nibble is a dish of stir-fried green beans with caramelized walnuts.

SUMMARY AND COMMENTS In one sense, this Wolfgang Puck–created spot suggests that the celebrity chef has been spending too much time in Las Vegas lately; it's extremely loud, beginning with the music. However, it's worth remembering that Puck was among the first to dabble in Pan-Asian fare (along with Jean-Georges Vongerichten, mentor of on-site chef Scott Drewno and Oval Room's Tony Conte, among others). The spicing here is bold, even brash, but unusually balanced. The Source has been hot since day one, and with reason.

Spice Xing ★★½

INDIAN INEXPENSIVE QUALITY ★★★½ VALUE ★★★★

100-B Gibbs St., Rockville (Rockville Town Center); ☎ 301-610-0303; spicexing.com Maryland suburbs

Reservations Suggested on weekends. **When to go** Anytime; lunch buffet. **Entrée range** $11.95–$16.95. **Payment** VISA, MC, AMEX, DC. **Service rating** ★★★★. **Friendliness rating** ★★★★. **Metro** Rockville. **Parking** Pay lots, street. **Bar** Full service. **Wine selection** Fair. **Dress** Casual, business, informal. **Disabled access** Good. **Customers** Locals, area businesspeople. **Hours** *Lunch:* Daily, 11:30 a.m.–2:30 p.m.; *Dinner:* Sunday–Thursday, 5:30–9:30 p.m.; Friday–Saturday, 5:30–10:30 p.m.

SETTING AND ATMOSPHERE Instead of going for the Raj posh, this goes for the posh spice, so to speak: with bright jewel-toned walls, photos of spices and veggies, gold silk swooshes overhead, and custom cocktails designed to bring in the young-professional crowd. (The Friday night sing-along is called curry-oke.) All-you-can-eat lunch buffet is $8.95 weekdays, $10.95 weekends. Weekday happy hours feature drink and appetizer specials.

HOUSE SPECIALTIES Lamb and apricot stew; okra with dry mango powder; Malabari chicken in coconut curry; jumbo butterflied barbecue shrimp (one at a time); Persian-style lamb and apricot stew; French-influenced seared scallops with anise.

OTHER RECOMMENDATIONS Roasted eggplant; mini-*dosas* with coconut chutney; chili-rubbed and vinegar-marinated tandoori chicken wings; vegetarian dishes.

SUMMARY AND COMMENTS Owner Sudhir Seth, who founded the slightly more formal Heritage India in Glover Park and still owns Passage to India in Bethesda, wanted this kitchen to go a little beyond the regional Indian curries and tandooris of his more formal kitchen. This one, as the name suggests, shows how Indian cuisine assimilated influences from other cuisines (such as Portuguese, Chinese, and French).

Sushi-Ko ★★★½

JAPANESE MODERATE QUALITY ★★★★½ VALUE ★★★★

2309 Wisconsin Ave. NW; ☎ 202-333-4187; sushikorestaurants.com Georgetown
5455 Wisconsin Ave., Chevy Chase, MD; ☎ 301-961-1644
Maryland suburbs

Reservations Recommended. **When to go** Anytime. **Entrée range** $11.50–$20. **Payment** VISA, MC, AMEX. **Service rating** ★★★. **Friendliness rating** ★★★. **Metro** Friendship Heights (Chevy Chase). **Parking** Street, valet (dinner only). **Bar** Full service. **Wine selection** Good, particularly French. **Dress** Business, casual. **Disabled access** No. **Customers** Locals, ethnics. **Hours** *Lunch:* Glover Park: Tuesday–Friday, noon–2:30 p.m.; Chevy Chase: Monday–Friday, noon–3 p.m.; *Dinner:* Glover Park: Monday–Thursday, 6–10:30 p.m.; Friday, 6–11 p.m.;

Saturday, 5:30–11 p.m.; Sunday, 5:30–10 p.m.; Chevy Chase: Monday–Thursday, Sunday, 5–10 p.m.; Saturday, 5–10:30 p.m.

SETTING AND ATMOSPHERE   The Glover Park original is a sleek twist on classic sushi-bar decor—carefully unfrilly—downstairs, and more obviously modern and non-tradition-bound, upstairs. The newer Chevy Chase site is even edgier, with an all-white sunken lounge, brilliant abstract paintings, and primary-colored walls.

HOUSE SPECIALTIES   First-quality sushi and sashimi; seasonal "small dishes," either traditional or contemporary, involving and often combining fish, both cooked and raw, with seaweeds, wild greens, grains, herbs, caviar, and sometimes unexpected American touches. If you want to see what the chef can do, order the six-course (starting at $65) tasting menu: you'll be full but not stuffed.

OTHER RECOMMENDATIONS   Sushi, especially seasonal dishes such as *ankimo* (monkfish liver) and *toro* (fatty tuna); broiled eel; soft-shell crabs; octopus salad; delicate dumplings; grilled fish. Spring for real wasabi ($4).

SUMMARY AND COMMENTS   Thanks to its unusual seasonal dishes, Sushi-Ko attracts a broad, generally knowledgeable, and fairly affluent crowd. (It originally opened in 1976, making it DC's oldest sushi bar.) This has made it possible for owner Daisuke Utagawa and his team to offer a more flexible style of cooking, both traditional and improvisational—that is, based on market availability and traditional seasonal factors. (The menu reflects the philosophy rather than the letter of classic Japanese cuisine.) However, while the "ordinary" sushi is reasonable, those specials can make dinner somewhat pricier than a meal at most other sushi bars, so don't waste it on someone who's happy with a grocery-store California roll. Utagawa is also intrigued with the notion of matching French wines and Japanese food, and offering higher-quality sakes.

Sushi Taro   ★★★★

JAPANESE   VERY EXPENSIVE   QUALITY ★★★★½   VALUE ★★★★½

1503 17th St. NW; ☎ 202-462-8999; sushitaro.com   Dupont Circle

Reservations Recommended. **When to go** Anytime for kaiseki; lunch. **Entrée range** Sushi, $4.95–$14.95; kaiseki menus, $58–$100. **Payment** VISA, MC, AMEX, DC. **Service rating** ★★★½. **Friendliness rating** ★★★★. **Metro** Dupont Circle. **Parking** Pay lot (validated at dinner), street. **Bar** Beer, wine, and sake. **Wine selection** Good (sake). **Dress** Casual, business, informal. **Disabled access** Good. **Customers** Locals, area businesspeople. **Hours** *Lunch:* Monday–Friday, 11:30 a.m.–2 p.m.; *Dinner:* Monday–Saturday, 5:30–10 p.m.

SETTING AND ATMOSPHERE   Classic blond wood, split bamboo shades, pastel accents, soothing instrumental music; with only 70 seats, this is one of the quieter sushi spots in town.

HOUSE SPECIALTIES   After decades as a dependable but traditional haven for Japanese businessmen and sushi lovers, owner Nobu Yamazaki (son of the founder and long a stalwart of classic sushi-making) has gone aggressively upmarket, staking out a series of fixed-price kaiseki menus. The traditional version, which leans on cooked dishes, is $80, with a small-portion option at $58. The sushi kaiseki, which alternates between sushi and cooked dishes, is $75 ($58). The *suppon* menu, which centers around soft-shell turtle, a classic imperial dish (also considered the Asian version of Viagra), is $80 per person for a minimum of two diners. And the surf and turf, which includes Wagyu shabu-shabu and a whole lobster (part sashimi, part tempura) is $100 a person for the table.

OTHER RECOMMENDATIONS Marinated baby octopus; *uni* (always fresh); salt-grilled mackerel (lunch); soba noodles. Specials might be don't-misses: grilled fish and fresh bamboo with sake rice; Alaskan king crab; wild prawns and winter melon with snapping turtle "jelly."

SUMMARY AND COMMENTS This is not Japanese for the tentative; the quality is too high to be playing with your money. (At these prices, asking $5.50 for fresh wasabi seems like ungilding the lily; on the other hand, on some days if you order a tasting menu, you get a bottle of sake or bargain drinks.) Also, to those accustomed to oversize, Americanized sushi, these correctly bite-sized pieces may seem small. Happy hour specials are available at the bar with discount sake, *maki* rolls, and appetizers.

Tabard Inn ★ ★ ½

MODERN AMERICAN   MODERATE   QUALITY ★★½   VALUE ★★★

1739 N St. NW; ☎ 202-331-8528; tabardinn.com

Dupont Circle/Adams Morgan

Reservations Strongly recommended. **When to go** Anytime; brunch. **Entrée range** $23–$35. **Payment** VISA, MC, AMEX, D, DC. **Service rating** ★★★. **Friendliness rating** ★★★★. **Metro** Farragut North or Dupont Circle. **Parking** Street. **Bar** Full service. **Wine selection** Good. **Dress** Business, informal. **Disabled access** No. **Customers** Businesspeople, locals. **Hours** *Breakfast:* Monday–Friday, 7–10 a.m.; Saturday, 8–9:45 a.m.; Sunday, 8–9:15 a.m.; *Brunch:* Saturday, 11 a.m.–2:30 p.m.; Sunday, 10:30 a.m.–2:30 p.m.; *Lunch:* Monday–Friday, 11:30 a.m.–2:30 p.m.; *Dinner:* Sunday–Thursday, 6–9:30 p.m.; Friday–Saturday, 6–10 p.m.

SETTING AND ATMOSPHERE This almost theatrically Old English jumble of rooms has a courtyard at its heart (as all good English country inns should), a series of small dining rooms with surprisingly lighthearted decor (a garden-path mural up the stairs, for example), and a wood-lined library with couches and a fireplace, ideal for a winter afternoon, cocktail before dinner, or after-dinner cordial.

HOUSE SPECIALTIES Exotic mushroom ragu; oyster gumbo; scallop and ricotta-stuffed squash blossoms; macadamia-crusted halibut; and a mixed grilled of quail, lamb, and house-made duck sausage.

OTHER RECOMMENDATIONS House-cured charcuterie; beef *tataki;* grilled octopus. Weekend brunch is a banquet, with choices that range from eggs Benedict with house-cured tasso ham, omelets, and waffles, to the hanger steak, seafood gumbo, grilled sardine salad niçoise, and the currently trendy lobster burger, Cubano sandwich, fish tacos, and oyster po'boys.

ENTERTAINMENT AND AMENITIES Live jazz Sunday nights.

SUMMARY AND COMMENTS Although it's currently in a sort of hearty eclectic bistro style, the Tabard has gone through a series of chefs, and so the tone and quality can be erratic; but currently it's going strong. At all times, it's a favorite spot for locals, thanks to its picturesque setting.

Taberna del Alabardero   ★★★

SPANISH   EXPENSIVE   QUALITY ★★★   VALUE ★★★

1776 I St. NW (entrance on 18th Street); ☎ 202-429-2200; alabardero.com   Downtown

Reservations Recommended. **When to go** Happy hour for tapas, lunch for fixed-price meals. **Entrée range** Lunch, $21–$31.50; dinner, $28.50–$36.50; five-course tasting menu, $75; seven-course menu, $90. **Payment** VISA, MC, AMEX, D, JCB, DC. **Service rating** ★★★★. **Friendliness rating** ★★★. **Metro** Farragut West or Farragut North. **Parking** Free next door. **Bar** Full service. **Wine selection** Very good. **Dress** Jacket and tie suggested. **Disabled access** Good. **Customers** Locals, embassy personnel, ethnics. **Hours** *Lunch:* Monday–Friday, 11:30 a.m.– 2:30 p.m.; *Dinner:* Monday–Thursday, 5:30–10:30 p.m.; Friday–Saturday, 5:30– 11 p.m.; closed Sunday.

SETTING AND ATMOSPHERE Lace curtains and velvet old-world elegance, with ornate moldings and a magnificent private chapellike room.

HOUSE SPECIALTIES Luscious lobster paella at night ($36.50 for two), as well as traditional and wild mushroom paellas; squid in its own ink; grilled duck foie gras with dried fruit; lamb sweetbreads; pork cheeks in two wine sauces; roast suckling pig; braised quail.

OTHER RECOMMENDATIONS Daily specials, particularly game, and at least a half dozen seafood specials daily; quail or pheasant; halibut with mussels. The five-course tasting menu is $75; add wine pairings for an additional $45. There is also a vegetarian menu.

SUMMARY AND COMMENTS This is a very old-world-style restaurant and quite dignified. One alternative is to dabble in Taberna's riches via the tapas menu, a selection of a dozen smaller-size dishes (and you can linger as long as you like). Taberna has whole legs of Iberico ham on-site, sliced paper-thin to order. There is also a list of a dozen sherries by the glass and red or white sangria. And it's also getting into the special-events trend, with wine dinners and imported guest chefs who show off Spanish regional cuisine with monkfish in saffron ragout and cream of pumpkin porcini soup. Every weekday 3–6 p.m., tapas and pitchers of sangria are half price.

Tako Grill   ★★★½

JAPANESE   INEXPENSIVE   QUALITY ★★★½   VALUE ★★★

7756 Wisconsin Ave., Bethesda; ☎ 301-652-7030; takogrill.com Maryland suburbs

Reservations Recommended. **When to go** Before 7 p.m. **Entrée range** $11–$32. **Payment** VISA, MC, AMEX. **Service rating** ★★★★. **Friendliness rating** ★★★.

Metro Bethesda or Medical Center. **Parking** Street, public garages, free lot (dinner only). **Bar** Beer and wine. **Wine selection** House. **Dress** Casual, informal. **Disabled access** Very good. **Customers** Locals, businesspeople. **Hours** *Lunch:* Monday–Friday, 11:30 a.m.–2 p.m.; Saturday, noon–3 p.m.; *Dinner:* Monday–Thursday, 5:30–10 p.m.; Friday–Saturday, 5:30–10:30 p.m.; Sunday, 5–9:30 p.m.

SETTING AND ATMOSPHERE   A cool, hip, very 21st-century-Tokyo room, a study in white, black, and scarlet, but with deft artistic touches (the flower arrangements) and almost hallucinatory script versions of Japanese verses hung on the walls. (The chefs, particularly the younger ones, are very Tokyo-stylish too—check out the bleached and reddened hair.) The adjoining sake bar (where you may order food as well) is particularly smart.

HOUSE SPECIALTIES   Soft-shell crab tempura fried and chopped into hand rolls; grilled teriyaki king salmon; broiled freshwater eel on rice. In the sushi bar: sushi assortment of tuna, yellowtail, salmon, flounder, crab stick, shrimp, seawater eel, and shad roe. Also grilled whole red snapper or rainbow trout; glazed grilled eel; tiny candied whole octopus.

SUMMARY AND COMMENTS   In addition to some of the best and freshest sushi and sashimi in the area, and a fairly extensive sake bar, Tako has a hot-stone grill called a *robata,* on which whole fish, large shrimp, and a variety of fresh vegetables are cooked. Weekday lunches are a business special: soup, salad, rice, and a daily entrée (such as orange roughy or chicken teriyaki), plus a California roll, for $9.50. And because several of the waitresses are vegetarian or vegan, Tako is especially well equipped to satisfy customers with special diets.

TenPenh   ★★½

PAN-ASIAN   MODERATE   QUALITY ★★½   VALUE ★★½

1001 Pennsylvania Ave. NW; ☎ 202-393-4500; tenpenh.com
Downtown

Reservations Recommended. **When to go** Early dinner or bar. **Entrée range** $15–$28, market price higher. **Payment** VISA, MC, AMEX, D, DC. **Service rating** ★★★★. **Friendliness rating** ★★★. **Metro** Federal Triangle or Archives–Navy Memorial–Penn Quarter. **Parking** Valet, pay lots. **Bar** Full service. **Wine selection** Very good. **Dress** Business, casual, dressy. **Disabled access** Very good. **Customers** Businesspeople, food trendies, media, pols. **Hours** *Lunch:* Monday–Friday, 11:30 a.m.–2:30 p.m.; *Dinner:* Monday–Thursday, 5:30–10:30 p.m.; Friday–Saturday, 5:30–11 p.m.; Sunday, 5:30–9:30 p.m.

SETTING AND ATMOSPHERE   This is a famous old law-firm office building, and it looks it outside, but inside, TenPenh is like one of those simple Asian jewelry boxes that opens to reveal the subdued glitter of saffron and gold silk, patinated Buddhas, hammered-bronze flatware, teak lamps, curio trays as dessert buffets, incense coils dangling from the ceiling, and bamboo place mats. And no wonder: the owners took a three-week shopping trip to Bangkok, Hong Kong, Ho Chi Minh City, Macao, and Singapore to hand-pick $40,000 worth of furnishings.

HOUSE SPECIALTIES Peking duck roll; curried lump crab cakes; Hong Kong–style crispy catfish; steamed shrimp–scallion dumplings; spicy wok-seared calamari; a sort of tempura-fried California roll (all appetizers); grilled yellowfin tuna; udon noodle shrimp stir-fry with coconut milk; five spice/pecan-crusted halibut with port-ginger sauce; the signature Chinese smoked lobster with crispy fried spinach; red Thai curry prawns with pineapple.

OTHER RECOMMENDATIONS Oysters with sake-pickled ginger granita (another signature); house-smoked salmon and wonton "napoleon"; panko-crusted soft-shell crab ravioli; crispy fish of the day.

ENTERTAINMENT AND AMENITIES Great amuses-bouche, such as the Thai-spiked gazpacho.

SUMMARY AND COMMENTS The executive chef here is Jeff Tunks, also of D.C. Coast, assisted by Clift Wharton; his fearless handling of seafood is at the heart of this fun-fare bazaar. Both the appetizer and entrée lists run the gamut from simple to ornate, mild to spicy, light to heavy; it's really like dining in Bangkok, where the outdoor stalls are like a giant progressive dinner, only sitting in a mogul's tent. The wine list is thoughtful, unusual, and affordable; there are several fine sakes to try as well.

Tosca   ★ ★ ★ ½

ITALIAN   EXPENSIVE   QUALITY ★ ★ ★ ★   VALUE ★ ★ ½

1112 F St. NW; ☎ 202-367-1990; toscadc.com   Downtown

Reservations Recommended. When to go Lunch, late dinner. Entrée range $12–$42. Payment VISA, MC, AMEX, D, DC. Service rating ★ ★ ★ ½. Friendliness rating ★ ★ ★ ½. Metro Metro Center or Gallery Place–Chinatown. Parking Street, pay lots, valet. Bar Full service. Wine selection Good. Dress Business, Friday casual. Disabled access Good. Customers Businesspeople (especially power-lunchers), pre-theater, young trendy. Hours *Lunch:* Monday–Friday, 11:30 a.m.–2:30 p.m.; *Dinner:* Monday–Thursday, 5:30–10:30 p.m.; Friday–Saturday, 5:30–11 p.m.

SETTING AND ATMOSPHERE This decor is so cool—stony shades of gray and beige with only splashes of cream and teal—that many people find it cold, but it does have the effect of making the dishes themselves seem more vivid. If you are hungry for sensation, go for the tasting menus.

HOUSE SPECIALTIES Lobster salad with pickled celeriac; heirloom tomato ravioli; black truffle–stuffed *tortelli* with porcini sauce; lobster risotto; ravioli stuffed with veal and prosciutto; fettuccine with wild boar ragout; thyme-crusted turbot *en brode;* hazelnut-crusted halibut with heirloom cauliflower.

OTHER RECOMMENDATIONS Free-range rack of lamb with braised artichokes in oxtail sauce; crab cake with sautéed green peas, caramelized Vidalia onions, and pine-nut sauce; fresh pea and house-made pork-sausage risotto; choice of fresh grilled seafood.

SUMMARY AND COMMENTS Even in this bustling restaurant neighborhood, Tosca, which takes a Northern Italian stance, stands out for both its silken fresh pastas, its deceptive simplicity, and its dedication to quality ingredients. (Who ever heard of heirloom cauliflower?) Tourists might want to try the fast preset lunch for $35. Happy hour means free focaccia and nibbles at the bar. There is also a chef's table in the kitchen, which is particularly popular, so reserve early and often.

Chef Massimo Fabrri is also co-owner and executive chef of a less formal restaurant called **Posto** in Logan Circle, with a wood-burning pizza oven and 24-bottle Enomatic wine system, and which has already gathered a celeb-name clientele.

Trummer's on Main ★★★

MODERN AMERICAN   EXPENSIVE   QUALITY ★★★   VALUE ★★★★

7134 Main St., Clifton; ☎ 703-266-1623; trummersonmain.com
Virginia suburbs

Reservations Recommended. **When to go** Anytime. **Entrée range** $24–$36; three-course brunch, $32. **Payment** VISA, MC, AMEX, DC. **Service rating ★★★★**. **Friendliness rating ★★★★**. **Metro** None nearby. **Parking** Free lot. **Bar** Full service. **Wine selection** Very good. **Dress** Casual, informal. **Disabled access** Good. **Customers** Locals, foodies, businesspeople. **Hours** *Brunch:* Sunday, 11 a.m.–2 p.m.; *Dinner:* Tuesday–Saturday, 5–10 p.m.

SETTING AND ATMOSPHERE   A big, bright barn of a place with expanses of glass, exposed beams, stacked stone and marble, and paintings and walls of warm pumpkin orange. The wide open bar (which has its own menu) leads to a pretty bar/wine cellar into two main dining areas, the Gallery Room and the Atrium (Winter Garden) with palm-frond fans overhead and a view of the waterfall.

HOUSE SPECIALTIES   Bacon-wrapped sturgeon with apples and Brussels sprouts leaves; grilled brisket of lamb with oyster mushrooms; a Thanksgiving-nostalgic 12-hour roasted and honey-glazed pork shoulder with sweet potatoes and pineapple confit. Brunch dishes include duck confit and oyster hash, steak and eggs, pork belly with biscuits, and shrimp and grits.

OTHER RECOMMENDATIONS   Tomato salad with tomato sorbet; seared foie gras with pureed black beans and hush puppies; goat cheese agnolotti; pumpkin soup with lump crab; potato salad with smoked salmon tartare; tomato water risotto.

SUMMARY AND COMMENTS   For a fairly young restaurant, this has a serious résumé list: chef Clayton Miller, formerly of French Laundry and Daniel, was one of *Food & Wine's* Best New Chefs in 2010; pastry chef Chris Ford hails from ChikaLicious Dessert Bar in New York; and sommelier Tyler Packwood used to deal for the Inn at Little Washington. Even owners Victoria (a local) and Stefan (former cocktail-meister at Bouley, and one to reckon with) Trummer are veterans of the Manhattan restaurant whirl. So you'll see a bit of New Americana (froths and reductions); a little updated Trad-American (braised veal with vermouth cream); and a lot of wahoo! (seared, that is, with compressed cucumbers and teriyaki pudding).

2941 ★★★★

MODERN AMERICAN VERY EXPENSIVE QUALITY ★★★ VALUE ★★★★

2941 Fairview Park Dr., Falls Church; ☎ 703-270-1500; 2941.com
Virginia suburbs

Reservations Suggested. **When to go** Lunch; three-course prix fixe, $24.
Entrée range $34–$42. **Payment** VISA, MC, AMEX, DC, D. **Service rating** ★★★.
Friendliness rating ★★★½. **Metro** None nearby. **Parking** Complimentary valet.
Bar Full service. **Wine selection** Very good. **Dress** Business, casual. **Disabled
access** Very good. **Customers** Businesspeople, locals, foodies, special occasion
diners. **Hours** *Lunch:* Monday–Friday, 11:30 a.m.–2 p.m.; *Dinner:* Monday–Friday,
5–9:30 p.m., Saturday, 5–10 p.m.; closed Sunday.

SETTING AND ATMOSPHERE Extremely handsome, despite its apparently staid
office building address: a three-story atrium, huge glass windows and
doors, and even glass sculptures, Zen-like fish ponds with stone patio,
lake, and fountain view to boot. Inside it sparkles with warm wood (and
sometimes firelight from the two hearths), "Floribbean" blue and tangerine linens, and a vast U-shaped marble bar.

HOUSE SPECIALTIES Lobster with baby clams; saddle and leg of rabbit with
foie gras–stuffed ravioli; sturgeon with truffled cauliflower; veal loin
and sweetbreads with artichokes; dorado with preserved lemons and
Kalamata olives; Wagyu sirloin and short rib with Guinness sauce;
cheese-stuffed chestnut ravioli. Chef Bernard Chemel is also playing
with sashimi-grade fish and sources his food from all around the globe.

SUMMARY AND COMMENTS Though not exactly accessible to car-less visitors,
this may be one of the most fun fine restaurants in Washington. Chemel
was for a long time at the helm of New York's Café Bouloud, and his
style shows it, with truffle-studded food, traditional in concept but not
in construction. Chemel offers tasting menus at lunch (three courses for
$24) as well as dinner (four for $58, six for $110, wine $30–$65).

Vidalia ★★★½

MODERN AMERICAN MODERATE QUALITY ★★★½ VALUE ★★★

1990 M St. NW; ☎ 202-659-1990; vidaliadc.com
Dupont Circle/Adams Morgan

Reservations Recommended. **When to go** Anytime. **Entrée range** $29–$36.
Payment VISA, MC, AMEX, D. **Service rating** ★★★★. **Friendliness rating** ★★★.
Metro Dupont Circle or Farragut North. **Parking** Street, garage, valet (din-
ner). **Bar** Full service. **Wine selection** Very good. **Dress** Business, dressy, casual.
Disabled access Good. **Customers** Businesspeople, locals, tourists. **Hours** *Lunch:*
Monday–Friday, 11:30 a.m.–2:30 p.m.; *Dinner:* Monday–Thursday, 5:30–9:30
p.m.; Friday–Saturday, 5:30–10 p.m.; Sunday, 5–9 p.m.; closed Sundays in July
and August except during Restaurant Week.

SETTING AND ATMOSPHERE Although this is actually a below-stairs establishment (disabled access is through the office lobby elevators), it's remarkably bright for a basement and as new–Southern Revival as *Southern*

Living magazine: buttermilk walls, elegant green and blue upholstery, and displays of silk magnolias and bold ceramics.

HOUSE SPECIALTIES Depending on the season, the flavors are hearty or light, but the juxtapositions are always intriguing, and generally with a sense of humor (a pork belly Reuben sandwich). Expect the likes of veal sweetbreads with a crisp lobster roll; veal cheeks over cheese grits; mustard seed–crusted tuna, pan-seared; pan-roasted monkfish with a crayfish-rice fritter, tasso ham, mâche salad, and étouffée sauce; a Provençal-style round-bone lamb steak with artichokes, olives, and pork rib chop pan-fried with sweet potato soufflé, smothered onions, turnip greens, fried apples, and lemon-orange whiskey sauce at dinner; and a spiced-pork sandwich slow-cooked and served open-face with toasted corn bread, avocado, and black bean–relish at lunch.

OTHER RECOMMENDATIONS Shrimp and grits is the signature dish; pan-roasted hen with fingerling potatoes; at lunchtime, cornmeal-crusted catfish with succotash of butter beans, pearl onions, corn, bacon, and dumpling squash; buttermilk-fried chicken breast with black-pepper gravy, fingerling potatoes, and green bean and butter pea salad.

ENTERTAINMENT AND AMENITIES Complimentary wine tastings, Tuesday, 5:30–7:30 p.m.; amuses-bouche such as mushroom bouillon.

SUMMARY AND COMMENTS Executive chef Jeff Buben picks native American ingredients based on flavor rather than tradition. Though the name is Southern, the menu is fused with broader tastes. The luxuriant sauces aren't necessarily low-cal, but they're served with a light touch.

Westend Bistro by Eric Ripert ★★★

MODERN AMERICAN   VERY EXPENSIVE   QUALITY ★★★½   VALUE ★★★

1190 22nd St. NW (Ritz-Carlton Hotel); ☎ 202-974-4900; westendbistrodc.com Downtown

Reservations Recommended. **When to go** Early evening, late lunch. **Entrée range** $14–$40. **Payment** VISA, MC, AMEX, D, DC. **Service rating** ★★★½. **Friendliness rating** ★★½. **Metro** Foggy Bottom. **Parking** Valet at dinner, lot, street meters. **Bar** Full service. **Wine selection** Very good. **Dress** Business casual. **Disabled access** Good. **Customers** Local foodies, business entertainers, Manhattan expats. **Hours** *Lunch:* Monday–Friday, 11:30 a.m.–2:30 p.m.; *Dinner:* Sunday–Thursday, 5:30–10 p.m.; Friday–Saturday, 5:30–11 p.m.

SETTING AND ATMOSPHERE At once plain and elegant, with pastel booths under rosy lights, long window views, and patio seating in good weather. The huge U-shaped bar is packed at all times; the boring house music seems out of place for such a highbrow location, however, and the whole place is loud.

HOUSE SPECIALTIES Meltingly tender skate wing in brown butter with braised endive; a "fish "burger" of ground striped bass with fennel and oven-roasted tomatoes; poached duck egg over asparagus and pea-vine salad; miniature pork pâté pies studded with Cognac-laced chicken livers; 24-hour-roasted pork shoulder; roast chicken for two. There is a six-course vegetarian menu as well (includes potato-wrapped sunchoke "bone marrow" and bamboo tempura), which can even be made vegan.

OTHER RECOMMENDATIONS Soft-shell crab with artichoke and quail egg; tuna carpaccio; unusually light fried calamari; Chesapeake seafood stew.

SUMMARY AND COMMENTS Ripert, the photogenic chef at New York's Le Bernardin, is on the marquee and makes occasional checks on the restaurant, but during its tenure in the nation's capitol, this New York import has picked up a bit of a Southern accent, with shrimp and grits and fried okra. Local ingredients are key.

Zaytinya ★ ★ ★ ½

MIDDLE EASTERN   MODERATE   QUALITY ★ ★ ★ ½   VALUE ★ ★ ★ ½

701 Ninth St. NW; ☎ 202-638-0800; zaytinya.com   Downtown

Reservations Available evenings. **When to go** Late lunch–early dinner; late dinner. **Entrée range** $6.50–$14.50. **Payment** VISA, MC, AMEX. **Service rating** ★ ★ ★ ½. **Friendliness rating** ★ ★ ★ ½. **Metro** Gallery Place–Chinatown or Metro Center. **Parking** Street, pay lot, valet at dinner ($11). **Bar** Full service. **Wine selection** Good. **Dress** Business, casual. **Disabled access** Good. **Customers** Businesspeople, foodies, young bar trendies, pre–MCI Center crowds. **Hours** Sunday–Monday, 11:30 a.m.–10 p.m.; Tuesday–Thursday, 11:30 a.m.–11:30 p.m.; Friday–Saturday, 11:30 a.m.–midnight.

SETTING AND ATMOSPHERE A big, high, and airy but almost modern art–minimalist room, white and angular with a soaring atrium-style ceiling, cut-through shelving walls stocked with lit candles, a long (and very busy) bar, half-hidden dining nooks and niches, a fireplace and a mezzanine overlooking the Manhattan-style communal table in the center of the main dining room. It's loud, it's lively, and it's delicious.

HOUSE SPECIALTIES Lamb mini-meatballs with cinnamon oil and dried fruit; prawns in smoked tomato sauce; feta- and tomato-stuffed quail with fingerling potatoes; crab cakes with shaved fennel; flaming cheese; fried eggplant; veal cheeks with chanterelle puree.

OTHER RECOMMENDATIONS Pork and orange-rind sausage; braised rabbit with lentils; fried mussels with pistachios; giant favas with tomatoes and red onions; meat-stuffed *manti* dumplings; squid in a variety of treatments.

SUMMARY AND COMMENTS Not Middle Eastern in the usual sense, Zaytinya—which means "olive oil" in Turkish—is specifically Eastern Mediterranean. *Bon Appétit* 2004 Chef of the Year José Andrés, racking up international stars with restaurants across the country, launched this smart and sophisticated Greek/Turkish/Lebanese meze restaurant in between his Spanish tapas kitchens (Jaleo) and the Cuban Oyamel.

PART SEVEN

SHOPPING *in* WASHINGTON

WE USED TO THINK THAT SHOPPING ON VACATION was mostly a matter of souvenir hunting, *until* Eve ran into a lawyer from her hometown of Nashville who had come to White Flint to shop on "Black Friday," the now ubiquitous day-after-Thanksgiving holiday shopping kickoff. And that was even before the era of the supermall; nowadays there are people who plan their vacations around the shopping, not the other way around.

So it should come as no surprise that Washington, which has one of the highest median household incomes in the nation, is situated at a crossroads of interstate highways, and is home to an increasingly diverse population, offers visitors a wide variety of shopping opportunities. You can quite literally shop until you drop—malled to death, so to speak. On weekend afternoons, roads leading to the shopping centers are as congested as commuter routes during rush hour. The stretch of I-95 south of Washington around the Potomac Mills factory outlet complex in Dale City—far and away the largest tourist draw in the state of Virginia—is nearly always backed up to a crawl in both directions. Arundel Mills, from the same folks who brought you Potomac Mills, bookends the metropolitan area on the north side of the interstate. And the Leesburg Corner Premium Outlets on Route 7 west of Tysons Corner—itself a substantial spread of shopping options—has transformed that formerly bucolic area into a name-brand bonanza.

MALL SHOPPING

SERIOUS BUYERS AND BARGAIN HUNTERS (as opposed to those recreational window shoppers) will have to decide up front whether they are willing to bring, rent, or borrow a car (or something even larger) or stick to using public transportation. Although we have repeatedly recommended against driving in Washington, if one of the big outlet malls is a major part of your itinerary—if you have a college-bound kid, an eye for fashion, or just a case of SAD (Seasonal Acquisitive Disorder)—that would be one reason to override us. (You can still park outside the Beltway, though.) In most cases there are hotels and motels built nearby for just that reason.

But unless you really plan to load up—and if so, you'll have to budget a lot of time as well as money—there are plenty of malls within the District of Columbia itself and in the surrounding suburbs that you can reach by public transportation. And in addition to the formal malls, Washington has a growing number of neighborhoods with intriguing boutiques and stores, often the same neighborhoods that have trendy restaurant and entertainment options, so you can really make a day, or night, of it.

THE SUPERMALLS

WASHINGTON MAY HAVE ITS MILLION-DOLLAR HOUSES, expense-account restaurants, and pricey private schools—and if you want to see its answer to Manhattan, see the section on the neighborhood of Chevy Chase, below—but it also has a surprising number of discount outlets. For every socialite flashing a full-price Coach bag or CEO tugging at his Saville Row shift cuffs, there are savvy shoppers quietly gloating over their discounted Lancôme cosmetics or their Polo dress shirts. (And these days, the ratio is probably a lot more uneven.) After all, the reason to buy good quality items is that they last a long time, so why not buy leather goods from one season back, when you're going to use it for ten years? And if you only want something for a year or so, then a quirky boutique or bargain basement is definitely the way to go.

Forty-five minutes south of Washington off I-95 is **Potomac Mills Mall** in Dale City, Virginia, one of the world's largest outlet malls with more than 220 shops (**www.simon.com/mall**). Potomac Mills draws more visitors each year than any other Virginia tourist attraction—about 24 million shoppers. It's nearly impossible to hit all of the stores, which include the popular Swedish home-furnishings store **IKEA** (which has its own cafeteria-style restaurant and Swedish food market) and outlets for **Bloomingdale's, BCBG Maxazria, Nordstrom Rack, Banana Republic, Under Armour, Benneton, Guess, Ann Taylor, H&M, Levi's, Movado, Nike, Saks Fifth Avenue OFF 5TH, Gap, Polo,** and **Brooks Brothers.** It also has an 18-screen multiplex including a 3-D IMAX screen.

Northeast of Washington, at the intersection of the Baltimore-Washington Parkway and Route 100 near Baltimore-Washington Airport (about two miles east of I-95), is **Arundel Mills** in Hanover, Maryland (**www.simon.com/mall**). More than a million square feet of name brands echo its Virginia sibling but trump them with entertainment options, including a 24-theater multiplex (with XD) that looks like an Egyptian pyramid, a **Medieval Times** restaurant/theater that looks like an 11th-century castle, and a full-sized **Bass Pro Shops Outdoor World,** with a sort of medieval archery lane, a waterfall, and a rock-climbing wall. Oh, and a **Dave & Buster's Sports Café** with billiards, arcade games, and shuffleboard.

To the west of town, perhaps 15 or 20 minutes past the various Tysons Corner malls (see below) at the intersection of Route 7 and the Route 15 Bypass, is the **Leesburg Corner Premium Outlets** (**www .premiumoutlets.com**), with many of those same names but also **Michael Kors, Charlotte Russe, Juicy Couture, Kate Spade,** and **True Religon.** And instead of IKEA, it offers **Crate & Barrel, Restoration Hardware, Williams-Sonoma,** and **Pottery Barn.**

> *unofficial* **TIP**
> Is 50 the new 10? Well, maybe not, but many of the stores at Leesburg Premium Outlets cut 10% off the bill for over-50 customers on Tuesdays. Make your plans accordingly.

CITY MALLS

THERE ARE A FEW MALLS WITHIN THE DISTRICT LIMITS. The **Shops at Georgetown Park** (**www.shopsatgeorgetownpark.com**), which shoulders around the intersection of M Street and Wisconsin Avenue, is the most extravagant in appearance, featuring a lush Victorian design and some popular retailers, including **Anthropologie, Express, H&M, Phat Dog, J. Crew,** and an **Intermix** boutique. It is also home, at least for the next few years, to the **National Pinball Museum,** a collection of nearly 900 vintage (the oldest dates to 1871) and modern arcade games collected by Silver Spring landscape architect David Silverman. However, the mall has never quite taken off—after three years' wrangling, Bloomingdale's pulled out of a deal to build a three-story anchor there, and the Ralph Lauren Polo boutique moved out of the mall to a free-standing space on the other side of Wisconsin Avenue next to its Rugby store/café—so empty storefronts are not unusual. It has had full-service restaurants come and go as well, but it still fronts the original **Clyde's of Georgetown** and houses a food court in the lower level. (In any case, you cannot go hungry in Georgetown; most of the spaces that aren't shops are restaurants.) In addition to those profiled in Part Six, there are also several restaurant/bars on the waterfront just south of the mall in Washington Harbor that are particularly attractive in summer.

> *unofficial* **TIP**
> Though a little walk from a Metro station, Georgetown Park is just one sector of the greater M Street shopping scene; see "Great Neighborhoods for Window-shopping," below.

Two Washington landmarks have been reborn as shopping centers: the **Old Post Office Pavilion** (near the Federal Triangle Metro station) and **Union Station,** which has its own subway stop.

The Post Office Pavilion, on Pennsylvania Avenue just north of the Smithsonian, is not a particularly upscale collection of shops—it's best for stocking up on souvenirs, connecting with various tour companies (see Part Five), or grabbing a fast bite—but its tower offers a view that rivals the Washington Monument but with a fraction of the waiting line.

On the other hand, Union Station, the city's restored train station on Massachusetts Avenue, is a grand Beaux Arts building whose two-story arcade of shops now boasts a number of familiar names, including some that travelers might find particularly useful in the case of mislaid luggage: **Ann Taylor, Chico's, Lucy Sportwear, Victoria's Secret, White House/Black Market, Swatch,** and **Jos. A. Bank,** along with several purveyors of ties, jewelry, and accessories. Be sure to wander into the East Hall, which has kiosks selling one-of-a-kind jewelry, ethnic Russian and Afrocentric crafts, and other merchandise.

In addition to a large and quite varied food court, Union Station has several sit-down restaurants, including a branch of the New York neo-soul food restaurant **B. Smith's,** a **Pizzeria Uno, Thunder Grill** for Southwestern and upscale Tex-Mex, **America** (a restaurant that once claimed to have dishes from all 50 states but which has trimmed its menu to recession-era levels), a couple of elevated-view bars, and a multiplex cinema.

There is also a 500,000-square-foot big-box shopping complex at 14th and Irving streets NW in Columbia Heights, called **DCUSA,** that houses a **Target, Bed Bath & Beyond, Staples, Best Buy, Mattress Discounters, Radio Shack,** and **Marshalls,** but it's not accessible by public transportation and is not in one of the major tourist neighborhoods. However, if you're in town because your teenager is going to college in Washington or just got an internship, this might be a good one-stop spot for you.

SUBURBAN MALLS

WASHINGTON'S MAJOR SUBURBAN MALLS are probably similar to what you have back home, though perhaps a little bigger; and most of them are easily accessible by subway. (The major exception, the multi-mall Tysons Corner area just west of the Beltway, will be accessible by subway by 2013, if construction goes as scheduled.)

White Flint Mall (**www.shopwhiteflint.com**), just north of the Beltway, does have a named subway stop, although it's a block or so from the mall itself; nevertheless, shuttle bus service is continuous. White Flint houses **Bloomingdale's, H&M, Pottery Barn, Galerie Ingrid Cooper, Williams-Sonoma, Coldwater Creek, Caché, Ann Taylor, Lord & Taylor, Coach, Nine West, Banana Republic, Bruno Cipriani, Gap, Talbots,** and branches of the **Cheesecake Factory** (which hands out silent "beepers" so you can keep shopping while waiting for a table), **Bertucci's,** and **P.F. Chang's** restaurant chains, plus a better-than-average food court, a five-screen multiplex, and a huge, two-story **Borders Books & Music. Dave & Buster's,** a vast virtual-reality sports/billiard parlor/bar/restaurant complex, dominates the top floor (see the profile on

unofficial **TIP**
Though both Mazza Gallerie and the Chevy Chase Pavilion shopping malls are (just) within the District boundaries, and with easy Metro access, they are really part of the larger border-crossing shopping district in Chevy Chase; see the description in "Great Neighborhoods", below.

page 391 in Part Eight: Entertainment and Nightlife). There is also a European-style day spa, **Roxsan,** which offers everything from hair-styling to ornately painted (real or false) nails, mud baths, massages, and all-natural facials. (Shop till you droop?)

Montgomery Mall (www.westfield.com/montgomery) does not have subway access, but for serious shoppers, it's only a ten-minute cab ride from **White Flint Mall;** or on weekdays you can catch a Ride-On bus at the White Flint Metro ($1.50 with SmarTrip, $1.70 cash). (There is even an Avis Rent-a-Car at the Sears Auto Center if you're *really* shopping.) Mongtomery Mall is anchored by **Nordstrom, Sears,** and **Macy's,** and includes **A|X Armani Exchange, Apple, Eileen Fisher, J. Crew, J. Jill, Michael Kors, Nine West, Under Armour, Banana Republic, Bebe, Gap, Crate & Barrel, Abercrombie & Fitch, Disney Store, Forever 21, BCBG Maxazria,** and **White House/Black Market.** It also has a large food court, a full-sized **Legal Sea Foods, Nordstom Café, Noodles & Company,** and **California Pizza Kitchen,** as well as facial and wellness centers (read: massage), and a newly renovated **three-screen multiplex** for bored kids.

The formerly dowdy **Wheaton Mall (www.westfield.com/wheaton)**, one block from the Wheaton Metro stop, is now a corporate sibling to Montgomery Mall and offers a very similar line-up of stores: **J.C. Penney, Macy's, Victoria's Secret, G by GUESS, Old Navy, Aeropostale, Lane Bryant, and Nine West,** plus its own Giant grocery store, food court, **Costco, Target,** six-screen multiplex, and **Bally Total Fitness club.**

One of the area's most elaborate malls is **The Fashion Centre at Pentagon City (www.simon.com/mall)** in Arlington, Virginia—a beautiful conservatory-style building filled with 170 primarily high-end retailers: **Macy's, Nordstrom, Coach, Club Monaco, Tourneau, Swarovski, Apple, Sephora, Williams-Sonoma, True Religion, A|X Armani Exchange, Michael Kors, Frederick's of Hollywood,** and **Lucky Brand Jeans.** The Fashion Centre also leads (through the parking garage) to a second fairly extensive shopping and restaurant complex called **Pentagon Row** (for listings, go to **www.pentagonrow.com/dining**). At the other end, the Fashion Centre connects to the Ritz-Carlton Hotel, where you can have a refreshing elegant meal at **Fahrenheit** or high tea in the lounge. The Pentagon City Metro stop, on the Blue Line, deposits shoppers right into the mall.

The **Tysons Corner** neighborhood, just west of the Beltway, is so large it helped inspire one of the catchphrases of 1990s development, the "edge city." Centered on the intersection of Chain Bridge Road/Route 123 and Leesburg Pike/Route 7, between the towns of Vienna and McLean, Tysons is actually a sort of Siamese twin supermall, with the original Tysons Corner Center hosting the slightly more predictable list of stores (**www.shoptysons.com**) and the Galleria at Tysons II (**www.shoptysonsgalleria.com**) having a few more upscale names. Between the two, Tysons Corner offers nearly 400 shops, including **Nordstrom, Lord & Taylor, Free People, 7 for All Mankind,**

Bloomingdale's, Saks Fifth Avenue, Crate & Barrel, Max Mara (the only one left in the area), the **Disney Store, Macy's, Chanel, Cartier, Brooks Brothers, BCBG Max Azria, H&M, Ed Hardy, Abercrombie & Fitch, Salvatore Ferragamo, Coach, Eileen Fisher, Ermenegildo Zegna, Hugo Boss, Burberry, Movado, Talbots,** and the **A|X Armani Express.** (The "Corner" fills up the neighborhood between Routes 7 and 123.) There are about 18 sit-down restaurants of various flavors, not to mention the snack shops and food court. And the Galleria adjoins the Ritz-Carlton Hotel, whose restaurants include **Michel,** the newest outpost of super-chef Michel Richard.

There is actually a third shopping section in Tysons Corner, seriously upscale, known as the **Shops at Fairfax Square** (☎ 703-448-1830), a sort of mini-mall of super-label shops, including **Tiffany & Co, Gucci, Hermès of Paris** (the only one around), **Pierre Deux, Louis Vuitton,** a branch of the custom bridal couturier **Priscilla of Boston,** and an **Elizabeth Arden Red Door Spa** that you can hit after working out at the **Equinox Fitness Center** and before refueling at **Morton's of Chicago** and the newest branch of **Chef Geoff's.**

FLEA MARKETS

WASHINGTON IS NOT A GREAT FLEA MARKET TOWN in the way that New York City is, but it does have a few dependable gatherings, and browsing flea markets for bargain-hunters is like grazing for foodies. The best, or at least the most likely to yield a fancy find, is the **Georgetown Flea Market** (in the parking lot of Hardy Middle School on Wisconsin Avenue between 34th and 35th streets NW), open Sundays 8 a.m. to 4 p.m. It's manned by more than 50 vendors of vintage jewelry, rugs, sterling, flatware, architectural remnants, and occasionally political memorabilia; *Lonesome Dove* author Larry McMurty, who used to run a second-hand bookstore in the neighborhood, based parts of his novel *Cadillac Jack* on the market (**www.georgetownfleamarket.com**).

Other regular gathering spots include the **Bethesda Flea Market** at 7155 Wisconsin Avenue, an easy walk from the Bethesda subway (open Wednesday, Friday, Saturday, and Sunday, 7 a.m. to 5 p.m.; **www.farmwomensmarket.com**); the **Flea Market at Eastern Market** in the Hines School at Seventh and C streets SE, near the Eastern Market Metro station (open Sundays from 10 a.m. to 5 p.m.; **www.easternmarket.net**); and **Friends in the Marketplace,** which calls itself the "funky fleamarket," near the New York Avenue–Florida Avenue–Galludet University Metro stop (open Saturdays and Sundays from 8 a.m. to 5 p.m.; **www.thefunkyfleamarket.com**). Both the Bethesda and Eastern Market gatherings have extra attractions; Bethesda sets up around the old **Montgomery Farm Women's Co-op,** so there's good food, flowers, and preserves inside; and the **Eastern Market,** itself a source of fine foods and produce of all sorts, also hosts a neighborhood crafts and street fair most Saturdays.

MUSEUM SHOPS

IF BY SHOPPING YOU MEAN THE SORT OF SOUVENIRS you take home for the family, you can combine your sightseeing with your shopping. Some of Washington's greatest finds are in its museum gift shops. A museum's orientation is a good guide to its shop's merchandise: prints, art-design ties, and art books fill the **National Gallery of Art** shop; model airplanes and other toys of flight are on sale at the **Air and Space Museum,** and so on. The largest Smithsonian shops are at the **Museum of American History,** which sells toys, clothing, musical instruments, and recordings from countries highlighted in the exhibits; although all the museums have some items reflecting the collection. Some of the hippest gifts are currently on view—sort of—at the **International Spy Museum,** which stocks video and CD copies of old spy TV shows and themes, pens disguised as lipsticks, disguises for people, and miniature cameras. The **National Museum of Crime & Punishment** has similar but somehow cheesier stuff, plus handcuffs. (There aren't many souvenirs at **Madame Tussauds** except the photos you take of yourself with the "celebrities.")

Some good museum shops are often overlooked by tourists. Among the best are the **National Building Museum** shop, which sells design-related books, jewelry, architecturally inspired greeting cards, and gadgets; the **Arts and Industries** shop, a pretty, Victorian setting stocked with Smithsonian reproductions; the **National Museum of the American Indian** with its turquoise and silver jewelry, Zuni pottery, hand carvings, and rugs; the **Textile Museum,** stocked with silk saris, shawls, brocade bags, and quilts; the **National Museum of Women in the Arts,** with umbrellas imprinted with Frida Kahlo self-portraits and some unusual jewelry; the **National Museum of African Art** shop, a bazaar filled with colorful cloth, Ethiopian crosses, and wooden ceremonial instruments such as hand drums and tambourines; the **Arthur M. Sackler Gallery** shop, with cases full of brass Buddhas, Chinese lacquerware, jade and jasper jewelry, feng shui kits, and porcelain; the **Renwick Gallery,** which stocks unusual art jewelry and handblown glass; the Shakespeare-lovers' treasure trove at **Folger Shakespeare Library** (everyone ought to have a Shakespeare bobblehead doll); and the newly expanded shop at the **John F. Kennedy Center for the Performing Arts,** stocked with videos, opera glasses, and other gifts for performing arts lovers.

The **Hillwood Museum** has jewelry and ornaments inspired by Marjorie Merriweather Post's famous collection of Fabergé eggs and Russian porcelains. The expanded shop at **Mount Vernon** offers reproductions of Martha's cookbook, George's key to the Bastille, and period china and silver patterns. The shop at the **National Geographic Museum** offers clothing, jewelry, toys, and accessories from all around the globe.

GREAT NEIGHBORHOODS
for WINDOW-SHOPPING

IF MALLS MAKE YOU CRAZY, Washington has a number of neighborhoods made for window-shopping—in the case of the Chevy Chase–Friendship Heights neighborhood, almost entirely *re*–made for window-shopping. In Georgetown, for instance, you might find yourself inspired to remake not just your personal environment, in the sense of your wardrobe, but your whole living style: bath, kitchen, living room art, garden statuary, etc. It's not that you can go far in any part of town without seeing shops, but here are some of the more interesting.

GEORGETOWN

GEORGETOWN MAY NOT BE THE AFTER-HOURS HOTSPOT it once was, but it has become the city's largest walk-and-shop district, spread out like a half-covered supermall with a combination of chains, independents, and boutique shops. And thanks to the crowds of teens and 20-somethings that hang out on Georgetown's sidewalks on weekends, many of these keep late hours for impulse shopping (which is, after all, another type of after-hours entertainment).

The central point of Georgetown's consumer compass is the intersection of M Street and Wisconsin Avenue NW, so you can use the **Banana Republic** or **United Colors of Benetton** stores there as locators. Or you could use the gilded dome of the PNC Bank at the same intersection as a marker; it's hard to miss.

Among the boutiques on M Street east of Wisconsin are **Hu's Shoes** and **Hu's Wear** for women, **Kate Spade, Lacoste, Cusp** (which hands out cupcakes and free fortunes to customers), **American Apparel, Diesel, White House/Black Market, Steve Madden, J. Crew, Brooks Brothers,** and **Barneys Co-op,** along with a branch of **Urban Outfitters** and a huge two-story collection of **Juicy Couture**. Inside **Georgetown Tobacco** is a treasure trove of elaborate hand-painted carnival masks elaborate enough to make the Phantom of the Opera change his tune, so to speak.

This is also the stretch where you can play around with cosmetics and spa products to your heart's content, thanks to the very hot French chain **Sephora** (where you can try on nearly a hundred brands of lipstick), **MAC, Blue Mercury** (which is both a spa and a Merle Norman for the new millennium, stocked with custom creams, exotic oils, and lipsticks named for film stars), the all-organic London-based **Lush,** and New York's revered **Kiehl's. (Aveda** loyalists may want to know that the animal-free pioneer has a huge spa/salon/store around the corner on Wisconsin Avenue NW as well.)

At the corner of 29th and M streets are two independent boutiques worth a look: **Bobbie Medlin,** who makes statement pieces, especially necklaces, of fine stone beads with antique Asian silver elements (and also showcases visual artists); and **Celine de Paris,** which ranges from high-end lingerie to high-heeled luxuries.

To the west of Wisconsin Avenue on M Street, facing the Shops at Georgetown Park, are more name-brand stores, including **Club Monaco, Aldo, BCBG, Coach, the North Face, Tommy Hilfiger, Intermix, H&M, Lululemon,** and both **True Religion** and **Lucky Jeans,** as well as one of the few U.S. outposts of the popular European **Camper Shoes** and the high-end Las Vegas designer-resales boutique **Annie Creamcheese,** where Paris is a customer, not a destination.

Anyone interested in home design and accessories should be sure to make it to the 3300 block of M Street and cruise **Cady's Alley,** which is actually a sort of hidden semi-mall (parts of it old warehouse buildings) housing high-end stores that may upend your concept of environment. Among stops worth making are the artisanal **Thos. Moser Cabinetmakers,** cutting-edge Italian design store **Contemporaria, Baker Furniture** (and its bargain-basement annex), **Ann Sacks** (striking stone and tile), the two-story Danish-sleek **BoConcept,** the to-die-for **Bulthaupt Kitchen Architecture,** the super-designer (Le Corbusier, Josep Hoffmann, Alvar Aalto, etc.) **M2L, Waterworks, Poggenpohl, B&B Italia, Illuminations, Gore Dean,** the house and garden antiques collection of local Martha Stewart **Deborah Gore Dean,** and   **Yves Delorme.** (If you get hungry, the fine Austrian-style **Leopold's Kafe & Konditorei** is right in the Alley's pedestrian intersection.) A large **CB2** store, an offshoot of Crate & Barrel, is scheduled to open in 2011 just west of Cady's Alley on M Street.

Wisconsin Avenue north of M Street has also become an open-air parade of boutiques, including one of two **Ralph Lauren** stores on the street (the other, a **Rugby** shop with its own café, is south of M Street), **Zara, Bebe, Sugar, Bel Mondo, Abercrombie & Fitch, Sassanova Shoes, Reiss, Vineyard Vines** (which is not a wine store but a seersucker-preppy men's store—think Martha's Vineyard), **Madewell** (a boutique-ish branch of J. Crew), the organic kids' clothing **Yiro, Ed Hardy, Max Studio, Urban Chic,** the **Apple Store,** and one of only five **Adidas Originals** retro-repro boutiques.

The south side of M Street between 28th and 30th streets NW in Georgetown offers an intriguing array of antiques and decorative arts, particularly rich in Art Deco, Art Nouveau, and moderne pieces. At **Justine Mehlman,** you'll find silver, pewter, and glass, and ceramic vases, the majority of them attributed, from Liberty Arts and Crafts and nouveau artists; plus fine Victorian rings and earrings, enamel, intaglio, and even Bakelite.

Grafix sells vintage posters—including Art Nouveau and Deco examples—antique hand-tinted maps, and collectible prints and illustration plates, while **Animation Sensations** has vintage Disney and Warner Bros. cels and drawings. A partitioned town house at

2918 M Street NW features **Michael Getz** and **Cherub Gallery** and offers a collection of works by such artists and studios as Tiffany, Lalique, Daum, and Icart. Here you can find heavy wrought irons, ivory-handled fish services and magnifying glasses, cream pitchers and perfume bottles, elegant cocktail shakers, nymphic candelabra, and ornate photo frames. In the back room is the largest collection of silver napkin rings outside a melting pot. Next door, **Keith Lipert** also displays art, glass, and silver, but its emphasis is on enamelware, ceramics, and heavier pieces.

Shops for antiques, both formal and more offbeat, stretch up Wisconsin toward Q Street, interspersed with collections of artwork, books, and shoes; see the section on "Antiques" in the "Specialty Shopping" section below.

ADAMS MORGAN AND MIDCITY

HISTORICALLY, ADAMS MORGAN AND U STREET NW—part of what local businesses are now promoting as the MidCity neighborhood—had little connection. Adams Morgan began as a wealthy white residential area adjoining the still-exclusive Kalorama, but with "white flight" to the suburbs after the unrest of the 1960s, emerged as the heart of the Hispanic and, a little later, the Ethiopian immigrant communities. Over the past 15 or 20 years, Adams Morgan has developed into an eclectic nightlife and dining area, especially along 18th Street NW.

U Street, at the north end of the Shaw neighborhood, was the closest thing Washington had to a Harlem, thanks to its national-circuit jazz and vaudeville venues and the proximity of Howard University. The restored Lincoln Theatre, where such black musical and theatrical luminaries as Duke Ellington and Cab Calloway performed, is one of the few surviving reminders of a time when U Street NW was known as the "Black Broadway." (Ben's Chili Bowl, the legendary diner in the same block, is nearly as old, having celebrated its 50th anniversary in 2008 with an all-star party.) An even more direct victim of the riots, Shaw only began to revive a decade ago, thanks partly to some timely government investment and partly to a wave of young couples willing to invest in renovating the old town houses as restaurants and small businesses.

In recent years, however, both these historically distinct and ethnically heterogeneous areas have become increasingly popular with younger, hip, and international crowds. Three particular developments—the increasing visibility of art galleries, performance venues, and trendy restaurants along 14th and U streets (which are to MidCity as Wisconsin Avenue and M Street are to Georgetown); the opening of the U Street–Cardozo subway station; and the commercial ripple effects from the construction of the Verizon Center sports and entertainment arena and the new Convention Center to the south—have increased that area's visibility and pedestrian traffic.

Although the two neighborhoods have not completely met in the middle, they are beginning to send out tendrils of development toward one another. But the characters of the two have changed a little: Adams Morgan is now more of a dining and nightlife area, while MidCity, which first attracted attention as a bar and restaurant frontier, has developed into a busy strip of popular stores, including a substantial number of home furnishings shops that cater to all kinds of style. Some shops have actually changed allegiance: **Meeps,** a popular vintage and designer boutique that spent 14 years as one of U Street's first destinations, has sidled west onto 18th Street. And while Adams Morgan used to be home to Washington's best Ethiopian restaurants, that title now belongs to the east end of MidCity.

In between Adams Morgan's melting pot of restaurants, which range from darkest pub to deepest trend, are African and Hispanic (and Rasta) clothing stores and craft boutiques, racks of Mexican wedding dresses, religious icons, and perhaps a medicinal herb or two.

The most intriguing boutique may be **Capitol Hemp,** which doesn't just stock clothes, shoes, and home furnishings made of hemp, it's actually constructed of hemp fiber board. **The Tibet Shop,** founded by a former Tibetan photographer and his journalist partner, stocks Himalayan jewelry, clothing, furnishings, crafts, and painted altars. **Toro Mata** is sort of its Peruvian counterpart, a South American Noah's Ark of animal art. **Tienda Santa Rosa** is a fairly high-end Latin women's boutique; **Oya's Mini-Bazaar** covers the African end.

unofficial **TIP**
Bargain hunters, note: Many Adams Morgan stores and restaurants celebrate the "First Tuesday" of the month with later hours and specials; MidCity vendors complement that with their own "Third Thursday" block party.

For architectural remnants—mantels, stained and leaded-glass windows, chandeliers, door handles, and columns—check out the **Brass Knob,** which has been a fixture on 18th Street for 30 years. The four-story **Skynear & Co.** trades in more modern, even luxurious hand-painted pillows, repro armoires and red China cabinets, whimsical wrought iron, acrobatic light fixtures, and the like. (The Gen-X, smart-set stuff is in the basement.) And **Beige** is more or less just what it sounds like, a haven for those who think "neutral" is a primary color.

MidCity, or the "new-U," is the commercial cluster that runs along U Street NW roughly between Ninth and 16th streets and down 14th Street from U south to P Street and Logan Circle.

On U Street from 16th to 14th are **Caramel,** which decorates its collection of designer clothing with local artists' works; **Stem,** which has a more Lower Manhattan basic-black style; **Junction,** a vintage couture boutique; **Legendary Beast,** which does up the jewelry end; and **Nana,** where you can find the vintage accessories to match. **Habitat** deals in primarily Mexican crafts and jewels, while the African and African American decorative arts and accessories, sculpture, and ceremonial items at **Zawadi Gallery** range from the fine and expensive to the simply attractive and affordable. **Millennium Decorative Arts** is one of several retro-kitsch shops in the area, mixing Waring blenders and fondue pots with the real retro stuff such as Eames chairs and a Saarinen pedestal table. **RCKNDY,** pronounced "rock candy," adheres to the sleek and minimal look—which extends to vowels, apparently. The style at **Goodwood,** on the other hand, is classic country—it specializes in 19th-century American furniture, including arts and crafts, andirons, and stained glass—but at Sunday-auction prices.

East of 14th along U Street is the neighborhood's restaurant and entertainment strip (and the African-American Civil War Museum and Memorial), but there are several notable stores. **Urban Essentials** puts the emphasis on "urban," as in cool: a soft-drink-machine-turned-CD rack, modular storage containers, mod-design home office pieces, etc. **4NX¢** handles both current and classic designer clothing. **Pink November** is yet another quality source for fun-funky urban styles ("cute" is the word most often used about it); and **Lettie Gooch** is an increasingly highly regarded eclectic boutique.

The rest of MidCity's shopping centers on 14th Street below U, including **Ruff & Ready,** an old-fashioned neighborhood antique store with great finds hidden all the way to the back, and which also offers increasingly desirable garden antiques; **Home Rule,** one of those shops that has figured out that home accessories don't have to be humorless; **Vastu,** a gallery of limited-edition furniture; **Hunted House,** which has a collection that could complete a *Mad Men* retro lounge; **Go Mama Go!,** which stocks smaller-scale but eye-catching ethnically flavored furnishings perfect for the chic dorm room, condo, or loft; **Well Built,** which promotes sustainable furniture (various icons tell you whether the piece is made using recycled material, low-energy techniques, etc.); and **Muléh,** filled with eco-friendly furnishings from Indonesia and the Philippines. Despite the vintage-sounding name (and some pieces are classic), **Reincarnations Furnishings** is the sort of stuff one dreams of finding at a European yard sale. **Room and Board** is almost its own big-box store, a four-story showcase for custom interiors from Arts and Crafts to midcentury modern and contemporary, also emphasizing green products. **Miss Pixie's Furnishings & Whatnot** is a treasure trove of fine and funky vintage furniture, whose owner frequently dispenses cookies or perhaps a winter warmer. **Rue 14** is a small designer boutique founded by a pair of New York corporate fashion veterans, while **Redeem** aims to bring swagger and a little urban grit to luxury casualwear.

The lower part of the 14th Street strip, closer to Logan Circle, is also home to a number of fine art galleries: See the section on art in "Specialty Shopping," below.

CHEVY CHASE

A HYBRID D.C.–MONTGOMERY COUNTY NEIGHBORHOOD—and a commercial gold mine—has been emerging around the Friendship

Heights Metro station for several years. At the intersection of Western and Wisconsin avenues, which also serves as the boundary between the two jurisdictions (and the multi-exit Friendship Heights Metro station), there are now two substantial shopping malls, a third complex anchored by **Bloomingdale's** and a huge **Whole Foods,** full-sized **Lord & Taylor, Saks Fifth Avenue,** and **Brooks Brothers stores**, several trendy new restaurants, a couple of mini shopping strips, and a one-block complex containing some of the most luxe shops in Washington.

On the southwest corner of Wisconsin and Western Avenues is **Mazza Gallerie** (www.mazzagallerie.com), home to **Neiman Marcus, Saks Fifth Avenue for Men, Ann Taylor, Williams-Sonoma,** and a branch of **Filene's Basement,** as well as a multiplex to park the kids. Across the street is the **Chevy Chase Pavilion** (www.ccpavilion.com), which has its own Embassy Suites Hotel (so you can certainly shop till you drop for a nap), as well as **J. Crew, Stein Mart, Ann Taylor Loft, CVS, Cheesecake Factory, Alpaca, World Market,** and **Pottery Barn.**

A little north of Mazza Gallerie on Wisconsin Avenue between Western and Willard avenues is the **Shops at Wisconsin Place,** which includes **Bloomie's, Anthropologie, BCBG Maxazria, Eileen Fisher, White House/Black Market, Talbots, Cole Haan, MAC,** and **Sephora.** Facing Bloomingdale's is **Saks Fifth Avenue,** with all its designer collections; and another block up Wisconsin past Willard Avenue are **Chico's, Banana Republic,** and **Gap. Brooks Brothers** is on the next corner.

But in the 5400 block of Wisconsin on the east side is a little bit of Manhattan in Maryland—specifically, the corner of Fifth Avenue and 55th Street—where the jewelry royalty cluster of **Tiffany & Co., Bulgari,** and **Cartier** are studded amid the complex called **The Collection at Chevy Chase,** across from the local direct-from-Africa diamond powerhouse **Mervis.** (Four other dependable local jewelers are also in the neighborhood, if you want to do some serious comparison shopping: **Boone & Son** and **Adam Keshesian,** as well as **Pampillonia** and **Chas Schwartz & Son** in Mazza Gallerie.)

Ralph Lauren's two-story boutique—which looks like a European prince's hunting lodge downstairs and a Hollywood starlet's bedroom upstairs—rubs structural shoulders in the Collection at Chevy Chase with **Jimmy Choo, Gucci, Piazza Sempione, Louis Vuitton, Christian Dior,** and **Barney's Co-Op.** And sharing a parking lot is **Saks-Jandel,** which is not affiliated with the Fifth Avenue brand but carries many Fifth Avenue designer names, and houses a Vera Wang Bridal Boutique.

Not surprisingly, there are also several trendy restaurants in this neighborhood where you can take a break (**Indique Heights, Lia's, Famoso, Sushi-Ko,** and the more midstream but dependable **Clyde's**) as well as a number of chain choices.

Hint: The Friendship Heights Metro station is on the Washington side, so if you have to take a taxicab from downtown instead of the subway, make sure the driver lets you out in D.C.—at Neiman

Marcus, for instance. Similarly, if you're coming from the north (and again, it's only one stop from the Bethesda Metro), ask to get off in Maryland; specify the Dior building.

DUPONT CIRCLE

ALTHOUGH IT IS PROBABLY BEST KNOWN for its restaurants and nightlife, Dupont Circle is also a draw for shoppers looking to enrich the mind—it's full of fine art galleries and bookstores. Most of these are on the north side of the circle: the art galleries are generally clustered along R Street in the two blocks just west of Connecticut Avenue leading you gently toward the **Phillips Collection** (see "Specialty Shopping," below). There is a branch of the New York–based **Best Cellars** at Q Street, which aims not only to educate people as to their personal wine tastes by categorizing the wines as "soft," "juicy," "big," etc., but also to find the best affordable—i.e., mostly under $15—wines available. So, if you need a last-minute hostess gift, drop by.

One of the first (founded in 1976) combination bookstore/cafés in the country is **Kramerbooks & Afterwords,** at Connecticut and Q streets, which stays open 24 hours a day on weekends; just off the circle at 20th and P streets you'll find **Second Story Books,** a terrific source for used books.

There are also specialty furniture stores. The **Chao Phraya Gallery,** on Columbia Road a half block east of Connecticut Avenue north of the Circle, showcases Chinese and Southeast Asian art and antiques. And west of the circle near the Phillips Collection is the **Geoffrey Diner Gallery,** which specializes in American and British Arts and Crafts furniture, including Stickley, Mission, Deco, and Nouveau pieces.

If you want to dress for success without financial stress, or you get a sudden invitation to an embassy dinner, look into **Secondi,** a very upscale consignment store on Connecticut Avenue near R Street. South of the circle, on Connecticut Avenue NW, between N and K streets, are several high-end retailers that cater to the law-and-lobby offices in the area, such as **Burberry, Hugo Boss, Brooks Brothers, Talbots, Betsy Fisher, Rizik's** (a prominent local women's shop), **Proper Topper** (a dashing haberdasher), and **Pampillonia Jewelers,** which specializes in antique and estate pieces. There is also a fine estate-jewelry shop called the **Tiny Jewel Box.** (There are some bargains around here, too, since not all office workers are partners just yet. Check out **Filene's Basement** if you find yourself short of a clean shirt.)

QUICK STOPS

MOST SHOPS ON CAPITOL HILL ARE IN AND AROUND the **Eastern Market** (see "Flea Markets," above) on Seventh Street between Pennsylvania and Independence avenues SE. There are also a few stores in the blocks around the Library of Congress side of the Capitol. Otherwise, the major shopping center of the hill is **Union Station,** which has dozens of name chains.

Although the Penn Quarter neighborhood is prime dining and museum territory, its shopping tends to be mostly on the supply side: chain clothing stores (**H&M, Forever 21, Urban Outfitters, Banana Republic, Ann Taylor, Filene's Basement, Jos. A. Bank**) and a few trendier spots (**Zara, Peruvian Connection, American Apparel,** and **Mia Gemma Jewelers**). You'll generally find them along F and G streets NW between Ninth and 14th.

In Old Town Alexandria, the main intersection for tourists is Washington Street (the George Washington Parkway) and King Street; the more interesting shops are along King Street. See the description of Old Town Alexandria in Part Five: Sightseeing, Tours, and Attractions for transportation suggestions.

In addition, many other town centers built around Metro stops— Ballston, Clarendon, Rockville, Bethesda, Crystal City—have shopping options.

SPECIALTY SHOPPING

Antiques

The stretch of Wisconsin Avenue north of M Street in Georgetown, where the clothing boutiques cluster, is also home to several notable antiques dealers, especially between O and Q streets. Among the best are **Carling Nichols,** which specializes in 18th and 19th century Chinese pieces; **John Rosselli & Associates,** a branch of the old-line New York firm; **David Bell, Darrell Dean, Blair House, Miller & Arney, Marston Luce, Cherry Antiques,** and the longtime Georgetown secret, **Christ Child Opportunity Shop,** where, on the second floor, you'll find silver and silver plate, china, paintings, and other cherishables on consignment from the best Georgetown homes. **Cotes Jardin,** which deals in 18th- and 19th-century French furniture, and **Antiques of Georgetown** are on O Street NW just west of Wisconsin Avenue; **Jean Pierre,** whose $1,000-and-under room is the antiques version of Filene's Basement, is on P at 21st Street.

One of the largest concentrations of antiques shops, about 80 in all, is on "**Antique Row**" in Kensington, Maryland, about four miles from the D.C. line. Most are along Howard Avenue, with smaller shops east of Connecticut Avenue and larger warehouses west of Connecticut. Whatever your era, country, or style, you're likely to find it here.

However, Washington's *very* serious antique-seekers get out of town—driving an hour or more to the countryside of Maryland, Virginia, West Virginia, or Pennsylvania for the bargains. Frederick, Maryland, about an hour north of Washington, is particularly popular with area antiquers. The biggest single group is at the 130-dealer **Emporium Antiques** on East

*un*official **TIP**
While some antiques neighborhoods thrive on weekends, Sundays are a toss-up; do a little web surfing before you hit the road.

Patrick Street in Frederick (**www.emporiumantiques.com**), though walking the Main Street neighborhood and the streets just off it will turn up scores of others.

Art

One of Washington's most concentrated selections of art for sale—traditional, modern, photographic, and ethnic—can be found around **Dupont Circle.** The best shops are centered on a sort of crossroads of Connecticut Avenue and R Street and spread a couple of blocks in each direction—especially R Street around 20th and 21st streets, where there are a dozen galleries within two blocks. Gallery openings are generally on the first Friday of the month, and the galleries stay open until 9. Among the most reliable names are **Marsha Mateyka,** who represents local art celebs Sam Gillian and Gene Davis, among many others; the brazenly younger-school **Meat Market,** which signs mostly younger artists, many of them recent graduates of the Corcoran School of Art; **Jane Haslem,** celebrating its 50th year; and the **Kathleen Ewing Gallery,** which largely promotes local photographers and artists (and has a soft spot for animal art).

As such things go (cyclically), rising rents and the continual upscaling of Penn Quarter have driven out many of the independent artists and co-ops that helped make the neighborhood between the National Portrait Gallery and Pennsylvania Avenue chic to begin with. Among the few that have held on are the **Gallery at Flashpoint,** at Ninth and G streets NW, and **Civilian Art Projects** (which often mounts shows with social or political agendas) on Seventh Street near K Street NW. There are sometimes exhibits at the **Goethe-Institut** on Seventh Street as well.

Many of the former downtown galleries have moved north to around 14th and P streets NW (Logan Circle), including the **Adamson Gallery,** one of Washington's premier print and photography sources; **Curator's Office, G Fine Art,** and the high-end folk art specialist **Hemphill Fine Arts,** all of which share an address at 1515 14th Street NW. Nearby are **Irvine Contemporary, Gallery Plan B,** and the Warhol Foundation–endowed **Transformer.**

One of the largest art "warehouses" is the **Torpedo Factory Art Center** near the waterfront in Old Town Alexandria, where 82 artist studios feature a range of media—painting, sculpture, jewelry, and more. You can buy their work or simply watch them create; an estimated 700,000 visitors a year do just that. It also houses a space for national touring exhibitions.

Bookstores

It's little wonder Washingtonians are well read: almost everywhere you look, there is a bookstore. There are general-interest chains such as **Books-a-Million, Barnes & Noble,** and **Borders,** but you can find those at home (indeed, you can scarcely escape them); the fun part is to dig out the small independent stores, many with narrow specialties such as art, travel, Russian literature, or, of course, politics.

Although *Lonesome Dove* author Larry McMurtry long ago closed down his Georgetown bookstore, several good ones remain in that neighborhood (with, inevitably, a three-story Barnes & Noble). **Bridge Street Books** at 2814 Pennsylvania Avenue NW specializes in political writing and social commentary from both sides—education presumably being the bridge—along with avant-garde criticism and poetry. **Bartleby's Books** on 29th Street just below M Street, whose name salutes Melville, has both general-interest secondhand books and seriously antiquarian volumes. **Presse Bookstore** on Wisconsin Avenue between Q and 33rd Street carries many translated versions of international publications as well as a wide range of subjects. **Books Used and Rare** at 1660 33rd Street NW is for the more serious browser of hard-to-find items. And sales of the liberal-arts standards at the **Lantern** at 3241 P Street NW benefit the Bryn Mawr College scholarship fund.

Georgetown is also home to one of the branches of **Big Planet Comics** (3145 Dumbarton Street NW), a major source for graphic novels and comics.

Even Washingtonians tend to overlook the **Government Printing Office Bookstore** at 710 North Capitol Street, which carries more than 15,000 books, pamphlets, and CD-ROMs, as well as books of photographs—and sometimes the real things—from the Library of Congress (**bookstore.gpo.gov**).

The highbrow-literary **Chapters,** which has become a staple of the reading and signing circuit for well-known authors, is currently an online resource only but hopes to reopen a true store in the Penn Quarter in 2011.

Politics & Prose specializes in psychology, politics, and the works of local authors—and hosts many of their book-signing parties (5015 Connecticut Avenue NW; **www.politics-prose.com**). And although it's not widely advertised, the **Shops at Mount Vernon** claims to have the largest bookstore in the country dedicated to George Washington.

Furniture and Home Furnishings

For one-neighborhood shopping, it has to be MidCity or Cady's Alley in Georgetown; see descriptions in "Great Neighborhoods," above.

Political Memorabilia

While you can easily find GOP or Demo-leaning T-shirts and buttons in most quickie souvenir shops, or on the street, for that matter, serious collectors might want to check out **Capitol Coin and Stamp** in Farragut Square at 1001 Connecticut Avenue NW, seventh floor (entrance on K Street between 17th and 18th streets; **www.capitolcoin.com**), which carries a broad selection of campaign items, posters, and ephemera.

Prints and Photography

In addition to the **Kathleen Ewing Gallery** in Dupont Circle and the **Adamson Gallery** and **Hemphill Fine Arts** in Logan Circle, all mentioned above, check out the **Govinda Gallery** at 34th Street and Prospect Place in Georgetown (**www.govindagallery.com**), which specializes in photographs of and by rock 'n' rollers, from Annie Leibovitz to onetime Beatle-turned-artist Stu Sutcliffe and his photographer girlfriend Astrid Kirchherr. For antique maps, botanical prints, and vintage cartoons, try the **Old Print Gallery,** also in Georgetown on 31st Street just north of M Street NW (**www.oldprintgallery.com**). As mentioned above, Georgetown's **Animation Sensations** carries prime Disney cels, but it also has great fine art and advertising prints and posters.

In the burgeoning nightlife district of Silver Spring on Georgia Avenue is the **Washington Printmakers Gallery** (**www.washingtonprint makers.com**), which continues to encourage traditional hand-pulled artists prints. And **Emma Mae Gallery** at 14th and U streets NW salutes MidCity's history as the "Black Broadway" with a collection of vintage black-and-white photos of jazz, R&B, and gospel musicians as well as civil rights leaders (**www.emmamaegallery.com**).

Records and CDs

Adams Morgan and MidCity are home to a number of good independent record and music stores catering to vinyl vets as well as cutting-edge, indie, and world music, among them **Crooked Beat Records** (2318 18th Street NW; **www.crookedbeat.com**); **Smash Records** (2314 18th Street NW); **Red Onion Records and Books** (18th and T Streets NW; **www.redonionrecordsandbooks.com**); and **Som Records** (1843 14th Street NW; **www.somrecordsdc.com**).

Vintage Clothing

The largest concentration of vintage boutiques is along U Street NW; see the section on Adams Morgan and MidCity neighborhood shopping, above. Other good options for high-end recyclables include **Secondi** in Dupont Circle (1702 Connecticut Avenue NW; **www.secondi .com**) and **Second Chance** in Bethesda (4920 Fairmont Avenue; **www .secondchanceboutiques.com**).

Watches

Washington's answer to Tourneau is **Alan Furman & Co.,** which offers up to 50% off on Rolex, Patek Philippe, and Cartier, plus diamond studs, pearl chokers, and the like (12250 Rockville Pike, second level; **www.alanfurman.com**).

Wine

As mentioned in the discussion of Dupont Circle above, Washington has a branch of the keep-it-simple, keep-it-affordable **Best Cellars** wine stores. At the other end of the spectrum, and not Metro-accessible, is **MacArthur Beverages** (4877 MacArthur Boulevard NW), which invests heavily and intelligently in wine futures and offers a strong catalog. Originally owned by the well-liked purveyor Addy Bassin, MacArthur is still often called "Bassin's" by Washington natives.

Writing Implements

Fahrney's Pens (1317 F Street NW; **www.fahrneyspens.com**) has all the write stuff: for more than 75 years, Fahrney's has sold beautiful pens by the likes of Gran von Faaber-Castell, Waterman, Mercedes, Cartier, and Montblanc. They even supplied Pope John Paul II a gold-trimmed white enamel fountain pen to match his regalia. And when it comes to repair, that's in the bloodline; the store was founded as a fountain pen repair shop before expanding into those newfangled ballpoints.

Bertram's Inkwell in White Flint Mall (**www.bertramsinkwell.com**) may not have quite the history that Fahrney's has, but their stock of fine fountain pens, some as ornate as jewelry, is almost its equal.

PART EIGHT

ENTERTAINMENT *and* NIGHTLIFE

WASHINGTON NIGHTLIFE:
More Than Lit-up Monuments

WASHINGTON AFTER-HOURS USED TO BE AN OXYMORON. Public transportation set its clock by the bureaucracy, commuters had too far to go (and come back the next morning) to stay out late, and big expense-account money was lavished on restaurants and buddy bars. Besides, Washingtonians suffered from a persistent cultural inferiority complex that had them running to buy tickets to see touring theatrical companies while not-so-benignly neglecting homegrown troupes.

Nowadays, though, the joke about "Washington after-hours" being an oxymoron is just that: a joke. It's not that there's too little nightlife around, it's that there's too much. Or too many. Washington is a hodgepodge of big-city bustlers, bureaucrats, yuppies, journalists, diplomats, artists, immigrants, CEOs, and college students; and every one of these groups is trying to create, and then integrate, their own circles. The fact that many overlap, and others evolve, means you can dabble in a little of everything.

Washington's legitimate theatrical community is underestimated but excellent; ballet, Broadway, and cabaret are almost constant presences, opera less so but increasingly frequent. And the theatrical community is booming, both physically and intellectually. The expansions of Signature Theatre, Studio Theatre, and most impressively, Arena Stage, plus the opening of the Music Center at Strathmore in Bethesda, the Clarice Smith Performing Arts Center at the University of Maryland, and other multispace performance venues, has established Washington as one of the country's premiere arts centers. (See more details on each of these and other theaters, below.)

At least some form of sports, from major- and minor-league teams to racetracks, are in season whatever time of year you visit (see "Spectator Sports" in Part Nine).

And nightclubs come in as many flavors as their patrons: dance halls, live-music venues, comedy showcases, salsa bars, specialty bars, sports bars, espresso bars, gay bars, singles scenes, and "second scenes" for re-entering singles. There are even a couple of strip joints around for boys'-night-out sentimentalists and plenty of brewpubs for beer connoisseurs.

Just in the last couple of years, a kind of nightclub renaissance has revitalized whole neighborhoods, a shift that has been particularly visible in areas that once were nearly deserted after rush hour, or at least after cocktail hour. The H Street NE neighborhood between 12th and 15th streets, famously hard-hit by riots after the assassination of Rev. Martin Luther King Jr. and left desolate for nearly 30 years thereafter, has become one of the most idiosyncratic and entertaining nightlife areas in town—nicknamed the **Atlas District** after the restored cinema–turned–multispace performing arts center. The **New U/MidCity** corridor centered on 14th and U streets NW has become a lively nightclub, restaurant, and small-theatre center.

unofficial **TIP**
Drinking and dining are major elements of nightlife culture these days; check the "best" lists and neighborhood descriptions in Part Six: Dining and Restaurants.

Since **Penn Quarter** is the hottest dining neighborhood in the area, it follows that many of the hippest restaurants also have the hottest bar scenes—and since the Verizon Center sports and concert arena is smack dab in the middle of it, it's also a late-night celeb-spotting scene. **Adams Morgan** may be less exuberant than the intentionally show-stopping Atlas District, but it still has a major after-dark vibe—more than one, actually. And even though **Georgetown** isn't much of a live-venue center anymore, it still has a few draws for night owls. See more information on all these areas below.

THE BIG-TICKET VENUES

WASHINGTON BOASTS MORE THAN A DOZEN major theatrical venues (not even counting the Kennedy Center's eight venues separately) and more than a half dozen smaller residential and repertory companies, plus university theaters, small special-interest venues, and itinerant troupes (see the Atlas Performing Arts Center, page 369). The "big six" are where national touring companies, classical musicians, and celebrity productions are most apt to show up, and they have the most complete facilities for handicapped patrons. They are also likely to be the most expensive, thanks to a citywide cycle of expansion. Washington is in a performing arts boom, and even the "small" theaters are rapidly getting bigger and better. And although it's on the other side of the Mall, the biggest new theatrical venue on the block—in both senses—is the recently reopened **Arena Stage** on the Southwest Waterfront; see description page 370.

Downtown Destinations

On any given night at the **Kennedy Center for the Performing Arts,** you might see the resident National Symphony Orchestra under Christoph Eschenbach or a visiting philharmonic in the 2,500-seat **Concert Hall,** a straight drama or classic farce in the 1,100-seat **Eisenhower Theater,** and a Broadway musical, kabuki spectacular, or premier cru ballet company in the 2,300-seat **Opera House**—that is, when the Washington Opera is not in residence. Three smaller venues, the **Terrace Theater, Theater Lab,** and the **KC Jazz Club,** share the third floor with the Roof Terrace restaurant (which has a nice view if you can get it). Philip Johnson's steeply canted and gracious Terrace Theater, a gift from the nation of Japan, houses experimental or cult-interest productions, specialty concerts, and showcases; in the Theater Lab, designed to accommodate the avant and cabaret, the semi-improvised murder farce *Shear Madness* is well into its third decade (and well past its 10,000th performance). KC Jazz Club (actually just the Terrace level gallery, tricked out cabaret style) is open only on weekends but hosts such first-rate groups as the Roy Hargrove Quintet, Chick Corea Trio, and one-chance double-bills such as Branford Marsalis Quartet with the Terrance Blanchard Quintet. And the **Family Theater** in the lobby level is one of the most up-to-date venues in the complex.

Most remarkable, however, is the Kennedy Center's gift to Washington music lovers: the always free **Millennium Stage,** which provides national and top local acts in an indoor venue at 6 p.m. every day of the year, holidays included. The Kennedy Center is at Virginia and New Hampshire avenues NW, next to the Watergate; the closest subway station is Foggy Bottom, and the center operates a free shuttle from the station. For tickets and information, call ☎ 202-467-4600 or visit **www.kennedy-center.org.**

The other major downtown venues are in or near Penn Quarter and accessible by several Metro stations.

unofficial **TIP**
If you are considering taking a (free) tour of the Kennedy Center, wait until later in the afternoon and stick around for the (also free) Millennium Stage show.

Among the most important tenants is the critically acclaimed **Washington Shakespeare Company,** which moved first from its beloved but cramped home at Folger Shakespeare Library on Capitol Hill into the 450-seat **Lansburgh Theatre** on Seventh Street NW, which it still operates; and then a few years ago it migrated to the new multivenue complex, the **Sidney Harman Center for the Arts,** around the corner on F Street. The new building houses jazz, dance, film, and chamber music, as well as theatrical productions; the Lansburgh houses smaller touring shows or quirkier Shakespeare Company productions. Each season WSC produces four classic plays, three by Shakespeare, and regularly corrals major stage and screen stars to headline. It also puts on another of Washington's best freebies: the annual Shakespeare "Free for All" series in late August and early September. The Harman Center is across from the Verizon Center and the Gallery Place–Chinatown Metro; the Lansburgh Theater is close to the Archives–Navy Memorial–Penn Quarter stops; for information call ☎ 202-547-1122; TTY ☎ 202-638-3863; **www.shakespearetheatre.org.**

The **National Theatre,** which was thoroughly, if a little showily, restored in Miami-bright pastels a few years ago, is a not-for-profit venue but managed by the Shubert Organization, which books its touring Broadway productions there and often uses it for pre-Broadway tryouts. It also offers assorted free programs—films in summer, Saturday morning family shows, and so on. The National is at 13th and Pennsylvania Avenue NW, near the Federal Triangle or Metro Center subway stop (**www.nationaltheatre.org**).

The **Warner Theatre,** which survived a two-year restoration marathon, is now a rococo delight, complete with a few special boxes with food service. Although it is emphasizing more legitimate theatrical bookings and musicals, and is booked by the national powerhouse Live Nation, it still occasionally harkens back to the days when it was one of the best small-concert venues for popular music (the Rolling Stones played a surprise show here in the late 1970s, and the reclusive Brian Wilson chose the Warner for his *Smile* and final *Pet Sounds* tours) or big-name comedians. The Warner is at 13th and E streets NW, near Federal Triangle or Metro Center (**www.warnertheatre.com**).

And **Ford's Theatre,** where the balcony box in which Abraham Lincoln was shot remains draped in black (and spectrally inhabited, according to rumor), has emerged from a $9-million renovation with state-of-the-art audiovisual equipment and a museum in the basement. Its annual production of *A Christmas Carol,* which ranges from very traditional to extremely spectral, is a local tradition; on 10th Street NW between E and F streets; Ford's is near several subway stops on various lines (**www.fordstheatre.org**).

(Double your fun: see profiles on the Kennedy Center, Ford's Theatre, and the Folger Shakespeare Library—which also still mounts Shakespeare plays in its Globe-inspired stage—in Part Five: Sightseeing Tips, Tours, and Attractions.)

It's not of the same size or profile, but the long-itinerant but undiminished "new theater" **Woolly Mammoth,** which has won more than two dozen Helen Hayes Awards, many for premiering new works, now has a 265-seat courtyard-style venue near the Lansburgh at Seventh and D streets NW (**www.woollymammoth.net**).

Midtown Draws

Several of Washington's smaller, special-interest theaters are clustered around the revitalized 14th Street NW Logan Circle neighborhood, not a long walk from Dupont Circle, and specialize in new and progressive works. Among the most important are **Studio Theatre** (14th and P streets NW; **www.studiotheatre.org**), which a few years ago unveiled a three-stage expansion that now allows it to mount more than one production at a time, from dramas to musicals. (When we say the theater scene in Washington is expanding, we're not joking.) The longtime home of the highly regarded but financially strapped Source Theatre Company at 14th and R has been bought by the Cultural Development Corporation. Although still called **Source Theatre,** it's now home to several small organizations, including the multi-ensemble (and partly educational) Washington Improv Theater and the Constellation Theatre Company, which specializes in visionary reconceptions of both cutting edge and global theater and many special series (**www.sourcedc.org**).

The **Keegan Theatre,** which specializes in American and Irish plays (recent productions have included Sam Shepherd's *Fool for Love* and Odets' *Golden Boy*), has grown from a basement ensemble to having a permanent home and producing a dozen shows a year, as well as hosting occasional concerts, at the 115-seat **Church Street Theatre** (1743 Church Street NW; **www.keegantheatre.com**). Among the more niche-specific troupes are the Jewish-interest **Theater J,** a few blocks away at 16th and Q streets NW (**www.washingtondcjcc.org/center-for-arts/theater-j**). The fantastically restored **Historic Sixth and I Street (NW) Synagogue** has begun offering a wider array of music and dance to its lectures and "Jewish yoga" (**www.sixthandi.org**). And the 35-year-old Spanish-language (with subtitles) **GALA Hispanic Theater** has moved into the beautifully restored 270-seat Tivoli Theater at 14th Street NW and Park Road, two blocks north of the Columbia Heights Metro (**www.galatheatre.org**).

A little north in the U Street corridor is the revitalized **Lincoln Theatre** (**www.thelincolntheatre.org**), across the street from the U Street–Cardozo/African-American War Memorial Metro. This 1922 beauty, once the heart of the "Black Broadway" neighborhood, now hosts a range of theatrical productions, musicals, comedic filmings, and concerts; it's also a major venue for the annual Duke Ellington Jazz Festival in June.

The itinerant **Ganymede Arts,** which stages acts for the GLBT community (and which has launched shows that moved to New York, San Francisco, and Los Angeles clubs), plays at various venues, mostly in MidCity; go to **www.ganymedearts.org** for information.

Though not directly accessible by Metro, it's an easy free shuttle (from Gallery Place–Chinatown or Union Station) to the multistage **Atlas Performing Arts Center,** which is also in a restored Deco movie theater. The Atlas acts as home base for the Washington Savoyards, a Gilbert & Sullivan troupe; the African Continuum Theatre; the Capital City Symphony; Joy of Motion Dance Theatre; and several other community arts groups as well as special series (14th and H streets NE; **www.atlasarts.org**). **Scena Theatre,** which originally specialized in European theater but has branched out to modern-day resettings (*Women of Troy* in Bosnia) and reenactments (Orson

Welles' *War of the Worlds*), appears at Atlas and the nearby H Street Playhouse at 13th and H streets.

On the Waterfront

The biggest excitement in recent years among Washington (and rising-theater) audiences has been the late-2010 opening of the soaring and state-of-the-art **Arena Stage,** formally known as the Arena Stage at the Mead Center for the American Theater. Already one of the country's most influential theatres, founded 60 years ago as a haven for the preservation and encouragement of American theatre, Arena has emerged from the 2½-year, $135-million reconstruction— renovation is too small a word—as a towering, 200,000-square-foot glass and concrete vessel, the largest performing arts center in the region since the Kennedy Center. In fact, it's expected to revitalize not only the theater scene but also the entire Southwest sector.

The new Arena, which is more than twice the size of the old, has three venues: the 500-seat Kreeger Theater; the 680-seat Fichandler Stage, which was the original Arena Stage and which has been embedded in the new design; and the completely new, 200-seat Kogod Cradle, which is like a chambered nautilus, with a semicircular entrance ramp on the outside and a slat-sided "basket" of a stage within. Designed by Bing Thom, the complex includes bars and an upscale café, catered by local star José Andrés; glass walls, wood columns, sloping floors, and long steel elbow bars; a rock garden, lots of overhung walkways, and mysterious vistas. The inaugural schedule included *Oklahoma,* the world premiere of *every tongue confess* with Phylicia Rashad, *Who's Afraid of Virginia Wolf?* (part of an Edward Albee festival), *The Arabian Nights,* visiting productions by Anna Deavere Smith and others, and a version of John Grisham's *A Time to Kill.*

Arena Stage is only a couple of blocks from the Waterfront-SEU Metro stop. The entire stretch of the waterfront in that area, with Arena as the catalyst, is being redeveloped with hotels and apartment buildings, a marina, and more transportation options. Visit **www .arenastage.org** for more information.

Superb Suburbanites

As dominant as the downtown theatrical scene may seem, the suburbs on all sides of the District have more opportunities than we can list here. Check the "Guide to the Lively Arts" in the *Washington Post* Friday "Weekend" section or the free *City Paper,* but here are some of the most important.

In the past few years, a number of impressive performance venues have been developed in the Maryland suburbs, several accessible by subway. One of the most popular is the **Music Center at Strathmore Hall** in North Bethesda, which, happily for tourists, has a dedicated pedestrian overpass from the Grosvenor-Strathmore Metro station. A beautiful blond-wood space with comfortable chairs and first-rate acoustics, it seats 2,000, books national classical and pop singers, visiting symphony orchestras, and folk and blues society shows. The original Strathmore Hall Mansion hosts tea-time concerts (harp, Japanese koto, violin) on Tuesdays and Wednesdays, as well as summertime concerts and family films on the lawn; it also has art galleries and crafts shows. For information on programming, visit **www.strathmore.org.**

In addition, Maryland now boasts one of the area's most impressive performance arts complexes. The **Clarice Smith Performing Arts Center,** on the College Park campus of the University of Maryland, offers almost as many venues as the Kennedy Center (and in several cases, even more cutting-edge acoustical and recording technology): the 1,100-seat **Dekelboum Concert Hall,** with its modern-Gothic arches and choral loft; the 180-seat **Dance Theatre;** the 650-seat proscenium **Kay Theatre;** the 300-seat **Gildenhorn Recital Hall;** the intimate 100-seat **Cafritz Foundation Theatre;** and the 200-seat "black box"–style **Kogod Theatre,** named for the same amazing arts patrons as the Kogod Cradle at Arena Stage and the courtyard at the National Portrait Gallery–Smithsonian American Art Museum. Smith Center offerings have ranged from Chinese opera and the Shanghai Traditional Orchestra to Phillip Glass and Laurie Anderson, Liz Lerman Dance Company and Merce Cunningham Dance Company, the Kronos Quartet, and the Abbey Theatre—plus productions featuring the university's dance, music, theater, and voice departments. It also plays host to several national and international competitions every year. The Clarice Smith Center is at University Boulevard and Stadium Drive in College Park; you can take the Green Line Metro to the College Park station and take one of two free shuttles to the Stamp Student Union or the campus "Circuit" shuttle directly to the complex (**www.claricesmithcenter.umd.edu**).

Closer in, and also Metro accessible, are the dual facilities of the **Round House Theatre,** one on East-West Highway across from the Bethesda Metro station and the other on Colesville Road near the Silver Spring Metro (**www.roundhousetheatre.org**). Round House mounts a mix of family, experimental, classic, and premiere productions.

Just a bit farther from the Bethesda Metro, a ten-minute walk at most, is one of the area's most important children's and family theaters, **Imagination Stage,** which began as a school for the performing arts and moved into its two-stage complex, with rehearsal and classroom space, in 2003 (**www.imaginationstage.org**).

And although they require cars (or friends), there are two other prominent venues in Montgomery County. The historic **Olney Theatre** on Route 108 in Olney, Maryland, started out in 1938 producing high-quality summer stock (over the years, its marquee has listed Tallulah Bankhead, Lillian Gish, Helen Hayes, Gloria Swanson, Jose Ferrer, Ian McKellan, John Carradine, Carol Channing, Hume Cronyn, and Jessica Tandy); now open year-round, it offers a variety of children's, classic, touring company, and musical productions, as well as free Shakespeare in the summer (**www.olneytheatre.org**). The increasingly popular **BlackRock Center for the Arts** in Germantown Town Center (**www.blackrockcenter.org**) also has three venues: a 210-seat main stage, a 130-seat dance theater, and an outdoor performance stage for theatrical productions, festivals, concerts, and outdoor family films. Among recent artists booked there are the Marcus Roberts Trio, Alvin Ailey II, the Baltimore Symphony Orchestra Chamber Players, Richie Havens, Janis Ian, top local acts the Nighthawks, Seldom Scene, and Mary Ann Redmond, and indie filmmakers and storytellers.

The Virginia suburbs are equally star-studded. In fact, two of Washington's most successful companies, **Signature Theatre** (which has sent several of its theatrical productions to Broadway) and the more idiosyncratic **Synetic Theater,** are based in Arlington. Signature, which moved into its stunning two-venue complex in the mini–new town Shirlington Village neighborhood in 2007, brings in national names for locally mounted productions of both established and avant-garde theater and cabaret (**www.sig-online.org**). Its collection of theatre awards, including the 2009 Regional Tony Award, is extensive.

Synetic (**www.synetictheater.org**) calls itself "D.C.'s premier physical theater," rethinking fantastic and often supernatural stories—Shakespeare, Edgar Allen Poe, *Don Quixote, King Arthur,* even *Dracula*—as intensely visual dream works mixing ballet, modern dance, artscapes, multimedia, and mime; its series of "Silent Shakespeare" plays are a local favorite. Its home stage is about a block from the Crystal City Metro.

unofficial **TIP**
Synetic's Crystal City home is Metro-friendly; however, it presents many of its shows at the Lansburgh Theatre downtown.

The newest multispace venue in Virginia is also in Arlington, just over the Potomac in Rosslyn, one block from the Rosslyn Metro station (and in nice weather, not an unpleasant stroll across the Key Bridge from Georgetown). The four-stage **Artsphere** campus (**www.arlingtonarts.org/venues**), which opened in late 2010, serves as home base to the National Chamber Ensemble and the Washington Shakespeare Company. It also includes several juried visual art and artisan galleries, a retail outlet of Fashion Fights Poverty, and a café.

The Center for the Arts at George Mason University in Fairfax is not Metro accessible, but if you have access to a car, it also hosts opera, jazz, popular music, symphony performances, and world music (**www.cfa.gmu.edu**).

SAVING AT THE BOX OFFICE

ALTHOUGH MANY OF THESE PROFESSIONAL PRODUCTIONS can be pricey and often sell out, there are ways to trim the ticket tab for less popular or longer-running shows. **Ticket Place,** operated by the Cultural Alliance of DC, sells half-price tickets (plus a service charge amounting to 17% of the face value) for same-day shows and concerts, and some half-price advance tickets as well. The office is in Penn Quarter at 407 Seventh Street NW; open Wednesday–Friday 11 a.m.–6 p.m., Saturday 10 a.m.–5 p.m., and Sunday noon–4 p.m. Cash, traveler's checks, and debit cards are accepted. You can also buy online at **www.culturecapitaltix.com.**

In addition, several venues offer their own discounts to students, seniors, patrons with disabilities, or patrons willing to stand or stand by. Arena Stage, for example, offers a variety of special opportunities: "Metro Mondays," when half-price tickets for the week's shows are available after noon on Mondays to patrons carrying a SmarTrip card or Metro pass; $15 tickets to patrons under 30, also on sale Mondays for the rest of the week; half-price "Hottix" available an hour before curtain, and so on. (Go to **www.arenastage.org/shows-tickets** for information.) Signature Theatre offers $30 "rush tickets" an hour before curtain when available; tickets are limited to two (**www.signature-theatre.org**).

The Kennedy Center also sells a limited number of same-day tickets at half price for some performances and offers half-price tickets for students, seniors, military, fixed-income families, and those with permanent disabilities. For more information call ☎ 202-467-4600. A limited number of standing-room passes at reduced prices and occasional returned seats may be available as well. Check the website (**www.kennedy-center.org**) or call the box office and just say you're from out of town and don't really know all the ins and outs of ticket pricing; operators will do the best they can for you.

Meantime, don't overlook the myriad freebies available, particularly during good weather. In addition to the several mentioned above—the Washington Shakespeare Company's "Free For All" series, the nightly Millennium Stage performances at the Kennedy Center, Olney Theater's free summer Shakespeare, the National Theater's Saturday mornings, and so on—several public sites frequently hold concerts of classical, jazz, pop, and folk music, and

*un*official **TIP**
The bottom line is, always ask if there's a way to boost your bottom line. What's to lose?

even some medieval consorts, among them the **Washington National Cathedral, National Gallery of Art**, and the **Library of Congress.** For information on these, plus the handful of smaller theaters and itinerant companies, check their websites, or the *Washington Post* on Friday or online.

If you are visiting in midsummer, be sure to investigate the Smithsonian's answer to the Millennium Stage (in terms of gifts to the public): the Folklife Festival, which for two weeks every year, around the last week of June and the first week of July (culminating around the Fourth of July fireworks celebration), celebrates a region of the United States and at least one foreign culture, complete with all-day live concerts and performances and food demonstrations.

There are several other outdoor music venues downtown, including the **Woodrow Wilson Plaza** at 13th and Pennsylvania Avenue NW, which hosts free noontime concerts all summer; **Freedom Plaza,** at 14th and Penn, is home to numerous free music and ethnic festivals during the summer; and of course the **Mall,** which is the site of many festivals during the year in addition to the Folklife Festival—notably on Memorial Day, the Fourth of July, and Labor Day, when the National Symphony Orchestra headlines family concerts.

Also in summertime, **Fort Dupont** in Anacostia hosts very popular free shows, primarily jazz and R&B, that draw up to 20,000 people; it's not completely Metro-accessible (about a mile from Benning Road), but there are buses.

Washington is also home to another type of free concerts: the **armed-services bands.** From about Memorial Day to Labor Day, ensembles from the four branches perform Monday, Tuesday, Wednesday, and Friday at 8 p.m. at the east or west side of the Capitol; Tuesday, Thursday, Friday, and Sunday at 8 p.m. at various locations; and Tuesday at 8 p.m. at the Navy Memorial at 7th and Pennsylvania Avenue NW. Programs include patriotic and martial numbers, country, jazz, pop, and some classical music; visit **www .army.mil/armyband** for details. You're welcome to bring picnic bags, but as with all National Park Service concerts, including the NSO concerts on the Mall, alcohol is not permitted.

LIVE MUSIC

ALTHOUGH IT ISN'T WIDELY ADVERTISED, Washington is a haven for music lovers of all types, from classical to college-radio rock, from hole-in-the-wall to the Washington Mall. Rock, revival, and pop will always move between the huge arenas and the mid-size ex-movie houses; multivenue centers need mid-draw acts to fill the smaller boxes. And credit for the rise in live-music clubs in the Washington area is split between the booming third-world community, used to later hours and different music styles; the large 20-something and 30-something population looking for entertainment close to home; the increasing number of those 20- and 30- and even 40-somethings who live in the suburbs and don't want to go downtown for a good time; the more assertive gay and faux-prole communities seeking accommodation; and the fair number of stubborn musicians and underground entrepreneurs who have established venues and support networks for themselves and one another.

The Larger Venues

As in many big cities, the downtown sports arenas do double duty as mega–rock concert venues, most often the 20,000-plus-seat **Verizon Center** downtown, home to the Washington Wizards and Mystics NBA and the Capitals NHL teams: that's where Lady Gaga, Springsteen, the Police, James Taylor, Carole King, and those orchestral music/light show spectaculars (Trans-Siberian Orchestra, *Star Wars* in concert) tend to land. Verizon Center has its own entrance from the Gallery Place–Chinatown Metro.

Both the **Washington Nationals ball park,** at the Navy Yard Metro, and the old **RFK Stadium,** at the Stadium-Armory stop, are still used as occasional entertainment venues—2010 dates included Billy Joel and Elton John and Dave Matthews at Nats Park, while Stone Temple Pilots and the Roots played RFK. (Nats Park is also used for live simulcasts of the Washington Opera.)

More progressive rock acts, which draw strong college and post-grad audiences, tend to be booked into college sports spaces such as George Washington University's **Smith Center** (**www.gwsports.com**), which usually goes through Ticketmaster; or Georgctown's **Gaston Hall.** National acts with mid-sized audiences— revived rockers (including John Mellencamp and the Allman Brothers), R&B, gospel, soul, and folk—are often booked into the **DAR Constitution Hall** alongside the Ellipse (**www .dar.org/conthall**). And the woods-lined, 3,700- seat **Carter-Barron Amphitheatre** in Rock Creek Park hosts occasional gospel, soul, jazz, ska, and R&B concerts in summer, along with some family film nights (**www.nps.gov/rocr**). Several other smaller city parks, museums, and federal building plazas stage concerts that are listed in the newspapers.

unofficial **TIP**
If you intend to book tickets for big shows, don't be confused by the name of the website; make sure you are dealing directly with the venue whenever possible, not being shuffled onto a secondhand or resale site which will cost more.

Outside the city are several of the area's largest venues, which are not so easily accessible but are regular summer commutes for Washingtonians. Perhaps the most sentimentally popular outdoor commercial venue, and the only one with any sort of Metro connection, is the most sophisticated of them: **Wolf Trap Farm Park** off Route 7 in Vienna, Virginia, which offers almost nightly entertainment—pop, country, jazz and R&B, MOR (middle-of-the-road) rock, and even ballet and Broadway musical tours—and picnicking under the stars during the summer at its **Filene Center** amphitheater. (It also operates a full-service restaurant.) During the winter season, Wolf Trap shifts to its small (220 seats) but acoustically great Barns, literally two rebuilt barns, where it books everything from small opera to the Flying Karamazov Brothers to Chris Smither; it also books some of the best local acts (☎ 877-WOLF-TRAP; **www.wolftrap.org**). On summer nights, the Metro operates a $3 round-trip shuttle service from the West Falls Church station to the Filene Center, but watch your watch: the return shuttle leaves either 20 minutes after the final curtain or at 11 p.m., whichever is earlier, in order to ensure that riders don't miss the Metro.

The gorilla in the Beltway backyard is **Jiffy Lube Live** pavilion just off Interstate 66 outside Manassas, Virginia. It's a surprisingly attractive amphitheater with 10,000 covered seats and lawn seating for another 15,000 people (and parking lots and hillsides for tailgates and picnicking). Operated by Live Nation, the largest promoter in the country, it books the full range of big-ticket acts: Pearl Jam, Tom Petty, Iron Maiden, Rush, Kiss, Taylor Swift, Tim McGraw, Kanye West, and Mary J. Blige. And since Live Nation and Ticketmaster are now one, it's all booked through the Ticketmaster network (☎ 202-397-SEAT; **www.livenation.com**)

Merriweather Post Pavilion in Columbia, Maryland, which also mixes under-cover and lawn seating, has the busiest pop-rock outdoor arena and mixes old-favorite rock and pop tours with younger-draw and cult acts (Virgin Fest, Lilith Fair, Phish, Snoop Dogg, Norah Jones, Kid Rock, Incubus, Béla Fleck). Keep in mind it is some distance from Washington and can only be reached by car. It's more likely to have some of the multiact, all-day festivals, and partly for that reason, perhaps, has upgraded its concessions. MPP, which is booked by locally based IMP Productions, which also owns the prestigious 9:30 club, sells tickets through Ticketfly (☎ 877-4FLYTIX; **www.ticketfly.com**).

The 10,000-seat **Patriot Center** college arena at George Mason University in Fairfax tends to carry the big-name country concerts as well as college-draw rock and pop. The adjoining GMU Center for the Arts, described above, is a lovely midsized venue for classical and jazz music and drama. Shows at these venues may be booked through a variety of promoters; check the web or newspaper listings.

Mid-sized Settings

Here we mean the smaller theaters and largest clubs, between, say, 300 and 2,000 seats. As mentioned above, the 1,800-seat Warner Theater still occasionally books musical acts. The Music Center at Strathmore Hall holds nearly 2,000; George Washington University's **Lisner Auditorium** (**www.lisner.org**) seats 1,500. Wolf Trap's cold-weather facility, the Barns, holds nearly 400, but occasionally pulls up the main-floor seats for "dance parties."

The **9:30** club holds 1,200 ("seats" not being exactly the word); the **Birchmere** in Alexandria holds about 500; the **State Theater,** a renovated movie house in Falls Church, holds about 215 upstairs but has cocktail tables and standing room on the ground floor; and the **Hard Rock Café** downtown, though primarily a restaurant, can hold 600 for its occasional live-music shows. (All these clubs are profiled below.)

More midsized venues are on the horizon. A new 2,000-seat venue is under construction on Colesville Road near the Silver Spring Metro stop; plans call for it to be operated by Live Nation, the national promotion and ticketing giant, as the Fillmore Silver Spring. But at press time Montgomery County's deal with Live Nation for the long-delayed big-name rock club was being contested by local promoter IMP. In theory, it will open in the fall of 2011.

In addition, D.C.-based Clyde's restaurant group has bought a former Border's Books at 14th and F streets NW in downtown D.C., which it plans to turn into a restaurant with a separate 500-seat concert venue in the basement; scheduled to open in 2011, it expects to book more "adult" entertainers with an emphasis on singer-songwriters in the folk, country, jazz, and perhaps even gospel fields.

Specialty Clubs

Jazz has a long history in Washington, and the old "Black Broadway" is a very good place to start. Just along U Street, near the U Street/African-American Civil War Memorial/Cardozo station and the old **Lincoln Theatre,** are several clubs offering jazz nearly every night: **Bohemian Caverns** (**www.bohemiancaverns.com**), an old revitalized jazz club (11th and U streets NW), which also spins occasional funk and go-go dance music; **Twins Jazz Lounge** at 1344 U (**www.twinsjazz .com**), which has live jazz every night; the younger-edge **U-Topia** at 1418 U (**www.utopiaindc.com**); and the very smooth **JoJo** at 1518 U (**www.jojorestandbar.com**). The nonprofit **HR-57** at 14th and Q hosts live jazz jam sessions every Wednesday and Thursday, and Sunday nights bring in established and hopeful local musicians as well as established combos (**www.hr57.org**).

Among other nice places to hear live jazz are **Blues Alley** in Georgetown (profiled); the nearby **Saloun in Georgetown** at 3239 M Street; **Zoo Bar** on Connecticut Avenue (**www.zoobardc.com**), a couple of blocks south of the Cleveland Park Metro stop just across from the main gate of the National Zoo; **Columbia Station** in Adams Morgan (**www.columbiastationdc.com**); the coffee bar–lounge **Tryst**, also in Adams Morgan (**www.trystdc.com**); and **Basin Street Lounge** above the 219 Restaurant in Old Town Alexandria (**www.219restaurant.com**). In addition, many restaurants have jazz at happy hour or during brunch; check newspaper listings or restaurant websites for more details.

For R&B and blues, best bets include **Madam's Organ** in Adams Morgan (get it?), with a nightly lineup of local and occasionally national acts (**www.madamsorgan.com**), and the venerable **Vegas Lounge** at 14th and P streets near Logan Circle (**www.newvegasloungedc.com**).

Irish bars do a flourishing business in Washington with the help of a resident community of performers. Among the Metro-accessible pubs with live music at least a couple of times a week—and preferably at least one fireplace— are the **Dubliner** on Capitol Hill (see profile, below) and its near neighbor **Kelly's Irish Times** (which doesn't have live music but is missing nothing else in the way of atmosphere); **Ireland's Four Fields** by the Cleveland Park Metro (**www .irelandsfourfields.com**) and **Nanny O'Brien's** across the street (**www .nannyobriens.com**); **Irish Channel,** a block from the Verizon Center in Penn Quarter (**www.irishchannelpub.com/dc**), and the theatrically "authentic" **Fado Irish Pub** in the old Chinatown (**www.fadoirishpub .com/Washington**). In Old Town Alexandria, **Murphy's Grand Irish**

unofficial **TIP**
Nobody ever wants to go to just one Irish bar, so we've dealt you a handful of deuces.

Pub on King Street has nightly entertainment and a famous fireplace (**www.murphyspub.com**), and **Pat Troy's Ireland's Own,** just off King on North Pitt Street, is owned by one of Murphy's favorite musicians (**www.pattroysirishpub.com**).

Despite its name, and a sophisticated take on Irish fare, **Flanagan's Harp and Fiddle** in Bethesda (**www.flanagansharpandfiddle.com**) has a lineup that includes not just Irish and folk but a wide range of blues, jazz, pop, and rock acts, including Eve's fave Mary Ann Redmond. A few blocks away is **Ri-Ra,** which is more likely to have rock cover bands than Irish troubadours, but the vintage look is very good.

Though Washington once claimed to be the bluegrass capital of the country, the bluegrass scene is down to one last stronghold, the **Tiffany Tavern** in Old Town Alexandria (**www.tiffanytavern.com**). And the best clubs for seeing national rock, indie, alternative, retro, and almost anything else are **9:30** and **Black Cat** in MidCity, **Iota** in Arlington, and **Jammin' Java** in Vienna, Virginia (all profiled below).

SWING YOUR PARTNER

COUNTRY AND DISCO DANCING HAVE BEEN BIG FOR YEARS in Washington, but ethnic and folk dancing—klezmer, polka, contra, Cajun—as well as swing dance and big-band boogie are also popular, especially in the suburbs. Their venues are also nonthreatening and hospitable spots for singles, even novices, since many have pre-dance "workshops" for learning the steps, and all seem well supplied with tolerant and deft "leaders."

However, not many of the locations are easily accessible. The closest major venue is **Glen Echo Park** just outside Washington near Bethesda, which hosts a variety of waltz, folk, swing, square, salsa, contra, and most anything else several times a week. Though for many years all dance parties were held in the restored Deco **Spanish Ballroom,** a second venue, the old **Bumper Car Pavilion,** also houses a few events. Go to **www.glenechopark.org/dancing** for information or to the **Folklore Society of Greater Washington,** which hosts many of them (☎ 202-546-2228 or **www.fsgw.org**). For an easy list of other swing-dance events in the area, most with classes, go to **www.gottaswing.com**.

Also check the Folklore Society site for folk, Cajun, and contra dances (**www.fsgw.org**). Though you'll have to get a ride, country dance and music fans should try **Nick's** (642 South Pickett Street, Alexandria, Virginia; ☎ 703-751-8900) or **Spurs** (2106 Crain Highway, Waldorf, Maryland; ☎ 301-843-9964).

And while it requires a car to get to, **Blob's Park** in Jessup, Maryland, between the District and Baltimore, is so over-the-top an experience—a biergarten, polka club, and best-of-the-wurst Bavarian restaurant–cum–theme park—that it might make for a really hilarious excursion if you happen to be inclined that way (**www.blobspark .net**). Just check the calendar—you probably had no idea there was such a polka circuit.

COMEDY IN WASHINGTON

WASHINGTON IS FULL OF JOKES—and that's the first one. Despite being an unending source of humor for TV talk show hosts and commentators, the nation's capitol itself seems to have a fairly limited tolerance for hearing its own favorite sons (of whichever party) skewered. Where there were once a dozen regular venues for comedians, now there are only a few. The major stop for touring comedians is the **DC Improv** (profiled below), though hip gay and straight comics with a larger audience—Paula Poundstone, Judy Tenuta, Dennis Miller—are more likely to be booked into the midsized theatrical or concert venues.

Capitol comedians divide very roughly into three generations and styles: the cabaret performers (those "Washington institutions" whose satires are usually musical and relatively gentle); the sketch and improvisational troupes from the post-Watergate *Saturday Night Live* era; and the stand-up artists who are the anti-establishment baby-busters—in some cases, the urban guerrillas. The first two groups are almost unavoidably political; the stand-up comedians range from political podium to locker room.

The most famous of the cabaret comedians is PBS irregular **Mark Russell,** whose residency at the Omni Shoreham lasted about four senatorial terms and who still swings through Ford's Theatre for a few weekends a year.

The most loyal opposition is offered by the **Capitol Steps** (**www .capsteps.com**), a group of former and current Hill staffers who roast their own hosts by rewriting familiar songs with punishing lyrics. In addition to entertaining at semi-official functions (which may be one reason why their barbs are a tad blunted compared to some more outspoken satirists), the Capitol Steps are a popular tourist attraction and perform every Friday and Saturday at the Ronald Reagan Building and International Trade Center at 13th Street and Pennsylvania Avenue NW; the Metro stop is Federal Triangle.

The raucously disloyal (in all directions) **Gross National Product** (**www.gnpcomedy.com**), a D.C.-based underground resistance movement that went above ground after Reagan's election, is now a national act and returns to Washington only for limited runs at various venues, most recently the Atlas Performing Arts Center, with 90-minute song, dance, and skit revues titled "Son of a Bush" or "Don't Tea on Me." Politics, especially the executive power structure, is its obsession: it skewers snoops, creeps, and veeps with gusto and, despite its long tenure, a hint of childish glee.

Another resident troupe is **Washington Improv Theater** (**www .washingtonimprovtheater.com**), actually a coalition of six ensembles that both entertain and teach classes. The regularly scheduled shows, about an hour long, are Thursday through Saturday at the old Source Theatre in Logan Circle; it also pays visits to other local venues and hosts occasional open improv jams. Other comedy troupes sometimes drop in as well.

Not surprisingly, there's at least one regular snipe session in the H Street corridor: **Twelve** restaurant and lounge at 12th and H streets NE holds Monday night comedy night with sometime BET and HBO star Chris Thomas as host (**www.twelve.com**).

GENTLEMEN'S (AND LADIES') CLUBS

WASHINGTON IS NOT THE SINGLES CAPITAL OF THE WORLD, but it does have many of the ingredients for a busy meet-market scene: frequent turnovers in power, a dozen colleges and universities, a continual influx of immigrants and corporate hires, and what until recently was considered a recession-proof economy. (Also considered bullet-proof, the sex industry seems to be slowing down as well.)

Although what was Washington's old strip-club strip—in retrospect, rather respectable—has long succumbed to redevelopment, there are still a few of the old-fashioned, and subway accessible, gentlemen's clubs downtown, including **Archibald's** on K Street just off MacPherson Square (**www.archibalds.com**); **Camelot Show Bar** near Farragut North (**www.camelotclub.com**); and the **Royal Palace** at the north end of Dupont Circle (**www.royalpalace-dc.com**). Though it's more of a hike, one must tip the, uh, hat to the longstanding **Good Guys** (**www.goodguysclub.com**) on Wisconsin Avenue above Georgetown, oft-embattled but soldiering on.

As to the other sort of gentlemen's club, and the ladies' own, even the "ordinary" singles bars around Washington are relatively benign. Many of them are dance clubs as well, so there's something to do besides discuss astrological incompatibilities. And since the District has been home to a strong gay community for decades, most nightclubs and bars attract at least a slightly mixed, albeit unobtrusive, crowd; several mainstream lounges host particular gay nights once a week or so. (And of course, no trendy area would be complete without at least a hangout or two.)

However, there are many well-established and easily Metro-accessible gay nightspots, especially around Dupont Circle and Capitol Hill. At the corner of P and 22nd streets, the seven-bar **Apex** (**www.apex-dc.com**), nee Badlands, can boast of being the city's longest-running gay dance club. In addition to Apex, some of the most popular Dupont Circle spots are **Cobalt/Level One** at 1639 R Street NW (**www.cobaltdc.com**), with Level being the restaurant on the ground floor; the all-comers-welcome **JR's** (**www.jrswdc.com**), which has long been known as the "gay Cheers"; the long-burning **Fireplace** (**www.fireplacedc.com**); and the *Hustler*-look billiards parlor **Omega** (**www.omegadc.com**).

Around Capitol Hill, check out the pointy-toe and big-buckle **Remington's** (**www.remingtonswdc.com**); the primarily black **Bachelor's Mill** (**www.thebachelorsmill.com**); the all-inclusive **Banana Café** piano bar (**www.bananacafedc.com**); and the lesbian billiards hall **Phase 1** (**www.Phase1dc.com**), all near the Eastern Market Metro.

Even the Convention Center has a handy hangout: the soft-core leather-and-Levi's **DC Eagle** (**www.dceagle.com**).

The long-running, high-profile **Ziegfeld's/Secrets** (**www.secretsdc .com**) has long been the most famously flamboyant of the outer hang-outs, featuring uproarious and often astonishingly polished drag shows and nude dancers, and used to book big-name cabaret stars. However, the old club was in the way of the new Nationals MLB stadium, and the new digs are some way from a Metro; it's best to go with a group or take a cab.

unofficial **TIP**
Mace, incidentally, is now legal in Maryland, Virginia, and the District of Columbia.

If you can't dance but hate to eat alone, try **Annie's Paramount Steak House,** at 17th and Q streets in Dupont Circle, or **Perry's** on Columbia Road off 18th Street in Adams Morgan, home of what must be the most straight-friendly drag brunch ever. Take the in-laws.

NIGHTLIFE NEIGHBORHOODS

AS SUGGESTED EARLIER, NIGHTCLUBS AND RESTAURANTS have a tendency to form clusters, which makes cruising or cocktailing relatively easy for visitors. This also means that in general you'll have plenty of company, and if you're not in easy reach of the Metro you won't have much trouble hailing a cab. However, in some cases, it may also mean that the price is tight: several of the more celebrity-conscious clubs and VIP-wannabe lounges will definitely put a dent in your platinum card. Just make sure you know which bubbly you're ordering, and ask exactly what "table service" means.

In terms of live entertainment, the two brightest strips in Washington are along H Street, in the sometimes rowdy but sweet-tempered Atlas District, and the slightly more sedate U Street/ MidCity neighborhood.

MidCity: "U" R There

As described in the previous chapter, the edgy-cum-trendy area along 14th Street and U Street NW, which locals are trying to brand the MidCity neighborhood, has been for the last several years evolving from fly-by-fortnight bars to boutiques that suggest more stabil-ity (home decor and accessories, import furniture, etc.) and lots of nightclubs and restaurants. Among the more important musical addresses in Washington are two MidCity attractions, which actually helped launch the neighborhood revival: the nationally known **9:30** club (which is actually on V Street) and the less widely recognized but sharp-eyed **Black Cat,** both profiled in depth below.

As described in Part Six, the MidCity area has become very busy in terms of cafés and restaurants, which of course is nightlife in itself. And, as pointed out above, U Street is the old Black Broadway, and home to a number of everything-old-is-new-again jazz clubs. But MidCity also has several nightspots with quite different characters; and the entire area is accessible via the U Street/African-American Civil War Memorial/Cardozo Metro, which has entrances at 13th and 10th streets.

At the corner of Eighth and U streets NW is **Town Danceboutique** (**www.towndc.com**), a lighthearted but technically serious two-level, 20,000-square-foot gay club that offers both upscale drag shows and DJs. At the corner of Ninth and U, you'll find **Nellie's Sports Bar** (**www.nelliesdc.com**), which may not have been the first gay sports bar in the area, but it's the most fun, with Tuesday drag bingo, Wednesday "smart-ass trivia," and weekend back-slapping football on the flatscreens; the **Velvet Lounge** (**www.velvetloungedc.com**), which is drink-spilling tight downstairs (stand-up bar and DJ) and up (prog-metal, dream-state rock, and indie-lounge rockers squeezed into a living room–size space); and around the corner on Ninth Street, **DC9** (**www.dcnine.com**), a much more upscale and larger space for indie rock and late-night DJs, with a roof deck.

At the corner of 11th and U next to Bohemian Caverns is the four-level dance club **LIV** (**www.livdc.com**), which isn't live but spins a mix of old school, reggae, R&B, and '80s and '90s dance pop. Across 11th Street you'll hit the **U Street Music Hall** (**www.ustreetmusichall .com**), which not only serves up some of Washington's favorite dance parties—Bliss has been rolling for more than a decade in various venues before coming home to roost—but also some of the most unusual late-night fare around (kosher pho dog, anyone?). The nightclub has a 1,200-square-foot, 300-capacity dance floor, dueling bars, dark charcoal walls, and two prohibitions: no bottle service and (at least in the blind-your-neighbor sense) no photos.

At 14th and U is the Jamaica-me-crazy, rum punch and reggae **Patty Boom Boom** (**www.pattyboomboomdc.com**), with mostly DJs but occasionally live music. And at the far end of the strip past 16th Street is **Chi-Cha Lounge** (**www.latinconcepts.com/chi-cha**), which also deserves some founding-father praise; here the schtick is hookah and South American snacks.

We've already pointed out that the cocktails at the Gibson are prime (and pricey), but there are a couple of other just bars worth checking out. The **Saloon** at 12th and U is famous for its three rules: "no standing, no TVs, no martinis." In other words, you're there to enjoy a drink and conversation with your neighbor. Really.

You'll have to climb four stories to get to the roof of **Tabaq Bistro** between 13th and 14th, but the glassed-in terrace has views of the Washington Monument and offers a baker's dozen martinis to get you back on your feet. (And no, that's not the only bar in the building.) Also at 13th is **Alero,** where you can choose from over 100 tequilas and mescals. And it would be hard to overlook the intentionally old-fashioned **Solly's Tavern,** if for no other reason than the Tuesday deaf happy hour (4 p.m. to close) with a signing bartender and the odd full-dress karaoke.

Get Your "H" in Gear

The **Atlas District,** a three-block stretch of H Street NE centered around the **Atlas Performing Arts Center** and its neighbor, the **H Street Playhouse** (which has survived incarnations as a garage, roller rink, furniture store, and diner to become a 100-seat theater), is without question the quirkiest entertainment district in the Washington area. Bars mix DJs and games—mini-golf, tabletop shuffleboard, skeeball—while nightclubs tender burlesque, rock bands, and dress-up. Even some of the restaurants are gamesters: **Sticky Rice** offers speed bingo and karaoke along with the offbeat sushi.

Some of the more irresistible attractions are clustered between 11th and 15th streets NW (just to get you started). Starting at the 11th Street end, there's **Little Miss Whiskey's Golden Dollar** (**www.littlemiss whiskeys.com**), which looks like a bit of fine New Orleans decadence, complete with wrought iron benches, a courtyard fountain, DJs ranging from yacht rock to '80s alternative—and Kostume Karaoke on alternate Wednesdays. In the next block is the new **Red Palace** (**www .redandblackbar.com**), which has risen like a phoenix from the merged ashes of two of the neighborhood's most popular nightspots: the fabulously weird Palace of Wonders, a house of carnie bizarrities (a five-legged dog, shrunken heads, preserved who-knows-what's) combined with a burlesque house; and the Red and the Black, another New Orleans–look music spot (though more of the roadhouse variety), which showcased up-and-coming talent. Just opening at press time, Red Palace promised to have both indie-circuit bands and neoburlesque and vaudeville, although (generally) on separate nights.

Between 13th and 14th is the H Street playgroundus maximus, the **H Street Country Club** (**www.hstreetcountryclub.com**), which boasts a two-level, nine-hole indoor mini-golf course—with miniature D.C. landmarks, including the Lincoln Theater, a gantlet of lobbyists, and a graveyard full of zombie Presidents among the traps—skeeball, shuffleboard, and, logically for H Street, Mexican food. The nearby **Star and Shamrock,** as the name suggests, is a combination Jewish deli and Guinness-Harp pub; it doesn't have entertainment except for the concept. Up from that is the **Rock and Roll Hotel** (**www.rockandrollhoteldc .com**), a funeral home renovated not as an overnighter but as a midsized (capacity 400) rock venue with VIP suites and pool tables upstairs. This is another gamesters' hangout: to stay in the Friday night spelling bee, you have to down a brew or a shot between rounds. And then there's the **Biergarten Haus** (**www.biergartenhaus.com**), which can make space for 300 mug-huggers in the (obviously) beer garden at long wooden tables *and* the strolling accordion players and tuba bands. The rest of it looks like an Alpine lodge, more or less. Fortunately for those more inclined

EASY ACCESS TO THE ATLAS DISTRICT

ALTHOUGH THE ATLAS DISTRICT IS NOT DIRECTLY ACCESSIBLE BY SUBWAY, local businesses and arts companies have banded together to run the free H Street Shuttle, a fleet of vans with a green-and-white logo that begins running at 5 p.m. daily and runs about every 5 minutes until midnight Sunday–Thursday and until 3 a.m. Fridays and Saturdays. The route runs between the Gallery Place–Chinatown Metro station and the Minnesota Avenue station (approximately a 30-minute circuit). Designed to open the Atlas District to a broader section of Washington, the shuttle stops between Fifth and Sixth streets NE; at 11th and H; at the Atlas Theater; at 14th and H; and at Bladensburg Road and L street NW before arriving at the Minnesota Avenue Metro.

to live jazz and blues and soul food, there's also **Majestic by Gwen** (**www.majestic-by-gwen.tripod.com**).

Cross 14th and you can play pool, foosball, or "booze clues" trivia at the **Argonaut.** (If you're afraid of dogs, duck Saturday afternoons: it's mutts happy hour on the patio.) And despite the wine bar-vibe, **Sova** has picked up on the "game night" craze and on Mondays throws out board games, card decks, word puzzles, strategy contests, or a twister.

Adams Morgan: The Big Mixer

Adams Morgan is a combination carnival midway and meet-market madhouse, and there's no way tourists, or even locals, can hit more than a few of its popular lounges in a night. But it does have a sort of multiple personality syndrome—part of which reflects its mixed ethnic, young hip, and not-quite-so-young marrieds—that might make it easier to narrow down the choices. There are the trendier, lounge-life nightclubs, the sort with white sofas, pastel drinks, and DJs; the truculently retro beer bars and dives; and the live-music and dance venues. Here are a few examples (and since they lie along 18th Street NW between Kalorama and Columbia roads, we'll just drop off a few addresses):

The grandmother of all Adams Morgan music clubs is **Madam's Organ** at 2461 18th Street, which has live music (blues, jazz, R&B, bluegrass) every night and a famously, um, robust eponymous mural, in whose honor all redheads pay half price for Rolling Rock. The jazz staples are **Tryst** at 2459 18th, which has live music Monday–Wednesday; and **Columbia Station** at 2325 18th (Sundays).

Among the best bets for cocktails and couture wars are **Town Tavern** at 2323 18th Street, a branch of a Greenwich Village singles mixer that requires men to be 23 and women 21; the multilevel, minimalist warehouse-chic, and gay-friendly **District** at 2473 18th; the white-banquette sushi bar above/dance hall below **Saki,** just up at 2477 18th; and, just around the corner, the simultaneously intimate and groupish **Perry's**, at 1811 Columbia Road, **Evolve** at 1817 Columbia, and the **Metropolitan,** the below-stairs champagne bar at Napoleon Bistro at 1847 Columbia Road. The liveliest mixer is the three-level **Reef** at 2446 18th Street, part jungle-theme disco, part aqua-wall bar (five huge salt-water tanks), occasional game room (Monday slot-car racing), and part deck party.

Among the very deliberately baseline bars are the venerable West Virginia-homey **Millie and Al's** at 2440 18th Street; the 1950s gas station–look **Toledo Lounge** at 2435 18th; and the rock 'n' roll detritus **Rendezvous** at 2226 18th. **Chief Ike's Mambo Room** at 1725 Columbia Road NW is probably the oldest compatriot-rival of Madam's Organ: the quintessential beer hall–basement-rec-room goof, it attracts one of the most mixed crowds (age, sex, and race) in town.

Long a center of Washington's Central and South American communities, Adams Morgan also has some of the area's nicer Latin jazz and samba joints: **Rumba Café** at 2443 18th Street, **Bossa Bistro** at 2463 18th, and **Habana Village** at 1834 Columbia Road all have full calendars of samba, Brazilian jazz, rhumba, and so on. (Habana Village has salsa lessons Wednesday through Saturday.)

Adams Morgan also has a high percentage of roof and deck bars per capita. The busiest are at the Reef, partly because it's open to the sky in warm weather but enclosed for year-round drinking; the tiki bar atop Madam's Organ; and Perry's, which isn't large (it's also a dining space) but is very pretty and a neighborhood fixture.

Midtown Redux

Downtown's new nightlife began with the turn-of-the-millennium revival of downtown Connecticut Avenue south of Dupont Circle, long a strictly commercial-business area, and one that regularly defeated attempts to push the expense-account-restaurant envelope. The five-pointed-star intersection at Connecticut, M, Jefferson, and 18th streets NW, just above Farragut North, marks the heart of what emerged in the mid-1990s as one of Washington's first semi-underground-luxe nightlife neighborhood.

The grandfather of the area is the outwardly low-key, inwardly delicious **18th Street Lounge** across the open triangle from Connecticut Avenue (**www.eighteenthstreetlounge.com**), true to its turn-of-the-20th-century mansion with languorous couches, three (working) fireplaces, a warm-weather deck, and with both DJs and live entertainment (reggae, Brazilian jazz, eclectic) nightly. Look across Connecticut and you'll see the swank all-white and sushi-chic bar-cum–dance hall **Current** (**www.currentsushi.com**), where the VIP "Captain's Table" of the yacht-look decor costs $2,000, and the see-through restroom doors steam up once you enter; and its much more casual sports-bar neighbor **Lucky Bar** (**www.luckybardc.com**). At the opposite end of the style spectrum is the underground "fly me" aero-look **Fly** (**www.the flylounge.com/dc**) and **Ozio** (**www.oziodc.com**), which got on the cigar and martini over-aged boy-bar bandwagon in the mid-90s and is still in the rut. (If you're networking with a stogie-sucking stockbroker, here's your spot.)

If lounge life is too much effort (or bucks) for you, just turn up Connecticut and as you move north toward Dupont Circle, there's the edgy-sketchy **Steve's Bar Room** (**www.stevesbar.com**) and the intentionally retro frat-boy beer-bar **Big Hunt** (**www.thebighunt .net**), where you might stumble over some off-the-record pols. Several of Washington's most venerable GLBT clubs are in the Dupont Circle area; and there are even a couple of neo-hip strip joints; see "Gentlemen's (and Ladies') Clubs," above.

But more recently, as part of the ripple effect of the Penn Quarter redevelopment, the stretch of K Street NW east of Connecticut Avenue, also previously a canyon of office buildings largely empty at night, has come to life, with landlords now looking to lure in after-hours crowds at the street and even basement level. (It's also trying to brand itself as Washington's "East End," à la "MidCity," though neither phrase is as yet in general use.) Most are using VIP bottle service and reasonably serious food, rather than pub grub, to promote a high-class dress code—and also to boost the tabs, all of which are likely to be serious.

The Park at 14th (**www.park14.com**) is a perfect example, an expensive and primarily word-of-mouth four-story Deco luxe-look lounge and so-called supper club created by some of Washington's most experienced club owners for, let us say, slightly more experienced patrons. (During Obama's Inauguration celebrations, it was packed round the clock.) From the second- and especially the fourth-floor balconies (what the website calls the "upper echelon"), VIP drinkers can lord it over the mere mortals below. The money, at least, is quite serious: a table for four to eight will cut you a couple of centuries, minimum; ditto the expected tab for a sofa. (After all, you're paying for celebrity sightings as well—more recently, John Legend, Donovan McNabb, Biz Markie, etc.) The "members-only" (as far as reservations are concerned) **Kstreet Lounge** (**www.kstreetdc.com**), catty-corner across Franklin Square, is even more expensive, but is popular with local sports and media types. The Asian fantasy **Lotus Lounge** (**www.lotusloungedc.com**) transforms its basement setting with a 14-foot waterfall and a Buddha (who probably wouldn't approve of or be able to afford the sushi). The three-level Nuevo Latino **Lima** (**www.limaloungedc.com**) separates the fine dining at the top from the luxe lounge in the basement via the bar in between, and keeps its heated sidewalk patio, furnished more like a rec room, open all year. And the chrome and black biker-look **Tattoo Bar** (**www .tattoobardc.com**) spins classic '80s and '90s dance music—all the

*un*official **TIP**
The "invitation list" is just about the only way around a hefty cover charge at many clubs these days; if you Twitter or Facebook, find yourself a friend on the guest list or ask about a "password."

while offering the faux-tattoo options of VIP tables. Here, too, opposites attract: Around the corner on Vermont Avenue is the boho-bordello **Josephine** (**www.josephinedc.com**), named for Napoleon's beloved and just as expensive.

Penn Quarter

Since this is mostly a dining mecca, that means primarily cocktail culture; and since the Verizon Center is at the heart of the neighborhood, at least a half dozen of the non–white linen hangouts are sports bars. (You can't miss them.) But of course, if you're not a home-towner, or a hockey fan, you need more than adrenalin. To pick out a couple of options: At the two-level **Iron Horse Tap Room** (**www .ironhorsedc.com**), a block from the arena at Seventh and E streets NW, the steeds referred to are not locomotives but vintage motorcycles, several of which hang about the place. It's not

unofficial **TIP**
It's not quite in Penn Quarter, but the POV rooftop bar at the W Hotel at 15th and F streets NW has a famously fabulous view of the White House, Washington Monument, and so on.

a biker bar except in name, however; upstairs it's lounge-a-lot territory; downstairs are skeeball machines, shuffleboard tables, and a few unfamiliar time-killers, plus a plentiful supply of TVs, 20 beers on tap, and as many bourbons. Iron Horse shares ownership with the even more games-away-from-the-game **Rocket Bar** at Seventh and G (**www.rocketbardc.com**), which sports a subterranean vibe with 17 flatscreens.

Though a few years ago many of the classic bank and federal buildings in the area had been turned into glitzy nightspots, there are only a couple of nightclubs in the DJ and dress code class left in Penn Quarter: **UltraBar** at Ninth and F (**www.ultrabardc.com**) mixes mode and mood: the VIP dance bar Chrome, the Latin-music "bedroom," the pop basement "vault," and the Top-40 main bar. And **Muse** at Seventh and F (**www.museloungedc.com**) is three stories (latin, hiphop, electronica) of slick and table-service come-ons. Dress to regress.

Georgetown

It's had as many nightlives as cats (or generations); and although Georgetown has lost most of its live-music venues to chain stores catering to its college and post-grad population, it still has a handful of hangouts left, including **Blues Alley** (profiled below).

Most of the other clubs (and bars) are along M Street near Wisconsin Avenue. Look for the live jazz/R&R survivor **Saloun** at 3239 M Street NW; the old standby **Mr. Smith's,** with its piano bar and year-round patio downstairs (where Tori Amos once worked) and a larger music club upstairs at 3104 M; the funky-disco DJ **Modern** at 3287 M, with its hipster circular sunken bar and VIP bottle service; the members-first poseur bar **L2** in Cady's Alley (3307 M); and such decor-heavy meet-market lounges as **Mie N Yu** at 3125 M.

And just above M Street on Wisconsin is **Third Edition,** which has been slinging cocktails and (pre-trend) burgers since 1969—and which served as the backdrop for the 1985 Brat Pack classic, *St. Elmo's Fire.*

PROFILES *of* CLUBS *and* NIGHTSPOTS

Birchmere

LIVE FOLK, NEW ACOUSTIC, NEWGRASS, HIP ROCKABILLY/OUTLAW, LIGHT JAZZ AND COUNTRY, AND OCCASIONAL OFF-PEAK POP MUSIC

3701 Mt. Vernon Avenue, Alexandria; ☎ 703-549-7500; www.birchmere.com   Virginia Suburbs

Cover Varies with entertainment; generally $20–$45, though big names can cost a lot more. **Minimum** None. **Mixed drinks** $5–$8. **Wine** $6.50–$8.50. **Beer** $6.50–$7. **Dress** A few suits, a lot of flannels, universal jeans (beat and pre-beat), neo-farm country wear and boots of all sorts—cowboy, hiking, motorcycle. **Food available** After years of getting by on potato chips, Birchmere patrons can now get more serious tavern fare, including barbecue, burgers, and hot nibbles, from the folks at Union Street Pub and King Street Blues. **Hours** Show nights only, from 5 p.m.; music curfew is 12:30 a.m. Shows start at 7:30 p.m. **Metro** None nearby.

WHO GOES THERE Gracefully aging boomers and a few recalcitrant rednecks; unreconciled folkies; local musicians.

WHAT GOES ON This is one of the major clubs in town, a serious eclectic venue and easily the biggest for new acoustic, alternative, and country acts, such as Rosanne Cash, Shelby Lynn and sister Allison Moorer, hometown heroine Mary Chapin Carpenter; Indigo Girls, Los Lonely Boys, and Steeleye Span; cult faves Lyle Lovett, Delbert McClinton, and Jerry Jeff Walker; femme fronters Linda Ronstadt, Kristin Hersh, Christine Lavin, k.d. lang, Maria Muldaur, and Shawn Colvin; jazz alters Keiko Matsui and John McLaughlin; quirk rockers Fountains of Wayne and Nick Lowe; Irish heartbreaker Mary Black and chanteuse Barbara Cook; bluegrass patriarchs David Grisman and Doc Watson (for 20 years, the Birchmere was the Seldom Scene's weekly home stand); singer-songwriters Patty Loveless, Suzanne Vega, and Don McLean; and a few old rockers such as Robin Tower, Jon Anderson, Frank Marino and Mahogany Rush, and Ian Anderson. Not to mention the odd comedian and trio of tenors. If you can't find something here, you can't find it.

SETTING AND ATMOSPHERE Once a sort of glorified roadhouse, and still not the most impressive-looking building from the outside, the Birchmere is now a multiroom venue with a 500-seat main stage with communal dining tables, a bandstand room for dance shows, a 150-seat New Orleans roadhouse-look side stage/café (where smoking is allowed), a nostalgic wood "tap room" with "real" pub food, plus a combination souvenir shop and record store.

Nightclubs by Type

NIGHTCLUB | DESCRIPTION | NEIGHBORHOOD | TYPICAL COVER

BAR AND GRILLS/BUFFETS

Dave & Buster's | **Adult game-room bar** | MARYLAND SUBURBS | **$5 weekends**

Hard Rock Cafe | **Bar and grill with memorabilia** | NATIONAL MALL | **None**

COMEDY CLUB

The Improv | **Pro-circuit comedy dinner club** | DOWNTOWN | **$10–$35**

LIVE JAZZ/BLUES

Blues Alley | **National-circuit jazz dinner club** | GEORGETOWN | **$18–$75**

LIVE POP/ROCK

Birchmere | **Live folk and rockabilly bar and brewery** | VIRGINIA SUBURBS
  $20 and up

Black Cat | **Live rock/pop venue with some DJs**
  DUPONT CIRCLE/ADAMS MORGAN | **$5–$20**

IOTA | **Tavern with live pop/roots rock** | VIRGINIA SUBURBS | **About $10–$20**

Jammin' Java | **All-ages alt-rock coffeehouse to the max**
  VIRGINIA SUBURBS **$5–$20**

9:30 | **Big-name alternative, hiphop, rock, and punk venue** | DOWNTOWN
  $5–$40

State Theatre | **Restored Deco movie house turned music venue**
  VIRGINIA SUBURBS | **$10–$35**

PUBS/BILLIARDS BAR

Dubliner | **Traditional Irish pub** | CAPITOL HILL | **None**

IF YOU GO Go early: parking is tight (but free); the line is long; and even with
the advance tickets sales (via Ticketmaster or at the box office), all seating is first-come, closest-in. Although most of the food is on the heavy,
American-bar-food side, there are a few lighter options these days.
Remember to take off your big hat so the folks behind you can see. And
take thankful note of the sign that asks for quiet during performances;
this really is a listening club.

Black Cat

MAJOR LIVE ROCK-POP VENUE WITH DJS FOR BACKUP

1811 14th Street NW; ☎ 202-667-4490; www.blackcatdc.com
Dupont Circle/Adams Morgan

Cover Varies with entertainment, $5–$20. **Minimum** None. **Mixed drinks** $5–$8.
Wine $5.50. **Beer** $4–7. **Dress** Ranges from grungy to nightclub-hip, depending

on the act. **Food available** Vegan and vegetarian fare from the relocated Food for Thought. **Hours** Sunday–Thursday, 8 p.m.–2 a.m.; Friday and Saturday, 7 p.m.–3 a.m. **Metro** U Street/African-American Civil War Memorial/Cardozo.

WHO GOES THERE 20–40; local and out-of-town music fans.

WHAT GOES ON A mix of hot regional and early-national alternative rock, funky-punk, post-punk, Brit-pop, etc. Some of the most fun dance nights are sort of like pop heavyweight bouts: Outkast vs. Prince or Madonna vs. Michael Jackson.

SETTING AND ATMOSPHERE This is physically, though perhaps not nominally, the area's largest indie-rock venue, with four separate areas, including the main stage, which holds nearly 1,000. The first-floor Red Room Bar is a combination watering hole (with a great jukebox) and pool and pinball game room; behind that is the Backstage, which can handle only about 150 for up-and-coming bands, so that's usually turned over to DJs on the weekends, with a mix of synth pop, film, Brit-indie, and even some mod and cult garage. The other space is Food for Thought, which is a veggie and vegan-friendly café that coexists with Black Cat because the original café, then an acoustic music hangout in Dupont Circle, was founded by the club owner's father.

IF YOU GO A who's-who of indie rock has passed through the Black Cat—and more recently, some rediscoveries, such as the Little Steven–inspired revival tour of the Zombies, Fleshtones, et al—so buy advance tickets for major concerts and expect some sweating crowds at the louder acts. Three things to remember here: First, you can buy tickets through Ticket Alternative (**www.ticketalternative.com**), but if you can make it to the box office, you'll save the ticket fee. Second, it's all cash-only with an ATM on site. And third, get there early for a concert; the check-in system is fairly slow because Black Cat is always an all-ages club, so IDs are closely scrutinized and 21-and-over hands have to be stamped for alcohol consumption (and stamped again to show you've paid your ticket). Oh, and fourth: wear comfortable shoes. There are a handful of tables and chairs in Food for Thought and around the bar, but most of the club is standing room only.

Blues Alley

NATIONAL-CIRCUIT JAZZ DINNER CLUB

1073 Wisconsin Avenue NW (in the alley); ☎ 202-337-4141; www.bluesalley.com   Georgetown

Cover Varies with entertainment; $18–$75. **Minimum** Two drinks or $10 food. **Mixed drinks** $6–$9.50. **Wine** $4.50–$7. **Beer** $5–$7. **Dress** Jacket over jeans, business attire, musician chic. **Food available** Full menu of Creole food (named for jazz stars): gumbo, chicken, steak. **Hours** Daily, 6 p.m.–12:30 a.m. **Metro** Foggy Bottom–GWU.

WHO GOES THERE 20–60; locals and tourists, especially jazz aficionados from other countries; other jazz pros; neo-jazz fans.

WHAT GOES ON For 40 years, whenever the big-name jazz performers have come to town—and despite the name, it's a rare blues or R&B show that makes the marquee—this is where they've played. Look back through the clips, and you'll see the names Dizzy Gillespie, Wayne Shorter, Ramsey Lewis, Ahmad Jamal, Gil Scott-Heron, Jerry Butler, Stanley Jordan, Earl "Fatha" Hines, Mose Allison, Charlie Byrd, Sarah Vaughn, Arturo Saldoval, Diane Schuur, Marcus Johnson, and every member of the Marsalis family—sometimes in combination.

SETTING AND ATMOSPHERE A fairly simple lounge, with exposed brick walls, a platform at one end and the bar at the other, and smallish dinner tables scattered between. It's not the most comfortable venue (there's not much room to expand), and the old and cramped restrooms that are barely accessible upstairs are a drawback, but the acoustics are fine.

IF YOU GO Get there early; it's first come, first served, so the line often goes around the block. Having a dinner reservation helps, but seating for that too is first-come and squeeze-'em-together.

Dave & Buster's

ADULT ENTERTAINMENT À LA SPIELBERG, PART HIGH-TECH, PART RETRO-REGRESSIVE

White Flint Mall, Bethesda; ☎ 301-230-5151; www.daveandbusters.com
Maryland Suburbs

Cover $5 weekends after 10 p.m. **Minimum** None. **Mixed drinks** $5–$7. **Wine** $5.75–$7. **Beer** $4–$6. **Dress** Upper shopping mall–quality: casual, but no tanks, cutoffs, etc. **Specials** Half-price well drinks and beer and wine specials at happy hour and after 9 p.m. **Food available** A full range of familiar upscale suburban fare: from artichoke dip and stuffed jalapenos to pastas, grilled salmon, Santa Fe chicken pizza, and ribs and ribeyes. **Hours** Sunday–Wednesday, 11:30 a.m.– 11 p.m.; Thursday–Saturday, 11:30 a.m.–1 a.m.; Sunday, 11:30 a.m.–midnight. **Metro** White Flint.

WHO GOES THERE Late-20s couples bored with disco; traveling salesmen nostalgic for Vegas; some computer geeks and groups of mixed-sex hangers-on looking for post-movie action.

WHAT GOES ON This is a carnival of the business animals: a half dozen pocket billiard tables, skeeball, hockey, pinball and video games, a couple of simulated "19th hole" golf games, shuffleboard, and four full-size virtual-reality pods, interlinked for games and sports simulation. There are also casino games, with fully trained blackjack dealers and tables— but the poker chips are "on loan" only. No actual gambling is allowed. Everything is played by token (actually a prepaid swipe card). Eat and play combos are an entrée and $10 card for $16.

SETTING AND ATMOSPHERE This is unabashedly a bar as well as a playroom, with two sideline bars: the double-sided, 40-foot bar that partners the "mid-way" (a stretch of interactive video and carny attractions) and the elevated, square "Viewpoint" bar (not to mention the private "showroom" with its own stage, bar, dining tables, and even audio-visual equipment, which is bound to become the status CEO party room of D.C.).

IF YOU GO Dave & Buster's has more than 50 such complexes around the country, and they've got it down smooth. Besides offering nearly every sort of game, it has polished service, fairly strict rules about drinking and dressing, and even stricter rules about under-21-year-olds being with an adult. Even better in this cigar-crazed era, smoking is extremely limited (even cigarettes are only where allowed). On the other hand, if you're not careful, you (or the kids) can rack up points for the house bank pretty quickly. Being in a shopping mall, wheelchair access is very good.

Dubliner

520 North Capitol Street NW; ☎ 202-737-3773; www.dublinerdc.com
Capitol Hill

Cover None. **Minimum** None. **Mixed drinks** $3.25–$6; Dubliner coffee is an Irish coffee with Bailey's added. **Wine** $4–$5.50. **Beer** $3–$4. **Dress** No cutoffs or tank tops. **Specials** Reduced light-fare prices, 11 p.m.–1 a.m.; daily specials Monday–Friday for lunch and dinner. **Food available** Irish-pub classics, from stew to hot sandwiches. **Hours** Monday–Thursday, 7 a.m.–1:30 a.m.; Friday, 7 a.m.–2:30 a.m.; Saturday, 7:30 a.m.–2:30 a.m.; Sunday, 7:30 a.m.–1:30 a.m. **Metro** Union Station.

WHO GOES THERE Hill workers, both upwardly mobile (staffers) and established (senators and lobbyists).

WHAT GOES ON This is not the oldest Irish bar in town (though it is more than 35 years old), but it has become the clan leader—centrally located, pol-connected, and providing the training ground for founders of a half dozen other bars, including the semi-sibling-rival Kelly's Irish Times next door—and one of the few places in Washington to find live music seven nights a week. Fittingly, the Dubliner also has one of the most colorful histories, filled with romantic intrigue, boom-and-bust bank troubles, and riotous St. Patrick's week parties.

SETTING AND ATMOSPHERE Owner Danny Coleman comes by the publican's role naturally; his father had a pub in Syracuse, New York, which his brother still runs. Now part of the pricey and hunt-country gracious Phoenix Hotel complex, the Dubliner is filled with antiques, such as the 1810 hand-carved walnut bar in the back room. The front bar is louder and livelier, often populated by the surviving members of the Dubliner's Irish football and soccer teams; the snug is a discreet heads-together, take-no-names hideaway in the finest tradition; and the parlor is where the tweeds gather. In warm weather, there's patio seating; and if you like a hearty brunch, this is a pretty good one. In fact, the entire menu is better than you might expect.

IF YOU GO Be sure to have at least one Guinness on draft: The Dubliner pours an estimated quarter-million pints a year. (If that's not your choice, there's a baker's dozen others on tap and an equal number in the bottle—and the ten or so various vintage Irish whiskies.) Drop by Irish Times next door for a breather (the high ceilings carry smoke away) and the *Finnegans Wake* crazy-quilt of literary pretense, political conversation, and interns' raves downstairs. Then call a cab. Please.

Hard Rock Cafe

SOUVENIR SHOP DISGUISED AS BARBECUE BAR

999 E Street NW; ☎ 202-737-7625; www.hardrock.com National Mall

Cover None. **Minimum** None. **Mixed drinks** $7–$18. **Wine** $6–$15. **Beer** $3–$7. **Dress** To be seen: leather, denim, sports or rock-and-roll tour jackets, creative black tie, Bermuda shorts (on tourists). **Food available** Surprisingly good and extensive but fairly predictable: steaks, burgers, etc.. **Hours** Sunday–Thursday, 11 a.m.–11 p.m.; Friday and Saturday, 11 a.m.–midnight. **Metro** Metro Center.

WHO GOES THERE 12–55; tourists and locals; Hard Rock memorabilia collectors; air-guitar experts.

WHAT GOES ON Despite the name, this is more of a restaurant than a club—nor does it rock on anything like a regular basis, though there is more live music than there used to be. However, it's big with kids, well located for families doing the museum thing, and with a whole generation of semi-serious radioheads who collect Hard Rock T-shirts from every city they can find. One of 100 Hard Rocks around the world, this is the "Embassy" and sometimes the "Smithsonian of Rock 'n' Roll," taking its turn rotating the nearly 7,000 pieces of music history in the HRC collection. (Most recently, these included Michael Jackson's red "Beat It" jacket and a shirt worn by Mick Jagger during the "Steel Wheels" tour.) The rest of the wall space is taken up with photos, posters, playbills, etc. The souvenir shop, with its signature T-shirts, is as busy as the bar, which is often stand-in-line packed—a doorman passes judgment on the hopeful.

SETTING AND ATMOSPHERE This is ersatz nostalgia for the second *Rolling Stone* generation, with a guitar-shaped bar, a trio of stained glass rock god windows (Elvis on his, um, throne in between Chuck Berry and Jerry Lee Lewis), and a lot of fed suits from nearby buildings trying to look cool. Hard Rock also makes a point of being Lollapalooza-era PC, supporting the Walden Project and nuclear freezes and hosting radio-chic benefits and post-concert VIP receptions, usually without the star. Although the Hard Rock motto is still "Love all, serve all," you can make reservations in advance and pass the line.

IF YOU GO Pick up the guidebook, formally known as the "Hard Rock Cafe Self-Motivating Non-Nuclear-Powered Memorabilia Tour of the World's Foremost Rock 'n' Roll Museum" and start circling the balcony.

The Improv

NATIONAL-CIRCUIT COMEDY CLUB

1140 Connecticut Avenue NW; ☎ 202-296-7008; www.dcimprov.com Downtown

Cover $10–$35, according to performer. **Minimum** Two items. **Mixed drinks** $6–$9. **Wine** $7–$8. **Beer** $5–$6. **Dress** T-shirts with jackets, suits, casual yup attire. **Specials** Tuesday, free admission to anyone wearing an Improv T-shirt ($15 in the lobby). **Food available** Full menu available before the 8:30 p.m. show, but light fare available whenever. **Hours** Shows Sunday and Tuesday–Thursday at 8 p.m.; Friday and Saturday at 8 and 10:30 p.m.; doors open 90 minutes before show time. **Metro** Farragut North or Dupont Circle.

WHO GOES THERE Visiting business types; 30ish suburbanites; 25–45 midlevel managers.

WHAT GOES ON Standard Improv franchise fare: a short opening act, often local; a semi-established feature act; and a headliner from the national club/cable showcase circuit. Most headliners are in for two to five nights; however, like many comedy clubs, the Improv is increasingly dependent on extended bookings of more theatrical comics such as Rob "The Caveman" Becker or Jack Gallagher, who perform alone for 90 minutes or so.

SETTING AND ATMOSPHERE This is the one dependable venue for national-name comedians—Jerry Seinfeld, Chris Rock, Ellen DeGeneres—and alums of *SNL*, Comedy Central, late-night talk shows, etc. Again, this goes with the franchise—a "brick wall" stage sentimentally recalling the original no-frills Improvisation, and the black-and-white checkerboard floor and trim that is practically a logo design. TV screens hang overhead for those with obscured views, but they're not big enough to be terribly useful. The wait staff wear tux-material Bermuda shorts.

IF YOU GO Don't bother to come early, at least on weeknights, when being seated in order of arrival isn't apt to be a problem. Since latecomers are usually seated amongst the diners, you have no real reason to seek early reservations. Besides, nibbling through the appetizers list is a more satisfying experience than sitting down to dinner (Tex-Mex) and then sitting through the show. (The later Friday and Saturday night shows have only a light menu anyway.) The Improv, though below sidewalk level, has wheelchair access via the elevator in the building lobby. Online ticketing is via Symphonee (**www.symphonee.com**), which also has Droid and iPhone aps for hip travelers, but there's a $3 charge; no service fee at the box office.

IOTA

NEIGHBORHOOD JOINT WITH SMART CONVERSATION AND LIVE NEW-POP ROOTS ROCK

2832 Wilson Boulevard, Arlington; ☎ 703-522-8340; www.iotaclubandcafe.com Virginia Suburbs

Cover About $10–$30; some shows free. **Minimum** None. **Mixed drinks** $3–$10. **Wine** $5.50–$7.50. **Beer** $3–$7. **Dress** Jeans, with or without bolo; hog leathers; baggy athletic wear; and frayed button-down collars. **Specials** Happy hour 5–8 p.m., $1 off rail and draft prices. **Food available** The menu is nice but fairly limited: mostly entrée salads and wraps and a handful of comfort foods such as pasta and fried chicken. **Hours** Daily, 5 p.m.–2 a.m. **Metro** Clarendon or Courthouse.

WHO GOES THERE Messengers; students; 30-something T-shirts; microbrew-savvy beer buddies; indie-music saveurs; other musicians.

WHAT GOES ON On a regular basis, this has the best lineup of acoustic rock, neo-roots, soft psychedelic, and eclectic melodic rock in town, and that's not just a couple of nights but every night of the week. Over the last 15 years or so, this rather surprising survivor—off the beaten track in Clarendon, it began as a sort of anti-establishment local musicians' showcase—has hosted any number of stars at the start of their careers (Norah Jones, John Mayer, Jason Mraz, Jack Johnson) as well as indie and alt-rock faves such as Drive-by Truckers, John Doe, Alejandro Escovedo, Bottle Rockets, and so on. A number of now-established regional acts are loyal regulars, including Emmet Swimming and Eric Brace & Last Train Home.

SETTING AND ATMOSPHERE In a time when a lot of Washington bars have an intentionally mismatched rec-room random look, IOTA's decor is unusual but intelligent—murals, geometric eye-catchers chiseled into the exposed brick walls, and beams that show the age of the neighborhood (especially nice, since there's so little of it left otherwise). The room used to be only half this size (hence the name), but giving the performers some extra elbowroom has not made either the musicians or their audiences self-conscious. There's still no "green room" or backstage, though, and not a lot of seats, either; so the musicians are even more up close and personal.

IF YOU GO You can plan to go in advance, but you can't do anything more than that: there are no advance ticket sales, and admission is first come, first served—which, since it only holds about 160 people, means you'd best be prepared to make friends. Actually, this is a good place to strike up a conversation at the bar before the music gets loud: you run into crossword-puzzle freaks, novelists, doctoral candidates, musicians, roadies, and ponytails of the friendly sort. It's the sort of bar that makes hanging out a pleasure. If you're taking the Metro, be sure you know what time the last train home leaves, no pun intended.

Jammin' Java

ALL-AGES ALT-ROCK COFFEEHOUSE TO THE MAX, WITH ROCK, A LITTLE PUNK, COUNTRY, FOLK, AND BLUES, AND EVEN THE ODD JUG BAND

227 Maple Avenue, East Vienna; ☎ 703-255-1566; www.jamminjava.com
Virginia Suburbs

Cover $8–$30, according to performer. **Wine** $7. **Beer** $4–$5. **Dress** Easy listening, mostly jean therapy. **Food available** Wraps and sandwiches, "gourmet chilis" and salads, plus espresso drinks. **Hours** Daily, 9 a.m.–midnight.

WHO GOES THERE Unreconstructed hard-folk boomers; family diners; midlife musical hopefuls; eclectic-minded 20-somethings.

WHAT GOES ON Two or three sets of music per night, mostly local but with some good regional and college-circuit acts; cult favorites such as Marshall Crenshaw, former Squeeze frontman Glenn Tilbrook, Peter Himmelman, Enter the Haggis, and the Kennedys; and open-mike Mondays. Heavy interest in alt-rock, alt-country, and singer-songwriters (local boy Eric Brace, Dan Navarro, Daniel Lanois, and so on).

SETTING AND ATMOSPHERE This is one of the area's most relaxed venues, a comfortably snug L-shaped room with bar and food counter in front with a handful of tables and the music room (also a recording studio)

around the side. But in terms of atmosphere, you have to remember that this really is a coffeehouse during the day, so no rock-frills here. This is an all-ages, no-smoking, family-friendly version of a music club, and in fact it's owned by three brothers, including popular local musicians Luke and Owen Brindley, who are recording their own alt-country album there. Unfortunately, it's nowhere near a Metro station.

IF YOU GO There is somewhat limited seating (first come, first seated) in the music room, and the crowd is often SRO, but nobody's a stranger here; it's a nice mix. Since you can eat all day, it may be better to come early, eat (maybe grab a table), and save the espresso for the show. Note that when we say family-friendly, we're serious; there are frequent kids' (Rocknocerous) and tweeners' shows, and even on concert nights, there's likely to be small children dancing around the stage.

9:30

NATIONAL-NAME LIVE ALTERNATIVE, PROGRESSIVE, SEMI-PUNK, HIPHOP, AND RETRO AND ROCK MUSIC CLUB

815 V Street NW; ☎ 202-265-0930; www.930.com Downtown

Cover Varies with entertainment, $5–$40. **Minimum** None. **Mixed drinks** $4–$5.25. **Wine** $4.50–$6.50. **Beer** $3.25–$4.25 (about 30 beers on tap and nearly as many bottles). **Dress** Grunge, imitation grunge, rhinestone cowboy, leftover business wear, knife-customized athletic wear, black jersey, black spandex, black denim, and black baggies. **Food available** A fairly nice menu of mostly wraps and pizzas, a substantial portion of which is vegan. **Hours** Sunday–Thursday, 7:30 p.m.–until close; Friday and Saturday, 9 p.m.–until close. **Metro** U Street/African-American Civil War Memorial/Cardozo.

WHO GOES THERE 18–35; new music hopefuls; postgrads; young media and political types; couriers; cowpunks.

WHAT GOES ON "9:30" is the name, it used to be the address (before the former F Street club moved into an old gospel-music hall and radio-broadcast site on V), and it used to be the showtime, but thanks to workday hangovers, midweek music now starts at 8:30. Thirty years on, this is arguably Washington's—perhaps the region's—most important music club, the loss-leader indulgence of major concert promoter Seth Hurwitz (he also owns IMP, which books Merriweather Post Pavilion, among other venues), who, with daring and eclectic booking of breaking acts, fosters loyalty from new bands as their reputations rise. Promising local bands fight to get work as first acts here; a headliner contract is a real prize. In any given month, you might see Liz Phair, Five for Fighting, Joan Jett, Richard Thompson, Sergio Mendes, the BoDeans, funk patriarch George Clinton, or neo-funk wannabe Justin Timberlake. If you were around a little longer (or longer ago), you might have seen James Brown, too, or Suzanna Vega, Smashing Pumpkins, Elvis Costello, Squeeze, Dwight Yoakam, Radiohead, Fugazi, or the Damned.

SETTING AND ATMOSPHERE A slightly trendy mix of leftover cornices, pilasters, virtue-of-necessity exposed steel trusses, and dropped lighting—but still theatrically dark, with great sight lines. The balconies are fine, and there are several bars, including one "quiet room" and a nostalgic, grungier one downstairs. The straightforwardly named Backbar is decorated with fliers from 9:30's early, grungy, great days. Club shows are all-ages unless otherwise marked, and alcohol consumption is pretty carefully monitored.

IF YOU GO The best views are from the three-sided balcony, but don't mistake the tiers for seats or you won't be seeing anything but, um, pants legs. Actually, the whole club is pretty much SRO (except for the Backbar), though you might find an odd ledge or two to lean on. The dress code is pretty expansive, but the club recommends against spiky jewelry (for good reason). And before you go, find out who's playing: The crowd that pays up for Ice-T isn't the same as the one for Marshall Crenshaw, Happy Mondays, They Might Be Giants, or even Anthrax. Never accuse Hurwitz of lacking a sense of humor. Tickets are available through Ticketfly or at the box office.

State Theatre

RESTORED DECO MOVIE HOUSE TURNED ROCK, BLUES, REGGAE, JAM, ALT-COUNTRY, FOLK, AND OCCASIONALLY, IRONIC VENUE

220 North Washington Street, Falls Church; ☎ 703-237-0300; www.statetheatre.com Virginia suburbs

Cover Varies according to performer, but generally $10–$35. **Minimum** None. **Mixed drinks** $6–$10. **Wine** $7. **Beer** $4–$6. **Dress** Depending on the show, anything from Texas-jack boots to tie-less suits to flannels. **Food available** Full menu with a variety of sandwiches and entrées. **Hours** Depends on showtime but generally 7 or 8 p.m–2 a.m. **Metro** East Falls Church.

WHO GOES THERE Young professionals, parents with older kids, old music fans, second-time-around jeans and boots, corduroy blazers, and blues-loving ponytails of both sexes.

WHAT GOES ON This is a popular venue for indie bands, been-there-done-that and hope-to-again dinosaurs and long-standers, and the occasional comic tour looking for a mid-sized venue, but in a satellite radio–worthy range of styles: Smithereens, Leon Russell, Johnny Winter, Asleep at the Wheel, Hanson, Toots and the Maytalls, Wu-Tang Clan, Radiators, and the increasing flood of high-quality tribute bands (Pink Floyd, Bee Gees, Journey, Led Zeppelin, Stones). State has also picked up on the wave of retro-jokey dance parties, hosting '80s and Michael Jackson nights.

SETTING AND ATMOSPHERE The bones of this 1930s Art Deco movie house are clearly visible and lovingly restored; there are about 200 old-style plush seats upstairs in the balcony (first come, first seated) and a handful of tables downstairs that can be reserved for dinner service; but it's mostly standing room. Occasionally all the seats are pulled up for dancing, in which case capacity doubles to 1,000. There are also four rather nice bars, although most shows are 18-and-up, so expect to be carded.

IF YOU GO Remember to wear shoes you can stand up in. Please note that although the state of Virginia allows concealed weapons, the State Theatre exercises its option to forbid all guns.

PART NINE

EXERCISE *and* RECREATION

WORKING *a* WORKOUT *into* YOUR VISIT

MOST OF THE FOLKS IN THE *Unofficial Guides* family work out routinely, even when (or perhaps especially when) we're traveling. Some bike, some run, some lift weights or do aerobics—the more "transportable" sports, which we've tried to master in addition to the more formal stuff back home. It's not just a matter of offsetting calories (although those of us who review restaurants need extra help) but of easing stress and jet lag. But it doesn't take long to realize that exercising in Washington's summer heat and humidity presents some problems, at least when it comes to outdoor exercise.

Washington is also prone to high levels of allergens, especially in spring and fall, and of pollution, especially in the summer. On those days, local authorities may declare Code Orange days, during which anyone with respiratory problems should limit exertion and outdoor exposure as much as possible; or Code Red, an even stronger warning that everyone should limit outdoor activities—including mowing the lawn, though unless you're paying off your rental by doing yard work, that's probably not an issue—avoid driving, and use public transportation as much as possible. (On Code Red days, certain Metrobus routes are free, to discourage the use of cars.) If you are sensitive to bad air or allergens, ask the hotel concierge or check news reports.

The best months for outdoor exercise are March through June and September through December. In July and August, you must get up very early to beat the heat, though the humidity won't ease up much. During those months, it might be safer to move your workout indoors—unless you have nothing else planned until dinner and can spend the rest of the day recuperating. January and February can bring quite cold weather, although snow usually isn't a problem in the major tourist areas because of aggressive snow removal. However, cold air can also be hard on those with respiratory trouble, so take it easy.

The good news is, exercise these days has less to do with the "work" part of "workout" and more to do with the "create" part of "recreation." Trapeze flying, zip lines, climbing walls, rowing and rafting, hiking and horseback riding, the Washington region—whose sweep includes rivers, lakes, mountains, battlefields, and an admirable amount of public parkland—has plenty to entice you.

The BASIC DRILLS

WALKING AND RUNNING

THE MOST OBVIOUS METHOD OF EXERCISE—in fact, the almost unavoidable form for tourists—is walking. With its wide-open public spaces, long museum corridors, picturesque neighborhoods, even its tourist queues, Washington is a walker's haven. (In both senses of the word: security is very good along the Mall and Potomac Park, making for a safe walking environment at all hours of the day and night.)

A long walk down the Mall and through **East** and **West Potomac Parks** offers grand views of the **Lincoln, Jefferson,** and **FDR** memorials and the **Washington Monument,** as well as the **Tidal Basin** and the **Potomac River.** To give you an idea of the length, it's almost two miles from the Capitol Steps to the Lincoln Memorial, so if you swing around the Mall—that is, using Independence Avenue going one way and Constitution the other—you'll have your deuce.

For a longer excursion, cross Arlington Memorial Bridge and explore **Arlington National Cemetery** (approximately two miles from the Capitol, so a four-mile loop). You can also walk north along the river past the **Kennedy Center** and the **Thompson Boat Center** to the **Georgetown waterfront.** (This is really nice when the cherry blossoms are in flower; plan to have a drink or dinner at one of the Georgetown waterfront restaurants.) And within Georgetown, the waterfront and portions of the Chesapeake and Ohio Canal Towpath are very popular; from the canal's beginnings near the Four Seasons Hotel to Fletcher's Boathouse is about three miles. It's also three miles from the trailhead to Union Station, going through the Mall and skirting the Capitol grounds, so round about is six miles.

The Mall and its surrounding areas are fairly flat, and you're never far from a restaurant (or restroom). But if you're not an habitual pedestrian, you might want to carry enough money not only to buy refreshments en route but for cab or Metro fare back to your hotel in case you wear out before you make it back.

continued on page 403

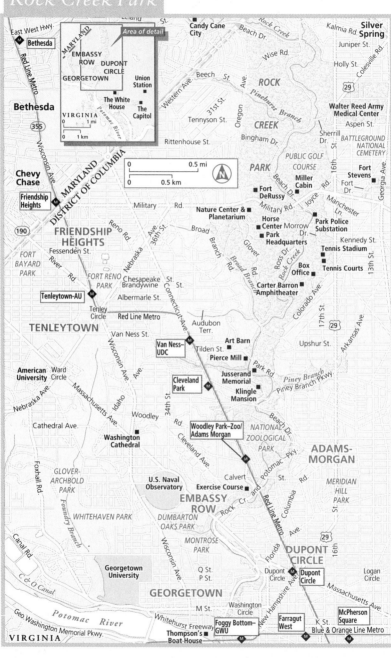

Rock Creek Park

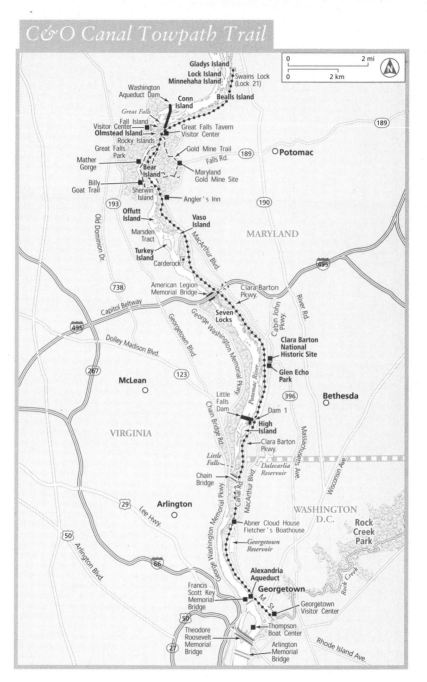

C&O Canal Towpath Trail

Mount Vernon Trail

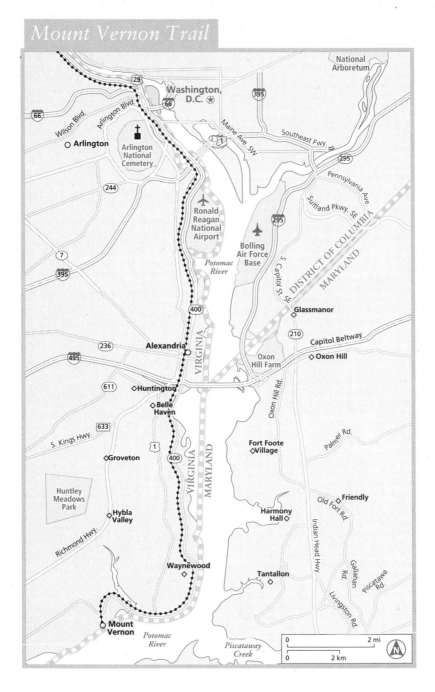

continued from page 399

Washington's wealth of parks offers plenty of options to both casual and serious joggers. Most of the better running areas are relatively flat but visually stunning. Many of the best paths are centrally located, close to major in-town hotels and other attractions, making either a morning or late-afternoon run easy to fit into a busy business or touring schedule. In fact, more and more hotels offer marked route maps; check with the hotel concierge. (And of course, if you master the road grid, as explained in Part Four, you can just take off and sidewalk-surf at will.)

Not surprisingly, the heart of Washington is also its most popular running location: the **Mall,** edged with packed-dirt and/or gravel paths. Nearby, the **Ellipse** (behind the White House) and the **Tidal Basin** offer paved pathways to run on as well. For some of the more popular walking/jogging routes in that area, see the section above.

Tree-shaded **Rock Creek Park,** the Central Park of Washington—and twice the size of the New York landmark—is a lovely retreat during hot weather. A good starting point is where Connecticut Avenue crosses over Rock Creek Parkway in Northwest Washington. Run north to **Pierce Mill** and retrace your steps for a four-mile jog. (For more information, go to **www.nps.gov/rocr.**)

With its southern terminus in Georgetown, the **Chesapeake & Ohio (C&O) Canal Towpath** offers what is probably the best running surface in town. Runners, cyclists, and hikers love this wide, dirt-pack trail that runs between the scenic Potomac River and the canal. The river views are spectacular in places; the placid canal reflects the greenery alongside; and historic lockhouses and locks appear at regular intervals. Mileposts along the towpath keep you informed of your distance.

Along the C&O are several landmarks. **Fletcher's Boathouse** is about three miles from Georgetown; **Glen Echo Park** (see Part Five: Attractions) is about seven miles out. (If you're not too tarty or sweaty, you may be able to get a restorative meal and/or drink at the Irish Inn at Glen Echo; sit outside or wash up a little in the restrooms.) Another seven miles out, near mile marker 14, the enormous cataract at **Great Falls,** also accessible from the Virginia side, attracts hikers and picnickers.

Spring through fall, given sufficiently high water levels, National Park Service rangers, dressed in 1870s period costume, lead mule-drawn boat tours between Georgetown and Great Falls. Tickets are $5; for information go to **www.nps.gov/choh/planyourvisit/publicboat rides.htm.**

In all, the C&O Canal, the entire stretch of which is now a national park (thanks primarily to the efforts of U.S. Supreme Court Justice William O. Douglas), runs 184.5 miles to Cumberland, Maryland, offering hikers, bikers, and joggers another way to enjoy several scenic and historic areas, including White's Ferry, where car commuters and recreational visitors still cross the Potomac toward Leesburg, Virginia; Harpers Ferry, where John Brown made his war-inciting stand; Sharpsburg, Maryland—aka Antietam—and the ¾-mile-long Paw Paw Tunnel, built with more than 6 million bricks over 12 years, on the way to Cumberland, Maryland.

There's a second recreational path, also part of the greater C&O park, that follows the C&O Towpath from Georgetown to near Fletcher's Boathouse but then turns east toward Bethesda and Silver Spring. The **Capital Crescent Trail,** based on the old Baltimore and Ohio Railroad right-of-way (and including a bridge over the canal), has both a wide biking trail and in many places a separate parallel running path. It has become so popular (more than a million walkers, runners, in-line skaters, and bikers every year) that it is now recognized as the most heavily used rail head in the country. From Georgetown to Fletcher's Boathouse, where you can use the restrooms and grab something from the concession stand, is three miles. To Bethesda—where the trail emerges at a convenient restaurant neighborhood not far from the Metro—is about seven miles; the leg from Bethesda to Silver Spring is another four miles, but you can catch the Metro there as well if you aren't up to the return trip.

Yet another riverside route, this one on the Virginia side of the Potomac River, is the **Mount Vernon Trail,** a paved path that starts near **Theodore Roosevelt Island** off the George Washington Memorial Parkway, goes downriver through Old Town Alexandria, past wildlife refuges and marinas, monument views, jet takeoffs, etc., and winds up 18.5 miles later at Mount Vernon. (If you start at the Lincoln Memorial and cross Arlington Memorial Bridge, it's about 16 miles.) You can run from the Lincoln Memorial to Ronald Reagan National Airport and back, a little over seven and a half miles each way; or plan to jump off at one of the Metro stations along the route. (Roosevelt Island itself is a sweet little wildlife and woodlands refuge designed by Frederick Olmstead, with a 1.6-mile easy walking loop.)

Serious exercise freaks can also cross Arlington Memorial Bridge and use the Rock Creek Trail to connect from the Mount Vernon Trail to the C&O Canal Towpath and Capitol Crescent Trail mentioned above; for details go to **www.nps.gov/gwmp/mtvernontrail.htm.**

Closer to downtown and the Mall, you can take a shorter but very picturesque turn through **West Potomac Park,** which is particularly beautiful (and busy) in the spring, when the Japanese cherry trees are blooming around the Tidal Basin. Start near the Jefferson Memorial, head down Ohio Drive, and make the loop at the end of the park. If you like, you can continue past the Jefferson Memorial and loop around the Tidal Basin, or even circle back past the reflecting pool and Korean and Vietnam War memorials toward the Washington Monument. Go early in the morning to beat the crowds.

For somewhat more strenuous walking, you can certainly stick to the above; but there are additional possibilities. At **Great Falls Park** (mentioned above), on the Virginia side, hiking trails follow the river and offer views of **Mather Gorge. Rock Creek Park** in Northwest Washington offers 15 miles of hiking trails, plus bridle trails you can hike. For a more extensive guide to hikes in the area, check out author Paul Elliott's *60 Hikes within 60 Miles: Washington, D.C.* published by Menasha Ridge Press (**www.menasharidge.com**).

FITNESS CENTERS AND AEROBICS

ALMOST ALL OF THE MAJOR HOTELS HAVE A SPA or fitness room with weight-lifting equipment. For an aerobic workout, most of the fitness rooms offer at least a stationary bicycle or two, a StairMaster, treadmill, or an elliptical trainer. However, if you are a member of one of the national chains, or are willing to buy a day pass, you have scores of options; and many clubs have massage therapists, yoga instructors, and even hair stylists on hand (not to mention pick-me-ups).

The **Vida Fitness** in the Verizon Center is the flagship of a very trendy local chain, now with four branches downtown (**www.vida fitness.com**). The Verizon Center location has the arena's sporting events on its TV screens, so if you can't get tickets, at least you can work out with the team; and it has a salon on site, so if you want to break a sweat before that breakfast meeting, you're covered ($25 for a day pass). **Results Gym** (three D.C. locations; **www.resultsthegym .com**) and **Sports Club/LA** in the Ritz-Carlton Hotel at 22nd and M streets NW ($35; **www.mpsportsclub.com**) are very hip, and the Sports Club also boasts a handy deluxe spa for taking the ache out.

There are 11 **Bally Total Fitness Clubs** in the Washington area (about $15 for a day pass; **www.ballyfitness.com**) and two dozen **Sport & Health Clubs,** some with golf and tennis facilities ($20, $10 ages 15 and under; **www.sportandhealth.com**). (If you check the companies' websites, you can sometimes find free trial memberships.) **Fitness First** (**www.fitnessfirstclubs.com**) has 17 locations in the Washington area; **Gold's Gym** has three dozen (**www.goldsgym.com**).

Washington Sports Club, with 18 area locations, is part of a company that also operates chains in Philadelphia, Boston, and New York City, and gets high marks for high-tech ($25; **www.mysportsclubs .com**). One of its biggest claims to fame, however, is that one of the employees once asked member (and U.S. President) Barack Obama for ID—"and your first name is…?"

RECREATIONAL SPORTS

TENNIS

WASHINGTON'S THREE PUBLIC TENNIS CLUBS are popular, making it difficult to get a court during peak hours without a reservation.

Rock Creek Tennis Center (**www.rockcreektennis.com**), which is home to an ATP pre–U.S. Open Tournament every August that draws many of the sport's biggest stars (Andre Agassi was a five-time champion, Andy Roddick a three-timer), has 25 total courts—10 hard and 15 clay; it's located at 16th and Kennedy streets in Upper Northwest. Five courts are heated during the winter. The club accepts reservations up to a week in advance. The club is open from 7 a.m. to 11 p.m. (clay courts open till 8 p.m.).

East Potomac Tennis Club (**www.eastpotomactennis.com**), located on Ohio Drive in East Potomac Park, has 24 hard courts, including five under a year-round bubble. Reservations for prime-time hours go fast, and you need to make reservations a week in advance; but walk-ups have a pretty good chance of getting a court weekdays between about 10 a.m. and 3 p.m. Open daily, 7 a.m.–10 p.m.

GOLF

WASHINGTON, D.C., HAS THREE PUBLIC GOLF COURSES operated on National Park Service land and open from dawn to dusk. Fees start at $10 for 9 holes; reservations can be made seven days in advance. All three courses feature snack bars, pro shops, rental clubs, and gas-powered golf carts. For more information on all three parks, visit **www.golfdc.com.**

East Potomac Golf Course, located near the Tidal Basin, offers one 18-hole course, two 9-hole courses, a driving range, and a very picturesque 1930 18-hole miniature golf course (no cartoon characters here). It's the busiest of the National Park Service courses; plan to arrive at dawn on weekends if you don't want to wait. East Potomac has wide-open fairways, well-kept greens, and great views of surrounding monuments. The park also offers tennis, an outdoor pool, plus a playground, bathroom, and picnic facilities, so it's a good choice for family outings.

Langston Golf Course, near RFK Stadium, features an 18-hole course, including remodeled back-nine holes, and a driving range. Langston, the only public course with water holes, is located along the Anacostia River.

Rock Creek Golf Course, 15 minutes north of the White House on 16th Street NW, offers duffers a hilly and challenging 18-hole course through rolling hills and wooded terrain. Both Langston and Rock Creek courses were picked as best-play sites by *Golf Digest* magazine in 2008.

There are also many suburban courses—nine of them operated by Montgomery County, Maryland, alone (**www.montgomerycounty golf.com**); and eight by Fairfax County, Virginia (**www.fairfaxcounty .gov/parks**). However, you'll have to know somebody—and maybe somebody she knows too—to get into Bethesda's famed **Congressional Country Club,** which lists scores of politicos and power brokers among its members; if you have a marker to call in, this would be the time.

Especially if you have dreams of seeing Tiger Woods at his annual tournament there.

Trumping even Tiger (sorry!), The Donald has bought and renovated the old Lowes Island course and turned it into the 600-acre Trump National Golf Club near Sterling, Virginia, and hopes to lure an LPGA tournament. But you have a better chance of winning on *The Apprentice* than scoring a free pass.

SWIMMING

THE LIAISON CAPITOL HILL SOMETIMES has Sunday afternoon swim parties open to outsiders for $20, but you need a reservation (**www.dcpoolparty.com**). And the Capitol Skyline Hotel just off South Capitol Street (**www.capitolskyline.com**) is often open on weekends to outsiders for $15 at the door—a fee that sometimes features "Top Chef" Spike Mendelsohn at the burger grill.

Local waters are polluted to one degree or another, so unless you have friends with a rental along the Atlantic beaches, stick to your hotel swimming pool, ask the hotel concierge to direct you to the nearest pool or gym, or check out one of these popular aquatic centers.

unofficial TIP
There are only a few hotels that offer pool passes to outsiders (and most of those, of course, are open only between about Memorial Day and Labor Day).

One of the nicest (though the lockers are small) is the free Olympic-sized pool at **East Potomac Park**, open June through early October (☎ 202-727-6523). The year-round pool **Rumsey Aquatic Center** near the Eastern Market Metro Station on Capitol Hill (also called the Capitol Hill Natorium) is also free to D.C. residents, so ask your friends to treat you like family . . . or pay the $4 non-resident fee (☎ 202-724-4495). For information on both of these pools and others in the District go to **dpr.dc.gov.**

For those staying in Bethesda or Rockville, the completely accessible **Montgomery Aquatic Center** is walking distance from the White Flint Metro station (☎ 240-777-8070).

ROPES AND ROCKS

THERE ARE ALREADY THREE OF THE NEW-STYLE ELEVATED-ROPE adventure parks in the Washington area: **Calleva** in the National Harbor development on the Potomac River south of town; **Go Ape** at Lake Needwood in Rockville, Maryland, a few minutes off I-270 or Route 355; and **Terrapin Adventures** in Savage, Maryland, about equidistant from Washington, Baltimore, and Annapolis.

Each park has restrictions involving minimum age, height, waist size (for harnesses), weight, minimal fitness levels, and so on. (Pregnant women may have to sign a waiver.) For the more challenging routes you will have preliminary instruction, and most have courses that range from beginner to advanced. Prices start at about $50; individual attractions start at about $10.

Calleva, the attraction at National Harbor, includes a "pirate ship" tower, a 400-foot zip line course, rope obstacle course, 30-foot climbing wall, and a giant swing. For information call ☎ 301-216-1248 or go to **www.calleva.com.**

Go Ape is the first American course from a company that already owns more than two dozen such attractions in the United Kingdom. In a space the size of seven football fields, it scatters zip lines, Tarzan Swings, rope ladders, trapezes, and so on; for specific information call ☎ 888-530-7322 or go to **www.goape.com.**

The most elaborate of the adventure parks is Terrapin Adventures, which includes high ropes, a 330-foot zip line 30 feet in the air, a giant tandem swing with an 80-foot arc, a multilevel rope course, and a 43-foot climbing tower. The Savage site also offers kayaking, tubing, fly fishing, wind surfing, horseback riding, and geocaching. For information and tickets call ☎ 301-725-1313 or go to **www.terrapinadventures.com.**

For rock climbing alone, check out the **Results Gym** Capitol Hill location at 315 G Street SE, which has a 38-foot wall (among many other options). Day passes are $19; call ☎ 202-234-5678 ext. 2 or go to **www.results thegym.com.**

Earth Treks Rockville, four blocks south of the Rockville Metro station in the Marlo Furniture building (725 Rockville Pike; ☎ 340-283-9942; **www.earthtreksclimbing.com**), is a huge complex, with 16,000 square feet of rock walls 40 feet high, plus a bouldering cave and more than 100 top-rope climbs. A day pass is $18.

unofficial **TIP**
Want to get in the swing—seriously? Take a class at Trapeze School New York's offshoot at the Navy Yard Metro (**www.washington dc.trapezeschool.com**). They also teach juggling and trampoline for the fainter of heart.

BICYCLING

ANY OF THE TRAILS MENTIONED ABOVE AS IDEAL for walking or running should be high on the lists of on- and off-road cyclists, and there are many more challenging routes in the rolling countryside of nearby Virginia and Maryland.

Fall is the best season for cycling around Washington, with cool, crisp weather and a riot of color as the leaves turn in mid- to late October. Even in winter, Washington's mild climate offers at least a few days a month that are warm enough to induce cyclists to jump on their bikes.

Adult cruiser bikes (plus helmets, baskets, locks, etc.) are available for rent on a first-come, first-served basis at **Thompson Boat Center,** located between the Kennedy Center and Georgetown on the Potomac River ($7 an hour or $28 a day; **www.thompsonboatcenter.com**). Rentals are available 8 a.m.–5 p.m., and bikes must be returned by 6 p.m. **Fletcher's Boathouse,** two miles north of Georgetown on Canal

Road, also rents single-speed cruisers and 21-speed train bikes ($7 per hour for up to four hours or $28 a day; **www.fletcherscove.com**). Fletcher's is open 7 a.m.–7 p.m., and the last rentals are at 5 p.m.

Bike the Sites rents mountain bikes (as well as strollers, mobility scooters, and wheelchairs) from its offices behind the Old Post Office Pavilion (☎ 202-842-2453; **www.bikethesites.com**).

In terms of great scenery and enough distance to really get a workout, the **Mount Vernon Trail** is Washington's premier bike path. In addition to pedaling the 16 paved miles to Mount Vernon, cyclists can make side trips to Dyke Marsh Wildlife Preserve, explore fortifications at Fort Hunt, and see a 19th-century lighthouse at Jones Point Park.

Another good out-and-back ride is the **Washington and Old Dominion Railroad Regional Park (W&OD),** a 45-mile-long paved linear bikeway that connects with the Mount Vernon Trail upriver of Arlington Memorial Bridge on the Virginia side of the Potomac. The trail intersects with a series of "bubble" parks in urban Northern Virginia and provides access to the rural Virginia countryside beyond the Capital Beltway. Both the Mount Vernon Trail and the W&OD trail are easily reached from Washington by bicycle by riding across the Arlington Memorial Bridge, at the Lincoln Memorial.

Road riders itching to see beautiful countryside outside the Washington metropolitan area (but within a day's drive) should go to either **Middleburg, Virginia,** or **Frederick, Maryland.** Middleburg, about 30 miles west of D.C., is in the heart of Virginia's horse country. Beautiful rolling countryside in the foothills of the Blue Ridge Mountains and low-traffic roads bordering thoroughbred horse farms make this area a fantastic place to spin the cranks.

Frederick is about an hour's drive north of Washington. North of town along US 15, covered bridges, narrow back roads, fish hatcheries, and mountain vistas evoke images of Vermont. The **Covered Bridge Cycle Tour** starts at Frederick Community College. From D.C. take I-270 north to Frederick and get on US 15 north; then exit on Opposumtown Pike going north to the college, about a mile on the left. To the south of Frederick, a 25-mile loop around **Sugarloaf Mountain** is a favorite with local road cyclists.

Hammerheads looking for challenging singletrack and some steep climbing have to do some driving to find it, but it's worth it. The **Frederick Municipal Watershed** offers the best technical singletrack this side of West Virginia—and it's a lot closer. Located an hour's drive from Washington near Frederick, Maryland, the 6,000-acre mountaintop forest is riddled with narrow trails and well-maintained dirt roads. Since there are hardly any signs or trail markers, the Catoctin Furnace Quadrangle topographic map and a compass are a must. Local knowledge helps too; call the **Wheel Base,** Frederick's pro bike shop, at ☎ 301-663-9288 for maps and advice.

ROWING, CANOEING, AND KAYAKING

IF YOU'RE ANYWHERE ALONG THE POTOMAC RIVER early in the day or around dusk, you'll have seen the area's school rowing crews doing drills. The George Washington University Invitational Regatta, which draws teams from all over the country during the Cherry Blossom Festival, is only one of the many contests. And all forms of rowing are increasingly popular in the Washington area; some high-level competitors come here to train.

Canoes and rowboats are available for rent on the C&O Canal and the Potomac River at **Thompson Boat Center** (see above). Single kayaks rent for $10 an hour or $28 a day, and double kayaks for $17 an hour or $40 a day; canoes are $12 per hour or $24 a day.

Fletcher's Boat House (also mentioned above) rents single and double kayaks for the same rates as Thompson's, but also rents canoes for $11 an hour or $22 a day and rowboats for $12 an hour or $22 a day.

unofficial **TIP**
Inspired by those rowing crews you see on the river? Or maybe you're just a fan of those British-historical romance movies? Thompsons's offers private rowing lessons ($75 an hour), sculling courses ($150 for a week's course), and even sweep rowing courses, which draw out-of-town Olympic team wannabes ($250 for two weeks).

Jack's Boats (**www.jacksboathouse.com**), located in a particularly lovely old building at the foot of Key Bridge in Georgetown, has two- and three-person canoes and single and double kayaks for rent at $12 per hour with a maximum of three hours. Reservations are available only for parties of 15 or more, but Jack's also has picnic and grilling spaces.

Paddle boats can be rented at the **Tidal Basin** across from the Jefferson Memorial (**www.tidalbasinpaddleboats.com**); rent for a two-passenger paddle boat is $12 an hour, $19 for a four-passenger boat.

If paddle boats sound like a stationary bike to you, you can kick it up any number of notches. Whitewater enthusiasts need go only a few miles north of the Capital Beltway to find excellent Class I through Class VI rapids year-round on the Potomac River. Local boaters boast that it's the best urban whitewater experience in the United States, featuring a very remote, wilderness feel; some Olympic competitors have trained here. One of the most popular trips is the Class II Seneca rapids section. The put-in is at **Violets Lock,** located on River Road (MD 190), north of Potomac, Maryland. Violets Lock is also the take-out, meaning you don't have to run a shuttle: it's a round-trip that lets you return to your starting point by paddling up the C&O Canal, about one and a half miles below Violets Lock. Below the Seneca rapids, the river is very scenic, featuring many islands and no rapids. But you must make the next take-out on the left bank at Maryland's Great Falls National Park or become another statistic—we're quite serious—as the river drops through Great Falls.

Seasoned paddlers may want to try running the Class II/III+ rapids that start below Great Falls and end at the Old Angler's Inn. As with Seneca rapids, no shuttle is required: park across the road from the Old Angler's Inn on MacArthur Boulevard on the Maryland side of the Potomac and follow the trail to the put-in. Paddle upstream on the C&O Canal to below Great Falls (at least 100 yards) for the return.

ICE SKATING

THERE ARE A FEW YEAR-ROUND ICE RINKS in the Washington area, but the two that would be the most fun for out-of-towners are seasonal: one on the Mall and the other at the heart of official Washington within sight of the White House.

Come skating weather—generally mid-November through mid-March—the **Sculpture Garden** of the National Gallery of Art between Seventh and Ninth streets NW and Constitution and Madison avenues (**www.nga.gov/skating**) is transformed into a fantasy ice rink in the middle of the Mall, with the U.S. Capitol and all the Smithsonian museums lit up as a backdrop. It's open from 10 a.m. to 9 p.m. Monday through Thursday, from 10 a.m. until a romantic 11 p.m. Fridays and Saturdays, and from 11 a.m. to 9 p.m. on Sundays. A two-hour session is $7 for adults or $6 ages 50 and over, ages 12 and under, and students with ID; skate rental is $3, and locker rental is 50¢ (but with a $5 refundable deposit).

The **Pavilion Café,** a lovely retro-Deco glass-sided eatery alongside the garden, stays open late during skating season, serving sandwiches, pizzas, salads, hot chocolate, coffee and tea, and wine and beer until 8 p.m. Sundays and weekdays and until 9 p.m. Fridays and Saturdays.

A few blocks away, **Pershing Park,** just east of the Treasury Building and the White House at 14th Street and Pennsylvania Avenue NW, with a view of the Washington Monument and many federal buildings, also gets a wintertime coat of ice (**www.pershingparkicerink .com**). It's lit and late, too, so that you can skate from 11 a.m. to 9 p.m. on weekdays and until 11 p.m. on Fridays and Saturdays. Skate rental is $2.50, and a two-hour ticket is $6.50 for adults and $5.50 for ages 12 and under; there are often early-bird discounts as well.

Several public rinks are accessible by Metro—and at Metro developments, in fact. The plaza atop the Bethesda Metro is iced during winter, as is the outdoor-café area at the **Shops at Pentagon Row,** part of the Pentagon City complex; and the town square at **Rockville Town Center.**

For hockey fans, however, the most intriguing facility might be the new, year-round **Kettler Capitals Iceplex,** atop a seven-story office building at Ballston Common Mall (at the Ballston Metro) in Arlington; it's also the practice rink for the NHL Washington Capitals (**www.kettlercapitalsiceplex.com**). Adults are $8, skate rental $4.

SKIING

MODERATELY GOOD DOWNHILL SKI SLOPES are within a couple hours' drive from Washington and offer dependable, machine-made snow and night skiing from November through March. **Whitetail**, a $25-million ski area in nearby Pennsylvania, features a vertical drop of almost 1,000 feet, 20 trails, and plenty of lift capacity (**www.ski whitetail.com**). Jointly-owned **Ski Roundtop** (**www.skiroundtop.com**) and **Liberty Mountain Resort** (**www.skiliberty.com**), also located in south-central Pennsylvania, are about a two- to three-hour drive from Washington. Both offer 600-foot verticals, 16 trails, and 100-percent snowmaking.

HORSEBACK RIDING

Rock Creek Park Horse Center (**www.rockcreekhorsecenter.com**) offers guided rides for ages 12 and up on the equestrian trails located in Rock Creek Park. Rates are $40 for an hour, but there is a limited schedule; reservations are required (and you should book well in advance). Rock Creek also offers 10–15-minute pony rides for children (ages 2 to 12 and at least 30 inches tall) for $20. The center, which is open all year, is located at Military and Glover roads in Northwest Washington.

unofficial **TIP**
If you want an overnight city-slicker excursion, check out the Marriott Ranch in Hume, Virginia, a B&B with trail ride options, western-style cookouts, and a variety of outdoor adventures. Or go equestrian A-class at the Inn at Kelly's Ford (**www .innatkellysford.com**) in the battlefield country of Virginia.

For indoor riding, the **Potomac Horse Center** in North Potomac (**www.potomac horse.com**) has several indoor as well as trail facilities and hosts kids' pony parties as well as dressage and hunter-jumper training. **Wheaton Park Stables** in Wheaton (**www .wheatonparkstables.com**) offer one-hour trail rides on Sundays ($40) as well as group or private lessons.

▐ SPECTATOR SPORTS

BASEBALL

IN 2005, AFTER A 30-YEAR DROUGHT, Washington finally welcomed a Major League Baseball home team—the **Washington Nationals,** formerly the Montreal Expos. In 2008 the team moved into an elaborate new stadium complex with 49 concessions stands (including those selling local names such as Dogfish Head and Flying Dog beers as well as Ben's Chili Bowl dogs, Five Guys Burgers and Fries, and Hard Times Cafe); an interactive Kids Area with a Sony PlayStation Pavilion, Build-a-Bear Workshop, and batting and pitching cages; and for adults, fine views of the Anacostia River and the federal monuments. It's located at the Navy Yard Metro, is entirely accessible, and is environmentally friendly to boot. Serious tickets can range well into the hundreds, but singles in the upper gallery start at $10—and all sight lines here are good.

Serious fans can also take an hour-long behind-the-scenes tour of Nationals Park on home game days when the game itself is at night; or a 75-minute tour on nongame days in season. (During the extra 15 minutes, you get to see the Nationals dugout and clubhouse, because the team isn't in.) All tours are accessible, but you should expect to spend two hours in total. Tours are $15 for adults; $12 for seniors, kids 12 and under, and military personnel; and free for infants and toddlers. Depending on the day and whether the team is at home, tours start at 10:30 and 11:30 a.m. and 1:30 and 2:30 p.m.; for information on tickets and tours go to **www.nationals.com.**

In those three decades between teams, however, many Washingtonians developed a fierce devotion to the **Baltimore Orioles,** only an hour north. Visitors to D.C. can make the trek by train to catch the Birds, as they are known, playing at home in Oriole Park at Camden Yards, near Baltimore's downtown Inner Harbor. Check the sports section of the *Washington Post* for information on both teams' home games and tickets.

If you're one of the growing number of fans of minor-league baseball, the Washington area is worth a minitour. The Orioles' Class A farm team, the **Frederick Keys** (named in honor of Francis Scott Key, a rural Maryland native), play in the historic town of Frederick, Maryland, about an hour to the northeast. The closest option for baseball is Prince George's Stadium, where the **Bowie Baysox,** a Class AA team belonging to the same group as the Keys, have been steadily building a crowd. The Class A **Potomac Nationals,** a farm team for the Nats, play just outside Fairfax County. And the **Hagerstown Suns,** a little west of Frederick, are the Single-A Nationals affiliate. For information on all of these teams, and ticket prices, go to **www.minorleaguebaseball.com.**

Fans of Hall of Famer and longtime Oriole Brooks Robinson may want to trek to Waldorf, Maryland, to see the **Southern Maryland Blue Crabs,** also known as the Crustaceans, part of the Atlantic League of Professional Baseball (**www.somdbluecrabs.com**).

Actually, the closest-in minor league team (which is really part of the Cal Ripken Collegiate Baseball League) is the **Potomac Big Train,** named for Washington Senators pitching great Walter "Big Train" Johnson, and winners of back-to-back league championships in 2009 and 2010. The CRCBL plays a short season, pretty much June and July, but it's great fun, and even the most expensive tickets are only $7. The team plays at home at Cabin John Regional Park just outside the Beltway in Bethesda, Maryland; go to **www.bigtrain.org** for information.

For those who see baseball as a stepchild of cricket, Washington's international community supports more than two dozen accredited teams, and one of the most popular fields is in West Potomac Park near the Jefferson Memorial, where you can often see white-suited teams bowling away on a weekend. For information go to **www.wclinc.com.**

BASKETBALL

WASHINGTON'S PROFESSIONAL BASKETBALL TEAMS, the NBA **Washington Wizards** and its sister team, the WNBA's **Mystics**, play at home at the Verizon Center, located downtown (right above the Gallery Place–Chinatown Metro). For schedules and tickets, call ☎ 202-397-SEAT (7328) or visit the teams' respective websites: **www .nba.com/wizards** and **www.wnba.com/mystics.**

The **University of Maryland Terrapins** (**www.umterps.com**) offer topflight college basketball at Comcast Center on the school's campus in suburban College Park. **Georgetown University** (**www.guhoyas .com**) plays its home games at Verizon Center.

The **George Mason University Patriots,** who made it into the NCAA Final Four in 2006, play on their college campus in Fairfax, but tickets may be hard to come by (**gomason.cstv.com**). The **George Washington University Colonials** (**www.gwsports.com**) have many devoted fans (watch for celebs and media faces); the team's Smith Center home is very near the Foggy Bottom–GWU Metro stop.

FOOTBALL AND SOCCER

LOTS OF LUCK GETTING TICKETS to see professional football in Washington: the **Washington Redskins** have sold out various stadiums for years, and the team holds the reputation as the hardest ticket to acquire in pro sports. Still interested? Scalpers regularly charge three to four times regular ticket price—more if the 'Skins are playing Dallas. (But it's worth checking out StubHub for the odd single seats; **www.stubhub.com.**)

FedEx Field in Landover has nearly 92,000 seats, so tickets are slightly easier to obtain than they used to be. On the other hand, they're among the most expensive in the NFL (VIP parking spaces cost $1000 a year). Following suit, Baltimore built a new football stadium for the Ravens, née Cleveland Browns. For Redskins schedule and ticket information, go to **www.redskins.com.** For the Ravens, visit **www.baltimoreravens.com.**

The Washington area is also home to one of the full-tackle Independent Women's Football League franchises, the **D.C. Divas** (**www.dcdivas.com**), who play on an outdoor field adjacent to the Redskins' FedEx field.

College football is extremely popular in the Washington area. The **Maryland Terrapins** play in Byrd Stadium at College Park (**www .umterps.com**). **The Naval Academy** in Annapolis, Maryland, and **Howard University** in Washington also field teams; check the *Post* for home game information.

Pro soccer, which is "football" to the rest of the world, comes to Washington when **D.C. United** play 16 home games each season

(March through September) at RFK Stadium. Tickets for evening and Sunday-afternoon games range from $28 to $59. For schedule information go to **www.dcunited.com. The Washington Freedom,** part of the professional Women's Soccer League, play at home at the Maryland SoccerPlex near Boyds, Maryland (**www.washingtonfreedom.com**).

HOCKEY AND RACQUET SPORTS

WASHINGTON'S PROFESSIONAL HOCKEY TEAM, the **Washington Capitals** (**capitals.nhl.com**), shares ownership with the Wizards and Mystics, and also plays at the Verizon Center in downtown D.C. near Gallery Place.

Washington has a World Team Tennis franchise, the **Washington Kastles,** but they have a very short (three-week) season; when they do play at home, it's in a temporary stadium at City Center, 12th and H streets NW (**www.washingtonkastles.com**). The **U.S. Open** circuit does play a major tournament here in August, the Legg-Mason, at the Fitzgerald Tennis Center in Rock Creek Park. Daily tickets are available as well as series packages (**www.leggmasontennisclassic.com**).

Unhappily, the **Chesapeake Bayhawks** pro lacrosse team (formerly the Washington Bayhawks), the MLL's most successful lacrosse franchise with three league championships and four division titles, now plays primarily at home in Annapolis at the Navy-Marine Corps Memorial Stadium. But for followers of this rapid-paced game, it's worth the drive (**www.thebayhawks.com**). After all, Annapolis on a summer's day, crabs and beer on the waterfront . . .

HORSE RACING AND POLO

RACING HAS A LONG HISTORY IN THE WASHINGTON AREA, particularly in Maryland, and both thoroughbred and harness racing are available at a number of tracks around Washington. (Pimlico is farthest from the city, and not in a particularly scenic neighborhood, but though endangered, it's still home to the Preakness Stakes, the middle contest of thoroughbred racing's Triple Crown, and the third Saturday in May is part of a huge celebration there.) Check the *Washington Post* to see which track is in season during your visit and for handicapping. The thoroughbred track at **Charles**

Harness:
  Rosecroft Raceway—Fort Washington, MD; **www.rosecroft.com**
Thoroughbred:
  Hollywood Casino at Charles Town Races—Charles Town, WV;
    www.hollywoodcasinocharlestown.com
  Laurel Race Course—Laurel, MD; **www.laurelpark.com**
  Pimlico Race Course—Baltimore, MD; **www.pimlico.com**

Town, West Virginia (**www.hollywoodcasinocharlestown.com**), has become a big draw because it also has slot machines, still a controversial issue in Maryland; it also offers simulcasts of harness racing and dog races. (And once you get through the racket of the casinos, it's quite a pretty track.)

There are several major steeplechase courses in the Washington region. The most famous is probably the **Gold Cup** lineup every October (**www.vagoldcup.com**). Also check **www.vasteeplechase.com** for other dates.

The **Potomac Polo Club** has been playing since 1956, with regular matches on Thursday evenings and Saturdays at noon; visit **www.americaspolocup.com.** You never know when a royal might drop by.

INDEX

Unofficial Guide Reader Survey

If you'd like to express your opinion about traveling in Washington, D. C. or this guidebook, complete the following survey and mail it to:

> *Unofficial Guide* Reader Survey
> P.O. Box 43673
> Birmingham, AL 35243

Inclusive dates of your visit:_____

Members of your party:

	Person 1	Person 2	Person 3	Person 4	Person 5
Gender:	M F	M F	M F	M F	M F
Age:_____

How many times have you been to Washington, D. C.?_____
On your most recent trip, where did you stay?_____

Concerning your accommodations, on a scale of 100 as best and 0 as worst, how would you rate:

The quality of your room?	The value of your room?
The quietness of your room?	Check-in/checkout efficiency?
Shuttle service to the airport?	Swimming pool facilities?

Did you rent a car?_____   From whom?_____

Concerning your rental car, on a scale of 100 as best and 0 as worst, how would you rate:

Pickup-processing efficiency?____	Return processing efficiency?____
Condition of the car?____	Cleanliness of the car?____
Airport shuttle efficiency?____	

Concerning your dining experiences:

Estimate your meals in restaurants per day? _____

Approximately how much did your party spend on meals per day? ____

Favorite restaurants in Washington, D. C.: _____
_____

Did you buy this guide before leaving? _____ While on your trip?_____

How did you hear about this guide? (check all that apply)

☐ Loaned or recommended by a friend   ☐ Radio or TV
☐ Newspaper or magazine   ☐ Bookstore salesperson
☐ Just picked it out on my own   ☐ Library
☐ Internet

What other guidebooks did you use on this trip?_____

_____

_____

_____

On a scale of 100 as best and 0 as worst, how would you rate them?

_____

_____

_____

Using the same scale, how would you rate the *Unofficial Guide*(s)?

_____

Are *Unofficial Guides* readily available at bookstores in your area?_____

Have you used other *Unofficial Guides*? _____

Which one(s)? _____

_____

_____

Comments about your Washington, D. C. trip or the *Unofficial Guide*(s):

_____

_____

_____

_____

_____

_____

_____

_____

_____

_____

_____

_____

_____

_____

_____

_____

_____

_____

_____